Computer Programming with C++

This textbook provides in-depth explanation of C and C++ programming languages along with the fundamentals of object oriented programming paradigm. Essential concepts including functions, arrays, pointers and inheritance are explained in a coherent manner.

The book follows an example-driven approach, to facilitate easy comprehension of theoretical concepts. Common concepts of C programming language are also elaborated wherever necessary. The text provides detailed explanation on complex topics including Dynamic Memory Allocation, Object Slicing, VTABLEs, Up Casting and Down Casting.

The concepts are explained using line diagrams, notes, conversation themes and flow charts. The book offers useful features including error finding exercises, quiz questions and points to remember. Necessary comments to explain the logic used to implement particular functionality are provided for the ease of readers. Plenty of computer programs, review questions and useful case studies are interspersed throughout the text.

The book is intended for undergraduate and graduate students of engineering and computer science.

Kunal Pimparkhede is an adjunct faculty at the Vidyalankar Institute of Technology, Mumbai. As a software professional, he has development experience in technologies such as Adobe Flex, Informatica; database systems like Oracle, Sybase; Java based frameworks like Spring, Struts, etc. His areas of interest include Microprocessors, Automata Theory, Data Structures, Analysis of Algorithms, Artificial Intelligence and Computer Programming.

Computer Programming with C++

Kunal Pimparkhede

CAMBRIDGE
UNIVERSITY PRESS

CAMBRIDGE
UNIVERSITY PRESS

University Printing House, Cambridge CB2 8BS, United Kingdom
One Liberty Plaza, 20th Floor, New York, NY 10006, USA
477 Williamstown Road, Port Melbourne, vic 3207, Australia
4843/24, 2nd Floor, Ansari Road, Daryaganj, Delhi – 110002, India
79 Anson Road, #06–04/06, Singapore 079906

Cambridge University Press is part of the University of Cambridge.

It furthers the University's mission by disseminating knowledge in the pursuit of
education, learning and research at the highest international levels of excellence.

www.cambridge.org
Information on this title: www.cambridge.org/9781316506806

First published 2017

Printed in India by Thomson Press India Ltd.

A catalogue record for this publication is available from the British Library

Library of Congress Cataloging-in-Publication Data
Names: Pimparkhede, Kunal, author.
Title: Computer programming with C++ / Kunal Pimparkhede.
Description: New York : Cambridge University Press, 2016. | Includes index.
Identifiers: LCCN 2015051227 | ISBN 9781316506806 (paperback)
Subjects: LCSH: C++ (Computer program language) | C (Computer program
    language) | Object-oriented programming (Computer science) | Computer
    programming. | BISAC: COMPUTERS / Programming Languages / General.
Classification: LCC QA76.73.C153 P469 2016 | DDC 005.13/3--dc23 LC record available at
http://lccn.loc.gov/2015051227

ISBN 978-1-31-650680-6 Paperback

Additional resources for this publication at www.cambridge.org/9781316506806

Contents

PART-I Structured Programming

PART-II Object Oriented Programming

Preface

A computer program is a set of instructions which is followed by a machine to generate the required output. The language in which a computer program is written is called a computer programming language. Several computer programming languages are in use in the IT industry today, for developing diverse software applications.

The study of C and C++ is considered an important step towards mastering computer programming fundamentals. Hence, C and C++ are included in the syllabus of any computer science course.

This textbook provides in-depth explanations of C and C++ programming languages along with the fundamentals of the object oriented programming paradigm.

About the Book

This book will be of use to anyone who is a beginner and aspires to learn the fundamentals of computer programming using C and C++. It has been primarily written for students of academic courses which include the study of C, C++ and object oriented programming paradigm. Simple and lucid language has been used to facilitate easy comprehension of complex topics.

Salient Features

- Example-driven approach illustrates application of theoretical concepts
- Theme of a conversation interspersed in the text, elucidate essential themes of the subject
- Each program includes necessary comments to explain the logic used to implement a particular functionality
- Several line diagrams and flow charts facilitate easy comprehension of theoretical concepts
- Student-friendly pedagogical features include:
  - ✓ Error Finding Exercise
  - ✓ Solved Problems

✓ Objective Questions
✓ Review Questions

Chapter Organization

This book comprises 17 chapters. **Chapter 1** gives an overview of computer organization and architecture. It also explains the C/C++ development environment. **Chapters 2** to **5** discuss the basic features of C/C++ including data types, variables and different control statements which are supported by the language. **Chapter 6** describes the creation of multivalued data types (also referred to as collection types) using arrays in C/C++. **Chapter 7** explains modular programming using functions. **Chapter 8** elucidates the fundamentals of memory management using pointers in C/C++. **Chapter 9** discusses the creation of composite data types using structures and unions in C/C++. Chapter 10 explains the principles of memory management and Dynamic memory allocations in C++ style. **Chapters 11** to **17** provide in-depth coverage of object oriented features supported by C++.

NOTES

Chapters 1 to 9 cover features which are common to C as well as C++. Hence programs written in these chapters will work with C as well as C++ compilers unless specified otherwise. Whereas Chapters 11 to 17 cover object oriented features which are supported only by C++ and not by C. Chapter 10 explains dynamic memory allocation in C++ style. Hence programs written from Chapter 10 to 17 will work with C++ compilers only.

Does this book also explain the underlying systems which are involved in the execution of a computer program ? **?**

Chapter 1 gives an understanding of computer organization, operating system and other system programs which make up the underlying platform required to execute any C/C++ program. Chapter 1 also gives an overview of many areas which are relevant for understanding computer programming fundamentals using C/C++. The specific features of individual topics have been explained in detail in the later chapters of this book.

I have put my best efforts to make this book as illustrative and interactive as possible. Any suggestions to further improve this book are always welcome. You can write to me at *kunalp84@rediffmail.com*.

Acknowledgements

Contribution and support of many people in my life has made this book possible. I am indebted to Vishwas Deshpande, Chairman, Vidyalankar Institute of Technology for giving me a wonderful platform to showcase my learnings. I am grateful to Professor N. H. Dubey for his constructive feedback, which added significant value to this project. I owe special thanks to my dear dearer dearest daughter Swara for allowing me to work long hours while I was writing this book.

I am thankful to Professors V. S. Padmakumar, Sanjeev Dwivedi, Sachin Bhojewar, Pankaj Vanwari from Vidyalankar Institute of Technology; Professors Kalpana Sagvekar, Sunil Surve and Brijmohan Daga from Fr. Conceacao Rodrigues College of Engineering, Mumbai; Professor Asawari Dudwadkar, Vivekanand Institute of Technology, Mumbai; Professors Prasad Kulkarni, Vinayak Shinde, Leena Thakur, Surbhi Crasto and Ajit Parab from Babasaheb Gawde Institute of Technology, Mumbai; Professor Yogesh Prabhu, Dr A. K. Pathak, Professor Sameer Velankar and Professor Yogesh Rajadhyaksha for their excellent support at different stages which helped me to present my learnings so well in the form of this book.

I am thankful to Ruhi Bajaj, Thadomal Shahani Engineering College, Mumbai and Shweta Loonkar, D. J. Sanghavi College of Engineering, Mumbai for their valuable suggestions which helped mould this script to meet the needs of a wide range of audience.

I sincerely acknowledge the contribution of all my teachers, who have played a vital role in developing my understanding of the subject and broadening my perspectives. They have strongly influenced me in building a positive attitude towards creative learning.

I would also like to thank every member of the team at Cambridge University Press, including Rachna Sehgal, who supported me throughout the publishing process to actuate timely release of this book.

I express heartfelt gratitude to my family for their moral support and patience. I am thankful to Pradeep Pimparkhede, Shalaka Pimparkhede, Dipti Pimparkhede, Swara Pimparkhede, Prabhavati Pimparkhede, Nivedita Bakre, Rajgopal Pai and Jayanti Pai for their patience while I was writing this script.

PART-I

Structured Programming

Chapter 1

Introduction

1.1 Overview

A *program* is a set of instructions, which are followed by the machine so as to generate a desired output. This means that writing a computer program is giving instructions to a processor, so as to delegate a particular job to the hardware of the computer system. Every instruction is a command given to the computer hardware to perform a specific job. Computer hardware is a digital system (collection of functional switches) and hence every instruction must be converted into the form of 0's and 1's (where a symbol 0 represents open switch and a symbol 1 represents closed switch). As an example, let us assume that we want the computer system to perform the addition of two numbers say 15 and 25. The instruction to perform addition of two numbers could be written in the machine language as shown below:

```
10000011  00001111  00011001
```

In this case, the first eight bits represent the code informing the hardware that the addition of the two numbers is to be performed. This is called as an *opcode* (operational code) of the instruction. Different instructions would have different opcodes and their purpose is to convey the meaning of the instruction to the internal hardware circuitry. In this case, we have assumed an arbitrary opcode of ADD instruction as 10000011. Different processors have different decoders and internal designs, hence the length and format of the opcode will certainly differ from processor to processor. Some processors have eight bit opcodes (e.g., intel 8085), some have 16 bit opcodes (e.g., intel 8086). Today's generation processors have 32 bit/64 bit opcodes or even 128 bit opcodes. We need not look into the hardware configurations and designs at this stage, but the key point to understand is that every instruction has an opcode and in this case, we just assume an arbitrary opcode of 8 bits as 10000011, which represents ADD operation. A different combination of 8 bits, say 11001010, may represent subtraction and so on. In theory, the variety of instructions any processor can offer is indirectly dependent on the length of its opcode. A processor with an opcode length of 8 bits can just offer $2^8 =$ 256 distinct instructions whereas a processor with an opcode length of 16 bits can offer $2^{16} = 65536$ distinct instructions. We cannot just increase the length of opcode arbitrarily, the internal hardware and the instruction decoders must support it too. A processor that has a rich-instruction set certainly has highly effective internal circuitry and decoders to support it. In today's generation, we are working with processors having 32 bit opcodes or 64 bit opcodes giving us rich- and high-performing instruction set, and this facilitates the execution of even complex programs in an optimized way. The next bits are the binary translations of the data values 15 and 25 over which addition is to be performed. The sample format of the ADD instruction is shown in Figure 1.1. We need not go too much in detail about computer hardware, however, the rationale of this discussion was just to make us clear that every processor has a digital circuitry, which only understands the language of 0's and 1's. This language is called as *machine language*.

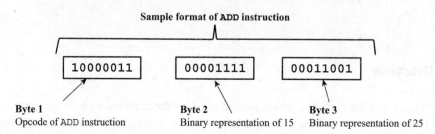

Sample format of ADD instruction

| 10000011 | 00001111 | 00011001 |

Byte 1
Opcode of ADD instruction

Byte 2
Binary representation of 15

Byte 3
Binary representation of 25

Figure 1.1: Representation of instruction in a machine language

Writing every instruction using *machine language* could be very complex when there are a large number of operations to be performed in the program as it requires us not only to work with 0's and 1's but also to understand hardware specifications of the processor. In today's generation, computer programs are written to design many complex applications having business challenges in itself, hence, it is practically impossible for a human being to write such programs in machine language.

To make the programmers life easy, an assembly language is designed, which codes every instruction using a *mnemonic*. For example, an instruction to perform the addition of 15 and 25 could be written in the assembly language as

```
ADD 15, 25
```

The symbol ADD is called as a mnemonic, which represents addition, whereas the constants 15 and 25 represent the data (also called as operands) over which the 'add' operation is to be performed. It is important to note that mnemonics are English symbols and hence they cannot be directly understood by the machine. Therefore, there is a need for a translator, which can translate the assembly language into a language of 0's and 1's. This will ensure that the hardware of the computer system can understand the meaning of the instruction, which is actually written in the assembly language by the programmer. The unit that performs the translation of assembly language into the machine language is called as an *assembler*. Therefore, the instruction ADD 15, 25 will be first translated by the assembler into the machine language as shown in Figure 1.2. After the translation process is completed, the hardware of the computer system can execute the instruction, which will actually perform the addition of constants 15 and 25.

The assembly language program can still be tedious to create if the program has a large number of operations to be performed. So as to make the programmer's life simple, the *high-level programming* languages are designed. A high-level programming language is an '*English-like*' programming language wherein the programmer can make use of user

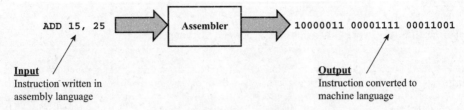

Figure 1.2: Assembler

friendly words and symbols to code an instruction. For example, we can write the following high-level instruction so as to perform the addition of two numbers:

$$Z = 15 + 25$$

Note that we have directly used a user friendly symbol + instead of coding the instruction in a machine language or an assembly language. Hence, the value of Z will be evaluated as 40, which is the addition of 15 and 25. High-level language is a set of 'English-like' symbols and hence these symbols cannot be directly decoded by the hardware of the system. Therefore, the high-level language is first converted into an assembly language by a unit called as 'compiler'. The assembly code can then be further converted into the machine code using the 'assembler as shown in Figure 1.3. It is important to reinforce on a point that the processor can execute a particular instruction only after it is translated into the machine language.

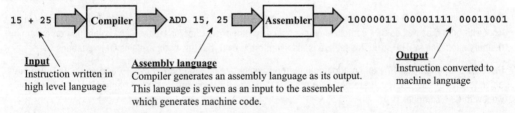

Figure 1.3: Translation of high level language to machine code

As the instructions in high-level programming languages are very user friendly and easy to code, they facilitate the creation of complex programs in a much more readable and maintainable then assembly or machine level languages. Hence, the programs written in high-level languages are easy to create, edit, debug and maintain. There are several high-level programming languages, which are currently being used in the software industries for creating different applications. Some of the high-level programming languages include C, C++, Java, Visual basic, FORTRAN, COBOL, etc. In this text book, we discuss computer programming using 'C and C++'.

C programming language is designed by Dennis Ritche in 1973 and C++ is designed by Bjarne Stroustrup in 1980 as an extension of C. Both C and C++ are designed in AT&T Bell Laboratories. C++ is an extension of the 'C' language, which means that all the features supported by 'C' are also supported by C++. Furthermore, C++ adds many useful features such as object orientation and template management, which are not supported by 'C'.

What is the difference between Assembly Language and Machine Language? **?**

Processor (CPU) is an integrated circuit that responds to a specific set of instructions. Instruction set for any processor is packaged along with its release and can be understood referring to hardware manuals of the processor. The instruction set of any processor is very much coupled and dependent on its internal circuitry. Every CPU has an instruction decoder which decodes the input instruction and passes it to the relevant architectural blocks for activating necessary hardware components to generate required results. Since an instruction needs to be ultimately decoded and executed by hardware, it must have a representation in binary form **(in the form of zeroes and one's)**. This language of zeroes and one's which is directly executed by the processor is called as **machine language or Binary language**.

It is technically impossible for Human beings to communicate with processor directly using machine language. Hence any release of processor is also packaged with the mnemonics to each of the instructions it supports. These mnemonics are readable by human beings and is called as the assembly language of a particular processor. Remember, since the mnemonics are English like symbols, they cannot be passed directly to the hardware. It is the responsibility of system programmers to design an assembler which can convert assembly language into machine language. Assembler is a software utility and it is packaged along the system programs required to compile and execute any High Level language.

In practice, both Assembly and machine languages are categorized as Low Level Languages from **Application programmers perspective**.

ROADMAP OF THE BOOK

This text book is divided into two parts

Part 1: Chapters 1 to 9 are the topics, which are common with C and C++. The programs given in these chapters will work with both C as well as C++ compilers unless specified otherwise. Chapter 10 gives an explanation on dynamic memory allocation in C++ style. This feature is also supported by C but this book explains C++ notations.

Part 2: Chapters 11 to 17 explain additional features, which are only supported by C++ and not by C. These are object-oriented features, which are not supported by C, hence the programs given in Chapters 11 to 17 will only work with C++ compiler.

It is impossible for a reader to understand the features of object orientation without having a thorough knowledge of structured programming, hence we should be extra careful when reading Chapters 1 to 10 as they become the prerequisite for Chapters 11 to 17.

NOTES

We have been saying that assembly and machine languages are very complex and it is practically impossible for a programmer to use these languages for application programming. Whilst this statement is very true, the *portability of programs* is another big problem in these languages. This is because assembly and machine languages are specific to a particular processor. For example, the assembly/machine language of an intel processor is very different from that of an AMD processor. Hence, even if we manage to write a program in assembly/machine language, our program may only be specific to our own platform and it cannot work if the hardware of the system is changed. It is absolutely not a good practice to design programs, which are very much dependent on hardware, because computer hardware often gets upgraded with technology improvements. It should not happen that the program runs well on current system and fails after processor or hardware/operating system is upgraded or changed. C/C++ programs do not have a direct dependency on platform (hardware/operating system), once designed they could run on different platforms without major changes. We have used the phrase 'without major changes' because C/C++ is not fully platform independent, there are changes that programmer has to make the program while migrating the program from one platform to another. Note that C/C++ programs are just *platform dependent* and not *hardware dependent*; intermediate system programs such as operating system, compilers, loaders, and linkers make a cohesive architecture so that C/C++ programs can run on any hardware with almost no change in the code as shown in Figure 1.4. Because of the additional layer introduced by operating system, loaders, compilers, linkers (in general called as a *layer of system programs*), we can be sure of the fact that the C/C++ programs we create can run without any changes when just hardware of the system is changed or upgraded. This layered architecture gives hardware independence *to application programs*. Now the next question is, What if there are any changes in the system program? For example, what if we decide to change our operating system from windows to Linux? This is called as a change in platform and in this case, we are not sure that a C/C++ program which runs on a windows platform will also run on Linux. This is because the C/C++ compiler for windows is different than that of Linux. So, in practice, we will also have to change the compiler if we change the platform. Clearly, C/C++ languages have removed the hardware dependency on the programs but not the platform dependency and this is because compiler is different for different platforms. Whilst platform dependency remains one of the challenges with C/C++ programs, it is also a settled situation in software industries that platforms are not changed very often. Hence, C/C++ languages are still used at an extensive scale in the world of application development. In this discussion, we have mentioned names of some system programs such as loaders and linkers and we will debrief about them in section 1.3, for now just understand that these are some of the system programs which help to keep our code independent of the underlying hardware.

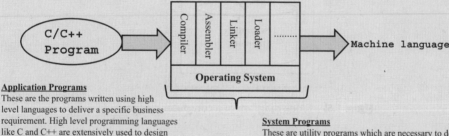

Application Programs
These are the programs written using high level languages to deliver a specific business requirement. High level programming languages like C and C++ are extensively used to design application programs.
These applications designed by programmers are used by business users who may not have any technical expertise. Few examples of Application programs are program for online shopping used to design an online shopping website, a banking program used to perform banking transactions online, online railway reservation system used over the web, web site for booking movie tickets etc. Application programs need not be always **web based**, they can also be **Desktop applications** like Microsoft paint, Microsoft office, desktop games etc. All these applications are designed in some high level programming languages like C/C++. A web based program is a program which can be accessed over internet without a need of any prior installation whereas a desktop application is always accessed locally and needs to be installed on the machine before it can be used. All applications designed in this book are desktop based applications.

System Programs
These are utility programs which are necessary to develop and execute application programs. For example, operating system, compiler, assembler, loader, linker, etc.
Some of programs are tightly coupled with the hardware of the system and hence you must have knowledge about system hardware and configuration before you could design such programs
The scope of this text book is to learn application programming using C/C++. Design of system programs is out of scope of this text book, we may mention about them as and when needed to understand certain application programming concepts though.

Figure 1.4: Layered architecture of application program, system programs, and computer hardware

1.2 Computer System Architecture

Before deep diving into the intricacies of C/C++ programming, we need to first understand the general flow of data and instruction in a computer system. Figure 1.5 shows the basic building blocks of a system, which consist of the following units:

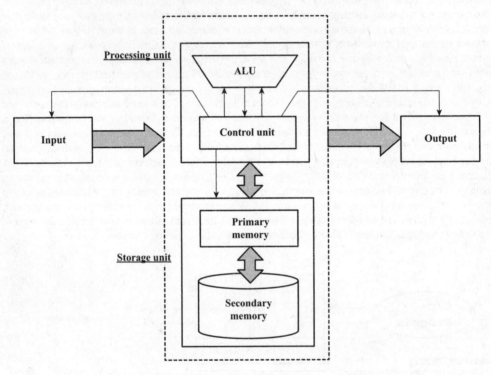

Figure 1.5: Block diagram of a computer system

1. Input unit
2. Processing unit
3. Output unit
4. Storage unit

1.2.1 Input to the system

'Data' and 'instructions' are given as input to the system so as to perform a particular operation. Here, the term 'instruction' represents the operation to be performed, whereas the term 'data' represents the information over which an operation is to be performed. For example, if we want the system to perform the addition of two numbers say x and y then we could write a statement as shown below:

$$x + y$$

The symbol + in this case, will be translated into an instruction ADD which will inform the underlying hardware to actually perform the addition of two numbers. The numbers x and y represent the 'data' over which the instruction ADD operates to generate the required output. We can give multiple instructions as input to the system, so as to get a consolidated result. Let us consider that we want the computer system to give us a result of sequence of instructions say I1, I2, ..., In which operate on a series of data values d1, d2, ..., dn, respectively as shown in Figure 1.6. These instructions can be stored in the file and can further be processed by the CPU thereby giving the required result as an output.

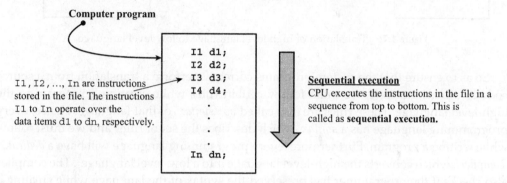

Figure 1.6: Computer program

The sequence of instructions that the system can process so as to generate the required output is called as *program* and the language in which a program can be written is called as a *computer programming language*. Although, we can write multiple instructions in a single file, the CPU can only process one instruction at a time. Hence, in reality, the processor runs just one instruction at a time in a sequence from first to last until all the instructions present in the file are fully executed.

This process of executing instructions in a file one by one is called as *sequential execution*.

1.2.2 Translation

As the hardware of a computer system is ultimately built up of electronic and semiconductor devices, it can only understand a binary language of 0's and 1's. However, it is impossible for us to write programs in machine language as this will involve a detailed study on the circuitry over which the system is built upon. In addition, as the fabrication of the machine changes, every machine will have a different machine language. This is because every machine is built up using different hardware technologies and circuitry. In summary, we do not understand machine language and machine does not understand the language we speak. This means that there is a need of a translator that can translate the 'human language' into the 'machine language'. The language that we can understand is called as high-level language whereas the language that only machines understand is called as a low-level language.

The set of programs that perform a translation of high-level language into a low-level language are called as *system programs*. The system programs take the high-level code (also called as source code) as input and generate an equivalent machine code at the output, as shown in Figure 1.7. The language compilers, assemblers, loader, linkers, etc. are examples of system programs, which are involved in translation of source code to machine code.

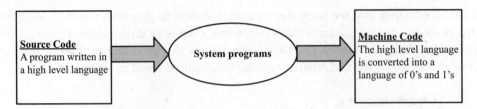

Figure 1.7: Translation of high level language to low level language

So as to ensure that the system programs correctly perform a translation from a source code to a machine code, we must follow certain rules while creating a program in the high-level language. These rules are also called as *'syntax'* of that language. Hence, every programming language has a *syntax*, which describes the set of rules and we must follow while writing a program. Furthermore, every programming language will have a *dedicated 'compiler'*, which converts the high-level language into a low-level language[1]. The compiler also checks if the programmer has preserved the syntax of the language while creating a program before it starts the translation process. The compiler will throw an 'error' message to the programmer if any of the syntax rules are violated, and the translation process is immediately terminated if at least one error is located in the input program. Hence, it becomes easy for the programmer to apply necessary corrections to the code and restart the compilation process after necessary fixes have been applied.

1.2.3 Processing unit

After the high-level language is translated into a language of 0's and 1's, the machine starts running each instruction one by one, so as to generate required output. The processing stage is called as *'execution stage'* of the program. Of course, the output of the code will be generated at the time when the code is under execution and not at the time when the code is getting translated or compiled. The process of translation or compilation just converts the program from one language to another while the process of execution actually runs the program thereby generating the results on output device. It is ultimately the hardware that performs the execution of the program. The hardware that executes the instructions written in the program one by one is called as *'processing unit'* of the computer system. The processing unit consists of two major blocks in it:

1. Arithmetic and logical unit (ALU)
2. Control unit

The ALU performs all the arithmetic and logical operations on the input data whereas the control unit is a circuitry that manages and controls the overall flow of data and instructions within the computer system. The control unit also consists of a set of decoders that can

---

[1] The output of compilation process is called as a target code. The target code differs from language to language as every language has its own compiler. The output of C/C++ compiler is called as object code which is a low level language.

understand the input instruction; it also passes the data to the ALU if the execution of the instruction requires any arithmetic or logical operation to be performed. The unit is responsible for reading the data and instructions from the 'input' devices, processing the instructions and sending the final results to the 'output' device so as to generate the output of the program.

1.2.4 Storage unit

The storage unit comprises of the memory devices, which are present in the computer system where instructions and data are stored. The area of the memory where instructions of the program are stored is called as a *'code segment'* whereas the area of the memory where the data required for the program is stored is called as a *'data segment'*. These memory segments are managed by the memory management unit (MMU) of the operating system in the primary memory of the computer system. In general, the memory units of a computer system are categorized as follows:

1. Primary memory (e.g. RAM)
2. Secondary memory (e.g. hard disk)

Hard disk or a secondary memory is generally a magnetic memory that stores the information persistently. The primary memory or RAM is a semiconductor memory that can store the information only for the time when the computer is powered ON. This means that RAM cannot store any information when the system is switched off and hence RAM is a 'volatile memory whereas a hard disk can store the information persistently even if the power is lost, therefore, hard disk as a 'non-volatile' memory.

Processor can directly access the data and information only if it is available in RAM, this is because CPU is also a semiconductor device, which is a very large-scale integrated circuitry (often abbreviated as VLSI). Hence, it is the duty of the MMU (unit part of operating system) to get the necessary data and information from hard disk to RAM when needed for CPU to access it, as shown in Figure 1.8. The transfer of information content from secondary memory to primary memory is also controlled by the MMU. The key point to note is that any program can be executed by the CPU if only the code and data referred by the program are brought into RAM.

When we 'open' any file for read or write operation, the file is actually copied from the hard disk to RAM by the operating system. This facilitates the CPU to directly access the data and instructions stored in the file. Once the MMU brings the file into the primary memory, CPU can then perform read /write operations on the file as shown in Figure 1.9. Therefore, once the file is opened, there are two copies of the file maintained in the system. The first copy of the file is in RAM whereas the second copy of the file is the original file present in the hard disk as shown in Figure 1.9.

When CPU writes any information only the file in RAM will be modified whereas the copy of the file in the hard disk will still represent an older version as shown in Figure 1.10. Hence, this is a state where the data in RAM is modified; however, the file in hard disk is stale. Such a write operation to a file is called as 'uncommitted' (or 'unsaved') write operation, which is performed by the CPU as shown in Figure 1.10.

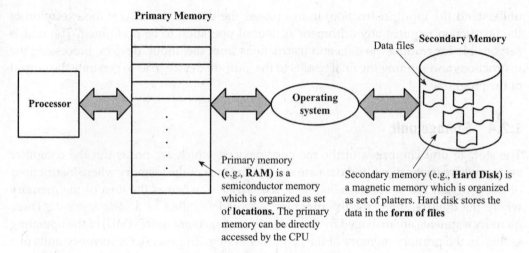

Primary memory (e.g., **RAM**) is a semiconductor memory which is organized as set of **locations**. The primary memory can be directly accessed by the CPU

Secondary memory (e.g., **Hard Disk**) is a magnetic memory which is organized as set of platters. Hard disk stores the data in the **form of files**

Figure 1.8: CPU accessing RAM

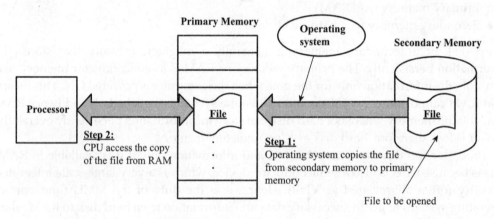

Step 2:
CPU access the copy of the file from RAM

Step 1:
Operating system copies the file from secondary memory to primary memory

File to be opened

Figure 1.9: CPU accessing the file

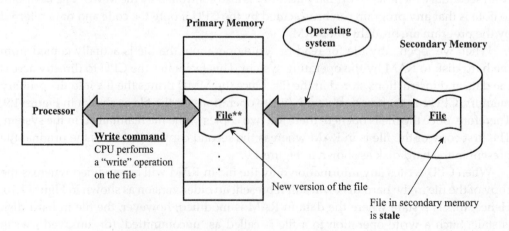

Write command
CPU performs a "write" operation on the file

New version of the file

File in secondary memory is **stale**

Figure 1.10: Uncommitted writes done to the file

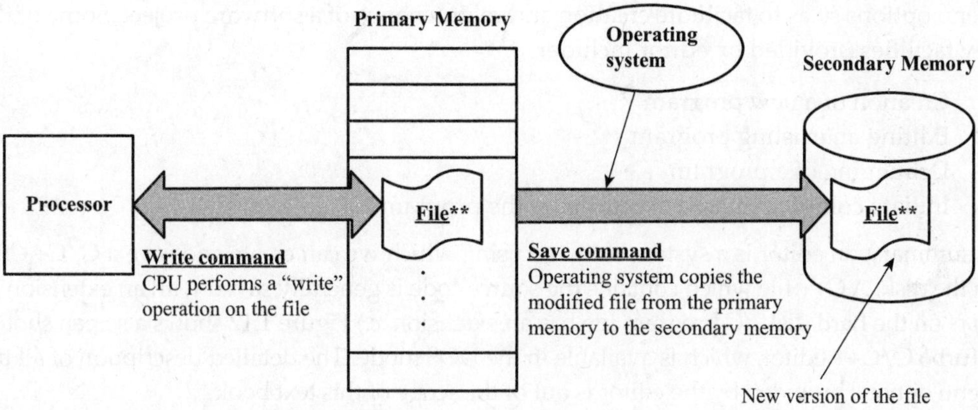

Figure 1.11: Saving the file

When we save the file using 'save' command (a command of operating system) operating system copies the file from RAM back to the hard disk. This ensures that the file in hard disk gets modified with the recent data as shown in Figure 1.11. Therefore, when we open the file next time, new changes will be reflected in the file. However, if we do not 'save' the file, which was modified by the CPU in the RAM space then any changes made to the file in RAM will not be copied to the hard disk and hence the file in the hard disk will not be modified. Therefore, when we 'open' the file next time, we will see the older version of the file. This means that all the uncommitted writes to the file will be lost as the file in the hard disk was never modified with the updates made by the CPU in RAM. In summary, every program that is 'opened' for execution at a particular instant of time must be brought into the RAM space; whereas, every program that is 'inactive' or 'closed' can be presented in the secondary memory or hard disk. Therefore, a hard disk memory is typically very large in size when compared to the RAM space of the computer system (the size of the hard disk is specified in Giga bytes whereas the size of RAM is specified in megabytes as a part of computer system configuration).

1.3   C/C++ Development Environment

So as to fully translate the high-level language into the machine language every C/C++ program has to go through the set of system programs before the machine can execute the code to generate the required output. The list of system programs involved in the process of translating the high-level language into a low-level language is as given below:

1. Editor
2. Pre-processor
3. Compiler
4. Linker
5. Loader

1.3.1   Editor

Editor provides an integrated development environment (IDE) to create and develop a C/C++ program. An editor is a system program that provides the programmer with multiple menu options so as to facilitate creation and maintenance of a software project. Some of the key facilities provided by editor include:

1. Creation of a new program
2. Editing an existing program
3. Debugging of a program
4. Initiate compilation and execution of the program

In summary, an editor is a system software using which we can create and save a C/C++ file on the disk. A C++ file which contains the source code is generally saved with an extension as '.cpp' on the hard disk. (C program file has an extension .c.) Figure 1.12 shows a screen shot of a Turbo C/C++ editor, which is available in the DOS mode. The detailed description of all the menu options provided by the editor is out of the scope of this text book.

Figure 1.12: Turbo C/C++ editor screen

1.3.2 Pre-processor

We can give an abbreviation for group of instructions to be executed in a C/C++ program. Such an abbreviation is called as a *macro*. The macro facility enables us to attach a name with the sequence of instructions, which are to be executed repeatedly in the program. The advantage of such naming is that we can now use a name of a macro each time we need to execute the sequence of instructions instead of actually typing the same instructions again and again in the program.

A *macro pre-processor* is a system program that resolves the macro references by substituting a 'macro name' with its 'definition'. All the macro references made by the programmer in the source code will actually be substituted by the sequence of instructions and the data which are defined by the macro. The pre-processor runs just before the compilation of the program starts. Hence, the compiler will not see any abbreviations or macros because they would already be expanded by pre-processor before the compilation of the code kicks off. The pre-processor creates a file without macros on the disk which is used by the compiler for the translation of the code as shown in Figure 1.13.

The instructions within the program that are understood by the pre-processor are called as *pre-processor directives*. The pre-processor directives are generally prefixed by a symbol # in C/C++. Some of the pre-processor directives are:

1. #include – The directive is used to include a header file in the C/C++ program.
2. #define – The pre-processor directive is used to define macros in the C/C++ program.

We will discuss the details of these directives in Chapter 2 of this text book.

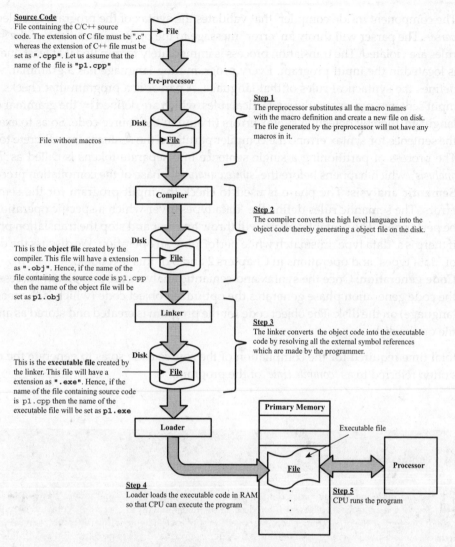

Source Code
File containing the C/C++ source code. The extension of C file must be ".c" whereas the extension of C++ file must be set as **".cpp"**. Let us assume that the name of the file is **"p1.cpp"**

File

Pre-processor

Disk

File without macros ──── **File**

Step 1
The preprocessor substitutes all the macro names with the macro definition and create a new file on disk. The file generated by the preprocessor will not have any macros in it.

Compiler

Disk

This is the **object file** created by the compiler. This file will have a extension as **".obj"**. Hence, if the name of the file containing the source code is p1.cpp then the name of the object file will be set as **p1.obj**

File

Step 2
The compiler converts the high level language into the object code thereby generating a object file on the disk.

Linker

Disk

This is the **executable file** created by the linker. This file will have a extension as **".exe"**. Hence, if the name of the file containing source code is p1.cpp then the name of the executable file will be set as **p1.exe**

File

Step 3
The linker converts the object code into the executable code by resolving all the external symbol references which are made by the programmer.

Loader

Primary Memory

Executable file

File

Processor

Step 4
Loader loads the executable code in RAM so that CPU can execute the program

Step 5
CPU runs the program

Figure 1.13: C/C++ development environment

1.3.3 Compiler

The compiler is a system program that converts the source code into the machine language. The machine language is also called as an object code, which is generated as an output of the compilation process. The compiler generates an '*.obj*' file on the disk after the successful compilation of the source code as shown in Figure 1.13. There are three major tasks, which are performed on the source code as a part of compilation process. These are the key phases of the compilation process and they are as explained below:

1. **Syntax analysis:** Program can be translated into the machine code only if the source code written by the programmer does not violate any of the syntactical rules defined by the language. The syntax phase is used to check if the syntax of the source code is correct.

The component inside compiler that validates the syntax of the program is called as a *parser*. The parser will throw an 'error' message to the programmer if any of the syntax rules are violated. The translation process is immediately terminated if at least one error is located in the input program. Every programming language has a grammar, which defines the syntactical rules of that language. A parser is a program that checks if the input sentence preservers the syntactical rules, which are defined by the grammar of the language, thereby detecting syntax errors (if any) in the source code. So as to examine the sentence for syntax errors, the compiler partitions the sentence into discrete tokens. The process of partitioning a single sentence into separate tokens is called as '*lexical analysis*', which happens before the '*syntax analysis*' phase of the compilation process.

2. **Semantic analysis:** The phase is used to check the input program for the semantic errors. The semantic rules define the 'data types' over which a specific operation can be performed. The semantic phase will throw an error and stop the translation process if there is a 'data type' mismatch while performing an operation. We discuss the details of 'data types' and operations in Chapters 2 and 3 of this text book.

3. **Code generation:** Once the syntax and semantic analyses are completed successfully, the code generation phase generates the optimized object code (which is the machine language) on the disk. The object code for the program is created and stored as an '*.obj*' file on the disk.

The total time required for the compilation of the source code so as to generate the object file is often referred to as '*compile time*' of the program.

What is Lexical analysis?

Before initiating translation, compiler needs to ensure that the programmer has not violated any of the syntactical rules which are defined by the language. To check the syntax of each of the statements written by the programmer, compiler needs to split each statement into different tokens. A token is a smallest indivisible part of each statement. For example, if value of z is to be calculated as addition of x and y the statement must be written as:

```
z = x+y;
```

This statement has 6 different tokens z , =, x, +, y and ;. Splitting of this statement into different tokens is as shown below.

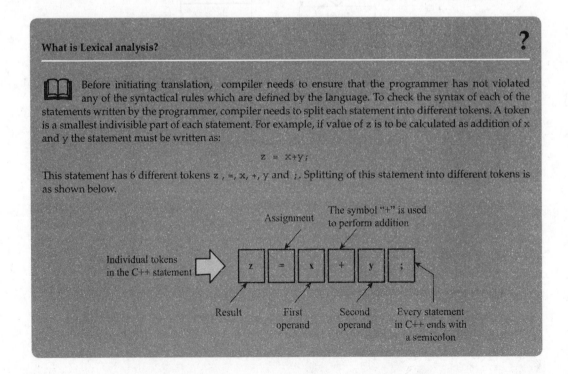

This process of splitting a instruction into set of tokens is called as Lexical analysis. The syntax analysis phase now determines if all the tokens are organized correctly in the statement. The syntax analysis will throw an error if there is any incorrect formation of tokens detected in particular statement. For example, the following statement would result into an compilation error.

z = x y+;

This is because, it organizes the tokens incorrectly according to the syntax defined by the language. The syntax of C/C++ is such that the operator + must be written exactly in between the two operands x and y which are to be added. Compiler does not allow writing the symbol + at the right side (or left side) of both the operands whose values are to be added.

1.3.4 Linker

It is possible that the C/C++ program contains references to functions or data, which are actually defined in the external libraries. These libraries can provide the definitions of the common functions or the data required throughout the development of the project and hence the program may be required to refer to functions and data present in multiple such libraries. Creation and usage of libraries facilitate reusability of the code in the project. The object file generated by the compiler will contain certain 'gaps' due to such external references present in the source code. The *'linker'* is a system program, which links the object code produced by the compiler with the object code for the external libraries by resolving all the external symbol references thereby filling the gaps present in the object file. Once all the external references are resolved, the linker generates an *executable code* (which is named as an '.exe' file) on the disk as shown in the Figure 1.13.

1.3.5 Loader

The linker generates the executable code (.exe file) on the disk. Recall from the section 1.2.4 that CPU cannot make a direct access to the code present in the hard disk. Therefore, the executable code must be first placed in RAM. A loader is the system program that loads the executable code in the main memory of the computer system (in RAM) so that the code can be executed by the CPU.

After the code is loaded into RAM, the processor can start executing the program, thereby generating the output. The time required to execute the 'executable code' of the program is often referred as *'run time'* of the program.

1.4 Evolution of Programming Languages

Along with the growth in hardware systems, the features provided by the programming languages are also being enhanced with time. In general, the computer programming paradigms can be categorized as 'structured programming' and 'object-oriented programming'. The type of the programming style to be used is dependent on the type of the application to be developed. In this section, we understand the difference between a 'structured programming' paradigm and an 'object-oriented programming' paradigm.

1.4.1 Structured programming (supported by both C and C++)

Structured programming is also referred to as modular programming or procedural programming where the program to be developed is organized into different procedures. Each of the modules defined in the program is called as a *function* or a *procedure*. A structured programming paradigm solves a large problem by dividing the problem into small pieces known as functions. Each of the small pieces are considered as different problems and solved independently by writing different functions. The results produced by each of the small functions are consolidated at the end, so as to derive the solution for the large problem. For example, let us consider that we need to create a program to sort 100 numbers stored in a file in an ascending order. The structured programming may divide the large problem statement into the following functions:

1. Function to read the 100 numbers from the file.
2. Function to arrange the numbers in the ascending order.
3. Function to write the result back to the file.

Hence, we have now divided a large problem to sort the data in the file into three different problems as listed above.

In general, the structured programming paradigm divides the large program into different modules based on the 'algorithm' or the 'function' that the module performs. A function A can call another function B if A needs service which is offered by B. For example, if the job of function A is to calculate factorial of a number and job of function B is to perform multiplication, function A would need to call function B multiple times because factorial requires performing multiplication multiple times with different data values. Figure 1.14 shows a typical structured programming behaviour with five functions A, B, C, D and E. Execution flow with functions are explained in detail in Chapter 7, at this stage, we just define structured programming as a collection of different building blocks called as functions such that each function is dedicated to perform a specific operation. We will just note a few points about function calls at this stage:

1. After the 'called function' completes its execution, the control is 'returned' to the calling function. For example, function A calls function B and after function B completes the control is returned to function A. Similarly, D calls E and hence after E completes, the control is returned to D.

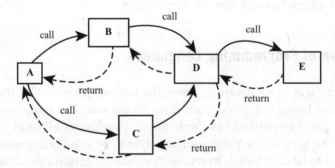

Figure 1.14: Structured programming

2. Function calls are always handled sequentially. This means that, if function A calls two functions B and C, they will be executed one by one depending on which is called first. If B is called before C, B will be executed before C.

3. All called functions complete before the execution of calling function can complete. In this example, function B calls D and D further calls E, this means that D will complete only after E completes and B will complete only after D completes.

4. The structure given below has two branches of function execution:

$$A \rightarrow B \rightarrow D \rightarrow E$$
$$A \rightarrow C \rightarrow D \rightarrow E$$

The function A completes its execution only when execution of both the mentioned branches completes. Here, we assume A calls B before calling C and hence the branch A → B → D → E is executed before A → C → D → E.

Calling function can pass values to the called function. These values passed from 'calling' function to the 'called' function are called as *parameters* or *arguments*. On the other hand, the 'called' function can also return the result of operation to the 'calling' function. This value which is returned from the 'called' function to the 'calling' function is called as *return value*. Parameter-passing and return values are very useful when the results produced by one function are required by some other function so as to perform the required set of operations to solve a given problem.

One of the major drawbacks of a structured programming paradigm is that the maintenance and support of the code becomes difficult as the size of the code increases. Hence, in many cases, 'object-oriented programming' is preferred over structured programming because the object orientation facilitates much better organization of the code thereby making the program easy to maintain and support. The 'C' programming language is an example of a structured programming paradigm whereas C++ supports many additional object-oriented features along with supporting structured programming features.

1.4.2 Object-oriented programming (only in C++)

Many applications and software systems to be developed require to operate with complex data elements such that each of the data elements in the program simulates one object in the real world. Object-oriented programming paradigm is an approach of programming that can correctly simulate a real world, such that one 'object' created in the program represents the data about one entity in the real world. C++ supports object orientation by allowing the creation of 'classes' in the C++ program. Unlike the concept of structured programming, the object orientation gives an emphasis on the 'data' on which the functions operate on rather than the 'algorithm' of the functions. Object-oriented program is organized as a set of 'classes', such that each class combines related 'data' elements and the 'functions' that operate on these data elements. In summary, a class is a combination of 'data' and related 'functions' into a single unit.

As an example, if we consider the development of a website for a particular educational institute, we will be required to maintain data about the following real world objects:

1. Students studying in the institute
2. Professors in the institute

3. Courses offered by the institute
4. Departments of the institute, etc.

So as to store the data about these real world entities, we can create different classes in the C++ program such that each of the class combines the 'data' and 'functions' required to manage the information about one entity in the real world as shown in Figure 1.15. Hence, we can create classes named as `Student`, `Professor`, `Course` and `Department` so as to store representing each of the respective real world entities.

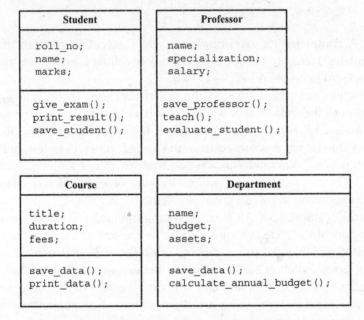

Figure 1.15: Example of classes in C++

Note that, each class combines related 'data' and 'functions' together. For example, the class `Student` contains the data elements named as `roll_no`, name and `marks` which indicates that for every student in the institute we will be storing the roll number, name and marks of the student object in computer memory. Further, the functions defined in class `Student` represent the operations that a student object can perform in the real world. The function `save_student()` indicates that the student object can save his/her details online by registering on the website of the institute. The presence of the function `give_exam()` in the class Student indicates that the student in the real world can appear for an online exam which is deployed on the web site of the educational institute and the function `print_result()` indicates that student can take a printout of his/her result, which prints the marks obtained by the student in the online examination. Similarly, we can imagine the meaning of data and functions which we have shown in other classes as shown in Figure 1.15.

The object-oriented program organizes the code based on the 'data' and hence it makes the large programs easy to maintain and support. The details of object-oriented programming paradigm along with its features are discussed in Chapters 11 to 14 of this text book. The key features of the object-oriented programming paradigm are as listed below. We have just given one liners for each of these features, however, understanding these features is understanding object-oriented programming. They are quite vast to explain in the first chapter, we will find each of these features explained in detail along with the real world examples throughout from Chapters 11 to 17. At this point, we would not worry about them much other than just the core definitions.

1. **Abstraction:** It is an ability of the program to hide the logical complexities and only reveals the necessary details to the programmer to progress with the software development. This feature is discussed in detail in Chapter 11.
2. **Message passing:** It is an ability of the object-oriented program to facilitate communication between different objects by passing data values (also called as messages) to each other. This feature is discussed in detail in Chapter 11.
3. **Polymorphism:** It is an ability of an operator or a variable to take multiple forms. This feature is discussed in detail in Chapters 11, 12, 13 and 14.
4. **Data hiding:** It is to ensure that critical data items in the program are secured from accidental updates. Such critical data variables belonging to a business object can be made private to a class and they are hidden from outside world to avoid any updates to these items. This feature is discussed in detail in Chapter 11.
5. **Encapsulation:** The process of wrapping variables and related functions is called as encapsulation to access these variables in a single logical unit called as a class. This feature is discussed in detail in Chapter 11.
6. **Inheritance:** A parent–child relationship between classes such that selective features of parent class are made available to child class to facilitate the reusability of the code is called as inheritance. Child class can define additional features of its own and by default inherit all the features from its parent classes. This feature is discussed in detail in Chapter 14.

Quiz

1. Which of the following is done before compilation?
   (a) Translation of source code to object code
   (b) Linking
   (c) Loading
   (d) Macro substitution
   (e) None of the mentioned options.
2. Which of the following statements are true?
   (a) Compiler generates output of the program as the result of the compilation process
   (b) Linker transfers the machine code from secondary memory to primary memory
   (c) Loader transfers the machine code from primary memory to secondary memory
   (d) Pre-processing happens after the code is compiled
   (e) None of the above statements are true
3. Assembler generates _____ language as its output.
   (a) Language of mnemonics
   (b) High-level language
   (c) Machine language
   (d) Middle-level language
4. Which of the following is not the function of compiler?
   (a) Syntax analysis
   (b) Lexical analysis
   (c) Semantic analysis
   (d) Code generation
   (e) Resolving external symbol references

5. Structured programming is a way to organize program as collection of _____.
   (a) Classes
   (b) Objects
   (c) Functions
   (d) Structures
6. Wrapping of data and related functions together is called as
   (a) Data hiding
   (b) Encapsulation
   (c) Inheritance
   (d) None of the mentioned options.
7. Inheritance facilitates
   (a) Data hiding
   (b) Security to the code
   (c) Reusability of the code
   (d) Modular programming
8. Which of the following statements is true
   (a) C/C++ programs are hardware dependent
   (b) C/C++ programs are operating system independent
   (c) C/C++ programs are operating system dependent and hence they cannot execute cross platforms
   (d) C/C++ programs are hardware and processor independent
9. Object-oriented features are supported by:
   (a) Both C and C++
   (b) Only by C
   (c) Only by C++
   (d) Neither by C nor by C++
10. Opcode represents
    (a) Operations performed by the instruction
    (b) Data used by instruction
    (c) Both A and B
    (d) None of the above
11. Which of the following statements is true
    (a) Calling function may complete before called function
    (b) Called function may complete before calling function
    (c) Called function always completes before calling function
    (d) Called function and calling function completes at the same time
    (e) Function calls are resolved sequentially
12. Program written in which language is easy to maintain?
    (a) Machine language
    (b) Assembly language
    (c) High level language

Review Questions

1. What is the difference between the structured programming and the object-oriented programming?
2. Write a short note on the functions performed by the compiler.
3. Explain the C/C++ development environment in detail. Give the functions of each of the system programs involved in the translation of C/C++ into a machine code.
4. Explain the difference between system programs and application programs with appropriate examples of each type.
5. Write a short note on object-oriented programming paradigm. List different properties of object-oriented programming in C++.
6. Explain the difference between compile time and run time of the program?

2 Fundamentals

2.1 Overview

C++ is an extension of C. This means that all the features of C are also available in C++. Furthermore, C++ has certain additional features of object-oriented programming, which makes it superior to the conventional C language. The details of object orientation and other features of C++ are covered in the later chapters of this text book.

In this chapter, we will study some fundamentals, which build the foundation to understand the advanced features of C and various object-oriented features supported by C++.

2.2 The First C/C++ Program

Recall from Chapter 1 that every C/C++ program has to be compiled and linked so as to convert the high-level language into the machine code. All the instructions written in the program are executed one-by-one by the processor in a sequence as they appear in the program file. Therefore, it is the job of the programmer to inform the processor about the exact starting point from which the execution of the program should begin. The main() function in C/C++ is used to represent the start and end points of the program execution. Hence, every program must have exactly one main() function, which is shown in Figure 2.1.

CPU will execute all the instructions where we write inside the body of the main() function in a sequence as they appear. The presence of empty round parenthesis after a special word main() informs the compiler that the function main() does not take any arguments. By default, every function in C/C++ is expected to return a value to the one who invokes the function. We can use a keyword void if we do not want to return any value to the calling function. The complete details of functions with arguments and return values are discussed in Chapter 7 of this text book and hence the details about 'function arguments' and 'return types' can be ignored at this point of time.

At this stage, we need to understand that a main() function is to be created using a template shown in Figure 2.1. The function main() defines the 'start point' and the 'end point' of the program, as the execution of any program starts from a point where the main() function begins and the execution of the program terminates at a point where the `main()` function ends. The opening and closing of the curly brackets are used to represent the start and end of the `main()` function as shown in Figure 2.1.

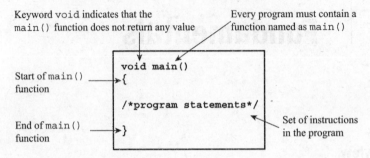

Figure 2.1: Template for creating the `main()` function

As an example, let us create a first program that prints a text message on the computer screen. Figure 2.2 gives the full source code to print a text message I like Computer Programming on the computer screen.

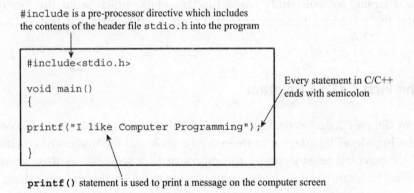

Figure 2.2: Source code to print a message on the computer screen

The statement

```
printf("I like Computer Programming");
```

is used to print a message I like Computer Programming on the computer screen. `printf()` is a built-in function available in C as well as C++ and this function is declared in the header file `stdio.h`. Therefore, we have written the first statement of the program as,

```
#include<stdio.h>
```

The statement includes the contents of the header file `stdio.h` into the program, so as to facilitate the programmer to call (or use) the built-in function `printf()` directly within the program. Recall from Chapter 1, `#include` is a pre-processor directive, which is used to include the contents of a particular header file into the program before the compilation of the code starts. This ensures that the complete declaration of `printf()` is included in the program before the compiler starts compiling the code.

As stated before, execution of any program always starts from `main()` function. Given that this program has only one statement in the `main()` function (which is the `printf()` statement), the output of the program is shown below.

```
I like Computer Programming
```

NOTE: Following is applicable to C++ and not to C

The program shown in Figure 2.2 executes in C as well as C++. This is because the `printf()` function is supported by both the languages. Along with support to `printf()` statement, C++ supports another way to print a message on the computer screen. `cout` is a built-in object available in C++ but not in C, which is used to stream messages on an output device. The program written in Figure 2.3 shows the usage of `cout` object to print the message on the computer screen.

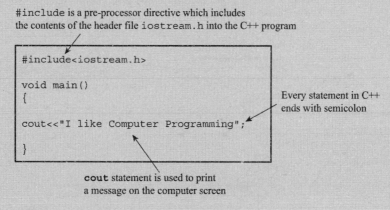

`#include` is a pre-processor directive which includes the contents of the header file `iostream.h` into the C++ program

```
#include<iostream.h>

void main()
{

cout<<"I like Computer Programming";

}
```

Every statement in C++ ends with semicolon

`cout` statement is used to print a message on the computer screen

Figure 2.3: Source code to print a message on the computer screen

The statement

```
cout<<"I like Computer Programming";
```

is used to print a message `I like Computer Programming` on the computer screen. Note that every statement ends with a semicolon. The operator `<<` is called as an *insertion operator*, which actually inserts a text message on the computer screen. We have also explained in Chapter 4 of this text book that the operator `<<` is also used as 'left shift operator', which can be used to shift the bits of a binary number in the left direction. However, in this case, we have used the operator `<<`, which acts as an insertion operator and prints a message on the screen because it is internally overloaded by C++ in one of the built-in classes which is named as ostream. The class `ostream` is fully defined inside the header file `iostream.h`. Also, `cout` is an object of class `ostream`, which is created inside the file `iostream.h`. Therefore, we have written the first statement of the C++ program as,

```
#include<iostream.h>
```

The statement includes the contents of the header file `iostream.h` into the program, so as to facilitate the programmer to use the built-in object of class `ostream`, which is named as `cout` directly in the code. Remember, `#include` is a pre-processor directive, which is used to include the contents of a particular header file into the C++ program before the compilation of the code starts. This ensures that the complete definition of the class `ostream` and the insertion operator `<<` is included in the program before the compilation. Details about classes and objects are discussed in Chapter 11 of this text book. *The only point we must understand at this stage is that the statement*

```
cout<<"I like Computer Programming";
```

is used to print a message as `I like Computer Programming` *on the computer screen as shown in Figure 2.4. And we must include the contents of header file* `iostream.h` *before making use of* `cout` *in our program.*

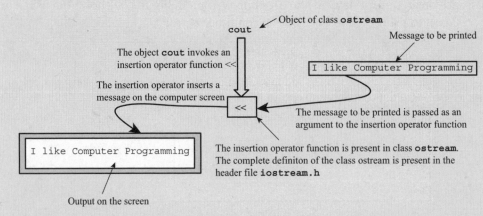

Figure 2.4: Usage of `cout`

C++ supports *streaming outputs*, which are not supported by C. In general, the word stream refers to the flow of data in the computer system. The *'output stream'* of C++ allows the programmer to perform a 'write' operation on the output devices such as 'screen', 'file', and 'disk'. The header file `iostream.h` defines the necessary classes and functions to support the streaming input and output. We will discuss the *input streams* of C++ in the later sections of this chapter. As we have written the `cout` instruction inside the main function, the processor will now execute the instruction after translating the instruction into a machine code, thereby printing a message specified on the computer screen as seen in the output of the program.

NOTES

The program given in Figure 2.2 uses `printf()` statement to print a message on the computer screen. The `printf()` function is declared in header file `stdio.h` which is included in the program. The program using `printf()` works with C as well as C++ because the header file `stdio.h` and `printf()` function are supported by both the languages. However, the program using `cout` shown in Figure 2.3 works with C++ but not with C. This is because the object `cout` and header file `iostream.h` are only supported by C++ and not by C. This clearly means that C++ supports streaming output operations whereas C does not. We will learn more about streams supported by C++ in Chapter 15.

Can I write C/C++ programs in upper case?   **?**

The answer is NO; because C/C++ is a **case sensitive language**. This means that, upper case and lower case characters have different meaning for the language. For example, `printf()` and `PRINTF()` will be considered as two different identifiers by the compiler. `stdio.h` declares the function `printf()` in lower case and hence compiler will not be able to recognize a symbol `PRINTF()`. Therefore, we cannot just write the complete C/C++ program in the upper case, rather we have to preserve the syntax of the language along with the case. Syntax of C/C++ is such that most of the built-in keywords and reserved words are in **lower case**. There are still some built-in macros which are to be written in **upper case**.

2.3   Writing Comments

Comment is a part of the code, which is ignored by the compiler. However, programmers may still write comments in the program to give documentation for the complex logic implemented using a particular piece of code. Although, comments do not contribute in generating the output of the program (comments are not even compiled), it is always recommended to comment the source code wherever possible. This makes the code easy to read and understand if any part of the code is to be referred in future for editing or debugging purpose. There are two different types of commenting styles that can be applied to the program:

1. Single line comments (only supported by C++ and not by C)
2. Multi-line comments (supported by both C and C++)

A single line comment starts with two slash symbols written back to back without any space in between two slash symbols as shown below:

```
// This is a single line comment
```

The compiler will ignore any text that is written within the line after two slash (//) symbols. Note that, a single line comment can be stretched until the end of current line only. This means that, if we wish to write a comment across multiple lines then we must begin each of the lines by the two slash symbols as shown below:

```
// This is the first line of the comment
// This is the second line of the comment
// This is the third line of the comment
```

Along with a support to // symbol for single line comments, compiler also ignores any text which is written in between /* and */ so as to support creation of multiline comments in the program. Hence, we can write a multiline comment in the code, such that, it begins with a token /* and ends with a token */ as shown below:

```
/*This is the first line of the comment
This is the second line of the comment
This is the third line of the comment*/
```

REMEMBER

Single line commenting style is only supported by C++ but not by C

```
//This commenting style is only supported in C++
```

Multi-line commenting style is supported by both C as well as C++

```
/*This commenting style is supported by C as well as C++*/
```

Given below is an example that includes comments in the program that we have created to print a text message on the computer screen.

```
/*This is a program to print a message
I like Computer Programming
on the computer screen*/
#include<stdio.h>
void main()
{
/*The below statement prints the text message on the screen*/
printf("I like Computer Programming");
}
```

Output:

```
I like Computer Programming
```

2.4 Constants or Literals

A constant or a literal is a part of the program that cannot change its value. The constants in C/C++ are classified as:

1. Integer constants
2. Real number constants
3. Character constants
4. String constants

We can directly create/use any of the above constants in the program, so as to perform operations with the constant values. Given below is the description for each of the above categories of constants giving the examples of each type of constant values which are supported by both C and C++.

2.4.1 Integer constants

These are numbers without a decimal point which can be written directly in the program. The integer constants can be positive or negative, without any fractional component present as a part of the constant value.

Given below are some valid and invalid examples of integer constants

```
10   /*This is a VALID integer constant*/
-95  /*This is a VALID integer constant which represents
      a negative  value*/
45.9  /*This is an INVALID integer constant as there is a decimal
      point in the number*/
25,000  /*This is an INVALID integer constant as there is a comma
          used in between the digits of the number*/
```

Note that the integer constants must be written as a combination of digits 0 to 9 in the code without any special characters like comma, space in between the digits.

2.4.2 Real constants

These are numbers with decimal point which can be written directly in the program. A real constant can be positive or negative and can also include a fractional component present as a part of the constant value. *Real* constants are also called as *float* constants or *double* constants in C/C++.

Given below are some valid and invalid examples of real constants.

```
10.5  /*This is a VALID floating point constant*/

−90.832  /*This is a VALID floating point constant*/
25,000.976  /*This is an INVALID floating point constant as there
              is  a comma used in between the digits of the number*/
```

Note that just like integer constants, real constants must be written as a combination of digits 0 to 9 in the code without any special characters like comma, space in between the digits. The real constants may contain exactly one decimal point in between the digits so as to represent a floating point value.

2.4.3 Character constants

A character constant is a single symbol enclosed in the single quotes. Given below are some valid and invalid examples of character constants in C/C++.

```
'e' /*This is a VALID character constant which represents a letter e*/
'1' /*This is a VALID character constant which represents a symbol 1*/
'$' /*This is a VALID character constant which represents a symbol
      dollar*/
' '  /*This is a VALID character constant which represents a blank
      space*/
'10' /*This is an INVALID character constant as it encloses two
      different symbols (1 and 0) within the single quotes*/
'ad' /*This is an INVALID character constant as it encloses two
      different symbols(letters 'a' and 'd') within the single quotes*/
```

Note that '1' is not same as a number 1. In a sense, a '1' represents a character constant whereas a number 1 represents an integer constant. Generally, we use only numbers and not characters in any of the arithmetic operations. For example, the below operation

```
1 + 5
```

will perform the addition of two integer constants 1 and 5, thereby giving a result of the arithmetic operation as 6. However, we would get indifferent results in the program if we perform the arithmetic operations with characters instead of integers. This is because C/C++ maps every character constant with an integer code so as to store the character constant in the computer memory. A unique integer code which is associated with every character constant is called as an *ASCII code* of that character. ASCII stands for **American standard code of information and interchange**. Although we attempt to store a character constant in the memory, C/C++ internally stores the ASCII code corresponding to that character in the memory. Whenever, we attempt to output the character on the screen, the internally stored integer value is converted back to the original character and hence we always get the result in terms of character symbols on the computer screen. Appendix I gives the complete list of ASCII codes for each of the characters relevant to C/C++. As seen from appendix I, the ASCII values of upper case characters from 'A' to 'Z' are 65 to 90, whereas the ASCII values of the lower case characters from 'a' to 'z' are 97 to 122 and the ASCII values for digits from '0' to '9' are 48 to 57, respectively. In all, the ASCII values range from 000 to 127 wherein the remaining ASCII values are assigned for the special characters.

As an example, if we attempt to store an character constant '*b*' in the computer memory, internally a value 98 will be stored which is the ASCII value of character '*b*' as shown in Figure 2.5. Furthermore, if we attempt to print the character value, the code 98 will be converted back into a character constant and then printed on the computer screen. Due to this translation, we always get the output in a character format as shown in Figure 2.5.

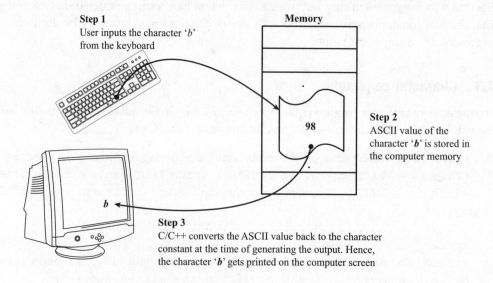

Step 1
User inputs the character '*b*' from the keyboard

Memory

Step 2
ASCII value of the character '*b*' is stored in the computer memory

98

Step 3
C/C++ converts the ASCII value back to the character constant at the time of generating the output. Hence, the character '*b*' gets printed on the computer screen

Figure 2.5: Storing characters in memory

2.4.4 String constants

Collection of characters is called as a string. A string constant is formed by enclosing multiple characters in double quotes.

Given below are some valid and invalid examples of string constants in C/C++

```
"Computer"  /*This is a VALID string constant which is a collection
            of eight characters*/
"C"  /*This is a VALID string constant which contains just a single
     character*/
'com'  /*This is an INVALID string constant. This is because a
       string cannot be enclosed in single quotes*/
"45+6"  /*This is a VALID string constant which is a collection  of
        4 characters*/
```

Every string in C/C++ terminates with a special character called as a NULL character, which is represented by '\0'. For example, the string "Computer" will be internally stored in the memory as shown in Figure 2.6.

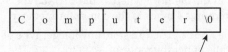

A string always ends with a NULL character \0

Figure 2.6: Memory representation of a string

Note that, the last character of the string is automatically added as '\0', which is the end of the string marker and is called as a NULL character. The details of string constants and their processing are discussed in Chapter 6 of this text book.

Why do we store the ASCII values for character constants in the memory? **?**

Recall from the Chapter 1 that, every symbol written in the high level language must be converted into the machine language before it can be processed by the CPU. Integer or real constants can be directly converted into the machine language by representing them into a "binary number system". So as to facilitate the storage of the character constants in the computer memory, every character constant is internally assigned an integer code which is called as the ASCII value of that character. Hence, we can now store a character constant in the computer memory by simply representing the ASCII code of that character in "binary number system".

2.5 Variables and Data Types

A variable is a place holder for a particular value to be stored in the memory. This means that variable is a reserved area in the computer memory wherein we can store a value. The process of creating a variable is called a '*declaration*' of a variable whereas the process of storing a particular value inside a variable is called as '*initialization*' of the variable.

Every variable is associated with a particular data type. A data type of a variable determines the type of value that can be stored inside the variable. The list of basic data types which are supported by C/C++ is given below:

Data type	Description	Size in bytes[1]	Range of values
int	A variable of type int can store any integer type of constant which falls under the range of −32,768 to +32,767	2 bytes[1]	−32,768 to +32,767
float	A variable of type float can store any number with a decimal point which falls under the range of −3.4e−38 to +3.4e+38	4 bytes	−3.4e−38 to +3.4e+38
char	The data type char is used to store character constant which is single symbol enclosed in the single quotes	1 byte	−128 to +127
double	A variable of type double can store any number with a decimal point which falls under the range of −1.7e−308 to +1.7e+308. This data type has higher precision when compared to float. Hence a double type variable requires 8 bytes in the memory whereas the float type of variable just requires 4 bytes in the computer memory	8 bytes	−1.7e−308 to +1.7e+308
short int	A variable of type short int can store any integer type of constant which falls under the range of −128 to +127. The keywords short int define a smaller version of the int type in C++. Hence, the short int type of variables just requires 1 byte in the computer memory, whereas the int variable actually requires 2 bytes in the computer memory	1 byte	−128 to +127
long	A variable of type long can store any integer type of constant which falls under the range of −2147483648 to +2147483647. The keyword long represents the larger version of the int type in C++. Hence, the long type of variables requires 4 bytes in the computer memory whereas the int variable just requires 2 bytes in the computer memory	4 bytes	−2147483648 to +2147483647

[1] We assume 16 bit compiler throughout this text book where size of an integer is 2 bytes (16 bits). If you get the size of integer as 4 bytes it means you are working on a 32 bit compiler.

2.5.1 Evaluating the range of data types

The range of values which can be stored inside a variable of a particular type is dependent on the size of that 'data type' in the computer memory. The range of a particular data type can be decided by considering the total number of permutations that can be represented by the bit values assigned to the variable. As an example, let us consider an integer type variable which requires 2 bytes in the computer memory. As each byte is formed using eight bits, we can say that an integer variable requires 16 bits in the computer memory. Therefore, the total number of permutations (X) that can be represented using 16 bits can be calculated as shown below:

$$\text{Number of permutations (X)} = 2^{16} = 65,536$$

Out of the total number of states that can be represented using 16 bits, half of the permutations must represent negative numbers in the high-level language and remaining half of the permutations must represent positive numbers in the high-level language. Also, one of the permutations of 16 bits must represent a value zero in the high-level language. Therefore, we divide the total number of permutations by two as shown below:

$$X/2 = 65,536/2 = 32,768$$

As one of the permutations of 16 bits is used to represent zero (this is when all the bit positions become 0), the range of integer constants in C/C++ is $-32,768$ to $+32,767$ as shown in Figure 2.7. This theory is used to convert a number in the high-level language into the machine language thereby storing the machine language in the computer memory as seen in Figure 2.7. The most significant bit (which is the left most bit) represents the sign bit which is 1 when a negative number is translated into the machine language and 0 when a positive number is translated into the machine language.

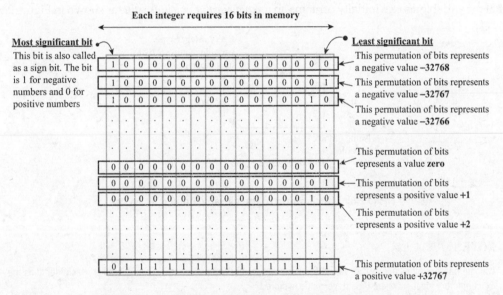

Figure 2.7: Translation of integers into machine language

The range for other data types such as short, long, and char can be calculated using a similar approach. Evaluating the range of floating point types such as double and floats is out of scope of this text book, as it requires a detailed study on IEEE formats in which the mantissa and exponent are internally stored in the computer memory.

What will happen if we give a value to a variable which is out of the range specified by its data type? **?**

This situation is called as overflow/underflow of values. We will not get any compilation error in this case; however program will produce unpredictable results. For example, if we assign a value say 66990 to a 2 byte integer; results produced by the program would be erroneous and unpredictable.

2.5.2 Declaration of variables

As we have mentioned above, a variable creates a place in memory where we can store a value of a particular type. The process of creating a variable in memory is called as *'declaration'* of the variable. Every variable must be declared before it is used in the program. Given below is the syntax to declare a variable in C/C++:

```
<DataType> variableName;
```

For example, the statement

```
int marks;
```

creates an integer type variable named as `marks` in the computer memory. The compiler allocates the memory for the variable when it is declared in the program. Hence, the above statement allocates a memory of 2 bytes for the variable which is named as `marks` as shown in Figure 2.8. Note that the initial value of any variable is *undefined* in C/C++ and hence we say that the variable `marks` initially contains an *unknown value or a junk value* as shown in Figure 2.8.

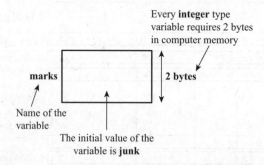

Figure 2.8: Declaration of the variable named as `marks`

NOTES

Variable name is also called as an **identifier**. For example, in this case `marks` is an identifier which identifies the exact memory location where the integer value is stored.

Figure 2.9 gives examples of declaring three variables named as a, b, and c of type integer, float, and character, respectively. As shown in Figure 2.9, the compiler allocates 2 bytes in memory for variable a because it is declared as integer. Whereas, the compiler allocates 4 bytes in memory for variable b because it is declared as float and 1 byte for the variable c because it is declared as character as shown in Figure 2.9. Note that, each of the variables initially contain junk values as shown in Figure 2.9.

If all the variables to be declared are of the same type, then we can also use a *comma operator* as a separator between the variable names so as to create multiple variables using a single C/C++ statement. For example, the below statement creates three different variables named as `marks`, `salary`, and `score` of type `float`:

```
float marks,salary,score;
```

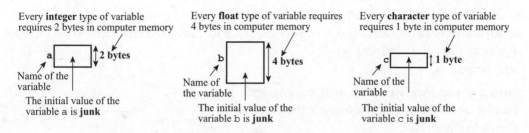

Figure 2.9: Example of declaring three variables a, b and c

2.5.3 Initialization of variables

The process of storing a value inside a variable is called as *initialization* of the variable. Given below is the syntax to initialize a variable with the value returned by the expression.

```
variable-name = expression;
```

Note that, every variable must be declared before it is initialized using the above syntax. The operator = is called as an assignment operator, which is used to initialize a value of the expression to a particular variable. A key point to note here is that the declaration of any variable always happens at the time of compilation of the program whereas the initialization of the variable happens at the time of execution of the program. This means that it is compiler who allocates the memory for the variable which is created in the program; however, the value will actually be stored inside the variable at the time of execution of the program. For example, let us consider the two statements given below:

```
int age; /*Declaration of the variable named as 'age'*/
age=10; /*Initialization of the variable 'age' with a value 10*/
```

The first statement declares a variable named as age, which is of type integer and hence the compiler will allocate 2 bytes for the variable age in the main memory (RAM) of the computer system as shown in Figure 2.10. Furthermore, it is important to note that the variable age will contain junk value at the time of compilation as shown in Figure 2.10.

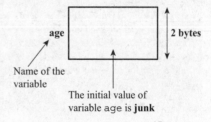

Figure 2.10: Declaration of the variable named as age

The next statement stores the value 10 inside the variable age as shown in Figure 2.11. Note that the constant 10 will be stored inside the variable a at the time when the program executes and not at the time when the program compiles. Therefore, it is important to remember that, the value of any variable will always be unknown to the compiler because every initialization made in the program always happens when the program starts executing.

The variable once declared can be initialized multiple times as and when the program executes. It is important

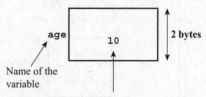

Figure 2.11: Initialization of the variable named as age

to understand that the new value initialized to the variable will overwrite the previous value, which was stored in the variable before. For example, if we initialize a new value to the variable age as 20 using the statement below,

age = 20;

then, the previous value 10 will be lost and the variable age will now store 20 inside the memory as shown in Figure 2.12.

We can also declare and initialize a variable using a single statement with a syntax as given below:

<DataType> variableName = expression;

For example, the below statement declares a variable named as salary of type float and initializes its value to 600.25

float salary = 600.25;

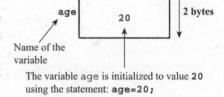

The variable age is initialized to value **20** using the statement: **age=20;**

Figure 2.12: Re-initialization of the variable named as age

Note that although the declaration and initialization of the variable salary are made in the single statement, it is important to recollect that the memory of 4 bytes will be allocated to the variable salary at the time of compilation of the program whereas the value 600.25 will be actually stored in salary when the program executes as shown in Figure 2.13.

Figure 2.14 gives the examples of declaration and initialization statements by creating the variables of type integer, float and character, respectively.

Why are variables not initialized at the time of compilation of the program? **?**

Recall from the Chapter 1 that, compiler is a system program that translates the source code into the machine code. The compiler does not perform any operations like "addition", "subtraction" or even "assignment" which we specify in the program. It is important to understand that compiler does not perform execution and hence compiler does not give us the output of the program. Rather, a compiler is just a translator that translates the program from one language to another. The operations specified in the program are actually performed when the CPU executes the program. As, the compiler does not perform any operations, it does not initialize the values of the variables. Compiler allocates the memory for the variables which are defined by the programmer whereas the value of each of the variables is initialized by the CPU at run time of the program.

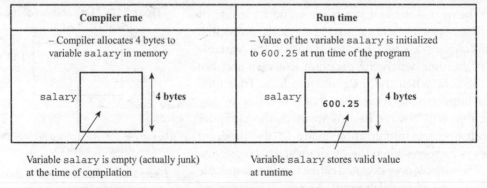

Compiler time	Run time
– Compiler allocates 4 bytes to variable salary in memory	– Value of the variable salary is initialized to 600.25 at run time of the program
Variable salary is empty (actually junk) at the time of compilation	Variable salary stores valid value at runtime

Figure 2.13: Declaration and initialization of the variable salary

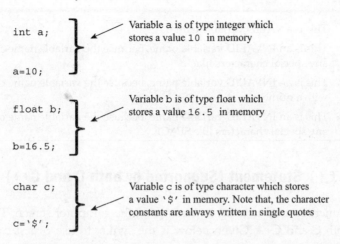

Figure 2.14: Sample declaration and initialization statements

2.5.4 *unsigned* keyword

The range of the values that a variable stores can be extended if the variable is required to store only the positive values instead of storing positive as well as negative values. For example, the range of integer variable can be increased from 0 to 65535 instead of –32768 to +32767, if we support storage of positive numbers only. C/C++ supports a keyword unsigned which informs the compiler that the programmer will not be storing any negative numbers in the variable. For example, the below statement creates an unsigned integer type of variable which is named as marks.

```
unsigned int marks;
```

This informs the compiler that the value of variable marks can never be negative. The keyword unsigned can be similarly applied to other data types as well.

2.5.5 Rules for naming variables

A variable name is a sequence of letters and digits. Given below are a set of rules that the programmer must follow while naming variables:

1. Variable name cannot contain special characters such as comma, semicolon, and space, however, we can have a underscore (symbol _) as a part of the variable name.
2. The variable name cannot begin with a number. This means that the first symbol of the variable name can be a letter or an underscore.
3. A variable name cannot be same as that of a built-in keyword of C/C++. Appendix II gives the list of keywords supported by C and C++.

Given below are the examples of valid and invalid variable names of variables

Variable name	Remark
roll_no	This is a VALID variable name.
Sum	This is a VALID variable name.

`Data12`	This is a VALID variable name.
`student's`	This is an INVALID variable name, because the variable name cannot contain any special characters like '.
`8bat`	This is an INVALID variable name, because the variable name cannot start with a number.
`Roll no`	This is an INVALID variable name, because the variable name cannot contain any special characters like SPACE.

2.6 `printf()` Statement (Supported by both C and C++)

printf() is a function used to print a message on the computer screen. The function is supported by both C and C++. Given below is the syntax to use `printf()` function to print a message on the screen

printf("message");

The function is declared in a header file `stdio.h`, hence this header file must be included in the program before using the `printf()` function.

`#include<stdio.h>`

For example, the program given below prints a message I like computer programming on the screen

```
#include<stdio.h>
void main()
{
printf("I like computer programming");
}
```

Output:

I like computer programming

2.6.1 Formatting the message using escape sequences

C/C++ supports different escape sequences to format the message to be printed on the screen. Each of the escape sequences begin with a backslash (\). Given below is the list of escape sequences supported by C/C++

\n – new line character

\n is used to transfer the cursor position to a new line. To understand the need of this escape sequence, consider the following two `printf()` statements

printf("I like");

printf("computer programming");

The output of the two statements is shown in Figure 2.15.

Complete message is printed on single line even if there are 2 different `printf()` statements responsible to print the message. Note that, there is no space between words "like" and "computer" because we have not printed a space while coding the `printf()` statements

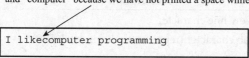

```
I likecomputer programming
```

Figure 2.15: Output of `printf()` statements

Note that, the string `computer programming` is printed on the same line as that of the string `I like`. There is not even a space printed in between the words `like` and `computer`. This is because compiler does not add space in the data unless there is a space explicitly specified by the programmer. Similarly, don't expect the compiler to print the strings `I like` and `computer programming` on new line. If you need to transfer the cursor to a new line on the screen, you must explicitly specify a new line character **\n**. For example,

```
printf("I like\ncomputer programming");
```

will generate the output as shown in Figure 2.16.

Cursor is transferred on a new line after printing the word "like" due to presence of **\n**

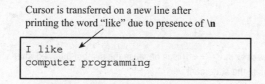

```
I like
computer programming
```

Figure 2.16: Output of `printf()`

Note that, the string `computer programming` is printed on the new line because \n appears before it in the `printf()` statement. \n instructs to transfer the cursor position on new line before printing anything further.

\t – TAB space character

\t is an escape sequence used to print a TAB space on the screen. For example, the statement

```
printf("I like\tcomputer programming");
```

will generate output as shown in Figure 2.17.

Alternatively, we can also break a single `printf()` statement into three different `printf()` statements as shown below:

```
printf("I like");
printf("\t");
printf("computer programming");
```

TAB space between words "like" and "computer"

```
I like        computer programming
```

Figure 2.17: Output of *printf()* statements

Table 2.1: List of escape sequences supported by C/C++

Escape sequence	Description
\n	New line character
\t	Tab character (represents a horizontal TAB)
\b	Backspace character
\a	Sound of a computer beep (one single beep)
\v	TAB character (represents a vertical TAB)
\\	Prints a single slash symbol \
\"	Prints double quotes

These three statements will produce the same output as shown in Figure 2.17; hence, they are equivalent to a single statement written before.

Whilst \n and \t are most frequently used escape sequences, Table 2.1 gives some more escape sequence supported by C/C++.

NOTES

\ is called as a **wild character** in C/C++. This is because the symbol followed after \ is an instruction and not a normal character. For example, the statement

```
printf("n");
```

will just print a symbol n on the computer screen. Whereas, the statement,

```
printf("\n");
```

is an instruction to take the cursor to the new line. We won't see any specific symbol as output of this statement on the screen apart from cursor position being shifted to the next line for subsequent print operations.

2.6.2 Format specifiers supported by C/C++

Format specifiers are used when we want to print a value of a particular variable within the message to be printed on the screen. For example, if there is a variable named as x as shown below

```
int x=3;
```

and if we need to print the value of x in the message as shown in Figure 2.18. Then, we need to write the printf() statement as shown below

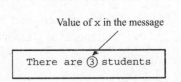

Figure 2.18: Printing value of x as a part of output message

```
printf("There are %d students",x);
```

The %d in the statement indicates that the value to be printed must be taken from the variable as shown in Figure 2.19.

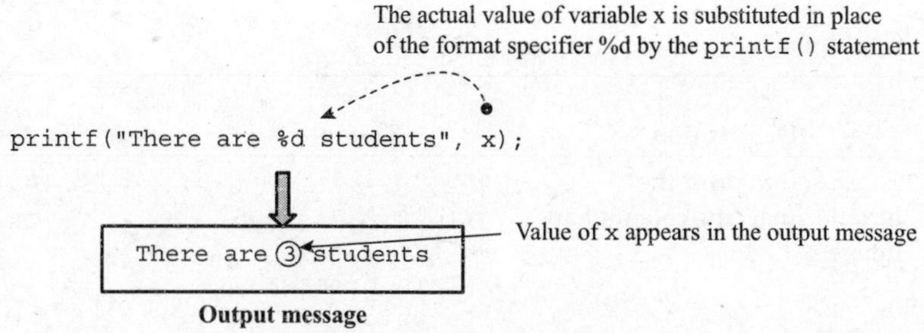

The actual value of variable x is substituted in place
of the format specifier %d by the printf() statement

```
printf("There are %d students", x);
```

There are ③ students ————— Value of x appears in the output message

Output message

Figure 2.19: Working of printf() statement that prints value of x as a part of output message

NOTES

As variable x is of type integer, we have used the format specifier %d. There are different format specifiers supported by C/C++ for each of the different data types. For example, %f is used to print a floating point value, %c is used to print character value and so on. Table 2.2 gives the list of all format specifiers supported by C/C++.

Table 2.2: Examples of format specifiers

Format specifier	Description	Example	Output
%d	%d is used to print a value of integer variable. We can also use %i to print integer value. %d and %i have same meaning	int v = 320; printf("Value is %d",v);	Value is 320
%c	%c is used to print a value of character variable	char ch='$'; printf("Value is %c",ch);	Value is $
%f	%f is used to print a value of floating point variable in a decimal form	float v=32.8; printf("Value is %f",v);	Value is 32.8
%u	%u is to print the value of an unsigned integer variable	unsigned int v = 65532; printf("Value is %u",v);	Value is 65532
%ld	%ld is used to print a value of long variable. We can also us %li to print long value. %ld and %li have same meaning	long v = 3200000; printf("Value is %ld",v);	Value is 3200000

%o	%o is used to print the octal equivalent of an integer	int v = 320;
		printf("Value is %o",v);
		/*This prints 500 which is an octal equivalent of decimal value 320*/
			Value is 500

(Continued)

Table 2.2:   Continued

Format specifier	Description	Example	Output

%x	%x is used to print the hexadecimal equivalent of an integer	`int v= 320;`
		`printf("Value is`
		`%x",v);`
		`/*This prints`
		`140 which is`
		`an hexadecimal`
		`equivalent`
		`of decimal`
		`value 320*/`
			`Value is 140`

%e	%e is used to print a value of floating point variable in exponential format with lower case e appearing in the output	`float v= 32000.9;`
		`printf("Value is`
		`%e",v);`
			`Value is`
			`3.200090e+004`

%E	%E is used to print a value of floating point variable in exponential format with lower case e appearing in the output	`float v =`
		`32000.9;`
		`printf("Value is`
		`%E",v);`
			`Value is`
			`3.200090E+004`

%lf	%lf is used to print a value of double variable in a decimal form	`double v =`
		`320001200.9;`
		`printf("Value is`
		`%lf",v);`
			`Value is`
			`320001200.900002`

%le	%le is used to print a value of double variable in exponential format with lower case e appearing in the output	`double v =`
		`320001200.9;`
		`printf("Value is`
		`%le",v);`
			`Value is`
			`3.200012e+008`

%lE	%lE is used to print a value of double variable in exponential format with upper case E appearing in the output	`double v =`
		`320001200.9;`
		`printf("Value is`
		`%lE",v);`
			`Value is`
			`3.200012E+008`

Let us assume that there is another variable y as shown below,

```
int y=5;
```

If we need to print the value of both x and y in the message as shown in Figure 2.20. then, we need to write the printf statement as shown below

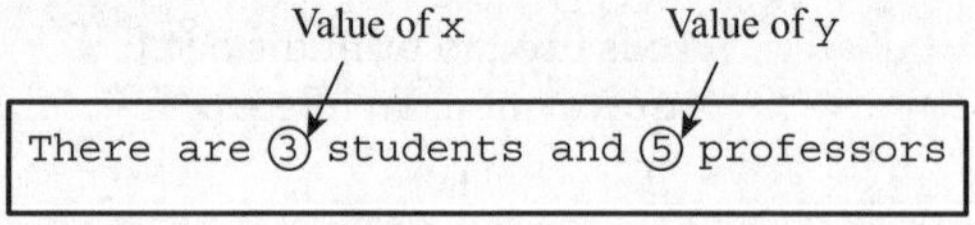

Value of x   Value of y

There are ③ students and ⑤ professors

Figure 2.20:   Required output message

```
printf("There are %d students and %d professors",x,y);
```

Format specifiers are resolved with variable values in a direction from left to right. In place of first %d the function prints the value of x because x is specified first in the comma separated list of variables. And in place of second %d the function prints the value of y as shown in Figure 2.21. We can print any number of variables/expression results using printf() statement provided to have one format specifier for each variable/expression result in the message.

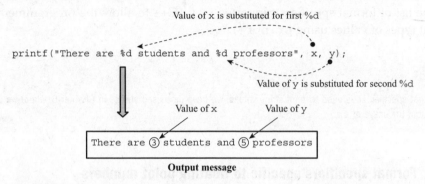

Figure 2.21: Execution of *printf()* which prints the value of two variables

NOTES

The number of format specifiers should exactly match with the number of expressions to be printed. For example, if we have two variables a and b

```
int a=10,b=20;
```

and if you want to print the following message on screen

```
Addition of 10 and 20 is 30
```

you actually need three format specifiers, the first one for 10 (value of a), second one for 20 (value of b), and third one for 30 (value of a+b). Hence, the printf() statement should be written as shown below

```
printf("Addition of %d and %d is %d", a, b, a+b);
```

Note that we have performed the evaluation of expression a+b within the printf() statement. This is allowed and works without any issues as shown in Figure 2.22.

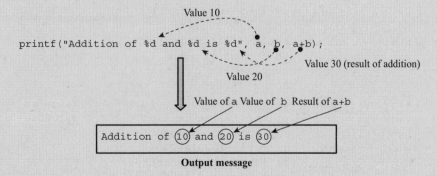

Figure 2.22: Execution of printf("Addition of %d and %d is %d", a, b, a+b);

The value of a will be printed for first occurrence of %d, b will be printed for second occurrence of %d, and the value of a+b will be printed for third occurrence of %d as shown in Figure 2.22.

Remember %d is a format specifier if we want to print integer types. In reality, there are different format specifiers for different types of data values to be printed. Table 2.2 gives the list of format specifiers supported by C/C++ to allow the programmer to print different types of values using printf().

NOTES

The format specifier %s is used to print string values. We have discussed strings in Chapter 6, where we will also learn about the usage of %s.

2.6.3 Format specifiers specific to floating point numbers

C/C++ supports additional format specifiers (for float and double types) which correctly choose either decimal or scientific way of the output format whichever is smaller to represent on screen.

Format specifier	Description	Example	Output
%g	%g prints the value of float variable in the form of %f or %e whichever is smaller to represent on screen	float v = 32000.9; printf("Value is %g",v); /*prints in decimal format(32000.9) because it is smaller to represent when compared to exponential format(3.200090e+004)*/	**Value is 32000.9**
%G	%G prints the value of float variable in the form of %f or %E whichever is smaller to represent on screen	float v= 32000.9; printf("Value is %G",v); /*prints in decimal format(32000.9) because it is smaller to represent when compared to exponential format(3.200090E+004)*/	**Value is 32000.9**
%lg	%lg prints the double variable in the form of %lf or %le whichever is smaller to represent on screen	double v= 32000120000.9; printf("Value is %lg",v); /*prints in exponential format(3.20001e+010) because it is smaller to represent when compared to decimal format(32000120000.9)*/	**Value is 3.20001e+010**

| %lG | %lG prints the double variable in the form of %lf or %lE whichever is smaller to represent on screen | `double v= 32000120000.9;` `printf("Value is %lG",v);` `/*prints in exponential` `format(3.20001E+010)` `because it is smaller` `to represent when` `compared to decimal` `format(32000120000.9)*/` | **Value is** **3.20001E+010** |

NOTES

C/C++ also supports format specifiers %Lg and %LG to print a long double value. Note L must be in upper case to print long double type of variables.

2.6.4 Specifying width and precision of output with *printf()* statement

Width and precision of the output can also be controlled using `printf()` statement. We know that %d in control string is used to print an integer value. By default, an integer value is printed in a left justified format. It is possible to specify the width of the output field to print the value in a right justified form. In order to get a right justified output, the integer control string must be specified as follows:

`"%[width]d"`

where [width] represents symbol width to be reserved for printing the output. For example, consider variable x with a value 100

`int x=100;`

The statement

`printf("%6d",x);`

will reserve six symbol spaces for printing the value of x on the screen. This means that although x is a three-digit number, there are six spaces reserved for printing its value on the screen. The value 100 will be printed in a right justified form by keeping the first three symbol spaces on the screen as blank as shown in Figure 2.23.

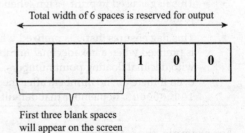

Total width of 6 spaces is reserved for output

First three blank spaces
will appear on the screen

Figure 2.23: Right justified printing of x

If the width specified is less than the number of digits in the number, the width specification is ignored and the full number will be printed without any loss of data on the screen. In this case, x is a three-digit number and accidently if we specify the width as 2 in the printf() statement as shown below

`printf("%2d",x);`

the width specification is simply ignored and full value of x (which is 100) is printed on the screen as shown below

100

C/C++ provides a some more flags, which can be applied to the control string to further format the output. For example, 0 flag is used to populate the blank spaces reserved for the output with zero values when output is right justified.

The statement,

```
printf("%06d",x);
```

will reserve six symbol spaces for printing the value of x on the screen and populate the first three unused spaces with zero as shown in Figure 2.24.

The below table gives the list of flags supported by printf() statement. The flags to be applied must be specified immediately after the % sign in the control string. Hence, the control string to print an integer can be specified in a format as shown below

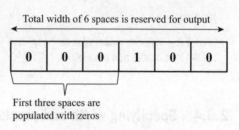

Figure 2.24: Output of `printf("%06d",x);`

```
"%[flag][width]d"
```

where, [flag] represents the optional flag to be applied to the value and [width] represents the optional symbol width specification for the output.

Flag	Description
0	0 flag is used to populate the blank spaces reserved for the output with zero values when the output is right justified. This flag has no meaning when output is left justified.
–	This flag is used to produce left justified output.
+	This flag is used to print + sign when printing positive numbers, for example, 100 will be printed as +100.
#	This flag ensures that 0 is prefixed when an octal number is printed on the screen and 0x is prefixed when a hexadecimal number is printed on the screen. When this flag is used with decimal floating point numbers, it ensures that decimal point appears in the output even if there are no numbers after the decimal point. For example, 100 will be printed as 100.000000. Remember that default precision is 6.

For example, the statement

```
printf("%-6d",x);
```

applies – flag and hence the output will be left justified as shown in Figure 2.25.

It is possible to apply more than one flag at a time. The statement below

```
printf("%-+6d",x);
```

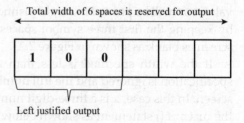

Figure 2.25: Left justified output

applies two flags – and + to print the value of x . Symbol – indicates that the output is left justified and + indicates that the + sign should appear in the output if the number is positive. Hence, the output of the statement is shown below. Note that, this time only two symbol spaces (out of 6) are left empty because one symbol space is consumed for printing + sign as shown in Figure 2.26.

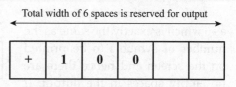

Total width of 6 spaces is reserved for output

Figure 2.26: + and – flags together

We know that control string %o is used to print the octal value and %x is used to print hexadecimal value. The statement,

```
printf("%o",x);
```

prints 144, because it is an octal equivalent of decimal value 100. We can apply a # flag if we need to prefix 0 to the output when an octal number is printed. For example, the statement

```
printf("%#o",x);
```

prints 0144 on the screen

Similarly, the statement

```
printf("%#x",x);
```

will print 0x64 on the computer screen because 64 is an hexadecimal equivalent of decimal 100. Note that 0x appears in the output because we have used # flag in printf() statement.

It is also possible to configure the precision of floating point numbers using printf statement. Precision of a floating point number is number of digits that can appear after the decimal point. As we have done with printing integer values, we can also specify flags and width of the output when printing floating point numbers. The full format of control string for printing floating point number is as follows

```
"%[flags][width].[precision]f"
```

Remember, all of the three parameters **[flags]**, **[width]**, and **[precision]** are optional so we can specify any of them, all of them or none of them. Let us first write statements using **[width]** and **[precision]** only and we will apply some flags to it later to show their usage with floating point values.

Let y be a floating point variable

```
float y = 100.56453;
```

The statement,

```
printf("%6.2f",y);
```

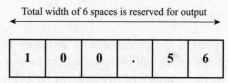

Total width of 6 spaces is reserved for output

Figure 2.27: Output of
`printf("%6.2f",y);`

sets the width of the output as 6 and precision as 2. The number will be rounded after two decimal places and hence, the output is 100.56 as shown in Figure 2.27.

In this case, the width is specified as 6 which is exactly the same as the number of symbols to be printed on the screen and hence there are no empty spaces in the output. If we specify width greater than the number of symbols to be printed, the output will be right justified as shown in Figure 2.28.

The statement,

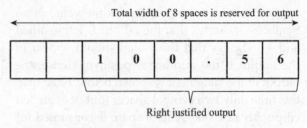

Figure 2.28: Output of `printf("%8.2f",y);`

```
printf("%8.2f",y);
```

sets the width of the output as 8 and precision as 2. The first two spaces are empty because output will be right justified. As before, we have specified precision as 2 and hence number will be rounded after two decimal places, thereby printing 100.56 on the screen as shown in Figure 2.28.

We can always apply flags mentioned in section 2.6.4 with floating point values in a similar way as we applied them while printing integers. For example, to make the output in Figure 2.28, left justified we can apply a – flag as shown in the statement below

```
printf("%-8.2f",y);
```

The output will be left justified, leaving last two symbol spaces as blank as shown in Figure 2.29.

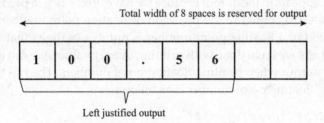

Figure 2.29: Output of `printf("%-8.2f",y);`

Similarly, other flags such as +, 0, and # can also be applied to floating point values. We can still specify the precision if we do not want to specify any width. For example, the statement,

```
printf("%.2f",y);
```

specifies the precision as 2 but does not specify any width. This means that the floating point value will be rounded up to two decimal places and the width will be same as that of the number of symbols to be printed on the screen. The output of the statement is shown in Figure 2.30.

The statement,

```
printf("%20f",y);
```

| 1 | 0 | 0 | . | 5 | 6 |

Figure 2.30: Output of `printf("%.2f",y);`

only specifies the width as 20 but no precision, in this case, the full number will be printed in right justified form (leaving first 11 spaces blank) as shown in Figure 2.31.

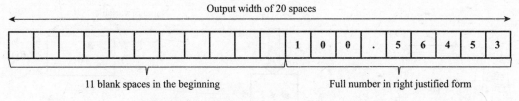

Figure 2.31: Output of $printf("\%20f",y);$

2.7 C++ Style of Printing the Value on Computer Screen

Recall, cout statement is supported by C++ (not by C) to print a message on the computer screen. Along with the text message, we can also print the value of a particular variable using a cout statement in a C++ program. The only difference between printing a text message and the value of a variable is that the text message to be printed must always be surrounded in double quotes whereas if we wish to print the value of a variable using a cout statement then the variable name must be written without double quotes. This facilitates the C++ compiler to differentiate between the parts of the cout statement which represents the direct text message to be printed on the screen and the parts of the cout statement which represent the variable name(s) whose values are to be printed on the computer screen.

Given below is the syntax to print the value of the N variables defined in the C++ program using a single cout statement:

```
cout<<variable1<<variable2<<variable3............<<variableN;
```

As shown in Figure 2.32, we have created an integer type variable named as a and initialized it to 10. Therefore, the statement,

```
cout<<a;
```

will actually print a value 10 on the computer screen as shown in Figure 2.32.

We can also invoke the insertion operator function multiple times using a single cout object. This feature of C++ called as cascading of insertion operations. The cascading of insertion operator (<<) can also be used when we wish to combine different elements so as to form a message to be printed on the computer screen. For example, the below cout statement,

```
cout<<"The value of variable is "<<a;
```

will print the following message on the computer screen.

```
The value of variable is 10
```

Note that, there are two parts in the above message. The first part is a plain text (The value of variable is) which is surrounded in the double quotes whereas the second

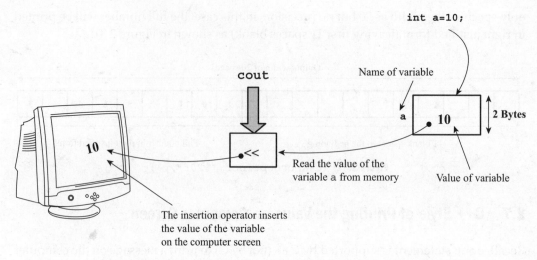

Figure 2.32: Printing the value of a variable using cout statement

part of the message is the name of the variable (variable a) which is not surrounded in the double quotes. Further, it is important to note that we must use the insertion operator separately so as to insert every part of the message on the computer screen. The working of the cout statement is shown in Figure 2.33.

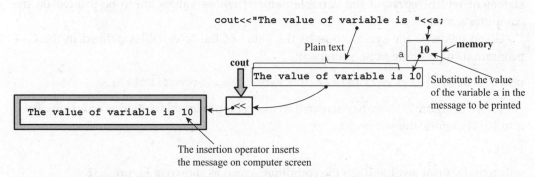

Figure 2.33: Execution of cout << "*The value of variable is* "<<a;

As an example, let us consider that x and y are variables of type integer with a value of 10 and 20 as shown below:

```
int x=10,y=20;
```

Similarly, the cout statement,

```
cout<<"Value of x is:"<<x<<" Value of y is:"<<y;
```

will print the following message on the computer screen.

```
Value of x is:10 Value of y is:20
```

2.8   `endl` Modifier (Supported by C++ not by C)

`endl` is a keyword in C++ which is used to transfer the cursor on the new line of the computer screen. The modifier `endl` is also called as a carriage return operator in C++. To understand the requirement of `endl` modifier, let us consider the two C++ statements given below:

```
cout<<"I like C++";
cout<<"I like Computer programming";
```

Although, we have written two different `cout` statements, the messages I like C++ and I like Computer programming will be printed on the same line of the computer screen as shown in Figure 2.34. Note that the streaming output of C++ will not even insert an additional space in the two messages. Therefore, the two messages will appear as if they are concatenated as shown in Figure 2.34.

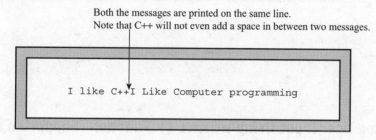

Both the messages are printed on the same line.
Note that C++ will not even add a space in between two messages.

```
I like C++I Like Computer programming
```

Figure 2.34:   Output

The C++ supports a modifier `endl` which can be written as a part of the `cout` statement. The modifier `endl` is used to end the current line and transfer the printing cursor on the new line. This ensures that the next message (which is printed after the occurrence of `endl`) will be printed on the new line of the computer screen. Let us modify the above C++ statements to use an `endl` modifier as shown below:

```
cout<<"I like C++"<<endl;
cout<<"I like Computer programming";
```

The first `cout` statement prints the message I like C++ on the computer screen following which the cursor is transferred on the new line and hence the next message I like Computer programming will be printed on the new line of the screen as shown in Figure 2.35.

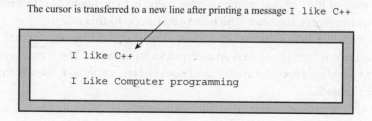

The cursor is transferred to a new line after printing a message I like C++

```
I like C++
I Like Computer programming
```

Figure 2.35:   Output

NOTES

Along with modifiers, it is also possible to make use of conventional escape sequences given in Table 2.1 with `cout` in order to format the message.

For example, the following `cout` statement is also valid

```
cout<<"I like C++ \n I like \t Computer programming"<<endl;
```

The output on the screen is shown below.

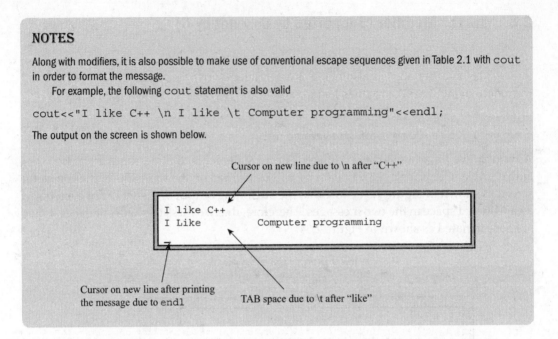

2.9 Accepting User Input Using `scanf()` Function (Supported by both C and C++)

`scanf()` is a function used to accept input data from keyboard and store the data values in program variables as shown in Figure 2.36. `scanf()` is declared in a header file `<stdio.h>` and defined in internal libraries of C/C++. The function is supported by both C and C++.

Given below is the syntax of the function to accept input data from keyboard

```
scanf("control string", &var1, &var2,......... &varn);
```

`var1, var2, ........ varn` are n different variables. The presence of & symbol before each variable indicates that the function requires the exact memory location of each of the variables to store the input data. & is called as an address-of-operator in C/C++, which gives the address of the location in memory where the variable is stored. For now, just remember & as a part of syntax to use `scanf()`. Don't worry much about & right now, we will discuss operating with memory addresses in detail in Chapter 8. Just remember to add & before each of the variable names whose value is to be taken as input from keyboard (we will learn strings in Chapter 6 which are exceptions to this rule).

Control string is a list of format specifiers. There should be one format specifier for each of the variable which is to be taken as input from the user. The format specifier to use depends upon the data type of variable and some of the generally used format specifiers are as listed in Table 2.2.

Consider an integer variable x

```
int x;
```

instead of initializing its value we can accept the value of x as input from keyboard using the statement,

```
scanf("%d",&x);
```

Notice we have used %d as a format specifier because variable x is of type integer. The & sign is added before x as mentioned before which is the requirement of the scanf() function. On this statement, the CPU waits for user to enter a value using keyboard. After the value is entered by the user; the user should hit a ENTER (or a SPACE BAR) key which indicates that the user input is completed. After the user hits the ENTER (or a SPACE BAR) key, the input value is stored in variable x by the scanf() function. Let us assume that user inputs a value as 10, then x will store 10 as shown in Figure 2.36. After the value of variable x is initialized, the execution of the program continues from the next statement after scanf().

We can also accept multiple input values using a single scanf() statement. For example, consider three variables a, b and c as described below

```
int a,b;
float d;
```

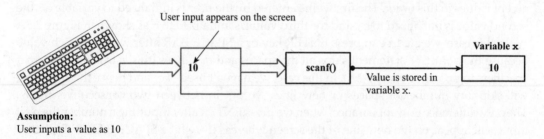

Assumption:
User inputs a value as 10

Figure 2.36:   Execution of scanf("%d",&x);

The statement,

```
scanf("%d %d %f",&a,&b,&c);
```

accepts three values as input from the user and assigns them to the respective variables. Notice that we have used the format specifier %d for accepting a and b because both of them are integers whereas we have used %f to accept the value of c as input because it is of type float. The format specifiers are delimited by space in the control string. We can also rewrite this statement without putting a space in between the control strings as shown below

```
scanf("%d%d%f",&a,&b,&c);
```

In this case, both the statements are equivalent because there is no character type input (we will discuss special case with character input shortly). However, it is strongly recommended to separate the format specifiers by space as it improves the readability of the code. As the scanf() statement is written to accept three values, the control will not move to the next statement until the user inputs all the three values. User can press an ENTER key (or a SPACE BAR) after inputting each value. It is the responsibility of the user to input first two

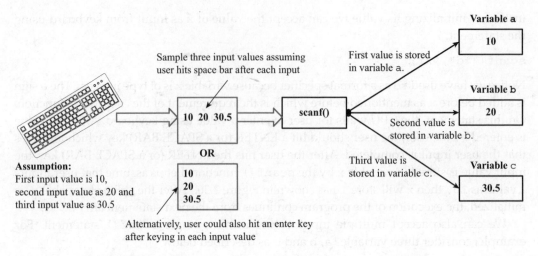

Figure 2.37: Execution of scanf("%d %d %f",&a,&b,&c);

values as integer and the third value as float because the scanf() statement is designed to accept values in this order. The first value entered by the user is initialized to variable a, the second value is initialized to b, and the third value is initialized to c as shown in Figure 2.37.

In this case, we are free to press ENTER key or a SPACE BAR after we input each value because the scanf() statement skips all the spaces and new lines (this is true for all format specifiers in scanf() except %c). In this case, we haven't used %c and hence the statement will skip any number of spaces or new lines we put in between two consecutive inputs. The only difference is in appearance, when we press ENTER after inputting a number the next input will appear on the new line of the screen whereas if we hit a SPACE BAR or TAB after inputting the number, the next input will appear on the same line as shown in Figure 2.37.

scanf() statement that inputs a character (written with format specifier %c) works slightly different then the scanf() written without %c. scanf() that inputs a character does not skip space and new line by default, because they are also valid characters (although not visible to us). This sometimes creates a problem because accidently space or new line gets assigned to a character variable instead of the actual input value. For example, let us declare two variables e and f of type int and char, respectively

```
int e;
char f;
```

If we write the scanf() statement to accept the values of e and f as input from the user as shown below

```
scanf("%d%c",&e,&f);
```

And let us assume that user input values are 10 z.

We might be at an impression that variable e is initialized with 10 and variable f is initialized to z. We are correct that the first value (which is 10) is initialized to e but the second value z is not initialized to f. This is because the user has input a SPACE after 10. Remember SPACE is also a valid character and hence it gets initialized to f instead of symbol z.

Hence, when we print value of e, we will get 10 in the output but if we print the value of f we will get nothing on screen. This is because SPACE is not visible on the screen but it is what is stored in variable f in memory. This indeed is technically incorrect because the input value z is lost which should have been initialized to variable f. To solve this problem, the trick is that %c must always have a leading space in the control string.

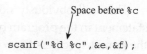

Space before %c

```
scanf("%d %c",&e,&f);
```

Figure 2.38: scanf() statement with a space before %c

The leading space informs scanf() to skip all the space and new lines even for character input. Hence, we rewrite the scanf() statement by putting a space before %c as shown in Figure 2.38.

In this case, if the input is,

```
10 z
```

variable e will be set to 10 whereas variable f will be correctly set to value z. This is because scanf() will skip all the spaces and new lines that occur in the input. A single space before %c informs scanf() to skip all spaces and new lines that occur in input. Hence, variable f will be correctly initialized to value z even if we put a multiple space and new lines between 10 and z while giving input as shown in Figure 2.39.

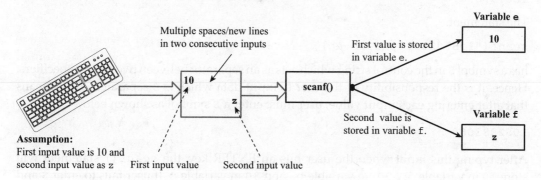

Figure 2.39: Multiple spaces in input

This is not only the case with a multi-input scanf() statement; but is also true for the scanf() statement which takes a single character value as input. For example, the statement,

```
scanf("%c",&f);
```

just accepts the value of single character variable f as input from the user. If the user inputs

```
z
```

there is a possibility that f will not be initialized correctly. This is because scanf() statement might pick up the ENTER key hit (new line character) or SPACE BAR hit (blank space character) which was made by the user in previous input activity (may be from the previous scanf() statement written somewhere before in the program). To overcome this problem, we should add a space before %c while accepting character input even if the scanf() statement is written to accept just one value as shown in Figure 2.40.

Space before %c

```
scanf(" %c",&f);
```

Figure 2.40: scanf() accepting single character input

This will obviously not be an issue if this scanf() statement is the very first input statement in the program but it is always better to keep a habit to put a SPACE before each of the format specifiers to avoid scanning of incorrect inputs.

NOTES

Always ensure that there is a SPACE before %c in the control string while reading character input using scanf().

All the other format specifiers such as %d, %f, and %ld (including %s which is for strings) skip the new line and spaces at input and hence it is not necessary to put a space before them in the control string. But it is always a better programming practice to separate the format specifiers within the control string of scanf() function by space as it improves the overall readability of the statement.

2.9.1 Delimited input using *scanf()*

It is possible to use any other delimiter apart from space in the control string of scanf(). For example, consider three variables a, b, and c declared as below

```
int a,b,c;
```

The statement,

```
scanf("%d$%d$%d$",&a,&b,&c);
```

has a symbol $ in the control string which acts as an separator between two format specifiers. Hence, it is the responsibility of the user to input data which is $ separated. This means that after entering each input value, user must enter a $ symbol as shown below

```
10$20$30$
```

After typing this input when the user hits an ENTER key, the scanf() statement will store 10 in variable a, 20 in variable b, and 30 in variable c. If user fails to enter $ and inputs data in any other format, the scanf() will crash. Remember when we put $ as a separator in format specifiers, it actually informs scanf() to skip $ in the input string and hence variables a, b, and c are correctly initialized to 10, 20, and 30, respectively. This feature is rarely used in programs because there is a risk that scanf() will crash if the user does not input data exactly in the same format as needed by scanf(). For example, in this case, if the user enters input in any other format say space delimited input

```
10 20 30
```

scanf() will fail to produce desired results. This is because, in this case, scanf will not skip spaces because we have explicitly written the statement to skip exactly one $ symbol between two input values. Remember, when we keep space as a delimiter between two format specifiers, scanf() will skip any number of spaces and new line characters that appear in between two consecutive input values. But when we set the delimiter to anything other than space (like dollar in this case) scanf() will not skip its multiple occurrences between two consecutive inputs. The below input

```
10$$$20$$$$$$$30$$
```

will fail the scanf() function because the input is not in the desired format as that of the control string. This is because, as per the control string, the input must have exactly one $ symbol that separates two values.

Given below is the full source code that accepts $ delimited input values of variables a, b, and c and prints the values back on the screen

```
#include<stdio.h>
void main()
{
int a,b,c;
printf("Enter three values delimited by $\n");
scanf("%d$%d$%d$",&a,&b,&c);
printf("a=%d\tb=%d\tc=%d\n",a,b,c);
}
```

Output

```
Enter three values delimited by $
10$20$30$
a=10      b=20      c=30
```

2.9.2 Specifying width of input data

Just like we can specify the width of output in printf(), it is also possible to specify maximum width of input data in the scanf() statement. For example if a and b are variables of type integer, the statement,

```
scanf("%2d %4d",&a,&b);
```

sets the width of first input as 2 digit number and the width of second input as 4 digit number. Hence, it is the responsibility of the user to enter value of a as 2 digit number and value of b as 4 digit number. Hence, if user inputs the data as

```
23 4520
```

then the value of a is initialized to 23 and the value of b is initialized as 4250.

CAUTION

Given scanf() will not produce desired results if user inputs a number containing more than two digits as first input. For example, if input is

```
2380 459
```

only the first two digits of 2380 will be assigned to variable a. Hence variable a will be initialized to 23. The remaining two digits (80) will be assigned to variable b and hence the value of b will be set as 80. The blank space after 80 in the input makes scanf() to stop performing any further initialization because both the input variables are initialized at this point of time. Hence the value 459 inputted by the user is simply ignored by the scanf() statement.

Clearly, this is an incorrect initialization due to wrong input provided by the user. This also has an adverse effect if the program has another scanf() statement at any place later in the program. For example, if there is one more scanf() statement later in the program to accept the integer variable c as input,

```
scanf("%d",&c);
```

then it won't let the user input any value and simply continue the execution to the next statement. In this case, user is not given any opportunity to input the value for c because 459 was already in the input stream and was left uninitialized by previous scanf() statement. Hence, CPU initializes variable c with 459 without waiting for user to input anything else.

NOTES

To avoid these complexities, it is strongly recommended not to specify any input widths with scanf() statement, unless it is absolutely necessary to do so.

2.10 *cin* Object in C++ (Only in C++ not in C)

C++ supports streaming input to read the data from an input device such as keyboard. The operator >> is called as an extraction operator in C++ which is used to read (extract) the data from the input device. The extraction operator function is defined in the class istream (istream is an abbreviation of input stream) which is defined in the header file `iostream.h`. Hence, we need to use the extraction operator along with the built-in object of class `istream` which is named as `cin`. As the object `cin` and the extraction operator function `>>` are defined in the header file `iostream.h`, we must include the contents of `iostream.h` in the C++ program before we can use the object `cin` in the C++ program. The pre-processor directive `#include` can be used to include the contents of the header file in the C++ program as discussed in Section 2.2.

The `cin` statement reads the value from keyboard and stores the extracted value inside a particular variable as shown in Figure 2.41.

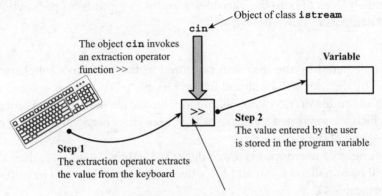

Figure 2.41: Working of `cin`

For example, let us assume that variable a is declared in the program then the following `cin` statement,

`cin>>a;`

can be used to read the value of variable a from the keyboard. If the user of the program enters the value as say 20, then the value 20 will be stored in the variable a as shown in Figure 2.42.

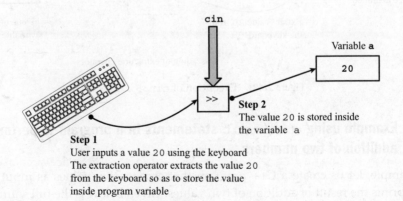

Figure 2.42: Execution of `cin>>a;`

We can also accept the values of multiple variables created in the program using a single cin statement by cascading the extraction operator >> just like we can cascade the insertion operator << as shown in the syntax below:

```
cin>>variable1>>variable2>>variable3 ... >>variableN;
```

As an example to understand the cascading of extraction operator, let us assume that variables x and y are declared in the C++ program as shown below:

```
int x,y;
```

We can read the values of both the variables x and y as input from the keyboard using a single cin statement as shown below:

```
cin>>x>>y;
```

The first value entered by the user will be stored in the variable x whereas the second value entered by the user will be stored in the variable y. The values entered by the user can be 'space' delimited or 'new line' delimited. This means that, user can enter the values of x and y which are separated by space or user may enter each value on the new line by using a 'enter' key of the keyboard.

Let us assume that user input is space delimited values 10 and 20, then the value of variable x will be initialized to 10 and the value of the variable y will be initialized to 20 as shown in Figure 2.43.

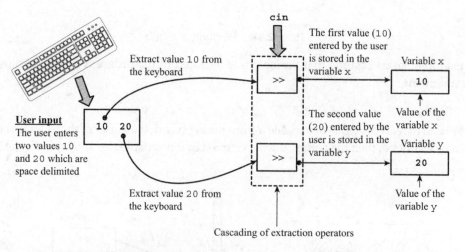

Figure 2.43: Execution of cin>>x>>y;

2.10.1 Example using *cin*/cout statements in a program to perform addition of two numbers

As an example, let us create a C++ program that accepts two values as input from the user and prints the result of addition of two values. Given below is the full source code to perform the addition of two numbers:

```
#include<iostream.h>
void main()
{
int a,b,c;
cout<<"Enter the two numbers"<<endl;
cin>>a>>b;
c= a+b;
cout<<"The result of addition is: "<<c;
}
```

Output:

```
Enter the two numbers
100 200
The result of addition is: 300
```

The first statement

```
int a,b,c;
```

creates integer type variables named as a, b, and c in the memory as shown in Figure 2.44. Note that, each of the variables initially store junk values.

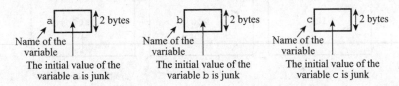

Figure 2.44: Variables a, b, and c

The statement,

```
cout<<"Enter the two numbers"<<endl;
```

prints the message Enter the two numbers on the computer screen which is followed by a modified endl. Hence, the cursor is transferred to the new line after printing the specified message on the screen.

The statement,

```
cin>>a>>b;
```

reads two values from the keyboard and stores them in variables a and b, respectively. Let us assume that user enters the two values as 100 and 200, then the first value which is 10 will be stored in the variable a whereas the second value which is 200 will be stored in the variable b as shown in Figure 2.45.

The statement,

```
c= a+b;
```

performs the addition of the two numbers a and b, thereby storing the result of addition in the variable c. As, the variables a and b are already initialized to the values 100 and 200, respectively. The variable c will now store the result as 300 as shown in Figure 2.46.

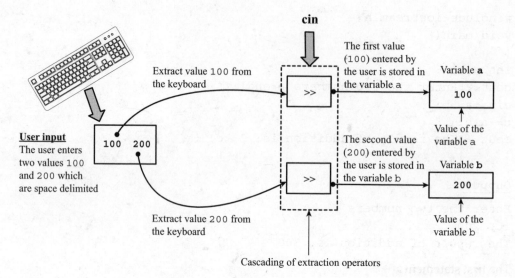

Figure 2.45: Execution of `cin>>a>>b;`

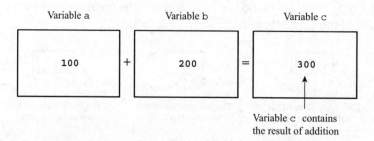

Figure 2.46: Execution of `c = a + b;`

The last statement,

```
cout<<"The result of addition is: "<<c;
```

cascades the insertion operator so as to print the following message on the computer screen:

```
The result of addition is: 300
```

NOTES

The given program to perform addition of two numbers works only with C++ compilers and not with C compilers. This is because it uses `cout/cin` objects which are only supported by C++ and not by C. The program given below uses `printf()` and `scanf()` statements and hence works with both C as well as C++ compilers. It is acknowledged that `printf()` and `scanf()` statements are much complex to write compared to `cout/cin` statements, but if we want our program to work with both C and C++ we have no choice but to use them.

```
#include<stdio.h>

void main()
```

```
{
int a,b,c;
printf("Enter the two numbers\n");
scanf("%d %d",&a,&b);
c = a + b;
printf("The result of addition is: %d\n",c);
}
```

Output:

```
Enter the two numbers
100 200
The result of addition is: 300
```

2.11 Manipulator `setw`

The manipulator `setw` is used to set the width of the output which is generated by the `cout` statement. By default, the field width of the `cout` statement is set to the number of symbols produced as the output of the statement.

As an example, let us consider the following `cout` statement,

```
cout<<"Hello";
```

The field width of the output generated by the `cout` statement is 5 and the output contains five symbols as shown in Figure 2.47.

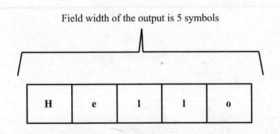

Figure 2.47: Field width of "Hello"

We can explicitly set the custom field width of the `cout` statement using the `setw` manipulator as shown below:

```
cout<<setw(10)<<"Hello";
```

The above `cout` statement sets the field width of the output as `10`. However, the actual length of the output required is just five symbols (since the string `Hello` just contains five characters in it). In such a scenario, the string `Hello` will be right aligned in the output leaving the space for first five symbols as blank, as shown in Figure 2.48.

The manipulator `setw` is generally used when we wish to right align a text or number which is generated at the output of the program using a `cout` statement. Given below is the sample C++ program that illustrates the usage of the `setw` manipulator which prints the addition of two numbers in the right justified form. The values 10, 20, and 30 are right aligned on the screen as seen in the output of the program

The manipulator `setw` is defined in the header file `iomanip.h`. Hence, we must include the contents of the header file `iomanip.h` before we use the manipulator `setw` in the C++ program.

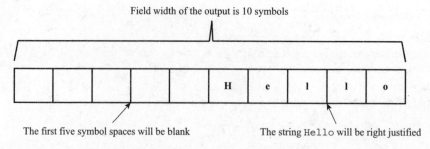

The first five symbol spaces will be blank

The string Hello will be right justified

Figure 2.48: Output using field width of 10

```
#include<iostream.h>
#include<iomanip.h>
void main()
{
int a = 10,b = 20,c;
c = a + b;
cout<<"a="<<setw(5)<<a<<endl;
cout<<"b="<<setw(5)<<b<<endl;
cout<<"c="<<setw(5)<<c<<endl;
}
```

Output:

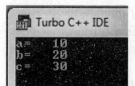

NOTES

We have studied two different techniques of giving input to the program, scanf() and cin. Likewise, we have studied two different ways for output generation, which are printf() and cout. Here is the summary of what we have discussed about these approaches

scanf()/printf() functions	cin/cout objects
These are formatted input/output functions supported by both C and C++. These functions are declared in header file stdio.h.	These are streaming input/output objects which are supported only by C++ and not by C. These objects are declared in header file iostream.h.
These functions need the programmer to specify format specifiers for each value to be inputted or outputted.	These are streaming objects and they do not need format specifiers for input/output operations.
Does not support modifiers(like setw) for formatting data. All the formatting must be done using escape sequences such as \n and \t.	They can support modifiers for formatting data as well as escape sequences.

2.12 Defining Constants using #define—A Pre-processor Directive

#define is a pre-processor directive which is used to define the constant values which are not going to change throughout the execution of the program. The constants defined by #define directive are also called as macros in the C/C++ program. Recall from Chapter 1, the pre-processor replaces every occurrence of a macro name in the program with the macro definition before the compilation of the program starts.

As an example, let us consider a pre-processor directive below:

#define PI 3.14

This means that, we have defined a constant PI (name of the macro is PI) with a value as 3.14. Remember that the #define statements are not compiled rather they are pre-processed before the compilation of the program starts. Hence, the pre-processor will replace every occurrence of PI with 3.14 before compilation of the program. Given below is the program to find the volume of a cone using #define directive to define the constant value 3.14.

```
#include<stdio.h>
#define PI 3.14
void main()
{
float radius, height,volume;

printf("Enter the radius  and height of the cone\n");
scanf("%f %f",&radius,&height);

volume = 0.3333*PI*radius*radius*height;
printf("Volume of the cone is %f\n",volume);

}
```

Output:
```
Enter the radius and height of the cone
10 2.3
Volume of the cone is 240.709259
```

The above given code defines a constant PI using the pre-processor directive #define. Hence, the statement,

volume = 0.3333*PI*radius*radius*height;

will be translated by the pre-processor to:

volume = 0.3333*3.14*radius*radius*height;

by substituting the value 3.14 instead of constant PI. Once the pre-processor completes substitution, a temporary file is generated on the disk which is then compiled by the compiler.

2.12.1 *NULL*—a built-in macro

NULL is constant defined in C/C++ with a value set as zero. NULL is a name given to a built-in macro which is defined inside C/C++ libraries using #define statement shown below:

```
#define NULL 0
```

This means that we can use a symbol NULL or an integer constant 0 interchangeably in the C/C++ program.

The statement,

```
int a = NULL;
```

is same as ,

```
int a=0;
```

Therefore, when we attempt to initialize a variable with a NULL value, the value of the variable will actually get initialized to zero.

Although, either using a symbol 0 or a using a symbol NULL will not affect the output of the program, the symbol NULL is often used when working with **pointers**. A pointer which is initialized to NULL (also called as **NULL pointer**) does not point any location in the computer memory. The exact usage of NULL pointers will be discussed in Chapters 8 and 10.

2.13   Character Specific Input/Output

We know that we can use scanf()/printf() as well as cin/cout for input/output operations for different type of data values including character types. C/C++ supports getchar() and putchar(), which are functions specifically used for character input and output operations.

getchar() is a function used to read a character from the keyboard and putchar() is a function to print the character on the computer screen. Although their job cannot be done by scanf()/printf() as well as cin/cout; the functions getchar() and putchar() are much simple to use compared to scanf()/printf() or cin/cout. Only point to note is that they can input or print only 1 character at a time. Consider the following program as an example:

```
#include<stdio.h>
void main()
{
char x;
printf("Enter a character\n");
/*getchar() is used to get a character as input*/
x=getchar();
printf("Character you entered is\n");
/*putchar(x) prints the value of character variable x*/
putchar(x);
}
```

Output:

```
Enter a character
$
Character you entered is
$
```

The statement,

```
x=getchar();
```

waits for user to input a character. The character inputted by the user is stored in variable x. In reality, the function stores the ASCII value of the input character in the variable x and hence the function getchar() returns an integer value (as ASCII values are integers). All we need to note at this stage is that the character inputted by the user is not stored in variable x, so if user inputs say $ then x will contain $. Remember, the function can take only 1 character as input at a time, so if you need to input another character we need to use another getchar() function.

The statement,

```
putchar(x);
```

prints the character value stored in variable x on the computer screen. So, for example, if the value of x is $, then $ will appear on the computer screen.

> **NOTES**
>
> The functions getchar() and putchar() are declared in the header file stdio.h. Hence, this header file must be included before using these functions in the program.

Quiz

1. Fill in the blank spaces:
    If a size of a particular data type is 10 bytes, _____ is the range of signed values and _____ is the range of unsigned values that can be stored in the variable of this type. Assume that the data type supports only numerical values without any fractional components.
2. Determine the output of three printf() statements given below assuming value of variable z as initialized
    ```
    int z = -2000;
    printf("%020d",z);
    printf("%-+20d",z);
    printf("%#o",z);
    ```
3. Consider the scanf() statement to input values of variables a and b
    ```
    int a,b;
    scanf("%3d %2d",&a,&b);
    ```
    Give the values of variables a and b in each of the following cases of user input
    Case 1: User input is 32000 42000
    Case 2: User input is 333 10000
    Case 3: User input is 12 1

4. Write a combination of `printf()` and `scanf()` statements to
   (a) Print the following message on screen
   ```
   Enter a number
   ```
   (b) Input a `float` value in exponential format and store it in variable named b
   (c) Print the value of b in decimal format

5. If p and q are variables of type `float`, write a `printf()` statement to print the result of following expressions
   (a) `p+q/100-p*q+q`   (b) p^3 (c) `(p/q+1)*100`

6. Determine the output of following `printf()` statement
   ```
   printf("\vI\vLike\tProgramming\tIn\vC++\v");
   ```

7. cout is a:
   (a) Keyword of C++
   (b) Built-in function of C++
   (c) Object of a built-in class of C++
   (d) Special word

8. Insertion operator `<<` is a:
   (a) Keyword of C++
   (b) Built-in function of C++
   (c) Object of a built-in class of C++
   (d) Special word

9. Which of the following statements is true?
   (a) Compiler allocates memory for the variables.
   (b) Compiler assigns values to the variables.
   (c) Linker assigns values to the variables.
   (d) Loader assigns values to the variables.

10. Which of the following statements are true?
    (a) Insertion operator cannot be cascaded.
    (b) Extraction operator cannot be cascaded.
    (c) Both insertion as well as extraction operators can be cascaded.
    (d) Only insertion operator can be cascaded.

11. Which of the following is not a pre-processor directive?
    (a) `include`
    (b) `define`
    (c) `cout`
    (d) None of the mentioned options.

12. Correct the errors if it exists and/or determine the output of the following program
    ```
    #define DATA=15
    void main()
    {
    int a=10,b=15,c;
    c = a+b+DATA;
    cout<<"Result of addition is <<c;
    }
    ```

13. Identify valid and invalid integer/float constants from the list given below
    (a) `3.5A`   (d) `34,000`   (g) `-12k`
    (b) `12`   (e) `12.4.2`
    (c) `12e2`   (f) `79,00,000`

14. Correct the errors if it exists and/or find the output of the following program
    ```
    #define NUMBER 15;
    void main()
    {
    ```

```
int x=76,y=90,z;
z=x+y+NUMBER-10+25+NULL;
printf("The value of variable z is %d",c);
}
```

15. Identify the valid/invalid variable names from the list below:
    (a) `Apple`   (d) `MAX`   (g) `_Bat-61`
    (b) `1_orange`   (e) `float`   (h) `Wild-life`
    (c) `Data123`   (f) `12k`   (i) `Sur;name`

16. Determine the output of each of the following `printf()` statements
    ```
    char a ='A';
    printf("%d",a);
    printf("%c",a);
    printf("%u",a);
    ```

17. Which of the following are valid constants? Specify the data type of those constants which are valid.
    (a) `'a'`   (h) `"'"`   (o) `0xFFF`
    (b) `-100e10`   (i) `'1'`   (p) `'\"'`
    (c) `-2.5E55`   (j) `'\t'`   (q) `548,000`
    (d) `35000L`   (k) `'\n'`   (r) `5,000`
    (e) `'10'`   (l) `'\0x34'`   (s) `1`
    (f) `"Ship123@#"`   (m) `044`   (t) `"100"`
    (g) `"Goal:'of'Life"`   (n) `876432282345231`

    What is the output of the following program.
    ```
    #include<stdio.h>
    void main()
    {
    int a=55;
    printf("Outer printf: %d\n", printf("Inner printf %d\n",a) );
    }
    ```

HINT

`printf()` returns number of characters it has printed on the computer screen. For example, `printf("Hi");` will return 2 because it has printed 2 characters on the screen. On this basis try to execute the above program and understand its output.

Review Questions

1. Explain the significance of the `main()` function in C/C++.
2. Correct the below C++ statement to print the values of variables a and b
   ```
   cout>>"value of a is a">>"value of b is b";
   ```
3. Explain and correct the errors in the following program.
   ```
   include>>iostream.h
   main()
   {
   ```

```
cout<<"Hello";
cin>>a;
cout>>"Value of a is"<<a;
}
```

4. Write a short note on the pre-processor directives.
5. List the different primitive data types along with their memory requirement and the range of values supported in each of the data type.

Chapter

3 | Operators and Type Casting

3.1 Overview

C/C++ has a dedicated set of special characters which can be used to perform operations on the data items. Each of these special characters represent as a specific operation to be performed to the compiler. For example, a symbol + is used to perform addition, and the symbol * is used to perform multiplication and so on. There are two properties associated with each of the operators so as to define the approach used for its evaluation:

1. Priority of the operator
2. Associativity of the operator

A **Priority** of the operator is a precedence associated with the operator. Every Operator is assigned a specific priority using which an operator must be resolved, so as to generate the result of the expression. Assigning priority to an operator helps in avoiding the **ambiguity** that may arise in the order of evaluation when a given expression consists of multiple operators. So as to understand the exact meaning of operator precedence, let us consider the expression below:

```
int p=10,q=5,r=2,s;
s=p+q*r;
```

After substituting the values of variables p, q, and r the expression that calculates the value of variable s can be rewritten as shown below:

```
s=10+5*2;
```

In the absence of operator precedence, the compiler will have two different options to generate the result of the above expression.

3.1.1 Option 1: Perform addition before multiplication (wrong option)

First perform the addition of two numbers 10 and 5, and then perform multiplication of the result with value 2. Hence, we will get the result of the expression as 30 as shown in Figure 3.1. Note that, this is a case where,we have evaluated the result of 'addition' before evaluating the result of 'multiplication'. The order of evaluation is as shown in Figure 3.1.

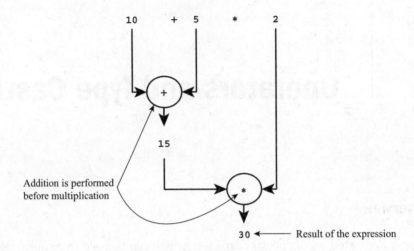

Figure 3.1: Option 1: Order of evaluation

3.1.2 Option 2: Perform multiplication before addition (correct option)

As a second option to generate the result of the expression, we could first perform multiplication of two numbers 5 and 2 and then perform addition of the result with value 10. Hence, we will get the result of the expression as 20 as shown in Figure 3.2. Note that, this is a case where, we have evaluated the result of 'multiplication' before evaluating the result of 'addition'. The order of evaluation is as shown in Figure 3.2.

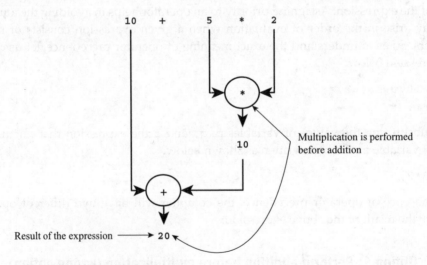

Figure 3.2: Option 2: Order of evaluation

Therefore, we can say that, there exists a situation, wherein the evaluation of a single expression can be done in different approaches such that each of the options will give us a different result. This problem in the evaluating the result of the expression is called an **ambiguity** in the compilation process.

It is very clear that, the second option gives us the correct mathematical result of the expression (which is value 20) whereas the first option gives us the incorrect result. So as to ensure correct order of operator evaluation, every operator is assigned a priority or precedence. The compiler ensures that the result of all the operators with the higher priority is evaluated before evaluating the result of any of the operators with a lower priority in the expression. For example, the priority of multiplication is HIGHER whereas the priority of addition is LOWER and hence C/C++ will always execute 'multiplication' before performing 'addition'. This also resolves the ambiguity or confusion that may arise in determining the order in which the operators within the expression are to be evaluated. This means that C/C++ will always follow the second option and correctly generate the result of the expression as **20** as shown in Figure 3.2.

REMEMBER

When there are multiple options available to the compiler to evaluate a result of particular operation then this situation is called '**ambiguity**'. Compiler of every language has its own way to eliminate ambiguity in the expression. The unit within the compiler that eliminates ambiguity within an expression is called a **parser**. Out of all the options available compiler must be in position to choose the correct evaluation tree which procures the mathematically correct result. To facilitate a **mathematically correct** result for each expression, every operator has a predefined **priority and associativity**.

In general, if we consider the precedence of arithmetic operators, multiplication, and division operators have a higher precedence whereas addition and subtraction have lower precedence. This ensures that the results of all the multiplication/division operators used in the expression are evaluated before evaluating the results of any addition/subtraction operators in the expression. The exact operator precedence of all the operators in C/C++ is as given in Figure 3.6.

Also, every operator has an **associativity** which specifies the direction in which a particular expression must be evaluated. Associativity of an operator can be from 'Left to Right (L→R)' or from 'Right to Left (R→L)'. In general, case associativity comes into picture when we attempt to use 2 or more operators with same priority within a single expression.

For example, let us consider the statements below:

```
int p=10,q=5,r=3,s;
s=p+q-r;
```

After substituting the values of variables p, q, and r, the expression that calculates the value of variable s can be rewritten as shown below:

```
s=10+5-3;
```

Note that both + and - are operators with same priority. In such a case, C/C++ determines order of evaluation using the associativity of arithmetic operators which is 'Left to Right (L→R)'. Hence, the system evaluates the expression in a direction from Left to Right, such that, the addition of 10 and 5 will be performed before evaluating the result of subtraction. Hence, the final result of the expression will be evaluated as 12 as shown in Figure 3.3.

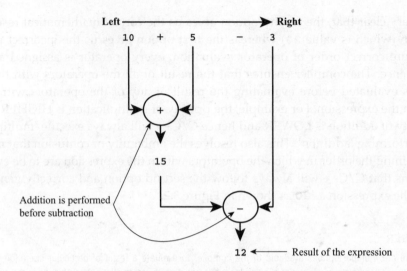

Figure 3.3:   Evaluation of expression $10 + 5 - 3$

To get a clear understanding of the concept of **'associativity'**, let us change the expression for evaluating the value of variable s as shown below:

s=p-q+r;

By applying substitution we have,

s=10-5+3

Again, we know that the operator - and + are of same priority. Hence, C/C++ determines order of evaluation using the associativity of arithmetic operators which is 'Left to Right (L→R)'. Therefore, we will evaluate the complete expression in a direction from Left to Right, such that, the subtraction of 10 and 5 will be performed before evaluating the result of addition. Hence, the final result of the expression will be evaluated as 8 as shown in Figure 3.4.

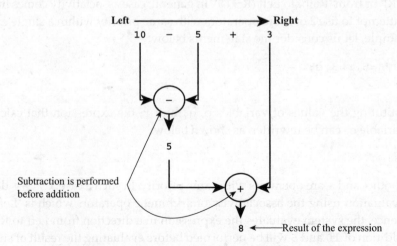

Figure 3.4:   Evaluation of expression $10 - 5 + 3$

The associativity of some operators in C/C++ can also be 'Right to Left' instead of 'Left to Right'. For example, consider the below statement which assigns the value of variable a to variables b and c.

```
int a=10,b,c;
```

```
c=b=a; /*Assignment operator has an associativity from Right to left*/
```

The statement c=b=a; uses the assignment operator =two times. Also, the value of variable a is already set to 10 at the time of declaration of the variable. The requirement here is that, the value of a must first be assigned to b and the value of variable b must then be assigned to c. Hence the associativity of the assignment operator is set as 'Right to Left' by compiler as shown in Figure 3.5.

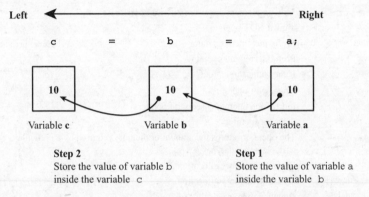

Figure 3.5: Evaluation of expression c = b = a

This ensures that, the value of variable a is copied into b before the value of b is copied into c. Therefore a value 10 is stored in all the three variables a, b and c after the evaluation of the expression.

Who assigns priorities to the operators? ?

The compiler of the language assigns priority and associativity to each of the operators supported by the language. Although, the actual evaluation of the operations is done at runtime of the program, the order in which the operators in an expression are to be evaluated is decided at the time compilation itself. The compiler decides the order of evaluating the operators based on the predefined priority and associativity of each of the operators used in the expression. This avoids possibility of any ambiguity that may arise at run time of the program when the expression is actually evaluated.

C/C++ supports rich collection of operators and each operator has a well defined associativity and priority as shown in Figure 3.6. In this chapter we will discuss different operators in C/C++. The operators can be broadly classified as below.

1. Arithmetic operator
2. Relational operator
3. Logical operator(will be discussed in chapter 4)

4. Bitwise operator
5. Shorthand operator
6. Increment/decrement operators

Rank / Precedence	Operator	Description	Associativity
1.	::	Scope resolution operator	Left to right
2.	[]	The operator to access array elements	Left to right
	()	The function call operator	
	.	Operator to access the members of the object using the object name	
	–>	Operator to access the members of the object using a pointer	
	++	Postfix increment operator	
	--	Postfix decrement operator	
3.	~	1's Complement operator (Bitwise operator)	Right to left
	!	logical NOT operator	
	++	Prefix increment operator	
	--	Prefix decrement operator	
	–	Unary minus operator	
	+	Unary plus operator	
	*	Indirection operator(used with pointers)	
	&	Address operator	
	sizeof	The operator returns the amount of memory required by a particular variable or a datatype	
	new	Dynamic memory allocation	
	new []	Dynamic memory allocation	
	delete	Dynamic memory deallocation	
	delete[]	Dynamic memory deallocation for arrays	
	(datatype)	Explicit type cast operator	
4.	.*	Pointer to a member using object	Left to right
	–>*	Pointer to a member using a pointer	
5.	*	Multiplication operator	Left to right
	/	Division operator	
	%	Modulo division operator	
6.	–	Subtraction operator	Left to right
	+	Addition operator	
7.	>>	Right shift operator	Left to right
	<<	Left shift operator	
8.	<	Less than operator	Left to right
	<=	Less than or equal to	
	>	Greater than	
	>=	Greater than or equal to	
9.	==	Equal to	
	!=	Not equal to	
10.	&	Bitwise AND operator	Left to right
11.	^	Bitwise XOR operator	Left to right
12.	|	Bitwise OR operator	Left to right
13.	&&	Logical AND operator	Left to right
14.	||	Logical OR operator	Left to right

(Contd)

Figure 3.6: (Contd)

15.	?:	Ternary conditional (if-then-else)	Right to left
16.	Shorthand operators	Assignment/Compound assignment operators	Right to left
17	,	Comma operator	Left to right

Figure 3.6: Priority and associativity of operators

3.2 Arithmetic Operators

Arithmetic operators are special symbols which can be used to perform arithmetic operations like addition, subtraction, multiplication, and division. An arithmetic operator is called a unary operator if the operator operates over a single operand. Whereas, an operator is called a binary operator, if it operates over two different operands.

Given below is the list of arithmetic operators supported by C/C++:

Operator symbol	Description
+	The symbol + is used to perform the addition of two numbers when it is used in the binary form. The symbol + can also be used in a unary form to represent a positive sign of a particular data value.
-	The symbol - is used to perform the subtraction of two numbers when it is used in the binary form. The symbol - can also be used in a unary form to represent a negative sign of a particular data value.
*	The symbol * is used to perform the multiplication of two numbers when it is used in the binary form.
/	The symbol / is used to perform the division of two numbers when it is used in the binary form.
%	The symbol % is used to perform modulo division of two numbers when it is used in the binary form. The difference between operators / and % is that the operator / returns the quotient of division of the two numbers whereas, the operator % returns the remainder of division of the two numbers.
=	The operator = is called an assignment operator. The operator is used to assign the value of the expression which is written on the right hand side of the statement to a variable which is present on the left hand side of the statement.

Let us consider a few example statements which describe the usage of arithmetic operators

3.2.1 Example 1: Using the operator – (minus) in an unary form

We can use the operator minus in the unary form so as to negate the value of a particular variable. As an example, let us consider the statements given below, where we declare two variables 'a' and 'b' of type integer. The value of the variable 'a' is initialized to 10 whereas the value of the variable 'b' is initialized by applying the 'minus' operator over a value of variable 'a' as seen below:

```
int a=10,b;
```

```
b=-a;
```

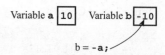

Figure 3.7: Values of the variables a and b

The statement `b=-a;` assigns the negated value of a to the variable b. Hence, the value of variable b is set to `-10` as shown in Figure 3.7. Note that, value of variable a will still be `+10` because the negated value of a is actually assigned to the variable b and not back to the variable a.

The syntax is such that, we can also use the operator + in a unary form. However, using the operator+ in unary form may not give any useful purpose to the programmer because all the data values are by default considered as positive in C/C++ unless any of the data value is explicitly specified as negative in the program.

3.2.2 Example 2: Using the operators +, −, *, /and % in binary form

Figure 3.8 gives the code which creates two variables a and b with values 20 and 5, respectively. The code applies all the binary arithmetic operators on the two variables a and b and stores the result of each of the operations in the variables p, q, r, s, and t.

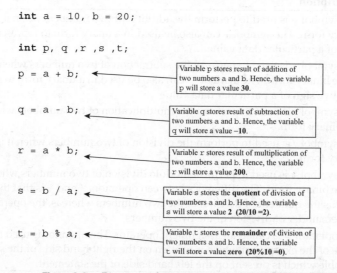

Figure 3.8: Binary arithmetic operators in C/C++

Can we use the remainder operator % with floating point constants? ?

We cannot use the operator % with the floating point or the double constants. This is because, the float/double constants contain fractional components and hence the result of dividing two floats or two doubles should also contain a fractional component without any remainder. Usage of a % operator with float or double variables will result into an compilation error in the program. Hence, the statement below will give a compilation error:

```
float a=100.7, b=22.5,c;
c=a%b; /*compilation ERROR: Illegal usage of float operands*/
```

3.2.3 Program to evaluate the area of a triangle: An example

As an example to understand the usage of operators, let us write a program that accepts the values of `length` and `breadth` as input from the user and prints the area of the triangle as the output of the program. Given below is the full source code that evaluates the area of the triangle:

```
#include<stdio.h>
void main()
{
float length, breadth, area;
printf("Enter length and breadth of the triangle\n");
scanf("%f %f",&length ,&breadth);
area= 0.5*length*breadth;
printf("The area of the triangle is %f",area);
}
```

Output

```
Enter length and breadth of the triangle
10.5 20
The area of the triangle is 105.000000
```

The program declares three variables named as `length`, `breadth`, and `area` of type float as seen from the first statement in the code. Further, the program reads the values of `length` and `breadth` from the keyboard using the `scanf()` statement. Let us assume that, the user gives the values of variables `length` and `breadth` as `10.5` and `20`, respectively. The value of the variable `area` is calculated using an expression given below:

```
area= 0.5*length*breadth;
```

As `*` is the only operator which is used for evaluation of the value of variable `area`. The complete expression will be evaluated with an associativity of **left to right**. Therefore, the value of the variable `area` will be initialized as `105`. The calculated value of the variable `area` is then printed on the computer screen using a `printf()` statement as seen in the output of the code.

3.2.4 Program to calculate the slope of the line: An example

Let us write a program to calculate the slope of the line which is given as below:

Slope of line = Difference in Y coordinates/Difference in X coordinates;

Let us declare four variables in the program named as `x1`, `y1` and `x2`, `y2` such that, `x1` and `y1` represent the x and y coordinates of the first point of the line and `x2`, `y2` represent the x and y coordinates of the second point of the line.

Given below is the full source code that reads the values of `x1,y1` and `x2,y2` from the user and calculates a floating point value m which represents the slope of the line.

```
#include<stdio.h>
void main()
{
float x1,y1,x2,y2,m;
printf("Enter the first point\n");
scanf("%f %f",&x1,&y1);
printf("Enter the second point\n");
scanf("%f %f",&x2,&y2);
m=(y2-y1)/(x2-x1);/*We assume (x2-x1) does not evaluate to zero*/
printf("Slope of the line is %f",m);
}
```

Output
```
Enter the first point
100 200
Enter the second point
10 20
Slope of the line is 2.000000
```

Note the presence of parentheses in the statement,

```
m=(y2-y1)/(x2-x1);
```

As we have performed the operations y2-y1 and x2-x1 in parenthesis the 'subtractions' in the expressions will be performed before the result of division is evaluated. This is because, the parenthesis has a highest priority when compared to the priority of division. It is always important to remember that everything inside the brackets will be evaluated before evaluation of any operator which is written outside the parenthesis in a particular expression. Therefore, the difference between x and y values will be evaluated before the division is performed as shown in Figure 3.9. It assumes that the user enters the values of (x1,y1) as (100,200) and the values of (x2,y2) as (10,20), therefore the value of the variable 'm' will be evaluated as **2** which is the slope of the line from point (100,200) to point (10,20).

3.2.5 Understanding the precedence of arithmetic operators: An example

As an example to understand the operator precedence with arithmetic operators, let us evaluate the result of variable Z using the following expression:

```
Z = (40+5)*10-60/2+4-(12+4)*3+4*2;
```

At first step, system evaluates the result of all the operations which are performed in parenthesis. This is because the parenthesis operator has a highest priority as compared to other arithmetic operators in C/C++. Therefore, the operations 40+5 and 12+4 will be evaluated at the initial stage as shown in Figure 3.10.

Hence, the expression for the variable Z can now be represented as shown below

```
Z = 45*10-60/2+4-16*3+4*2;
```

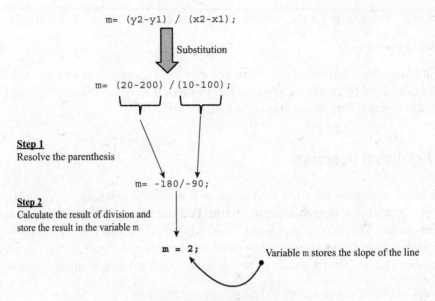

Figure 3.9: Evaluation of slope

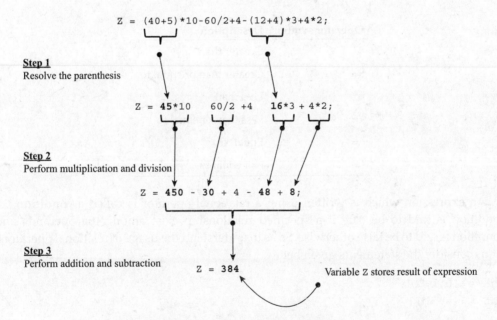

Figure 3.10: Evaluating an expression

Note that, the values 45 and 16 are results of addition which is performed in the parentheses as shown in Figure 3.10. Now, the distinct operators remaining in the expression are *,/, + and - out of which * and / have a higher priority whereas + and - have a lower priority. Therefore, the multiplication and division will be performed before the results of addition of subtraction can be evaluated. The further evaluation of the expression is as shown in Figure 3.10.

Hence, the expression for the variable Z can now be represented as shown below:

```
Z = 450-30+4-48+8;
```

As the only operators which are now remaining in the expression are + and - the value of Z will be evaluated by resolving the operators from left to right, thereby storing the final value of the variable Z as 384 as shown in Figure 3.10.

3.3 Relational Operators

The relational operators are used to determine if a specific relationship exist among the operands. The relational operators always return Boolean values as **true** or **false** as the result of the expression. The value 1 represents 'true' whereas the value 0 represents false. Every relational operator is always a binary operator which means that we must always use a relational operator with exactly 2 operands. Given below is the syntax of using relational operators

```
<operand1> <relationalOperator> <operand2>
```

The list of relational operators supported by C/C++ are as given below:

Operator symbol	Description
>	Greater than
>=	Greater than or equal to
<	Less than
<=	Less than or equal to
==	Equal to
!=	Not equal to

An expression which is written using a relational operator is called a **condition**. A condition is said to be true if a specified relationship exist among the operands and condition is said to be false otherwise. So as to understand the usage of relational operators, let us consider the statements given below.

```
int a=10,b=20;
int k=(a>=b);
```

Here, we have created two variables a and b of type integer with values 10 and 20 respectively and we store the result of the condition (a>=b) in a variable k. The value of the condition in this case will be zero because the value of a is neither greater than nor equal to the value of b. This means that the value of variable k will be set as zero because the condition a>=b is **false**, as shown in Figure 3.11.

Figure 3.12 gives the full source code which shows the output of all the relational operators by creating two variables p and q with values 100 and 200, respectively.

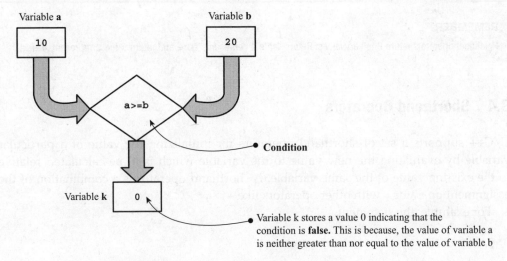

Figure 3.11 Relational expression returning Boolean result

```
#include<stdio.h>

void main()
{
int p=100,q=200;

printf("Result of p>q is %d \n", (p>q));

printf("Result of p>=q is %d \n", (p>=q));

printf("Result of p<q is %d \n", (p<q));

printf("Result of p<=q is %d \n", (p<=q));

printf("Result of p==q is %d \n", (p==q));

printf("Result of p!=q is %d \n", (p!=q));

}
```

This statement will print **0(false)** on the computer screen. This is because, the value of variable p is not greater than the value of variable q.

This statement will print **0(false)** on the computer screen. This is because, the value of variable p is not greater than or equal to the value of variable q.

This statement will print **1(true)** on the computer screen. This is because, the value of variable p is less than the value of variable q.

This statement will print **1(true)** on the computer screen. This is because, the value of variable p is less than the value of variable q.

This statement will print **0(false)** on the computer screen. This is because, the value of variable p is not same as value of variable q.

This statement will print **1(true)** on the computer screen. This is because, the value of variable p is not same as the value of variable q.

Figure 3.12: Source code of relational operators

The output of the code shown in Figure 3.12 is as given below:

```
Result of p>q is 0
Result of p>=q is 0
Result of p<q is 1
Result of p<=q is 1
Result of p==q is 0
Result of p!=q is 1
```

REMEMBER

Relational operators return Boolean values. Return value 1 represents **true** and return value 0 represents **false**.

3.4 Shorthand Operators

C/C++ supports a set of shorthand operators for initializing the value of a particular variable by evaluating the new value to the variable which is to be calculated relative to the existing value of the same variable. A shorthand operator is a combination of the assignment operator = with other operators like +, -, *, /, %, etc.

For example, the statement,

```
a=a+100;
```

can be written in a shorthand notation as

```
a+=100;
```

Note that the result of both of the above statements is exactly same as both the statements will add a value 100 to the value of variable a and store the result of addition back in the variable a itself. It is important to understand that, every shorthand statement as an equivalent longhand statement. Hence, the compiler internally converts every shorthand notation used by the programmer into its long form so as to get the result of the shorthand operator. Assuming that a and b are two variables; the table below gives a meaning of few shorthand operators used ith the variables a and b:

Shorthand operator	Example	Equivalent longhand statement
+=	a+=b;	a=a+b;
-=	a-=b;	a=a-b;
*=	a*=b;	a=a*b;
/=	a/=b;	a=a/b;
%=	a%=b;	a=a%b;

As seen from the table above, we understand that writing a statement a+=b in the program will have a same effect as writing a statement a=a+b; writing a statement a*=b; in the program will have a same effect as writing a statement a=a*b; and so on. In summary, the shorthand operators just provides short cut to the programmers so as to make a longer statement short.

Hence a statement,

```
a=a*(b+c+d);
```

will be equivalent to

```
a*=(b+c+d);
```

3.5 Bitwise Operators in C/C++

The bitwise operators are used to support bit level operations with integer values. C\C++ supports the following bitwise operators to perform bit level operations:

Operator	Description
&	AND operator
|	OR operator
~	1's complement operator
^	Ex-OR operator
<<	Left shift operator
>>	Right shift operator

Let us create 2 variables p and q of type integer so as to understand the usage of bitwise operators. Further, let us set the values of p and q as 20 and 13, as shown below:

```
int p = 20;
int q = 13;
```

Hence, the binary translated values for the variables p and q will be as shown below:

```
p = 0000 0000 0001 0100
q = 0000 0000 0000 1101
```

Note that we represent every integer using 16 bits because every integer is 2 bytes in size. We will now perform the bit level operations over operands p and q as discussed in sections below.

3.5.1 Bitwise AND Operation (&)

The operator & is used to perform a bitwise AND operation. Hence, the statement,

```
a = p & q;
```

will perform the bit-by-bit logical AND operation over the operands p and q, thereby storing the result of AND operation in the variable a. We know that the result of the AND operation is 1 when all the input bits are 1. Given below is the truth table of the AND operation.

Input bit 1	Input bit 2	Result of AND operation
0	0	0
0	1	0
1	0	0
1	1	1

Given below is the evaluation of the statement a = p & q; using the truth table of AND operation:

$$
\begin{array}{lcl}
p & = & 0000\ 0000\ 0001\ 0100 \\
q & = & 0000\ 0000\ 0000\ 1101 \\
a & = & 0000\ 0000\ 0000\ 0100
\end{array}
$$

Hence, the value of the variable a will be set to 4 in decimal number system, because a binary number 0000 0000 0000 0100 is equivalent to a decimal number 4.

3.5.2   Bitwise OR Operation (¦)

The operator ¦ is used to perform a bitwise OR operation. Hence, the statement,

```
b=p|q;
```

will perform the bit-by-bit logical OR operation over the operands p and q, thereby storing the result of the OR operation in the variable b. We know that the result of the OR operation is 1 when any one of the input bits is 1. Given below is the truth table of the logical OR operation:

Input bit 1	Input bit 2	Result of OR operation
0	0	0
0	1	1
1	0	1
1	1	1

Given below is the evaluation of the statement b=p|q; using the truth table of the logical 'OR' operation:

$$
\begin{array}{lcl}
p & = & 0000\ 0000\ 0001\ 0100 \\
q & = & 0000\ 0000\ 0000\ 1101 \\
b & = & 0000\ 0000\ 0001\ 1101
\end{array}
$$

Hence, the value of the variable b will be set as 29 in the decimal number system, because the binary number 0000 0000 0001 1101 is equivalent to a decimal value of 29.

3.5.3   Bitwise Ex-OR Operation (^)

The operator ^ is used to perform a bitwise Ex-OR operation. Hence, the statement,

```
c = p^q;
```

will perform a bit-by-bit logical Ex-OR operation over the operands p and q, thereby storing the result of Ex-OR operation in the variable c. We know that the result of Ex-OR operation is 1 when the ODD number of input bit is 1. Given below is the truth table for the logical Ex-OR operation:

Input bit 1	Input bit 2	Result of Ex-OR operation
0	0	0
0	1	1
1	0	1
1	1	0

Given below is the evaluation of the statement c = p^q; using the truth table of the bitwise Ex-OR operation:

$$
\begin{aligned}
p &= 0000\ 0000\ 0001\ 0100 \\
q &= 0000\ 0000\ 0000\ 1101 \\
\hline
c &= 0000\ 0000\ 0001\ 1001
\end{aligned}
$$

Hence, the value of the variable c will be set as 25 in decimal number system, because a binary number 0000 0000 0001 1001 is equivalent to a decimal number 25.

3.5.4 One's complement operator (~)

One's complement of any binary number is obtained by bit inversion. Bit inversion is a process to replace every occurrence of 1 by 0 and every occurrence of 0 by 1 in a binary number.

The operator ~ is a unary operator and hence it must be associated with exactly one operand. As an example, let us consider a variable x with a value 0, as shown below:

```
int x = 0;
```

Now, let us apply a l's complement operator (~) over x and store the l's complement of variable x in the variable x itself. This can be done using the statement below:

```
x = ~x;
```

As the original value of the variable x is zero, the initial value of x can be represented in binary as shown below:

```
x = 0000 0000 0000 0000
```

After applying 1's complement operator on the variable x, the new value of the variable x will be as shown below:

```
x = 1111 1111 1111 1111
```

Hence, the new value of x will be set as 65535, which is the decimal equivalent of the resultant binary number.

3.5.5 Left shift operator (<<)

The left shift operation is used to shift the bits of the binary number in the left direction by padding 0s from the right direction, as shown in Figure 3.13. Therefore, the left shift operator will delete the Most significant bits (MSBs) of the number because the extra 0s are padded as the least significant bits (LSBs) of the number.

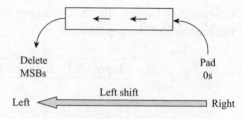

Figure 3.13: Working of left shift operator

For example, let the value of the variable x be initialized to 4 using the statement below:

```
int x = 4;
```

The statement,

```
l = x << 3;
```

will shift the bits in number x by padding three extra 0s at the LSB side of x.

The resultant number obtained after shifting the bits of x will be stored in the variable l, as shown in Figure 3.14 below.

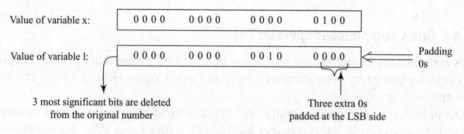

Figure 3.14: Example of left shift operator

Hence, the value of the variable *1* will be 32, which is a decimal equivalent of the binary number 100000.

Note that the value of the variable x is 4 and after shifting 3 bit positions in x, we get the value of the variable *l* as 32, which can also be obtained from the original value 4, as shown below:

$$4 \times 2^3 = 32$$

This means that when we apply a left shift operation on any number x by k bit positions, the result of the left shift operation is equivalent to $x \times 2^k$.

3.5.6 Right shift operation (>>)

The right shift operation is used to shift the bits of a binary number in the right direction by padding 0s to the number from the left direction, as shown in Figure 3.15. Therefore, the right shift operation will delete the least significant bits of the number because the extra 0s are padded as the most significant bits of the number.

For example, let the value of the variable x be initialized to 32, as shown below:

```
int x = 32;
```

The statement,

```
r = x >> 3;
```

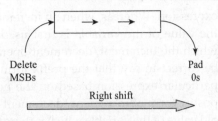

Delete
MSBs

Pad
0s

Right shift

Figure 3.15: Working of right shift operator

will shift the bits in the number x by padding 3 extra 0s at the MSB side of x. The resultant number obtained after shifting the bits of x will be stored in the variable r, as shown below in Figure 3.16.

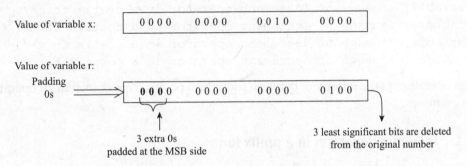

Value of variable x:

| 0 0 0 0 | 0 0 0 0 | 0 0 1 0 | 0 0 0 0 |

Value of variable r:

Padding
0s

| 0 0 0 0 | 0 0 0 0 | 0 0 0 0 | 0 1 0 0 |

3 extra 0s
padded at the MSB side

3 least significant bits are deleted
from the original number

Figure 3.16: Example of right shift operator

Hence, the value of the variable r will be set as 4, which is the decimal equivalent of the binary number 100.

Note that the value of the variable x is 32 and after shifting 3 bit positions in x, we get the value of the variable r as 4, which can also be obtained from the original value 32, as shown below:

$$\frac{32}{2^3} = 4$$

This means that when we apply a right shift operation on any number x by k bit positions, the result of the right shift operation is equivalent to the expression $x/2^k$.

3.6 Increment/Decrement Operators

The increment operator is used to increase the value of the variable by 1 whereas the decrement operator can be used to decrease the value of the variable by 1. The symbol ++(two consecutive plus signs without a space) represents an increment operation over a variable and the symbol, --(two consecutive minus signs without a space)represents a decrement operation over a variable. The increment/decrement operators can be used in **prefix** or **postfix** form.

When an increment/decrement operator is used in the prefix form the value of the variable is incremented/decremented before it is used to evaluate the result of a particular expression. Whereas, when an increment/decrement operator is used in the postfix form, the value of the variable is first used to evaluate the result of the expression following which the increment/decrement operation is performed over the variable. Hence, it will be correct to say that the prefix form of increment/decrement evaluates the result of a particular expression based on the newly calculated value of the variable whereas, the postfix form of increment/decrement evaluates the result of the expression based on the old value of the variable which is there before applying the increment/decrement operation on the variable.

Given below is the syntax of using the increment operator ++ and the decrement operator--over a particular variable

```
++Variable; /*usage of increment operator in a prefix form*/
Variable++; /*usage of increment operator in a postfix form*/
--Variable; /*usage of decrement operator in a prefix form*/
Variable--; /*usage of decrement operator in a postfix form*/
```

Let us now discuss the difference between prefix and postfix from of increment operations with examples.

3.6.1 Increment operator in a prefix form

So as to understand the usage of increment operator in the prefix form, let us create two variables a and b as shown below:

```
int a =10,b;
```

Note that, the value of variable a will be set as 10 and the value of the variable b will be junk at this stage as shown in Figure 3.17.

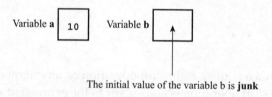

The initial value of the variable b is **junk**

Figure 3.17: Value of variables a and b

Let us now apply a prefix increment operation on the variable a and initialize the result of the operation to the variable b. This can be done using a following statement:
```
b=++a;
```

As we have used the increment operation in the prefix form, that value of the variable a will be first incremented to 11. Further, the value 11 will now be initialized to the variable b. Therefore, as a result of the above statement the values of variables a as well as b will be set to 11 as shown in Figure 3.18. Hence, it will be correct to say that the prefix form of the increment variable assigns the newly calculated value of the variable a to the variable b.

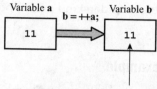

The incremented value of the variable a will be stored in variable b because we have used the increment operator in the prefix form.

Figure 3.18: Value of variables a and b

3.6.2 Increment operator in a postfix form

So as to understand the usage of increment operator in the postfix form, let us create two variables x and y as shown below:

```
int x =10,y;
```

As per the above statement, the value of variable x will be set as 10 and the value of the variable y will be junk at this stage as shown in Figure 3.19.

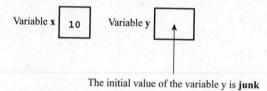

The initial value of the variable y is **junk**

Figure 3.19: Value of variables x and y

Let us now apply a postfix increment operation on the variable x and initialize the result of the operation to the variable y. This can be done using a following statement:

```
y=x++;
```

As we have used the increment operation in the postfix form, that value of the variable x will be first assigned to the variable y. Hence, the value of the variable y will be set as 10. After the assignment operation is completed, the value of the variable x will be changed to 11 as shown in Figure 3.20. Hence, it will be correct to say that the postfix form of the increment variable assigns the older value of the variable x to the variable y.

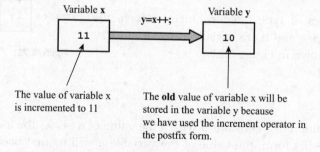

The value of variable x is incremented to 11

The **old** value of variable x will be stored in the variable y because we have used the increment operator in the postfix form.

Figure 3.20: Value of variables x and y

A similar theory can also be applicable to understand prefix/postfix form of decrement operations.

3.6.3 Evaluating the output: An example

As an example to have a clear understanding of increment/decrement operators, let us determine the output of the given code by calculating the value of each of the variables whose value is printed on the computer screen.

```
#include<stdio.h>
void main()
{
int a=10,b=20 ,r1,r2,r3;
r1 = 5 + a++;
r2= b--;
r3 = --r2;
printf("a=%d \n",a);
printf("b=%d \n",b);
printf("r1=%d \n",r1);
printf("r2=%d \n",r2);
printf("r3=%d \n",r3);
}
```

Output

```
a=11
b=19
r1=15
r2=19
r3=19
```

Let us trace the output of the code starting from the first line in the main function.

The statement,

```
int a=10,b=20,r1,r2,r3;
```

creates 5 variables of type integer. Out of which, the values of variables a and b are initialized to 10 and 20 respectively as shown in Figure 3.21.

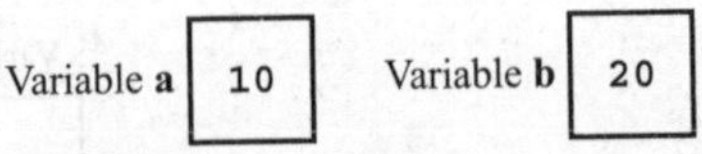

Variable a | 10   Variable b | 20

Figure 3.21: Variables a and b

The statement,

```
r1 = 5 + a++;
```

performs the addition of a constant 5 with a the value of a++. As the increment operator is used in the postfix form, the value of the variable a will be first used to evaluate the result of the expression following which the value of the variable a will be incremented to reflect a new value as 11. Hence, the expression to calculate the value of variable r1 can be rewritten as shown below:

```
r1=5+10; /*old value of the variable a is used to calculate the
result of the expression*/
```

Note that, the value of a is considered as 10 for calculating the value of variable r1 because the postfix form of the increment operation always uses the older value of the variable to calculate the result of the expression. Hence, the value of the variable r1 will be evaluated as 15 and then the value of a will be incremented to 11 as shown in Figure 3.22.

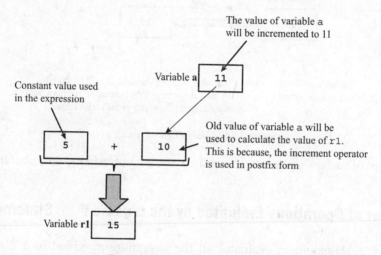

Figure 3.22: Variables r1 and a

The next statement,

```
r2= b--;
```

initializes the value of the variable r2 by applying a post decrement operator to the variable b. This means that the value of the variable b will be first assigned to the variable r2 following which the value of variable b will be decremented. Hence, the value of variable r2 will be set to 20 following which the value of variable b will be decremented to 19 as shown in Figure 3.23.

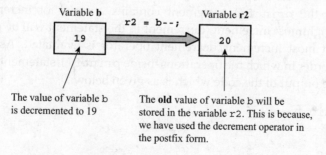

Figure 3.23: Variables r2 and b

The statement,

```
r3 = --r2;
```

initializes the value of the variable r3 by applying a pre decrement operator to the variable r2. This means that, the value of the variable r2 will be first decremented to reflect the new value as 19 (since the value of r2 was previously set as 20 as per Figure 3.23) and the new value of r2 will then be assigned to the variable r3. Therefore, the values of the variables r2 as well as r3 will be set to 19 as shown in Figure 3.24.

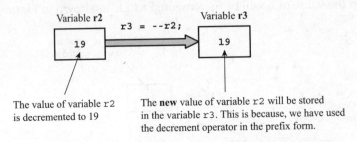

Figure 3.24: Variables r2 and r3

The values of variables a, b, r1, r2, and r3 are as shown in the output of the program.

3.7 Order of Operations Evaluated by the `printf()` Statement

The `printf()` statement in evaluates all the operations specified in a direction from **right to left (R→L)**. For example, if 'op1' and 'op2' are two different operations and if the `printf()` statement is written as below,

```
printf("control string", op1, op2);
```

then the operation 'op2' will be executed before the execution of the operation 'op1'. This is because, the operation 'op2' is the right most operation in the `printf()` statement. However, keep a note that the order of printing will still be 'left to right' which is exactly opposite to the order of execution. This means that, although the operation 'op2' is executed before 'op1', the result of operation 'op1' will be printed on the computer screen before printing the result of operation 'op2'.

Therefore, if the `printf()` statement contains a series of increment/decrement operations, the rightmost increment/decrement in the statement will be evaluated before the result of left most increment/decrement operator is evaluated. As an example, to understand the order in which the operations inside `printf()` statement are executed, let us determine the output of the code which is as given below:

```
#include<stdio.h>
void main()
{
int a=10;
```

```
printf("%d %d %d\n",a++,++a,--a);
printf("The last value of a is %d",a);
}
```

Output

```
10 10 9
The last value of a is 11
```

The statement,

```
int a=10;
```

creates an integer type variable named as a with value 10 stored inside it.
   The second statement,

```
printf("%d %d %d\n",a++,++a,--a);
```

prints the following output on the computer screen:

```
10   10   9
```

The order in which the increment/decrement operators will be evaluated is from **right
to left** whereas the order of printing the result on the computer screen will be from
left to right. As there is a difference between the order of evaluation and the order of
printing, we trace the output of the statement in reverse order as seen in the Figures
given below.

   Firstly, the operation - -a will be executed which will decrement the value of variable
a to 9 and hence print 9 on the computer screen as shown in Figure 3.25. Note that, the
value of variable a is first decremented to store 9 following which it is printed on the
screen. This is because we have used the decrement operator in the **prefix** form as shown
in Figure 3.25.

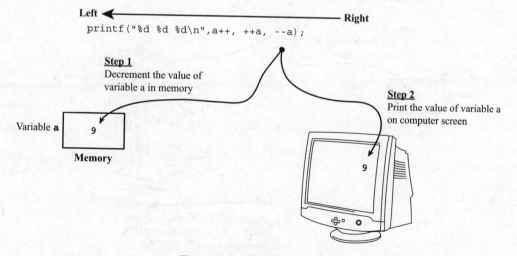

Figure 3.25:   Execution of --a

Secondly, the operation ++a will be executed which will increment the value of variable a to10 and hence print 10 on the computer screen as shown in Figure 3.26. Note that, the value of variable a is first incremented to store 10 following which it is printed on the screen. This is because we have used the increment operator in the **prefix** form as shown in Figure 3.26.

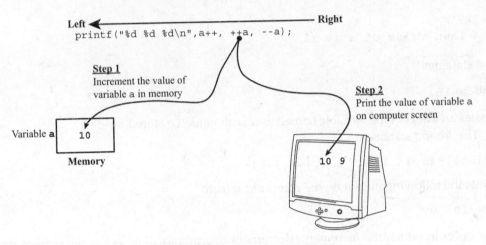

Figure 3.26: Execution of ++a

Thirdly, the operation a++ will be executed which will first print the value of variable a which is 10 on the computer screen following which the value of variable a will be incremented to 11 as shown in Figure 3.27. Note that, the old value of variable a is first printed on the screen following which it is incremented in the memory because the increment operator is used in the **postfix** form as shown in Figure 3.27.

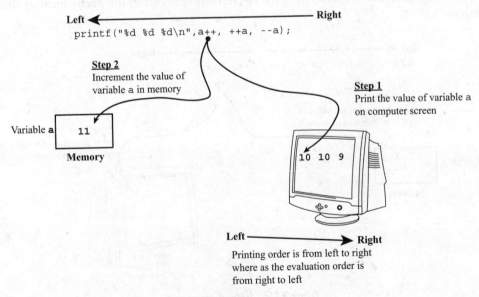

Figure 3.27: Execution of a++

Hence, when we read the output in a direction from left to right the **printf()** statement prints the output as

```
10 10 9
```

on the computer screen. Note that, as shown in Figure 3.27, the value of variable a is updated to 11 in the memory and hence the last statement prints the final value of the variable a as 11 on the computer screen, as seen in the output of the program.

NOTES

Needless to mention if you use cout instead of a printf() you will still get the same output. The operations in cout are also executed from right to left as with that of printf(). Hence the output of both the statements will be exactly identical.

```
printf("%d %d %d\n",a++,++a,--a);
cout<<a++<<" "<<++a<<" "<<--a<<endl;
```

3.8   Implicit Type Casting/System Casting

We can perform operations in C/C++ by mixing the operands of different data types in the expression. For example, let us consider the expression below:

```
12.9+40
```

The result will be evaluated as an addition of values 12.9 and 40. We understand that, the value 12.9 is a float type constant whereas the value 40 is an integer type constant. In such a case, the data type of the result will be automatically converted to the data type of that operand which requires the highest memory among all the operands used in the expression. In this case, the data type of the first operand is **float** and the data type of the second operand is **integer**, therefore the data type of the result of the expression will **float**. This is because, the size of float is 4 bytes and the size of integer is 2 bytes, which means that the 'float' is the data type of the operand which requires highest memory among all the operands used in the expression. Such a conversion of the data type that is applied by the compiler so as to get the result of the expression which contains the values of heterogeneous data types is called '**Implicit type casting/system casting**'. Figure 3.28, gives the rules that compiler follows for generating the result of the expression when the data values used in the expression are of heterogeneous types.

3.9   Explicit Type Casting

C/C++ also allows the programmer to explicitly convert the data type of the result generated by the expression to a specific type which is required by the programmer. The programmer may require to perform 'explicit type casting' over the value of the result, if the data type of the result does not match with the data type of any of the operands used in the expression. C/C++ support the following syntax for explicit type casting:

```
(New-datatype)expression;
```

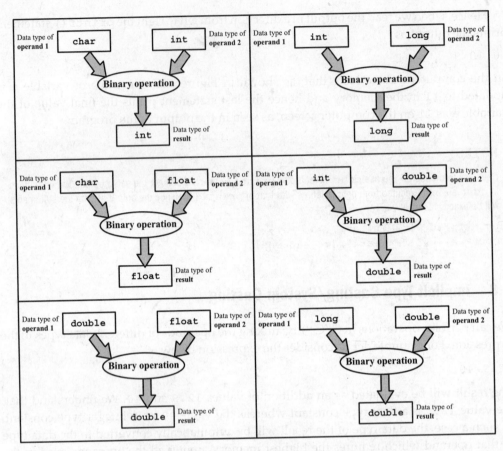

Figure 3.28: Rules for implicit type casting

As an example, to understand the requirement to explicit type casting, let us consider the code given below

```
#include<stdio.h>
void main()
{
int a=7, b=2;
float result;
result = a/b;
printf("Result is %f",result);
}
```

Output

```
Result is 3.000000
```

As seen in the code, the data type of the variables a and b are integer and the values of a and b are initialized as 7 and 2, respectively. Further, we divide the value of variable a by the value of variable b and store the result of the division in the variable named as result as seen in the code. As we expect the result to contain the fractional component, we have created the variable `result` of type `float` as seen in the code. However, dividing the variables a and b will always produce a integer value because the data type of both the operands is integer. This is because compiler follows a rule that `int/int=int`. This means that, when both the operands are of same type then the data type of the result will be same as that of the data type of the operands.

Therefore, the statement,

```
result = a/b;
```

will truncate the result of the expression to `3` instead of `3.5` as shown in Figure 3.29. Therefore, the value of variable `result` will be printed as `3.000000` as seen in the output of the code.

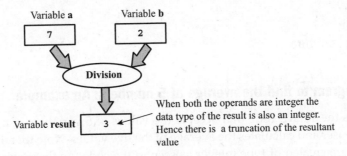

Figure 3.29: Truncation of the result

So as to solve this problem, we can convert the data type of the result to `float` by explicitly type casting the result of division of two integers into a `float` using the statement below:

```
result = (float)a/b;
```

The type casting informs the compiler that the user expects a `float` result after the division of two integers is performed. Hence, the compiler reserves 4 bytes in memory to store the result of division even if both the operands are of type integer. Therefore, the value of variable `result` will now be initialized as `3.5` as seen in Figure 3.30.

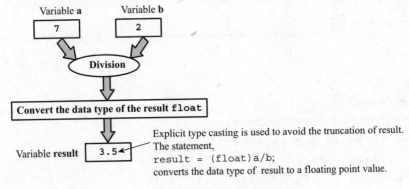

Figure 3.30: Explicit type casting

Given below is the full source code that explicitly converts the data type of division of two integer values into a float value thereby printing the result as 3.5 on the computer screen.

```
#include<stdio.h>
void main()
{
int a=7, b=2;
float result;
result = (float)a/b;
printf("Result is %f",result);
}
```

Output

```
Result is 3.500000
```

3.9.1 A program to find the average of 5 numbers: An example

Given below is the source code that accepts the values of 5 variables a, b,c,d, and e as input from the user and calculates the average of the five values. Note that the variables a, b, c, d, and e are created of type integer as seen in the code. As there exists a possibility that the average of the 5 numbers may contain a fractional component in it, we have created the variable named as average of type float as seen in the code.

Further, we recollect that, when all the operands are of type integer the division operator/always returns an integer value. So as to avoid truncation of the fractional component of the result value we explicitly type cast the data type of the result to float as seen in the statement below:

```
average=(float)(a+b+c+d+e)/5;
```

Note that the addition of variables a, b, c, d, and e is performed in the parenthesis so as to ensure that all the numbers are added before performing the operation of division.

The source code to calculate the average of five numbers is as given below:

```
#include<stdio.h>
void main()
{
int a,b,c,d,e;
float average;
printf("Enter the five numbers\n");
scanf("%d %d %d %d %d",&a,&b,&c,&d,&e);
average=(float)(a+b+c+d+e)/5;
printf("Average is %f",average);
}
```

Output

```
Enter the five numbers
12 33 45 6 7
Average is 20.600000
```

3.10 `sizeof` Operator in C/C++

The `sizeof` operator returns the number of bytes that a particular data type requires in the memory. Given below is the syntax of using the `sizeof` operator in C/C++

```
sizeof(dataType);
```

For example, the statement below,

```
k = sizeof(int);
```

will initialize the value of the variable k as 2 because every integer requires 2 bytes[1] in the computer memory. We can also pass a variable name to the `sizeof` operator instead of the data type as shown below.

```
float a= 32;
printf("%d",sizeof(a));
```

The `sizeof` operator in this case will return 4 because the variable a requires 4 Bytes in the computer memory.

Given below is the sample code which demonstrates the usage of the `sizeof` operator. The program prints the size of variables a and ch and the size of the data types **int** and **double** in bytes as seen in the output of the code.

```
#include<stdio.h>
void main()
{
double a=12.5;
char ch='$';
printf("size of variable 'a' is %d bytes\n",sizeof(a));
printf("size of variable 'ch' is %d bytes\n",sizeof(ch));
printf("size of any integer is %d bytes\n",sizeof(int));
printf("size of any float is %d bytes\n",sizeof(float));
}
```

Output

```
size of variable 'a' is 8 bytes
size of variable 'ch' is 1 bytes
```

---

[1] We assume 16-bit compiler. If you get size of integer as 4 bytes it means you are working on a 32-bit compiler.

```
size of any integer is 2 bytes
size of any float is 4 bytes
```

NOTES

Just as a practice and to be 'hands on' with cout statement, given below is the full source code which uses cout statements instead of printf() to print size of each item in memory using sizeof operator. Note that, cout does not need any format specifier and hence it is much simpler to use compared to printf(). The output of the below program is exactly the same as that of the one using printf(). Keep in mind that if you are using cout your program will work only with C++ compilers and not with C compilers.

```
#include<iostream.h>
void main()
{
double a=12.5;
char ch='$';
cout<<"size of variable 'a' is "<<sizeof(a)<<" bytes"<<endl;
cout<<"size of variable 'ch' is "<<sizeof(ch)<<" bytes"<<endl;
cout<<"size of any integer is "<<sizeof(int)<<" bytes"<<endl;
cout<<"size of any float  is "<<sizeof(float)<<" bytes"<<endl;
}
```

Output

```
size of variable 'a' is 8 bytes
size of variable 'ch' is 1 bytes
size of any integer is 2 bytes
size of any float is 4 bytes
```

3.11 Scope Resolution Operator(::)| Only in C++ not in C

The scope resolution operator (::) is used to access the global value of the variable when the variable with the same name is defined globally as well as locally in the same C++ program. A global variable is a variable which can be accessed by all the functions in a program whereas a local variable is a variable which can only be accessed by the function in which the variable is defined.

Given below is the syntax of using the scope resolution operator in the unary form:

```
::variableName;
```

As seen in the C++ program given below, we have defined a variable named x two times in the program. At a first place the variable x is defined outside the main() function with a value as 100, this definition is called a global definition of the variable x. At a second place, the variable x is defined within the main() function with a value as 50, such a definition of a variable x is called local definition of the variable x.

```
#include<iostream.h>
/*Global definition of variable x*/
int x=100;
void main()
```

```
{
/*local definition of variable x*/
int x=50;
cout<<"Value of x is: "<<x<<endl;
cout<<"Global Value of x is: "<<::x;
}
```

Output

```
Value of x is: 50
Global Value of x is: 100
```

When we access the value of variable x directly inside the `main()` function then the local value of the variable 'x' will always be accessed. This means that, the following statement,

```
cout<<"Value of x is: "<<x<<endl;
```

will print the value of x as 50 because it will always access the local value of the variable x. Whereas, the statement,

```
cout<<"Global Value of x is: "<<::x;
```

will print the global value of the variable x which is 100 because we have applied the scope resolution to the variable x before accessing its value.

NOTES

We have used `cout` instead of `printf()` in this program, because scope resolution operator is anyways supported only by C++ and not by C. Hence this program must be executed only on C++ compilers. Reason we have used `printf()`/`scanf()` functions in most of the other programs in Chapters 1 to 9 is that `printf()`/`scanf()` are supported by C as well as C++. Hence most of the programs from Chapter 1 to 9 can work on C as well as C++ compilers unless mentioned otherwise. However, programs from chapter 10 onwards are exclusive to C++ and hence you will find that we have used `cout`/`cin` statements instead of `printf()`/`scanf()` statements in the programs from chapter 10 onwards. Syntax of `cout` statement is explained in Chapter 2 Section 2.7 and the syntax of `cin` statement is explained in Section 2.10

3.11.1 Creating blocks to define scope of variables

We can create new scope for the variables in C++ by simply opening and closing curly brackets as shown in Figure 3.31. Note that, the life time of a particular variable is limited within the scope in which the variable is created. This means that, the value of the variable can only be accessed till the time the control of execution is in the same scope in which the variable is declared. Also, if a variable is declared inside the outer scope it can be accessed in all the inner blocks which are created inside the outer block.

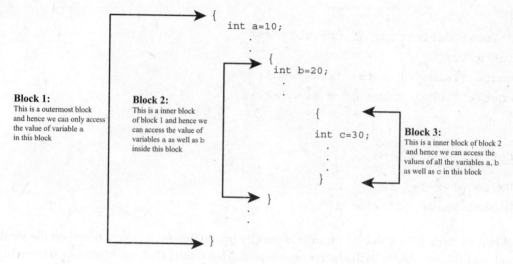

Block 1:
This is a outermost block and hence we can only access the value of variable a in this block

Block 2:
This is a inner block of block 1 and hence we can access the value of variables a as well as b inside this block

Block 3:
This is a inner block of block 2 and hence we can access the values of all the variables a, b as well as c in this block

Figure 3.31: Creating blocks

However, a variable which is defined inside the inner scope can only be accessed till the time the control of execution is within the inner scope. The variable which is created inside the inner scope cannot be accessed by the outer scope once the control of execution exits the inner block.

Figure 3.31 shows the creation of variables a, b and c in three different scopes as 'Block 1','Block 2', and 'Block 3'. As seen from Figure 3.31 the variable a is defined in the outer most scope and hence it can be accessed inside all the blocks. The variable b is defined in 'Block 2' and hence it can only be accessed in 'Block 2' and 'Block 3'. Note that, the variable b cannot be accessed inside 'Block 1' because it is the outer block of 'Block 2'. Further, the variable c is defined inside the 'Block 3' and hence we can access the value of variable c only inside the 'Block 3' because the 'Block 3' is the innermost block as seen in Figure 3.31.

We can also create a variable with a same name inside outer block as well as the inner block. Figure 3.32 gives a source code which defines the variable p in three different scopes. Note that, applying the scope resolution operator on the variable p will always access the global value of variable p as seen in Figure 3.32.

When we attempt to access the value of the variable p without applying a scope resolution operator, the CPU will access the variable p which is defined in the current scope which is under execution. For example, the statement,

```
cout<<"Value of variable p in main is "<<p<<endl;
```

will print the value of variable p as 10 as shown in Figure 3.32.

It is important to understand that, although the name of the variable is same in all the three scopes, these are actually three different variables created in the computer memory. This means that, the three variables created in the program below will be stored in three

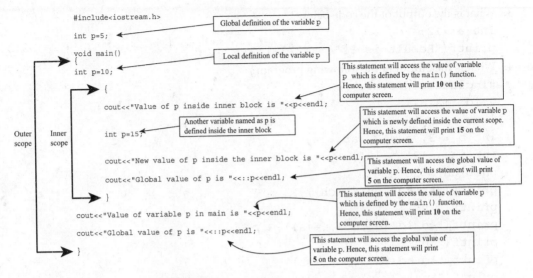

Figure 3.32: Scope and life time of a variable

different locations in RAM and hence they can store different values as 5, 10, and 15, respectively.

REMEMBER

Scope resolution operator is only supported by C++ compilers and not by C compilers.

Quiz

1. What is the output of the following program?

```
#include<stdio.h>
void main()
{
int k=3, l=4, m;
m=++k + l--;
printf("Value of m %d\n",m);
m=k++ + -- l;
printf("Value of m %d\n", m);
}
```

2. Select the correct answer

```
int a = 29, b = 10; float c;
c = (float)(a/b);
```

The correct value of c is

(a) 2.9

(b) 2

(c) 3

(d) None of the mentioned options.

3. What is the output of the code below?

```
int a =12;
printf("Result is %f", a+2/3-1/2);
```

4. What is the output of the following program?

```
#include<stdio.h>
void  main()
{
int b = 3, a = 2, ab = 4;
int in = '2' * '2';
char ch = 'c' ;
printf("%c %c",ch,(++ch));
printf("\n");
printf("%d %d %d",a,a,(++a));
printf("\n");
printf("%d %d %d",b,b,(++b));
printf("\n");
printf("%d %d %d",ab,ab,(++ab));
printf("\n");
printf("%d %d",a,!!a);
printf("\n %d %d",in ,  ch);
}
```

5. What will be the output of the following code:

```
#include<stdio.h>
void main( )
{
int a = 3;
printf("%d %d %d %d\n",a,a++,++a,(--a)--);
}
```

6. What will be the output of the following code:

```
#include<stdio.h>
void main( )
{
int x = 4, y = 9;
int z, r;
z = (x++) + (-- y) + y || y--  & ++y && --x;
printf("Value of z = %d\n" , z );
r = (--x) + x + (y--) | y--;
printf("Value of r = %d\n" , r );
}
```

7. What will be the output of the following code:

```
#include<stdio.h>
void main()
```

```
{
int a, b, c;
a = 2 ; b = 5 ; c = 10 ;
printf("First Value = %d\n", (a + b *- c));
printf("Second Value = %d\n", (-- c/b * c- a));
printf("Third Value = %d\n", (-- a + ++b%a));
}
```

8. Explain the evaluation of following expressions and determine errors, if any

```
int x = 4, y = 9,z=55,r=22,p,q,t,v,w;
char a ='a',b='B',c,d;
int e =10,f=3,g=2;
c=a+b+'\n';
d=b--;
p=(x+y++-z--)*(z++ -y )/x*2+(x-y);
q = p*x+y%(z++ - x--);
t = x | y|z--|y++& d;
v =x && y ||z | p;
w=e^f^g;
```

Error Finding Exercise

Given below are some programs which may or may not contain errors. Correct the error(s) if exist in the code and determine the output.

Program 1

```
#include<stdio.h>
void main()
{
int a=10,b;
b=++a++;
printf("Value of b is %d\n",b);
}
```

Program 2

```
#include<stdio.h>
void main()
{
int a=10,b=10,c;
c=++a>=---b++;
printf("Value of c is %d\n",c);
}
```

Program 3

```c
#include<stdio.h>
void main()
{
int y=10,z;
z=::y;
printf("Value of z is %d\n",z);
}
```

Program 4

```c
#include<stdio.h>
void main()
{
int a=10,b=20;
printf("Value of a is %d\n",a);
printf("Value of b is %d\n",b);
a=+b;
b=*a;
printf("Value of a is %d\n",a);
printf("Value of b is %d\n",b);
}
```

Program 5

```c
#include<stdio.h>
void main()
{
float p=100.365,q=200.98,r;
r=sizeof(sizeof(sizeof(p+q)));
printf("Value of r is %f\n",r);
}
```

Program 6

```c
#include<stdio.h>
void main()
{
int a=75,b=90,c;
c=++a>>b++<<--b;
printf("Value of c is %d\n",c);
}
```

Review Questions

1. Explain the problem of ambiguity in expression evaluation. How is it resolved?
2. Explain the rules of implicit type casting in C/C++.
3. What is the need for explicit type casting. Explain with an example.
4. Write a short note on Bitwise operators.
5. Explain the use of scope resolution operator in the unary form.
6. What are the relational operators? Give one example of each of the relational operators by writing a program.
7. List the priorities of all the arithmetic operators. Explain the evaluation of an expression which is formed using following operators +,–,%,*, and ().
8. List and explain any two operators which have an associativity of right to left.
9. What is the difference between prefix and postfix form of increment/decrement operators? Explain with examples.

Chapter 4

Decision Making Control Statements

4.1 Overview

We understand from Chapters 1 and 2 that instructions in a program are executed in a sequence in which we write them in the `main()` function. Such an execution is called a sequential execution. In many cases it is required to change the sequence of executing instructions based on some condition. The statements that can be used to alter the sequence of executing instructions at run time of the program are called **branching or decision making** control statements.

C/C++ supports a following branching/decision making control statements:

1. `if - else` statement
2. `else-if` ladder
3. `switch` statement
4. Ternary operator (`? :`)
5. `goto` statement

In this chapter we discuss the syntax and working of each of the above decision making control statements supported by C/C++.

4.2 `if else` Statement

The if-else statement is used to change the sequence of execution by evaluating a specified condition at run time of the program. The condition to be evaluated must be specified in round parenthesis when defining the `if` block as shown in Figure 4.1. The `if-else` statement defines two blocks, the first block is called `if` block and the second block is called `else` block. The control of execution is transferred inside the `if` block if the condition specified in the parentheses is evaluated as **true**, whereas the control of execution is transferred inside the `else` block if the condition specified is evaluated as **false**.

A condition is generally written using relational operators and hence an evaluation of a condition can result into two possible outcomes as **'true'** or **'false'**. Therefore, it will be correct to say that, in any of the given scenario the control of execution will always be transferred to **at least one** of the two blocks (`if` block or the `else` block). Also, the control of execution will be transferred to **exactly** one of the two blocks (`if` block in case the

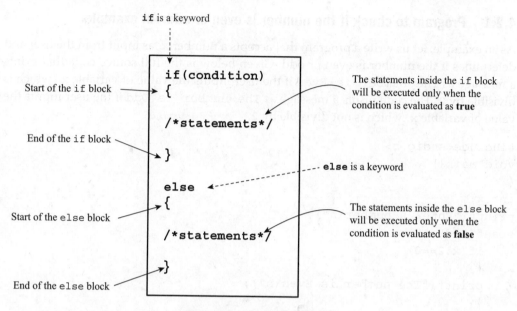

Start of the if block

End of the if block

Start of the else block

End of the else block

The statements inside the `if` block will be executed only when the condition is evaluated as **true**

`else` is a keyword

The statements inside the `else` block will be executed only when the condition is evaluated as **false**

Figure 4.1: Syntax of if-else

condition is evaluated as true or it can be a `else` block in case the condition is evaluated as 'false'). Figure 4.2 gives the workflow which describes the working of `if-else` statement

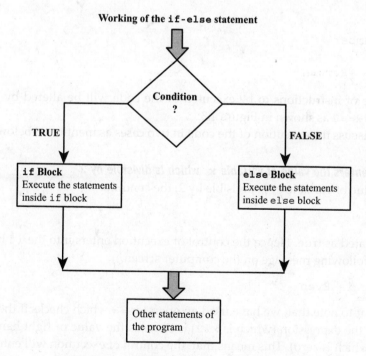

Figure 4.2: Working of the `if-else` construct

4.2.1 Program to check if the number is even or odd: An example

As an example, let us write a program that accepts a number x as input from the user and determines if the number is even or odd. Given below is the full source code that prints a message as The number is Even if the user inputs the value of variable x which is divisible by 2. The code prints a message as The number is Odd if the user inputs the value of variable x which is not divisible by 2.

```
#include<stdio.h>
void main()
{
int x;
printf("Enter a number\n");
scanf("%d",&x);
    if(x%2==0)
    {
    printf("The number is Even\n");
    }
    else
    {
    printf("The number is Odd\n");
    }
}
```

Output

```
Enter a number
10
The number is Even
```

The sequence of instructions to be executed in the code will be altered by the result of condition x%2==0 as shown in Figure 4.3.

We will discuss the execution of the code in two cases as mentioned below:

Case 1: User enters the value of variable x which is divisible by 2

When the value of variable x is divisible by 2, the condition,

```
x%2==0
```

will be evaluated as **true.** Hence the control of execution enters into the if block thereby printing the following message on the computer screen.

```
The number is Even
```

It is important to note that, we have used an operator == which checks if the value of left hand side of the expression (which is x%2) is same as the value of right hand side of the expression (which is zero). This means that, the control of execution will enter into the if block provided that the remainder of x with respect to 2 is zero. For example, if the user

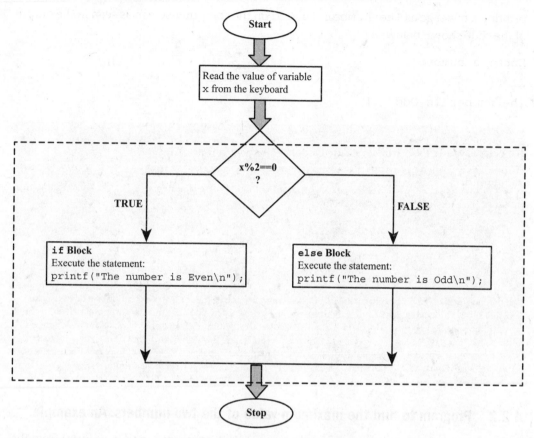

Figure 4.3: Execution of the code

enters the value of variable x as 10 then the condition will be evaluated as **true** because the remainder of 10 and 2 is zero, thereby printing a message as The number is Even on the computer screen as seen in the output of the code shown below:

```
Enter a number
10
The number is Even
```

Case 2: User enters the value of variable x which is not divisible by 2

When the value of variable x is not divisible by 2, the condition,

```
x%2==0
```

will be evaluated as **false**. Hence, the control of execution enters into the else block thereby printing the following message on the computer screen.

```
The number is Odd
```

For example, if the user enters the value of variable x as 21 then the condition will be evaluated as false because the remainder of 21 and 2 is one (which is not zero), thereby printing a message as The number is Odd on the computer screen as seen in the output of the code shown below:

```
Enter a number
21
The number is Odd
```

Can we have a if block without a else block in a C++ program? **?**

Yes, we can have a if block in the program without a corresponding else block. As an example, consider the construct given below:

```
if(condition)
{
printf("Inside if block \n");
}
printf("Outside if block\n");
```

If the condition specified as a part of the if block is evaluated as true the control of execution will be transferred inside the if block thereby printing the message as "Inside if block" on the computer screen. If the condition specified by the if block is evaluated as false, the control of execution will not enter inside the if block and hence the printf() statement which is present inside the if block will not be executed. Note that, the printf() statement written outside the if block will always be executed even if the condition is true or false. Hence, the message "Outside if block" will always be printed on the computer screen.

4.2.2 Program to find the maximum value of the two numbers: An example

As an example, let us write a program that accepts two numbers a and b as input from the user and prints the greatest value on the computer screen. Given below is the full source code that prints the value of variable a, if the value of a is greater than the value of b and prints the value of variable b otherwise.

```
#include<stdio.h>
void main()
{
int a,b;
printf("Enter two numbers\n");
scanf("%d %d",&a,&b);
    if(a>b)
    {
        printf("The maximum is %d\n",a);
    }
    else
    {
        printf("The maximum is %d\n",b);
    }
}
```

The sequence of instructions to be executed in the code will be altered by the result of condition a>b as shown in Figure 4.4.

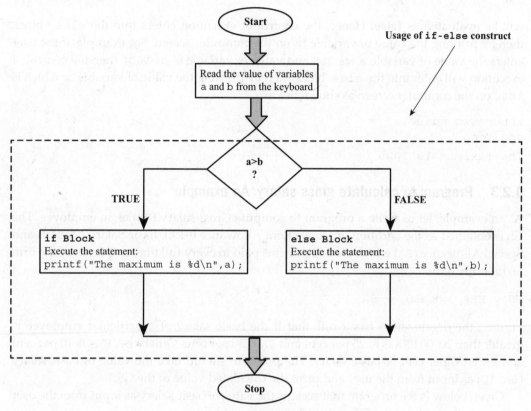

Figure 4.4: Execution of the code

We will discuss the execution of the code in two cases as mentioned below:

Case 1: User inputs the values such that, value of a is greater than value b

When the value of variable a is greater than the value of variable b the condition,

```
a>b
```

will be evaluated as **true**. Hence, the control of execution enters into the if block thereby printing the value of variable a on the computer screen. For example, if the user enters the value of variable a as 20 and value of variable b as 10 then the control of execution will enter into the if block thereby printing the value of variable which is 20 on the computer screen as shown below:

```
Enter two numbers
20 10
The maximum is 20
```

Case 2: User inputs the values such that, value of a **is not greater than value of** b

When the value of variable a is not greater than the value of variable b the condition,

```
a>b
```

will be evaluated as **false**. Hence, the control of execution enters into the else block thereby printing the value of variable b on the computer screen. For example, if the user enters the value of variable a as 200 and value of variable b as 1000 then the control of execution will enter into the else block thereby printing the value of variable b which is 1000 on the computer screen as shown below:

```
Enter two numbers
200 1000
The maximum is 1000
```

4.2.3 Program to calculate gross salary: An example

As an example, let us write a program to compute Gross salary (GS) of an employee. The GS is obtained as the addition of House Rent Allowance (HRA), Basic Salary (BASIC) and Special Allowance (SA) which are components paid to every full time employee of the firm on monthly basis.

```
GS = HRA + BASIC + SA
```

Further, the organization has a rule that if the basic salary of a particular employee is greater than 20000 HRA is to 25 per cent and SA is 30 per cent. Otherwise, HRA is 10 per cent and SA is 50 per cent of basic salary. The program should take the value of basic salary (BASIC) as input from the user and print the calculated value of the GS.

Given below is the program that accepts the value of basic salary as input from the user and prints the value of the GS of the employee.

```
#include<stdio.h>
void main()
{
float BASIC, HRA, SA, GS;
printf("Enter the basic salary of the employee\n");
scanf("%f",&BASIC);
    if(BASIC>20000)
    {
    HRA=0.25*BASIC;
    SA=0.3*BASIC;
    }
    else
    {
    HRA=0.1*BASIC;
    SA=0.5*BASIC;
    }
```

```
GS=BASIC+HRA+SA;
printf("Gross salary of the employee is %f\n",GS);
}
```

We will discuss the execution of the code in two cases as shown in Figure 4.5:

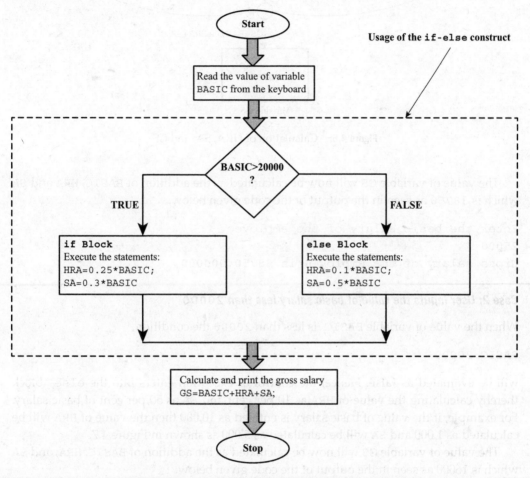

Figure 4.5: Execution of the salary calculation code

Case 1: User inputs the value of basic salary higher than 20000

When the value of variable BASIC is greater 20000 the condition,

```
BASIC>20000
```

will be evaluated as **true**. Hence, the control of execution enters into the if block thereby calculating the value of HRA as 25 per cent and SA as 30 per cent of basic salary. For example, if the value of basic salary is entered as 25,000 then the value of HRA will be calculated as 6,250 and SA as 7,500 as shown in Figure 4.6.

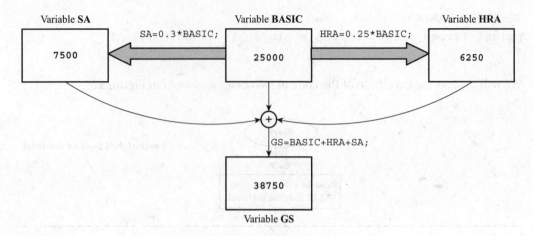

Figure 4.6: Calculation of HRA, SA, and GS

The value of variable GS will now be calculated as the addition of BASIC, HRA and SA which is 38750 as seen in the output of the code given below:

```
Enter the basic salary of the employee
25000
Gross salary of the employee is 38750.000000
```

Case 2: User inputs the value of basic salary less than 20000

When the value of variable BASIC is less than 20000 the condition,

```
BASIC>20000
```

will be evaluated as **false**. Hence, the control of execution enters into the else block thereby calculating the value of HRA as 10 per cent and SA as 50 per cent of basic salary. For example, if the value of basic salary is entered as 10,000 then the value of HRA will be calculated as 1,000 and SA will be calculated as 5,000 as shown in Figure 4.7.

The value of variable GS will now be calculated as the addition of BASIC, HRA, and SA which is 16000 as seen in the output of the code given below:

```
Enter the basic salary of the employee
10000
Gross salary of the employee is 16000.000000
```

4.2.4   Program to find the maximum value of the three numbers: An example

Let us now write a program that accepts three numbers a, b, and c as an input from the user and prints the greatest of the three numbers. For example, if the user enters the values of variables a, b, and c as 10, 30, and 20 respectively, then the program should print the value of variable b which is 30 as it is the greatest among all the values.

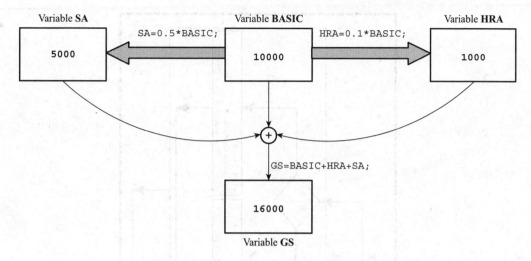

Figure 4.7: Calculation of HRA, SA and GS.

To find the greatest of three numbers, every number must be compared with the other two numbers before we conclude that it is the greatest among all the numbers. For example, so as to conclude the value of variable a to be greatest, we must compare the value of a with the value of b as well as with the value of c. If the value of a is greater than both b as well as c, then we can say that the value of variable a is greatest of all the values. This means that, even if the condition **a>b** is evaluated as true we must further check another condition **a>c** to conclude if variable a is greatest as shown in Figure 4.8.

If the condition **a>b** is true but the condition **a>c** is false, it indicates that the value of variable a is greater than the value of variable b but the value of a is not greater than the value of variable c. This means that, the value of variable c is greatest as shown in Figure 4.8.

Further, if the condition a>b itself is evaluated as false, it means that the value of variable a can never be the greatest value. Hence, only candidates for the maximum value are b and c. Therefore, we find the maximum of variables b and c if the condition a>c is false as shown in Figure 4.8.

It is clear that, to write a code that implements the above solution we need to check some other condition based on the result of a particular condition (say C1). For example, let us consider a situation where, we need to check the condition C2 only if the condition in C1 is evaluated as true and we need to check the condition C3 only the condition C1 is evaluated as false. Such a scenario can be implemented by embedding an if-else block inside another if-else block as shown in Figure 4.9. The implementation in which an if-else block is written inside another if-else block, is called nesting of if-else. The format for nesting if-else blocks, is as shown in Figure 4.9.

In this case, we need to check the condition a>c only if the condition a>b is true and we need to check the condition b>c only if the condition a>b is false. Therefore, we can nest the if-else blocks as shown in Figure 4.10.

Given below is the full source code that prints the greatest of the three numbers on the computer screen.

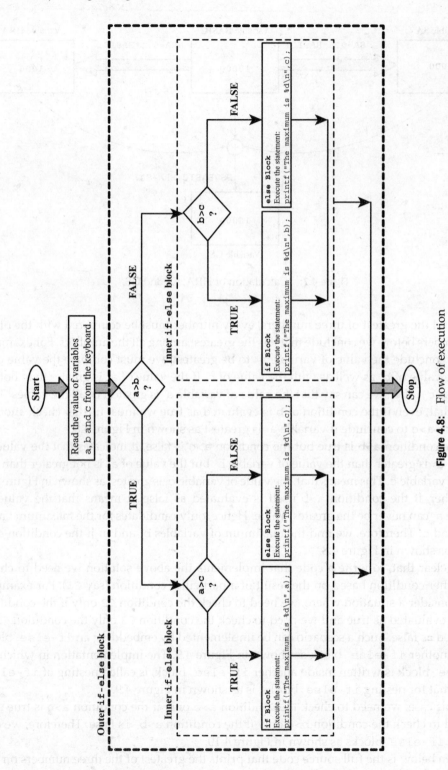

Figure 4.8: Flow of execution

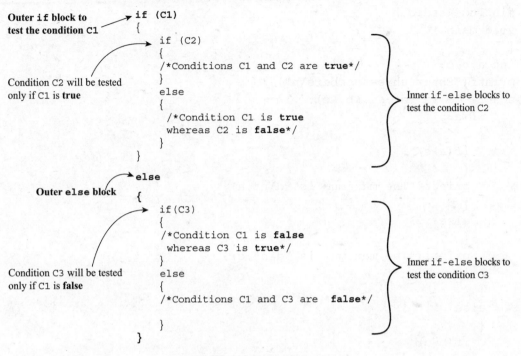

Figure 4.9: Nesting of if-else

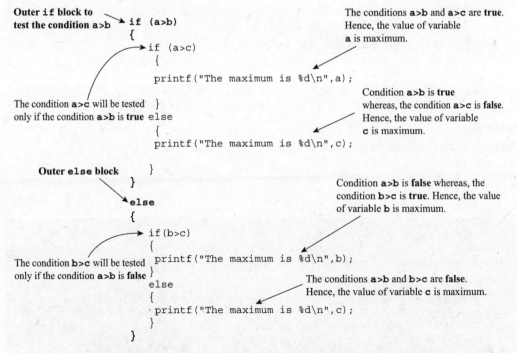

Figure 4.10: Nesting of if-else to find the greatest of the three numbers

```
#include<stdio.h>
void main()
{
int a,b,c;
printf("Enter three numbers\n");
scanf("%d %d %d",&a,&b,&c);
    if(a>b)
    {
        if(a>c)
        {
        printf("The maximum is %d\n",a);
        }
        else
        {
        printf("The maximum is %d\n",c);
        }
    }
    else
    {
        if(b>c)
        {
        printf("The maximum is %d\n",b);
        }
        else
        {
        printf("The maximum is %d\n",c);
        }
    }
}
```

Output

```
Enter three numbers
10 20 30
The maximum is 30
```

Can I write the condition in the program as:
a>b>c
so as to compare the value of variable a with b as well as c?

?

a>b>c is a **wrong** way to write the condition. This is because, the associativity of the relational operators is from left to right. Hence, the condition a>b will be evaluated first; which will return a value as true(1) or false (0). Hence, the expression,

a>b>c

will compare the result of condition a>b with the value of variable c. This means that, the above expression will compare the value 0 or 1 with the value of variable c, thereby generating incorrect results. Therefore, we must write two different conditions as a>b and a>c so as to individually compare the value of variable a with b and c respectively. Hence, we have used nesting of if-else statements in the given program. This is because, we need to check two different conditions such that, the first condition compares the value of variable a with the value of variable b and the second condition compares the value of variable a with the value of variable c.

4.3   Logical Operators

The logical operators are used to connect multiple conditions so as to form a single expression. C/C++ supports three logical operators as listed below:

&&	Logical AND operation
||	Logical OR operation
!	Logical NOT operation

4.3.1   Logical AND operation

Given below is the sample expression that connects conditions C1 to CN using a logical AND operation.

C1 && C2 && C3 && C4......... &&CN

The complete expression will be evaluated as true if each of the conditions C1, C2, C3 .... CN are individually evaluated as true. Note that, the whole expression will be evaluated as false if at least one condition from C1 to CN is evaluated as false.

As an example, if we consider the if block given in Figure 4.11, we combine two different conditions a>b and a>c using a logical AND operation. This means that, the control of execution will enter into the if block if and only if both the conditions a>b and a>c are true.

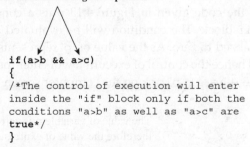

Conditions connected using && operator

```
if(a>b && a>c)
{
/*The control of execution will enter
inside the "if" block only if both the
conditions "a>b" as well as "a>c" are
true*/
}
```

Figure 4.11: if block using && in the condition

4.3.2   Logical OR operation

Given below is the sample expression that connects conditions C1 to CN using a logical OR operation.

C1 || C2 || C3 || C4......... ||CN

The complete expression will be evaluated as true if at least one of the conditions C1 to CN is evaluated as true. Note that, the whole expression will be evaluated as false if none of the conditions from C1 to CN is true

As an example, if we consider the if block given in Figure 4.12, we combine to different conditions y==15 and y==20 using a logical OR operation. This means that, the control of execution will enter into the if block if the value of variable y is either 15 or 20.

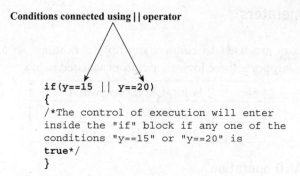

Conditions connected using || operator

```
if(y==15 || y==20)
{
/*The control of execution will enter
inside the "if" block if any one of the
conditions "y==15" or "y==20" is
true*/
}
```

Figure 4.12: if block using || in the condition

4.3.3   Logical NOT operation

Unlike the logical AND/logical OR which are binary operators, the logical NOT is a **unary** operator which works only with a single operand. We recollect that, any expression whose result is zero is considered as false whereas the expression whose result is nonzero is considered as true in C/C++. The logical NOT operator (!) is used to complement the result of the given condition. This means that, if the condition C1 is true then the condition !C1 will be evaluated as false, and if the condition C1 is false then the condition !C1 will be evaluated as true.

As an example, the code given in Figure 4.13 puts a condition as !p in the round parenthesis of the if block. The condition will be evaluated as true, because the value of variable p is initialized to zero. As the value of 'p' represents false, the value of !p will represent a true and hence the control of execution will enter the if block thereby printing the message Inside the if block on the computer screen.

The value of variable p is zero (**false**),
therefore the value of expression !p is **true**

```
int p=0;

if(!p)
{

printf("Inside the if block");

}
```

Figure 4.13: if block using ! in the condition

4.4 `else if` Ladder

Nesting of `if-else` blocks can sometimes increase the lines of code thereby making the program difficult to develop and maintain. `else-if` ladder can be used as an alternative to the nesting of multiple `if-else` blocks in the program thereby making the code more readable and easy to maintain when compared to 'nesting' of `if-else` statements.

Figure 4.14 gives the syntax of using else-if ladder in the program. The ladder consist of a single `if` block, multiple `else-if` blocks and a single `else` block as shown in Figure 4.14. The ladder evaluates conditions from top to bottom and as soon as the first condition from top is found to be true the control is transferred in the respective block of the `else-if` ladder and the rest of the ladder is skipped. The `else` block of the ladder will be executed only if all the conditions which are mentioned above in the ladder are evaluated as false.

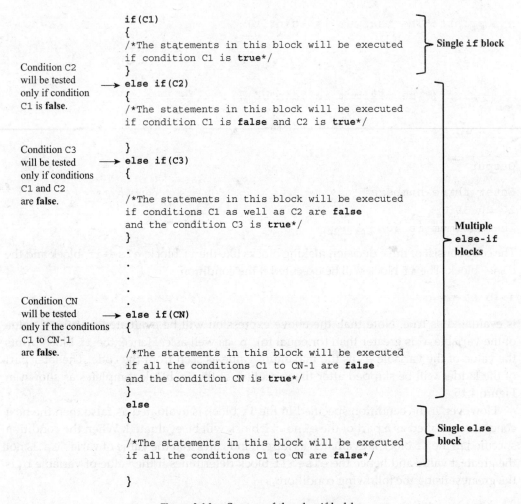

Figure 4.14: Syntax of the else-if ladder

Given below is the full source to find the greatest of three numbers a, b and c using the else-if ladder and the logical operators:

```
#include<stdio.h>
void main()
{
int a,b,c;
printf("Enter three numbers\n");
scanf("%d %d %d",&a,&b,&c);
    if(a>=b && a>=c)
    {
    printf("The maximum is %d\n",a);
    }
    else if(b>=a && b>=c)
    {
    printf("The maximum is %d\n",b);
    }
    else
    {
    printf("The maximum is %d\n",c);
    }
}
```

Output

```
Enter three numbers
10 20 30
The maximum is 30
```

The code consist of three decision making blocks like the if block, else-if block and the else block. The if block will be executed if the condition,

```
a>=b && a>=c
```

is evaluated as true. Note that, the above expression will be evaluated as true, if value of the variable a is greater than (or equal to) b as well as c. Hence, the if block prints the value of the variable a as the maximum value as seen from the code. The later part of the ladder will be skipped after the execution of the if block completes as shown in Figure 4.15.

However, if the condition specified in the if block is evaluated as **false** then the next condition specified as a part of the else if block will be evaluated. When the condition specified in the if block is evaluated as false, it indicates that the value of variable a is not the greatest value and hence the else if block determines if the value of variable b is the greatest using the following condition:

```
b>=a && b>=c
```

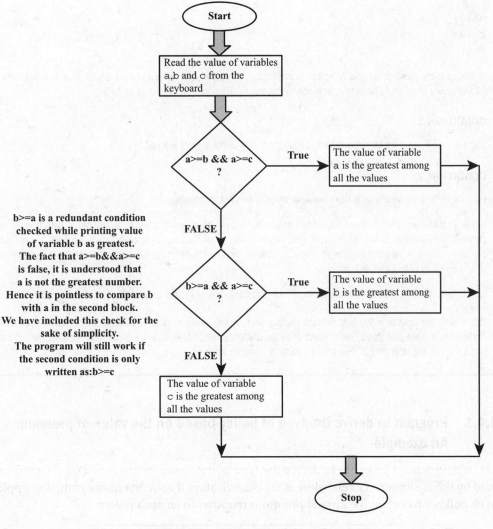

Figure 4.15: Execution of the code

Similarly, if both the conditions which are specified by the `if` as well as the `else-if` blocks are evaluated as false, it indicates that the value of variable `c` is the maximum among all the values. Hence, the `else` block at the end prints the value of variable `c` as seen in the code.

NOTES

Note that, we have used operator `>=`(greater than or equal to) rather than `>` (greater than) while framing conditions. This makes the program intelligent to handle equalities in some specific cases. For example, let us consider the values of `a`, `b` and `c` as under

```
a=10;
b=10;
c=5;
```

In this case the greatest value is 10 but it is duplicated in two variables a and b. Had it been that we would have written conditions using operator >, both the below conditions would be evaluated as false.

CONDITION 1

a>b && a> c [Condition is false because value of a is not greater than b]

CONDITION 2

b>a && b>c [Condition is false because value of b is not greater than a]

Hence in this case control would have been in the last else block printing value of variable c (which is 5) as greatest. This is certainly wrong! To avoid generation of wrong results in such specific cases we have framed the conditions using>= operator instead of > operator. Hence the first condition itself is evaluated as true because value of a is equal to b and greater than c.

a>=b && a>=c [Condition is true because a is equal to b and greater than c]

This makes the control in the first if block thereby printing the value of variable a as greatest, which is correct. Remember, it is the fact that 10 is greatest of all the distinct values anyways. Since the control has entered into the first if block the later part of else-if ladder is correctly skipped.

4.4.1 Program to derive the type of policy based on the value of premium: An example

Let us now write a program to derive the type of insurance policy based on the premium paid by the customers. Given below is the classification that an insurance company applies to its policies based on the annual premium required to create a policy.

Annual premium	Type of policy
≥1 lakh	Platinum policy
75,000 to 99,999	Gold policy
50,000 to 74,999	Silver policy
<50,000	Regular policy

The program should accept the value of the annual premium as input from the user and print the type of policy on the computer screen.

Given below is the complete source code to derive the type of policy based on its premium. Note that, we have created a variable 'premium' of type long because it is required to store values which are beyond the range of int type.

```
#include<stdio.h>
void main()
```

```
{
long premium;
printf("Enter the annual premium of the policy\n");
scanf("%d",&premium);
    if(premium >=100000)
    {
    printf("This is a PLATINUM policy\n");
    }
    else if(premium >=75000)
    {
    printf("This is a GOLD policy\n");
    }
    else if(premium >=50000)
    {
    printf("This is a SILVER policy\n");
    }
    else
    {
    printf("This is a REGULAR policy\n");
    }
}
```

Output

```
Enter the annual premium of the policy
85000
This is a GOLD policy
```

The code consist of four decision making blocks like one if block, two else-if blocks and the last else block.

The statement inside the if block will be executed if the condition,

```
premium >=100000
```

is evaluated as true. If the value of the variable premium is greater than or equal to 100000 it indicates that the type of the policy is PLATINUM and hence we print a message as This is a PLATINUM policy inside the if block as seen from the code. The later part of the ladder will be skipped after the execution of the if block completes as shown in Figure 4.16.

If the condition premium >=100000 is evaluated as false, the next condition which is specified as a part of the else if block will now be evaluated. The condition of the first else if block is as given below.

```
premium >=75000
```

Note that, at the time of evaluation of this condition, we already have a conclusion that the condition premium >=100000 is false. This is because, the else-if ladder will not evaluate any condition which is written below in the ladder unless all the conditions written above are evaluated as false. This means that if the condition premium >=75000 is evaluated as true it indicates that the value of the premium is between 75,000 and 99,999 because we necessarily know that the value of the variable premium is not greater than or equal to 100000. Hence, the else-if block prints the type of policy as GOLD as seen in the code.

Similarly, the other type of policies can be derived based on the value of variable premium as we see in the code. The working of the full source code is as shown in Figure 4.16.

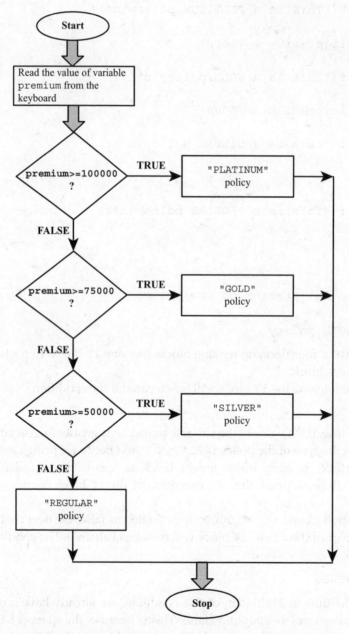

Figure 4.16: Execution of the code Program to determine the type of policy: an example

4.4.2 Program to determine the type of character – An Example

Let us write a program that accepts a character value as input from the user and prints the type of character which is read from the keyboard. The program classifies each character into one of the following categories:

1. Upper case character
2. Lower case character
3. Digit
4. Special character

Given below is the full source code that reads the value of character variable named as ch from the keyboard and prints the type of character on the computer screen.

```c
#include<stdio.h>
void main()
{
char ch;
printf("Enter a character\n");
scanf(" %c",&ch);
/*note the space before %c, revisit scanf() function described in
chapter 2 for a detailed explanation if needed */
    if(ch>=65 && ch<=90)
    {
    printf("Upper Case\n");
    }
    else if(ch>=97 && ch<=122)
    {
    printf("Lower Case\n");
    }
    else if(ch>=48 && ch<=57)
    {
    printf("Digit\n");
    }
    else
    {
    printf("Special Character\n");
    }
}
```

Output

```
Enter a character
B
Upper Case
```

As we recollect from Chapter 2 that, the ASCII value of the character is actually stored in the computer memory. Hence, we compare the value of character variable ch with the corresponding integer ASCII values so as to determine the category of the character which is stored in the variable ch. Further, we see from the Appendix I that the ASCII values from 65 to 90 represent a upper case character, whereas the ASCII values from 97 to 122 represent the lower case characters, the ASCII values from 48 to 57 represent digits and all the remaining ASCII values are assigned to the special characters. Hence, if the ASCII value of a character does not fall in between any of the ranges of upper case, lower case or digit we then print the category of the character as a 'Special Character' as seen in the code.

4.5 `switch` Statement

Consider a scenario wherein a 'expression' written in the code can give any one of the values v_1, v_2, v_3, ..., v_n as a result of its evaluation. In many cases, we may require to execute different statements based on the different results generated by the expression. For example, we may require executing statement(s) s_1 if the result of the expression is v_1, we may require executing statement(s) s_2; if the result of the expression is v_2 and so on, as shown in Figure 4.17. The requirement in general is that, for any value v_i generated by the expression, we need to execute the statement(s) s_i as shown in Figure 4.17. Further, if the expression generates a result which is other than the values v_1 to v_n then by default we will execute the statement s_d as shown in Figure 4.17.

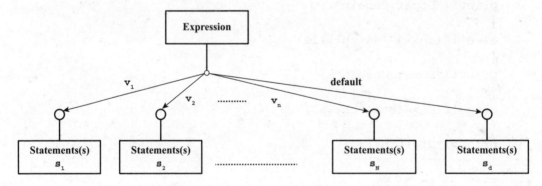

Figure 4.17: Executing statements based on the result of an expression

The given scenario can be implemented using `switch` statement. A switch consists of a set of `case` blocks such that each `case` block corresponds to one of the distinct values v_1 to v_n that the expression can generate. The statements written inside a particular `case` will be executed if the result of the expression is same as that of the value specified in that `case`. This means that, the statements written inside `case` v_1 will be executed if the result of the expression is v_1, the statements in `case` v_2 will be executed if the result of the expression is v_2 and so on. In general, the statements written inside the `case` v_i will be executed if the result of the expression is v_i. If the result of the expression does not match with the values specified by any of the case blocks then the statements written inside the default case will be executed, Figure 4.18, gives the syntax of switch statement. Note that, a break statement must be written as a last statement in every case so as to transfer the control of execution outside the switch block after a particular case is executed. The break statement need not be written after the last case (generally the default case) because, as such the control of execution will be transferred outside the switch as there is no other case defined after the last case.

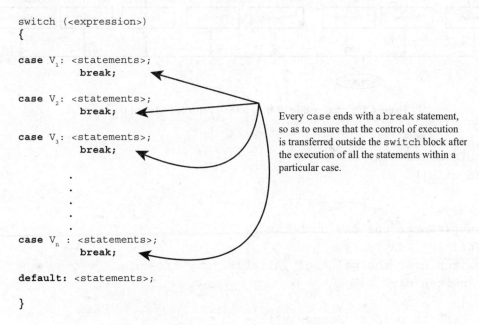

Figure 4.18: Syntax of switch statement

As an example, let us write a program to accept the day number as input from the user and print the calendar day on the computer screen. This means that, if the user enters the number 1 then the code should print "Sunday", if the user inputs the number 2 then the code should print "Monday" and so on. In general, if the user enters any i the code should print i^{th} day of the week as shown in Figure 4.19. Also, if the user enters any number which is not between 1 and 7 then we will print a message as "Invalid day number" on the computer screen as shown in Figure 4.19.

Given below is the full source code that takes an integer variable day as input from the user and prints the corresponding day of the week on the computer screen based on the value of variable day. As seen in the code, we use a switch statement that compares the value of variable day with each of the cases and if the value of variable day is 1 then statements written in the case 1 will be executed thereby printing "Sunday" on the computer screen. Similarly, if the value of variable day is 2 then statements written in the case 2 will be executed thereby printing "Monday" on the computer screen and so on.

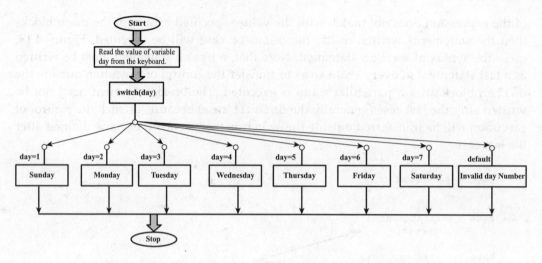

Figure 4.19: Execution of the code to print the 'day of the week'

```c
#include<stdio.h>
void main()
{
int day;
printf("Enter the day number\n");
scanf("%d",&day);
/*switch over the value of variable "day"*/
    switch(day)
    {
    case 1: printf("Sunday\n");
      break;
    case 2: printf("Monday\n");
      break;
    case 3: printf("Tuesday\n");
      break;
    case 4: printf("Wednesday\n");
      break;
    case 5: printf("Thursday\n");
      break;
    case 6: printf("Friday\n");
      break;
    case 7: printf("Saturday\n");
      break;
    default: printf("Invalid Day Number\n");
    }
}
```

Output

```
Enter the day number
2
Monday
```

Why do we write a break statement at the end of every case inside a switch block? **?**

When a particular case is satisfied, the `switch` is considered as **closed**. This means that, the control of execution does not come out of `switch` block even after all the statements in a particular `case` are executed. In the absence of `break` statement, the flow of execution falls through all the case statements written after the `case` which was satisfied by the expression. Hence, we explicitly write the `break` statement inside each of the `case` block so as to avoid the **fall through** in the execution flow. For example, in the above program if we do not write a `break` statement and set the value of variable `day` as 4, then the execution flow falls through each case block (starting from case 4) and gives the following output:

```
Wednesday
Thursday
Friday
Saturday
Invalid Day
```

Hence, a `break` statement is required to be written inside each `case` block in order to generate the desired output.

4.6   Ternary Operator/Conditional Operator

The conditional operator is an alternative to an if-else statement. The operator is also called an ternary operator, which operates on three operands as shown in the syntax below:

```
condition? expression1:expression2;
```

The operator first evaluates the condition and if the condition is found to be 'true' then the result of the ternary operation is same as the result returned by the 'expression1'. If the condition is found to be 'false' then the result of the ternary operation is same as the result returned by the 'expression2'.

As an example, to understand the working of the ternary operators, let us consider the `if-else` statement given below which stores the minimum of the two numbers x and y into the variable res.

```
if(x<y)
{
res=x;
}
else
{
res=y;
}
```

This means that, the variable res is set to the value of variable x if the condition x < y is 'true' and the value of variable res is set to variable y if the condition x < y is 'false' as shown in Figure 4.20. As an alternative to the given if-else statement, we can also use a ternary operator to initialize the value of variable res as shown below:

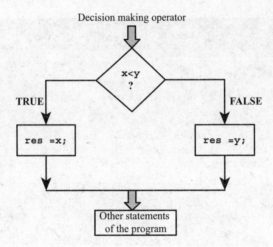

Figure 4.20: Find minimum of two numbers x and y

```
res= (x<y)?x:y;
```

Given below is the full source code that finds the minimum of two numbers x and y using the ternary operator.

```
#include<stdio.h>
void main()
{
int x,y,res;
printf("Enter the two numbers\n");
scanf("%d %d",&x,&y);
res= (x<y)?x:y;
printf("Minimum is %d\n",res);
}
```

Output

```
Enter the two numbers
10 30
Minimum is 10
```

NOTES

Nesting of conditional operator

It is possible to nest conditional operators. For example, consider a situation where we need to find greatest of three numbers a, b, and c using conditional operator. In this case we can nest conditional operator as follows:

```
res = a>=b && a>=c ? a : b>=a&&b>=c ? b : c;
```

This statement is equivalent to the else if ladder as shown in illustration below:

The conditions in `else-if` ladder are very much identical to those in example in Section 4.4. Hence, the variable `res` will store the value which is greatest of all the three variables. Given below is the full program which finds maximum of three numbers using nesting of conditional operator instead of `else-if` ladder

```
#include<stdio.h>
void main()
{
    int res,a,b,c;
    printf("Enter 3 nos\n");
    scanf("%d %d %d",&a,&b,&c);
    res = a>=b && a>=c ? a : b>=a&&b>=c ? b : c;
    printf("Greatest number is %d\n",res);

}
```

Output
```
Enter 3 nos
10 55 22
Greatest number is 55
```

You could also write the same condition differently by changing the way in which the conditional operators are nested. For example, the following statement will also store the greatest of values `a`, `b` and `c` in variable `res`.

`res = a>=b ? a>=c ? a :c : b>=c? b : c;`

Whilst the statement does the same job, the only difference is that, this statement internally translates to **nested if-else** blocks instead of an else if ladder. The main condition `a>=b` is tested first, if this condition is true the following part is executed

`a>=c ? a :c`

whereas, if the main condition **`a>=b`** is false the following part of the statement is executed

`b>=c? b : c`

The working of the statement is as shown in the following figure

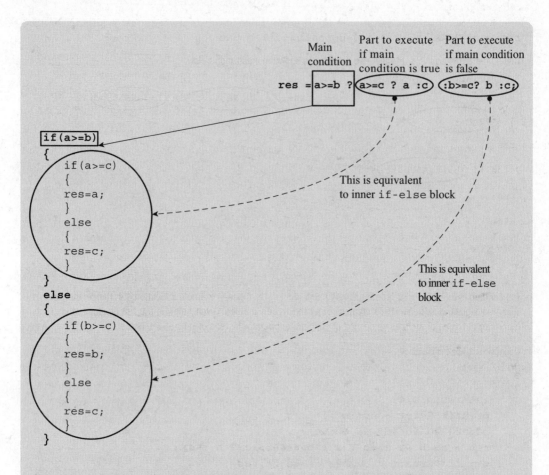

Given below is the full source code to find greatest of three numbers by nesting conditional operators using this approach

```
#include<stdio.h>
void main()
{
    int res,a,b,c;
    printf("Enter 3 nos\n");
    scanf("%d %d %d",&a,&b,&c);
    res = a>=b ? a>=c ? a :c : b>=c? b : c;
    printf("Greatest number is %d\n",res);
}
```

Output

```
Enter 3 nos
10 55 22
Greatest number is 55
```

4.7 goto **Statement**

goto statement is used to implement an unconditional jump in a program. When a goto statement is encountered the normal sequential execution of the program is discontinued and the control of execution is transferred to the statement which is identified by the label specified as a part of the goto statement.

Given below is the syntax of the goto statement

```
goto <label>;
```

The label is a unique name in the program which is given to a statement to which the control of execution is to be transferred using the goto statement. Such a unique name to the statement must be given as a prefix of the statement in the program using a colon (:) operator as shown below:

```
label: Statement;
```

Given below is the modified program to print the day of the week by accepting the day number as input from the user. As seen, the code uses a else-if ladder to print the day of the week based on the value of integer variable day. At the beginning, we have written the following if construct which checks if an invalid day number is provided as an input by the user

```
if(day<=0 || day>7)
    {
    printf("Invalid Day Number\n");
    goto END;
    }
```

This means that if the value of variable day is not between 1 and 7 (both inclusive) then we print a message as "Invalid Day Number" on the computer screen. Also, the following goto statement present inside the if block will transfer the control to the statement labelled as END in the program.

```
goto END;
```

Hence the goto statement transfers the control to the last statement of the program which is,

```
END: printf("End of the program\n");
```

Thereby skipping the complete else if ladder and avoiding any unnecessary operations as user has entered the invalid day number

```
#include<stdio.h>
void main()
{
int day;
printf("Enter the day number\n");
```

```
scanf("%d",&day);
    if(day<=0 || day>7)
    {
    printf("Invalid Day Number\n");
    goto END;
    }
    if(day==1)
    {
    printf("Sunday\n");
    }
    else if(day==2)
    {
    printf("Monday\n");
    }
    else if(day==3)
    {
    printf("Tuesday\n");
    }
    else if(day==4)
    {
    printf("Wednesday\n");
    }
    else if(day==5)
    {
    printf("Thursday\n");
    }
    else if(day==6)
    {
    printf("Friday\n");
    }
    else
    {
    printf("Saturday\n");
    }
    END: printf("End of the program\n");
}
```

Output

```
Enter the day number
2
Monday
End of the program
```

Output (Case: Invalid Day number)

```
Enter the day number
```

```
-1
Invalid Day Number
End of the program
```

Quiz

1. Translate the given if-else construct into a switch statement
   (Assume variable x is of type integer)

```
if(x>1000)
{
printf("Condition is true\n");
}
else
{
printf("Condition is false\n");
}
```

2. What is the output of the following code? (Choose the correct option)

```
#include<stdio.h>
void main()
{
    if(NULL)
    {
    printf("Inside the if block \n");
    }
    printf("Outside the if block\n"):
}
```
   (a) This is a compilation error
   (b) This is a runtime error
   (c) Output is:
      ```
      Inside the if block
      Outside the if block
      ```
   (d) Output is
      ```
      Outside the if block
      ```

3. What is the output of the following code? (Choose the correct option)

```
#include<stdio.h>
void main()
{
    int a=25;
    if(a)
    {
    printf("Inside the if block \n");
    }
```

```
        printf("Outside the if block\n"):
    }
```

(a) This is a compilation error

(b) This is a runtime error

(c) Output is:

```
    Inside the if block
    Outside the if block
```

(d) Output is:

```
    Outside the if block
```

4. Translate the given if-else construct using a conditional operator? :
   (Assume a, b and c are integer type variables defined in the program)

```
if(a>b)
{
printf("Condition 1 is true\n");
    if(b>c)
    {
    printf("Condition 2 is true\n");
    }
    else
    {
    printf("Condition 2 is false\n");
    }
}
else
{
printf("Condition 1 is false\n");
}
```

5. What is the output of the following code? (Choose the correct option)

```
#include<stdio.h>
void main()
{
    int x=10,y=20,z=30;
    if(++(++x>y++<z--))
    {
    printf("The condition is true\n");
    }
    else
    {
    printf("The condition is false\n");
    }
}
```

(a) This is a compilation error

(b) This is a runtime error

(c) Output is:
```
The condition is true
```
(d) Output is:
```
The condition is false
```

6. What is the output of the following code
```c
#include<stdio.h>
void main()
{
int a=55,b=90,c=81,d=22,r;
r =a>b&&c>d?a>c?c<d?a:b:c:d;
printf("Result is %d\n",r);
}
```

Error Finding Exercise

Given below are some programs which may or may not contain errors. Correct the error(s) if exist in the code and determine the output.

Program 1
```c
#include<stdio.h>
void main()

{
int a=NULL;
    if(printf("Value of a is %d\n",a))
    {
    printf("Inside the if block\n");
    }
    else
    {
    printf("Inside the else block\n");
    }
printf("End of the code\n");
}
```

Program 2
```c
#include<stdio.h>
void main()
{
    if("A">> "B")
    {
    printf("A is greater than B\n");
    }
```

```
        else
        {
        printf("A is not greater than \n");
        }
}
```

Program 3
```
#include<stdio.h>
void main()
{
int a,b,c;
printf("Enter the values of a b\n");
scanf("%d %d",&a,&b);
        if(c=a>b>NULL?NULL:-1:-2);
        {
        printf("Condition is true\n");
        };
        else
        {
        printf("Condition is false \n");
        };
}
```

Program 4
```
#include<stdio.h>
void main()
{
int x=10,y=20,z=30;
        if(x<y>z>10>20<30)
        {
        printf("The condition is true\n");
        }
        else
        {
        printf("The condition is false\n");
        }
}
```

Program 5
```
#include<stdio.h>
void main()
{
        int a,b,c;
        printf("Enter the values of a b\n");
        scanf("%d %d",&a,&b);
```

```
if(a=b==b)
{
printf("TRUE\n");
}
else
{
printf("FALSE\n");
}
}
```

Review Questions

1. Explain a need of decision making control statements in the program with an example.
2. Write a short note on the else-if ladder in C/C++. Compare `if-else` construct with the `else-if` ladder using an example of your choice.
3. Write a program to take a character as input from the user and to check if it's a vowel or not. The program should recognize vowel characters in upper as well as lower case.
4. Write a program to find the greatest of five numbers using a decision making operator(?:)
5. Explain the use of `switch` statement with an example.
6. Write a program to show the usage of `goto` statement. Write a program to print a message "Hello World" n times using `if` construct and a `goto` statement (where n is the value to be taken as input from the user).
7. Write a program to take a month number as input from the user and to print the name of the month. For example, if user inputs a value 2 the program must print February. Make use of `switch` statement.
8. Write a program to take a number as input from the user and to determine if the number is even or odd using `switch` statement
9. Write a program to take the `year` as input from the user and to check if it's a leap year or not.

Chapter 5

Iterative Control Statements: Loops

5.1 Introduction

Often we come across requirements where same set of operations need to be executed multiple times to generate the required output. For example, we need to repeatedly perform multiplication to calculate factorial of a number; we need to repeatedly draw lines to construct a polygon and so on. Each time the operation may use different data sets for evaluation; hence, results of each of the individual operations may be different, but the expression that defines the operation is always the same. To give an example, although lines are drawn repeatedly to construct a polygon, the [x, y] coordinates (data values) giving start and end of a line may be different each time. Immaterial of the data used in each stage, we will still consider this as an repetitive execution of the same operation. We can form an expression to draw line from (x1, y1) to (x2, y2) in terms of variables x1, y1, x2 and y2. We can change the value of these variables each time before repeating draw line operation so as to ensure that each line is created at a different position and the consolidated result is a polygon.

To elaborate what we just said, let us try to construct a triangle using a series of drawLine operations. A triangle can be visualized as a consolidated effect of three lines drawn at correct positions. Hence, the execution of the drawLine operation must be repeated thrice. Before we proceed further, readers are requested to note that the detailed study of computer graphics is out of the scope of this textbook, however, we still give an example to draw a triangle using some abstract operation drawLine to understand the concept of loops in C/C++.

Let us assume that the expression to draw a single line from point (x1, y1) to point (x2, y2) be as shown below:

```
drawLine[(x1,y1),(x2,y2)]
```

Drawing a triangle using this operation will now be a three-step process, which is elaborated as below:

Stage 1: Initialize variables x1=50, y1=0, x2=0, y2=50 and execute the operation

```
drawLine[(x1,y1),(x2,y2)]
```

The line drawn in this step is shown in Figure 5.1.

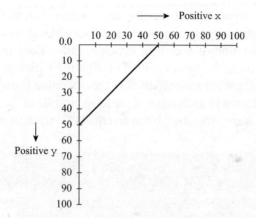

Figure 5.1: Output after first drawLine
operation

Stage 2: Initialize variables `x1=50, y1=0, x2=100, y2=50` and again execute the operation
`drawLine[(x1,y1),(x2,y2)]`

The line drawn in this step is shown in Figure 5.2.

Stage 3: Initialize variables `x1=0, y1=50, x2=100, y2=50` and again execute the operation
`drawLine[(x1,y1),(x2,y2)]`

The line drawn in this step is shown in Figure 5.3.

Note that in all the three stages we repeat the following expression:

`drawLine[(x1,y1),(x2,y2)]`

However, the data used in each stage is different (the actual values of variables `x1`, `x2`, `y1`, and `y2` are different at each stage). When working with loops, our focus should be in understanding

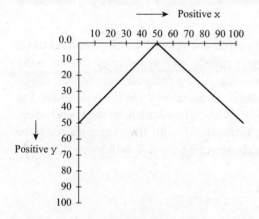

Figure 5.2: Output after second drawLine
operation

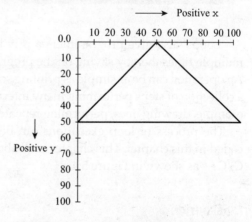

Figure 5.3: Output after third drawLine
operation

that the expression to be repeated is always the same, rather than the data values involved at each stage, because we can easily change the values of variables at each iteration.

We can put such operations in a control structure called **Loop** instead of repeating it in the program. The only thing we need to ensure is that the variables x1, y1, x2, and y2 correctly change their values at each stage before the operation is executed. This will ensure that different lines are drawn in each stage of the loop, in spite of the same expression being executed in each of the stages thereby giving an effect of a triangle on the graphical screen.

But, I can also draw a triangle by writing three different drawLine statements. Why are we trying to have a single drawLine statement and repeat it three times using loop? **?**

If we explicitly write three different drawLine statements, it will be hard coding which is a bad programming practice. Because in such a case, your program will not be configurable to draw any other shape. The program in this case can only draw a triangle because we have written drawLine three times. But, if user wants to draw other shapes like square, hexagon, etc., the program will fail, as these shapes need different number of lines. By using loops we can achieve configurable programs, i.e., we can accept the name of the shape as input from the user and repeat drawLine operation for the required number of times, to draw a particular shape. So if user needs "square" we can repeat drawLine 4 times, if user needs "hexagon" we can repeat drawLine 6 times and so on.

How can we change the values of variables x1, y1, x2, y2 at each stage before executing the statement drawLine[(x1,y1), (x2,y2)]? **?**

This is the responsibility of the programmer, to develop a logic of the program such that the values of the variables are changed at each stage before the execution of operation is repeated. This will ensure at different lines are drawn at each stage thereby giving a net result as a polygon at the end of the loop. In this chapter, we have many examples where we will understand on how to develop such a logic. We again reiterate saying that, implementing the above example to draw polygon is out of scope of this text book, however we have just used this real world example as a base to understand **concept of "Loops"**

'Loops' also give programmers a privilege to write the operation once and execute it multiple times thereby saving on the programmer's time as well as reducing lines of code. An operation can be as simple as printing some message onto a computer screen, or it can be a collection of steps performing many intermediate computations to get the final result. For example, drawing lines, performing repeated multiplication to calculate factorial and so on.

The process of loop executions can be best understood with the examples we have coded in this chapter. This chapter is all about understanding the different loops offered in C/C++ as shown in Figure 5.4.

DEFINITION

Loop is an **iterative control structure** used to repeat a block of statements for a given number of times.

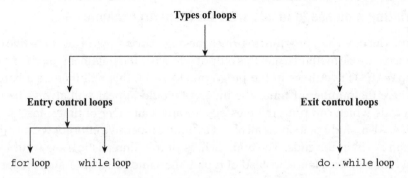

Figure 5.4: Types of loops in C/C++

5.2 while Loop in C/C++

The while loop is used to repeat the execution of an operation as long as a specific condition is satisfied. An operation to be repeated can be a single statement or a block of statements. The while loop executes the operation specified in its body repeatedly and requires a condition for terminating its execution. The condition is checked each time before repeating the execution of operation. The operation is executed if and only if the condition is evaluated as true. After executing the operation, the control is again transferred back to check the condition, thereby resulting in a cyclic flow of control to repeat the execution of block of statements. while loop terminates its execution once the condition specified is evaluated as FALSE, following which the control is transferred to the first statement outside the loop. As the condition is evaluated before entering the loop, it is categorized as 'Entry Control' type of loop in C/C++. Figure 5.5 shows the detailed execution flow and syntax of while loop.

> **DEFINITION**
>
> **while loop** is a **entry control loop** which repeats the execution of an operation as long as a specific condition is satisfied.

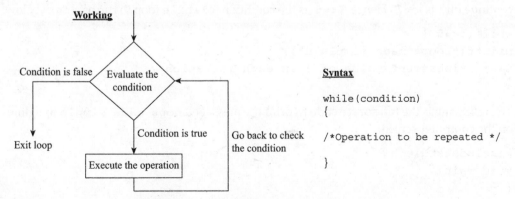

Figure 5.5: Workflow and syntax of while loop

5.2.1 Printing a message inside `while` loop: An example

As an example, let us write a program to print a message *Loops made simple* five times on a computer screen. One method to get this output is to write the statement: **printf ("Loops made simple\n");** five times in the program. However, this will then be a hard-coded program where the number of times the message would appear will always be five. Let us design a code which can print the message for any k number of times, instead of hard coding to five. Also, study of loops is all about avoiding repetitive effort of writing the same line again and again in the code. The approach is simply unrealistic if we want to print a message say 1000 times. Hence, instead of typing the same **printf()** statement multiple times we shall write it only once and put it in the loop so that it is executed multiple times.

We can put the printf() statement in the while loop as shown below:

```
while(<condition>){
printf("Loops made simple\n");
<code to control the condition>
}
```

while loop will repeat the execution of printf() statement as long as the condition is evaluated as true. Hence, we need to design a condition such that the condition is evaluated as true for the first five iterations and becomes false later on as we need to print the message only five times on the screen.

To design such a condition, we maintain a counter variable say i with an initial value of 1.

```
int i = 1;
```

Each time the operation is performed, we increment the value of i by 1. This will ensure that we always store the count of times **printf()** is executed in the variable i. This means that any iteration of while loop can determine the progress by looking at the value of variable i. To clarify further, when value of i is 2, it will imply that the operation is executed two times, when value of i is 3, it will imply that the operation is performed three times and so on. In general, when the value of i is **k**, we can say that operation is performed **k** times. Here, we need to perform the operation 5 times, i.e., we need to print a message for values of variable i = 1,2,3,4, or 5, once i crosses 5 the loop shall terminate. In other words, the loop must continue till i is <= 5. Hence, **i<=5** is the condition for while loop to run as shown below:

```
while(i<=5){
printf("Loops made simple\n");
i++; /*increment value of i in each iteration*/
}
```

The following is the full source code to print the message **Loops made simple** five times on the computer screen:

```
#include<stdio.h>
void main()
{
int i=1;
```

```
int k=5;
while (i<=k)
        {
        printf("Loops made simple\n");
        i++;
        }
}
```

Output of the program is as follows:

```
Loops made simple
Loops made simple
Loops made simple
Loops made simple
Loops made simple
```

5.2.1.1 Execution of the code

while loop has five iterations as shown in Figure 5.6. The loop performs the following two tasks with each iteration:

1. Print the message "Loops Made Simple" on the screen.
2. Increment the value of variable i.

Loop will repeat the operation as long as the condition i<=5 is true. Given that the initial value of i is set to 1, the loop has five iterations, thereby printing the message five times, as shown in Figure 5.6. The loop terminates when the value of i becomes 6, because this is the first value which is greater than 5.

This is great! I got a message "Loops made Simple" 5 times on my screen even if there is only one printf() statement in the program. But how is this program configurable? Can I print the message as many number of times as I want or do I have to always print the message 5 times? **?**

Currently the value of variable k is initialized to 5 hence the code is executing the printf() statement 5 times. If you change the value of k to say 10 the loop will execute the printf() statement 10 times. Remember the condition of the loop is specified as i<=k. Hence, you can change the number of times you want to perform the operation by simply changing the value of variable k. To make this code further configurable you can also accept value of variable k as input from the user instead of initializing it in the program, so that user can input the actual number of times the operation is to be performed.

The initial value of variable i is set to 1 in the program. Is it possible to get the same result with any other initial values? **?**

There is no rule to set the initial value of variable i. Note that variable i is just used as a counter to determine the number of times we need to be execute an operation. The only requirement is that the operation must get executed five (value of k) times. In this case we have initialized the value of i as 1 and each time the operation executes, we increment the value of i until it crosses 5. As an alternative to this, we could have also have given the initial value of i as 5, and decrement it each time we perform the operation. In this case, to perform an operation 5 times, we must execute printf() statement for following values i=5;i=4;i=3;i=2;i=1. Hence the condition for termination of the loop will now be `i>=1` which means that we must execute the statements inside the loop until value of `i` is greater than or equal to 1. This is because we are setting the initial value of `i` as 5 instead of 1. The point to be noted here is that variable `i` is just counting the number of times the operation is to be repeated, moving `i` from `1 to 5` executes the loop 5 times which is same as moving `i` from `5 to 1` which will also execute the loop 5 times without affecting the output. In fact, you can set any arbitrary initial value of `i` as say 101 and keep incrementing it until it crosses 105 (100+k); this will also work to perform the operation 5 times. All that is needed from you is to ensure that loop has 5 iterations, and it is up to you how to ensure this. Here we have step size of increment as 1, because we are executing `i++`; in the program however you can also have different step sizes if needed. So, if you want to perform the operation 5 times, you may have initial value of `i` as 100, terminating condition as `i<=110` (k+10) but a step size of 2. This means that at each step you increment `i` by 2 hence `i` progresses as

`i=100,i=102,i=104,i=108,i=110`

Hence this arrangement of condition will also perform the operation 5 times. In summary, changing the initial value of `i` will require some change in your logic of counting the iterations and the terminating condition itself, but it is still possible to perform the operation desired number of times without affecting the output. Of course you don't want to make your program unnecessarily complex so we have kept initial value if `i=1` and terminating condition as `i<=k` which makes it easy to read, understand and maintain the loop.

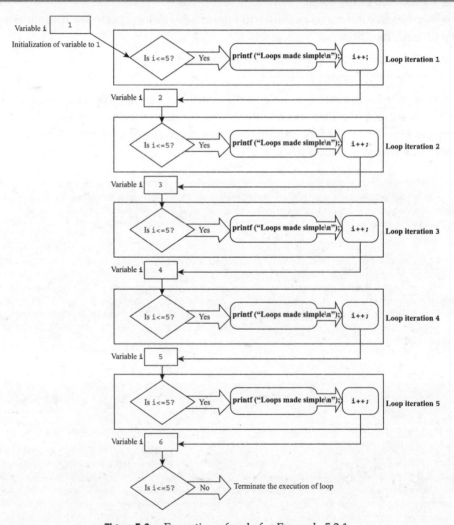

Figure 5.6: Execution of code for Example 5.2.1

5.2.2   Printing even numbers using `while` loop: An example

As another example, let us write a program which prints all the even numbers from 0 to n. If we assume a value of n say 10, then we must print all the even numbers from 0 to 10 which are 0, 2, 4, 6, 8 and 10. We can take the value of n as input from the user which will give us the upper bound up to which the program needs to print even numbers. Hence, the value of variable n will be required to determine the number of iterations the loop should execute to print the even numbers.

We maintain a counter variable i so as to determine the number of times the printf() is to be executed. We set the initial value of variable i as zero.

```
int i=0;
```

Note that if any number x is even then x+2 is also even. This would mean that if we start a counter i with an even value then we can simply increment i by 2 each time, so as to represent the next even value.

At each stage of the loop, program executes the statement **i=i+2** so that i takes 0, 2, 4, 6, 8, . . . , n (if n is even) [or 0, 2, 4, 6, 8, . . . , n-1 (if n is odd)] at each stage. Note that as we are incrementing value of i by 2 at each stage, i will always represent even values. And as we need to print the numbers only up to n, we must terminate the execution of loop when value of i crosses n. In other words, we must print the even numbers till i is <=n. Hence, the condition to run loop will be **i<=n**.

```
while(i<=n)
{
printf("%d\n",i);
i=i+2; /*Generate next even number*/
}
```

5.2.2.1   *Execution of the loop*

Figure 5.7 shows the execution of the loop assuming the value of n as 10. while loop has six iterations as shown below. The loop performs the following two tasks with each iteration:

1. Print the value of i.
2. Increase the value of variable i by 2.

Since the initial value of variable i is set to zero in the program, each time you increase the value of i by 2 you will get the next even number as shown in Figure 5.7. Hence, the program prints even number in every iteration. The loop terminates as the value of i becomes 12, because this is the first value which is greater than 10.

The following is the full source code to print even numbers from 1 to n, where the value of variable n is taken as input from the user.

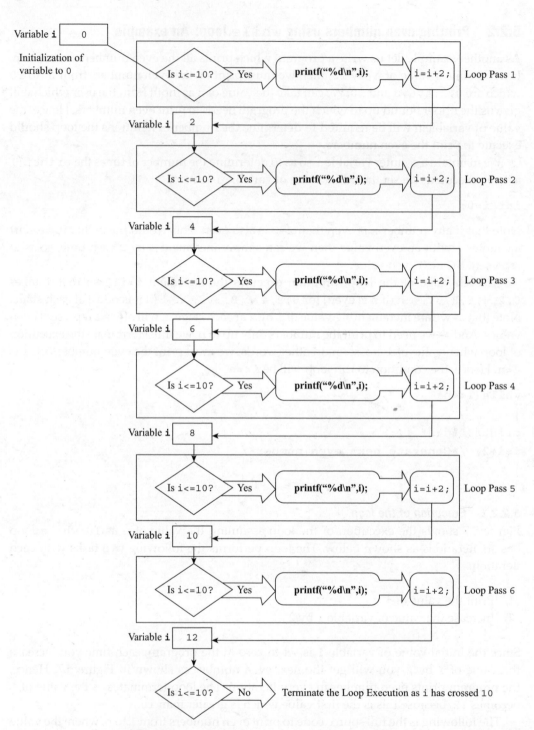

Figure 5.7: Execution of the code to print even values

```
#include<stdio.h>
void main()
{
int n,i=0;
printf("Enter the upper bound");
scanf("%d",&n);
printf("Even numbers are\n");
    while(i<=n)
    {
    printf("%d\n",i);
    i=i+2;/*Generate next even number*/
    }
}
```

Output:
```
Enter the upper bound: 10
Even numbers are
0
2
4
6
8
10
```

5.2.3   Calculating factorial using `while` loop: An example

Let us write a program to take a number as input from the user and compute the factorial of the given number. Before we start working on this problem statement, we must answer to the following questions:

1. Is there any operation to be executed repeatedly to calculate the factorial of a number x?
2. If yes, how many times do we need to repeat the execution of that operation?

We start with answering question 1, as factorial of any number x is calculated by repeated multiplication as shown below:

```
=x*(x-1)*(x-2)*(x-3)*(x-4)···*1
```

From the expression, we find that multiplication is performed repeatedly but the data used in each of the multiplications is different. For example, at the first stage we multiply x and (x-1) and we may store the result in some temporary variable, going forward in the expression we multiply this result with another number (x-2) thereby creating another temporary result and so on. The point to understand here is, for large values of x, we have x temporary results created, one formed at each stage of evaluation of the expression. Obvious point to note here is that each temporary result generated is the multiplication of the previous result with the next number in the expression. And the last multiplication of the formed result with 1 gives the factorial of x. In any case, you will not be able to create x temporary variables to store each of the intermediate results, this is because value of variable x is not known at the time of compilation. This is also not needed because, once the ith result is generated the (i-1)th result is not required to be stored in the system memory as the expression only needs to keep moving in one direction. Therefore, we can store all the temporary results in a single variable such that the new result generated overwrites the previous result stored in the variable. Hence, we create a variable **f** which can store the different temporary results generated during the evaluation of expression.

```
int f=1;
```

Note that the initial value of f is set to 1, which means that the first number in the expression will always be multiplied by 1 as there is no previous result available at the time of first multiplication. As an example, let us apply this logic to calculate factorial of 4.

```
4! = 4*3*2*1
```

The first number in the expression is 4, which can be multiplied with the previous temporary result defaulted to 1; hence, at the first stage we perform multiplication of 1 and 4, i.e., we perform f*x and generate a temporary result 4(1*4=4). We have already concluded that once the new result is generated we do not need the previous temporary result. Hence, we can store the new result in the same variable **f** thereby overwriting the value of f to 4. This evaluation can be performed using the following statement:

```
f = f * x;
```

The statement multiplies the value of variable f which stores the previous temporary result with the value x and stores the result back in f which overwrites the previous temporary result with the new value.

The new result in variable **f** needs to be multiplied with the value 3 (the number x-1), which is the next number in the expression. As we have already stored the temporary result generated till now in variable f, it is now safe to reduce x by 1 to generate the next number required in the expression. Also, as the current value of x which is 4 is no longer required in the expression ahead we can execute a statement x-- to reduce the value of x which then makes x = 3.

Now on execution of f=f*x, we multiply 4 (current value of f) with 3 (current value of x) and generate a new temporary result 4*3=12 which is stored back in f overwriting the previous value of variable f.

The same process can be followed to multiply the newly generated result 12 with the next number in the expression which is 2 and so on. Figure 5.8 shows the execution of the following statements at each stage of loop:

```
f=f*x;
x--;
```

Executing statement x-- after each multiplication ensures that when the loop repeats the execution of f=f*x in the next stage, the new reduced value of x is multiplied with the previous result to form a new result for the next stage of the loop as shown. Also, as we reduce

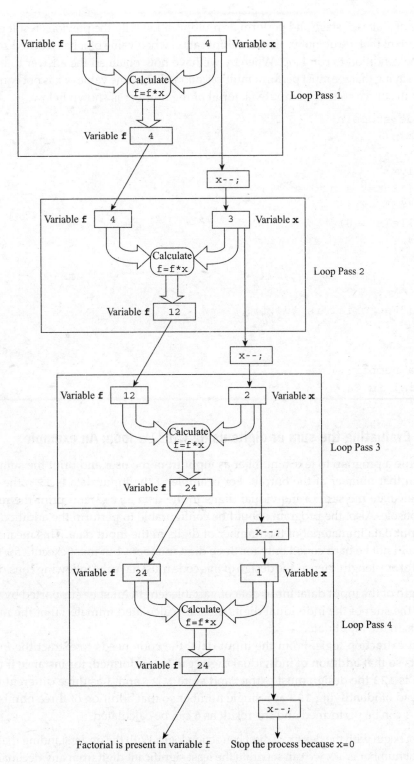

Figure 5.8: Calculating factorial of a number

the value of x at each stage and perform its multiplication with the previous result generated, it is important that we do not perform multiplication when value of x has reached zero, hence x>0 is the condition to run loop. Whereby we have now obtained the answer to the second question saying that we must perform multiplication till the time value of x is not equal to zero.

The full source code to compute factorial of the number is shown below:

```
#include<stdio.h>
void main()
{
int f=1,x;
printf("Enter a number:");
scanf("%d",&x);
    while(x > 0)
    {
    f=f*x;
    x--;
    }
printf("Factorial is %d",f);
}
```

Output
```
Enter a number: 4
Factorial is 24
```

5.2.4 Evaluating the sum of digits using `while` loop: An example

Let us write a program to take a number as input from the user and print the sum of digits present in that number at the output. For example, if the input data is 123, the program should calculate the sum of individual digits in the data 1+2+3 and print the result as 6 on the console. Also, the program should be configurable to perform the addition of digits in the input data immaterial of the number of digits in the input data. This means that the logic should not be hard coded only for three digit numbers, but must execute for the input numbers of any length. Hence, the design of this code must have the following considerations:

1. Length of the input data: Input data of variable length must be supported by the code, and the sum of the individual digits must be calculated immaterial of the number of digits in the input data.

2. Digit extraction logic: From the input data, the code needs to extract the individual digits so that addition of individual digits can be performed, for instance if the input data is 123 the design must extract and store 1, 2, and 3 as three different numbers instead of identifying 123 as a single number so that addition of three numbers 1, 2, and 3 can be performed and the result as 6 can be calculated.

Let us first begin with the design of digit extraction logic. With the understanding that the base of decimal number is 10, we can separate the least significant digit from any decimal number by calculating the remainder of the number with respect to 10. That is, if the input number is

123 and remainder of 123 with respect to 10 is **3** and the quotient is **12,** which also means that the remaining most significant digits are left as a quotient of division. Hence, the quotient obtained as **12** can be further used to extract the next digit in the number which is 2, because 2 is the least significant digit of 12 we can obtain the digit 2 as a remainder of 12 and 10. Thus, in summary the quotient calculated in the current division can be used to obtain the next most significant digit from the input data. The full process of digit extraction is shown in Figure 5.9, and note that after extracting the last digit from the number the quotient of the division with respect to 10 becomes zero which indicates that the digits in the input data are fully extracted. Hence, the digit extraction logic given in Figure 5.9 will work for input data of any length.

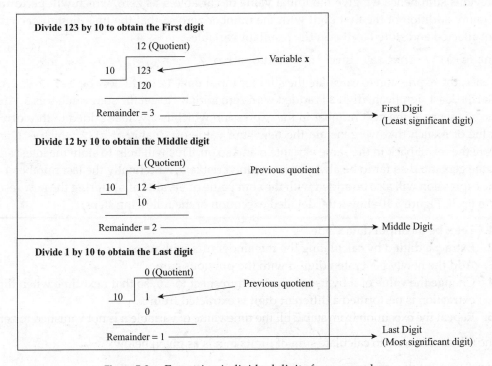

Figure 5.9: Extracting individual digits from a number

Also, as the digit extraction logic evaluates the remainder and quotient of a number x (input data) with respect to 10 multiple times, we can insert this operation in the loop because the execution of the same block of statements can be easily repeated using while loop. The next point is to store the individual digits extracted in memory variables, so that we can add the individual digits to get the required output. That is, if the input data is 123 the individual digits 1, 2, and 3 must be stored in variables say d1, d2, and d3 so that we can perform the addition of d1+d2+d3 to obtain the result as 6. However, as the program is configurable in terms of number of digits, the number of digits in the input data cannot be anticipated at the time of compilation of the program; hence, the option of storing each digit in the separate variable cannot be implemented in practice. We will therefore come up with an idea to store all the digits in the same variable instead of creating a different variable for each digit. Let us then create a variable d, which can store the digits as and when they are generated such that when a new most significant digit is generated the previous least significant digit can be overwritten. Overwriting previous digit when a new digit is extracted will also mean that we need to keep performing addition of digits as and when the digits are generated so that the previously generated digit is already included in the sum that we evaluate before the digit is fully lost in the process of calculating the next digit. Let us create a variable s to store the 'sum' evaluated each time a new digit is extracted. This would mean that every new digit extracted would be added to variable s which stores the previous sum, thereby storing the complete sum value in variable s itself once all the digits are extracted.

At the time of extracting the first least significant digit, there cannot be any value of previous sum hence we give the initial value of variable s as zero, which will perform a dummy addition of the first digit with the number zero so that the first digit extracted is not affected and stored as it is in the resultant variable.

```
int s=0; /*initial sum is set to zero*/
```

Hence, the expression to calculate the sum for input data 123 will now be 0+3+2+1. Note that the least significant digit **3** is added with zero initially to get the sum value s as 3. After the s is set as 3, the next number in the expression which is **2** will be added to the current value of s such that we generate the new sum value of 3(value of s)+2 which is **5** and store the result back in the same variable s and so on. This will help to store the latest sum value generated so far to be always present in variable s. And finally the last number 1 in the expression will also be added with the sum value of 5(value of s) storing the new result in s itself. Figure 5.10 shows the detailed execution of the following steps:

1. Let x be the input data value.
2. Extract a digit d by calculating the remainder of x with respect to 10.
3. Add the newly generated digit d with the previous sum s.
4. Change the value of x by its quotient with respect to 10, so that next time when digit extraction is performed a different digit is extracted from x.
5. Repeat the execution from step 2 till the time value of variable x is not vanished to zero.

The full source code to calculate sum of digits in x is as given below:

```
#include<stdio.h>
void main()
{
int s=0,x,d;
printf("Enter a number:");
scanf("%d",&x);
    while(x!=0)
    {
       d=x%10; /*extract the individual digit*/
       s=s+d;  /*perform addition with previous sum*/
       x=x/10;  /*Use quotient for the next iteration*/
    }
printf("Sum of digits is %d",s);
}
```

Output
```
Enter a number: 123
Sum of digits is 6
```

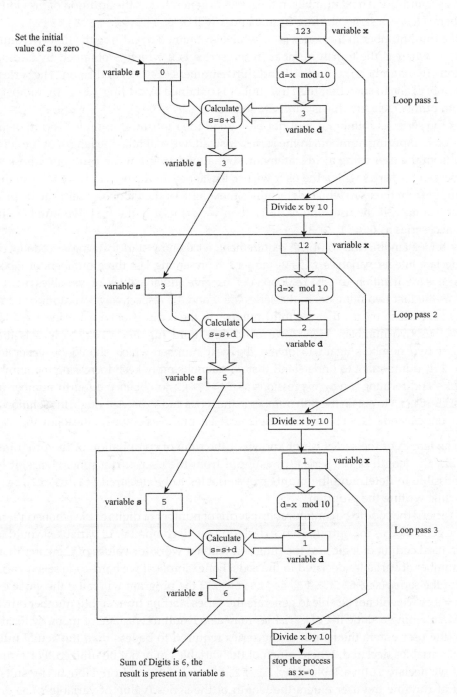

Figure 5.10: Calculating the sum of digits

5.2.5   Generating the Fibonacci series using `while` loop: An example

Fibonacci series requires two numbers to start, the starting two numbers are generally taken as 0 and 1, the next number in the series is generated as the addition of previous two numbers. Hence, a series starting from 0 and 1 will be 0,1,1,2,3,5,8,13,21,.... Note that the third number in the series is 1, which is obtained by adding the first two numbers 0 and 1, whereas the fourth number in the series is 2 which is obtained by adding the previous two numbers, i.e., second and third numbers (1+1=2) and so on. The series gets the numbers ahead such that the ith number is obtained by adding (i-1) th number with (i-2)th number, clearly this is a infinite series.

As the series is infinite, it will not be a good idea to run an infinite loop that simply keeps on computing numbers in the series. Instead, we will take the length of the series as input from the user using a cin statement, so that our program can print only those many numbers in the series which the user wishes to. Hence, in the program we take an integer n as input from the user, which determines the length of the Fibonacci series to be printed. So, for example, if the user enters n=5, then we print only the first five numbers in the Fibonacci series as **0 1 1 2 3**.

By understanding the complete requirement, let us now start focusing at code level. We will declare integer variables f1, f2, and f3 representing last three numbers of Fibonacci series at each iteration of `while` loop. Let us give initial values of variables f1=0 and f2=1 as the first two numbers in the series are 0 and 1, respectively. We can now compute f3=f1+f2, which means that the third number in the series is obtained using the addition of previous two numbers. Hence, we obtain the third number f3=1. Now it is time to add last two numbers again to obtain the next number which should be generated as 1+1 = **2**. It is important to understand that we cannot simply keep increasing the number of variables and forming a new expressions as f4=f3+f2 to obtain the fourth number in the series, f5=f4+f3 to obtain the fifth number in the series and so on. Although, the solution looks easy to understand it is not possible to implement it in practice because of the following reasons:

1. The length of the series is not known at the time of compilation of the program. We take the length of the series (n) as input from the user at run time. Hence, it is not possible to determine the number of variables to be declared (f1, f2, f3, f4, etc.) while writing the program.

2. We need the code to be configurable in terms of number of digits of the Fibonacci series to be generated as the output. Hence declaring the fixed number of variables would result in hard coding of logic and the program will not work for values of n greater than the number of variables declared in the code. For example, if we hard-code seven variables for the series (say, f1, f2, f3, f4, f5, f6, f7) the program will fail if the value of n is >= 8 as we will not be able to generate the series starting from eighth number onwards.

3. Maintaining a static list of variables may also result in wastage of memory locations, if the user enters the length of the series required to be less than the actual number of variables declared, where much of the variables may not be utilized. For example, if we declare 100 variables (say, f1, f2, f3, ..., f100) to store Fibonacci results, but if at runtime the user enters the length of the series (value of variable n) as only 5 indicating that the user needs only first 5 numbers in the series, the remaining 95 variables may go waste as they will still contain junk values.

To avoid the implications of hard coding, we should develop the design of the code such that all the required number of Fibonacci digits are generated using just three variables f3=f1+f2. In this case, f3 will store all the numbers in the Fibonacci series starting from the third number onwards. Hence, the fourth number in the Fibonacci series will overwrite the third number in f3 and the fifth number of the Fibonacci series will overwrite the fourth number and so on.

As the ith Fibonacci number will be overwritten when (i+1)th number is generated, it is important that we print the ith number in the Fibonacci before we generate (i+1)th number which is done by putting the statement **printf("%d",f3);** inside the loop. Furthermore, the next question would be how to generate the fourth number, fifth number, and so on, using an expression f3=f1+f2? The answer is simple, similar to how the third number is generated using first two numbers the fourth number will be generated using third and the second numbers of the series hence before we execute the expression f3=f1+f2 for generating fourth number we will copy the value of second number in f1 and value of third number in f2 and recompute f3 as the addition of f1 and f2. In this way, the variable f3 will now represent the fourth number in the Fibonacci series as shown in Figure 5.11. In summary, to generate the ith number of Fibonacci series we will copy the (i-2)th number in f1 and (i-1)th number in f2 and then execute the expression f3=f1+f2. Therefore f3 will represent the ith number of the series which is the addition of previous two numbers. The detailed design of this logic is shown in Figure 5.11.

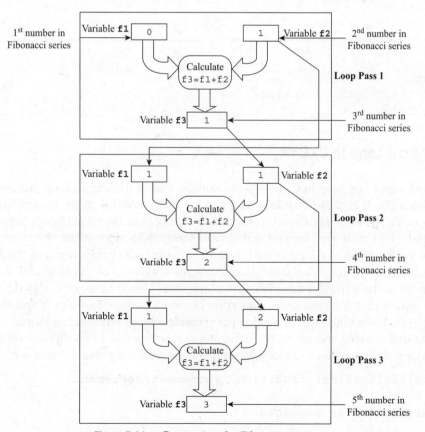

Figure 5.11: Generating the Fibonacci series

The following is the source code for generating the Fibonacci series:

```
#include<stdio.h>
void main()
{
int f1,f2,f3,i=1,n;
printf("Enter the length of series:");
scanf("%d",&n);
/*First two numbers of the series are f1=0 and f2=1*/
f1=0;
f2=1;
/*print the first two digits 0 and 1*/
printf("%d %d",f1,f2);
/* 2 numbers are already printed hence only n-2 numbers are
    required to be printed*/
    while(i<=n-2)
    {
    f3=f1+f2;
    printf(" %d",f3);
    /*substitution*/
    f1=f2;
    f2=f3;
    i++;
    }
}
```

Output
```
Enter the length of series: 5
0 1 1 2 3
```

5.3   `for` Loop in C/C++

The working of `for` loop in C/C++ is the same as that of the `while` loop discussed in the previous section, because `for` loop is a similar **'entry control'** type of loop similar to a `while` loop. The loop has a much compressed syntax than the `while` loop, hence it helps to keep the C++ code well formed and easy to maintain in many cases.

The syntax of `while` loop is such that it puts the basic components of the loop (i.e., initialization of the loop variable, terminating the condition of the loop and increment/decrement of the variable) into different statements. Hence Lines of Codes (LOC) in the C++ program may increase and a C++ code becomes difficult to support and maintain if the program has a high level of nesting (loop inside a loop) with `while` loops.

Note that working and execution of the program with a `for` loop will have no significant difference as compared to `while` loop, the only change is the compressed syntax as given below:

```
for(initialization; condition; increment/decrement)
{
//operation to be repeated
}
```

The `for` loop first performs initialization of the variable(s) specified in initialization part of its syntax. After initialization is completed, the loop checks for the result of condition specified. Only if the condition is evaluated as '**true**', operations within the loop will be executed. After the specified operations are fully executed, the loop performs 'increment/decrement'. After performing 'increment/decrement', the condition is again evaluated to determine if execution of operation must be repeated. In summary, the execution of operation is repeated as long as the condition is evaluated as 'true'. The control is transferred inside the body of the loop only if condition is true hence `for` loop is also **entry control type of loop**, similar to a `while` loop.

If the condition is evaluated as 'false', the execution of loop terminates and the control is transferred to the first statement outside the body of the loop.

Figure 5.12 illustrates the working of `for` loop in detail, followed by examples to understand `for` loop:

> **NOTES**
>
> `for loop` is also a **entry control loop** like `while` loop.
>
> The syntax of `for` loop is simple and it helps improve the **readability of the program** when compared to `while` loop.

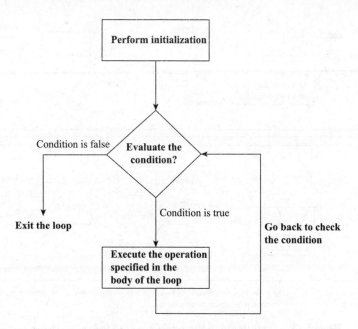

Figure 5.12: Working of `for` loop

5.3.1 Program to compute the series $1^2+2^2+3^2+4^2+\ldots x^2$ using `for` loop: An example

As seen, the series starts from 1 and ends at a value x. The end value x is required to be configurable and will be taken as input from the user. Similar to all the examples discussed earlier, we will use a counting variable k that will take all the values from 1 to x step by step as the loop proceeds its execution. For each value of k from 1 to x, we perform addition of k^2 with the sum of previous squares as shown. Note that as with previous examples when k=1, there is no previous value of sum hence the initial value of sum (say variable s) is set to zero and each time variable s is updated so that it represents the latest computed sum so far as shown in Figure 5.13.

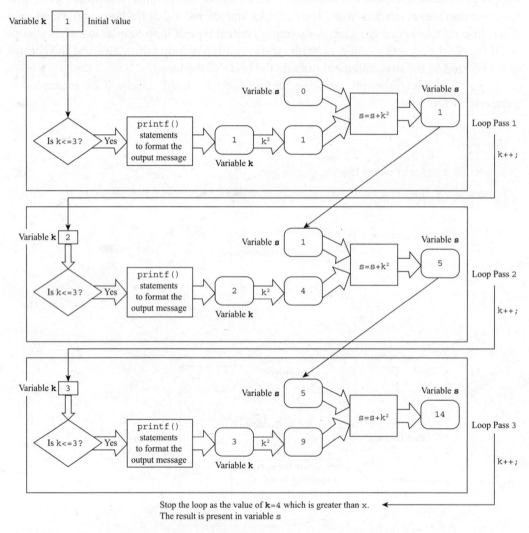

Figure 5.13: Evaluation of the series $1^2+2^2+3^2+4^2+\cdots x^2$ using for loop

Also note the presence of if else that formats the output to print a message "1*1+2*2+3*3+···+x*x" where a symbol + is to be printed for all the numbers except the last number and symbol = is required to be printed after the last number. As the loop runs from k=1 to x, in the last iteration of loop will k will be same as x where we can print the symbol =

```
#include<stdio.h>
void main()
{
int k,x,s;
s=0;
printf("Enter x:");
scanf("%d",&x);
    for(k=1; k<=x; k++)
    {
    printf("%d*%d" ,k,k);
      if(k!=x)
            printf("+");
      else
            printf("=");
    s= s + k*k;
    }
printf("%d",s);
}
```

Output
```
Enter x:3
1*1+2*2+3*3=14
```

5.3.2 Calculating the series $1/2!+1/4!+1/6!+1/8!...1/n!$ using `for` loop: An example

Although the series looks slightly complex, evaluating the given series involves the following two operations:

1. Calculating the factorial of each even number starting from 2 to n (2 to n-1 if n is odd).
2. Reciprocating the factorial and calculating the sum of all the n fractions in the series.

This means that we will generate each of the even numbers one at a time from 2 to n using a counting variable say k. For each number k, we need to calculate the factorial of k and use k! as a denominator part of the fraction. As seen, the numerator part of the fraction is always 1 which can be hard coded in the program.

In the place of denominator we need to calculate the factorial of the number k. As discussed in Example 5.2.3, the factorial of any number x can be computed using the following simple `while` loop:

```
f=1.0;
while(x>0)
    {
    f=f*x;
    x--;
    }
```

We have already proved that variable f will contain the factorial of x, hence we can reuse the above while loop to calculate the factorial of k by putting the value of k in variable x. Each time we have a new value of k, the above while loop should run so as to compute its factorial. Also, before we start calculating factorial of any number k, we must reset the value of f=1.0 as this is a primary requirement of the logic to calculate factorial of any number as per Example 5.2.3.

We now need to make sure that the above while loop runs for every even value of k from 2 to n, so that the factorial of each of the denominators is calculated before adding the result of the fraction to the previous sum. Hence, we can simply put the above logic to calculate factorial of variable k in a for loop such that the code to calculate factorial runs for each even value of k as the for loop progresses its execution.

When it comes to calculating the sum of fractions, we can always store the sum of all the fractions evaluated in variable s, such that when factorial of k is being calculated, variable s will store the sum of reciprocals of all the factorials from 2 to (k-1) as this is the previous sum when the factorial of (k-1) was being calculated.

Also as with the earlier examples there will be no value of previous sum present when the result of first fraction (1/2!) is calculated. Hence, we set the initial value of sum (say variable s) to zero. Variable s will always store the sum of all the previously calculated fractions similar to Examples 5.2.4 and 5.3.1.

Figure 5.14 shows the execution of the above design assuming the value of variable n as 6. Hence, the loop stops when value of k crosses 6 and variables represents the final result of series as shown below:

```
#include<stdio.h>
void main()
{
int k,n;
double f,s=0.0,x;
printf("Enter n:");
scanf("%d",&n);
    for(k=2; k<=n; k+=2)
    {
        x=k;
        f=1.0;
            while(x>0)
            {
            f=f*x;
            x--;
            }
```

```
        s=s+1/f;
    }
printf("Result of the series is %f",s);
}
```

Output

```
Enter n: 6
Result of the series is 0.543056
```

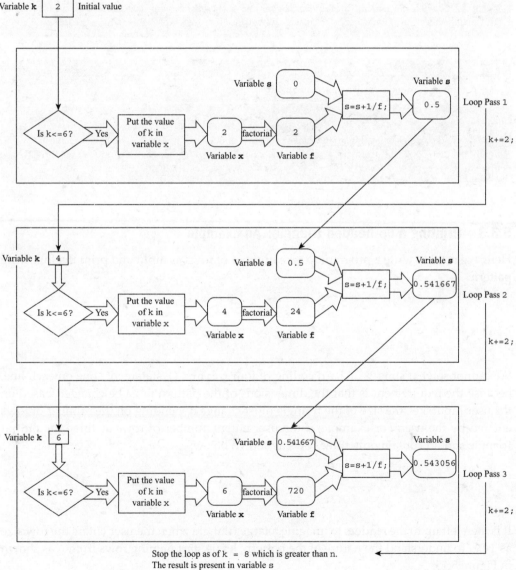

Figure 5.14: Evaluation of the series $1/2!+1/4!+1/6!$ using for loop

In the above program, we are storing the value of variable k in variable x and then calculating the factorial of x. Instead, why are we not directly calculating the factorial of k itself? Wont this avoid creation of an additional variable named x? **?**

The for loop is required to increase the value of variable **k** at each step. On the other hand, the inner while loop used to calculate the factorial of variable decreases the value of variable at each Step. The while loop in the code performs x--; till the time x is not equal to zero. In the absence of variable x while loop would have calculated factorial of k directly and performed k--; thereby making k as zero at the end of while loop. This will hence give incorrect results because the normal working of for loop will now be impacted as while loop will always reset k to 0. Therefore for loop will always get k as 1 when it executes k++; in any of its iteration. This will result in an infinite for loop. Hence we create a separate variable x so that the while loop can safely make x as zero after its factorial is calculated without affecting the logic of for loop which uses k as a counter.

In the above program, we have created a loop inside another loop. Is there any maximum limit on the number of inner loops we can create inside an outer loop? **?**

Executing a loop inside another loop is called as Nesting of loops. Theoretically there is no limit to the degree of nesting. In the above program the degree of nesting is two. You can have any number of inner loops inside an outer loop and the inner loops can further have any number of loops inside it. There is no obvious restriction imposed by the language on the degree of nesting.

5.3.3 Printing a up-headed triangle: An example

Here, we need to write a program to take number of rows as input and print the following pattern:

```
*
*    *
*    *    *
*    *    *    *
```

We cannot solve it simply by hard coding of four **printf()** statements one on each line, because the requirement is that the dimensions of the pattern must be changed based on the user input, i.e., the size of the triangle must change depending on the number of rows entered by the user. For example, if the user enters number of rows as three the output triangle should contain only three rows as shown below:

```
*
*    *
*    *    *
```

It is then left up to the readers to imagine a large triangle when the user enters the row size as 100. To understand the nature of the pattern, let us start naming rows from 0 as shown in Figure 5.15.

As seen, row number 0 (which is the first row) contains 1 star, row number 1 (which is the second row) contains 2 starts and so on. The number of stars required in each row is

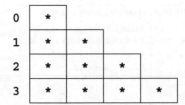

Figure 5.15   Required pattern of stars with four rows

documented in the table. From the table, it is clear that in any row number i there are i+1 stars to be printed.

Row number	No. of stars
0	1
1	2
2	3
3	4
i	i+1

Therefore, the statement printf ("*") must be executed i+1 times for each row i. Below is the for loop which is used to print i+1 stars

```
for(j=1; j<=i+1 ; j++)
{
    printf("*");
}
```

Given that we need r rows in the output, it means that the process of printing stars must be executed for each row i, such that the range of i is from 0 to r-1. (Setting the range of i from 0 to r-1 will result in r distinct iterations, thereby printing r rows at the output.)

The for loop shown below gives different values to variable i starting from 0 to r-1 (from row number 0 to row number 3 when r=4). Note that the presence of printf ("\n") which will move the cursor on the new line after all the stars in the current row are printed and before the row number i is changed to the next value.

```
for(i=0; i<=r-1; i++)
{
```

> Print i+1 starts in each
> row number i.

```
printf("\n");,
}
```

Figure 5.16 gives the detailed understanding of the program for generating the required pattern.

The following is the full source code to print the required pattern.

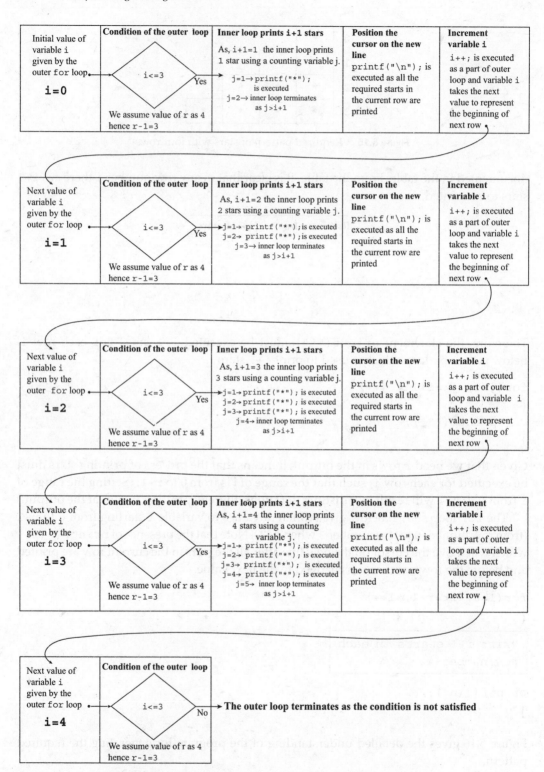

Figure 5.16: Execution of the code to print up headed triangle

```
#include<stdio.h>
void main()
{
int i,j,r;
/*Take number of rows as input*/
printf("Enter the number of rows:");
scanf("%d",&r);
/*Range row numbers from 0 to r-1*/
    for(i=0; i<=r-1; i++)
    {
/*For each row number i , print i+1 stars*/
        for(j=1;j<=i+1; j++)
        {
            printf("*");
        }
/*Transfer the cursor on new line after current row is printed*/
    printf("\n");
    }
}
```

Output

```
Enter the number of rows: 4
*
* *
* * *
* * * *
```

NOTES

You can skip the curly brackets from the syntax of the loop, if the loop just has a single statement to execute in its body. But it is always a better coding practice to explicitly specify the curly brackets, this way you are always cautions on when each loop starts and ends. As far as this program is concerned you can omit the curly brackets from the inner loop because it just has a single statement to execute. The loops given below will work correctly; however it is not a very good coding practice. Hence it is strongly recommended to always have curly brackets in your program even if your program, even if the loop contains just 1 statement. This helps improving maintainability of the code and makes the program easy to read

```
for(i=0; i<=r-1; i++)
{
        for(j=1;j<=i+1; j++)    ←——————  Curly brackets are not needed
        printf("*");                     for the inner loop because it
printf("\n");                            just contains a single statement
}                                        printf("*");
```

5.3.4 Printing an down-headed triangle: An example

Here, we need to write a program to take number of rows as input and print the following pattern:

```
*   *   *   *
*   *   *
*   *
*
```

The above pattern is very much similar to the previous example; hence, we can solve this by the earlier method. Let us document the pattern for r=4, where r is the number of rows.

Assuming number of rows (r) as 4. We number the rows from 0 to r-1 as shown in Figure 5.17.

As seen, row number 0(which is the first row) contains four stars, row number 1(which is the second row) contains three starts and so on. The number of starts required in each row is documented in the following table. From the table, it is clear that in any row number i there are r-i stars to be printed.

Figure 5.17: Required pattern of stars with four rows

Row number (i)	Numbers of stars in i^{th} row
0	4
1	3
2	2
3	1
i	r-i

Therefore, the statement printf("*") must be executed r-i times for each row i. Below is the for loop which is used to print r-i stars

```
for(j=1; j<=r-i ; j++)
{
    printf("*");
}
```

The outer loop required to increment the row numbers is same as that of the previous example, we can represent it as follows. Figure 5.18 gives the execution plan of the source code.

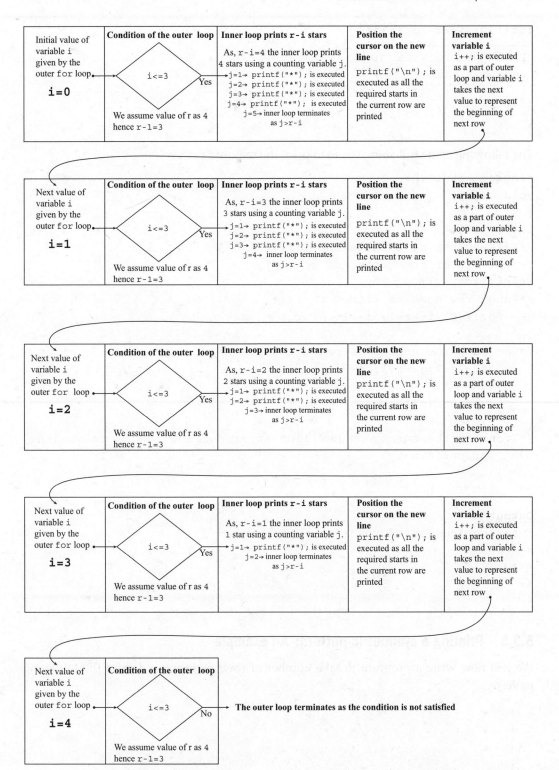

Figure 5.18: Execution of the code to print down headed triangle

```
for(i=0; i<=r-1; i++){
```

```
Print r-i starts in
each row number i.
```

```
printf("\n");

}
```

The following is the full source code to print the required pattern.

```
#include<stdio.h>
void main()
{
int i,j,r;
/*Take number of rows as input*/
printf("Enter the number of rows:");
scanf("%d",&r);
/*Range row numbers from 0 to r-1*/
    for(i=0; i<=r-1; i++)
    {
/*For each row number i, print r-i stars*/
      for(j=1;j<=r-i; j++)
      {
       printf("*");
      }
/*Transfer the cursor on new line after current row is printed*/
      printf("\n");
    }
}
```

Output
```
Enter the number of rows: 4
****
***
**
*
```

5.3.5   Printing a symmetric pattern: An example

We will now write a program to take number of rows as input and print the following pattern:

```
*   *   *   *   *   *   *   *
*   *   *           *   *   *
*   *                   *   *
*                           *
```

Let us understand the above pattern by separating its individual components, because the pattern is formed using a combination of stars and spaces. Printing spaces at right points will split the pattern into two symmetrical parts as shown in Figure 5.19. Also needless to say, the pattern must be generated dynamically wherein the user has a choice to enter any number of rows.

The pattern shown above is for the number of rows(r) equal to 4.

For pattern analysis, we can say that each row in the above pattern has x starts followed by y spaces and then again x stars. Again, we will start numbering the rows from 0 as shown in Figure 5.19. Note that for the first row which has no spaces hence value of y should be 0 and x should be 4. So in summary, the topmost row (row number 0) has 4 stars followed by 0 spaces and again followed by 4 stars. The next row (row number 1) has 3 stars followed by 2 spaces and the again 3 stars and so on. In general, the ith row has (r-i) stars followed by 2*i spaces again followed by (r-i) stars. The following table shows the pattern analysis assuming the number of rows(r) as 4.

0	*	*	*	*	*	*	*	*
1	*	*	*	space	space	*	*	*
2	*	*	space	space	space	space	*	*
3	*	space	space	space	space	space	space	*

Figure 5.19: Printing symmetric pattern

Row number (i)	Number of stars before space	Number of spaces between star	Number of stars after space
0	4	0	4
1	3	2	3
2	2	4	2
3	1	6	1
i	r-i	2*i	r-i

Let i be the current row number, we need the following three loops to complete a single row:

1. **Left loop:** This is the loop used to print r-i stars as shown below:

```
for(j=1;j<=r-i; j++)
{
printf("*");
}
```

2. **Middle loop:** This is the loop to print 2*i spaces as shown below:

```
for(j=1;j<=2*i; j++)
{
printf(" ");/*space*/
}
```

3. **Right loop:** This is the loop to print r-i stars as shown below:

```
for(j=1;j<=r-i; j++)
{
printf("*");
}
```

Given that we need r rows in the output, it means that the process of printing stars and spaces must be executed for each row i, such that the range of i is from 0 to r-1. (Setting the range of i from 0 to r-1 will result in r distinct iterations, thereby printing r rows at the output.)

The following for loop gives different values to variable i starting from 0 to r-1 (from row number 0 to row number 3 when r=4). Note that the presence of printf ("\n") ;, which will move the cursor on the new line after all the stars in the current row are printed and before the row number i is changed to the next value.

```
for(i=0; i<=r-1; i++)
{
```

```
1. Print r-i stars.
2. Print 2*i spaces
3. Print r-i stars.
```

```
printf("\n") ;,
}
```

Figure 5.20 gives the full execution plan for the program.

The following is the full source code to print the required pattern.

```
#include<stdio.h>
void main()
{
int i,j,r;
printf("Enter the number of rows\n");
scanf("%d",&r);
    for(i=0; i<=r-1; i++)
    {
        for(j=1;j<=r-i; j++)
        {
        /*printing left star*/
        printf("*");
        }
        for(j=1;j<=2*i; j++)
        {
        /*printing space*/
        printf(" ");
        }
        for(j=1;j<=r-i; j++)
        {
        /*printing right star*/
        printf("*");
        }
```

```
        printf("\n");
    }
}
```

Output

```
Enter the number of rows: 4
*   *   *   *   *   *   *   *
*   *   *       *   *   *
*   *           *   *
*               *
```

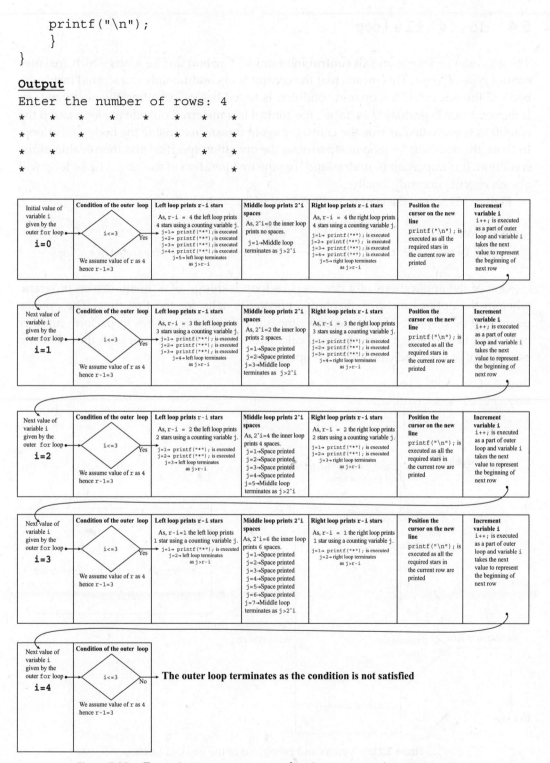

Figure 5.20: Execution trace to generate the given symmetric pattern

5.4 `do..while` Loop

The `do..while` loop is an **exit control loop** unlike `for` and `while` loops which are entry control type of loops. This means that the control is unconditionally transferred inside the body of the `do..while` loop and condition is tested before executing the next iteration. If the condition is evaluated as 'false', the control is transferred outside the loop and if the condition is evaluated as true the control is again transferred inside the body of the loop. In short, the `do..while` loop first performs the operation specified and then evaluates the condition. It is important to understand that the first iteration of the `do..while` loop will always execute unconditionally.

Figure 5.21 shows the syntax and working of `do..while` loop.

> **DEFINITION**
>
> `do..while` **loop** is a **exit control loop** unlike `while` or `for` loops which are **entry control** type of loops.

One of the applications of a `do..while` loop is design of a 'menu-driven program' wherein the options menu is displayed unconditionally for the first time. The options menu will be displayed in the second time, only if the user wishes to perform another operation. Let us design a menu-based calculator that gives the menu with the following assignment of keys dedicated for each operation:

```
Key 1 for addition
Key 2 for subtraction
Key 3 for multiplication
```

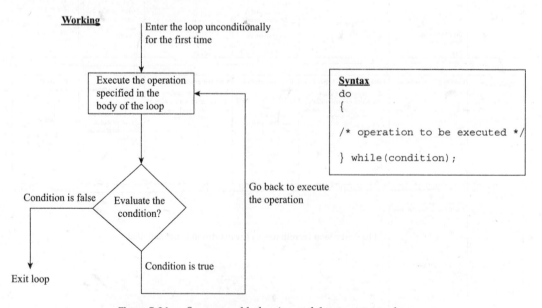

Figure 5.21:   Syntax and behaviour of the `do-while` loop

The user will then enter a choice looking at the menu options and the program must then take a decision on which operation to perform depending on the choice entered by the user. Say, if the user enters the choice as **3**, then the program should take two numbers as input and perform the multiplication of two numbers. After displaying the result of multiplication, the calculator must ask the user if he/she wishes to perform any other operation.

```
Do you want to continue(Y/N)?
Y
```

If the user enters **Y**, then the program shall again display the menu options for the user to determine what is the next operation the user wishes to perform and so on. The execution of the program must terminate when the user enters **N** as an answer to the above question. The typical behaviour of the code is shown in Figure 5.22. The complete source code for this calculator is shown below the figure:

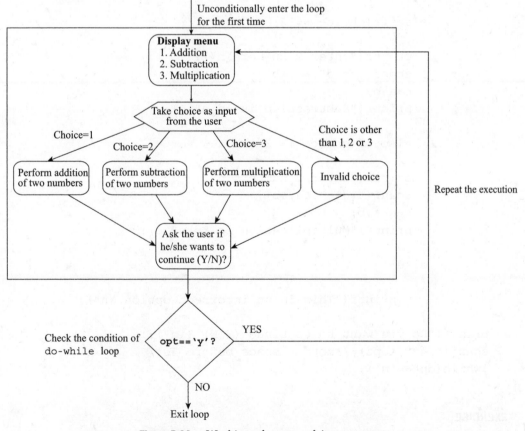

Figure 5.22: Working of a menu-driven program

```
#include <stdio.h>
void main()
{
    int choice,a,b,c;
    char opt='y';
    do{
      printf("Welcome to the calculator screen\n");
      printf("Please enter your choice\n");
      printf("1. Add\n2.Subtract\n");
      printf("3. Multiply\n");
      scanf("%d",&choice);
          if(choice == 1)
              {
                printf("enter 2 numbers\n");
                scanf("%d%d",&a,&b);
                c=a+b;
               printf("Addition is %d\n",c);
              }
              else if(choice == 2)
              {
                printf("enter 2 numbers\n");
                scanf("%d%d",&a,&b);
                c=a-b;
                printf("Subtraction is %d\n",c);
              }
              else if(choice == 3)
              {
                printf("enter 2 numbers\n");
                scanf("%d%d",&a,&b);
                c=a * b;
                printf("Multiplication is %d\n",c);
              }
              else
              {
                  printf("This is an incorrect option.\n");
              }
    printf("Do you want to continue (Y/N) ?\n");
    scanf(" %c",&opt);/*note a space before %c*/
    }while(opt=='n');
}
```

EXERCISE

Trace the output of the program assuming user first wants to perform multiplication and then addition. Assume input data of your choice for each of the operations.

5.5 `break` and `continue` Statements

The `break` and `continue` statements are used to modify the default behaviour of loops.

The `break` statement is used to exit the loop execution and it passes the control to the first statement after the loop. The exit of loop using `break` statement is often called early exit, because it terminates the execution of the loop even if the condition for running the loop ahead is true. Execution of break statement should always be conditional inside the loop. Executing `break` statement unconditionally within a loop would mean that loop will just have one iteration that too partially terminated due to `break` statement. Figure 5.23 shows the effect of `break` statement executed conditionally within the loop.

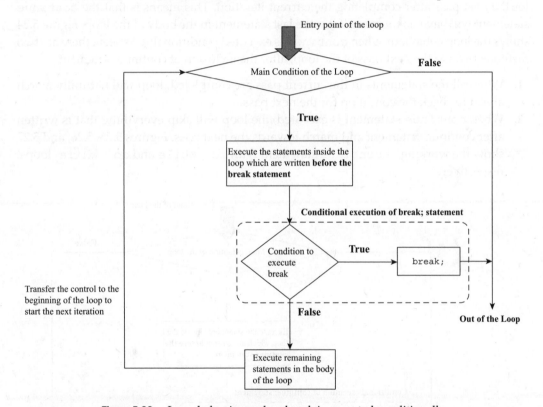

Figure 5.23: Loop behaviour when break is executed conditionally

As seen from Figure 5.23, there are two methods to come out of the loop after inclusion of `break` statement. First, when main condition of the loop is itself false, the loop terminates itself naturally. And the second is when the `break` statement is executed (when the condition to execute break statement is true). Note that when the `break` statement is executed the loop is terminated abruptly thereby skipping all the other statements which are written after `break;` statement inside the loop. On execution of `break`, there will be no further iterations even if the main looping condition is still true. As seen from the figure, once `break` is executed, there will be no check to examine the main looping condition at all. It is very important to note that execution of `break` statement may result in the current iteration of the loop terminating partially, if there are some statements written after break. This is because the statements which were written before break will be executed fully, whereas the statements after break will be skipped.

On the other hand, continue statement is used to start the next pass of the loop immediately by skipping all the statements in the current pass which appear after the continue statement. Hence, the execution of continue statement should always be conditional, otherwise the statements which are written after continue will not have any meaning. Logically, there should be some operations that are performed in the body of the after the conditional block of in which continue is executed; otherwise there will be nothing for continue statement to really skip as the loop anyways goes back to check the condition for the next pass after completing the current iteration. This means is that the continue statement will have no meaning if it is the last statement in the body of the loop. Figure 5.24 shows the loop behaviour when continue is executed conditionally. As seen, there are two methods to do to the next pass of the loop, after the inclusion of continue statement.

1. When all the statements in the current pass are completed, loop will naturally march ahead to check the condition for the next pass.
2. When continue statement is executed, the loop will skip everything that is written after continue statement and march towards the next pass. Figures 5.25, 5.26, and 5.27 show the working of continue statement with for, while and do..while loops, respectively.

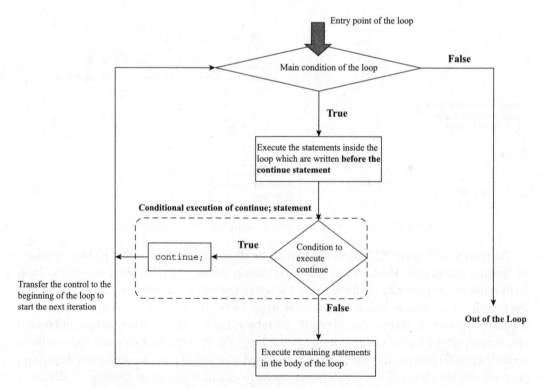

Figure 5.24: Loop behaviour when continue is executed conditionally

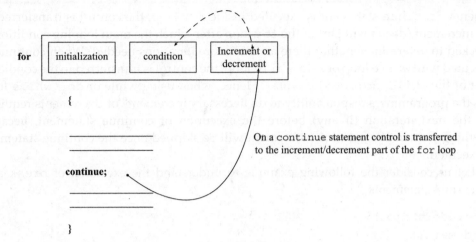

On a continue statement control is transferred
to the increment/decrement part of the for loop

Figure 5.25: continue statement with for loop

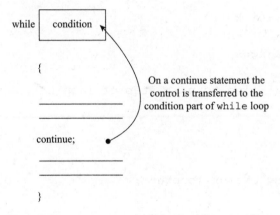

On a continue statement the
control is transferred to the
condition part of while loop

Figure 5.26: continue statement with while loop

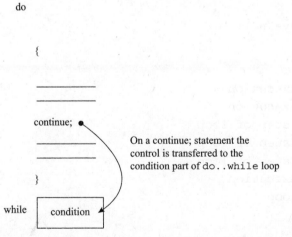

On a continue; statement the
control is transferred to the
condition part of do..while loop

Figure 5.27: continue statement with do..while loop

When a continue statement is executed inside for loop, the control is transferred to the increment/decrement part of the for loop after which the main looping condition is checked to determine whether there are any more iterations needed. When continue is executed with while loop or a do while loop, the control is transferred to the condition part of the while/do..while syntax. Hence, when using while or do..while loop it is the programmers responsibility to do necessary increments or decrements required for the next iteration (if any) before the execution of continue statement, because anything written after continue statement will be skipped once the continue statement is executed.

Let us consider the following example to understand the execution of break and continue statements.

```
#include<stdio.h>
void main()
{
int k;
    for(k=1; k<=10; k++)
    {
      if(k>=3 && k<=5)
        {
          printf("Going to next step of loop\n");
          continue;
        }
        if(k>=7)
        {
    printf("Going out of loop\n");
    break;
        }
    printf("Default loop execution\n");
    }
printf("Good Bye\n");
}
```

Output
```
Default loop execution
Default loop execution
Going to next step of loop
Going to next step of loop
Going to next step of loop
Default loop execution
Going out of loop
Good Bye
```

The above program has a loop that runs from k=1 to 10 as its default behaviour.

However, this behaviour is modified using break and continue statements which are conditionally inserted inside the body of the for loop. When the loop starts with the initial value of 1 and for k=1 and 2, none of the two if blocks will be executed and the statement printf("Default loop execution\n"); is executed. Furthermore, when k gets the value as 3 the condition in first if block is satisfied and after printing the message "Going to next step of loop" the continue statement is executed. Hence, the control is immediately transferred to the **for loop control** statement changing the value of k as 4. Note that all the statements pending their execution in the current pass are skipped by the continue statement. Similarly, the loop is continued for values of k as 4 and 5. Hence, the message "Default loop execution" will never be printed when value of k is 3, 4, or 5 as the loop skips this statement and goes to the next pass after execution of *continue* statement.

When k=6, the loop again executes normally as no if block is satisfied, thereby printing a message "Default loop execution".

Now when k takes a value as 7, the condition specified in second **if block** present in the body of the loop is satisfied which contains a *break* statement. Hence, after printing a message "*Going out of loop*" the control is immediately transferred to the first statement outside the loop and the execution of the loop is terminated immediately. Hence, after executing break; machine prints "Good Bye", which is the very first statement outside the loop. The following table explains the detailed execution of the loop at each pass.

Value of loop variable (k)	Statement executed by the machine
k=1	Condition specified in none of the if blocks is satisfied hence the loop executes normally. The message "*Default loop execution*" is printed.
k=2	Condition specified in none of the if blocks is satisfied hence the loop executes normally. The message "*Default loop execution*" is printed.
k=3	The condition of the first if block is satisfied and hence the message "Going to next step of loop" is printed on the computer screen. Following which a continue statement is executed which skips all the remaining statements and makes the value of k as 4 by transferring control to the for loop statement.
k=4	The condition of the first if block is satisfied and hence the message "Going to next step of loop" is printed on the computer screen. Following which a continue statement is executed which skips all the remaining statements and makes the value of k as 5 by transferring control to the for loop statement.
k=5	The condition of the first if block is satisfied and hence the message "Going to next step of loop" is printed on the computer screen. Following which a continue statement is executed which skips all the remaining statements and makes the value of k as 6 by transferring control to the for loop statement.
k=6	Condition specified in none of the if blocks is satisfied hence the loop executes normally. The message "*Default loop execution*" is printed.
k=7	The condition specified in the second if block is satisfied, hence the message "Going out of loop" is printed on the computer screen, following which a break; statement is executed and hence the execution of the loop terminates and the control is immediately transferred to the first statement outside the loop which is printf("Good Bye\n");

NOTES

break statement is also used to break the switch block as discussed in Chapter 4. Hence break statement, in C/C++ can be used to break the **switch block** or it can be used to break the **loop**. However, continue statement is designed to operate only with loops and it will make no sense to use it with any of the decision making control structures like switch block for example.

Will the break statement terminate if it is written within the switch block which is inside the loop? **?**

If the switch block is present inside the loop and if the break statement is written within the switch block, it will only exit the switch block and not the loop. For example, consider pseudo code below:

```
while(Looping condition )
        {
                switch(expression)
                {
                case Value 1: operation 1;
                        break;
                case Value 2:operation 2;
                        break;
                ......
                default: default operation;
                }
        }
```

If you intend to terminate the loop, in this case, you must write the break statement outside the switch block. Similarly, if there is a nesting of loops in your program, the break statement will only terminate the inner most loop in which it is written. Do not expect the break statement to terminate all the loops together. As shown below, there are three while loops one inside another and the break statement is written in the innermost loop. In this case, the break statement will only terminate the inner most loop and the execution of outer loops will continue as usual

```
    while(Looping condition 1)
    {
                while(condition 2)
                {
                        while(condition 3)
                        {
                        ........
                        ........
                        break;
                        ........
                        ........
                        }
                }
    }
```

5.5.1 To check if the number is prime or not: An example

Let us write a program to take a number as input from the user and to check if the number is prime of not.

We know that any number x is a prime number if it is divisible by exactly two numbers 1 and x itself. Hence, for a given number x we will generate all the numbers from 2 to x-1 in our code, and we can easily conclude that "x is prime" if it is divisible by no number between 2 and x-1. It is very important to note that the decision of whether a number x is prime or not prime can be taken only after checking the divisibility of number x with all the numbers between 2 and x-1. If the number x is divisible by no number between 2 and x-1 we can conclude that the number is prime, on the other side if we find at least one divisibility of variable x with any number i, such that i is in between 2 and x-1 then there is no point checking the divisibility of number x with any other number, thus when x is already found to be divisible with one of the numbers we can conclude that x is not prime and break the execution of the loop so as to avoid unnecessary iterations. We therefore need a divisibility indicator or a flag to determine whether the number x is divisible by at least one number between 2 and x-1 or not, this can be implemented by a character variable **flag** which takes two values 'y' or 'n' such that if flag is 'y' it may represent that the number is prime and if flag is 'n' it may represent that the number is not prime.

For implementing this process, we can use a counter variable, say i, with a initial value of i as 2 and increment the value of i till the time it does not cross a value which is one lesser than x (x-1). The variable i now takes each value between 2 and (x-1) as the loop progresses, at each value of i we can now check if x is divisible by any one of the values of i. If yes, then we will set some character flag to say n indicating that the number is not prime. Naturally, if x is divisible by no value that variable i is taking between 2 and x-1, the character flag will never be set to **n** which will indicate that the number is prime given the initial value to the character flag as 'y'. This would mean that the loop that takes the counter variable i from 2 to (x-1) can be terminated because of the following two reasons:

1. The upper bound of variable i is reached, and the number x is not divisible by any number between 2 and x-1. In this case, value of character flag will be retained to 'y' at the end of loop, hence the number will be correctly identified as a prime number by the code.

2. The divisibility of variable x with some value of i is found; hence the break statement is executed by the machine. Before executing the **break** statement, we set the value of the character flag as 'n' indicating that the number is not prime.

Hence at the end of the loop, we can check just the value of flag. If the value of flag is 'y', then the number x is prime and if its 'n', the number x must have been divisible by some number between 2 and x-1 and loop must have terminated due to break statement. Hence we can say that the number is not prime.

The following is the complete source code for checking if the given number is prime or not.

```c
#include<stdio.h>
void main()
{
int x,i;
char flag='y';
```

```
printf("Enter a number\n");
scanf("%d",&x);
/*note the creation of a character flag with a default value of
    'y'*/
/*set initial value of counter as 2*/
i=2;
    while(i<=x-1)
    {
        if(x%i==0)
        {
        flag='n';
        break;
        }
    i++;
    }
    if(flag=='n')
    {
    printf("Number is not prime\n");
    }
    else
    {
    printf("Number is prime\n");
    }
}
```

Output
```
Enter a number
13
Number is prime
```

5.6   Infinite Loops

A loop which never terminates till the time the program is terminated is called infinite loop. Till now, we have seen loops which have finite number of iterations, however in some cases we need to keep the loop in running state for ever. The condition of the loop should be designed such that it is always true and never goes to false. For example, consider the following loop:

```
while(1)
{
............ .
}
```

The condition of the while loop is 1, which means true. This means that this loop will never terminate. You can also make for loop to have infinite iterations by not specifying anything in its condition. Note that the below `for` loop contains no initialization condition or increment/decrement blocks and hence the loop will keep running and never terminate itself. You will still have to put in two semicolons as shown below:

```
for(;;)
{
-----
}
```

The only way to terminate such loops is to terminate the execution of the program itself. There are a multiple examples wherein you would need infinite loops. For example, if you want to write a program for a bouncing ball, the requirement is to keep the ball moving up and down continuously. Hence, the loop should move the ball up and down and never terminate. The pseudo code of the `while` loop responsible for bouncing ball (assuming ball is initially UP) will be as follows:

```
while(1)
{
1. Code to move the ball DOWN.
2. Code to move the ball UP.
}
```

Another example could be screen saver programs. These programs keep repeating a defined set of movements till the time you actually hit the keyboard and terminate the screen saver run. While discussion of computer graphics is beyond the scope of this textbook, the following code is a simple example of infinite loop which runs forever producing an effect of blinking text.

The `for` loop has no condition for termination and performs the following two steps in each iteration:

1. Prints a text message `Hello`....
2. Clears the screen using `clrscr();` function.

Hence, the program prints the message and clears the screen after printing. As this is done in an infinite loop, it gives an effect that the message is blinking on the screen as the message is printed and cleared alternatively.

```
#include<stdio.h>
#include<conio.h>
void main()
{
    for(;;)
    {
        printf("Hello....");
        clrscr();
    }
}
```

NOTES

`clrscr()` is a function in Turbo C/C++ which clears the output screen by making it blank. This function is defined in header file **conio.h** which needs to be included in the program before using this function.

5.7 Comma Operator with `for` Loop

We know that `for` loop has three parts in it, initialization, condition, and increment/decrement. At times, there is a need to perform a multiple initializations or increments/decrements for the attaining the required results. For example, see the following code:

```
k=1; /*Initialize k to 1*/
for (j=10; j<50; j++)
{
..............

..............
k++; /*increment k*/
}
```

The looping variable in this case is `j` and the loop runs from `j=10` to `50`. However, you can see that variable `k` is initialized to `1` before entering the loop and k is incremented at the end of each iteration. Hence, it would be correct to say that this loop actually needs two initializations and increments one for variable `i` and other for variable `j`. We can use the comma operator to perform multiple initializations and increments/decrements. The code above can be simplified as follows:

```
/*Multiple initializations and increments using comma operator*/
for (k=1, j=10; j<50; j++, k++)
{
..............

..............
}
```

Needless to say, the execution principle of `for` loop will remain the same. The initializations `k=1` and `j=10` will happen only once before the first iteration of the loop, whereas the increments `j++` and `k++` will happen at the end of each iteration.

NOTES

You **cannot** connect multiple conditions in `for` loop using a **comma operator**. If you need to connect multiple conditions, you must make use of logical operators discussed in Chapter 4 Section 4.3 of this text book.

5.8 Creating Variables Local to Loops (Possible in C++ but not in C)

When a variable is declared within the loop, it is called local variable of the loop. Such variables cannot be accessed outside the loop in any manner, because they are alive only for the time the loop is running. For example, let us try to print a message Loops Made Simple 5 times using for loop. The sample code is as given below:

```c
#include<stdio.h>
void main()
{
    for(int i=1; i<=5; i++)
    {
    printf("Loops Made Simple\n");
    i++;
    }
    /*Value of variable i cannot be accessed outside the loop*/
}
```

Note that variable i is within the loop and its job is only to count the number of iterations of the loop. The loop has five iterations because it is executed from i=1 to 5. The value of variable i reaches 6, the loop terminates and hence the variable i is destroyed. This is because the variable was declared within the loop and it cannot be accessed outside the loop in any manner.

If you want to access the value of variable i even outside the loop, you should not create it as a local variable of the loop. This means that you have to declare variable i, outside the loop as shown in the following program:

```c
#include<stdio.h>
void main()
{
    int i; /*variable i is declared outside the loop */
      for(i=1; i<=5; i++)
      {
            printf("Loops Made Simple\n");
            i++;
      }
    /*Value of variable i can be accessed outside the loop*/
    printf("Value of variable i outside the loop is %d",i);
}
```

Given that variable i is declared outside the loop, we are able to print its value even after the execution of the loop is completed. The last printf statement prints the value of i as 6, as 6 is the first value of i when the loop terminates.

```
Value of variable i outside the loop is 6
```

5.9   Empty Loops

A loop that has no operation to perform is called an empty loop. For example, see the following loop:

```
int k;
for (k=1;k<=5;k++)
{
}
printf("Value of variable k outside the loop is %d",k);
```

The loop has an empty body (nothing in between the curly brackets). The job of this loop is only to keep incrementing the value of variable k. The loop terminates when k=6. Hence, when we try to access variable k outside the loop, we will get the value as 6. The last printf() statement will print the following output:

```
Value of variable k outside the loop is 6
```

Such empty loops which are only responsible to take a variable up to a certain value can be written by putting a semicolon at the end of loop. The empty loop shown above can be simply written as

```
int k;
for (k=1;k<=5;k++); /*Note the semicolon, which represents this is
    an empty loop*/
printf("Value of variable k outside the loop is %d",k);
```

When you put in a semicolon at the end of for statement, the for loop is considered as empty and you do not have to open and close curly brackets after that. The next statement after the for will be considered as if the statement is occurring after the loop. Hence, the last printf() statement will print the following output, even in this case:

```
Value of variable k outside the loop is 6
```

It is difficult to mention the application of empty loops at this stage; you will see empty loops in the next chapter wherein we calculate the length of the array elements.

Solved Example 5.1

Write a program to print all the numbers which are divisible by 4 in the range from 4 to 100. For example, the program should print 4, 8, 12, 16, 20, 24, ..., 100

```
#include <stdio.h>
void main()
{
    int i;
printf(" The list of numbers divisible by 4 are \n");
    for(i=4;i<=100;i++)
    {
        if(i%4==0)
        {
```

```
        printf("%d",i);
        }
    }
}
```

Output

```
The list of numbers divisible by 4 is
4 8 12 16 20 24 28 32 36 40 44 48 52 56 60 64 68 72 76 80 84 88 92
96 100
```

SCRATCH PAD

The below `for` loop runs for each value of variable `i` from 4 to 100:

```
for(i=4;i<=100;i++)
{
    if(i%4==0)
    {
    printf("%d",i);
    }
}
```

We calculate the remainder of `i` and 4 at each iteration of the `for` loop. The value of variable `i` is printed on the computer screen only if its remainder with respect to 4 is zero. Hence we print only those numbers from 4 to 100 which are divisible by 4 .

Solved Example 5.2

Write a program to take the number of rows as input from the user and to print the following vertically symmetric pattern on the computer screen:

```
  *
 **
***
****
***
**
*
```

```
#include <stdio.h>
void main()
{
    int  rows, w,i,j, spaces=1;
```

```
printf("Enter the number of rows for the upper triangle:");
scanf("%d",&rows);
/*Loops for the upper triangle*/
    for(i=1; i<=rows; i++)
    {
/*Print spaces required in each row*/
        for(w=spaces; w<=rows; w++)
        {
            printf(" ");
        }
/*Print stars required in each row*/
        for(j=0; j< i; j++)
        {
            printf("*");
        }
        spaces = spaces + 1;
        printf("\n");
    }
/*Loops for the lower triangle*/
    spaces = 1;
    for(i=rows-1; i>=1; i--)
    {
        for(w=spaces; w>=0; w--)
        {
            printf(" ");
        }
        for(j=i; j>=1; j--)
        {
            printf("*");
        }
        spaces = spaces + 1;
        printf("\n");
    }
}
```

Output

```
Enter the number of rows for the upper triangle:4
   *
  **
 ***
****
 ***
  **
   *
```

SCRATCH PAD

The above pattern is a symmetric figure with `r` rows (including the middle row) on the top and `r-1` rows at the bottom. Hence, we can divide the pattern into two parts:

Upper triangle
- The variable `rows` stores the value of number of rows required in the upper triangle.
- Each row of the upper triangle consist of spaces followed by stars.
- For example, if rows=5 then the first row consist of 5 spaces followed by 1 star. The second row consist of 4 spaces followed by 2 starts and so on. Therefore, the last row consist of 1 space followed by 5 stars.
- Hence, we have written two for loops inside the outer loop as seen below. The first `for` loop prints spaces using the counter variable w and the second `for` loop prints stars using the counter variable j.

```
for(i=1; i<=rows; i++)
    {
        for(w=spaces; w<=rows; w++)
        {
            printf(" ");
        }
        for(j=0; j< i; j++)
        {
            printf("*");
        }
        spaces = spaces + 1;
        printf("\n");

    }
```

This is a `for` loop for incrementing **row numbers**. The value of variable i represents the current row number at each iteration of the loop.

This is a `for` loop to print **spaces** in the current row. Note that, the number of spaces to be printed will **reduce** as the row number **increases**.

This is a `for` loop to print **stars** in the current row. Note that, the number of stars to be printed will **increase** as the row number **increases**. As seen from the pattern, we need i starts to be printed in every i^th row.

The `for` loops for **lower triangle** can be similarly understood from the code

Solved Example 5.3

Write a program to take the number of rows as input from the user and to print the following pattern on the computer screen:

```
#include<stdio.h>
void main()
{
```

```
int i,j,r;
printf("Enter the number of rows\n");
scanf("%d",&r);
    for(i=0; i<=r-1; i++)
    {
      /*Loop for printing spaces */
      for(j=1;j<=r-i; j++)
      {
      printf(" ");
      }
      /*Loop for printing stars */
      for(j=1;j<=2*i+1; j++)
      {
      printf("*");
      }
    printf("\n");
    }
}
```

SCRATCH PAD

In order to print the given pyramid we need to print spaces followed by a stars in each row. It is not required to print any spaces to the right of stars, this is because, the screen to the right of starts will be left blank any which ways when the control is transferred to the new line. Hence we can solve the problem, by designing two loops for each now:

  Inner Loop 1: To print spaces that appear to the left of starts in each row.

  Inner Loop 2: To print stars in each row.

The above two loops will now have an ability to print 1 full row as required on the screen. This means that, the execution of these loops must be repeated r times, if we need to print r rows at the output. Therefore, the limits of the outer most loop are from $i=0$ to r-1 as seen in the code. Note that, the outermost loop is responsible to increment row numbers hence it repeats the execution of two inner loops for each row. To understand how the limits of inner loops are decided, let us assume the value of r (no. of rows) is 4. Hence the pattern would be imagined as follows:

space	space	space	*			
space	space	*	*	*		
space	*	*	*	*	*	
*	*	*	*	*	*	*

When the value of the outer loop variable i is 0, we are required to print the first row which has 3 spaces followed by 1 star. After which the control is transferred to new line by execution of statement `printf("\n");` When outer loop increments the value of variable i to 1, we are ready to print the second row which has 2 spaces followed by 3 starts. Hence, in general, if number of rows are r, for any row number i, we are required to print $r-i$ spaces followed by $2*i+1$ starts.

Hence, the first inner loop (Inner Loop 1) is responsible to print $r-i$ spaces and the second inner loop is responsible to print $2*i+1$ starts as shown below

```
for(i=0; i<=r-1; i++)←
```

This is a `for` loop for incrementing **row numbers**. The value of variable i represents the current row number at each iteration of the loop.

```
        {
                /*Loop for printing spaces*/
                for(j=1;i<=r-i;j++)
                {
                printf(" ");
                }
                /*Loop for printing stars*/
                for(j=1;j<=2*i+1;j++)
                {
                printf("*");
                }
        printf("\n");
        }
```

Inner Loop1: This is a `for` loop to print **spaces** in the current row. Each row has `r-i` spaces, hence the loop runs from `j=1` to `r-i`

Inner Loop2: This is a `for` loop to print **stars** in the current row. Each row has `2*i+1` stars, hence the loop runs from `j=1` to `2*i+1`

To transfer control on new line after printing each row

Solved Example 5.4

Write a program to take a number as input from the user and to check if it is an Armstrong number.

Note: Armstrong number is a number whose sum of cube of digits is same as the number itself. For example, if we consider a number as 153, the sum of cube of digits of 153 is:

$1^3 + 5^3 + 3^3$

= **153** itself.

Hence, when we extract individual digits of 153 and find the sum of cube of its digits we get the number 153 back. Therefore, 153 is an Armstrong number.

```c
#include <stdio.h>
void main()
{
int sum=0,x,d,temp;
printf("Enter a number:");
scanf("%d",&x);
temp=x;
    while(x!=0)
    {
    d=x%10; /*get the individual digit*/
    sum=sum+d*d*d;  /*sum of cube of digits*/
    x=x/10;  /*Use quotient for the next addition*/
    }

    if(sum==temp)
    {
    printf("The number is a Armstrong number\n");
    }
```

```
        else
        {
        printf("The number is not a Armstrong number\n");
        }
}
```

Output

```
Enter a number:153
The number is a Armstrong number
```

SCRATCH PAD

The logic for the program is same as that of calculating "sum of digits" as discussed in Section 5.2.4 with a only difference that instead of calculating the sum of individual digits of the input number x we now calculate the "sum of cube of digits" of x using the following statement:

```
sum = sum +d*d*d;
```

Where, d represents digit within x extracted by a particular iteration of the while loop.

Further, the sum of cube of digits must be compared with the input number so as to determine if the input number x is an Armstrong number. However, we know that the while loop makes the value of x as zero after its execution. Hence, we store the value of variable x in a variable temp before starting the loop. This maintains a backup of the input data before starting the while loop as shown below:

```
temp=x;
```

Therefore, even if the value of variable x becomes zero after the while loop completes, the value of variable temp will still represent the input data. Hence, we compare the calculated value of sum of cube of digits with temp to determine if the number is Armstrong or not, as seen in the code.

Solved Example 5.5

Write a program to take the number of rows as input from the user and to print the following pattern on the computer screen:

```
1
1    2
1    2    3
1    2    3    4
```

```
#include <stdio.h>
void main()
{
int i,j,r,value=1;
printf("Enter the number of rows:");
printf("%d",&r);
    for(i=0; i<=r-1; i++)
    {
    value=1;
```

```
        for(j=1;j<=i+1; j++)
        {
                printf("%d",value);
        value++;
        }
    printf("\n");
    }
}
```

Output

```
Enter the number of rows: 4
1
1   2
1   2   3
1   2   3   4
```

SCRATCH PAD

Instead of printing a pattern of stars, we now need to print the pattern of integer values as seen in the question. Therefore, we create a variable named `value` with the initial value as 1. We also set the value of variable as 1 at the beginning of each row. This can be done by writing the following statement inside the body of the outer `for` loop:

```
value=1;
```

Further, the inner `for` loop increments the variable `value` each time a number is printed on the computer screen. Thereby printing the consecutive numbers within a single row of the triangle using the statements as shown below:

```
printf("%d",value);
value++;
```

Hence we get a pattern as,

```
1
1       2
1       2       3
1       2       3       4
```

because we reset `value` to 1 each time we start the processing for a new row.

Solved Example 5.6

Write a program to take the number of rows as input from the user and to print the following pattern on the computer screen:

```
a   a   a   a
b   b   b
c   c
d
```

```
#include<stdio.h>
void main()
{
int i,j,r;
char v ='a';
printf("Enter the number of rows:");
scanf("%d",&r);
    for(i=0; i<=r-1; i++)
    {
       for(j=1;j<=r-i; j++)
         {
                printf("%c",v);
         }
    v=v+1;
    printf("\n");
    }
}
```

Output

```
Enter the number of rows:4
aaaa
bbb
cc
d
```

SCRATCH PAD

Instead of printing a pattern of stars, we now need to print the pattern of characters starting from 'a' as seen in the question. Therefore, we create a variable named v with the initial value as 'a'. Further, we also increment the value of variable v at the beginning of each row. This can be done by writing the following statement inside the body of the outer for loop:

```
v=v+1;
```

The inner for loop prints the value of variable v in every iteration on the computer screen. Thereby printing the same character within the a single row of the triangle using the statement as shown below:

```
printf("%c",v);
```

Hence we get a pattern as,

```
a     a     a     a
b     b     b
c     c
d
```

Note that, we can increment characters same as that of integers. This is because C/C++ actually stores the **ASCII** value of the character in the memory. A new character is printed on each line of the pattern because we increment the value of v at the beginning of each row.

Solved Example 5.7

Write a program to take the value of n as input from the user and to print the result of following series:

2!-4!+6!-8!+10!....n!

```
#include<stdio.h>
void main()
{
int k,n;
float f,s=0.0,x,sign=-1;
printf("Enter the value of n:");
scanf("%d",&n);
    for(k=2; k<=n; k+=2)
    {
      x=k;
      f=1.0;
    /*Calculate the factorial of 'x'*/
    while(x>0)
        {
        f=f*x;
        x--;
        }
    sign=sign*(-1);
    s=s+f*sign;
    }
printf("Result of the series is %f",s);
}
```

Output
```
Enter the value of n:6
Result of the series is 698.000000
```

SCRATCH PAD

So as to obtain an alternate pattern of "+" and "-" in the series we create a variable named as `sign` with a initial value as -1. At each iteration of the `for` loop we further multiply the value of variable sign with -1. Hence, every multiplication with -1 that happens in a even iteration will result into a positive value of `sign` and every multiplication with -1 that happens in a odd iteration will result into a negative value of `sign`. Thereby, evaluating the value of series with alternate + and - signs.

Solved Example 5.8

Write a program to take the value of n as input from the user and to print the result of following series:

$x^2/2!-x^3/3!+x^4/4!-x^5/5!+x^6/6!....x^n/n!$

```
#include<stdio.h>
#include<math.h>
void main()
{
int k,n,t;
float f,s=0.0,x,sign=1;
printf("Enter the value of  n:");
scanf("%d",&n);
printf("Enter the value of x:");
scanf("%f",&x);
    for(k=2; k<=n; k++)
    {
    t=k;
    f=1.0;
/*Calculate the factorial of 't'*/
        while(t>0)
            {
            f=f*t;
            t--;
            }
    sign=sign*(-1);
    s=s+ pow(x,k)/f*sign;
    }
printf("Result of the series is %f",s);
}
```

Output
```
Enter the value of n:5
Enter the value of x:3
Result of the series is -1.350000
```

SCRATCH PAD

The function **pow(x,k)** can be used to calculate the value of x to the power of k. The function is defined in the header file math.h which we have included in the code. Further, the value of variable sign is multiplied with the ratio **pow(x,k)/f** so as to evaluate the series with alternate "+" and "-" signs as seen in the code. Therefore, on executing following statement in each iteration of the for loop:

```
s=s+pow(x,k)/f*sign;
```

we will get the result of the required series in variable s after the loop completes.

Solved Example 5.9

Write a program to take the number of rows as input from the user and to print the following pattern on the computer screen:

```
*   *    *    *
   *    *    *
       *    *
           *
```

```c
#include<stdio.h>
void main()
{
    int rows,i,j,w,spaces=1;
    printf("Enter the number of rows:");
    scanf("%d",&rows);
    for(i=rows; i>=1; i--)
    {
/*Print spaces required in each row*/
        for(w= spaces; w>=0; w--)
        {
        printf(" ");
        }
/*Print stars required in each row*/
        for(j=i; j>=1; j--)
        {
        printf("*");
        }
        spaces = spaces + 1;
        printf("\n");
    }
}
```

Output

```
Enter the number of rows:4
****
 ***
  **
   *
```

Solved Example 5.10

Write a program to take the width and height of the rectangle as input from the user and to print the following rectangular pattern on the computer screen:

```
*    *    *    *
*    *    *    *
*    *    *    *
*    *    *    *
*    *    *    *
*    *    *    *
```

```
#include<stdio.h>
void main()
{
    int width,height,i,j;
    printf("Enter the width and height of the rectangle:");
    scanf("%d%d",&width,&height);
/*Print a rectangle*/
    for(i=0; i<height; i++)
    {
      for(j=0; j<width; j++)
      {
            printf("*");
      }
    printf("\n");
    }
}
```

Output
```
Enter the width and height of the rectangle: 10 3
**********
**********
**********
```

SCRATCH PAD

The number of rows to be printed are specified by the `height` of the rectangle whereas, the number of columns to be printed are specified as the `width` of the rectangle. Hence total iterations of outer for loop is same as `height` of the rectangle whereas the total iterations of inner for loop is same as `width` of the rectangle. In each row, `width` number of stars are to be printed and hence the loops are nested as seen in the code.

Solved Example 5.11

Write a program to perform addition of all the integer-type values that are entered by the user at runtime of the program. The program should stop performing the addition and print the final result when the user enters a value 0.

```
#include<stdio.h>
void main()
{
int number, s = 0;
printf("Enter a number:\n");
scanf("%d",&number);
/*Take a number as input until user enters 0*/
    while(number!=0)
    {
    s=s+number;
```

```
        printf("Enter next number:\n");
        scanf("%d",&number);
        }
printf("Result of addition is %d",s);
}
```

Output
```
Enter a number:
10
Enter next number:
20
Enter next number:
30
Enter next number:
40
Enter next number:
0
Result of addition is 100
```

SCRATCH PAD

We accept the value of the variable `number` at each iteration of the `while` loop as seen in the code. Each value of the variable `number` which is read by the program is added to the value of variable s which represents the sum of the numbers entered by the user so far. The `while` loop terminates when the user inputs the value zero which represents the end of incoming data.

Solved Example 5.12

Write a program to print Floyd's triangle. The program should read the number of rows as input from the user and print the Floyd's triangle which is given as below (The below triangle is drawn assuming the height as 5.):

```
1
2       3
4       5       6
7       8       9       10
11      12      13      14      15
```

```
#include<stdio.h>
void main()
{
int i,j,r,value=1;
printf("Enter the number of rows:");
scanf("%d",&r);
    for(i=0; i<=r-1; i++)
```

```
    {
      for(j=1;j<=i+1; j++)
      {
       printf("%d",value);
       value++;
      }
    printf("\n");
    }
}
```

Output

```
Enter the number of rows: 4
1
2 3
4 5 6
7 8 9 10
```

Solved Example 5.13

Write a program to take two numbers as input from the user and to calculate the LCM and GCD of the two numbers.

```
#include<stdio.h>
void main()
{
int number1, number2, gcd,max,i;
printf("Enter  two numbers:");
scanf("%d%d",&number1,&number2);
    if(number1> number2)
    {
    max= number1;
    }
    else
    {
    max= number2;
    }
    if(number1!=0 && number2!=0)
      {
        for(i=max;i>=1;i--)
          {
            /*check if 'i' divides number1 as well as number2*/
            if (number1%i==0 && number2%i==0)
              {
```

```
                    printf("GCD is %d\n",i);
                    gcd=i;
                    break;
                    }
                }
        }
    else if (number1 == 0)
    {
    printf("GCD is %d\n",number2);
    gcd=number2;
    }
    else
    {
    printf("GCD is %d\n",number1);
    gcd=number1;

    }
    }
printf("LCM is %d\n",(number1*number2)/gcd);
}
```

Output

```
Enter two numbers: 20 30
GCD is 10
LCM is 60
```

SCRATCH PAD

GCD of any two numbers `number1` and `number2` is the maximum number `i` such that, `i` divides both `number1` as well as `number2`. Therefore, we start the iterations of the `for` loop from the value of `i` as `max` and break the `for` loop as we get the first number which divides both `number1` and `number2` as shown below:

```
for(i=max;i>=1;i++)
{
if(number1%i==0 && number2%i==0)
        {
        printf("GCD is %d\n",i);
        gcd=i;
        break;
        }
}
```

Hence, the value of variable `i` will represent the GCD of two numbers which we have also saved in variable named as `gcd`.

Further, the LCM of two numbers is calculated as shown below:
```
(number1*number2)/gcd
```

Error Finding Exercise

The following are some programs which may or may not contain errors. Correct the error
if it exist in the code and determine the output.

Program 1

```
#include<stdio.h>
void main()
{
int i;
    for(i=0, i<=10 , i++)
    {
    printf("Computer Programming");
    }
}
```

Program 2

```
#include<stdio.h>
void main()
{
int k=1;
    for(;k;)
    {
    printf("Hello\n");
    }
}
```

Program 3

```
#include<stdio.h>
void main()
{
    int k;
    for(i=k;i<=10;i++)
    {
    for(k=1;k<5; printf("Hello world"))
      {
      k++;
      }
    }
}
```

Program 4

```
#include<stdio.h>
void main()
{
```

```
int i=1;
    for(i>10;i++;++i)
    {
    printf("%d",i);
    }
}
```

Program 5

```
#include< stdio.h>
void main()
{
int i=6;
    while(--i<=0 && i++>=5);
    {
    printf("Hello\n");
    }
}
```

Program 6

```
#include<stdio.h>
void main()
{
int j=1,r=5;i=5;
    for(i=0; i<=r-1; i++)
    {
      value=25;
      for(NULL;j<i+1; j++)
      {
       printf("%d", value);
       value++;
      }
    printf("\n");
    }
}
```

Program 7

```
#include<stdio.h>
void main()
{
int i;
    for(i=0; i=10; i++)
    {
    printf("Animal Kingdom\n");
    }
}
```

Quiz

1. Determine the value of i after execution of the below statement

    ```
    for (int i=0;i<=10;i++);
    ```

    (a) This is an error as there cannot be a semicolon after `for` statement

    (c) `10`

    (b) `11`

    (d) `0`

2. What is the output of the below segment:

    ```
    for( ;  ; )
    {
    printf("Computer Programming");
    }
    ```

    (a) It will print "Computer Programming" exactly once on the screen

    (b) This is a compilation error as the initialization and condition part is mandatory when defining the `for` loop

    (c) The block results in an infinite loop

    (d) This is a runtime error

3. What will be the value of variable `counter` after the following block is executed?

    ```
    int counter = 100;
    for( ; ; )
    {
    if(counter-- == 95)
    break;
    }
    ```

    (a) This is a compilation error as the initialization and condition part is mandatory when defining the `for` loop

    (b) Value of counter will be 95

    (c) Value of counter will be 94

    (d) Value of counter will be 96

    (e) None of the above

4. What is the value of v after the execution of following segment?

    ```
    int v=1;
    while(v<=10)
    {
       if(v>8)
       {
       break;
       printf("%d\n",v);
       }
       else
       {
    ```

```
    printf("%d\n",v+1);
    continue;
    }
v++;
}
```

(a) 9   (c) 8
(b) 10   (d) None of the above

5. What is the value of i when the following code segment is executed:
```
int i;
for(i=10; 0 ; i--)
{
i--;
}
```

(a) Garbage value   (c) 9   (e) 7
(b) 10   (d) 8   (f) None of the above

6. Which of the following statements is true?
   (a) for loop is an entry control loop whereas while loop is a exit control loop
   (b) for and do-while loops are exit control loops
   (c) for and while loops are entry control loops
   (d) for loop is an exit control loop.

7. Given that l1, l2 and l3 are three different loops in the program, such that the loop l3 is written inside l2 and loop l2 is written inside l1. Which of the following statements is true:
   (a) l1 will be executed maximum number of times
   (b) l2 will be executed maximum number of times
   (c) l3 will be executed maximum number of times
   (d) We cannot comment on the loop that will be executed maximum number of times.

8. What is the value of i and j after the execution of the following code segment:
```
for(i=0;i<=6;i++)
{
for(j=i+1;j>=0;j--)
    {
    printf("$");
    }
}
```

(a) i=0 j=1   (c) i=5 j=0
(b) i=7 j=-1   (d) i=6 j=0

9. What will be the value of variable r after the execution of the given while loop, if the value variable x is 9856.
```
while(x!=0)
```

```
{
r=x%10;
x=x/10;
}
```

(a) 6   (c) 8   (e) 0
(b) 5   (d) 9   (f) None of the above

10. Choose a correct answer to complete the given code segment to print the following pattern for r rows. For example, if r=4 then the code should print the following output:

```
P
P Q
P Q R
P Q R S
char v;
for(i=0; i<=_____; i++)
{
v='P';
    for(j=___;j>=___;____)
    {
    printf("%c",v);
    v=v+1;
    }
printf("\n");
}
```

(a) i<=4 and j=0;j<=4;j++   (c) i<=3 and j=1;j<=i+1;j++
(b) i<=3 and j=0;j>=i-1;j--   (d) i<=3 and j=0;j<=i+2;j++

11. Consider the following code segment and choose the correct answer

```
int i,k=4;
for(i=0;k>0;k--)
{
i++;
}
```

(a) The value of k will be 1 and i will be 3 after the loop completes
(b) The value of k will be 0 and i will be 4 after the loop completes
(c) The value of k will be -1 and i will be 4 after the loop completes
(d) The value of k will be 0 and i will be 3 after the loop completes

Review Questions

1. Write a short note on entry control loops.
2. Explain the working of do..while loop.
3. Write a program to print all the prime numbers from 1 to 100.

4. Write a program to print all the Armstrong numbers from 1 to 100.
5. Write a program to display the following pattern:

```
*     *     *     *     *     *     *
   *     *     *     *     *
      *     *     *
         *
```

6. Explain the following with example
   (i) break   (ii) continue.
7. Write a program to display the following pattern using nested loops

```
            A
      A  B  A
   A  B  C  B  A
A  B  C  D  C  B  A
```

8. Write a program to generate all the possible combinations of three symbols 1, 2 and 3 using for loop.
   [Example, print 1 1 1 (1st row), 1 1 2 (2nd row), 1 1 3 (3rd row)... 3 3 3 (Last row)]
9. Write a program to give the following output:

```
        1
     2  2
   3  3  3
4  4  4  4
```

10. Select the correct answer
```
I=50;
do
{
.... Body of Loop ....
} while(I<50);
```
    (1) Loop will be executed at least once.
    (2) Loop will not be executed at all.
    (3) do-while loop is not valid in this case because condition should be true at least once.
    (4) none of the above.
11. Write a program to take a number as input from the user and reverse the position of digits. For example if user enters the integer value as 1234 the output should be 4321
12. Write a program to calculate the output of following series:
    1/2−1/4+1/6−1/8+1/10−1/12....1/n

Chapter

6 | Arrays

6.1 Overview

All the variables we created till now can store only one value at a time. If you re-initialize a variable, the new value overwrites the value which was already present in the variable. For example, let us consider an integer type variable a initialized with a value 10 as shown below:

```
int a=10;
```

While value of variable a is initialized as 10, we can always re-initialize its value. The statement

```
a=20;
```

re-initializes value of a to 20. This means that a no more contains 10 as shown in Figure 6.1. You can re-initialize a variable any number of times in the program; but each time a variable is re-initialized, its previous value is lost. This is because there is only a certain space in memory reserved for a particular variable having capacity to store just one value at a time. In this case, since a is of type integer, the compiler reserves only 2 bytes of memory for it. Since a single integer constant in itself is of 2 bytes, there is no scope for variable a to store two different values at the same time. Hence, when you re-initialize a value a with 20, its previous value is overwritten and there

Variable **a**

Figure 6.1: Re-initialization of variable

is no way to recover it unless it is backed up at some other place by the programmer. What if we want to store both the values 10 and 20 in memory? One of the simple solutions is to create two different variables, say a and b, such that a stores 10 and b stores 20. Although the solution sounds practical for storing two values, this is not something that could be implemented in every case. For example, what if you want to store 100 different values at the same time? In this case, creating 100 different variables in the program is simply not practical. Even if a programmer manages to create them, the program will become very cluttered and difficult to maintain. Also, what if we want to store 1000 different values at the same time? Creating 1000 different variables with different names is something that we could not even think of. C/C++ offers a data structure called **array** to solve such problems.

An array is a data structure which can store collection of values having same data type. Arrays are used to store logically related data values under a common name. For example, let us assume that we need to store the runs scored by each of the batsmen, in a cricket team of 11 players, in computer memory. The statement

```
int runs[11];
```

creates an **integer array** named `runs` with size 11 in memory, as shown in Figure 6.2. Elements of the array are indexed starting from 0 and are stored in physically adjacent memory locations. The first element of the array can be accessed as `runs[0]` where we can store the runs made by the first batsman. Similarly, the second element of the array can be accessed as `runs[1]` where we can store the runs made by the second batsman and so on. Since the array index starts from zero, the runs scored by 11th batsmen will be stored at position 10 and can be accessed as `runs[10]` as shown in Figure 6.2. Hence, the total score of the cricket team can be calculated by adding all the elements in the array `runs`.

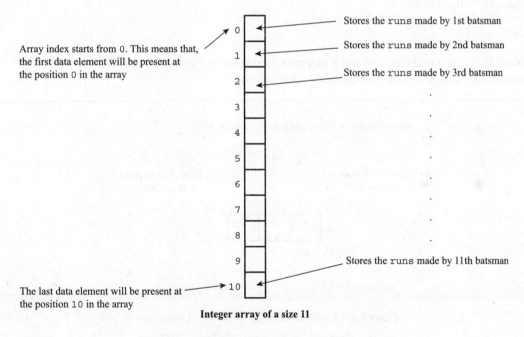

Integer array of a size 11

Figure 6.2: Structure of array in computer memory

NOTES

An array always has a **data type** associated with it. All the data items stored in an array must be of the same type that is specified at the time of creating an array. For example, if data type of array `runs` is `int`, it means that all the elements of the array (`runs[0]` to `runs[10]`) will be of type `int`. Remember, array is a collection of data items of same type and hence two values with different data types cannot exist in the same array.

6.2 Creating an Array

Given below is the syntax to create an array:

```
<DataType> array_name[SIZE];
```

Given below are some examples, showing creation of an array in computer memory:

Statement	Description
int p[10];	Creates an integer array named p with a size of 10 integers
float q[5];	Creates a float array named q with a size of 5 floats
char r[20];	Creates a character array named r with a size of 20 characters

To understand few more aspects, let us create an integer array a of size 3 as shown in the following statement:

```
int a[3];
```

Note that a is a collection of three integers as shown in Figure 6.3. All the array elements store junk values, unless they are individually initialized.

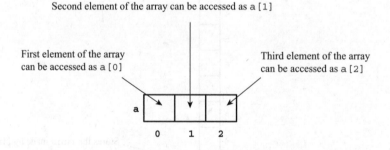

Initially, a[0], a[1] and a[2] will contain junk values

Figure 6.3: Creation of array a to store 3 integers

Each element of array a is indexed starting from 0. Hence, the first element should be accessed as a[0], second element should be accessed as a[1] and the third element should be accessed as a[2]. Let us now initialize these elements to values 10, 20 and 30, respectively; this can be done by using the following statements:

```
a[0]=10;
a[1]=20;
a[2]=30;
```

After execution of these statements, array elements will be initialized as shown in Figure 6.4.

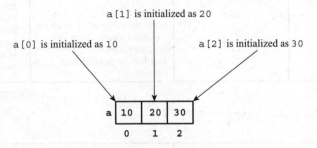

Figure 6.4: Initialization of an array a

We can print each of the values using the **printf()** statements as tabulated below:

Statement	Description
printf("%d",a[0]);	The statement prints the value of a[0] which is 10
printf("%d",a[1]);	The statement prints the value of a[1] which is 20
printf("%d",a[2]);	The statement prints the value of a[2] which is 30

Instead of writing three individual printf() statements to print the values of a[0], a[1] and a[2], we can also write a generic printf() statement and execute it three times by passing different values of index. We know that index ranges from 0 to 2; hence we can create a separate variable to represent an index value (say i) and put the statement printf("%d\n",a[i]); in a loop ranging the value of i from 0 to 2 as shown below:

```
for(i=0;i<=2;i++)
{
printf("%d\n",a[i]);
}
```

In the first iteration of the for loop the value of variable i will be 0 and hence the **printf()** statement will print the value of element a[0] which is 10. In the second iteration of the for loop, the value of variable i will be 1 and hence the **printf()** statement will print the value of element a[1] which is 20, whereas in the third iteration the value of variable i will be 2 and hence the **printf()** statement will print the value of element a[2] which is 30 as shown in Figure 6.5. Note that after printing each data element the cursor is transferred on the new line using the escape sequence \n as a part of printf() and hence each element of the array will be printed on the new line of the screen as seen in the output of the program.

Given below is the full source code to initialize and print an array a of size 3:

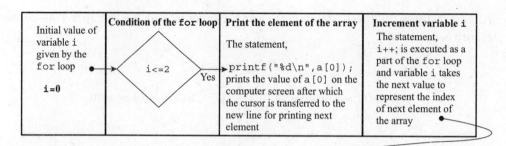

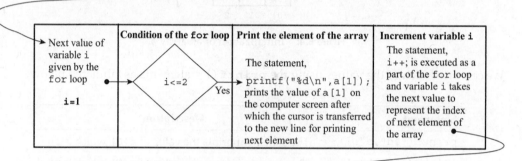

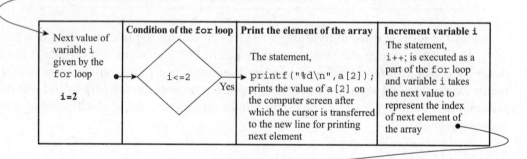

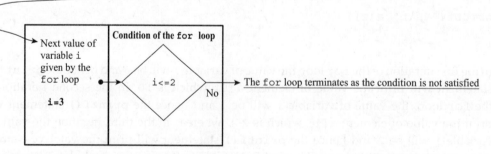

Figure 6.5: Execution of `for` loop responsible to print array elements

```
#include<stdio.h>
void main()
{
int a[3];
int i;
a[0]=10;
a[1]=20;
a[2]=30;
printf("Array elements are\n");
        for(i=0;i<=2;i++)
        {
        printf("%d\n",a[i]);
        }
}
```
Output
```
Array elements are
10
20
30
```

NOTES

All elements of the array are stored in **physically adjacent memory locations** and they are consecutively indexed starting from 0. In this case, elements of a are indexed from 0 to 2 because size of the array is 3. In general, if size of array is n, then indexes range from 0 to n−1. Given that indexes are consecutive, it makes traversing of an entire array possible using loops. In this chapter, we will learn several examples which explain traversing of an array using loops.

CAUTION

C/C++ does not perform any **boundary checks** when an array element is accessed. This means that, there is a possibility that, if programmer attempts to access some element by specifying an index which is outside the boundary of an array then this mistake may simply go **unnoticed** without any error getting generated. For example, consider array a of size 3 initialized as shown below:

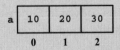

a[0], a[1] and a[2] are valid accesses that we can make to array because its size is 3. However, if the programmer genuinely makes a mistake of specifying wrong index (which is out of array bounds) while accessing an array element (may due to a typing error or a logical error): C/C++ is not going to generate any error to the programmer. For example, if you accidently access an element outside array say a[3]; you will get a junk value stored at location, without any error being generated. Indeed, if you pass any index to the array other than 0, 1 or 2 you will get a junk value from the corresponding location in memory without any error being generated by C/C++.

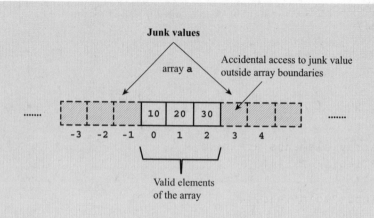

This is a very dangerous situation because you may continue doing operations with junk values without even knowing that index passed to the array is incorrect. Hence extra care must be taken when specifying index of array elements in the program to ensure that the index specified is not out of bounds.

6.2.1 Initializing an array at the time of creation

In the program given in Section 6.2, we have individually initialized each element of array a as shown below:

```
a[0]=10;
a[1]=20;
a[2]=30;
```

Instead of initializing one element of an array at a time, you can also initialize all the array elements together by specifying the values in curly brackets. However, such an initialization can only be applied at the time of creating an array and no later than that. For example, you could initialize array a at the same time when you created it as shown below:

```
int a[3] ={10,20,30};
```

Such an initialization is called **direct initialization** of the array and the array elements will be initialized as shown in Figure 6.6.

When an array is initialized at the time of creation, C/C++ keeps it optional to specify the size of the array. For example, the following statement which does not specify the size of an array will also work well:

a	10	20	30
	0	1	2

Figure 6.6: Direct initialization

```
int a[] ={10,20,30}; /*Specifying size is optional when array is
initialized at the time of creation*/
```

The compiler itself computes the size of this array, considering at the number of values initialized to it.

NOTES

Such an initialization can only be applied at the time of creation and no later than that. For example, the following code will give an error because it first creates an array and later attempts to initialize all its elements using direct initialization:

```
int a[3]; /*Array created*/
a={10,20,30}; /*Error: Direct initialization cannot be applied after
creation of an array*/
```

In this case, you have to rather initialize the array elements individually as done in the program given in Section 6.2.

6.2.2 Specifying size of an array

Size of the array must be specified at the time of its creation; this makes it possible for the compiler to allocate required memory for an array at the time of compilation of the program. The rule is that the array size must always be specified as a direct integer value and it cannot be specified in terms of another variable. For example, to create a float type array (named a) having a capacity of three elements, we must specify the size as direct integer 3 at the time of creating the array, as shown below:

```
float a[3];
```

As each floating point number requires 4 bytes in memory, the compiler will allocate the memory for array a as

```
4 × 3 = 12 Bytes
```

In general, if storing one value needs d bytes, the compiler allocates d*size bytes of memory for an array.

We cannot create an array by specifying its size indirectly, in terms of another variable. For instance, let us create a variable n with value 3 and then create an array a with the size of array specified in terms of n as shown below:

```
int n=3;
float a[n]; /*ERROR: value of "n" is not known at the time of
compilation*/
```

Logically, the statements float a[3]; and float a[n]; will have the same meaning because the value of variable n is initialized as 3. However, the later statement will not compile because the value of variable n will be initialized only when the program starts running and whereas the compiler allocates the memory for the array at the time of compilation. This means that the exact size of the array a will not be known at the time of compilation of the statement float a[n]; because value of n itself is not known at the time of compilation. Hence, compilation of the program fails because the compiler cannot allocate memory for the array.

NOTES

Memory is allocated for a variable at the time of compilation of the program, but its initialization happens at run time. For the statement

```
int n=3;
```

compiler allocates 2 bytes of memory for variable n, but the value 3 is initialized to n only when the program runs. Therefore, value of variable n is not known at the time of compilation. As memory for an array needs to be allocated at the time of compilation, array size must always be specified as direct integer value and it cannot be specified in terms of another variable. Hence the statement float a [n] ; does not compile because compiler cannot determine the amount of memory to be reserved for an array a. The only exception to above theory is when you create constant variables in the program. Constant variables are declared as well as initialized during compilation stage as there is no scope for their value to change later in the program. Hence, if we create variable n as constant, the following statements work correctly.

```
const int n=3;
float a[n]; /*This works fine because n is a constant variable*/
```

The memory for array a is correctly allocated as 12 bytes because compiler knows the value of constant variables.

6.2.3   To find sum and average on n numbers: An example

Let us create a program to accept different numbers as input from the user and to find their sum and average. Let us assume that the total number of inputs are n; we will store these n numbers in a float array a. In theory, we need an array with size n. However, as we recollect from section 6.2.2, we will not be able to specify the size of the array in terms of n because the value of variable n is not known at the time of compilation. Hence, we create this program by assuming the maximum limit of value of n as 100, thereby creating an array with a capacity of 100 elements as shown below:

```
float a[100];
```

This means that the array a can store at the most 100 floating point values (maximum capacity) inside it and the elements of the array will therefore be indexed from 0 to 99 as shown in Figure 6.7. Note that all the elements of the array will have junk values unless we initialize them explicitly.

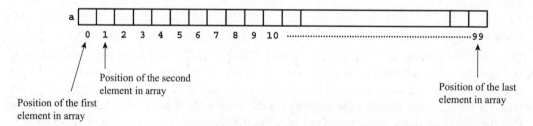

Figure 6.7:   Array a of size 100

Although we have created a space large enough to accommodate 100 floating point numbers, it should not mean that the user must always input 100 values. The user might actually require storing different number of elements each time the program is executed. Hence, before we start accepting the actual array elements as input from the user, we will ask the user about the number of elements that the user really wishes to input, for calculating their sum and average. Hence, we create an integer variable n which stores the 'number of elements' that the user will input. Hence, the first step of the program is to take the value of n as input from the user as shown below:

```
int n;
printf("How many numbers you want to enter?\n");
scanf("%d",&n);
```

Once the value of variable n is known, program can then be designed to accept only the required number of values as input from the user and store them in first n-locations of the array, while the remaining part of the array can still continue to hold junk values. For example, if user inputs the value of variable n as 4, then it means that the program should accept only 4 floating point numbers as input from the user storing them at first 4 positions of the array as shown in Figure 6.8. (The first floating point number entered by the user is stored in a[0], the second floating point number is stored at a[1] and so on. Hence, the last number entered by the user will be stored at a[3].) The remaining part of the array, that is, elements from position 4 to position 99 will still continue to hold junk values as shown in Figure 6.8.

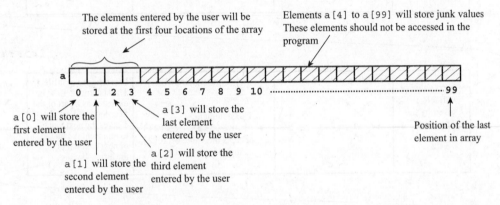

Figure 6.8: Initialization of first 4 elements of the array

This means that if we assume the value of n as 4 then we need to take elements a[0], a[1], a[2] and a[3] as input from the user. In general, for any value of n we need to take elements in the array at position 0 to position n-1 as input from the user. This process to take individual array elements as input from the user is implemented using the following for loop:

```
for(i=0;i<=n-1;i++)
{
  scanf("%d",&a[i]);
}
```

As seen, the for loop executes a statement scanf("%d",&a[i]); in each iteration for different values of variable i. Hence, when the value of variable i is zero, the for loop will execute a statement scanf("%d",&a[0]); thereby accepting the value of a[0] as input from the user and when the value of variable i is 1, the for loop will execute a statement scanf("%d",&a[1]); thereby accepting the value of a[1] as input from the user and so on. The detailed execution of the for loop to take first n-elements as input from the user is as shown in Figure 6.9. Note that when n=4 the for loop terminates its execution after taking the last number a[3] as input from the user. Hence, in general, the for loop will

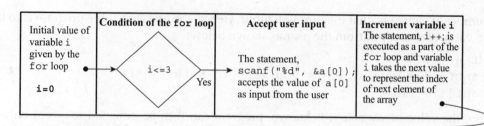

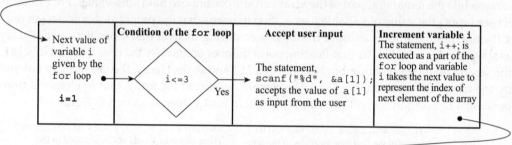

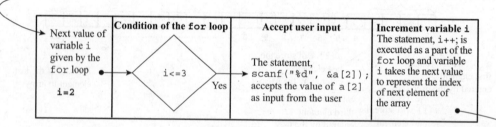

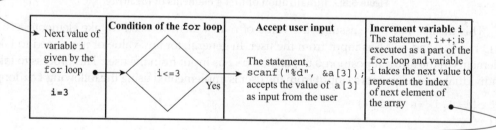

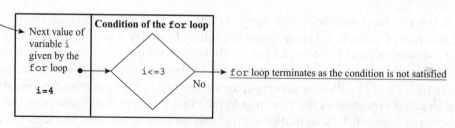

Figure 6.9: Execution of `for` loop to accept array elements as input from the user

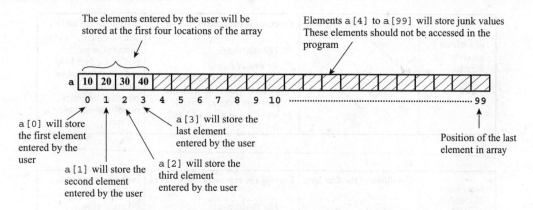

Figure 6.10: Actual initialization of array elements

run for the values of variable i from 0 to n-1, thereby taking all the elements of the array from position 0 to position n-1 as input from the user.

Let us assume that the user inputs the values 10, 20, 30 and 40. Hence, these values will be stored at a[0], a[1], a[2] and a[3], respectively, as shown in Figure 6.10.

As the required elements are stored in the array, we can start calculating the sum of n numbers. Let us create a variable s to store the resultant sum. This would mean that if the value of n is 4 then s should be calculated as

a[0]+a[1]+a[2]+a[3]

However, the valid number of elements in the array is not known at the time of compilation because user inputs the value of n only when we run the program. Hence, we cannot directly write such a hardcoded expression (a[0]+a[1]+a[2]+a[3]) for variable s. We, therefore, perform the addition by considering one element of the array at a time in a for loop such that every iteration of the for loop accesses one element of the array. At each iteration of the for loop, an array element accessed would be added to the value of variable s which stores the previous sum, thereby storing the complete sum value in variable s itself, once all the iterations of the for loop complete. In the first iteration of the for loop, we access the first element of the array and hence there cannot be any value of previous sum. Therefore, we give the initial value of variable s as zero which will perform a dummy addition of the first element of the array with the number zero, so that the first element of the array is not affected and stored as it is in the resultant variable.

```
float s=0; /*initial sum is set to zero*/
for(i=0;i<=n-1;i++)
{
s = s + a[i];
}
```

If n = 4, the loop will have 4 iterations and hence the full expression to calculate the sum of elements in the array will be as follows:

```
s = 0+a[0]+a[1]+a[2]+a[3];
```

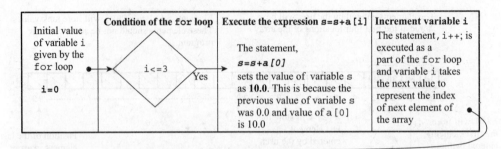

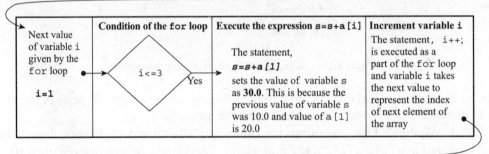

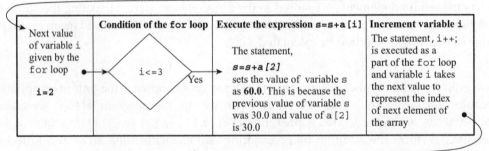

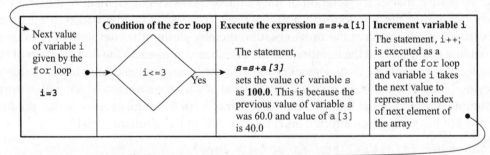

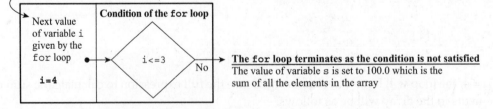

Figure 6.11: Execution of `s = s + a[i];` in a loop

On substituting values in the above expression, we have

```
s = 0+10+20+30+40
```

Note that in the first iteration of the `for` loop, the first element of the array is added with zero so as to get the initial sum as `10`. After the value of variable s is set as `10`, in the second iteration of the loop the second element of the array (which is `20`) is added with the previous sum (which is `10`) to get the new value of variable s as `30` and so on. The detailed execution of the `for` loop is as shown in Figure 6.11. As seen, at each iteration of the `for` loop, one element of the array is read and its value gets added to the sum variable s calculated by previous iteration of the loop, thereby giving the final sum value s as `100` at the end of the `for` loop as shown in Figure 6.11. Hence, the program prints the value of variable s, after the loop completes using the following statement:

```
printf("Sum is :%f\n",s);
```

After the sum is calculated, we divide the sum by total number of elements n to get the average as seen in the following statement:

```
printf("Average is %f\n",s/n);
```

Note that the value of variable s contains the sum of n elements only when the loop is fully executed which adds all the elements of an array stored from position 0 to position n-1. Hence, the `printf()` statements to print full sum and an average should be written outside the loop as seen in the program.

The complete source code to calculate the sum and average of n numbers is as given below:

```c
#include <stdio.h>
void main()
{
 int n,i;
 float a[100];
 float s=0;
 printf("How many numbers you want to enter?\n");
 scanf("%d",&n);
 printf("Enter %d numbers:\n",n);
    for(i=0;i<=n-1;i++)
    {
      scanf("%f",&a[i]);
    }
    for(i=0;i<=n-1;i++)
    {
      s=s+a[i];
    }
    printf("Sum is :%f\n",s);
    printf("Average is %f\n",s/n);
}
```

Output:
```
How many numbers you want to enter?
4
Enter 4 numbers:
10
20
30
40
Sum is :100.000000
Average is 25.000000
```

In this example, we have created an array of size 100. However, if user enters the value of n much lesser than 100, say n=3 than the remaining 97 elements in the array are unused and they will continue storing junk values. This clearly means that there is a wastage of memory. Is there a way we can avoid this wastage? **?**

Yes, there is a wastage of storage space because the value of variable n is known only at run time but the memory for an array is allocated at the compile time. Such a memory that is allocated at the time of compilation of the program is called as **static memory**. Wastage of storage space is one of the drawbacks of static memory allocation. To solve the problem, program must allocate the memory at runtime after knowing the value of n (to create an array of exactly n elements). This would be possible then because value of n would have been already entered by the user before the creation of the array. Such a memory that is allocated at runtime of the program is called as **dynamic memory**.

Compiler allocates static memory for all the arrays and variables which are created in this chapter; and hence there will be wastage of storage space but considering the rich memory configurations we have today this wastage is hardly of any concern.

We will discuss dynamic memory allocation in Chapter 10 which is used to avoid such a wastage of storage space.

6.2.4 Program to find minimum value in the array: An example

Let us create a program that accepts n different numbers as input from the user and finds the minimum element out of the n numbers. As discussed in the previous example, we will define an integer array a of size 100 and create a program with an assumption that the value of n is always less than or equal to 100. After accepting n elements as input from the user using a loop, we start the process to find minimum of n elements.

Let us assume the user inputs four elements in the array as 70, 40, 35 and 65 which will be then stored in a[0], a[1], a[2] and a[3], respectively, as shown in Figure 6.12.

We create a variable min which is required to store the minimum value present inside the array as a result of this program. Initially we will assign the value of a[0] to min and hence the initial value of variable min is set to 70, assuming the input values shown in Figure 6.12.

```
min=a[0]; /* set the initial value of min as a[0]*/
```

We will now find the minimum element stored in the array by comparing each element from position 1 to position n-1 with the value present in variable min. Note that there is

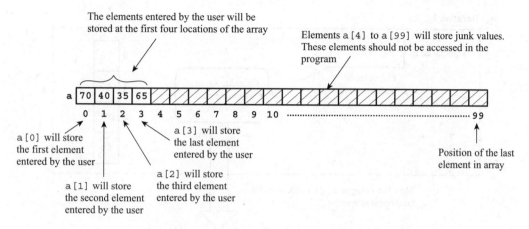

The elements entered by the user will be stored at the first four locations of the array

Elements a[4] to a[99] will store junk values. These elements should not be accessed in the program

a[0] will store the first element entered by the user

a[3] will store the last element entered by the user

Position of the last element in array

a[2] will store the third element entered by the user

a[1] will store the second element entered by the user

Figure 6.12: Initialization of array elements

no need to compare variable min with a[0] because we have ourselves initialized min to a[0] so we know that min and a[0] are indeed equal.

If the value present in variable min is greater than the value at next position in the array, it indicates that the value in variable min is not the minimum value and hence we overwrite min with the value of the array element which has lesser value than the current value of min. This way we keep comparing the value of variable min with each element of the array one by one starting from a[1] and ending at a[n-1] using a for loop. If the value of min is found to be greater than any element a[i] of the array, then we replace the value of variable min by the value stored in a[i]. Hence, the value of variable min will represent the minimum element of the array at the end of the for loop.

In our example, we have assumed number of elements in the array as 4 and hence we need to perform the following comparisons to find the minimum element in the array. In this case, the for loop will have following three iterations:

Iteration 1: Compare min with a[1]
The initial value of variable min is 70 (which is a[0]), whereas the value of a[1] is 40. Hence, the value of variable min is greater than a[1]. Therefore, the value stored in variable min cannot be the minimum value because at least one element of the array, specifically a[1], is having a value lesser than min. Hence, we set the new value of variable min as value of a[1], which overwrites min to 40 at the end of first iteration of the loop as shown in Figure 6.13.

Iteration 2: Compare min with a[2]
Similarly, we now compare the current value of min with a[2] as shown in Figure 6.14. In this iteration, we will again overwrite the value of variable min with the value of a[2] because the current value of min (which is 40) is greater than the value of a[2] (which is 35).

Iteration 3: Compare min with a[3]
The current value of variable min is 35, whereas the value of a[3] is 65. Hence, the value of variable min is less than a[3]. Therefore, we understand that the value stored in

Iteration 1

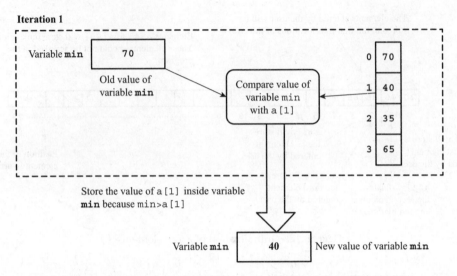

Figure 6.13: Iteration 1 to find minimum element from the array

Iteration 2

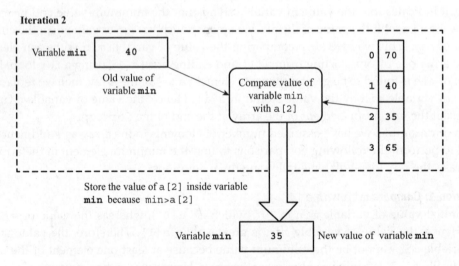

Figure 6.14: Iteration 2 to find minimum element from the array

variable a [3] cannot be the minimum and hence we do not change the value of variable min. The value of min is unaffected at this iteration and will remain 35, as shown in Figure 6.15.

There can be no more iterations as we have reached the end of array. As seen, the logic works fine and the value of variable min is set to 35 at the end of last iteration which is indeed the minimum value in the array. Hence, at the end of the loop the program simply prints the value of variable min because it is guaranteed to store the minimum value within the array.

Iteration 3

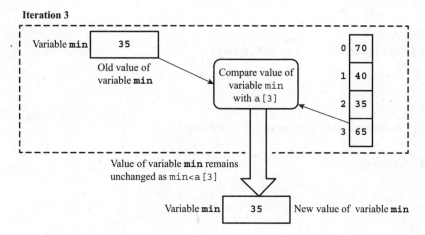

Figure 6.15: Iteration 3 to find minimum element from the array

NOTES

The **ith iteration** of the loop compares the value of min with value of a[i] and replaces min with a[i] only if current value of min is greater than a[i]. This way, at the end of all iterations, the program is guaranteed to store the minimum value within the array in variable min.

Given below is the complete source code to find minimum element of the array:

```
#include<stdio.h>
void main()
{
 int n,i,min;
 int a[100];
 printf("How many numbers do you want to enter? \n");
 scanf("%d",&n);
 printf("Enter %d numbers\n",n);
 for(i=0;i<=n-1;i++)
 {
  scanf("%d",&a[i]);
 }
min=a[0]; /*set the initial value of min as a[0]*/
for(i=0;i<=n-1;i++)
 {
  if(min>a[i])
  {
   min=a[i];
```

```
    }
  }
  printf("Minimum is : %d \n",min);
}
```

Output:

```
How many numbers do you want to enter?
4
Enter 4 numbers
70
40
35
65
Minimum is : 35
```

NOTES

Similarly, we can create a program to find **maximum element in the array** by defining variable (say max) which initially stores the value of a [0]

```
max=a[0]; /* set the initial value of max as a[0] */
```

We can compare value of max with each element of the array one by one starting from a [1] and ending at a [n-1] using a for loop as we did before. The only difference is that **max** should be replaced with a [i] only when the current value in max is **less than** a [i], as shown below

```
for(i=0; i<=n-1;i++)
  {
    if(max<a[i])
    {
      max=a[i];
    }
  }
```

With similar illustrations, we can prove that variable max will contain the maximum value in the array after the loop completes.

6.2.5 Program to arrange n numbers in ascending order: An example

Let us create a program that accepts n numbers as input from the user and arranges them in ascending order. As discussed in section 6.2.4, we will define an integer array a of size 100 and create a program with an assumption that the value of n is always less than or equal to 100. After accepting n elements as input from the user using the for loop, we start the process to sort the n elements.

Let us assume that the five values (user inputs) to be sorted are 15, 12, 19, 17 and 6 which will be stored at a[0], a[1], a[2], a[3] and a[4], respectively, as shown in Figure 6.16.

For simplifying the explanation, we will refer the element at lower index as a number above in the array and the element at higher index as a number below in the array. This means that element a[0] is present above a[1], element a[1] is present above a[2] and so on, as seen from Figure 6.16. In general, every element a[i] is to be considered above a[j], if i < j. The requirement of ascending order is that a number above in the array must not be greater than the number below in the array; this means that any number a[i] must not be greater than number a[j], if i < j. Hence, if we get a number a[i] which is greater than a[j] we swap the numbers a[i] and a[j] so that a[i] now becomes less than a[j].

The algorithm of sorting compares a number above with all the numbers below it. This means that the element at position 0 in the array will be compared with elements at position 1, 2, 3 and 4, whereas the element at position 1 in the array will be compared with elements at positions 2, 3 and 4 and so on. The complete comparison chart is as shown in Figure 6.17.

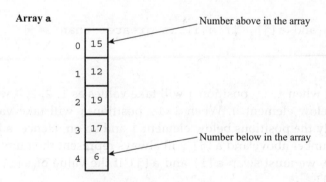

Figure 6.16: Integer array a

Element above (a[i])	All elements a[j] to be compared with element a[i], such that a[j] is below a[i]
a[0]	a[1], a[2], a[3], a[4]
a[1]	a[2], a[3], a[4]
a[2]	a[3], a[4]
a[3]	a[4]

Figure 6.17: Comparison chart

Let the variable i always represent the index of number above in the array and let variable j represent the index of number below in the array. As i needs to represent all the positions in the array which are **above** at least one element, the range of i will be from **0 to n-2**. Note that variable i has a maximum limit as n-2 because the last number is at position n-1 and the last number is not above any element of the array. Similarly, as j needs to represent all the positions in the array which are **below** at least one element, the range of variable j will be from **i+1 to n-1**. Note that the starting index of j is i+1 because variable j should always represent a position which is below the position represented by i. Hence, if i=0 then j should be 1 and if i is 1 then j should be 2 and so on. From these points, we clearly understand that variables i and j are position indicators in the array a such that i always represents the position of number above and j always represents the position of number below. We also understand from the comparison chart that an element above in the array is compared with all the elements below it and hence we organize the for loops for i and j as shown below:

```
for(i=0;i<=n-2;i++)
{
    for(j=i+1;j<=n-1;j++)
    {
    swap a[i] and a[j], if a[i] is greater than a[j]
    }
}
```

This means that when i=0, position j will take values as 1, 2, 3, 4 which are clearly the positions below element 0. When i=1, position j will take values as 2, 3, 4 which are clearly the positions below element 1 and so on. Hence, a[i] will always represent the number above and a[j] will always represent the number below in the array. Therefore, we must swap a[i] and a[j] if the value of a[i] is greater than the value of a[j].

The complete working of sorting algorithm for n=5 is as given in Figure 6.18:

Given below is the full source code to arrange n numbers in ascending order:

```
#include<stdio.h>
void main()
{
 int n,i,t,j;
 printf("How many numbers you want to enter ?\n");
 scanf("%d",&n);
 int a[100];
 printf("Enter %d numbers:\n",n);
 for(i=0;i<=n-1;i++)
 {
  scanf("%d",&a[i]);
 }
```

```
for(i=0;i<=n-2;i++)
{
  for(j=i+1;j<=n-1;j++)
  {
   if(a[i]>a[j])
   {
     /* Swap the 2 numbers */
     t=a[i];
     a[i]=a[j];
     a[j]=t;
   }
  }
}
printf("Ascending order is: \n");
for(i=0;i<=n-1;i++)
{
  printf("%d\n",a[i]);
}
}
```

Output:

```
How many numbers you want to enter ?
5
Enter 5 numbers:
15 12 19 17 6
Ascending order is:
6
12
15
17
19
```

> **What is the change that I can make in this program to arrange numbers in descending order, instead of ascending?** ?
>
> The program is arranging the numbers in ascending order because we are swapping the values of a[i] and a[j], if value of a[i] is greater than value of a[j]. As a[i] represents the number at a lower index in the array and a[j] represents the number at a higher index in the array, the swapping process ensures that the number at lower index is always less than number at higher index; thereby arranging the array in ascending order. In case of descending order we want the number at lower index of the array to be always greater than the number at higher index of the array. Hence we would swap a[i] and a[j] if a[i] is less than a[j] to arrange numbers in descending order. Therefore the only change that must be applied to the given program to arrange the numbers in descending order is that the condition in the if block responsible for swapping must now be specified as a[i]<a[j].

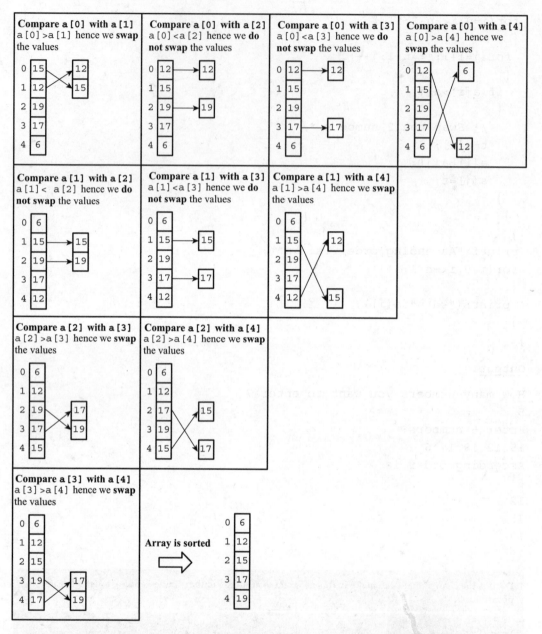

Figure 6.18: Sorting process

6.3 Array of Characters

Similar to any other type of array, we can create an array of characters as shown below:

```
char array_name[size];
```

For instance, let us create an array of characters named as a with a size 8 as shown below:

```
char a[8];
```

This means that the first element of the array can be accessed as a[0], the second element of the array can be accessed as a[1] and so on. The last element of the array can be accessed as a[7]. Also, every element of the array a will be of type character and it can be initialized using the following statements:

```
a[0] = 'c';
a[1] = 'o';
a[2] = 'm';
a[3] = 'p';
a[4] = 'u';
a[5] = 't';
a[6] = 'e';
a[7] = 'r';
```

Figure 6.19 shows the structure of array a in computer memory.

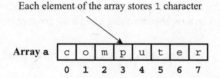

Figure 6.19: Initialization of a character array

The elements of the array can now be individually processed in the program similar to any other array.

C/C++ also supports an **alternative approach** to initialize array of characters as a **string** constant. A string constant is always surrounded in double quotes. For example, following is the valid notation to create a string constant:

```
"computer"
```

We can directly initialize a character array a with a string constant as shown in the statement below. In this case, there is no need to specify size of the array a explicitly because compiler derives the size of the array as **the number of characters in the string + 1**. This is because in the case of **string** initialization the end of the string is marked by the compiler by adding an additional character called NULL CHARACTER ('\0') as last character of the array, as shown in Figure 6.20.

```
char a[] = "computer";
```

This means that a[0] will be initialized to character value 'c', a[1] will be initialized to character value 'o' and so on, as shown in Figure 6.20.

Each element of the array stores 1 character

Array a | c | o | m | p | u | t | e | r | \0 |
        | 0 | 1 | 2 | 3 | 4 | 5 | 6 | 7 | 8 |

A string always ends with a NULL character \0

Figure 6.20: String initialization

CAUTION

Directly initializing an array of characters using a string constant is possible only at the time of creating an array. For example, the following approach will not work.

```
char a[9];
a ="computer"; /*Error cannot apply string initialization after creation
of an array*/
```

NOTES

If you need to, you can always specify the size of character array explicitly even if you are initializing it with string constant. For example, the following statement will work well

```
char a[9] ="computer";
```

But note that you have to specify the size as **number of characters in the string+1**. Remember additional space of 1 character is consumed for storing NULL character (\0) at the end. Anyways, C/C++ does not make it mandatory for the programmer to specify the size of an array when initializing it with string constant. Hence best is not to specify the size as shown below

```
char a[] ="computer"; /*Specifying size is optional for string
initialization*/
```

NOTES

Figure 6.19 shows character by character initialization of an array a. In this case, \0 will not be added automatically because we are initializing each of the array elements individually. Whereas, Figure 6.20 shows a string initialization of array a, where the compiler automatically adds a NULL character at the end of the array. Hence the size of the array shown in Figure 6.20 is one byte more than the size of the array in Figure 6.19, although the data contents in both the cases are exactly the same.

As a NULL character is automatically added as an end of string marker in the case of string initialization, Input/Output functions can correctly identify the position where the string ends. Hence, if we want to print the complete character array a we can write a single printf() statement as shown below:

printf("%s",a);

This statement will print all the characters stored in the array a from the first character up to the NULL character. Hence, the output of the **printf()** statement will be as shown below:

computer

Remember that \0 does not appear at the output because it is an internal escape sequence used by the language. Such a direct Input/Output is not possible with any other type of array because C/C++ adds an end marker only with strings. Similar to direct output we can also take a string value to be initialized to an array of characters directly as input from the user. The code below creates a character array b and illustrates the usage of direct Input/Output with the character array.

```
#include<stdio.h>
void main()
{
char b[100];
printf("Enter a String:\n");
scanf("%s",b);
printf("String is %s \n",b);
}
```

NOTES

Format specifier **%s** is used while inputting or outputting a string. In this case, we are using %s because b is a string type to be taken as input from the user and printed on the computer screen. Needless to say that, if you use pure C++ object oriented style of input and output (using `cin` and `cout` statements) you need not specify any of the format specifiers. Hence the above program can be rewritten using `cin` and `cout` statements without using any of the format specifiers as shown below.

```
#include<iostream.h>
void main()
{
char b[100];
cout<<"Enter a String:"<<endl;
cin>>b;
cout<<"String is "<<b<<endl;
}
```

Recall from Chapter 2 that we must include `iostream.h` when using objects `cin` and `cout`. Also we can use modifier `endl` instead of `\n` to transfer the cursor to the new line as mentioned in Chapter 2.

The first statement

```
char b[100];
```

creates an array of characters b of size 100 as shown in Figure 6.21.

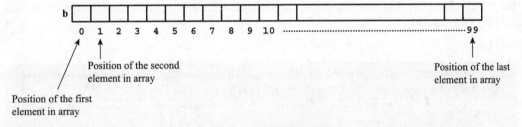

Figure 6.21: Creating an array b

We can directly take the string to be stored inside an array b as input from the user using a statement

```
scanf("%s",b);
```

because C/C++ supports direct input and output operations with an array of characters. Note that there is no need to specify ampersand symbol in `scanf()` statement while taking a string as input from the user. This is because strings in C/C++ are self-addressable. We will revisit the concept of self-addressability in Chapter 7 so do not worry about it right now, but for now just remember not to specify ampersand symbol when inputting strings using scanf() statement.

Let us assume that the user inputs a string as Hello, this will be stored in array b starting from position 0 as shown in Figure 6.22. Also, note that an end of the string marker '\0' (NULL character) will be automatically stored at position 5 of the array to represent the end, because this is a string input done using %s, as shown in Figure 6.22.

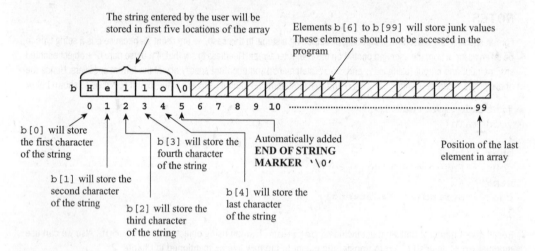

Figure 6.22: Direct input of character array b

The statement

```
printf("String is %s \n",b);
```

will print all the characters in string b from position 0 up to the NULL character. Note that the NULL character will not appear at the output. Hence, output on the computer screen will be as follows:

```
Hello
```

What is the advantage of NULL character getting added at the end of the string? ?

We know that NULL character is added to an array when we input the array in string mode (using %s) or when we directly initialize it using a string constant.

One of the advantages of NULL character is that we can perform direct Input and Output operations with the array, due to its presence. When we perform direct input or direct initialization of an array with a string constant, C/C++ automatically adds \0 at the end of the string. And, when we print an array (say a) using the statement,

```
printf("%s",a);
```

This will print all the valid elements of the array because the printf() function knows the exact point when the string ends due to the presence of \0.

6.3.1 Calculating length of a string: An example

Length of the string is defined as the number of characters present in the string. As an example, let us create a program that accepts a string as input from the user and calculates its length. For example, if user inputs a string as hat, then the program should calculate the length of the string as 3. Note that, the NULL character which is just the end of string marker should not be counted in calculation of length. As a first step, let us accept a string as input from the user and store it in the character array a. Recall from section 6.3 that the character array can be directly taken as input from the user, which means that we can directly write a statement **scanf("%s",a);** to take a string as input, and store it in array a. Also, similar to all the other examples, we create a character array of size 100, assuming that the user will not input a string whose length is greater than 100. The piece of code which creates a character array a and accepts a string as input from the user is as shown below:

```
char a[100];
printf("Enter String\n");
scanf("%s",a);
```

Let us assume that the user inputs a string value as hat, then the first 3 characters of the array a[0], a[1] and a[2] will be initialized to characters 'h', 'a' and 't', respectively, as shown in Figure 6.23. Note that the NULL character will be automatically stored at a[3] as shown in Figure 6.23.

Once all the array elements are initialized, we can start calculating the length of the string using an integer variable len as seen in the code. The initial value len is set to zero because we will be using it as a counter to count the number of valid characters in the array a.

Figure 6.23: Initialization of the array

```
int len=0;
```

The counting logic to count the number of valid characters can be implemented by comparing each character in a with the NULL character. We will search '\0' in array a starting from position 0 and till the time we do not get the NULL character we will keep incrementing the value of len using the statement

```
len++;
```

inside the loop. As the initial value of variable len is set to zero, its value will be incremented exactly till the time array a contains valid characters and hence len will store the length of the string at the end of the program. We can implement this logic using a simple for loop as shown below:

```
for(i=0;a[i]!='\0';i++)
{
    len++;
}
```

The for loop starts with setting initial value of variable i as 0 and hence it initially compares a[0] with '\0'. As the value of a[0] is h (which is not '\0') the control of execution is transferred inside the for loop, thereby incrementing the value of len as shown in Figure 6.24. After first iteration of the loop, the value of index variable i is

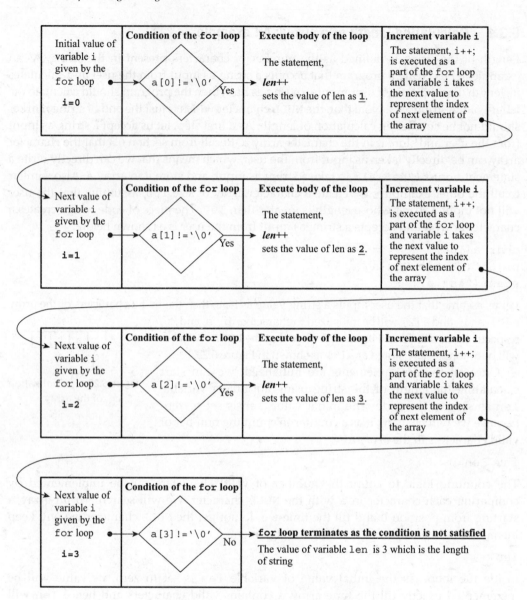

Figure 6.24: Calculating length of string

incremented to 1 to compare the next character stored in a[1] with '\0'; the execution of the for loop proceeds similarly for all the subsequent iterations. Note that the for loop terminates when the value of variable i is 4 because a[4] is storing '\0' and hence the value of variable len is incremented exactly three times as shown in Figure 6.24. Therefore, the value of len will always reflect the length of the string in a. In this case, variable len is set to 3 at the end of the loop because there are three characters in the string hat.

The complete source code to determine the length of the string is as given below:

```
#include<stdio.h>
void main()
{
 int len=0,i;
 char a[100];
 printf("Enter a String\n");
 scanf("%s",a);
 for(i=0;a[i]!='\0';i++)
 {
  len++;
 }
 printf("Length is: %d\n",len);
}
```

Output

```
Enter a String
hat
Length is: 3
```

NOTES

In the given program variables i and len are redundant. The only statement in the body of the for loop is

```
len++;
```

The loop anyways does i++ before going to the next iteration. Since the initial values of len and i are set to 0, the value of variable len will be exactly same as value of variable i when the loop terminates. In fact both the values i and len walk together. As seen in the Figure 6.24, when the loop terminates i and len both a have a value 3. This means that, with the presence of loop which anyways increment i, there is no need to define variable len at the first place. If we do not define len, there is really nothing to write in the body of the loop and hence we can convert this loop into an **empty loop**. As explained in Chapter 5 Section 5.9 an empty loop is a loop which has iterations but no body. We can write empty loop by putting a semi column at the end as shown below

```
for(i=0;a[i]!='\0';i++);
```

This loop will still have three iterations and the loop terminates when i=3 because a[3]='\0'. Hence the variable i itself contains the length of the string. Given below is the full source which gives an alternative approach to compute the length of string using an empty loop thereby avoiding creation of an additional variable len.

```
#include<stdio.h>
void main()
{
int i;
char a[100];
printf("Enter a String\n");
scanf("%s",a);
for(i=0;a[i]!='\0';i++); /* Empty loop */
printf("Length is: %d\n",i); /* variable i contains the length */
}
```

6.3.2 Program to compute reverse of a string: An example

Let us create a program to accept a string as input from the user and to compute its reverse. For example, if user inputs a string as `hello`, then the program should compute the reverse as `olleh`. We create two arrays a and b such that array a will store the original string entered by the user and array b to store the reverse. As with all the other examples, we create character arrays a and b of size 100 assuming that user will not input any string with length greater than 100. We accept the string a as input from the user using the statements shown below:

```
char a[100],b[100];
printf("Enter String\n");
scanf("%s",a);
```

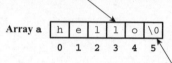

Let us assume that the user enters a string value as `hello`; then the array a will be initialized as shown in Figure 6.25.

A string always ends with a NULL character \0

Figure 6.25: Initialization of array a

Now, we need to calculate the reverse of array a and store it in array b. This means that a[4] must be copied to b[0], a[3] must be copied to b[1] and so on. Figure 6.26 gives the complete set of copy operations required to store the reverse of array a and in array b. Note that the NULL character should always be present as the last character of both the strings a and b as shown in Figure 6.26.

We perform these copy operations using a for loop that copies each character in array a at an appropriate position in array b. Obviously, this means that the array a must be read in reverse direction and the array b must be written in forward direction by the loop. Hence, the index of array a must start from the position of last character and should traverse it in the reverse order, whereas the index of array b must start from first position and traverse it in the forward direction. Let variable k represent the position of last character in array a. Note that if length of the string stored in an array is 5, then the position of last character is 4 as seen from Figure 6.26; in general, if length of array a is len then the position of last character in array a is len-1. Hence, we initialize the initial value of variable k as shown below:

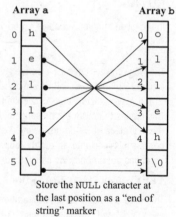

Store the NULL character at the last position as a "end of string" marker

Figure 6.26: Calculating reverse of the string

```
int k= len-1; /*k is the position of last character in array a*/
```

It is clear that to determine the position of last character in string a we need to calculate length of a. Length of a string a can be easily calculated as discussed in Section 6.3.1. Also, let variable i represent the index of array b and hence the initial value of variable i must be set to zero as we need to initially write to the first location in array b. As the index position k must move in reverse direction the for loop must perform **k--;** after each iteration.

Also, the index position i must move in forward direction and hence the for loop must perform **i++;** after each iteration. In each iteration, the loop copies the value of a[k] to b[i] as shown below:

```
for(i=0;k>=0;i++) /*increment i*/
{
  b[i]=a[k]; /*Copy a[k] to b[i]*/
  k--; /*decrement k*/
}
```

Figure 6.27 shows the detailed execution of the for loop that performs the copy operation.

As the index k starts from len-1 and decrements towards zero, the NULL character in array a is not copied in array b because the NULL character is present at position len which is after the last character in array a. Hence, we copy the NULL character explicitly as a last character of array b using the statement

```
b[len] = '\0';
```

after the for loop completes, as seen in the code.

The complete source code to calculate the reverse of the string is as given below:

```
#include<stdio.h>
void main()
{
 int len=0,i,k;
 char a[100],b[100];
 printf("Enter a String:\n");
 scanf("%s",a);
   for(i=0;a[i]!='\0';i++)
   {
    len++;
   }
 k=len-1;
   for(i=0;k>=0;i++)
   {
    b[i]=a[k];
    k--;
   }
 b[len] = '\0';
 printf("Reverse is: %s\n",b);
}
```

Output
```
Enter a String:
hello
Reverse is: olleh
```

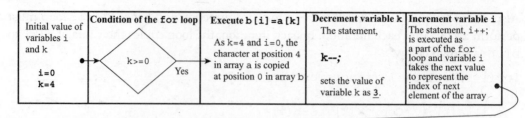

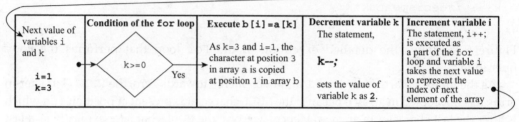

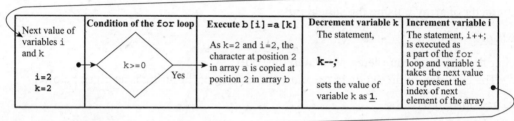

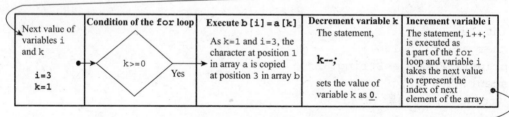

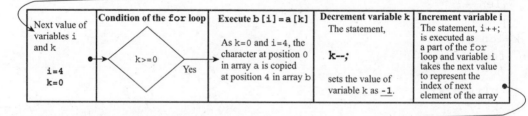

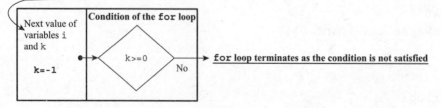

Figure 6.27: Execution of `for` loop

6.3.3 Program to check if the string is palindrome or not: An example

Let us create a program to accept a string as input from the user and check if it is a palindrome or not. A string is said to be a palindrome if the reverse of the string is same as the original string. For example, consider string mom its reverse is same as itself and hence the string is a palindrome. So, a program to check if the input string is palindrome or not must perform following steps:

- Take the string as input from the user and store it in array a.
- Calculate the length of the input string and store the length in variable len.
- Compute the reverse of array a and store the reverse string in array b.
- Check if original array a is exactly the same as the reverse array b. If this is the case, then we can conclude that the input string is a palindrome.

The first three steps will be implemented exactly in the same way as that of the previous examples. Hence, we start our explanation assuming that the array a contains the original string and the array b contains its reverse. Therefore, we now need to only check if each character in array a is exactly the same as the corresponding character in array b and if this is the case then we can conclude that the reverse of the string is same as the original string. To implement this comparison between two arrays, we need to compare character at a[0] with character at b[0] and if they are equal, then we can move ahead and compare character at a[1] with character at b[1] and so on. This means that we compare each character a[i] with the corresponding character b[i] till the end of the string as shown in Figure 6.28.

If any of the character in an array a is not equal to the corresponding character in array b, then we can immediately terminate the for loop using a break statement and conclude that the string is 'not a palindrome'. This means that if all the characters in a are exactly the same as all the characters in b, then the break statement will never be executed and the for loop will execute normally till the end of the string. This means that, we come out of the for loop in two specific cases.

Case 1: A character at position i in array a does not match with a corresponding character at position i in array b. This means that the string is not a palindrome and hence the break statement will be executed which transfers the control outside the for loop.

Case 2: All the characters in the array a are exactly same as corresponding characters in array b. This means that the string is a palindrome. Hence the control will be transferred outside for loop after all the characters are successfully compared.

Therefore, we need to determine the exact reason of why the control is transferred outside for loop. Hence, we create a variable flag with initial value as 0 and it will be set to 1 if break statement is executed. Therefore, if the value of variable flag is 1 it indicates that the control is transferred outside for loop because of the break statement and hence we can conclude that the string is not a palindrome when flag is set to 1. Further, if value of flag is zero after the for loop is completed, it indicates that the break statement was never executed within the for loop (and hence flag is retained as zero) which indicates that the string is palindrome.

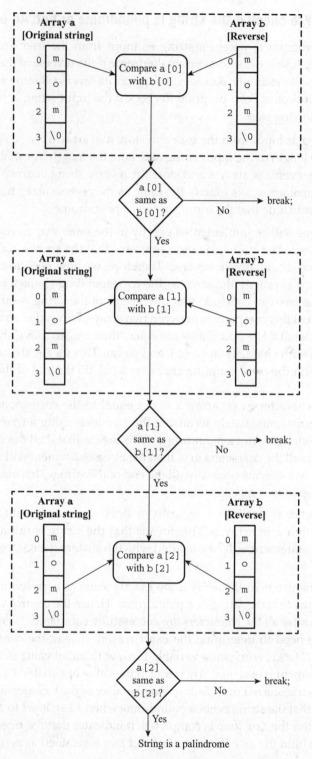

Figure 6.28: Comparisons needed to check if string in array a is same as that of string in array b

Given below is the full source code to check if the string is palindrome or not.

```c
#include<stdio.h>
void main()
{
 int len=0,i,k,flag=0;
 char a[100],b[100];
printf("Enter a string:");
scanf("%s",a);
   for(i=0;a[i]!='\0';i++)
   {
     len++;
   }
 k=len-1;
   for(i=0;k>=0;i++)
   {
     b[i]=a[k];
     k--;
   }
 b[len]='\0';
   for(i=0;a[i]!='\0';i++)
   {
     if(a[i]!=b[i])
     {
       flag=1;
       break;
     }
   }
   if(flag==0)
   {
     printf("The string is a Palindrome\n");
   }
   else
   {
     printf("The string is not a Palindrome\n");
   }
}
```

Output:

```
Enter a string: MOM
The string is a Palindrome
```

In this program we have applied a character by character comparison, to compare a string in array a with the string in array b. Can't we directly compare the complete array a with b using condition a==b? ?

Array is a collection of multiple characters. Hence, in order to determine if one collection is exactly same as the other, we need to compare each character in a with corresponding character in b as seen in the program. Operators in C/C++ work with primitive types like integer, float, character, double, etc., but they cannot work with collection types like arrays. Hence the program applies character by character comparison to check if both the arrays a and b are exactly same.

6.4 2D Arrays

Unlike a one-dimensional (1D) array which is organized as a vector, a two-dimensional (2D) array is organized as a matrix of rows and columns. The following statement creates an integer type matrix a of 3 rows and 4 columns as shown in Figure 6.29.

```
int a[3][4];
```

In general, if the matrix has r rows and c columns the rows will be numbered as 0 to r-1 and columns will be numbered as 0 to c-1 as shown in Figure 6.29.

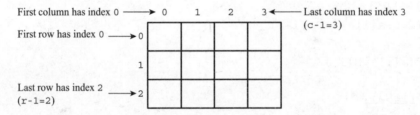

Figure 6.29: Matrix a of 3 rows and 4 columns

The individual elements of the matrix can be accessed by giving the row number and column number along with the array name. That is, the element at $(i+1)^{th}$ row and $(j+1)^{th}$ column can be accessed as a[i][j] in the program. As we have created an array of 3 rows and 4 columns, the row numbers range from 0 to 2 and column numbers range from 0 to 3. Hence, the element at first row and first column can be accessed as a[0][0], the element at third row and fourth column can be accessed as a[2][3], element at second row and first column can be accessed as a[1][0] and so on. Therefore, each element of array a can now be initialized as follows:

```
/*Initialize the element at row number 0 and column number 0*/
a[0][0]=10;
/*Initialize the element at row number 0 and column number 1*/
a[0][1]=20;
```

Similarly, every element of the array can be initialized in the program as shown in Figure 6.30.

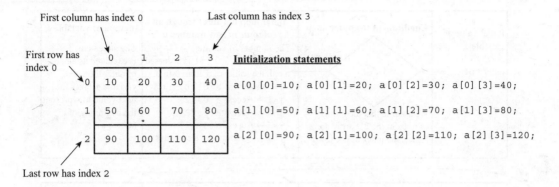

Figure 6.30: Initialization of the array a

We can also perform direct initialization of a 2D array using the following syntax:

```
<data_type> array_name [NumberOfRows] [NumberOfColumns] = {
                                        {first row},
                                        {second row},
                                        ...
                                        {last row}
                                        };
```

This means that instead of writing individual initialization statements for an array a as seen in Figure 6.30, we can also initialize the array with 3 rows and 4 columns as shown below:

```
int a[3][4] = {
              {10,20,30,40},
              {50,60,70,80},
              {90,100,110,120}
              };
```

Hence, the above statement is shorthand syntax when compared to the statements shown in Figure 6.30 and it will create an exactly similar array with the identical values. However, it is important to note that such a direct initialization can only be applied to an array at the time of declaration. We cannot apply such an initialization any time later in the program after the declaration statement is completed.

We can also access every element of a 2D array in a **loop** because an array with r rows and c columns will have row numbers ordered in a range from 0 to r-1 and column numbers ordered in a range from 0 to c-1. This means that to print all the values stored in a particular row we need to iterate over each of the columns number 0 to c-1 in that row. Figure 6.31 shows the process to access every element of a 2D array a using for loop. As the array a has 3 rows and hence the row for loop ranges from 0 to 2. Also, each row has 4 columns; this means that to access the values stored in the single row we need to iterate over all the column indexes from 0 to 3.

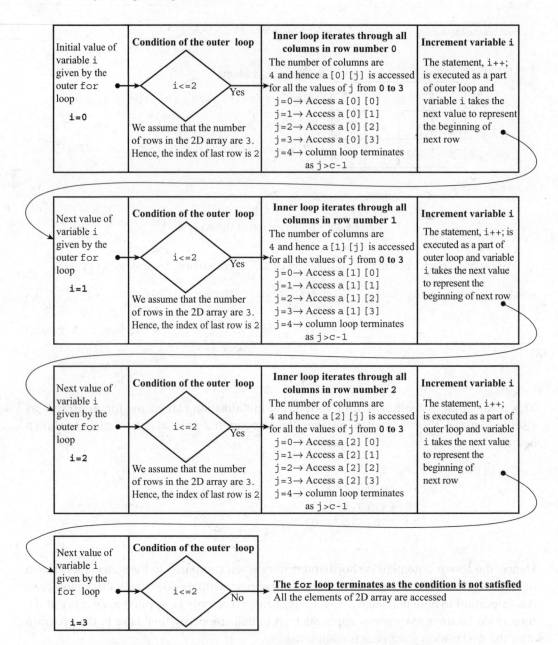

Figure 6.31: Execution of `for` loops to access all elements of 2D array

Let variable `i` represent the current value of the row number and variable `j` represent the current value of column number then to access the complete i^{th} row, `j` should range from 0 to `c-1` as shown in the code below.

```
for(i=0;i<=r-1;i++)
{
    for(j=0;j<=c-1;j++)
```

```
    {
    /*Process element a[i][j]*/
    }
}
```

We now implement this set of `for` loops to print all the elements of array a which has 3 rows and 4 columns as shown below:

```
for(i=0;i<=2;i++)
{
    for(j=0;j<=3;j++)
        {
        printf("%d",a[i][j]);
        }
printf("\n");
}
```

The initial value of variable i will be set to 0 by the outer `for` loop, and the inner `for` loop will start executing for different values of j from 0 to 3. At each iteration of the inner `for` loop, the element a[i][j] will be accessed as shown in Figure 6.31. Note the presence of the statement `printf("\n");` after the end of inner `for` loop which will transfer the cursor onto the new line when all the elements of the current row are completed.

6.4.1 Addition of two matrices: An example

As an example, let us create a program to accept two matrices a and b as input from the user and perform their addition, storing the result in another matrix named Res. We know that addition of two matrices can be performed if and only if they have the same order. Hence, we define each matrix with r rows and c columns, respectively. As we need to take the matrices a and b as input from the user, we take the number of rows (value of r) and number of columns (value of c) also as input from the user so that the program can perform the addition of matrices with any order. Also, because we do not know the row and column dimensions of the matrix at the time of compilation of the program, we create the matrices a, b and Res with 100 rows and 100 columns, assuming that the order of the matrix will not be higher than 100 rows and 100 columns at run time.

```
int a[100][100],b[100][100],Res[100][100];
```

We now take the number of rows (r) and number of columns (c) as input from the user to determine the order of each matrix. Once the values of r and c are known, we can now take each element of matrix as input from the user by ranging row number i from 0 to r-1 and column number j from 0 to c-1 as shown below:

```
for(i=0;i<=r-1;i++)
{
    for(j=0;j<=c-1;j++)
        {
```

```
/*Accept each element of matrix as input from the user*/
}
```

```
}
```

Let us assume that the user enters the number of rows as 3 and number of columns also as 3. Also, let us also assume that the user enters the values for each of the matrix elements a and b as shown in Figure 6.32.

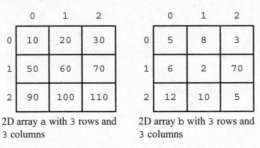

2D array a with 3 rows and 3 columns

2D array b with 3 rows and 3 columns

Figure 6.32: Matrices a and b

After the values of matrices a and b are taken as input from the user, we can now start performing addition to obtain the resultant matrix Res. The element at i^{th} row and j^{th} column of matrix Res will be evaluated as the addition of element at i^{th} row and j^{th} column in matrix a with the element at i^{th} row and j^{th} column in matrix b. For example, the element Res[0][0] is to be evaluated as shown below:

Res[0][0]=a[0][0]+b[0][0];

Similarly, for each value of row number i and column number j we evaluate Res[i][j] inside a for loop as follows:

Res[i][j]=a[i][j]+b[i][j];

The last set of for loops print each element stored in the resultant matrix Res which is shown in Figure 6.33:

	0	1	2
0	15	28	33
1	56	62	140
2	102	110	115

2D array Res with 3 rows and 3 columns
storing the result of addition of two matrices

Figure 6.33: Result of addition of matrices a and b

Given below is the source code to perform addition of matrices:

```
#include<stdio.h>
void main()
{
```

```
int r,c,i,j;
printf("Enter the order of the matrix ");
scanf("%d%d",&r,&c);
int a[100][100],b[100][100], Res[100][100];
printf("Enter Matrix a\n");
 for(i=0;i<=r-1;i++)
 {
  for(j=0;j<=c-1;j++)
  {
   scanf("%d",&a[i][j]);
  }
 }
printf("Enter Matrix b\n");
 for(i=0;i<=r-1;i++)
 {
  for(j=0;j<=c-1;j++)
  {
    scanf("%d",&b[i][j]);
  }
 }
/*perform addition*/
printf("Addition is \n");
 for(i=0;i<=r-1;i++)
 {
  for(j=0;j<=c-1;j++)
  {
   Res[i][j]=a[i][j]+b[i][j];
   printf("%d",Res[i][j]);
  }
 printf("\n");
 }
}/*end of main*/
```

Output:

```
Enter the order of the matrix 2 2
Enter Matrix a
10 20
25 15
Enter Matrix b
5    6
10   5
Addition is
15   26
35   20
```

6.4.2 Program to perform multiplication of matrix: An example

As an example, let us write a program to take two matrices a and b as input from the user and perform the multiplication of a and b, storing the result in another matrix Res. Let the matrix a have r1 rows and c1 columns and matrix b have r2 rows and c2 columns. Also, we know that the multiplication of two matrices can only be performed if number of columns in the first matrix is same as the number of rows in the second matrix. Hence, we perform the multiplication of the matrices only if the value of c1 is same as r2 as shown in the code. Before starting the multiplication process, we take the matrix a with r1 rows and c1 columns and matrix b with r2 rows and c2 columns as input from the user as seen in the code.

Let us assume that the matrices a and b are of order 3X3 and the user enters the following values in each of the matrices as shown in Figure 6.34.

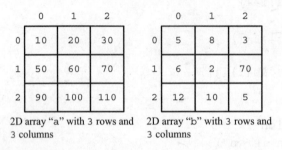

2D array "a" with 3 rows and 3 columns   2D array "b" with 3 rows and 3 columns

Figure 6.34: User input data for two matrices

Also, we know that if matrix a is of order r1Xc1 and matrix b is of order r1Xc2, then the order of resultant matrix Res which is the multiplication of a and b will be r1Xc2. Hence, the Res matrix is always iterated for 0 to r1-1 rows and 0 to c2-1 columns as shown in Figure 6.35.

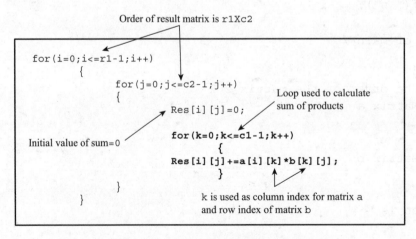

Figure 6.35: Multiplication of matrices

To understand the process of multiplication, let us evaluate the value `Res[0][0]` which is the first element of the resultant matrix. The value `Res[0][0]` will be evaluated as follows:

`Res[0][0] = a[0][0]*b[0][0] + a[0][1]*b[1][0] + a[0][2]*b[2][0];`

Substituting the values from Figure 6.34, we have

`Res[0][0] = 10*5 + 20*6 + 30*12`
`Res[0][0] = 5400`

Hence, for element at i^{th} row and j^{th} column, we can evaluate `Res[i][j]` as

`Res[i][j] = a[i][0]*b[0][j] + a[i][1]*b[1][j] + a[i][2]*b[2][j];`

Note that while calculating the sum of products the column number of the first matrix a is 0 in the first term, 1 in the second term and 2 in the third term. Similarly, the row number for the second matrix b is 0 in the first term, 1 in the second term and 2 in the third term. Also, the column number of first matrix/row number of second matrix ranges from 0 to 2 while calculating the sum of products. Hence, we have the innermost `for` loop that runs for the values of `k = 0, k = 1` and `k = 2` which iterate over columns of first matrix and rows of second matrix. The `for` loop for variable k must run exactly three times because the number of rows in the second matrix are 3 (which is also same as number of columns in the first matrix). Hence, the innermost `for` loop that increments the column number of first matrix/row number of second matrix using a variable k is as shown in Figure 6.35.

The complete source code to perform matrix multiplication is as shown below:

```c
#include<stdio.h>
void main()
{
 int a[100][100],b[100][100], Res[100][100];
 int r1,c1,r2,c2,i,j,k;
 printf("Enter the order of the matrix a ");
 scanf("%d%d",&r1,&c1);
 printf("Enter the order of the matrix b ");
 scanf("%d%d",&r2,&c2);
 if(c1==r2)
 {
  printf("Enter Matrix a\n");
  for(i=0;i<=r1-1;i++)
  {
   for(j=0;j<=c1-1;j++)
   {
    scanf("%d",&a[i][j]);
   }
```

```
    }
    printf("Enter Matrix b\n");;
    for(i=0;i<=r2-1;i++)
    {
      for(j=0;j<=c2-1;j++)
      {
      scanf("%d",&b[i][j]);
      }
    }
/*perform multiplication*/
printf("Multiplication is\n");
for(i=0;i<=r1-1;i++)
        {
                for(j=0;j<=c2-1;j++)
                {
                        Res[i][j]=0;
                            for(k=0;k<=c1-1;k++)
                            {
                                Res[i][j]+=a[i][k]*b[k][j];
                            }
                    printf("%d ",Res[i][j]);
                    }
            printf("\n");
        }
    }
    else
    {
    printf("Multiplication is not possible\n");
    }
}/*end of main*/
```

Output:
```
Enter the order of the matrix a 2 2
Enter the order of the matrix b 2 2
Enter Matrix a
10 2
1  0
Enter Matrix b
5    6
10   5
Multiplication is
70   70
5    6
```

6.5   2D Array of Characters

Similar to any other 2D array, we can also create a 2D array of characters. For example, the statement

```
char a[3][4];
```

creates a 2D array of characters with 3 rows and 4 columns. The array can be initialized character by character as shown in Figure 6.36. Note that we have stored NULL character \0 in each of the rows explicitly because C/C++ does not add \0 automatically in the case of character-by-character initialization.

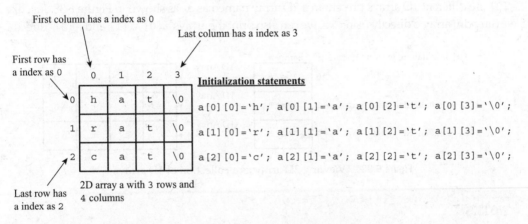

Figure 6.36:   Character-by-character initialization of a 2D array

As explained in section 6.3, an array of characters is also called a **string** when it is terminated by \0. The advantage of strings is that we can perform direct input and output operations with strings. As seen in Figure 6.36, each row in the 2D array a is terminated by \0 and hence we can view a 2D array a as an array storing 3 strings (instead of viewing it as an array of 12 different characters).

Let us compare the structure in Figure 6.36 with a single 1D array of characters. The statement

```
char b[4] = "rat";
```

creates a 1D array named b and stores a string rat in it as shown in Figure 6.37.

Due to the presence of NULL character, we can directly print the string b using the statement

```
printf("%s",b);
```

The 2D array specified in Figure 6.36 can actually be viewed as three different 1D arrays of characters, such that each 1D array contains one string. The next question is: what are the names of these individual 1D arrays? We know that when a row index as

```
      0   1   2   3
Array b │ r │ a │ t │\0│
```

Figure 6.37: String stored in 1D array named b

well as column index is specified to an array a, it will actually access one cell of the array. For example, the statement

```
printf("%c" ,a[0][2]);
```

prints the character t on the screen because it is stored at row =0 and column=2 in array a. In general, a[0][k] will access k^{th} column in row 0. Now, if you look at the structure in Figure 6.36, a[0][k] can be compared with b[k]. Just as b[k] gives the kth character in array b, a[0][k] gives the kth character in a[0]. Hence, we can say that a[0] in itself is an 1D array like b. The argument that we are trying to make here is that a[i][k] gives the kth character in the ith row, but any row a[i] of a 2D array in itself is a 1D array when the structure of single row in Figure 6.36 is compared with structure of 1D array shown in Figure 6.37. Therefore, a[0], a[1] and a[2] are different 1D arrays present in a 2D array named as a as shown in Figure 6.38. Just like we can print array b directly using %s, we can also print the arrays a[0], a[1] and a[2] directly.

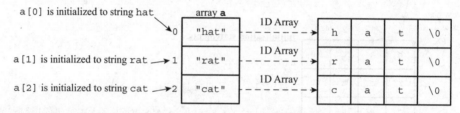

Figure 6.38: Viewing 2D array as a collection of 1D arrays

NOTES

A 2D array of characters is also called an 1D array of strings because it actually stores multiple strings. Remember, if you consider **character as a dimension** it's a 2D array for you but if you use **string as a dimension** you can actually access the 2D character array as if it is a 1D array of strings. For example, the statement

```
printf("%s", a[1]);
```

prints the string hat. Internally, the statement accesses character locations a[0][0], a[0][1], a[0][2] and a[0][3]. Since a[0][3] contains \0 it is not displayed on the computer screen. Hence, in a 2D array of characters **character-by-character access** is two dimensional, whereas a **string access** is just one dimensional.

6.5.1 Program to print the number in words: An example

Let us write a program which accepts any digit number as input from the user and prints the number in the word format. For example, if the user inputs the number as 1265, the output of the program must be One Two Six Five.

```
#include<stdio.h>
void main()
{
char words[][15]=
```

```
{"Zero","One","Two","Three","Four","Five","Six","Seven","Eight","Nine"};
int s=0,x,d, a[100];
int w;
printf("Enter a number: ");
scanf("%d",&x);
int i=0;
    while(x!=0)
    {
    d=x%10; //get the individual digit
    a[i]=d;
    i++;
    x=x/10; //Use quotient for the next addition
    }
    /*Traverse the array in reverse direction*/
    printf("The word format is: ");
    for(w=i-1;w>=0;w--)
    {
    printf("%s ",words[a[w]]);
    }
}
```

Output

```
Enter a number: 1265
The word format is: One Two Six Five
```

The statement

```
char words[][15]=
{"Zero","One","Two","Three","Four","Five","Six","Seven",
"Eight","Nine" };
```

creates an array of strings which stores each digit in the word format as shown in Figure 6.39.

The statements

```
printf("Enter a number: ");
scanf("%d",&x);
```

accept a number x as input from the user which is to be translated into words.

We have used division by 10 to extract individual digits of x. Each digit extracted by the while loop is stored in an array a. The digit extraction logic is very similar to what we have designed in Chapter 5, Section 5.2.4. Hence, the digits will be extracted in the reverse order. So, if the input value x is 1265 the array a will contain the digits in reverse order as shown in Figure 6.40.

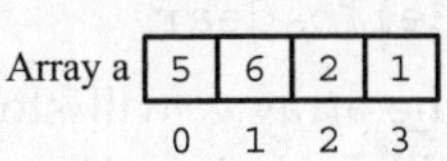

Therefore, to translate each of the digits into words, we will have to iterate over the array a in reverse direction (last element of the array must be visited first, so that we get the correct order back).

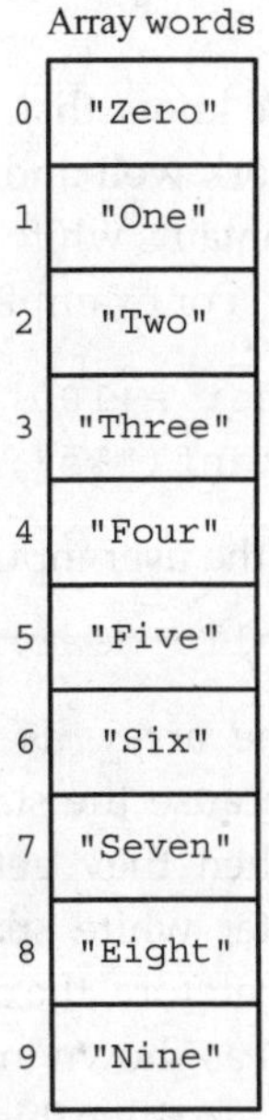

Array words	
0	"Zero"
1	"One"
2	"Two"
3	"Three"
4	"Four"
5	"Five"
6	"Six"
7	"Seven"
8	"Eight"
9	"Nine"

Figure 6.39: Array words

Array a	5	6	2	1
	0	1	2	3

Figure 6.40: Array a

This is done using a for loop as seen in the code. Note that the variable i is incremented by the while loop responsible for digit extraction each time a new digit is extracted. Hence, i will store the number of digits extracted from x. This means that the length of array a will always be i because each digit of x is stored as one element of a. We know that for any array whose length is i, the position of last element is i-1. As the for loop is required to traverse the array in reverse direction, it traverses the array from position i-1 to position 0. Each element of the array can be translated into words by using the array named words created in the program. For example, to translate 5 into words we must access the string words[5]. In short, to translate any number a[w] into words we must access a string words[a[w]] as seen in the code.

6.6   String-Specific Input and Output Operations: gets()/puts()

We know that string input can be taken using scanf() or cin. Both scanf() and cin work well and can accept a string as input, but they fail when the string to be accepted contains white spaces.

For example, let us consider following statements:

```
char a[100];
scanf("%s",a);              /*OR   cin>>a; in pure C++ */
```

If the user inputs a string as

```
Hello dear
```

The array a will only contain Hello. This is because the statements scanf() or cin terminate when they get a white space. Hence, everything after white space in the input is simply ignored. Therefore, the array a just stored Hello followed by \0 as shown in Figure 6.41.

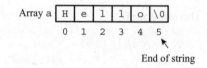

Figure 6.41:   Array a storing Hello

To solve this problem, C/C++ supports a function gets() which is specifically designed to take string inputs. The function gets() does not terminate on white spaces, but terminates when \n character is encountered. This means that the function gets() terminates when you hit an ENTER key after input.

If a is an array of characters, you can use gets() function to input the string and store it in a as shown below:

```
gets(a);
```

The function gets() will wait for the user to input a string and then store it in array a. If the user inputs a string as

```
Hello dear
```

the array a will store the full string because the function gets() does not terminate although there is a white space within the input data. Hence, the contents of array a are as shown in Figure 6.42.

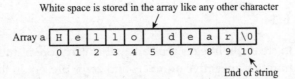

Figure 6.42: Array a storing Hello dear

gets() is used to input a string, whereas the function puts() is used to print the string on the computer screen. The statement

puts(a);

prints the contents of array a on the computer screen. Hence, it prints the following on the text screen:

Hello dear

Given below is the full source code that describes the usage of gets() and puts() functions to input and print a sentence:

```
#include<stdio.h>
void main()
{
char a[100];
printf("Enter a sentence\n");
/*Input a string*/
gets(a);
printf("Sentence you entered is\n");
/*Print the value of string stored in array a on computer screen*/
puts(a);
}
```

Output
```
Enter a sentence
Hello dear, world is nice!
Sentence you entered is
Hello dear, world is nice!
```

NOTES

The functions gets() and puts() are declared in the header file stdio.h. Hence this header file must be included before using these functions in the program.

Solved Example 6.1

Write a program to create an integer type array that can store n integers. Display the count of positive numbers, negative numbers and zeros present in the array.

```c
#include<stdio.h>
void main()
{
int a[100],i,n, positive=0,negative=0,zero=0;
printf("How many elements are to be stored in the array?\n");
scanf("%d",&n);
printf("Enter the %d elements\n",n);
/*Loop to input array elements */
    for(i=0;i<=n-1;i++)
    {
        printf("Enter element number %d\n",i+1);
        scanf("%d",&a[i]);
    }
/*Loop to count positives, negatives and zeros present in the array */
    for(i=0;i<=n-1;i++)
    {
        if(a[i]>0)
        {
        positive++;
        }
        else if(a[i]<0)
        {
        negative++;
        }
        else
        {
        zero++;
        }
    }
printf("The positive count is %d\n", positive);
printf("The negative count is %d\n", negative);
printf("The zero count is %d\n", zero);
}
```

Output
```
How many elements are to be stored in the array?
5
```

```
Enter the 5 elements
Enter element number 1
10
Enter element number 2
-2
Enter element number 3
-3
Enter element number 4
45
Enter element number 5
0
The positive count is 2
The negative count is 2
The zero count is 1
```

SCRATCH PAD

- We create three different counters named as `positive`, `negative` and `zero` to store the counts of positive, negative and zero's present in the array. Initial value of all the counters is set to 0.
- We iterate over each element of the array using a for loop so as to determine if that element is a positive number, negative number or a zero.
- Depending on the type of element stored we increment the respective counter variable at each iteration of the `for` loop as shown in the code below:

```
for(i=0; i<=n-1; i++)
{
    if(a[i]>0)
    {
    positive++;
    }
    else if(a[i]<0)
    {
    negative++;
    }
    else
    {
    zero++;
    }
}
```

- At the end of loop, the variable `positive` will contain the count of positive numbers, `negative` will contain the count of negative numbers and the variable `zero` will contain count of zeros present in the array.

Solved Example 6.2

Write a program to search a particular element in the array. The program should accept n integers as input from the user and store them in the array. The program should then accept a key x, and determine whether or not it is present in the array.

```
#include<stdio.h>
void main()
{
int a[100],i,n,x;
printf("How many elements are to be stored in the array?\n");
scanf("%d",&n);
/*Input n elements and store them in an array a*/
printf(" Enter the %d elements\n",n);
      for(i=0;i<=n-1;i++)
      {
      printf("Enter element number %d\n",i);
      scanf("%d",&a[i]);
      }
printf("Enter element to be searched in the array \n");
scanf("%d",&x);
/*The while loop below is used to determine whether or not value x
is present in the array a*/
i=0;
      while(i<n && a[i]!=x)
      {
      i++;
      }

      if(i==n)
      {
      printf("Element is not present in the array\n");
      }
      else
      {
      printf("Element is present at position %d in the array\n",i);
      }
}
```

Output
```
How many elements are to be stored in the array?
5
Enter the 5 elements
Enter element number 0
10
Enter element number 1
20
Enter element number 2
30
Enter element number 3
40
```

```
Enter element number 4
50
Enter element to be searched in the array
30
Element is present at position 2 in the array
```

SCRATCH PAD

We scan the full array sequentially and compare each element of a with x to determine whether or not x is present in a. The sequential scan should start from position 0 and end at position n-1; hence we set the initial value of the index variable i to 0 as shown below:

```
int i=0;
```

Given below is the while loop which traverses the array a to find the value x.

```
while(i<n && a[i]!=x)
{
i++;
}
```

The loop keeps incrementing the index variable i to compare each a[i] with x. The while loop terminates if any one of the following conditions is false.

1. **i<n**

   If this condition is false, it indicates that variable i has crossed the boundaries of an array a; hence there is no point searching ahead. Therefore, the while loop terminates because i is not less than or equal to n-1 (Remember n–1 is the last position in the array).

2. **a[i]!=x**

   If the condition **a[i]!=x** is **false**, it indicates that **a[i]==x** is **true**. This means that value x is present at position i in the array. Since the value x is found, there is no point searching ahead.

So, we can conclude the following after the while loop ends.

1. If the value of variable i is same as n after while loop terminates, it actually means that the while loop terminated because the condition i<n is false. It also means that the condition a[i]!=x was always true and element x was never found in the array a, thereby taking index i out of bounds. Hence, we print the message:

   ```
   printf("Element is not present in the array\n");
   ```

   If the condition i==n is true even after the while loop completes.

2. If the condition i==n is false when the while loop completes, then it means that the value of i is still less than or equal to n-1. In this case, it is obvious that the

while loop terminated because condition `a[i]!=x` is false, which means that `a[i]==x` is true and hence the element `x` is present at position `i` in the array. Hence, we print the following message in the `else` block:

```
printf("Element is present at position %d in the array\n",i);
```

CAUTION

Logical operators `&&` and `||` give a short circuit behaviour. When two conditions `C1` and `C2` are connected using `&&` operator such that `C1` is the first condition and `C2` is the second condition, as shown below:

`C1&&C2`

C2 will be evaluated only when C1 is true. This is because; when `C1` is false the ultimate outcome of `&&` is always going to be false immaterial of what `C2` is. Hence, optimizer of C/C++ does not evaluate `C2` if `C1` is false. This is called short circuit behaviour in evaluating logical `&&` operator. In the given program, we have connected two conditions using `&&` operator

`i<n && a[i]!=x`

Hence, condition `a[i]!=x` will not be evaluated if `i<n` is false. This is a very important point because if condition `i<n` is false, it indicates that `i` has crossed the boundaries of the array and hence `a[i]` should not be accessed. In case you access `a[i]` it is going to be a junk value and there is no point comparing junk with `x`. Hence, we must not change the order of conditions specified in the `while` loop of the given program.

Solved Example 6.3

Write a program to read an array of n integers and to reverse the order of elements in the array without using any temporary array.

For example, if the input array is

Array a | 10 | 20 | 30 | 40 | 50 |
         0   1   2   3   4

the order of elements in the array must be reversed as shown below:

Array a | 50 | 40 | 30 | 10 | 10 |
         0   1   2   3   4

```
#include<stdio.h>
void main()
{
int n, i, mid, temp, a[100];
```

```
printf("How many elements are to be stored in the array?\n");
scanf("%d",&n);
printf("Enter the %d elements\n",n);
/*Input the array elements*/
      for(i=0;i<=n-1;i++)
      {
      scanf("%d",&a[i]);
      }
/*Calculate the midpoint of the array*/
   if( n%2 == 0 )
      {
      mid = n/2 - 1;
      }
      else
      {
      mid = n/2;
      }
/*Swap the left side of the array with right side of the array*/
for ( i = 0 ; i < mid ; i++ )
   {
      temp = a[i];
      a[i] = a[n-i-1];
      a[n-i-1] = temp;
   }
printf("Reverse of the array is\n");
   for( i = 0 ; i < n ; i++ )
      {
      printf("%d ",a[i]);
      }
}
```

Output

```
How many elements are to be stored in the array?
5
Enter the 5 elements
10 20 30 40 50
Reverse of the array is
50 40 30 20 10
```

SCRATCH PAD

To reverse the ordering of elements in the array we swap the elements stored in the left half of the array with the corresponding elements in the right half of the array.

For example, if the size of array is 5 we swap a[0] with a[4] and a[1] with a[3]. Note that the position of the middle element, which is 30, is unaffected by the swap operation.

Given below is the for loop that performs the required swapping to reverse the array:

```
for( i = 0 ; i < mid ; i++ )
    {
        temp = a[i];
        a[i] = a[n-i-1];
        a[n-i-1] = temp;
    }
```

The variable mid represents the position of the element at the centre of the array. Variable mid will be calculated as n/2-1 (if the array is of even length) and n/2 if (array is of odd length). This is because the array index always starts from 0. For example, if length of array is 5, the midpoint will be calculated as

mid = 5/2 = **2**

On the other hand, if length of the array is 6, the position of mid will be calculated as follows:

mid =6/2-1 = **2**.

Solved Example 6.4

Write a program to take two vectors as input from the user and to calculate the scalar product of the two vectors.

```
#include<stdio.h>
void main()
{
int n, i, v1[100],v2[100],scalar_prod=0;
printf("Enter the number of elements in each of the vectors\n");
scanf("%d",&n);
/*Input the first vector from the user*/
printf("Enter the first vector\n");
    for(i=0;i<=n-1;i++)
    {
    scanf("%d",&v1[i]);
    }
```

```
/*Input the first vector from the user*/
printf("Enter the second vector\n");
      for(i=0;i<=n-1;i++)
      {
      scanf("%d",&v2[i]);
      }
      /*Calculate the scalar product of the vectors*/
      for(i=0;i<=n-1;i++)
      {
      scalar_prod = scalar_prod+v1[i]*v2[i];
      }
printf("Scalar product is %d",scalar_prod);
}
```

Output
```
Enter the number of elements in each of the vectors
4
Enter the first vector
10 20 30 40
Enter the second vector
5 10 15 20
Scalar product is 1500
```

Solved Example 6.5

Write a program to calculate the result of following expression if X and Y are two collections each containing n integers.

$$\sum X_i + \sum Y_i - \sqrt{|\sum X_i|}$$

```
#include<stdio.h>
#include<math.h>
void main()
{
int n, i, x[100],y[100], sumX=0,sumY=0, absX;
float result;
printf("Enter the number of elements to be stored in each of the
arrays\n");
scanf("%d",&n);
printf("Enter the %d elements of array x\n",n);
      for(i=0;i<=n-1;i++)
```

```
      {
      scanf("%d",&x[i]);
      /*calculate sum  of x in parallel*/
      sumX=sumX + x[i];
      }
printf("Enter the %d elements of array y\n",n);
      for(i=0;i<=n-1;i++)
      {
      scanf("%d",&y[i]);
      /*calculate sum  of x in parallel*/
      sumY=sumY + y[i];
      }
/*Find absolute of sum of X elements*/
absX = abs(sumX);
/*Calculate the resultant expression*/
result = sumX+sumY + sqrt(absX);
printf("Result is %f\n",result);
}
```

Output
```
Enter the number of elements to be stored in each of the arrays
5
Enter the 5 elements of array x
10 20 30 40 50
Enter the 5 elements of array y
12 45 67 88 2
Result is 376.247437
```

Solved Example 6.6

Write a program to take an array as input from the user and to rotate the elements of the array in the right direction by accepting the rotation factor as input from the user.

Suppose, the original array given as input to the program is as follows:

Array a | 10 | 20 | 30 | 40 | 50 |
        0   1   2   3   4

If we apply a right rotation to the array, the state of the array after one cycle of rotation will be as shown below:

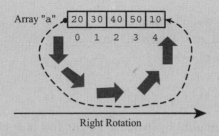

Figure 6.43: State of the array after the first cycle of right rotation

Note that 10, which was the first element of the array, has become the last element and rest of the elements are shifted ahead as seen in Figure 6.43. If you apply another cycle of right rotation, the new state of the array will be as shown below:

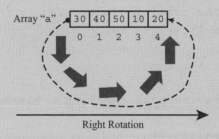

Figure 6.44: State of the array after the second cycle of right rotation

Hence after two cycles, 30 becomes the first element of the array and 20 becomes the last element as seen in Figure 6.44. Number of cycles to be applied to an array is specified by a rotation factor. The program should apply m cycles of rotation to an array a if the rotation factor is m. The program should take the following as input from the user:

1. Size of an array a.
2. Elements of an array a.
3. Rotation factor m to specify number of cycles of right rotation to be applied to array a.

Program should print the resultant array a on the computer screen after applying m rotation cycles.

```c
#include<stdio.h>
void main()
{
int n, i,k, m, temp[100], a[100];
printf("How many elements are to be stored in the array?\n");
```

```
scanf("%d",&n);
/*read the array of n- elements*/
printf("Enter the %d elements\n",n);
      for(i=0;i<=n-1;i++)
      {
      scanf("%d",&a[i]);
      }
printf("Enter the amount by which rotation is to be applied\n");
scanf("%d",&m);
      /*copy the first m elements of the array into temp folder*/
      for(i=0;i<=m-1;i++)
      {
      temp[i] =a[i];
      }
      /*left shift the remaining elements*/
      for(i=0;i<=n-m-1;i++)
      {
      a[i] =a[i+m];
      }
      /*copy the array temp as the last m elements of the array*/
      k=0;
      for(i= n-m;i<=n-1;i++)
      {
      a[i] =  temp[k];
      k++;
      }
      /*Print the result*/
      printf("The array elements after rotation are \n");
      for(i=0;i<=n-1;i++)
      {
      printf("%d ",a[i]);
      }
}
```

Output
```
How many elements are to be stored in the array?
5
Enter the 5 elements
10 20 30 40 50
Enter the amount by which rotation is to be applied
2
The array elements after rotation are
30 40 50 10 20
```

SCRATCH PAD

The program performs the following steps:

1. Copy the first m elements of the array a into a temporary array named temp.
2. Left shift the positions in array a by m. This will overwrite the first m positions in the array a.
3. Copy the m positions stored in array temp as the last m positions of the array a.

As an example, let us consider that we need to rotate array a shown below with a factor of 2

Array a
10	20	30	40	50
0	1	2	3	4

As per step 1, we will copy the first two elements of the array a in array temp as shown below:

Array temp
10	20
0	1

After the copy operation, we shift the elements of the array a by two positions in the left direction. Hence, the new state of the array a is as shown below:

Array a
30	40	50	40	50
0	1	2	3	4

As a last step, we copy the array temp into the last two positions of the array a as shown below:

Array a
30	40	50	10	20
0	1	2	3	4

The program prints the resultant array as seen in the output.

Solved Example 6.7

Write a program that performs a string copy operation. Take a string in array a as input from the user and then copy the string in array a to another array b.

```c
#include<stdio.h>
void main()
{
 int len=0,i,k;
 char a[100],b[100];
/*Input string in a from the user*/
 printf("Enter a source string: ");
```

```
 scanf("%s",a);
/*Calculate the length of string in a*/
 for(i=0;a[i]!='\0';i++)
 {
  len++;
 }
/*Copy String in a to array b including the null character */
 for(i=0;i<=len;i++)
 {
  b[i]=a[i];
 }
printf("Destination string is: %s ", b);
}
```

Output
```
Enter a source string: Computer
Destination string is: Computer
```

Solved Example 6.8

Write a program to accept two strings as input from the user and to perform concatenation of the two strings. For example, if the user enters the first string as Com and the second string as puter the result of the program should be Computer. Store the concatenated string in a character array named c.

```
#include<stdio.h>
void main()
{
 int lenA=0,lenB=0,i,k;
 char a[100],b[100],c[200];
 /*Take first string as input from the user in array a*/
 printf("Enter first string:");
 scanf("%s",a);
 /*Take second string as input from the user in array b*/
 printf("Enter second string:");
 scanf("%s",b);
 /*Calculate length of string in array a*/
     for(i=0;a[i]!='\0';i++)
     {
       lenA++;
     }
 /*Calculate length of string in array b*/
     for(i=0;b[i]!='\0';i++)
     {
```

```
    lenB++;
    }
/*Copy string a in array c*/
    for(i=0;i<=lenA-1;i++)
    {
     c[i]=a[i];
    }
/*Append string b to array c after the last character*/
k=0;
    for(i=lenA;b[k]!='\0';i++)
    {
     c[i]=b[k];
    k++;
    }
/*Store NULL character in array c*/
c[i]='\0';
printf("Concatenation of strings is: %s",c);
}
```

Output
```
Enter first string:Com
Enter second string:puter
Concatenation of strings is: Computer
```

Solved Example 6.9

Write a program to take a string as input from the user and to convert the string into uppercase. For example, if the user enters the string as hello123 the output must be HELLO123. Note that the numerical part in the string should not be affected; only the lowercase alphabets must be translated to uppercase.

```
#include<stdio.h>
void main()
{
char a[100];
printf("Enter a string in lower case: ");
scanf("%s",a);
/*Subtract 32 from the ASCII value only if the a[i] is in upper
case*/
    for(int i=0;a[i]!='\0';i++)
    {
```

```
    if(a[i]>=97 &&a[i] <=122)
      {
       a[i] = a[i]-32;
      }
  }
printf("Upper Case is: %s\n",a);
}
```

Output

```
Enter a string in lower case: hello123
Upper Case is: HELLO123
```

SCRATCH PAD

The ASCII values of the lowercase characters are from 97 to 122, whereas the ASCII values of the uppercase characters are from 65 to 90. This means that we can convert any lowercase character into an uppercase character by subtracting 32 from its ASCII value (Refer to Appendix 1 for ASCII values).

Hence, we traverse the array a and subtract 32 from its ASCII value as shown below:

```
for (int i=0;a[i]!='\0';i++)
{
        if(a[i]>=97 &&a[i] <=122)
          {
           a[i] = a[i]-32;
          }
}
```

Note that subtraction is done inside an if block to ensure that its not performed for special characters, numbers, etc. which may also be present in the input string. This way we ensure that only lowercase characters are affected by converting them into uppercase and there is no impact on digits, special symbols or already existing uppercase symbols in array a.

Solved Example 6.10

Write a program to take a sentence as input from the user and to determine the frequency of a particular character in a sentence. The program should take a sentence as well as a character as input from the user and should print the count of times the character occurs in a sentence.

For example, if the user enters the sentence as 'I like Cricket' and the character as 'i', then the output of the program must be 3 because the character 'i' occurs 3 times in the input sentence as shown in Figure 6.45.

I like cricket

Figure 6.45: I like cricket

Note that the program should count the presence of character in upper or lowercase in the input sentence immaterial of in what case the user inputs the character.

```c
#include<ctype.h>
#include<stdio.h>
void main()
{
 int i,count=0;
 char a[100];
char ch;
printf("Enter a sentence:");
gets(a);
printf("Enter a character:");
scanf("%c",&ch);
        for(i=0;a[i]!='\0';i++)
        {
        if(toupper(a[i])==toupper(ch))
            {
            count++;
            }
        }
printf("Character %c occurs %d times in the sentence.\n",ch,count);
}
```

Output
```
Enter a sentence:I like Cricket
Enter a character:i
Character i occurs 3 times in the sentence.
```

NOTES

As we need to take a sentence as input from the user, we have used the function gets(). We cannot use scanf() to input a sentence because it cant accept spaces as input. We store the character whose frequency needs to be determined in variable ch using a usual scanf() statement as seen in the code.

SCRATCH PAD

We traverse the complete sentence using a `for` loop and increment the value of the variable count each time the character `ch` is found in the sentence. Note that we have used a function `toupper()` while performing matching of `a[i]` and `ch`. This means that we forcefully convert the characters to be compared in upper case so as to ensure that the matching process is case insensitive and the case in which user inputs the data does not make any difference in comparisons. The loop used for comparison is as shown below:

```
for(i=0;a[i]!='\0';i++)
    {
    if(toupper(a[i])==toupper(ch))
        {
        count++;
        }
    }
```

Hence, the variable count will represent the frequency of the character in the input sentence.

NOTES

The function `toupper()` converts a character in uppercase if its currently not in uppercase. It does not affect the character if it is already in uppercase. Also the function does not affect digits and special symbols. As we have applied `toupper()` on both the sides in the comparison, it just ensures that the match is performed ignoring the case, which is the requirement given in the question. We could have also used `tolower()` function instead of `toupper()`, keep in mind the only requirement here is to forcefully get both the sides in an uniform case so that case differences between them(if any) do not hamper the results of comparisons. Both the functions are defined in the header file **ctype.h** which has to be included in the program.

Solved Example 6.11

Write a program to take a sentence as input from the user and to reverse the occurrence of words in the sentence. Note that the program should not reverse the characters inside the word. For example, if the user enters the string as "`I like computer programming`" the output must be:

```
programming computer like I
```

```
#include<stdio.h>
void main()
{
    char a[100];
```

```
    int len=0,i;
    printf("Enter a sentence: ");
    gets(a);
printf("*****Reverse is******\n");
/* Calculate the length of the string */
for(i=0;a[i]!='\0';i++)
 {
  len++;
 }
for(i= len; i>=0; i--)
 {
  if (i!= len && a[i]!=' ')
  {
  continue;
  }
  else
  {
    /*take the variable i to the beginning of a particular word*/
          while(a[i-1]!=' ' && i>=1)
            {
             i--;
            }
          //print the word in forward direction
          while (i< len && a[i]!=' ')
            {
             printf("%c",a[i]);
             i++;
            }
          printf(" "); //print the space
          i--; /*reduce value of i as space is already printed*/
  }
 }
}
```

Output

```
Enter a sentence: I like Cricket
*****Reverse is******
Cricket like I
```

SCRATCH PAD

The program to reverse the order of words in the sentence works as follows:

Step 1: Calculate the length of the sentence

The length of the input sentence is calculated and stored in the variable len using the following for loop.

```
for(i=0;a[i]!='\0';i++)
  {
   len++;
  }
```

Step 2: Traverse the sentence in reverse direction

Once the length is calculated, we start reading the sentence in reverse direction using another for loop which is shown below:

```
for(i= len; i>=0; i--)
{
-----------
-----------
-----------
}
```

The if block written inside this for loop executes continue; till the time counter variable i is not positioned after the end of a specific word. All the intermediate words in a sentence will have a space after them and hence it is clear that if a[i] is space then it means that we are just after the end of the word. The situation is different for the last word in a sentence, which does not have any space after it. In this case, variable i will cross the position len-1 (which is the position of last character in the sentence). Hence, when i is initialized to len it means that we have crossed the last word. In summary, we are at a position next to a specific word if:

1. a[i] is equal to space (for intermediate words in a sentence)

    or

2. Variable i gets a value len (which means i has crossed the position len-1). This will happen in the case of last word of a sentence.

If we are at a position after the end of a particular word, we have two while loops described in step 3 and step 4. The while loop in step 3 actually takes i to the beginning of the word and while loop in step 4 prints the word from its beginning. Remember, we don't have to reverse the individual words and hence when i is at a position after the end of the word, we fist take it to the beginning of the word and print the word in forward direction.

   If we are not at a position after the end of the word, there is really nothing to do. Hence, if both the conditions which detect end of the word are false, we simply continue the loop without performing any action. This is done using the if block in the for loop as shown below:

```
if (i!= len && a[i]!=' ')
     {
```

```
    continue;
    }
```

Step 3: Determine the start of the word

Beginning of the word is determined by traversing the sentence from end. Hence, the last word present in the sentence will be read in the first iteration of the `for` loop specified in Step 2; the second last word will be read in the second iteration and so on. Therefore, the first word of the sentence is read in the last iteration of the `for` loop. The starting of any word can be determined by searching the index of the space (which appears before every word) in the sentence, using the `while` loop as shown below:

```
while(a[i-1]!=' ' && i>=1)
    {
    i--;
    }
```

Note that the `while` loop also has a condition as `i>=1`; this is because the first word will never have a space before it.

Step 4: Read each word in the forward direction

Once the beginning of the word is determined, we print each word in forward direction using the `while` loop given below:

```
while (i< len && a[i]!=' ')
{
printf("%c",a[i]);
i++;
}
```

The following `printf()` statement ensures that the space appears after every word, while the reverse sentence is getting printed on the screen

```
printf(" ");
```

Step 5: Program repeats Steps 2, 3 and 4 until the beginning of the original sentence is reached using the `for` loop which is specified in Step 2.

Solved Example 6.12

Write a program to take a word as input from the user and to determine the count of vowels in the word. For example, if the user enters the word as "Computer" the output of the program must be 3 because the word contains 3 vowels in it.

```
#include<stdio.h>
void main()
{
int i,count=0;
char a[100];
printf("Enter a word:");
scanf("%s",a);
for(i=0;a[i]!='\0';i++)
{
if(a[i]=='a' || a[i]=='e'|| a[i]=='i'|| a[i]=='o'|| a[i]=='u'||
a[i]=='A'|| a[i]=='E'|| a[i]=='I'|| a[i]=='O'|| a[i]=='U' )
    {
    count++;
    }
}
printf("Number of vowels are %d\n",count);
}
```

Output
```
Enter a word:Computer
Number of vowels are 3
```

Solved Example 6.13

Write a program to accept a month number as input from the user and to print the month name. For example, if the user inputs the month number as 3 the program should print March.

```
#include<stdio.h>
void main()
{
 int mon,index;
 char a[][15]= {"January","February","March","April","May",
 "June","July","August","September","October","November",
 "December"};
printf("Enter the month number: ");
scanf("%d",&mon);
      if(mon<=0 || mon>12)
      {
      printf("In valid month number\n");
      }
      else
      {
      /*map the month number to the array index*/
      index=mon-1;
```

```
    printf("Month Name is %s",a[index]);
    }
}
```

Output

```
Enter the month number: 12
Month Name is December
```

SCRATCH PAD

The program to print the name of the month from the month number works in following steps:

Step 1: Create a 2D array of characters storing the month names. Each element of a 2D array stores one character as shown below. A single row of the 2D array stores the name of a particular month. For example, row number 0 stores a string January, row number 1 stores a string February and so on. Note that each of the strings is terminated by the NULL character.

Array a	0	1	2	3	4	5	6	7	8	9
0	J	a	n	u	a	r	y	\0		
1	F	e	b	r	u	a	r	y	\0	
2	M	a	r	c	h	\0				
3	A	p	r	i	l	\0				
4	M	a	y	\0						
5	J	u	n	e	\0					
6	J	u	l	y	\0					
7	A	u	g	u	s	t	\0			
8	S	e	p	t	e	m	b	e	r	\0
9	O	c	t	o	b	e	r	\0		
10	N	o	v	e	m	b	e	r	\0	
11	D	e	c	e	m	b	e	r	\0	

Step 2: Accessing strings from a 2D array: As we know that we can access the individual characters in the array by specifying the row number and the column number. For example, a[0][3] will give the value as 'u' because the character 'u' is stored at cell which is at row number 0 and column number 3. Along with accessing individual characters in the array, we can also access the whole string which represents the month name by specifying only the row index. For example, a[0] will read all the characters stored in

row number 0 up to the NULL character. Hence, a[0] will give us a string as January. Similarly, a[1] will read all the characters stored in row number 1; therefore, a[1] will give us a string February. To get the name of the ith month, we need to access the row a[i-1] which gives us all the characters in the row number i-1 up to a NULL character. Such a access of reading all the characters in a particular row by giving the row reference is possible **only with 2D array of characters**, because strings are **self-addressable**. This concept does not apply to any other data type apart from array of characters.

Solved Example 6.14

Write a program to take a matrix as input from its user and print its transpose.

```c
#include<stdio.h>
void main()
{
 int r,c,i,j;
 int a[100][100],result[100][100];
printf("Enter the order of the matrix\n");
scanf("%d%d",&r,&c);
printf("Enter the matrix\n");
 for(i=0;i<=r-1;i++)
 {
  for(j=0;j<=c-1;j++)
  {
   scanf("%d",&a[i][j]);
  }
 }
/*Compute the Transpose*/
for(i=0;i<=r-1;i++)
 {
  for(j=0;j<=c-1;j++)
  {
/*Note: j is used as a row index for result matrix which is actually
the column index of original matrix a and i is used as a column
index for the result matrix which is actually the row index of
original matrix a*/
   result[j][i] = a[i][j];

  }
}
```

```
printf("Transpose is \n");
/*As the original matrix as r rows and c columns, the result matrix
has c rows and r columns*/
for(i=0;i<=c-1;i++)
 {
  for(j=0;j<=r-1;j++)
  {
   printf("%d ",result[i][j]);
  }
printf("\n");
 }
}
```

Output

```
Enter the order of the matrix
3 4
Enter the matrix
10 20 30 40
50 60 70 80
90 100 110 120
Transpose is
10 50 90
20 60 100
30 70 110
40 80 120
```

Solved Example 6.15

Write a program to determine whether or not an integer x is present in a 2D array. The program should accept a 2D array as input from the user and print the position in the array which gives the first occurrence of x.

```
#include<stdio.h>
void main()
{
 int r,c,i,j,posRow=-1,posCol=-1,x;
 int a[100][100];
 printf("Enter the number of rows and columns of the array:\n");
 scanf("%d%d",&r,&c);
 printf("Enter a 2D array\n");
 for(i=0;i<=r-1;i++)
 {
  for(j=0;j<=c-1;j++)
```

```
    {
      scanf("%d",&a[i][j]);
    }
  }
printf("Enter the element to be searched:\n");
scanf("%d",&x);
  for(i=0;i<=r-1;i++)
  {
    for(j=0;j<=c-1;j++)
    {
        if(a[i][j]==x)
        {
        posRow=i;
        posCol=j;
        }
    }
  }
  if(posRow!=-1 && posCol!=-1)
  {
   printf("Element present at row %d and column %d \n" ,posRow,
   posCol);
  }
  else
  {
  printf("Element not found\n");
  }
}
```

Output
```
Enter the number of rows and columns of the array:
3 4
Enter a 2D array
10 15 20 25
30 35 40 45
50 55 60 65
Enter the element to be searched:
40
Element present at row 1 and column 2
```

Solved Example 6.16

Write a program to take a square matrix as input from the user and to calculate the sum of diagonal elements of the matrix.

```
#include<stdio.h>
void main()
{
 int r, i,j,s=0;
 int a[100][100];
printf("Enter the no of rows/columns of a square matrix\n");
scanf("%d",&r);
printf("Enter a Matrix\n");
 for(i=0;i<=r-1;i++)
 {
      for(j=0;j<=r-1;j++)
      {
      scanf("%d",&a[i][j]);
      /*Add the input value with sum if its a diagonal element*/
      if(i==j)
            {
            s=s+a[i][j];
            }
      }
 }
printf("Sum of the diagonal elements is %d",s);
}
```

Output
```
Enter the no of rows/columns of a square matrix
3
Enter a Matrix
10 20 30
40 50 60
70 80 90
Sum of the diagonal elements is 150
```

Solved Example 6.17

Write a program to take a square matrix as input from the user and to check if the matrix is symmetric or not.

```
#include<stdio.h>
void main()
{
 int r, i,j;
```

```
 int a[100][100];
 char symmetric='y';
printf("Enter the no of rows/columns of a square matrix\n");
scanf("%d",&r);
 printf("Enter a Matrix\n");
 for(i=0;i<=r-1;i++)
 {
  for(j=0;j<=r-1;j++)
  {
   scanf("%d",&a[i][j]);
  }
 }
/*Check if the matrix is symmetric*/
for(i=0;i<=r-1;i++)
 {
  for(j=0;j<=r-1;j++)
  {
      if(a[i][j]!=a[j][i])
      {
      symmetric='n';
      }
   }
 }
if(symmetric!= 'n')
 {
  printf("Matrix is symmetric\n");
 }
 else
 {
  printf("Matrix is not symmetric\n");
 }
}
```

output

```
Enter the no of rows/columns of a square matrix
3
Enter a Matrix
10 10 50
10 50 10
50 10 10
Matrix is symmetric
```

Solved Example 6.18

Write a program to take a 2D array as input from the user and find the greatest element in the 2D array.

```c
#include<stdio.h>
void main()
{
 int r,c,i,j;
 int a[100][100];
 int max;
 printf(" Enter the no. of rows and columns of the array:\n");
 scanf("%d%d",&r,&c);
 printf("Enter a Matrix:\n");
 for(i=0;i<=r-1;i++)
 {
  for(j=0;j<=c-1;j++)
  {
   scanf("%d",&a[i][j]);
  }
 }
max=a[0][0];
for(i=0;i<=r-1;i++)
 {
  for(j=0;j<=c-1;j++)
  {
      if(a[i][j]>max)
      {
      max=a[i][j];
      }
  }
 }
printf("Maximum is %d" ,max);
}
```

Output
```
Enter the no. of rows and columns of the array:
3 3
Enter a Matrix:
10 20 30
40 50 99
60 70 80
Maximum is 99
```

Error Finding Exercises

Given below are some program snapshots which may or may not contain errors. Correct the error(s) if exist in the code and determine the output.

Code 1

```c
#include<stdio.h>
void main()
{
int a[2];
int i;
a=40;
a=50;
a=60;
for(int i=0;i<3;i++)
        {
printf("%d\n",a[i]);
        }
}
```

Code 2

```c
#include<stdio.h>
void main()
{
int a[]={10,20,30};
printf("Enter array\n");
scanf("%d",a);
}
```

Code 3

```c
#include<stdio.h>
void main()
{
int a[5]={10,20,30,40,50};
int b[5]={1,2,3,4,5};
int t[5];
t=a;
a=b;
b=c
printf("Elements of the array 'a' are\n");
        for(int i=0;i<5;i++)
        {
```

```
    printf("%d\n",a[i]);
    }
    printf("Elements of the array 'b' are\n");
    for(int i=0;i<5;i++)
    {
    printf("%d\n",b[i]);
    }
}
```

Code 4

```
#include<stdio.h>
void main()
{
char a[]={'h','a','r','d','w','a','r','e'};
printf("%s",a);
}
```

Code 5

```
#include<stdio.h>
void main()
{
char a[]="misc";
char b[100];
b=a;
printf("The value of string a is %s\n", a);
printf("The value of string b is %s\n", b);
}
```

Code 6

```
#include <stdio.h>
void main()
{
char a[]="misc";
char b[]="misc";
    if(a==b)
    {
    printf("The two strings are same\n");
    }
    else
    {
    printf("The two strings are not same\n");
    }
}
```

Quiz

1. Choose a correct answer to complete the code segment that prints all the elements of the array a on the screen.
   ```
   int a[] ={10,15,20,45,32};
   for(int i=0; _____;i++)
   {
   prinf("%d\n",a[i]);
   }
   ```
   (a) i<4   (c) i<=4
   (b) i<6   (d) i<=5

2. Given that a is the array of integers as shown below:
   ```
   int a[] ={10,15,20,45,32};
   ```
   What will be the output of following printf() statement?
   ```
   printf("%d",a);
   ```
   (a) The statement will print all the elements of the array a.
   (b) This will give a compile time error as array a cannot be printed directly.
   (c) This will give a run time error.
   (d) The statement will print the starting address of the memory location of array a.

3. Consider an array of characters defined as below:
   ```
   char a[]={'a','b','c','d'};
   ```
   Which of the following statements are true?
   (a) The size of array a is 4 bytes.
   (b) The array a will contain NULL character as a last element.
   (c) We can directly print the elements of the array a using a statement printf("%s",a);
   (d) None of the above statements are true.

4. Every string in C\C++ is terminated by:
   (a) \0
   (b) \^
   (c) 0
   (d) Whatever is the actual last character in the string

5. Consider the following two initialization statements.
   ```
   i.    char a[]={'h','a','t'};
   ii.   char a[]= "hat"
   ```
   Which of the following statements are correct?
   (a) Both the initializations have a same effect and will store a constant hat inside array a.
   (b) The first initialization will not store '\0' as at the end, whereas the second initialization will store '\0' as a last character of the string.
   (c) We can print all the elements of the array using statement **printf("%s", a);** only in the case of first initialization.
   (d) We can print all the elements of the array using statement **printf("%s", a);** only in the case of second initialization.

6. Complete the following code segment to arrange the array a (of n elements) in descending order.
   ```
   for(_____;_____;_____)
   {
   ```

```
for(_____;_____;_____)
   {
   if(a[j+1]>a[j])
      {
      t=a[j];
      a[j]=a[j+1];
      a[j+1]=t;
      }
   }
}
```

7. Choose a correct statement
   (a) Compiler allocates static memory for every array declared in the program.
   (b) Size of the array may or may not be specified at the time of creating the array.
   (c) Array can store heterogeneous data values.
   (d) Memory for an array is always allocated dynamically.
8. Choose a correct statement:
   (a) It is mandatory to specify the number of rows while creating a 2D array.
   (b) It is mandatory to specify number of columns at the time of creating a 2D array.
   (c) It is mandatory to specify the number of rows as well as columns at the time of creating a 2D array.
   (d) None of the above is true.
9. If M is a square matrix with r rows and r columns, complete the following code segment to find the transpose of the matrix:

```
for(i=0;_____;i++)
   {
   for(j=0;_____;j++)
      {
      cout<<a[i][j];
      }
   }
```

10. Array a is a 4D array with size as shown in its declaration.
    `int a[10][5][4][11];`
    Write a program using `for` loops to accept each element of this array as input from the user and then to print it on computer screen.

Review Questions

1. What are arrays? Explain the usage of arrays in computer programming.
2. What are the drawbacks of array as a data structure?
3. Write a program to calculate the result of following expression, where X and Y are collections of integer values: $Z = \Sigma X_i + \Sigma Y_i$
4. Write a program to create two integer type arrays a and b such that if a[i] stores a value x then b[i] will store the factorial of x. Take all the elements of array a as input from the user and calculate the values to be stored in array b.
5. Write a program to create three arrays one to store the first name of the person, second to store the last name of the person and third to store the age of the person. Use the three arrays to store the details about n person objects and print the details in tabular format.

6. Write a program to find the inverse of a matrix.
7. Write a program to take a matrix as input from the user and to determine if it is a unit matrix or not.
8. Write a program to take a 2D array as input from the user and sort the array in ascending order.
9. Write a program to show the creation of 3D and 4D arrays.

Chapter

7 | Functions

7.1 Overview

Creation and maintenance of the program becomes difficult when the lines of code in the program increase. As the size of the program increases, the code becomes more prone to errors and the debugging of the program becomes difficult. The **line of code (LOC)** is considered as one of the metrics to determine the logical complexity of the program in the software development life cycle. Any program is a sequence of instructions and there can be a situation where a subsequence needs to be repeatedly executed at different places in the program. Repeating the subsequence at each place will not only increase the LOC but also make the program bulky and hamper its readability, thereby making **change management** cumbersome. Imagine a situation wherein a certain operation (say performing addition) is repeatedly written in the program at 100 different places, and suddenly you realize that you need to perform subtractions instead of additions. Making this change is going to be difficult because you need to ensure that all the addition operations at 100 different places need to change to subtraction. And what if you miss one of them to change? Or what if you change something else by mistake in a rush to make these 100 changes? The problem is that there is a lot of duplication of code (**redundancy of code**), and hence making one change requires making multiple changes.

In C/C++, it is possible to split a large program into multiple independent pieces. Each independent piece is called a **function** or a **method**. A function can define a single operation or a sequence of operations. You can invoke a function whenever you need to execute the operations it defines. Hence, the idea is to define an operation only once within the function and invoke the same function at multiple places where you need to perform the operation. A function can have multiple inputs (called **arguments**) and generate a single output (called **return value**) as shown in Figure 7.1.

For example, we can create a function to perform addition of multiple arguments passed to it such that it returns the result of addition as its output. In this way, instead of actually performing addition at 100 different places you could write the operation of addition only once within the function and invoke this function at 100 different places by passing different data values. Now, if you need to change this operation to subtraction all you need to do is just change it at one place within the function as all the 100 occurrences invoke the same function passing different values.

NOTES

It is also possible to create a function without any arguments and/or return value. We will learn creation and usage of functions with and without arguments and/or return values in this chapter.

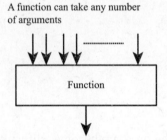

A function can take any number of arguments

Function

A function can return at the most one value

Figure 7.1: Function or a method

Just as we have taken an example of a function which performs addition, it is possible to create multiple functions in the program with each of them performing an independent operation. The operation a particular function performs is called a **service** provided by that function. Any function F_i in the program can invoke some other function F_j if F_i needs the services provided by F_j. A program can be viewed as collection of different pieces as shown in Figure 7.2. Such a programming is called **structured programming or modular programming**.

As an example to understand the concept of **structured programming**, let us refer to the main() function shown in Figure 7.3.

The main() function repeatedly executes a sequence S1, S2, S3. For the first time the sequence S1, S2, S3 is executed after the execution of instruction I2 and the second

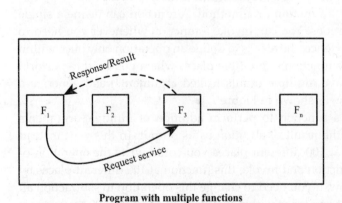

Program with multiple functions

Figure 7.2: Structured programming or modular programming

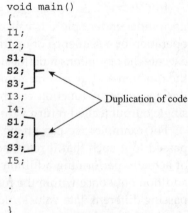

```
void main()
{
  I1;
  I2;
  S1;
  S2;
  S3;
  I3;
  I4;
  S1;
  S2;
  S3;
  I5;
  .
  .
  .
}
```

Duplication of code

Figure 7.3: Duplication of code in the main() function

time the sequence is again executed after the execution of instruction I4. Instead of writing redundant code, we can create a separate function, say, sub_seq() which contains the sequence S1, S2, S3. The programmer can simply invoke the function sub_seq(), whenever it is required to execute the instructions S1, S2, S3 in the program. Syntax to create the function sub_seq() is very much similar to the way we create main() function, except that the name of the function in this case is sub_seq() as shown below. Such functions are called **user-defined functions**. You are free to give any name to the function which is defined by you. The rules for naming functions are same as that of the rules for naming variables mentioned in Chapter 2, Section 2.5.5.

```
void sub_seq()
{
S1;
S2;
S3;
}
```

A function will not get executed until and unless it is invoked. We must explicitly call (invoke) the function sub_seq(), whenever we wish to execute the instructions S1, S2, S3. After the function is **called** the control of execution is transferred inside the function body and hence the statements S1, S2 and S3 will be executed in the sequence as we have written inside the function. Once the last statement of the function is executed, the control of execution will return to the **next statement after the function call** to continue the execution of the remaining part of the main() function.

In this case, the sequence S1, S2, S3 repeats twice in the main() and hence instead of actually writing it two times we can invoke the function sub_seq() at each place in the main() where we wish to execute the said sequence. As shown in Figure 7.4, we "call"

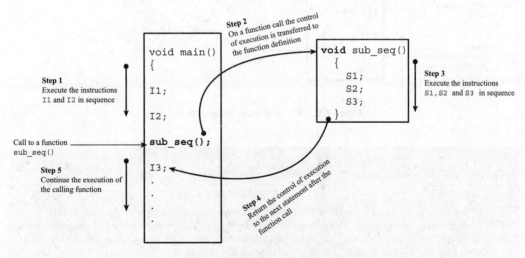

Figure 7.4: Calling sub_seq()

the function sub_seq() after instruction I2, because this is one of the places in main() function where we wish to execute the sequence.

After the function is 'called' the control of execution is transferred to the function sub_seq(), thereby executing the statements S1, S2, S3 after I2. After the execution of the function sub_seq completes, the control returns to main() at the next statement after the function call (which is I3) and resumes the execution of the main() function from I3. This means that the sequence S1, S2, S3 is executed exactly between the two statements I2 and I3, which is exactly our requirement.

The statements I3 and I4 are executed after the function sub_seq() completes its first execution. There is a second call made to the function sub_seq() after I4; hence, the execution of sequence S1, S2, S3 will be repeated after I4. Once the function sub_seq() is completed the control returns to the next statement after the function call which is this time I5. The execution of the main() function resumes from I5 as seen in figure 7.5. This flow of control ensures that the statements S1, S2, S3 are executed exactly between I4 and I5.

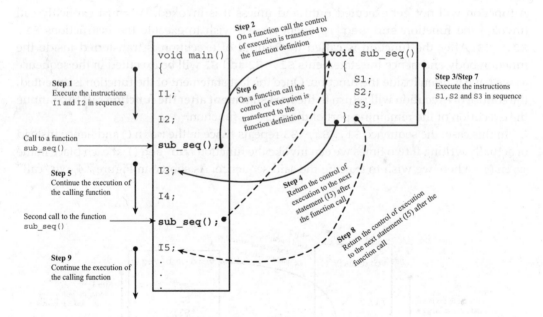

Figure 7.5: Calling sub_seq() twice

Is main() a user-defined function ?

Yes main() is also a user-defined function. The execution of every program always starts from the it. main() represents start and end of the program and it is a function which is recognized by the compiler. When you execute your program compiler invokes main() function and starts the execution of the code from the first line of main(). Other user defined functions should be invoked by the programmer explicitly; whereas `main()` is implicitly invoked by the compiler when you compile and execute your code. Hence `main()` must be written in a format which is recognized by the compiler. One of the formats in which `main()` can be written is what we have been using throughout this text book, as given below

```
void main()
{
/*operations*/
}
```

There are some more formats in which `main()` can be coded and they are discussed later in this chapter. However, we will always use the above style of creating `main()` in this text book, unless there is a specific need to use any other format

As execution always starts from `main()`, any other function that we wish to execute must be "called" either from the `main()` function or from some other function which can be reached through `main()` in at least one execution flow.

REMEMBER

♦ A function is a subroutine which contains sequence of statements to be executed to perform a specific operation.
♦ A function can have multiple inputs (called arguments) and generate a single output (called **return value**).
♦ Functions are used to avoid redundancy of code in the program, thereby reducing lines of code and simplifying change management process.
♦ Structured programming (also called modular programming) is a programming technique wherein a large program is splitted into different functions (modules) such that each of the functions perform a specific operation. The operation a particular function performs is called as **service** provided by that function. Any function F_i in the program can invoke some other function F_j if F_i needs the services provided by F_j.

7.2 Creating Functions

Figure 7.6 gives the syntax for creating user-defined functions.

As a first example to understand the syntax, let us create a simple function without any arguments and return values. We will work with arguments and return values later in this chapter. Let us create a function `add()` that prints the result of addition of the two

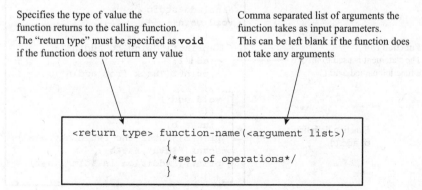

Specifies the type of value the function returns to the calling function. The "return type" must be specified as **void** if the function does not return any value

Comma separated list of arguments the function takes as input parameters. This can be left blank if the function does not take any arguments

```
<return type> function-name(<argument list>)
                {
                /*set of operations*/
                }
```

Figure 7.6: Syntax for creating a function

numbers on the computer screen. The syntax for creating a function add() is very similar to creating main() function with the only difference that the name of the function is given as add() instead of main() as seen in Figure 7.7. The keyword void indicates that the function add() does not return any value to the caller after its execution. The argument list is empty because we do not intend to pass any arguments to the add() function.

Remember, the execution of the program always starts from the main() function, hence add() will not be executed unless it is called from the main(). We create a main() function which calls the add() as shown in Figure 7.8.

The statement

```
add();
```

is a **function call** to add() function. The function is always called using its name followed by the parenthesis and then a semicolon. The parenthesis are empty because add() does not accept any arguments. Due to this call, the control of execution should ideally be transferred to the function definition of add(). However, this does not happen because function add() is defined after main() and C/C++ compiler makes it mandatory to

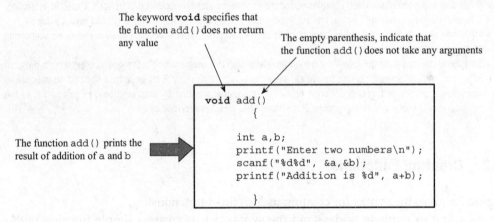

Figure 7.7:   Function definition of add()

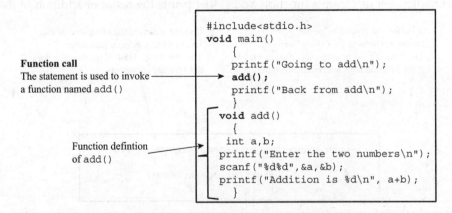

Figure 7.8:   main() function defined along with the add() function

declare every function defined after `main()` before it can be called. Hence, it is mandatory to declare `add()` as a function before making a function call. Declaration of a function is called **function prototype.** Prototyping a function is not necessary if we define the function before `main()`, it is mandatory only when the function is defined after `main()`.

Hence, we have two options to make the code work:

1. Include function prototype of `add()` in the program.
2. Define function `add()` before `main()`: In this case prototyping `add()` is not mandatory.

To understand option 1 we need to know what is a function prototype? We know that C/C++ does not support forward referencing. This means that you cannot use a variable in the program before its declaration. The general rule is that an identifier can be used only after its declaration. Same is true with functions. You cannot call a function `add()` without declaring (prototyping) it. The 'function prototype' informs the compiler about the exact way in which the function `add()` is defined later in the program.

Prototype includes the following information about the function:

1. Name of the function
2. Return type of the function
3. Data type and order of the arguments of the function

The syntax for function prototyping is as shown in Figure 7.9.

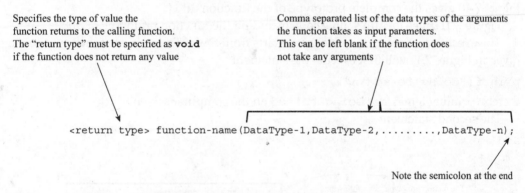

Figure 7.9: Syntax for function prototyping

C/C++ makes it mandatory that every function which is defined after `main()` must always be prototyped before `main()` function starts, so that the compiler has a complete understanding of the way in which the function is defined later in the program before its call. At the time of compilation, the compiler checks if the call made to the function follows the rules defined in the 'function prototype'. If the 'function call' correctly fulfils the rules of 'function prototype', then the compilation process is marked successful.

This means that before calling the function `add()` from the `main()` function, we must prototype the function `add()` to give the following information to the compiler:

1. **Name of the function:** The name of the function specified in the prototype should exactly match with the name that is given in the 'function definition' appearing after `main()`.

In this case, the 'function prototype' specifies the name of the function as add() which is same as what appears in the 'function definition'.

2. **Return type of the function:** Function add() does not give any value in return to the 'calling function' and hence its return type is set as void. We will discuss the functions that return a value in the later sections of this chapter.

3. **Data type and order of arguments:** As the function add() does not take any arguments, we have kept the argument section as blank in the prototype by simply opening and closing the parenthesis as shown in Figure 7.10. We will discuss the functions with 'arguments' in the next section. However, remember if the function takes any arguments, they should appear in the same order in the function prototype as they appear in the actual definition.

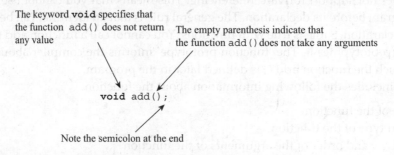

The keyword **void** specifies that the function add() does not return any value

The empty parenthesis indicate that the function add() does not take any arguments

void add();

Note the semicolon at the end

Figure 7.10: Prototype of the function add()

Figure 7.10 gives the complete prototype of the function add() .

Figure 7.11 gives the full source code including the function prototype of add()

The execution of any program always starts from the main() function; hence the code given in Figure 7.11 will first execute the statement

```
printf("Going to add\n");
```

thereby printing a message Going to add on the computer screen.

The second statement

```
add();
```

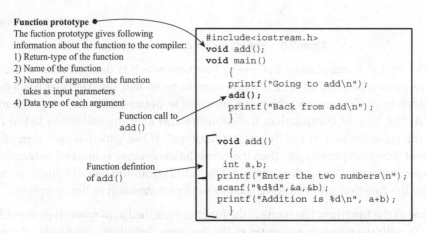

Function prototype
The fuction prototype gives following information about the function to the compiler:
1) Return-type of the function
2) Name of the function
3) Number of arguments the function takes as input parameters
4) Data type of each argument

Function call to add()

Function defintion of add()

```
#include<iostream.h>
void add();
void main()
{
    printf("Going to add\n");
    add();
    printf("Back from add\n");
}

void add()
{
    int a,b;
    printf("Enter the two numbers\n");
    scanf("%d%d",&a,&b);
    printf("Addition is %d\n", a+b);
}
```

Figure 7.11: Complete program with the function add() prototyped

calls the function add() and hence the control of execution will be transferred to the function definition of add() as shown in Figure 7.12. Remember, making a call to add() from main() is possible because we have already prototyped it before main(). The function definition of add() will now be executed which takes two numbers a and b as input from the user and prints the result of addition on the computer screen.

After execution of the function add() completes, the control will be returned back to main() at the next statement after the function call.

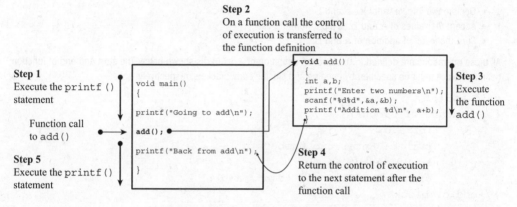

Figure 7.12: Call to function add()

Hence, the statement

```
printf("Back from add\n");
```

will get executed thereby printing a message, "Back from add" on the computer screen.

Obviously, there is no need to prototype a function if it is defined before main(). This is because there is no forward referencing whatsoever as the full definition of the function itself appears before making the function call. In this case, compilers are smart enough to extract the prototype function from the function definition and hence the code in Figure 7.13 works absolutely fine without prototyping add().

There is no need to prototype add() because it is defined before main() In this case, there is **no forward referencing** because the definition of the function appears **before its call**.

Function call to add()

```
#include<stdio.h>
void add()
    {
    int a,b;
    printf("Enter the two numbers\n");
    scanf("%d%d",&a,&b);
    printf("Addition is %d\n", a+b);
    }
void main()
    {
    printf("Going to add\n");
    add();
    printf("Back from add\n");
    }
```

Figure 7.13: Defining the function before main()

NOTES

Function call is a statement which transfers the control of execution to the function definition. For example, the statement

```
add();
```

is a function call to function named add().

Function definition is a block of code which defines all the operations that the function performs. For example, the operations that add() performs are as follows:

- Declare two integer variables a and b.
- Accept the values of a and b as input from the user.
- Print the result of addition of a and b.

All these operations are defined in the function definition of add() as shown below. The start and end of function definition block must be specified by opening and closing curly brackets, respectively

```
void add()
{    /*start of block*/
        int a,b;
        printf("Enter two numbers\n");
        scanf("%d%d",&a,&b);
        printf("Addition is %d\n", a+b);
} /*end of block*/
```

Function prototype is a declaration of the function which should be made by the programmer before calling the function. Prototyping a function is necessary only if function call appears before the function definition in the program. This is necessary because C/C++ compilers do not support forward referencing. Prototype includes following information about the function:

- Name of the function
- Return type of the function
- Data type and order of the arguments of the function

Function prototype is used by the compiler to validate if programmer has called the function correctly. If the 'function call' correctly fulfils the rules of 'function prototype', then the compilation process is marked successful.

In large projects, the function definitions are often placed in different files which are archived as external libraries. When you write your own function and call functions defined in external files from it, you must prototype each of the functions which you are calling. This gives compiler a notification beforehand about the names which can appear as function calls in the program and are defined externally. This is necessary because the function definition actually resides at a different place and compiler has not yet seen the function definition while compiling your file. In this case, prototyping a function is indeed like a promise made to the compiler that the function called in this file is actually present in some other file, so as to pass the compilation process. It is the job of the **linker** at the later stage to correctly resolve this **external function references** and provide all the needed function definitions to the program to generate the required output. Linker can only link different files if each of them are successfully compiled. Function prototype plays a vital role in this case, because it helps your file to compile without worrying about the function definition of the called functions. Remember, linking function calls to the external function definitions present in different libraries is a job of linker and not the compiler. The next question is how does the linker know where are the external libraries present? This needs to be configured by the programmer within the C/C++ editor. For example, in Turbo C/C++ editor the link director path is configured as shown in Figure 7.14.

Here, we have configured the link directory as D:\TC\LIB where linker would expect the external libraries to be present. You will find object files here because these are essentially compiled libraries. Remember that linker cannot link source codes; it can only work on compiled files and establish a link between them. It is the programmer's responsibility to ensure that all the needed libraries containing the required function definitions are present here. If they are not placed here, linking would fail giving a link error but compilation of the program might have still succeeded if function prototypes are specified correctly in the program.

Figure 7.14: Library configurations in Turbo C/C++ editor.

In some cases, you may not even have access to actually see the function definition; all you can do is just use its functionality. For example, we have used `printf()` function in almost every program we have written till now. Have you ever bothered where is `printf()` defined? No, because it is internally defined in C/C++ libraries which come along with the compiler. So by making a call to `printf()`, we are actually invoking an external function defined in some other file and we do not even know its definition. These libraries are usually present in a folder named LIB. The actual name of the folder may differ in your case but you should be able to track the correct folder in which libraries are stored looking at the library path configured in your editor as shown in Figure 7.14. In our case, the libraries which contain the definitions of the built-in functions, for example, `printf()` must be present in the `D:\TC\LIB` folder. These libraries usually come as compiled files so you cannot see the source code anyway.

We just said that every external function which we call must be prototyped. Where is `printf()` prototyped? The answer is the header file `stdio.h`. This header file contains prototypes of multiple input/output functions and they get included in your program when you include `stdio.h`. This saves programmers' efforts in prototyping built-in functions before using them. The next question is, how does pre-processor determine where is `stdio.h` present on the machine? The answer is this directory needs to be configured in the `include` directory path as shown in Figure 7.14. In our case, we have configured the `include` directory as `D:\TC\INCLUDE` and hence the macro pre-processor expects all the header files to be present at this location. If you browse this location you will find all the header files here. The directory configurations which we have discussed here are editor specific and in this case we have taken an example of Turbo C/C++ editor. If you have a different editor it might have a different way to configure `include` and `LIB` directories but conceptually all editors work the same way.

7.3   Local Variables of the Function

Any variable declared inside the function can be accessed only within the scope of that function. Such a variable which is defined within the function body is called a 'local variable'. To understand the concept of local variables, let us create two functions add() and sub() in the program to perform addition and subtraction of two numbers, respectively. The main() function will call the function add() and sub() as shown in Figure 7.15.

As seen in Figure 7.15, the function add() creates local variables a and b, accepts their values as input from the user and prints their addition on screen. Similarly, the function sub() also creates local variables a and b and prints the result of subtraction. The variables have been intentionally created with same name in functions add() and sub(); always remember they are not really the same in the memory. The variables defined in add() cannot be accessed in sub() and vice versa. Each of the functions has their own set of

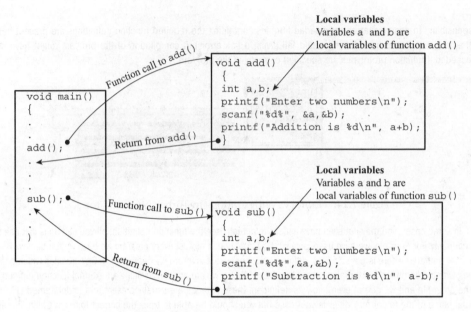

Figure 7.15: Functions `main()`, `add()` and `sub()`

variables local to that function. Even `main()` cannot access any variables defined in any of the other functions, such as `add()` and `sub()` because `main()` is also a function and like any other function it cannot access local variables of some other function.

Given below is the full source code that defines two functions `add()` and `sub()` to perform addition and subtraction, respectively.

NOTES

Each time a function is called, space is created in the memory for its execution. This space is called an **activation frame or an activation record**. The word 'activation' signifies the fact that the function actually gets activated when it is called. This memory gets destroyed when the function completes its execution (i.e., when the function is deactivated). This activation frame stores the local variables of the function and hence the lifetime of local variables is only till the time function is under execution.

Remember, program always executes sequentially. So if there are two back-to-back calls to a particular function they will always be handled one by one. For example, if `add()` is called two times as shown below:

```
add(); /*First call to add()*/
add();/*Second call to add()*/
```

Execution will happen considering one statement at a time. In response to the first call to `add()`, an activation frame will be created at runtime with space for local variables a and b and destroyed after execution of `add()` completes. In response to the second call to `add()`, a new activation frame will be created containing space for a and b. Notice that even if the same function is called twice the activation frame is not shared. The actual memory in which the first call executes is different from the second call; hence the scope of local variables is only for the time the function is under execution. We will discuss this concept with an example code given below. An activation frame contains many other details along with the values of local variables and its detailed structure is discussed later in Section 7.8.

```
#include<stdio.h>
void add();
void sub();
void main()
{
add();
sub();
add();
}
void add()
{
int a,b;
printf("Enter two numbers\n");
scanf("%d%d",&a,&b);
printf("Addition is %d\n", a+b);
}
void sub()
{
int a,b;
printf("Enter two numbers\n");
scanf("%d%d",&a,&b);
printf("Subtraction is %d\n", a-b);
}
```

Output
```
Enter two numbers
10 20
Addition is 30
Enter two numbers
90 50
Subtraction is 40
Enter two numbers
200 300
Addition is 500
```

As the execution always starts from the main() function, let us trace the output of the program starting from the first statement in main()

The first statement

```
add();
```

calls the function add() and hence the control of execution will be transferred inside the function body of the add() function. This creates an activation frame for add(). The function add() creates two local variables a and b by accepting their values as input from the user. Let us assume that the user inputs the values of variables a and b as 10 and 20, respectively; then the activation frame is as shown in Figure 7.16. The result of addition will be printed as 30 on the computer screen as seen in the output of the program. Note that the result of addition is stored temporarily in the memory only during the execution of printf() statement and cannot be accessed anywhere in the add() function later on. Certainly, the resultant value printed by the printf() statement will be on the screen and visible to us

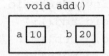

Figure 7.16: Activation frame for add()

After the execution of the function add() is completed, the activation frame is destroyed and the local variables can no longer be accessed. Hence, the variables a and b of add() function will no longer be present in the memory.

As the execution of add() is completed, the control returns to the next statement in main() which is

```
sub();
```

This statement calls the function sub() and hence the control of execution will be transferred inside the function body of the sub() function. This creates an activation frame for sub(). Like add(), the function sub() also creates two local variables a and b accepting their values as input from the user. Let us assume that the user inputs the values of variables a and b as 90 and 50, respectively; then the activation frame is as shown in Figure 7.17. The result of subtraction will be printed as 40 on the computer screen as seen in the output of the program.

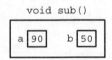

Figure 7.17: Activation frame for sub()

After the execution of the function sub() is completed, the activation frame is destroyed and the local variables can no longer be accessed. Hence, the variables a and b of sub() function will no longer be present in the memory.

As the execution of sub() is completed, the control returns to the next statement in main() which is

```
add();
```

This statement calls add() one more time and hence a new activation frame will be created for its execution. We will again have to input the values of variables a and b as a new copy of the local variables will be created each time the function is invoked. Let us assume that this time the user inputs the values of variables a and b as 200 and 300, respectively; then the activation frame for this call is as shown in Figure 7.18. Remember, this is a new activation frame created specific to this function call and is not related in any way with the activation frames shown in Figures 7.16 and 7.17. In fact the previous two activation frames have been already destroyed and are no longer present in the memory. Each time we call a function, a new copy of its local variables

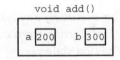

Figure 7.18: New activation frame for add()

will be created in the memory because the activation frames are indeed different for every call even if the same function is called multiple times. This time, the result of addition will be printed as 500 on the computer screen as seen in the output of the program.

NOTES

The local variables are created when the control of execution enters the function definition and they will be destroyed after the function execution is completed. The local variables of the function will not be available outside the scope of the function in which they are defined.

7.4 Functions with Arguments

If there is a requirement for **called** function to operate on the values of the variables defined in the **calling** function, we can pass the values or references of these variables as **arguments** to the **called** function. This helps the **called** function to get the access to the values which are actually defined inside the **calling** function.

DEFINITION

The values that we pass from the **calling** function to the **called** function are referred as **arguments**.

As an example, let us write a program that creates the functions add() and sub() to perform addition and subtraction of the values of variables a and b defined in the main() function. Note that the values of these variables a and b will not be accessible to functions add() or sub() because they are local variables of main as shown in Figure 7.19.

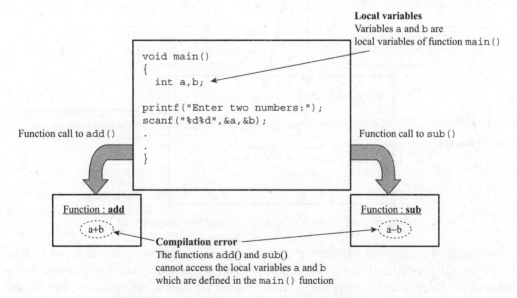

Figure 7.19: Function main() creating variables a and b

To perform the addition of the variables defined in the main(), we can pass the values of its local variables a and b as arguments to the 'add'. Let the values of the variables a and b in main() be 10 and 20, respectively; then these values will be passed from function main() to function add() as shown in Figure 7.19. The function add() stores the values passed by main() in variables p and q, respectively. The variables p and q which are created as a part of add() function to store the values passed by the 'calling' function are called **formal arguments.** In contrast, the **values** of variables a and b which are actually passed by the main() function at the time of calling add() are called **actual arguments.**

Remember, the 'actual arguments' are the arguments specified in the 'function call', whereas the 'formal arguments' are the arguments specified in the 'function definition' of the called function. The value of each of the actual arguments will be initialized to the corresponding formal argument in an order from left to right. This means that the value of variable a will be initialized to the first formal argument which is 'p' and the value of the variable b will be initialized to the second formal argument which is 'q'. Therefore, p stores 10 and q stores 20 as shown in Figure 7.20. Although we cannot access local variables a and b of main() in add(), we can still access their values using formal arguments p and q within the scope of add(). This means that addition of p and q will give the same result as adding the values of a and b. Hence, the function add() will give the result of addition as 30 as shown in Figure 7.20.

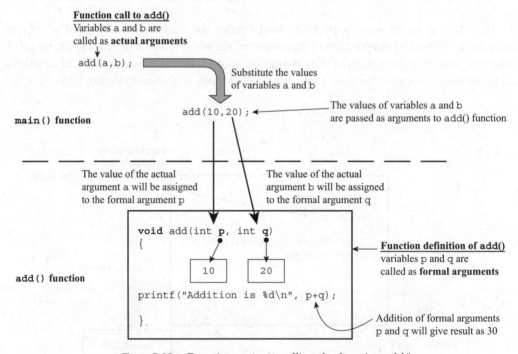

Figure 7.20: Function main() calling the function add()

Although the values of variables p and q are same as that of variables a and b, they are physically present at different locations in memory. Therefore, any change made to the value of variable p will not affect the value of original variable a and, similarly, any change made to the value of variable q will not affect the value of original variable b.

NOTES

Actual arguments are stored in the activation frame of calling function, whereas formal arguments are stored in the activation frame of the called function. This point will be clearer when we discuss detailed structure of activation frame in Section 7.8, but mentioning it here reiterates the fact that actual and formal arguments are physically different in memory although they are guaranteed to have same values.

As the function add() now takes two arguments of type integer we must prototype the function as shown below.

```c
void add(int,int);
```

It is mandatory for the function prototype to specify the data types of arguments in the same order as specified in the function definition. It is not required to specify the variable names p and q in function prototype as they are anyways created in function definition. As discussed in Section 7.2, function prototype is only required to give the following information so that the compiler can validate if the function is called correctly:

- Name of the function
- Return type of the function
- Data type and order of the arguments of the function

Given below is a full source code which shows the creation of functions with arguments. Similar to add(), we have also created a function sub() with two arguments to perform subtraction of two integers passed to it:

```c
#include<stdio.h>
void add(int,int);
void sub(int,int);
void main()
{
int a,b;
printf("Enter values of a and b:\n");
scanf("%d%d",&a,&b);
add(a,b);
sub(b,a);
add(400,100);
}
void add(int p,int q)
{
printf("Addition is %d\n",p+q);
}
void sub(int p,int q)
{
printf("Subtraction is %d\n",p-q);
}
```

Output
```
Enter values of a and b:
10 20
Addition is 30
Subtraction is 10
Addition is 500
```

As the execution always starts from main() function, we will trace the output of the program starting from the first statement of main()

The statements

```
int a,b;
printf("Enter values of a and b:\n");
scanf("%d%d",&a,&b);
```

create local variables a and b in the main() function and accept their values as input from the user. Let us assume that the input values of a and b are 10 and 20, respectively.

The statement

```
add(a,b);
```

calls the function add() by passing the values of a and b as actual arguments which are initialized to the formal arguments p and q created as a part of add() function. The function performs the addition of values p and q, thereby printing the result as 30 which is shown in Figure 7.20.

The statement

```
sub(b,a);
```

is a function call to sub(). Notice that the order in which the arguments are passed to sub() is different from that of add(). We have passed b as the first argument and a as the second argument. The function definition of the sub() creates the formal arguments p and q. As the value of variable b is passed as a first argument from left, it will be time initialized to formal argument p and the value of a which is passed as a second argument will now be initialized to the formal argument q as shown in Figure 7.21. This means that the value of p will be set as 20 and the value of q will be set to 10. Hence, performing the subtraction of p and q in the sub() function will give the result as **10** as shown in Figure 7.21.

NOTES

The order in which arguments are passed to the function could impact the result produced by the function if the function is performing at least one non-commutative operation. For example, call sub(b,a); is different from the call sub(a,b); The call sub(b,a); produces the result as +10, whereas sub(a,b); will produce a result as -10.

We can call the same function multiple times by passing different values to it. The statement

```
add(400,100);
```

Order of arguments specified in the function call to sub()
The values of actual arguments will be assigned to the formal arguments
with an associativity of **Left to Right**

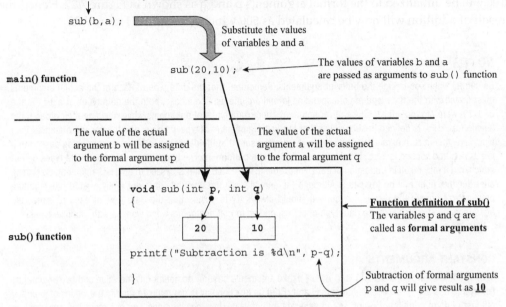

main() function

sub(b,a);

Substitute the values
of variables b and a

sub(20,10);

The values of variables b and a
are passed as arguments to sub() function

The value of the actual
argument b will be assigned
to the formal argument p

The value of the actual
argument a will be assigned
to the formal argument q

sub() function

```
void sub(int p, int q)
{
        20      10

printf("Subtraction is %d\n", p-q);

}
```

Function definition of sub()
The variables p and q are
called as **formal arguments**

Subtraction of formal arguments
p and q will give result as **10**

Figure 7.21: Calling the function sub()

Specifying direct values at the time of a function call
We can pass constant values at the time of a function call.
For example, the values 400 and 100 can be passed to the function add()
using the following function call

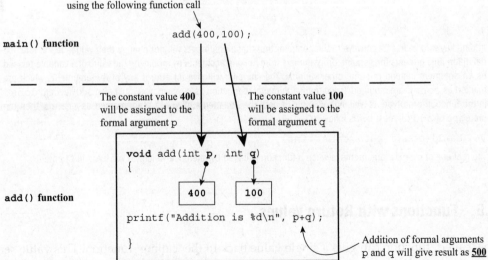

main() function

add(400,100);

The constant value **400**
will be assigned to the
formal argument p

The constant value **100**
will be assigned to the
formal argument q

add() function

```
void add(int p, int q)
{
        400     100

printf("Addition is %d\n", p+q);

}
```

Addition of formal arguments
p and q will give result as **500**

Figure 7.22: Calling the function add()

passes the hardcoded argument values as 400 and 100 to the function add(). This means that the function add() will be 'called' one more time and the actual arguments 400 and 100 will be initialized to the formal arguments p and q as shown in Figure 7.22. Hence, the result of addition will now be calculated as **500** which is shown in Figure 7.22.

NOTES

Be careful when you decide the order of arguments. Remember that the data type of each of the actual arguments must match with the data type of corresponding formal arguments. In our case, both the data types of add() and sub() were of type integer so we never bothered about data types of arguments while deciding their order. If the function add() is defined in such a way that the first argument is of type float and the second argument is of type int then it is programmers' responsibility to make sure that the data type of first argument being passed to it is float and second is int. In many cases, C/C++ can perform implicit type conversions when data types do not match, but it may result in truncation of data. For example, if float value is passed to an int argument, everything after decimal point will be truncated. Although the compiler will not complain, it is not really a good programming practice to truncate the results. Hence, you should always try to ensure that the data type of each of the actual arguments must match with the data type of corresponding formal arguments when working with primitive types.

CONSTANT ARGUMENTS

In this case, the functions add() and sub() take arguments but they do not modify the value of these arguments. For example, add() accepts arguments p and q but its functionality is not really to modify the values of p and q but just perform addition of p and q and generate a third value. In such situations, you can create an argument as a constant argument by adding a keyword const before the argument while defining the function

```
void add( const int p , const int q)
{
/*Function body*/
int res = p+q; /*Works fine*/
p=p+1; /*ERROR! Cannot modify constant argument*/
q=q+1; /*ERROR! Cannot modify constant argument*/
    . .
    . .
}
```

Adding keyword const conveys to the compiler that these arguments will not change their values in the function definition. This protects the genuine programmers from making accidents by modifying the value of a variable passed as an argument instead of some other variable. The compiler will give an error if any of the arguments which are marked as const are modified. If you mark arguments of function as const, you must also add keyword const in the function prototype as well. For example, if both the arguments of add() are marked as const, then the prototype of add() must be as follows:

```
void add(const int, const int);
```

The real use of const arguments is when a function is called by reference which we will learn in Chapter 8.

7.5 Functions with Return Values

The 'called' function can give a single value back to the 'calling' function. This value sent from the 'called' function to the 'calling' function is called a 'return value'. The 'return value' typically represents the result of the operations performed by the 'called' function.

The 'return' statement in C/C++ is used to send value back to the caller. Given below is the syntax of return statement:

```
return <expression>;
```

The statement will return the result of the expression back to the calling function.

As an example to demonstrate the usage of return statement, let us write a function add() that performs the addition of two arguments passed to it and returns back the result of the addition to the 'calling' function. If two formal arguments p and q store the values to be added, the statement

```
return p+q;
```

will return the result of p+q to the caller. As the arguments p and q are of type int, the result will also be an integer. As add() returns an integer value, we should prototype it as shown in Figure 7.23.

This means that the function add() takes two arguments of type int and returns one value of type int. Given below is the source code that creates a function add() returning the result of addition of two integers to the main() function.

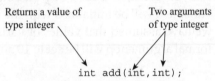

Figure 7.23: Prototype of function add() returning an integer

```
#include<stdio.h>
int add(int,int);
void main()
{
int a,b,c;
printf("Enter the values of a and b\n");
scanf("%d%d",&a,&b);
c=add(a,b);
printf("Addition of %d and %d is %d\n",a,b,c);
int d;
d= add(100,200);
printf("Addition of 100 and 200 is %d\n",d);
}
int add(int p,int q)
{
return p+q;
}
```

Output

```
Enter the values of a and b
10 20
Addition of 10 and 20 is 30
Addition of 100 and 200 is 300
```

As the execution always starts from main() function, we will trace the output of the program starting from the first statement of main().

The statements

```
int a,b,c;
printf("Enter the values of a and b\n");
scanf("%d%d",&a,&b);
```

create the local variables a, b and c inside the main() function, accepting the values of variables a and b as input from the user. Let the user input the values of a and b as 10 and 20, respectively.

The statement

```
c = add(a,b);
```

calls the function add() by passing the values of a and b as arguments. The value of variable c will be initialized with the value returned by add() as shown in Figure 7.24. As we have assumed that values of variables a and b as 10 and 20, respectively, value of the formal argument p will be set to 10 and the value of the formal argument q will be set to 20.

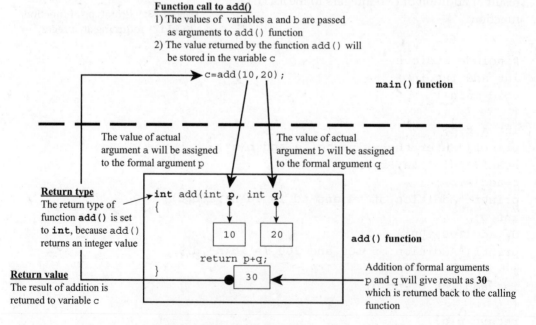

Figure 7.24: Calling function add()

The 'return' statement will return the result of addition as 30 back to the main() function which will be initialized to the variable c as shown in Figure 7.24.

The main() function prints the result of addition using the printf statement

```
printf("Addition of %d and %d is %d\n",a,b,c);
```

As the value of c is initialized to 30, the output of the statement is

```
Addition of 10 and 20 is 30
```

The next statement

```
d=add(100,200);
```

calls the function add() one more time by passing the hardcoded values 100 and 200 and storing the result of addition in variable d. This means that the function add() will again be executed (with a new activation frame) by setting the values of formal arguments 'p' and 'q' as 100 and 200, respectively. Therefore, add() will return the result of addition as **300** which will be initialized to the variable d.

What is a return type? ?

The return type of the function is the data type of a value returned by the function. In the above example, the function add() returns addition of two integers which is also a integer; and hence its return type is **int**.

To clarify further, consider function f1() which returns value of a as shown below. In this case the return type of the function f1() must be specified as **float** because the data type of variable a is float

```
float f1()
{
float a;
------------
------------
-----------
return a;
}
```

What will happen if, we do not specify the return type of a particular function in the program? ?

If we do not specify the return type its by default considered as int by the compiler. For example if we define a function f1() without specifying any return type as follows:

```
f1()
{
---------------
---------------
}
```

then, the compiler expects f1() to return an integer.

If we do not want to return any value from f1() then we must explicitly specify its return type as **void** as shown below

```
void f1()
{
--------
--------
}
```

void is a keyword that informs the compiler, that the function does not return any value

NOTE

When `return` statement is encountered, it ends the execution of the current function and transfers the control back to the caller immediately. Any code present after the `return` statement will not be executed because it is never reached.

In Figure 7.25, we have written a `return` statement without any expression as shown below:

```
return;
```

This statement is written when you don't want to give any value back to the caller but just want to exit the 'called' function immediately. This statement is essentially used in void type functions to terminate their execution if a certain condition is satisfied. As per Figure 7.25, if main() calls function f1() which is of type void, when return statement is executed in f1() the code which appears after return statement is skipped and the control is transferred back to the 'calling' function, resuming its execution. Such return statements are always executed conditionally, as we have done in Figure 7.25 wherein the `return;`

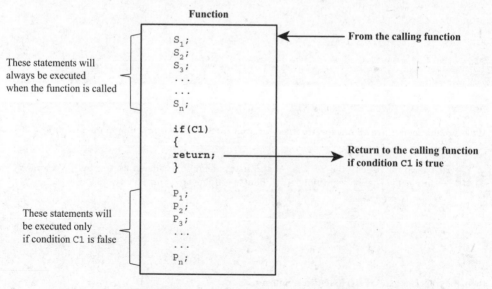

Figure 7.25: Execution of return statement

statement is only executed if condition of the `if` block is satisfied, thereby skipping the later part of the code in f1(). If the condition in `if` block is false, the `return;` statement will not be executed and the execution of f1() will continue till the end as usual. Hence, in this case, we have designed an execution flow that will terminate f1() abruptly if a specific condition is satisfied.

7.5.1 Program to find the maximum of six numbers using the function with two arguments: An example

Consider the function `max()` defined as follows. The function takes two integer arguments a and b and returns maximum of a and b:

```
int max(int a, int b)
{
        if(a>b)
        {
        return a;
        }
        else
        {
        return b;
        }
}
```

What if we need to make use the above function to find maximum out of more than 2 numbers? Since `max()` can just compare two values at a time, we need to make multiple calls to `max()` to get the maximum value out of all the numbers. Given below is the full source code to find the maximum of six numbers using the function `max()`:

```
#include<stdio.h>
int max(int, int);
void main()
{
int a,b,c,d,e,f,m;
printf("Enter 6 numbers:\n");
scanf("%d%d%d%d%d%d",&a,&b,&c,&d,&e,&f);
m =max( max( max(a,b), max(c,d) ) ,max(e,f) );
printf("Maximum is %d\n",m);
}
int max(int a, int b)
{
        if(a>b)
        {
        return a;
}
```

```
    else
    {
    return b;
    }
}
```

Output

```
Enter 6 numbers:
10 5 15 25 6 30
Maximum is 30
```

Let the user input values of six variables a, b, c, d, e and f as shown below:

Variable	a	b	c	d	e	f
User input	10	5	15	25	6	30

The program finds the maximum out of the six values using a function max() which takes two arguments. Remember that max() can take only two arguments at a time and hence we will call the function multiple times to find the maximum of all the six numbers. The statement

```
m =max( max( max(a,b) ,max(c,d) ) ,max(e,f) );
```

makes five different calls to function max(). The function calls will be made from left to right such that all the inner calls are resolved before the outer calls. The outer function calls will use the return values given by the inner function calls. For example, if we consider a subpart of the above statement as

```
max( max(a,b) ,max(c,d) )
```

then the innermost and leftmost function call max(a,b) will be resolved first, which returns the maximum of a and b which is **10**. After max(a,b), the function call max(c,d) will be resolved which will return maximum of c and d which is **25**. After both the inner function calls are resolved, the function max() will be 'called' one more time using the values returned by the inner calls as arguments. The outer function call shown in Figure 7.26 returns the maximum of values 10 and 25 which is **25**.

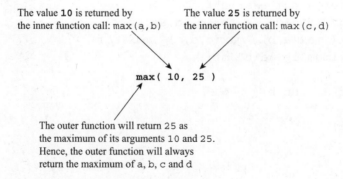

The value **10** is returned by the inner function call: max(a,b)

The value **25** is returned by the inner function call: max(c,d)

max(10, 25)

The outer function will return 25 as the maximum of its arguments 10 and 25. Hence, the outer function will always return the maximum of a, b, c and d

Figure 7.26: Outer function call

Figure 7.27 gives the complete execution of the statement

```
m =max( max( max(a,b), max(c,d) ), max(e,f) );
```

After the execution of the statement, the value of variable m will be initialized to **30** which is the maximum of the six numbers.

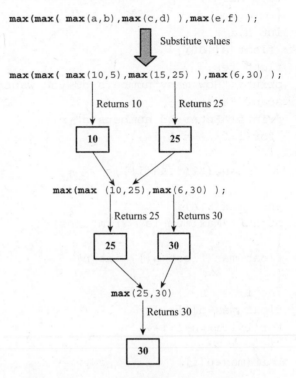

7.6 Passing Array as an Argument to the Function

It is possible to pass array as an argument to the function. Let a be an array of size n created in the main() function. We create a function max() which accepts an array as an argument and returns the maximum element from the array back to the caller.

When defining the function max(), we create an array p which is of type 'float' as a formal argument along with the integer n. Note that we should not specify the size of the formal array p because the array p will be the exact image of the actual

Figure 7.27: Execution of nested calls to max()

argument a passed to it by the 'calling' function. Hence, the size of the array p will be same as the size of the array a. In this case, since the size of array a is 100, size of p will also be 100. The function max() will find the maximum of all the elements in the array passed to it and return a resultant 'maximum value' back to the 'calling' function.

The function max() takes the following two arguments:

1. **Array of floats:** This is the array a which stores the actual data.
2. **Integer n:** Although size of the array a is 100, all 100 elements of a are not valid. As seen in main(), only n elements in a are valid, containing actual user inputs. As n is a local variable of main(), there is no way for function max() to determine how many elements in a are valid user inputs. Hence, we pass n as an argument from main() to f1() so that f1() knows the exact value of n.

Further, the function max() returns a floating point result, which is the maximum of n elements in the array. Hence, the function max() must be prototyped as

```
float max(float[] , int);
```

The logic to find the maximum of n elements from the array is same as discussed in Chapter 6, section 6.2.4. Given below is the full source code to find the maximum of n numbers using the function max().

```
#include<stdio.h>
float max(float[] , int);
void main()
{
int n,i;
 float a[100];
float res;
printf("How many numbers do you want to enter? \n");
scanf("%d",&n);
printf("Enter %d numbers\n",n);
 for(i=0;i<=n-1;i++)
 {
    scanf("%f",&a[i]);
 }
res= max(a,n);
printf("Maximum is  %f\n",res);
}
float max(float p[], int n)
{
int i;
float max=p[0];
for(i=1;i<=n-1;i++)
 {
  if(max<p[i])
  {
   max=p[i];
  }
 }
return max;
}
```

Output

```
How many numbers do you want to enter?
3
Enter 3 numbers
10 35 20
Maximum is 35.000000
```

7.6.1 Arrange n numbers in descending order using functions: An example

Let us create a function sort_desc() to arrange n numbers in descending order. Before we design the function, it should be noted that 'arrays' are always passed by address, unlike other variables which are passed by value. We will discuss a detailed difference between 'call by address' and 'call by value' in Chapter 8 of this textbook. However, the

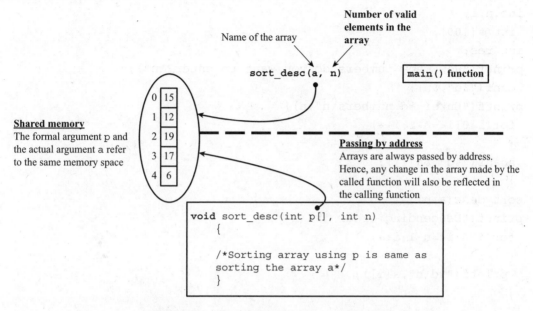

Figure 7.28: Call to function `sort_desc()`

key point to note is that when an array is passed as an argument, the 'actual argument' and the 'formal argument' share a **common data space** in the memory and hence any change made to the array by the 'called' function is also reflected in the 'calling' function (as the array is internally one and the same).

Let us assume that a is the array with n valid elements, created in the `main()` function containing integers to be sorted in descending order. We can pass this array to the function `sort_desc()` to arrange n numbers in descending order as shown in Figure 7.28. Note that p is a formal argument created inside the function `sort_desc()` which sorts the array using the sorting algorithm discussed in Chapter 6, section 6.2.5. The array p and the array a will share the same memory space and hence sorting array p is same as sorting array a. The changes in the array made by the function `sort_desc()` using p will be automatically reflected in the `main()` function as well. Hence, it is not required to have a return statement in the function `sort_desc()` as the results are as such available to `main()`. When the `main()` function prints the array after the `sort_desc()` function is executed it gets the descending order at the output of the program as seen in the code, because the array arranged by `sort_desc()` is same as that of the array used by `main()`.

The return type of function `sort_desc()` is set as void because it is not required to return any value to `main()` as both the functions share the same array space. Given below is the full source code to arrange n numbers in ascending order.

```c
#include<stdio.h>
void sort_desc(int[] , int);
void main()
{
```

```
int n,i;
 int a[100];
int res;
printf("How many numbers do you want to enter?\n");
scanf("%d",&n);
printf("Enter %d numbers\n",n);
 for(i=0;i<=n-1;i++)
 {
 scanf("%d",&a[i]);
 }
sort_desc(a,n);
printf("Descending order is:\n");
 for(i=0;i<=n-1;i++)
 {
  printf("%d\n",a[i]);
 }
}
void sort_desc(int p[],int n)
{
int t,i,j;
for(i=0;i<=n-2;i++)
 {
  for(j=i+1;j<=n-1;j++)
  {
   if(p[i]<p[j])
   {
     // Swap the 2 numbers
     t=p[i];
     p[i]=p[j];
     p[j]=t;
   }
  }
 }
}
```

output

```
How many numbers do you want to enter?
5
Enter 5 numbers
15 12 19 17 6
```

```
Descending order is:
19
17
15
12
6
```

> **NOTES**
>
> When an array is passed as an argument, the 'actual argument' and the 'formal argument' share a **common data space** in the memory and hence any change made to the array by the 'called' function is also reflected in the 'calling' function (as the array is internally one and the same).

> **NOTES**
>
> When arrays are passed as an argument they are always passed by address. This mechanism is called **call by address**. Call by address is discussed in detail in Chapter 8, you may want to revisit this explanation after you read Chapter 8. Chapter 8 also covers relationship between arrays and pointers. Some points which we have not touched in this section will be clarified in Chapter 8.

7.7 Recursion

Recursion is a programming construct implemented using stack which solves a large problem by dividing it into smaller parts. It is also called 'divide and conquer' technique to solve problems.

> **Recursive Function**
>
> A function that calls itself conditionally is called a recursive function. A simplest example of a recursive function would be function `f1()` as shown in Figure 7.29.

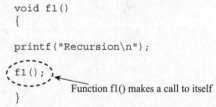

```
void f1()
{

printf("Recursion\n");

f1();

}
```
Function f1() makes a call to itself

Figure 7.29: Unconditional recursion

As seen in Figure 7.29, the function `f1()` keeps calling itself. This results into a similar effect as that of executing the operation defined before the function call (in this case `printf()`) in an indefinite loop. Each execution of `f1()` performs the following two steps:

1. Executes the statement `printf("Recursion\n");`
2. Makes another call to `f1()`

Due to another call made to function `f1()`, steps 1 and 2 above will keep executing in an infinite loop. Remember each function call creates a new activation frame on stack memory. As there is no condition to terminate this recursion, stack memory will go full at some point due to a large number of activation frames for `f1()` created in it. When stack overflows, the program crashes giving out of memory error.

To avoid this situation, every recursive function must have at least one **terminating condition**. Hence, we have defined a recursive function as a function which calls itself **conditionally** and not unconditionally.

NOTES

Every recursive function must have at least one terminating condition which terminates the recursion. This avoids crashing of program due to infinite number of activation frames being created on stack.

In this section, we will discuss different examples of recursive solutions which will work in both C and C++.

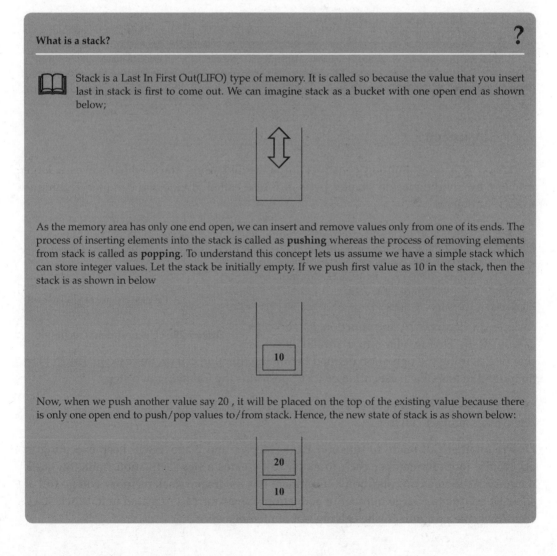

What is a stack?

Stack is a Last In First Out(LIFO) type of memory. It is called so because the value that you insert last in stack is first to come out. We can imagine stack as a bucket with one open end as shown below;

As the memory area has only one end open, we can insert and remove values only from one of its ends. The process of inserting elements into the stack is called as **pushing** whereas the process of removing elements from stack is called as **popping**. To understand this concept lets us assume we have a simple stack which can store integer values. Let the stack be initially empty. If we push first value as 10 in the stack, then the stack is as shown in below

Now, when we push another value say 20 , it will be placed on the top of the existing value because there is only one open end to push/pop values to/from stack. Hence, the new state of stack is as shown below:

Similarly, when we push 30 it will be placed above 20 as shown below

While popping out elements from the stack, we will have to remove 30 before we remove 20, this is because 30 is placed above 20. Similarly, we will have to pop out 20 before we pop out 10 because 20 is placed above 10. Notice that, 30 was last to go in the stack but is first to come out of stack. Hence stack is called as Last in First out (LIFO) type of data structure.

Stacks play a very important role in handling function calls. The requirement of recursive function calls is that, the function that is "called" at the end must be completed first and the function that is "called" at the beginning must be completed last. Due to its last in first out type of structure stacks are internally used to implement recursion. Hence, recursion is one of the important applications of "Stack". Stacks are also used to handle non recursive function calls. Section 7.8 describes how stack memory is used to handle function calls, so don't worry about it right now.

7.7.1 Calculating x^y using recursion: An example

Let us calculate the x^y using recursion where the values of x (base) and y (index) are taken as input from the user. We will create a recursive function named exp() which takes two arguments of type integer (x and y) and returns an integer value of x^y. The prototype of the function exp() should be such that it takes two integer values (x and y) and returns the integer result as shown below:

```
int exp(int,int);
```

To understand the calculation of x^y using recursion, let us assume the value of variable x as 2 and the value of variable y as 4. We now need to calculate the result of 2^4 in the program. To solve any large problem using recursion, we need to split the problem into different small problems and then consolidate the results given by the smaller pieces to derive the result of the large problem. Hence, we evaluate 2^4 as

$$2^4 = 2 * 2^3$$

This means that before we can get the result of the term 2^4, we should calculate the result of the term 2^3. Further, we can still split the calculation of the term 2^3 into smaller parts as shown below:

$$2^3 = 2 * 2^2$$

Similarly, we can split the term 2^2 as

$$2^2 = 2 * 2^1$$

The principle of recursion is to keep dividing the large problem until a stage where no further division is possible. Hence, we further split the term 2^1 as

$$2^1 = 2 * 2^0$$

There is no point in dividing the term 2^0 further because the index of the term is zero and we know that anything to the power of 0 is 1. Hence, we can simply return 1 from the `exp()` function if the value of `y` (index) is 0.

In general, for given values of `x` and `y` the calculation can be split as

$$x^y = x * x^{y-1}$$ equation (1)

Let us assume for a while that the function `exp(x,y)` correctly returns the value of x^y. Therefore, the equation 1 can be rewritten as

```
exp(x,y) = x * exp(x,y-1);
```
   equation (2)

All we have done is substituted x^y with `exp(x,y)` and x^{y-1} with `exp(x,y-1)`. This equation 2 indicates that in order to evaluate the result of `exp(x,y)`, we need to make another call to the same function `exp()` by passing arguments as `x` and `y-1`. Such a relation is called a **recurrence relation**. We have already proved that `exp(x,y)` can directly return `1` if `y=0`. Hence, as per equation 2, `exp(x,y)` should be calculated as

```
x * exp(x,y-1);
```

only when `y` is not equal to zero. If the index is zero, the result is always `1` and there is no need to perform any computations. Hence, `y==0` is the terminating condition for recursion.

Any iterative program written using loops can be converted into a recursive program and vice versa. Given below is the function `exp()` to compute x^y using recursion:

```
int exp(int x,int y)
{
      if(y==0)
      {
      /*If index is 0 we return 1*/
      return 1;
      }
      else
      {
      return x*exp(x,y-1);
      }
}
```

To understand the execution of the function, let us trace the evaluation for 2^4. As the base of the term is 2 and the index of the term is 4 we have invoked the function `exp()` from `main()` as

```
res= exp(2,4);
```

At this point, the activation frame for `exp()` is created with formal argument x initialized to 2 and formal argument y initialized to 4 as shown in Figure 7.30. The function `exp()` now starts executing and since the condition `y==0` is false the control is transferred in the `else` block of the `exp()` function, thereby executing the statement

```
return 2*exp(2,3);
```

The above 'return statement' makes another call to the exp() function before it can return any value to the 'calling' function. Hence, another activation frame for exp() is created with formal argument x initialized to 2 and formal argument y initialized to 3 as shown in Figure 7.30. The new instance of exp() starts executing with x=2 and y=3 which makes another call to exp() using the statement

```
return 2*exp(2,2);
```

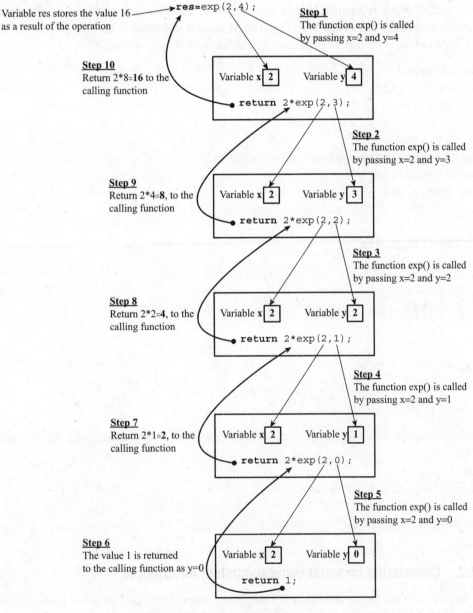

Figure 7.30: Execution of recursion

This process of recurring function calls continues till the last exp() function returns 1, when the value of y is passed as 0 (which is the terminating condition for a recursive function). After the last function return 1, each function then evaluates its return expression, thereby returning required results to the caller. There are total five activation frames in Figure 7.30; although all of the five frames belong to the same function, you have to treat them as five different function executions. When the fifth exp() function returns a value, it is returned to its caller (which is the fourth exp() function). In general, ith exp() function returns the value to (i-1)th exp frame which called it. This process continues till main() is reached, thereby returning 16 as a final result in variable res of main(). The detailed stepwise execution from step 1 to step 10 is as shown in Figure 7.30.

Given below is the full source code to calculate x^y using recursion:

```
#include<stdio.h>
int exp(int,int);
void main()
{
int x,y,res;
printf("Enter the values of x and y:\n");
scanf("%d%d",&x,&y);
res= exp(x,y);
printf("The result is %d \n",res);
}
int exp(int x,int y)
{
        if(y==0)
        {
        /*If index is 0 we return 1*/
        return 1;
        }
        else
          {
          return x*exp(x,y-1);
          }
}
```

Output

```
Enter the values of x and y:
2 4
The result is 16
```

7.7.2 Calculating factorial using recursion: An example

Let us calculate the factorial of number using recursion. Let x be a number whose factorial needs to be calculated. We create a recursive function named factorial() that takes an integer value x as an argument and returns a resultant integer which is the factorial of x. Hence, the prototype of the function `factorial()` will be as follows:

```
int factorial(int);
```

Mathematically speaking, `factorial(x)` is calculated as

$$\text{factorial(x)} = x* (x{-}1)*(x{-}2)*(x{-}3)...*1 \qquad \text{equation (3)}$$

The principle of recursion is to conquer a large problem by dividing it into multiple small problems. Hence, we rewrite the expression for `factorial(x)` as

$$\text{factorial(x)} = x*\text{factorial(x{-}1)}; \qquad \text{equation (4)}$$

This means that the factorial of any number x is multiplication of x with the factorial of the previous number which is (x–1). Actually, equation 4 is formed by substituting (x–1)*(x–2)*(x–3)........*1 in equation 3 with `factorial(x-1)` because this expression is indeed factorial of x–1.

To understand the calculation of factorial using recursion, let us assume x = 4. Factorial of 4 can be calculated as

$$\text{factorial(4)} = 4*\text{factorial(3)};$$

This means that we must calculate the factorial of 3 before we calculate the factorial of 4. We can further split the calculation of factorial(3) as shown below:

$$\text{factorial(3)} = 3*\text{factorial(2)};$$

We can continue this process until we reach a stage where no further split is possible. This means that we continue the splitting until we reach an expression:

```
factorial(1) = 1* factorial(0);
```

There is no point in dividing the term `factorial(0)` because we know that 0! is always 1. Hence, this is a stage where we terminate the recursion.

NOTES

In general, `factorial(x)` when x > 0 is calculated as

```
factorial(x) = x* factorial(x-1);
```

We know that zero factorial is 1. Hence, x==0 is a condition that can be used to terminate recursion.

Given below is the source code of the function to calculate the factorial of a number x.

```
#include<stdio.h>
int factorial(int);
void main()
{
int x,y,res;
printf("Enter the value of x\n");
```

```
scanf("%d",&x);
res=factorial(x);
printf("The factorial is %d\n",res);
}

int factorial(int x)
{
    if(x==0)
    {
    /*If x is 0 we return 1*/
    return 1;
    }
    else
    {
     return x*factorial(x-1);
    }
}
```

Output

```
Enter the value of x
4
The factorial is 24
```

To understand the execution of the function, let us trace the evaluation for x=4. To calculate factorial of x, we have invoked the function factorial(x) from main() as

```
res= factorial(4); /*Let x=4*/
```

At this point, the activation frame for factorial() is created with formal argument x initialized to 4 and as shown in Figure 7.31. The function factorial() now starts executing and since the condition x==0 is false the control is transferred in the else block of the factorial() function, thereby executing the statement

```
return 4 * factorial(3);
```

The above 'return statement' makes another call to the factorial() function before it can return any value to the 'calling' function. Hence, another activation frame for factorial() is created with formal argument x initialized to 3 as shown in Figure 7.31. The new instance of factorial() starts executing with x=3 which makes another call to exp() using the statement

```
return 3 * factorial(2);
```

This process of recurring function calls continues till the last factorial() function returns 1, when the value of x is passed as 0 (which is the terminating condition for a recursive function). After the last function returns 1, each function then evaluates its return expression, thereby returning required results to the caller. There are total five activation frames in Figure 7.31; although all of the five frames are of the same function, you have to treat them as five different function executions. When the fifth factorial() function returns a value, it is returned

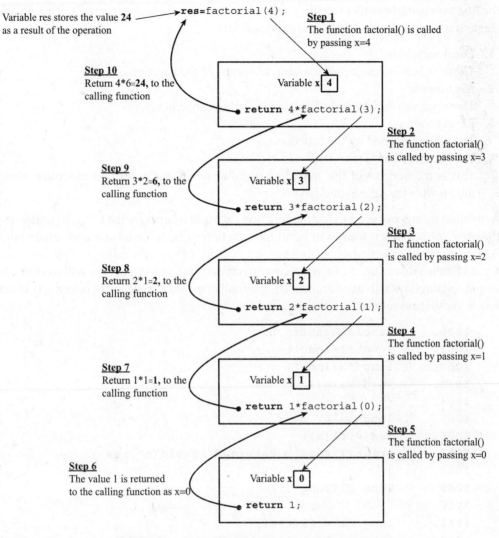

Variable res stores the value **24** as a result of the operation

res=factorial(4);

Step 1
The function factorial() is called by passing x=4

Step 10
Return 4*6=**24**, to the calling function

Variable x 4

return 4*factorial(3);

Step 2
The function factorial() is called by passing x=3

Step 9
Return 3*2=**6**, to the calling function

Variable x 3

return 3*factorial(2);

Step 3
The function factorial() is called by passing x=2

Step 8
Return 2*1=**2**, to the calling function

Variable x 2

return 2*factorial(1);

Step 4
The function factorial() is called by passing x=1

Step 7
Return 1*1=**1**, to the calling function

Variable x 1

return 1*factorial(0);

Step 5
The function factorial() is called by passing x=0

Step 6
The value 1 is returned to the calling function as x=0

Variable x 0

return 1;

Figure 7.31: Execution of factorial using recursion

to its caller (which is the fourth `factorial()` function). In general, ith `factorial()` function returns the value to (i-1)th factorial frame which calls it. This process continues till `main()` is reached thereby returning 24 as a final result in variable `res` of `main()`. The detailed stepwise execution from step 1 to step 10 is as shown in Figure 7.31.

7.8 Activation frames: How Function Calls and Returns are Internally Handled in C/C++

Each time a function is called, space is created in memory for its execution. This space is called an activation frame or an activation record. The word 'activation' signifies the fact that the function actually gets activated when it is called. The memory gets destroyed when the function completes its execution (i.e., when the function is deactivated). An activation frame is a data structure which contains four parts:

1. **Local variables**

   These are variables declared within the scope of the function.

2. **Arguments**

   These are values which the function accepts as arguments.

3. **Return value**

   The value returned by the function.

4. **Return location**

   This is the address of the statement of caller where the control of execution should return after the called function ends.

Activation frames are used to handle function calls and returns by the CPU. To understand the usage of activation frames in handling function calls, consider the code given below containing three functions: main(), f1() and f2(). The calling sequence is that main() calls function f1() which in turn calls function f2(). We will use this code to understand how activation frames are internally created at runtime to effectively handle function calls and returns at right places in the program

```
1000.      #include<stdio.h>
1001.      long f1(long);
1002.      long f2(long);
1003.      void main()
1004.      {
1005.      long a=10, res;
1006.      res = f1(a);
1007.      printf("Result returned is %ld\n",res);
1008.      }
1009.      long f1(long t)
1010.      {
1011.      long r1 = f2(t*t);
1012.      return r1;
1013.      }
1014.      long f2(long s)
1015.      {
1016.      long r2 = s*s;
1017.      return r2;
1018.      }
```

Every statement we write is actually stored in the memory at a specific address after converting it into machine language. The program we write is converted into machine language by multiple system utilities, such as compiler, linker, loader. Hence, it is not possible for us at this stage to determine the exact memory location of each of the statements written in the program. A single high-level statement we write is translated into a multiple machine instructions when the program is compiled. In actuality, these machine instructions are stored in the memory, which are executed by the CPU. At this stage, it is impossible for us to determine the exact memory addresses where each of our statements will be stored; hence, we have given line numbers to each of the statements in the program starting from 1000. Remember that these are line numbers we have given and not the real addresses of the statements in RAM; however, we will use these line numbers as if they are addresses to explain the concept of activation frames.

When a function is called, the activation frame for the function is created and pushed on the stack. When the function execution is completed, the activation frame for the function is popped out from the stack. When you run the program, operating system invokes the `main()` function to start the execution of program from `main()`. Since `main()` is the first function being invoked, its activation frame is pushed into stack as shown in Figure 7.32. There is no need to store return value in `main()` function's activation frame because we have crated it as a void type function.

There are two local variables a and `res` declared in `main()` which are present in the activation frame of `main()`. The function `main()` does not take any arguments (we have not use command line arguments in this program) and hence this section of activation frame is empty. C/C+ library code invokes the `main()` function and hence after `main()` completes the control returns to the library code and the operating system console. The activation frame also contains some temporary data needed by C/C++ runtime environment which is not shown in the sketches we have drawn. This information is not something we should worry about while learning programming, but this point should be mentioned for the sake of completeness.

The statement

```
res = f1(a);
```

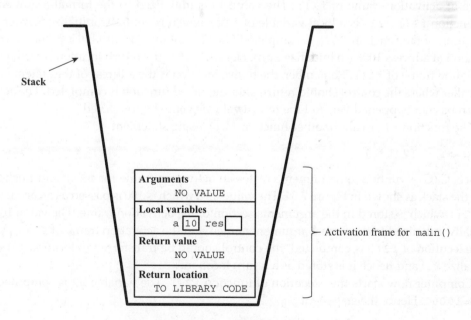

Figure 7.32: Activation frame of `main()`

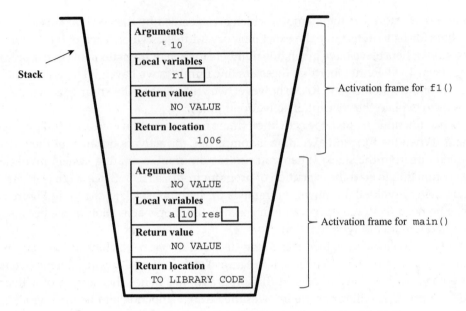

Figure 7.33 Stack storing activation frames of main() and f1()

invokes function f1() by passing value 10 as an argument. Since f1() is called, its activation frame is created and pushed into stack by the C/C++ runtime environment. The activation frame of f1() will be on the top of activation frame of main() as shown in Figure 7.33.

As the value of a is 10, which is the argument passed to f1, it is stored in the arguments space of activation frame of f1(). The value 10 is initialized to the formal argument t of function f1(). r1 is a local variable of f1() which is yet to be initialized. After the execution of the function f1() is completed, the control must return back to the main() function at address 1006 (to initialize res). Hence, 1006 is the return location stored in the activation frame of f1(). Remember, the return location is the address of the statement in the caller where the control should return after the called function is completed. The actual return has not happened yet, and the return value is yet to be computed.

The function f1() calls another function f2() using statement

```
long r1 = f2(t*t);
```

Hence, C/C++ runtime environment creates an activation frame for f2() and pushes it into the stack as shown in Figure 7.34. The value t*t which is 100 is passed as an argument to f2() which is stored in the arguments section of the activation frame. The value 100 is actually initialized to the formal argument named s in the activation frame of f2(). After the execution of f2() is completed, the control should be transferred to location 1011 (to initialize r1) and hence it is stored as a return location.

Computer now starts the execution of function f2(). The variable r2 is computed as s*s=10000. Hence the statement

```
return r2;
```

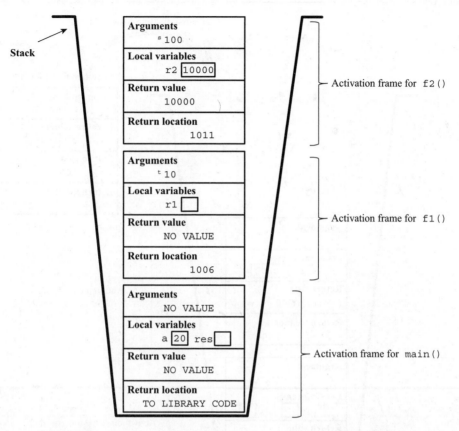

Figure 7.34: Stack storing activation frames of main(), f1() and f2()

will store 10,000 in the return value section of activation frame of f2() and pop out the activation frame of f2() from stack as shown in Figure 7.35.

As per the return location in activation frame of f2(), the control of execution is returned to address 1011 in function f1(). The variable r1 is initialized with the return value present in activation frame of f2(); this is very much possible because the activation frame of f2() is still present in the memory although it is popped out from stack. Hence, the variable r1 of function f1() is initialized with 10000. The statement

```
return r1;
```

is executed which pops out the activation frame of f1() by storing the return value 10000 in the return value section. As the execution of f1() is completed, the control of execution returns to the return location specified in the activation frame of f1() which is 1006. Similarly, variable res is initialized with the return value 10000 from the activation frame of f1(). The statement

```
printf("Result returned is %ld\n",res);
```

is executed which prints the following message on the computer screen:

```
Result returned is 10000
```

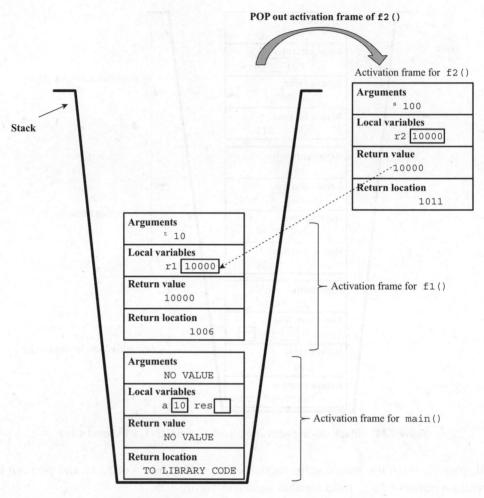

Figure 7.35:   Stack after f2 () completes its execution

The execution of main() function now completes popping out the activation frame of main () indicating that the program has been executed successfully. Remember that the call stack becomes empty when the program is completely executed.

7.9   Storage Classes in C/C++

The place in the memory where a variable is stored on its creation is called a 'storage class' of that variable. C/C++ supports following storage classes for each of its variables:

1. **auto** storage class
2. **register** storage class
3. **static** storage class
4. **extern** storage class

The compiler allocates memory to each of the variables declared in the program depending upon the 'storage class' specified at the time of declaration of the variables. Given below is the syntax of declaring variables by specifying the 'storage class' for the variables.

```
<StorageClass>  <DataType>  <VariableName>;
```

7.9.1 `auto` storage class

This is the default storage class for all the variables of C/C++. The variables of type `auto` are stored in the main memory (RAM) of the computer system as shown in Figure 7.36. If an `auto` variable is defined inside the function, then it is called a **local auto variable**. The local auto variables are stored in a part of RAM called **stack**. The local auto variables are created when the control of execution enters the function definition and they will be destroyed after the function execution is completed. The local auto variables will not be available outside the scope of the function in which they are defined. The statements below show the creation of `auto` variables b and c:

```
/*auto is a keyword in C/C++*/
auto int b =20; /* b is a "auto" variable*/
/*By default all the variables are "auto"*/
int c=30; /* c is a "auto" variable*/
```

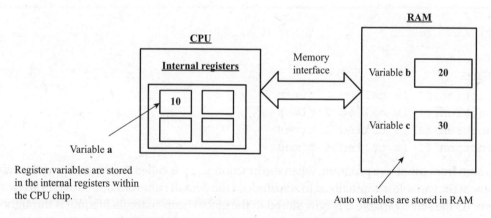

Figure 7.36: Register and auto-storage classes

7.9.2 `register` storage class

`register` refers to the internal memory integrated inside the chip of the processor. The variables with a storage class specified as `register` are stored in the internal registers of the CPU as shown in Figure 7.36, and hence they can be accessed faster when compared to the `auto` variables. As the number of registers present inside the processor memory are limited, we cannot create large number of register variables. The typical count of `register` variables can be 3 or 4 in C/C++ program. C/C++ supports a keyword `register` to create register type variables. Given below is a C/C++ statement that creates an integer variable a with a register storage class:

```
register int a = 10;
```

7.9.3 static storage class

The static variables are variables whose lifespan is throughout the C/C++ program. However, it is important to understand that the static variables can only be accessed within a function or a block in which they are defined. For example, let us consider the function f1() which defines a static variable c with an initial value as zero as shown in the code.

```
#include<stdio.h>
void f1()
{
static int c=0;
c++;
printf("Function f1 is called %d times\n",c);
}
void main()
{
f1();
f1();
f1();
f1();
}
```

Output

```
Function f1 is called 1 times
Function f1 is called 2 times
Function f1 is called 3 times
Function f1 is called 4 times
```

As seen from the above program, when the function f1() is called for the first time the value of the static variable c is initialized to zero, indeed the default value of static variables is always zero. As the static variable c is now stored in the global heap space its lifetime is throughout the C/C++ program. This means that the static variables will be initialized only once when the function is called for the first time and the variable c will not be initialized each time when the function f1() is called. Rather the value of variable c updated by previous function call will now be used by the new function call. Hence, the output of the program is as shown below. The output clarifies that each time we call a function, each of the function runs use the value of variable c that was last updated by the most recent execution of the function

```
Function f1 is called 1 times
Function f1 is called 2 times
Function f1 is called 3 times
Function f1 is called 4 times
```

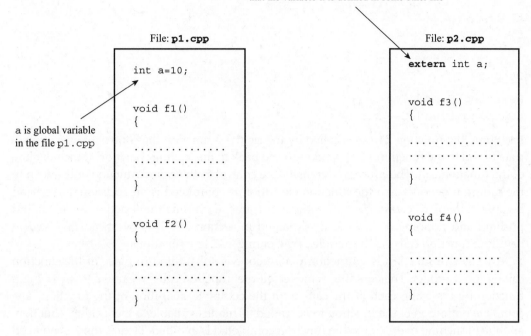

Figure 7.37: Extern variables

7.9.4 `extern` storage class

The variable which is defined in some other cpp file is called an external variable. We can access the value of such variables using the keyword 'extern' as shown in Figure 7.37.

As seen from Figure 7.37, the variable a is declared as a global variable in the file p1.cpp with a value initialized as 10. The value of variable a can also be accessed in some other file say p2.cpp provided that the variable a is declared as extern in the file p2.cpp. The keyword informs the compiler that the variable a is actually declared in some the file. Hence, we can now access the value of a variable which is defined in some other file using a keyword `extern`.

7.10 Inline Functions in C/C++

We understand that when a function is 'called' the control is transferred to the function definition. For example, let us consider a function f1() that prints a message Learning C and C++ on the computer screen as shown in the code below:

```c
#include<stdio.h>
void f1()
{
printf("Learning C and C++\n");
}
```

```
void main()
{
f1();
f1();
}
```

Output

```
Learning C and C++
Learning C and C++
```

Each time the function f1() is called by the main() function the control of execution is transferred to the function f1() and returned back to the 'calling' function at the next line of the function call. The process to transfer the control to the called function and return to the calling function when the function execution is completed is an additional overhead because it involves creating a new activation frame, each time the function is called, and pushing and popping it in stack as explained in section 7.7. This overhead involved in handling function calls can be avoided by creating inline functions.

An inline function is a function whose code is substituted in place of the function call by the compiler. The compiler removes all the 'function calls' we make to an inline function by replacing each of the calls with the complete definition of the function. The complete definition of the function to be 'called' is made available to the 'calling' function, and the branching overhead to the function completed is avoided. Hence, there is no need to push and pop new activation frames each time an inline function is called. Hence, the inline functions **speed up** the execution of the program.

A function can be made inline using a keyword inline in C/C++. As shown in the code below, we have created the function f1() as an inline function using a keyword inline while defining the function f1().

```
#include<stdio.h>
/*function f1 is a inline function*/
inline void f1()
{
printf("Learning C and C++\n");
}
void main()
{
f1();
f1();
}
```

Output

```
Learning C and C++
Learning C and C++
```

This means that every call to the function f1() will be replaced by the function definition of 'f1' in the calling function. As the function main() calls the function f1() two times,

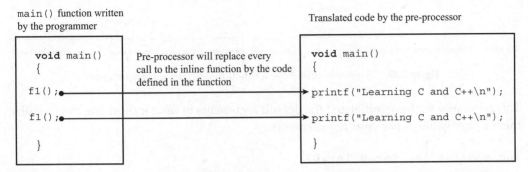

Figure 7.38: Substitution by pre-processor

pre-processor will replace both the calls in the `main()` by the function body of `f1()` which is `printf("Learning C and C++\n");` as shown in Figure 7.38. Hence, the program does not actually branch to the function 'f1' at runtime, thereby resulting into a faster execution as shown in Figure 7.38.

Although the inline functions result into faster execution of the program, they have a drawback that they need more memory when compared to the normal functions. This is because the code defined by the inline function is duplicated at all places where a function call is made. Hence, if memory is a constraint we should rather make use of non-inline functions in the program instead of the inline functions.

NOTES

Definition
An inline function is a function whose code is substituted in place of the **function call** by the compiler.

Advantage of using inline functions
Inline functions speed up the execution of the program by avoiding overhead involved in using stack for branching to the 'called function' and returning from it.

Disadvantage of using inline functions
Although inline functions speed up the execution of the program, they need more memory when compared to normal functions. Hence, if memory is a constraint we should rather make use of non-inline functions in the program instead of inline functions.

7.11 Function with Default Arguments (Only in C++ not in C)

A function argument which can take a default value if its value is not provided by the caller is called a **default function argument**. The default values of the arguments must be specified while prototyping the function. Figure 7.39 is the syntax to prototype a function which allows default arguments.

Let us consider a prototype of add which takes four arguments of type integer. The first two arguments are mandatory, whereas the later two arguments are optional. The optional arguments will automatically consider their value as 0 if it is not provided by the caller.

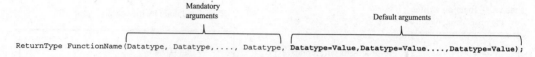

Figure 7.39: Syntax to prototype a function with default arguments

This is because we have initialized the default arguments to zero; indeed you can initialize them to any value as per your requirements.

```
int add(int,int,int=0,int=0);
```

The order of arguments should be such that all the mandatory arguments appear before the default once. Compiler does not allow programmer to specify any mandatory argument after the occurrence of default argument.

Given below is the full source code which defines a function add to perform addition of four integers with two of them as default arguments:

```
#include<stdio.h>
/*Prototype specifying two default arguments*/
int add(int,int,int=0,int=0);
void main()
{
int r1,r2,r3;
/*Call function add to add two integers*/
r1= add(10,20);
/*Call function add to add three integers*/
r2 = add(100,200,300);
/*Call function add to add four integers*/
r3 = add(1000,2000,3000,4000);
printf("r1=%d\n",r1);
printf("r2=%d\n",r2);
printf("r3=%d\n",r3);
}
/*Function definition of add*/
int add(int a,int b,int c, int d)
{
return a+b+c+d;
}
```

Output

```
r1=30
r2=600
r3=10000
```

Note that there are different ways to call function add(). The statement

```
r1= add(10,20);
```

invokes the function add by passing two values 10 and 20; these values are assigned to the first two mandatory arguments a and b. Since the values of c and d are not specified they will take a default value of zero as specified in the prototype of the function. Hence, the function returns addition as 30 which is stored in r1.

The statement

```
r2 = add(100,200,300);
```

performs addition of three values. The optional argument c will take up the value 300 while the argument d will use the default value 0. Hence, the add() function returns addition as 600 which is stored in variable r2.

The last call to add

```
r3 = add(1000,2000,3000,4000);
```

specifies all the four values and hence neither of the arguments c nor d take default values. In this case, the function add() performs addition of four values, thereby storing 10000 in r3.

NOTES

It is possible to have a function with all its arguments as default arguments. For example, you could prototype add() as

```
int add(int=0,int=0,int=0,int=0);
```

In this case, given below are the valid calls to add()

```
int r1= add(); /*Invokes add() with no arguments, adds all zeros and
     returns zero*/
int r2= add(10); /*Invokes add() by passing one argument, adds value
     10 with three zeros and returns 10*/
int r3= add(10,20); /*Invokes add() by passing two arguments; returns
     result 30*/
int r4= add(100,200,300); /*Invokes add()by passing three arguments;
     returns result 600*/
int r5= add(1000,2000,3000,4000); /*Invokes add()by passing four
     arguments; returns result 10000*/
```

7.12   Command Line Arguments

It is possible to pass arguments to the main() function from command line; these arguments are called **command line arguments**. There is an executable file (.exe file) created for every program by the compiler. This file contains a code (called machine code) which is ready to run on the machine. The executable file is stored in the output folder configured in the Turbo C/C++ editor. Every operating system offers some way to run the

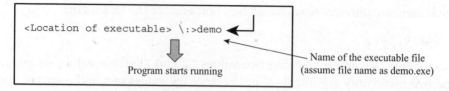

Figure 7.40: Running a program from command prompt

executable file (.exe file) of the program. For example, in DOS, the program starts running as and when you type in the name of the executable file on the command prompt as shown in Figure 7.40.

C/C++ provides a feature which facilitates the programmer to pass arguments to the program at the time of invoking its executable file. These arguments are passed directly to the main() function from command line just before program starts running. If you intend to facilitate passing arguments from command line, you must define the main() function with two formal arguments as shown below:

```
void main( int arg_c, char *arg_v[] )
```

The first argument is an integer variable named arg_c (you can give it any name, only rule is that it should be an integer type variable). This variable will store the count of number of arguments passed from command line. The second argument is an array of strings named arg_v. The * symbol before the array name indicates that it is an array of strings created using array of pointers. We have not discussed pointers yet, so do not worry about the * symbol as of now. We will learn about pointers in the next chapter, till then you can just remember it as a part of syntax. arg_v can be accessed as we access normal arrays arg_v[0], arg_v[1], arg_v[2] and so on. Each element of an array arg_v is a string. The first element of the array arg_v[0] will always give the name of the executable file (in this case 'demo'), whereas the remaining elements arg_v[1] onwards will store the arguments passed through command line. Hence, the size of the array will always be one more than the number of parameters passed from command line. As the variable arg_c stores the count of parameters passed through command line its value is same as

```
(size of array arg_v) - 1
```

because one value in the array is just the name of the executable file which is not counted by arg_c. The arguments to be passed must be delimited by space. For example, if the name of the executable file is demo.exe and if you execute it by passing values as Mickey, Jack, 10 and -50 then the variable arg_c will store 4 because you have passed four arguments to the program (along with the nsame of the executable file at its first location) and the array arg_v will store the actual four string values with \0 at the end of each of the strings as shown in Figure 7.41.

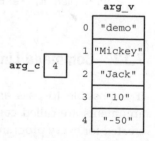

Figure 7.41: State of arg_c and arg_v

NOTES

Only string values can be passed as an argument from command line to the `main()` function. If you need to pass values of any other type, the conversion of string to appropriate types must be handled within the program. For example, in Figure 7.41 we have passed values `Mickey`, `Jack`, `10` and `-50`. You might want to consider the last two values `10` (stored in `arg_v[3]`) and `-50` (stored in `arg_v[4]`) as integers; but C/C++ still considers them as strings. This means that you will not be able to perform any mathematical compilations with these values even though they are fully numeric in nature. There is a built-in function named `atoi()` to convert an array of characters to an integer value. The statement

```
int x = atoi(arg_v[3]);
```

will convert the string value in `arg_v[3]` into an integer value. The resultant integer value is stored in variable `x`. Assuming `arg_v[3]` contains a string literal `"10"` followed by `\0`, `x` will store an integer constant `10`.

It is programmer's responsibility to ensure that the string value on which the conversion is applied is fully numeric before applying `atoi()` function on it. The function `atoi()` will return NULL if you try to convert any non-numeric value to integer. For example, the statement

```
int k=atoi("abc"); /*incorrect way of using atoi*/
```

attempts an invalid conversion of a string literal `"abc"` to integer. In this case, `k` will store zero. The statement below gives a valid conversion

```
int k=atoi("80"); /*correct way of using atoi*/
```

because the string `"80"` is fully numeric and hence variable `k` in this case will store an integer constant `80`. The function `atoi()` is declared in a header file `stdlib.h`. Hence this file must be included in the program if you need to use the built-in function `atoi()`.

Similarly, there is a function `atof()` used to convert a string to a double value.

7.12.1 Program to perform addition of values passed through command line: An example

Let us create a program that accepts values from command line and performs their addition. If we name the file as `pro1.cpp` (or `pro1.c` for C) the name of executable will be `pro1.exe`. The command

```
pro1 10 20 30 40
```

should perform addition of the four values and print 100 on the computer screen. The program should not impose any restriction on the number of values to be passed from command line. So, the statement

```
pro1 100 200 300 400 500 600 700 800
```

which passes eight values using command line to pro1, and the program prints the result of addition which is 3600.

Given below is the full source code that performs addition of all the integers passed to it from command line:

```
#include<stdio.h>
#include<stdlib.h>
```

```
void main( int arg_c, char *arg_v[] )
{
int sum=0;
int i=1;
printf("Name of the executable file is: %s\n",arg_v[0]);
/*Calculate the sum of all the parameters supplied from command line*/
     while(i<=arg_c)
     {
     sum = sum + atoi(arg_v[i]);
     i++;
     }
printf("Sum of values is: %d\n",sum);
}
```

Output

The statement

```
printf("Name of the executable file is: %s\n",arg_v[0]);
```

prints the name of the program as pro1 because this is the string stored in arg_v[0].

The initial value of variable sum is set to zero because the final sum of all the elements is to be accumulated in sum. The initial value of variable I is set to 1 because it is to be used as an array index to read the command line parameters; we know that the values are stored from index 1 onwards in the array arg_v. Assuming that the command is

```
pro1 10 20 30 40
```

Figure 7.42 shows the state of arg_c and arg_v.

The count of number of parameters, passed through command line is stored in arg_c and hence the while loop will have exactly arg_c iterations such that one value is accumulated in sum in each of iterations:

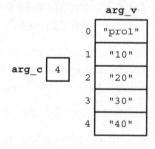

```
     while(i<=arg_c)
     {
     sum = sum + atoi(arg_v[i]);
     i++;
     }
```

Figure 7.42: State of arg_c and arg_v

Each value arg_v[i] is in string format and hence atoi() is used to convert every arg_v[i] into integer before performing addition. Hence, the final sum is printed as 100 which is the addition of four parameters (10 + 20 + 30 + 40) as seen in the output of the program. The code written is very generic to handle any number of parameters because the terminating condition of the while loop is in terms of arg_c as shown below:

```
i<=arg_c
```

The compiler guarantees that the value of `arg_c` will be correctly set to the count of parameters which are passed in command line. If the command is

```
pro1 100 200 300 400 500 600 700 800
```

the value of `arg_c` will be set to 8 and hence the `while` loop will have eight iterations each time accumulating one value in sum. Therefore, at the end of the `while` loop the value of sum will be correctly set to 3600.

7.13   Some Built-in Functions

C/C++ has a large set of library functions defined in different header files. The complete set of library functions and header files are document in the C++ documentation available with the editor. These library functions of C++ come along with the compiler of C++ and they are defined in the header files with '.h' as the extension. This means that if we wish to use any of the library functions we must include the corresponding 'header' file in which these functions are defined. As examples of built-in functions in C++, we discuss a few library functions of C++ in this section:

Library functions	Header file to be included	Description
`double sin(double)`	`#include<math.h>`	The function `sin()` computes the `sin()` value of the angle passed to it as an argument. The angle must be specified in radians.
		For example, consider the C/C++ statement below:
		`double res = sin(30.0);`
		The value of variables `res` will be -0.988032 which is the `sin()` value of 30 radians.
		The function takes an argument of type `double` and returns a `double` value.
`double cos(double)`	`#include<math.h>`	The function `cos()` computes the `cos()` value of the angle passed to it as an argument. The angle must be specified in radians.
		For example, consider the C/C++ statement below:
		`double res = cos(30.0);`
		The value of variables `res` will be 0.154251 which is the `cos()` value of 30 radians.
		The function takes an argument of type `double` and returns a `double` value.
`double atan(double)`	`#include<math.h>`	The function `atan()` computes the $\tan^{-1}$ of the expression passed to it as an argument.

Library functions	Header file to be included	Description
		For example, consider the C/C++ statement below: `double res = atan(0.5);` The value of variables `res` will be `0.463` which is the $\tan^{-1}$ value of `0.5`. The function takes an argument of type `double` and returns a `double` value.
`double sqrt(double)`	`#include<math.h>`	The function `sqrt()` computes the square root of the expression passed to it as an argument. For example, consider the C/C++ statement below: `double res = sqrt(9);` The value of variables `res` will be `3` which is the square root of `9`. The function takes an argument of type `double` and returns a `double` value.

`int strlen(string)`	`#include<string.h>`	The function `strlen()` computes the length of the string passed to it as an argument.
		
		For example, consider the C/C++ statements below:
		
		`char a[] ="hello";`
		`int res = strlen(a);`
		
		The value of variables `res` will be set to 5 because the number of characters in the string a is 5.
		
		The function takes an argument of type `"string"` and returns an `int` value which represents the number of characters in the string.

`void strcat`
`(string1,string2)`
	`#include<string.h>`	The function `strcat()` takes two arguments of type string as `"string1"` and `"string2"`. The function concatenates the two strings and stores the result in `"string1"`
		
		For example, consider the C/C++ statements below:
		
		`char a[] = "hat";`
		`char b[] = "rat";`
		`strcat(a,b);`
		
		The function will concatenate the strings stored in arrays a and b, thereby storing the result of concatenation in the array a. Hence, the new string value in array a will be `"hatrat"`.

Library functions	Header file to be included	Description
void strcpy (destination, source)	#include<string.h>	The function strcpy () takes two arguments of type string as "destination" and "source". The function copies the source string into the destination string For example, char a[] = "hat"; char b[100]; strcpy(b,a); will copy the complete string stored in array a into the array b. Hence, the string value in array b will also be "hat".
int strcmp (string1, string2)	#include<string.h>	The function strcmp () compares two strings passed to it as arguments. The string values are compared character by character based on their ASCII values. If the first character of the two strings is same then the function will compare the second character of the strings, if the second character is also same then the function will compare the third character of the two strings and so on. The comparison of the two strings continues until a differing character is found. The function returns an integer value as a result of the comparison. The value returned is <0 if string1<string2 >0 if string1>string2 =0 if string1 is same as string2 For example, consider the statements below: char a[] = "sight"; char b[]= "site"; int res= **strcmp**(a,b); As seen, the character at position 2 is the first differing character in the two strings a and b. The character at position 2 of the string a is 'g', whereas the character at position 2 of the string b is 't'. Also, the ASCII value of 'g' is less than the ASCII value of 't'. Hence, the value of variable res will be negative indicating that the string stored inside a is less than the string stored inside b.

Solved Example 7.1

Write a program to take the value of variable n as input from the user and to print the nth number in the Fibonacci series using recursion.

```
#include<stdio.h>
int fibo(int);
void main()
{
int n;
printf("Enter the value of n \n");
scanf("%d",&n);
printf("The number in the fibonacci series is %d\n",fibo(n));
}
int fibo(int n)
{
    if(n==0 || n==1)
        {
        return n;
        }
    else
        {
        return fibo(n-1)+fibo(n-2);
        }
}
```

Output

```
Enter the value of n
6
The number in the fibonacci series is 8
```

SCRATCH PAD

Every number in the Fibonacci series is calculated as the addition of the previous two numbers in the series. For example, consider the series below:

0, 1, 1, 2, 3, 5, 8, **13**..........

the number 13 in the series is calculated as the addition of previous two numbers. In general, every n[th] number in the series is calculated as addition of number at position $(n-1)$ with the number at position $(n-2)$. Therefore , if `fibo(n)` is a function that returns n[th] number in the Fibonacci series then the function call,

`fibo(n-1)`

will return the $(n-1)$[th] number in the series whereas the function call,

`fibo(n-2)`

will return the $(n-2)$[th] number in the series. Hence, the nth number in the Fibonacci series can be calculated using the function fibo() as shown below:

`fibo(n-1)+fibo(n-2);`

Solved Example 7.2

Write a program to take the value of variable n as input from the user and to calculate the result of following series using recursion.

1+2+3+4+...+n

```c
#include<stdio.h>
int sum(int);
void main()
{
int n;
printf("Enter the value of n: \n");
scanf("%d",&n);
printf("The value of the series is: %d \n",sum(n));
}
int sum(int n)
{
    if(n==1)
    {
    return n;
    }
    else
    {
    return sum(n-1)+n;
    }
}
```

Output
```
Enter the value of n:
4
The value of the series is: 10
```

Solved Example 7.3

Write a program to create a function average() that accepts an integer type array as an argument and returns the average of n elements stored in the array.

```c
#include<stdio.h>
float average(int[],int);
void main()
{
int a[100],n,i;
float mean;
printf("Enter the number of elements to be stored in the array\n");
scanf("%d",&n);
```

```
    for(i=0;i<n;i++)
    {
    printf("Enter element number %d\n",i+1);
    scanf("%d",&a[i]);
    }
mean= average(a,n);
printf("The average of elements is %f\n",mean);
}
float average(int a[], int n)
{
int i,s=0;
float result;
        for(i=0;i<n;i++)
        {
        s=s+a[i];
        }
result= (float)s/n;
return result;
}
```

Output

```
Enter the number of elements to be stored in the array
5
Enter element number 1
10
Enter element number 2
20
Enter element number 3
32
Enter element number 4
33
Enter element number 5
21
The average of elements is 23.200001
```

Solved Example 7.4

Write a program to create a function find() that can be used to search an element x in the array of integers. The function should accept an integer type array as an argument and return FALSE if the element x is not present in the array or return TRUE if the element is present in the array.

```
#include<stdio.h>
int find(int[],int,int);
```

```
void main()
{
int a[100],n,i,key,status;
float mean;
printf("Enter the number of elements to be stored in the array\n");
scanf("%d",&n);
    for(i=0;i<n;i++)
    {
    printf("Enter element number %d\n",i+1);
    scanf("%d",&a[i]);
    }
printf("Enter the element to be searched in the array\n");
scanf("%d",&key);
status = find(a,key,n);
    if(status==0)
    {
    printf("Element not found\n");
    }
    else
    {
    printf("Element found\n");
    }
}
int find(int a[],int x,int n)
{
int i=0;
    while(i<n && a[i]!=x)
    {
    i++;
    }
    if(i==n)
    {
    return 0;
    }
    else
    {
    return 1;
    }
}
```

Output
```
Enter the number of elements to be stored in the array
5
Enter element number 1
10
```

```
Enter element number 2
20
Enter element number 3
30
Enter element number 4
40
Enter element number 5
50
Enter the element to be searched in the array
30
Element found
```

Solved Example 7.5

Write a program to sort an array of strings. Take n strings as input from the user and arrange the n strings in ascending order. Write a function sort () which takes a two-dimensional array of characters as an argument to sort the strings stored in the array in ascending order.

```c
#include<stdio.h>
#include<string.h>
void sort(char[][100],int);
int isGreater(char[],char[]);
void main()
{
char a[100][100];
int i,n;
printf("How many words are to be stored inside the array\n");
scanf("%d",&n);
printf("Enter %d words\n",n);
    for(i=0;i<n;i++)
    {
    /*one row of a 2D array represents one string*/
    scanf("%s",a[i]);
    }
sort(a,n);
printf("Sorted order is: \n");
    for(i=0;i<n;i++)
    {
    printf("%s\n",a[i]);
    }
}
void sort(char a[][100],int n)
{
```

```
int i,j,k,max_length,lenI,lenJ;
char t;
for(i=0;i<=n-2;i++)
{
     for(j=i+1;j<=n-1;j++)
     {
      if(isGreater(a[i],a[j]))
          {
                  lenI=strlen(a[i]);
                  lenJ=strlen(a[j]);
                  if(lenI>lenJ)
                  {
                  max_length=lenI;
                  }
                  else
                  {
                  max_length=lenJ;
                  }
                  for(k=0;k<max_length;k++)
                  {
                  t=a[i][k];
                  a[i][k]=a[j][k];
                  a[j][k]=t;
                  }
          }
     }
}
} /*End of function  sort()  */
int isGreater(char p[],char q[])
{
 if(strcmp(p,q)>0)
     {
     return 1;
     }
   else
     {
     return 0;
     }
}
```

Output

```
How many words are to be stored inside the array
4
Enter 4 words
```

```
Orange
Mango
Chikoo
Apple
Sorted order is:
Apple
Chikoo
Mango
Orange
```

SCRATCH PAD

Logic to arrange the strings in ascending order is same as that of sorting integer values as discussed in Chapter 6 of this text book. The only difference is that, string is a array of characters and hence we cannot directly compare two string constants using relational operators as we do with integers. Therefore, we have written a user-defined function `isGreater()` that determines if string p is greater than string q as shown below:

```
int isGreater(char p[],char q[])
{
   if(strcmp(p,q)>0)
        {
        return 1;
        }
   else
        {
        return 0;
        }
}
```

The function returns 1 if the string constant stored in p is greater than string constant stored in q and the function returns zero otherwise. Note that, we actually check the relationship between two strings using a **strcmp()** function which is defined in **string.h.** When the result of **strcmp()** is positive it indicates that string p is greater than string q and if the result of **strcmp()** is negative it indicates that the string p is less than string q. Therefore, we return 1 if the result of the function **strcmp()** is positive as seen in the code.

Now, the requirement of ascending order is that we need to swap two strings s[i] and s[j] in the array, if the string s[i] is greater than string s[j]. Hence, the condition to swap s[i] with s[j] is written as:

```
isGreater(s[i],s[j])
```

Solved Example 7.6

Write a program to take two numbers as input from the user and to calculate the HCF of two numbers using recursion.

```
#include <stdio.h>
int hcf(int, int);
void main()
```

```
{
int result, no1, no2,i;
printf("Enter two numbers\n");
scanf("%d%d",&no1,&no2);
result = hcf(no1, no2);
printf("HCF of the  two numbers is %d\n",result);
}
int hcf(int p, int q)
{
    if (p%q == 0)
    {
    return q;
    }
    else
    {
    return hcf(q, p%q);
    }
}
```

Output
```
Enter two numbers
20 15
HCF of the  two numbers is 5
```

Solved Example 7.7

Write a program to calculate the value of variable `result` using the formulae given below, where X and Y are the arrays and each of them store n elements of type integer

$$result = \frac{n\sum(X_i \ Y_i) - \sum(X_i) \ \sum(Y_i)}{(\sum(Y_i))^2}$$

```
#include<stdio.h>
int sumArray(int[],int);
int sumOfProducts(int[],int[],int);
void main()
{
int n, i, x[100],y[100],sum=0;
float result;
printf("Enter the number of elements to be stored in each of the
    arrays\n");
scanf("%d",&n);
printf("Enter the elements of array x\n");
    for(i=0;i<=n-1;i++)
    {
```

```
    scanf("%d",&x[i]);
    }
printf("Enter the elements of array y\n");
    for(i=0;i<=n-1;i++)
    {
    scanf("%d",&y[i]);
    }
result= (float)(n*sumOfProducts(x,y,n)- sumArray(x,n)*
    sumArray(y,n))/(sumArray(y,n)* sumArray(y,n));
printf("Result is %f\n",result);
}
int sumOfProducts(int x[],int y[],int n)
{
int i,s=0;
    for(i=0;i<=n-1;i++)
    {
    s=s+x[i]*y[i];
    }
return s;
}
int sumArray (int x[],int n)
{
int i,s=0;
    for(i=0;i<=n-1;i++)
    {
    s=s+x[i];
    }
return s;
}
```

Output
```
Enter the number of elements to be stored in each of the arrays
4
Enter the elements of array x
10 20 30 40
Enter the elements of array y
5 10 15 20
Result is 0.400000
```

Solved Example 7.8

Write a program to take two strings S1 and S2 as input from the user. Create a function isPartOf() which takes both the strings as arguments and determines if the string S2 is contained in S1. For example, it S1="Computer" and S2="put" then we can say that string S2 is the part of string S1.

```c
#include<stdio.h>
void isPartOf (char[],char[],int,int);
void main()
{
char s1[100],s2[100];
int len1=0,len2=0,i;
printf("Enter a string S1\n");
scanf("%s",s1);
printf("Enter a string S2\n");
scanf("%s",s2);
    for(i=0;s1[i]!='\0';i++)
    {
    len1++;
    }
    for(i=0;s2[i]!='\0';i++)
    {
    len2++;
    }
    if(len2>len1)
    {
    printf("Length of substring cannot be greater than the main
    string\n");
    }
    else
    {
    isPartOf (s1,s2,len1,len2);
    }
}
void isPartOf (char s1[], char s2[],int len1,int len2)
{
int diff = len1-len2;
int i=0,k,flag,j;
    for(i=0; i<diff;i++)
    {
    flag=0;
    j=0;
        for(k=i;k<len2;k++)
        {
        if(s2[j]!=s1[k])
        {
        flag=1;
```

```
        }
        j++;
        }
        if(flag==0)
        {
        printf("String %s is a part of %s",s2,s1);
        return;
        }
    }
printf("String %s is NOT the part of %s",2,s1);
}
```

Output

```
Enter a string S1
Computer
Enter a string S2
put
String put is a part of Computer
```

Quiz

1. Choose the correct statement(s):
   (a) Inline functions reduce the execution time of the program.
   (b) Inline functions increase the execution time of the program.
   (c) Inline functions have a lesser memory requirement when compared to the normal functions.
   (d) Inline functions have a greater memory requirement when compared to the normal functions.
2. Choose the correct statement(s):
   (a) A function can return only one value at a time.
   (b) A function can return multiple values at a time.
   (c) A function should at least return one value to the calling function.
   (d) None of the above is true.
3. The default return type of any function is:
   (a) void
   (b) int
   (c) float
   (d) char
4. Consider the function f1() given below:
   ```
   void f1()
   {
   int ,x,y,m,n;
   printf("Enter two numbers\n");
   scanf("%d %d",&x,&y);
   /*Assume x>0 and y>0*/
   while(m!=n)
   ```

```
{
if(m>n)
{
m=m-n;
}
else
{
n-n-m;
}
}
printf("Result is %d",n);
}
```

The function is used to compute:

(a) x/y.

(b) GCD of x and y.

(c) x mod y.

(d) LCM of x and y.

5. Consider the code below:

```
void func1(int n,int total)
{
int p=0,j=0;
if(n==0) return;
p=n%10;
j=n/10;
total=total+p;
func1(j,total);
printf("%d ",p);
}
```

What will the given function print if it is called as func1(9076,0)?

(a) 9 0 7 6 22

(b) 9 0 7 6

(c) 6 7 0 9 22

(d) 6 7 0 9

6. Which is the storage class you will use to reduce the access time for accessing the value of the variable?

(a) auto

(b) static

(c) extern

(d) register

7. Which of the following storage class/classes you will use to store the value of a variable throughout the scope of the program?

(a) auto

(b) static

(c) extern

(d) register

8. Choose the correct statement:

(a) When an array is passed as an argument the data space that stores the elements of the array is shared between 'calling' function and the 'called' function.

(b) When an array is passed as an argument the data space that stores the elements of the array is local to each function.

(c) Array cannot be passed as an argument to the function.

(d) None of the above is true.

Error Finding Exercises

Given below are some programs which may or may not contain errors. Correct the error(s) if exist in the code and determine the output.

Code 1

```
#include<stdio.h>
void f1(int i)
{
i++;
}
void main()
{
int i;
        for(i=0;i<10; f1(i))
        {
        printf("Computer programming\n");
        }
}
```

Code 2

```
#include<stdio.h>
void main()
{
printf("start of main function\n");
display();
printf("End of main function\n");
}
void display()
{
printf("Inside the display function\n");
}
```

Code 3

```
#include<stdio.h>
void add(int,int)
void main()
{
int result;
result= add(10,20)+ add(50,60);
printf("Result of addition is %d\n",result);
}
void add(int p,int q)
```

```
{
        int result;
        result=p+q;
        }
```

Code 4

```
        #include<stdio.h>
        void main()
        {
        main(10);
        }
        void main(int p)
        {
        printf("Inside a user-defined main function\n");
        p++;
        printf(" The value of variable p is %d\n",p);
        }
```

Code 5

```
        #include<stdio.h>
        int i=0;
        int init_fn();
        int condition_fn();
        int change_fn();
        void main()
        {
              for(init_fn();condition_fn();change_fn())
              {
              printf("Computer programming\n");
              }
        }
        int init_fn()
        {
        i=1;
        }
        int condition_fn()
        {
        return i<=10;
        }
        int change_fn()
        {
        return ++i;
        }
```

Review Questions

1. Write a short note on functions in C/C++. Also, explain the need for creating functions with an appropriate example.
2. List the different types of storage classes supported by C/C++. Also, explain each of the storage classes with an appropriate example of each storage class.
3. Write a program to create a function that checks if a string is a palindrome or not. The function should return 1 (true) if the string passed to it is a palindrome or 0 (false) otherwise.
4. Write a program to create a function that takes a value of variable x as a parameter and returns the result of the following series: 2!+3!+4!+5! ⋯ x! such that value of x is always positive.
5. Write a short note on recursive functions. Give an example to illustrate the working of recursive functions.
6. What is the difference between 'actual arguments' and 'formal arguments' to the function? Illustrate your answer with an appropriate example.
7. Write a function that can calculate square root of a given number without using the built-in function sqrt(). The function should take an integer value x as argument and should return a float value which is a square root of x.
8. Write a function that can calculate a sine value of an angle without using the built-in function sin(). The function should take a double value x (angle) as argument and should return sin(x).
9. Define a function that checks if a given number x is a perfect cube or not. The function should return TRUE if x is a perfect cube and should return FALSE otherwise.
10. Create a function named table() that can be used to print the multiplication table of any number. The function should take a single argument say x as a parameter and should print the multiplication table of x on the computer screen.

Chapter

8 | Pointers

8.1 Overview

Every variable that we create is stored in the main memory of the computer system. This is the primary memory which is directly accessible to the CPU. It is a semiconductor implementation of a volatile memory that supports random access, hence it is also called Random Access memory, often abbreviated as RAM. As the memory is volatile in nature, the program variables are destroyed after the execution of the program completes. This justifies, why you need to again input the values of variables when you re-execute your program. It is important to note that, C/C++ cannot make its variables persistent. All the variables lose their value as soon as the execution of the program completes. Whilst, discussing about hardware structure and implementation of RAM is out of scope of this textbook, you must know that, the main memory (RAM) of the computer system is organized as set of locations. Each location of RAM is given a 'location number' also called address of that location, as shown in the Figure 8.1. This means that, every location in the memory can be uniquely identified by its address.

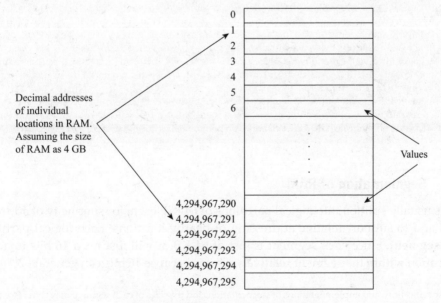

Figure 8.1: Basic structure of RAM

The size and speed of RAM that is supported by a particular computer system depends upon multiple hardware and software specifications of the system, and the detailed discussion on system configuration is out of scope of this textbook as it involves a detailed study of hardware and operating system parameters.

Figure 8.1 shows the basic structure of RAM assuming its size as 4 GB. This means that the number of locations in RAM will be 4,294,967,296 (2^{32}) because a single location in RAM is always of 1 byte in size. Therefore, 4,294,967,296 locations will form 4 giga bytes of RAM.

Further, the locations in RAM are always addressed starting from zero, hence the address of first location in RAM will be 0 and the address of last location in RAM in this case will be 4,294,967,295 as shown.

As a standard practice the location addresses are usually specified in hexadecimal format, however, in the figure we specify address of each location in decimal format for simplicity of understanding this topic.

How does the processor perform read or write operations at a specific location in RAM?   **?**

📖   Before performing a read or a write operation, a specific location must be selected (or activated) in the RAM chip. Address decoder circuitry is present on the motherboard to activate any specific set of locations for reading or writing purposes. Processor generates the address of a location using stream of bits called as **address bus**. The address carried by the address bus is then decoded by the **address decoder circuitry** to activate a specific location. Hence, the **decoder** is the one, which takes address generated by processor as input and generates a correct bit pattern required to activate a specific RAM location at the output. A typical **address decoder takes n bits as input** and **generates one of the combinations out of 2^n** at its output. (Since each bit can take two possible states 0 or 1, n bits in all can form 2^n possible states). In our example, wherein we assumed 4 GB of RAM, we would therefore need a decoder which can take 32 bits as input, because 2^{32} = 4,294,967,296. Hence, the processor should generate a 32 bit address which would give address decoder an ability to generate one of the 2^{32} distinct combinations at the output. Each of the combination will activate one location in RAM, after which read or write operation can be performed on that location. The **size of address bus** of the processor determines how much of the maximum RAM a system can support. For example, if the size of your address bus is just 24 bits, then your system will be able to support at the most 2^{24} = 16777216 (16 MB) distinct locations in RAM. Hence the maximum RAM your system can support is just 16 MB, if your address bus is 24 bits.

The detailed discussion of the hardware circuitry and address decodes is out of scope of this text book, but all we should understand from this is that, the amount of RAM that you can configure on your system heavily depends on multiple hardware and software parameters.

8.1.1   Segmentation of RAM

RAM is usually splitted into logical partitions of 64 KB[1] each, for simplicity of addressing modes and to support relative addressing of nearby locations. Each logical partition is called **segment**. Since each segment is just of 64 KB, it will just need 16 bits to address any location within the segment relatively. This is because 16 bits can generate 2^{16} (65536)

---

[1] Exact specifications and implementations of segmentation, and the sizes of each segment may differ from system to system. In this case, we assume an Intel x86 series of processors just to explain the concept of segmentation.

distinct addresses which can address 64 KBs of memory given that one location is of 1 byte in size. Segments partition the RAM logically as per the type of data that is to be stored. The actual way segmentation is implemented will vary from system to system, but there are basically three different types of segments, in general, with each having a specific logical purpose and is designed to store a specific type of data as shown in the Figure 8.2.

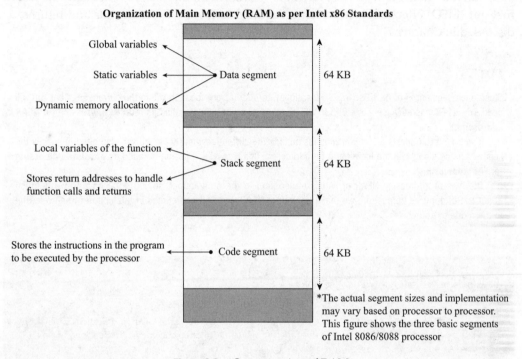

Organization of Main Memory (RAM) as per Intel x86 Standards

Global variables
Static variables → Data segment — 64 KB
Dynamic memory allocations

Local variables of the function
Stack segment — 64 KB
Stores return addresses to handle function calls and returns

Stores the instructions in the program to be executed by the processor — Code segment — 64 KB

*The actual segment sizes and implementation may vary based on processor to processor. This figure shows the three basic segments of Intel 8086/8088 processor

Figure 8.2: Segmentation of RAM

8.1.1.1 *Data segment*

The segment stores the data needed during the program execution. This segment actually stores the value of variables and constants declared in the program.

Data segment stores the following type of variables, created in the program

- Global variables having scope throughout the program execution.
- Static variables.
- Dynamically allocated memory (we will understand dynamic memory allocation in Chapter 9). Part of the data segment that is reserved for dynamic memory allocation is called **heap.**

Note that, **local variables** declared in any of the functions are not stored on heap.

8.1.1.2 *Code segment*

This segment stores the actual instructions that are to be executed during the program execution. This segment will store instructions which are converted to the machine language by the C or C++ compiler.

For example, this segment will store machine language codes which are equivalent to operations of program statements such as `printf()`, `scanf()`, `+`, `-`, `*` and `/`.

8.1.1.3 Stack segment

This segment stores the local variables defined in all the functions of the program, including local variables defined in `main()` function. This segment internally implements the **last in first out** (LIFO) effect of Stack which is required to handle function calls and returns, as discussed in Chapter 7.

NOTES

Since each segment is of 64 KBs (65536 locations), to address any location within the current segment you will need 16 bits (This is because 2^{16} = 65536). Such a way of addressing is called as **relative addressing (or NEAR addressing)**.

If you need to address a location which is outside the current segment then you will also need to specify the segment name along with the location to be addressed. This type of addressing is called as **absolute addressing (or FAR addressing)**.

The type of addressing NEAR or FAR is transparent to the programmer, so you don't have to worry much about it. But don't be confused if we make use terms **NEAR** and **FAR** sometimes in this chapter when referring to the mode of addressing.

Why are local variables stored on stack?

?

Stack is a **Last In First Out (LIFO)** type of memory as explained in Chapter 7 Section 7.7. In a case when function calls are nested, the function which is called at the end is the first one to finish its execution. As and when the function completes its execution, its local variables can be destroyed from the memory. This task becomes simple by using stacks, because the local memory of the function which is called at the end is always on the **top of the stack**.

8.1.2 Storage of variables in RAM

Since every location in RAM is of 1 byte, integer constant will require two consecutive locations in RAM because size of integer is of 2 bytes. Similarly character constant will require one location in RAM and a floating point constant will require four locations in RAM. So if size of a particular data type is n bytes, then storing a single value of that type will need n consecutive locations in RAM.

As an example, let us consider storage of an integer value, by creating an integer type of variable as shown in the following statement:

```
int a=5;
```

The statement creates a variable a of integer type with a value of 5, so a requires 2 bytes in computer memory (which would also mean that the variable a requires 2 locations in RAM).

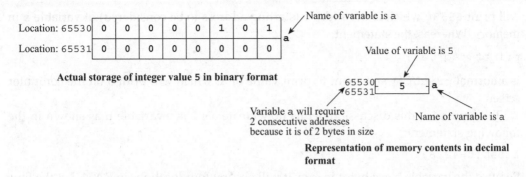

Figure 8.3:   Storage of integer variable in RAM

The exact place in RAM where the variable will be stored is not under the control of programmer and is fully at discretion of operation system. Hence we cannot decide the exact addresses where a variable will be stored in RAM, the memory management unit of Operating System (OS) makes this decision. To understand this topic we can just assume addresses, remember they are not in our control anyway.

Let us assume that the two consecutive addresses in RAM where value of variable a is stored by OS are 65530 and 65531. This means that the integer constant 5 will be placed at these memory locations as shown in the Figure 8.3. Actually a decimal value 5 can be stored in memory only after converting it into binary form as [0000 0000 0000 0101], where 1st byte of 5 is 0000 0101 (least significant bits) and second byte is of 5 is 0000 0000 (most significant bits). The actual storage of integer constant 5 in binary format is as shown in Figure 8.3, but it will become difficult to read such diagrams every time and hence we will represent storage of data in decimal format going forward in this chapter. The decimal format illustration which we will be using going forward is also shown in Figure 8.3.

Although the address in memory where a variable is stored is not in our control, we can always determine the address where OS has placed the variable by using & operator in C/C++. The ampersand (&) operator is pronounced as 'address of' operator, which is used to determine the address of the location in RAM where the particular variable is stored.

For example, if we need to determine the address of variable a, we can obtain it as &a in the program. The & operator always returns the starting address of a variable in RAM, which means that &a, in this case will be 65530, because it is the starting address of a in RAM. There is no need for & to return other addresses apart from starting address, because the later addresses that the variable takes will always be consecutive to the starting address of that variable. Hence &a only returns the address of variable a as 65530 and not 65531. In summary, we always work with the starting address of any variable and not with the later subsequent addresses taken up by the variable. So the term 'address' in this chapter will always means the 'starting address', unless any particular address to be considered is specified explicitly.

The statement,

```
printf("%d",&a);
```

will print 65530 which is the address (starting address to be considered) of variable a in memory. Whereas, the statement,

```
printf("%d",a);
```

is a normal `printf()` statement to print value of a, which will print 5 on the computer screen.

To summarize this discussion, let us now create a `float` variable b as shown in the following statement:

```
float b=42.8;
```

Because the variable b is 4 bytes in size, it will occupy four locations in RAM. Let the four addresses in RAM where b is stored be 2000, 2001, 2002, and 2003. The address of variable b in such a case should be considered as 2000 because it is the starting address of the variable as shown in the Figure 8.4.

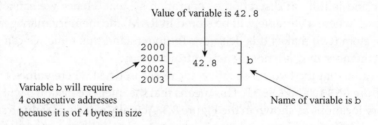

Figure 8.4: Storage of variable in RAM

The statement

```
printf("%d",&b);
```

will print 2000 which is the address of variable b. Note that we have used control parameter %d and not %f while printing address, because address of b will always be of type integer even if the value of b is of type `float`.

Whereas the statement

```
printf("%f",&b);
```

will print 42.8 because it is the value stored inside variable b. Note that we have used %f in printing the actual value of b.

How are character and floating point constants stored in computer memory? ?

We know that every character has an ASCII value which is in a range from 0 to 255. In order to store a character constant in computer memory, the ASCII value corresponding to the character constant is converted into binary and the resultant bit pattern is stored in computer memory. For example, if we want to store the character constant 'a', system will store the bit pattern as 01100001, which is the binary equivalent of 97 (which is ASCII value of 'a').

Floating point numbers will also be converted into binary before they are stored in memory. There are certain floating point formats defined by IEEE which are used to represent floating point numbers in machine language. Discussion of various IEEE formats for floating point representation is out of scope of this text book.

8.2 Creating Pointers

A pointer is a variable which stores the address of some other variable. This means that the value of the pointer will be the memory address of location which stores the value of another variable. The variable whose address is contained in the pointer is called target variable. We can access the value of target variable by using a pointer that points to it, this process is called **indirection**. We will learn in the later sections of this chapter on how indirection is supported by C/C++.

The following is the syntax to create a pointer:

`Data-Type *<Pointer_Name>;`

Note the presence of asterisk (*) before the pointer name, which makes the syntax of declaring pointers different then the syntax for declaring of any other variable.

The statement,

`int a=10;`

creates a normal variable named as a with a value 10. Let us assume the starting address of variable a as 1000. Hence the variable a will be stored in memory as shown in the Figure 8.5.

Let us create a pointer that will store the address of variable a. Since the variable a is of type integer, the pointer must also be of type integer.

The statement,

`int *p;`

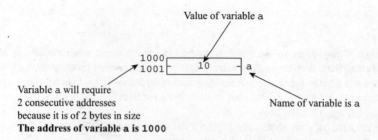

Figure 8.5: Storage of variable in RAM

will create a integer type pointer named as p. Pointer itself is a variable and it will also be stored in memory as that of any other variable. Any pointer is always of 2 bytes in size by default (applicable to near pointers), so pointer p will occupy two locations in RAM. Let the address of memory location where pointer p is stored be 5000 as shown in the Figure 8.6.

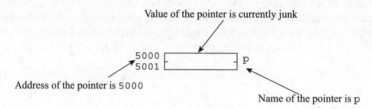

Figure 8.6: Storage of pointer in RAM

We have just declared a pointer p without storing any value inside the pointer. Hence, the pointer p will contain junk value initially and it will not point to any meaningful and relevant location in memory.

The statement,

```
p=&a;
```

will store the address of variable a in pointer p. We have assumed the address of variable a in memory as 1000, then the pointer p will contain 1000 after the execution of this statement. Since pointer p contains the address of variable a as shown in Figure 8.7, we say that the **pointer p points to variable** a.

We can now access the value of variable a by using pointer p with the help of **indirection operator** (*). When applied on a pointer, the indirection operator gives the value of a variable to whom it points to. For example, *p will give a value 10, because the pointer p

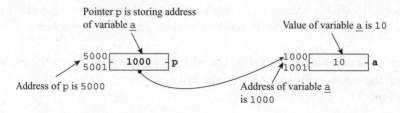

Figure 8.7: Pointer pointing to a variable

points to variable a having value 10. On execution of *p, the CPU will access the memory location whose address is contained in the pointer p and fetch the value stored in that location.

To understand this concept, we describe the output of a certain **printf()** statements in the following table. Cross refer to Figure 8.7 to understand the outputs described in the following table.

Statement	Description (as per Figure 8.7)
printf("%d",a);	This statement will print the value of variable a on the computer screen. Hence the statement prints **10** on the computer screen.
printf("%u",&a);	& is called 'address of' operator. Hence the statement prints the address of variable a. The output of the statement will be **1000,** as the variable a is stored at location 1000 in memory.
printf("%u",p);	This statement prints the value of pointer p. As the pointer p contains address of variable a, the output of this statement will be 1000. Note that, as per the definition of pointer, the value of pointer is always the address of some other variable (in this case it is address of variable a).
printf("%u",&p);	This statement applies & operator on a pointer, hence it will print the address in memory where the pointer p is stored. The output of this statement will be 5000, as the pointer p is stored at location **5000** as per Figure 8.7.
printf("%d",*p);	This statement applies an **indirection operator** (*) to a pointer p. The operator directs the CPU to access the memory location whose address is contained in the pointer and read the value stored in that location. As pointer p contains the address 1000, the CPU will access the contents of memory location 1000, which is value of variable a as per Figure 8.7. Hence the statement prints the **10** (value of variable **a**) on the computer screen.

Note that, as agreed in Section 8.1.2, we have used the control string %d when printing value and %u when printing address.

NOTES

While declaring a pointer, you can use operator * immediately next to the data type or just before the pointer name. It does not matter, when you hit the space bar. For example, both the declarations of the pointer p are valid

```
int* p; /*asterisk immediately after the data type*/

OR

int *p; /*asterisk just before the pointer name*/
```

In any case, the operator * should repeat with every declaration of a pointer when multiple pointers are declared in single statement. For example, if you want to create two pointers p and q in a single statement you must use * two times as shown in the statement below:

```
int *p, *q;
```

The statement,

```
int* p, *q;
```

is also valid and will create two pointers p and q. Notice that in any case, to create q as a pointer you must use asterisks just before the pointer name q.

The statement,

```
int* p, q;
```

creates p as a pointer but q as a normal integer variable. This is because no asterisk symbol is specified for q. Hence C/C++ compiler considers q as a simple variable of type integer. But since there is an asterisk symbol before p, it is created as a pointer of type integer.

In this text book, we will generally use asterisk symbol just before the pointer name when we create pointers; with an exception while creating **constant pointers** where we have to use a notation of asterisk immediately after the data type. **Constant pointers** are described in the later part of the text book.

What is the size of a pointer? ?

 C/C++ has two types of pointers.

  1. Near Pointer (used for relative addressing within the segment).
  2. Far Pointer (used for absolute addressing to address a location outside the current segment).

As mentioned in Section 8.1.1, the size of each segment and organization of main memory (RAM) depends upon a multiple hardware and software parameters. In a typical ×86 environment where 16 bit compilers are used the size of each segment is 64 KB and hence **near pointer** is of **2 bytes** in size whereas a **far pointer** is of **4 bytes** in size. As mentioned in Section 8.1.1, near and far addressing is transparent to the programmer so you don't have to worry about this point from programming perspective. When you store the address of a particular variable in a pointer, C/C++ will internally determine whether a near or far pointer needs to be created to point to the target variable.

In fact, with today's generation of computing, most of the C/C++ compilers are 32 bit and they do not have a concept of near and far pointers at all. A 32 bit compiler makes all the pointers declared in the program as **4 bytes** wide. Don't be surprised if you always get the size of a pointer as 4 bytes, it just means that you are working on a 32 bit compiler.

8.3 Data Type of Pointers

Although the memory addresses are always of type integer, the data type of pointer may not always be an integer. This is because the data type of the pointer depends upon the data type of the target variable whose address is contained in the pointer. In the absence of polymorphism, the data type of the pointer must be exactly same as the data type of the variable to whom the pointer points to. This is because the **indirection operator** (*) is to be used with pointers to fetch the value of the target variable. As the amount of memory required for a particular variable depends on the data type of that variable, giving a correct data type to the pointer helps the CPU to determine the number of memory locations to be fetched to access the complete data value of the target variable. For example, if the pointer is of type integer, then CPU will access only the first two locations in order to fetch the complete value of the variable from memory by using indirection. This is because every integer value is of 2 bytes in size. Or if the pointer is of type float, then CPU will access the first four locations in order to fetch the complete value of the variable by using indirection, because every float value is of 4 bytes in size. This means that, an integer type pointer can only point to an integer variable whereas a float type pointer can only point to a float variable and so on the concept can be similarly extended to other data types.

CONCLUSION

Data type the pointer must be same as the data type of the variable to which it points to.

Following is an example that creates two variables a and c of type int and float, respectively. To store the addresses of each of these variables, we create two pointers p and r of type int and float, respectively.

```
#include<stdio.h>
void main()
{
/*create variables*/
int a=10;
float c=42.9;
/* create individual pointers*/
int *p;
float *r;
/*store address of each of the variables in a corresponding
    pointer*/
p=&a;
r=&c;
/*print the values of a and c using pointers*/

printf("a=%d\n",*p);
printf("c=%f\n",*r);

/*print the address of a and c*/
printf("Address of a is %u\n",p);
printf("Address of c is %u\n",r);
}
```

Output

```
a=10
c=42.900002

Address of a is 1000
Address of c is 3000
```

The statements,

```
p=&a;
r=&c;
```

store the address of variable a in a integer pointer p and address of variable c in a floating point pointer r. Note that, the data type of each pointer is same as the data type of target variable which it points to. Figure 8.8 shows memory structure created by the code, assuming the starting addresses of variables a and c as 1000 and 3000, respectively.

As each of the pointers is associated with a particular data type, the indirection operator when applied to a particular pointer will accurately determine the number of locations required to be accessed by CPU in order to fetch the complete value of the target variable.

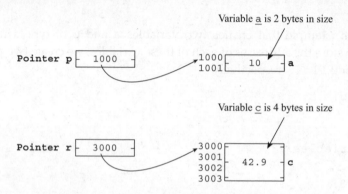

Figure 8.8: Pointers pointing to a variables a and c

The following table will help in understanding the outputs of each of the **printf()** statements.

Pointer usage	Description
*p;	The pointer p contains the address of variable a, hence *p will give the value of variable a, that is 10.
	As pointer p contains the address 1000, when an indirection operator is applied to a pointer p, CPU will read the two consecutive locations with addresses 1000 and 1001, to get the value of the variable which is pointed by p. The value stored at these locations in memory is 10, hence the operation *p gives a value 10.
	In this case, the CPU reads two locations in memory because the data type of pointer p is integer and every integer requires 2 bytes in memory.
	Hence the statement,
	`printf("a=%d\n",*p);`
	will generate the following output:
	`a=10`
*r;	Similar to how *p works, *r will give the value 42.9, which is the value of variable c. The only point to mention is CPU this time reads four locations in memory with addresses 3000,3001,3002, and 3003 to get the value by using indirection because this pointer is of type float.

Hence the statement,

```
printf("c=%d\n",*r);
```

will generate the following output:

```
c=42.9
```

p   Writing p in the code, will give the value stored inside the pointer p. We know that pointer p contains address of variable a, that is 1000. Hence, the result of this token will be 1000.
Hence the statement,

```
printf("Address of a is %u\n",p);
```

will generate the following output:
```
Address of a is 1000
```

r   Writing token r in the code, will give the address stored inside r that is 3000. Hence the statement,

```
printf("Address of c is %u\n",r);
```

will generate the following output:

```
Address of c is 3000
```

8.4 Types of Function Calls

8.4.1 Call by value

Consider the given code which consists of two functions main() and f1(). The function f1() takes one integer type argument and increments the integer value passed to it. The function main() calls a function f1() by passing the value of its local variable a which is created in main().

Due to the function call, value of variable a in main() is passed to variable p which is the formal argument of f1(). Since value of the variable is passed from calling function to the called function, the mechanism is named as '**call by value**'.

```
#include<stdio.h>
void f1(int);
void main()
{
int a=10;
printf("Before call a=%d\n",a);
f1(a);
printf("After call a=%d\n",a);
}
void f1(int p)
{
p++;
}
```

Output

```
Before call a=10
After call a=10
```

To understand the working of 'call by value' in detail, let us go through the above code line by line. The execution of code will start from the main() function. The following table explains the execution of each line in main().

Statement	Description
int a=10;	This statement creates a local variable a initialized to value 10. Note that, this is local variable of main() and cannot be directly accessed by function f1().
printf ("Before call a=%d\n",a);	The statement prints the value of variable a which is 10. Hence, the following message is printed on the computer screen : Before call a=10
f1(a);	This statement is a function call to f1() by passing a value of variable a as an argument to the function. On executing this statement, the control is transferred to the function definition of f1(), triggering its execution. The value 10 is assigned to the formal argument p which is the local variable of f1() as shown in the Figure 8.9. It is important to understand that, there are two variables being created in the memory, first is the variable a which is the local variable of main() function and the second is variable p which is the local variable of function f1(). Initially both the variables have same value which is 10 as shown in the Figure 8.9. Inside the body of function f1(), the statement p++ changes the value of p to 11. After the function completes its execution, the control is transferred back to the main() function.
printf ("After call a=%d\n",a);	The statement prints the value of variable a after execution of the f1() is completed. Note that the function f1() never changed the value of variable a but it had just changed the value of variable p. As shown in the Figure 8.9 the variables a and p are two different variables in memory and changing the value of variable p will not change the value of variable a in anyway. When the control returns to the main() function the value of variable a is still 10. Hence, this statement prints the following message on the computer screen: After call a=10

NOTES

Call by value creates two different variables one in the **calling** function, and the other in the **called** function. Updating the value of variable in **called** function will never update the corresponding variable in the **calling** function. This is because the two variables reside at different physical locations in memory.

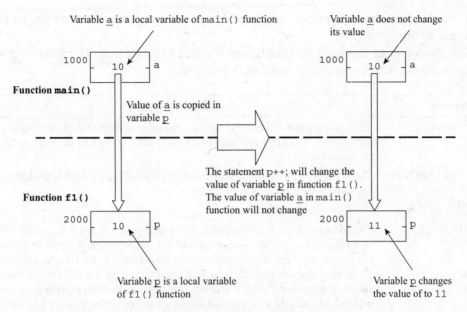

Figure 8.9: Call by value

8.4.2 Call by address

When a function is called by passing the address of the actual parameters instead of values, the mechanism is named as '**call by address**'.

Consider the given code to understand working of call by address. The function main() has a local variable a and its address is passed to f1() at the time when function call is made. Note that, the formal argument of function f1() is declared as a pointer, as it needs to store the address that is passed by main().

```c
#include<stdio.h>
void f1(int*);
void main()
{
int a=10;
printf("Before call a=%d\n",a);

f1(&a);
printf("After call a=%d\n",a);
}
void f1(int *p)
{
(*p)++;
}
```

Output

```
Before call a=10
After call a=11
```

To understand the working of 'call by address' in detail, let us go through the given code line by line.

The execution of the code will start from the `main()` function. The following table explains the execution of each line in `main()` function.

Statement	Description
`int a=10;`	This statement creates a local variable a initialized to value 10. Remember it is local variable of `main()` and cannot be directly accessed by function `f1()`.
`printf("Before call a=%d\n",a);`	The statement prints the value of variable a which is 10. Hence the following message is printed on the computer screen: `Before call a=10`
`f1(&a);`	This statement is a function call to `f1()` by passing the address of variable a as an argument. Let us assume the address of variable a as 1000 as shown in the Figure 8.10. The control will now be transferred to the function definition by storing the address of the actual argument a in the formal argument p which is a pointer. Hence it will be correct to say that the pointer p stores the address of variable a. Therefore the value stored in the pointer p is 1000 as shown in the Figure 8.10. The statement inside function `f1()`, `(*p)++;` applies an indirection operator to pointer p, hence increment (++) is applied to the contents of the variable whose address is contained in the pointer. This changes the value of variable a to 11. It is important to understand that because pointer p points to variable a, both a and *p will operate on the same memory location, hence adding 1 to *p is same as adding 1 to variable a as shown in the Figure 8.10. Also note the presence of parentheses in the statement `(*p)++;` which first applies the indirection operator to the pointer and then increments the value of the variable. This is necessary because in the normal course the priority of ++ is greater than the priority of * which we have to alter in this case. After the `f1()` completes its execution, the control is transferred back to the `main()` function.
`printf("After call a=%d\n",a);`	The statement prints the value of variable a after returning from the function `f1()`. Note that the function `f1()` has already changed the value of variable a by using a pointer. Hence, when the control returns to `main()` function the value of variable a is already changed to 11. Following message is printed on the computer screen as a result of this statement: `After call a=11`

NOTES

When a function is called by passing address of actual argument, the **called** function creates an additional ink (using pointer) to the variable defined in the **calling** function. This way, we can access the actual value of the variable in the **called** function using an **indirection operator**. This mechanism is named as **call by address**.

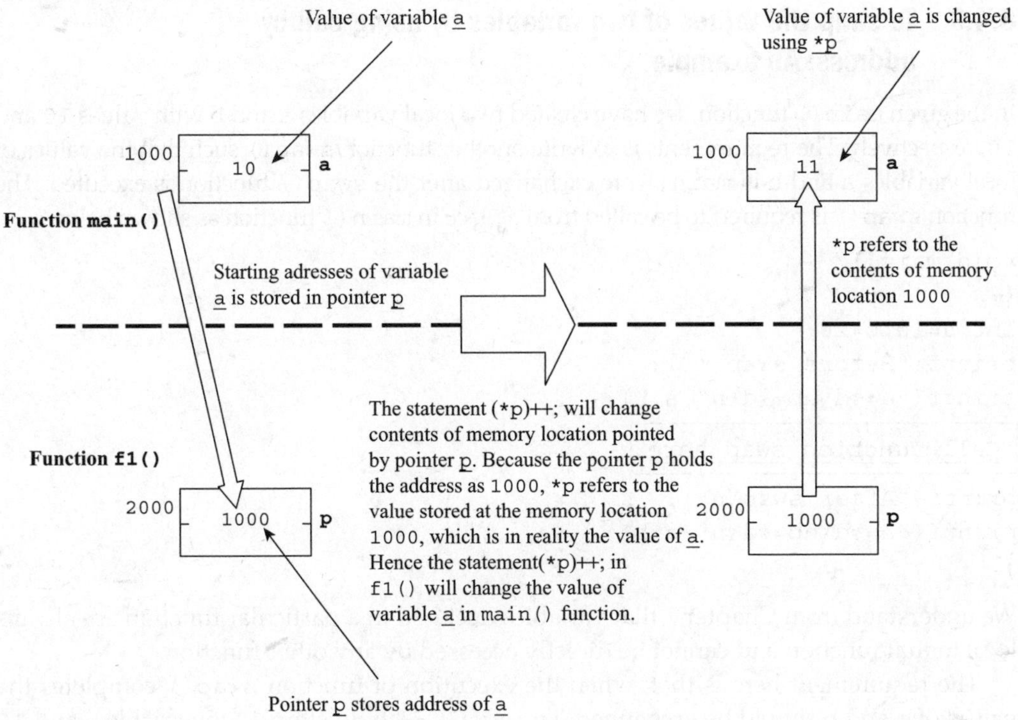
Value of variable a
Value of variable a is changed using *p
1000
10
a
1000
11
a
Function main()
*p refers to the contents of memory location 1000
Starting adresses of variable a is stored in pointer p
The statement (*p)++; will change contents of memory location pointed by pointer p. Because the pointer p holds the address as 1000, *p refers to the value stored at the memory location 1000, which is in reality the value of a. Hence the statement(*p)++; in f1() will change the value of variable a in main() function.
Function f1()
2000
1000
p
2000
1000
p
Pointer p stores address of a

Figure 8.10: Call by address

NOTES

Clearly, call by address gives additional access to the called function to modify the variable declared in the calling function by using the principle of indirection. Though this is required in some cases but it also creates a possibility of genuine programmers to accidently modify the memory location of the calling function from the called function. In this example, we have intentionally modified the memory location of the `main()` from `f1()`. This is ok, but in some cases, we may not want to do so. Under such circumstances you can declare the pointer argument as a `const`. For example, if we make pointer `p` as a constant argument of function `f1()` as shown in the following statement:

```
void f1(const int *p)
{
(*p)++; /*ERROR: Value pointed by p cannot be changed*/
}
```

then, we will not be able to modify the value which is pointed by pointer `p`. Hence the statement `(*p)++;` will give an error. This is because, making the argument as `const` in this case, conveys the compiler that the value pointed by pointer should not be modified. If this is the requirement, the keyword `const` must also be added while prototyping the function `f1()` as shown in the following statement:

```
void f1(const int*);
```

Further details about `const` pointers are discussed in Section 8.5. This note just explains one of the possible usage of `const` pointers. Please refer Section 8.5 to know more about `cost` pointers.

8.4.3　To swap the values of two variables by using call by address: An example

In the given `main()` function, we have created two local variables a and b with values 10 and 20, respectively. The requirements is to write another function `swap()` such that the values of local variables a and b in `main()` are exchanged after the `swap()` function is executed. The function `swap()` is required to be called from a place in `main()` function as shown below:

```
void main()
{
int a=10,b=20;
printf("Before swap\n");
printf("a=%d\nb=%d\n",a,b);
```

```
Call function swap here
```

```
printf("After swap\n");
printf("a=%d\nb=%d\n",a,b);
}
```

We understand from Chapter 7 that variables declared in a particular function are always local to that function and cannot be directly accessed by any other function.

The requirement here is that, when the execution of function `swap()` completes the values of a and b should be exchanged (i.e., `swap()` should store 20 in variable a and 10 in variable b). This means that the function `swap()` is required to modify the values of variables a and b which is against the concept of 'local variables' and 'call by value'.

Hence, the only option is to call the function `swap()` by address. Let us create two pointers in `swap()` function say p and q, so that these pointers can store the addresses of variables a and b, respectively. Also, we already understand that the contents of actual arguments in the 'calling function' can be modified by using the pointers in the 'called function' provided that the pointers store the addresses of the actual variables in 'calling function'. This means that we can now access the values of variables a and b in function `swap()` by applying the indirection operator to pointers p and q, respectively. Hence, swapping the values of a and b in `main()` function is same as swapping of *p and *q in `swap()` function, because the pointer p points to variable a pointer q points to variable b.

```
void swap(int *p,int *q)
{
    int temp;
    temp=*p;
    *p=*q;
    *q=temp;
}
```

As shown below, we call function `swap()` such that the first argument passed to `swap()` is address of variable a and the second argument is the address of variable b, this will ensure that p holds address of a and q holds address of b

```
swap(&a,&b);
```

NOTES

In summary, as pointers p and q point to variables a and b respectively, using *p in function swap() we can access the value of variable a of function main() and using *q in function swap() we can access the value of variable b of function main().

Given below is the full source code that performs exchange of variables in main() using swap() function:

```
#include<stdio.h>
void swap(int*, int*);
void main()
{
int a=10,b=20;
printf("Before swap\n");
printf("a=%d\nb=%d\n",a,b);
swap(&a,&b);
printf("After swap\n");
printf("a=%d\nb=%d\n",a,b);
}
void swap(int *p, int *q)
{
    int temp;
    temp=*p;
    *p=*q;
    *q=temp;
}
```

Output

```
Before swap
a=10
b=20
After swap
a=20
b=10
```

Let us go through the above code line-by-line to understand the approach of swapping values by using call by address. The execution will start from the main() function and the first line in the code creates two variables a and b with values 10 and 20 as shown in the Figure 8.11:

```
int a=10,b=20;
```

The next two printf() statements in the code will print the values of a and b as follows:

```
Before swap
a=10
b=20
```

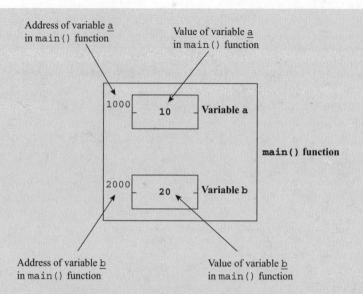

Figure 8.11: Local variables in `main()` function

The statement,

```
swap(&a,&b);
```

calls function `swap()`, by passing the addresses of actual arguments a and b which will be stored in pointers p and q, respectively.

Hence, pointer p in `swap()` now points to variable a in `main()` and pointer q in `swap()` points to variable b in `main()` as shown in the Figure 8.12.

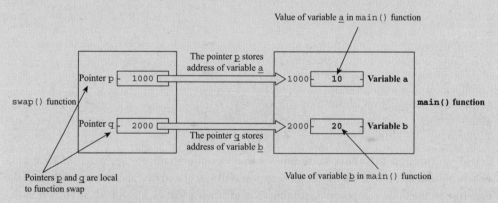

Figure 8.12: Initialization of formal arguments of `swap()` function

The first line of `swap()` function,

```
int temp;
```

declares a local variable named as `temp` as shown in Figure 8.13. The variable `temp` will give a temporary storage in memory which is required to `swap()` the values of variables a and b.

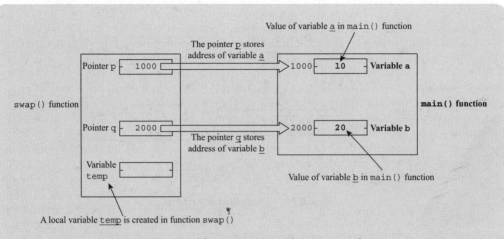

Figure 8.13: Variable `temp` is created in `swap()` function

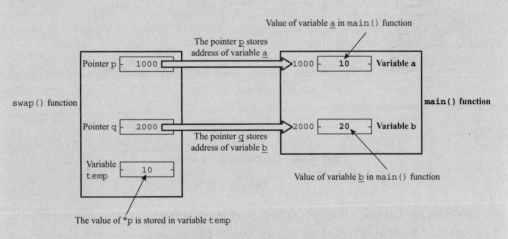

Figure 8.14: Execution of `temp=*p`

The next statement in function `swap()`,

```
temp=*p;
```

stores the value of the variable a in variable `temp` as shown in the Figure 8.14. Hence, we have accessed the value of variable a in `main()` by the principle of **indirection** using pointer p in `swap()`.

The next line in function `swap()`,

```
*p=*q;
```

puts the value of variable b inside variable a as shown in the Figure 8.15. This statement reads the value of variable b by applying the indirection operator to pointer q and writes the value to variable a by applying the indirection to pointer p.

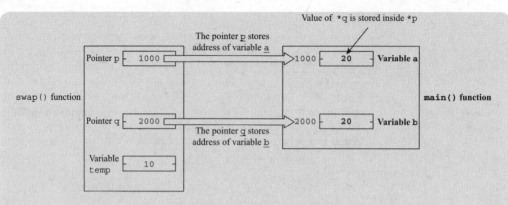

Figure 8.15: Execution of *p=*q

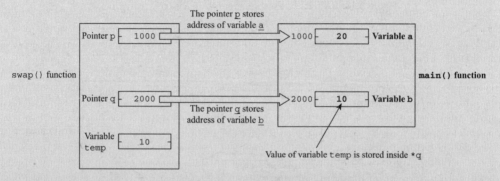

Figure 8.16: Execution of *q=temp

Similarly, the last line in swap function *q=temp; stores the value of local variable temp inside the variable b as shown in the Figure 8.16.

Thus, the values of variables a and b are exchanged using the pointers created in swap() function. Therefore when control of execution returns back to the main() function the printf() statement now prints the value of a as 20 and value b as 10 as shown below:

```
After swap
a=20
b=10
```

CAUTION

If a pointer is used in the program without initializing it to a valid memory location then such a pointer is called **wild pointer**. Wild pointers are dangerous because we never know to what memory location they are pointing to, then they may corrupt some location in RAM resulting the program to crash or make the system misbehave.

For example,

```
int *p; /*The pointer is not initialized and hence it points to some
    random unknown memory location*/
*p=30; /*changes the contents of some memory location which is not
    really known and hence it may crash the program of make the
    system misbehave*/
```

8.5   Arithmetic Operations with Pointers

C/C++ supports usage of following operators for performing operations with the address that is contained in the pointer:

- Unary operators: ++ (increment) and – – (decrement)
- Binary operators: + (addition) and – (subtraction)

Address inside a pointer will be changed as a result of pointer arithmetic's, hence it is the responsibility of the programmer to ensure that even after the arithmetic operation completes, the pointer continues to point to a relevant memory location that contains a meaningful data value.

The address inside a pointer is always changed in multiples of the size of its data type. This means that, if we attempt to change the address inside a pointer by a value k, then the address will actually be changed by a factor k*sizeof(d), where d is the 'data type' of the pointer. The factor k*sizeof(d), always ensures that the pointer never contains any address other than the starting address of the data value, in cases when a single data value is spread across multiple locations in RAM.

For example, let us consider an integer type pointer, pointing to a variable a as shown below.

```
int a=10;
int *p;
p=&a;
```

Let the address of variable a be 1000, which is also contained in the pointer p as shown in the Figure 8.17. Let us now perform an increment operation (++) to change the address inside the pointer. This can be done by the statement below:

```
p++;
```

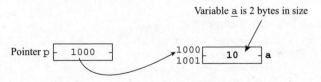

Figure 8.17:   Pointer pointing to variable a

Note that the increment operation will not be applied to the value of variable a, this is because the pointer is not used along with an indirection operator *. The statement p++; will change the address contained inside the pointer, by a factor **1*sizeof(int),** as the data type of the pointer is integer. Every integer takes two bytes in the memory, hence the statement will actually change the address by 1*2=2. This means that every change in address by 1 will change the address actually by 2 for integer type pointers. Hence the new address inside a pointer will now be 1002 and not 1001. Notice that 1001 is not the starting address of variable a, so it will never be contained in the pointer, this is because pointers should always store the starting address of any object in order to accurately point to the object in memory.

To get a thorough understanding of this concept, let us create four variables a, b, c and d of type integer, char, float, and double, respectively. Let us now create four pointers p, q, r, and s such that they point to the variables a, b, c and d, respectively as shown in the Figure 8.18.

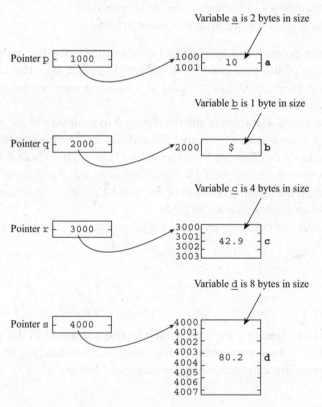

Figure 8.18: Pointer s, p, q, r, s pointing to variables a, b, c, and d, respectively

```
/*create variables in memory*/
int a=10;
char b='$';
float c=42.9;
double d=80.2;
```

```
/*create individual pointers*/
int *p;
char *q;
float *r;
double *s;

/*store the address of each of the variables in a pointer*/
p=&a;
q=&b;
r=&c;
s=&d;
```

Figure 8.18 assumes the starting address of variables a, b, c, and d as 1000, 2000, 3000, and 4000, respectively as contained in pointers p, q, r, and s, respectively.

The table below gives some **examples** on Pointer arithmetic's.

Example statement	Description
p+2;	This statement adds constant 2 to the address contained in the pointer p. Given that the current address contained in the pointer is 1000 and the pointer is of type integer, new address will be calculated as: =1000 + 2*sizeof(int) =1000 + 2*2 =1004 Hence, the next address generated by the expression is 1004.
q+6;	This statement adds constant 6 to the address contained in the pointer q. Given that the current address contained in the pointer is 2000 and the pointer is of type char, new address will be calculated as: =2000 + 6*sizeof(char) =2000 + 6*1 =2006 Hence, the next address generated by the expression is 2006.
r+3;	This statement adds constant 3 to the address contained in the pointer r. Given that the current address contained in the pointer is 3000 and the pointer is of type float, new address will be calculated as: =3000 + 3*sizeof(float) =3000 + 3*4 =3012 Hence, the next address generated by the expression is 3012.
s-5;	This statement subtracts constant 5 to the address contained in the pointer s. Given that the current address contained in the pointer is 4000 and the pointer is of type double, new address will be calculated as: =4000 - 5*sizeof(double) =4000 - 5*8 =3960 Hence, the next address generated by the expression is 3960.

Pointer arithmetic's will be heavily in the Section 8.6, which explains the process to access array elements by using pointers.

8.5.1 Keyword `const` with pointers

From Chapter 2, we understand that `const` is a keyword used to create constant variables. For example,

```
const int a=10;
```

creates a variable a with a constant value 10. As we have used a keyword `const` in the declaration of a, the value of variable a cannot change throughout the program. Any attempt to change the value of the variable a will raise a compile time error.

Keyword `const` can also be used with pointer declarations. `const` can be used to create following three types of pointers:

1. Constant pointer
2. Pointer that points to a Constant Data Value
3. Constant pointer that points to a constant variable (combination of both 1 and 2)

8.5.2 Constant pointer

A pointer which cannot change the address to which it points to is called a **constant pointer**. The following is the syntax of creating constant pointers.

```
DataType* const pointer_name=&Target_Variable;
```

Note the presence of keyword `const` which creates a constant pointer. The pointer named as `pointer_name` is initialized to hold the address of `Target_Variable`.

It is important to note that, when you declare a constant pointer it must always be initialized. The following declaration of a constant pointer is illegal,

```
int* const p;
```

because the pointer p is never initialized. The highlighted statement,

```
int a=10;
int* const p=&a;
```

is legal because it initializes the address of variable a in the constant pointer p. Hence, assuming address of variable a as 1000, pointer p, points to variable a as shown in the Figure 8.19.

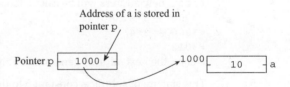

Figure 8.19: Address contained in pointer p

As p is a constant pointer, you cannot change the address stored inside p by any means. This means that you cannot reinitialize p to point to any other variable. For example, if b is another integer type variable, the following statement will give an error,

p=&b; /*This is an error because you cannot reinitialize p to point to any other variable*/

because it attempts to change the address stored inside p.

The following program will give a compile time error, because we are attempting to change the address contained inside a constant pointer. The program creates two variables a and b and a constant pointer p, which initially points to variable a. Later in the program, we attempt to make the pointer point to variable b, by using the following statement:

```
p=&b;
```

As p is a constant pointer, the compilation of this statement fails giving a **compile time error**.

Since compilation of the program itself failed, the program will **not produce any output**

```
#include<stdio.h>
void main()
{
int a=10, b=20;
int* const p=&a;
printf("a=%d",*p);
p=&b; /*ERROR - cannot change address inside the pointer*/
printf("b=%d",*p);
}
```

ERROR on compilation of this program is as follows:

Checking file dependency...
Compiling C:\Program Files\C-Free Standard\temp\Untitled5.cpp...
[Error] C:\Program Files\C-Free Standard\temp\Untitled5.cpp:7: assignment of read-only variable `p'

Complete Make Untitled5: 1 error(s), 0 warning(s)

NOTES

When declaring constant pointers we have to use a notation to specify asterisk immediately after the data type. The notation wherein we specify asterisk just before the pointer name will not give proper results.

The following statement is a correct declaration and initialization of a constant pointer

```
int* const p=&a;
```

whereas, the statement below will not give the desired results

```
int const *p=&a;
```

We will discuss the results of this statement shortly. But, at this point remember that if you need to create a constant pointer you must specify asterisk immediately after the data type.

8.5.3 Pointer that points to a constant data value

If you place the const keyword in the beginning of the pointer declaration statement, C/C++ creates a pointer that points to a constant data value. In this case, you can change the address that is contained in the pointer but you will not be able to change the value which is pointed by the pointer.

The following is the syntax to create a pointer that points to a constant data value:

```
const DataType* pointer_name=&Target_Variable;
```

In the following program, we have created a pointer p which holds the address of variable a

```
const int* p=&a;
```

This makes pointer p point to a constant data value, which means that you cannot change the value of the memory location pointed by p, using the pointer p.

Hence, the statement,

```
*p=(*p)+1;
```

gives a **compile time error** because it is an attempt to change the value pointed by the pointer.

However, if we would have written a statement

```
p=&b;
```

it would just work fine. Because, you can change the address contained in the pointer but only constraint is that you will not be able to change the value that the pointer points to.

Note that, you can always change the value of variable a directly by using a. For example, the following statement,

```
a=a+1;
```

will just work fine. This is because variable a is not declared as a constant variable. However, you will never be able to change the value of variable a by using pointer p, because pointer p is declared as a pointer that points to a constant value.

```
#include<stdio.h>
void main()
{
int a=10;
const int* p=&a;
printf("a=%d",*p);
*p=(*p)+1; /*ERROR - cannot modify value using pointer*/
printf("b=%d",*p);
}
```

ERROR on compilation of this program is as follows:

```
Checking file dependency...
Compiling C:\Program Files\C-Free Standard\temp\Untitled5.cpp...
[Error] C:\Program Files\C-Free Standard\temp\Untitled5.cpp:8: assignment of read-only location

Complete Make Untitled5: 1 error(s), 0 warning(s)
```

> **NOTES**
>
> To create a pointer that can point to a constant value, you can also put keyword **const** in between data type and asterisk symbol.
> The statement
>
> ```
> const int* p=&a;
> ```
>
> is equivalent to
>
> ```
> int const *p=&a;
> ```
>
> Both the statements create a pointer p that points to constant. You can use any one of the syntax in your program.

8.5.4 Constant pointer that points to a constant value

We can also create a constant pointer that points to a constant value. This means that we will neither be able to change address contained inside the pointer nor the value that the pointer points to. Such pointers can be initialized only once during their creation. In order to create such pointers, the keyword const must appear at two places in the pointer declaration as shown in the following syntax:

```
const DataType* const pointer_name=&Target_Variable;
```

The statement,

```
const int* const p=&a;
```

will create a pointer p as a constant pointer that points to a constant value. Hence, both the statements,

```
p=&b; /*Error - cannot change the address contained in pointer*/
*p=(*p)+1; /*Error - cannot change the value pointed by pointer*/
```

will give an error because you can neither change the address contained inside the pointer nor the value that the pointer points to.

> **NOTES**
>
> An array is internally created using a constant pointer which points to the first element of the array. This pointer has a same name as that of the name given to the array. Indeed, the array name is actually the name of the constant pointer, using which array elements are accessed.

For example, the statement

```
int a[3]={10,20,30};
```

creates a constant pointer named as a. This pointer stores the starting address of an array. Hence the statement,

```
printf("%u",a);
```

will print the starting address of an array a. If the starting address of an array is 1000 as shown in the figure below, the printf() statement will print 1000

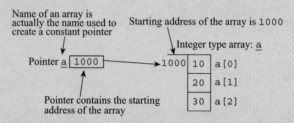

Obviously, the starting address of an array is actually the address of its first element which can also be obtained using &a[0]. Therefore, following two printf() statements will give exactly the same address

```
printf("%u",a);
printf("%u",&a[0]);
```

This means that, pointer a actually stores &a[0].

8.6 Accessing Array Elements using a Pointer

All the elements of an array can be accessed by using a single pointer, if the pointer stores the starting address of the array. To prove this statement, let us create an integer array of 3 elements as a shown below:

```
int a[3]={10,20,30};
```

Each element of a is an integer, hence every array element will require 2 bytes in memory. Hence total memory requirement for an integer array =2*n bytes, where n is the size of the array. Therefore array a will require 6 bytes of memory as it contains 3 elements. Also we understand from the Chapter 6, that all the elements in the array are always stored in **contiguous** memory locations, hence they will have **consecutive** memory addresses. Figure 8.20 shows the memory allocated for an array a assuming the starting address of array as 1000.

Let us now create a pointer p that stores the starting address of the array a. Note that the starting address of the array will always be the address of the first element of the array (written as &a[0]). As the array a is of type integer the pointer p must also be of type integer as shown below:

```
int *p;
p=&a[0];
```

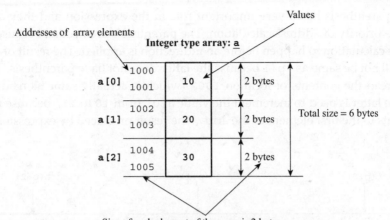

Figure 8.20: Memory allocation of array a

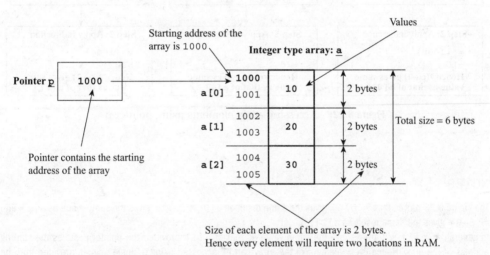

Size of each element of the array is 2 bytes.
Hence every element will require two locations in RAM.

Figure 8.21: Pointer p points to the first location in the array

The statement p=&a[0]; stores the address of the first element of the array inside the pointer, hence the pointer p now contains 1000. This is as shown in the Figure 8.21.

Figure 8.22, describes the results of some expressions based on the Figure 8.21. Let us take an example of an expression *(p+1). In this case, p+1 is surrounded in parenthesis, hence the expression first adds a constant 1 to the address contained in p and then applies indirection operator on the resultant address. The address contained in p is 1000 and because the pointer is of type integer 1000+ 1 is evaluated as 1002. We now apply indirection operation and fetch the value at memory location 1002 which gives 20 as seen in the Figure 8.21. (Applying indirection operator on memory address 1002 will read 2 consecutive bytes in memory stored at addresses 1002 and 1003, this is because every integer is 2 bytes). Hence, the expression returns a value 20 which is the value of a[1].

Note that, parenthesis has a very important role in the expression and they are used to increase the priority of address calculation. The parenthesis are needed because, we want the address calculation to happen before an indirection is applied. The result of expression * (p+1) will not be same as *p+1 because the latter does not have parenthesis. The former is used to read the contents of location 1002 (which is actually same as reading a[1]), whereas the latter is used to increment the value a[0] from 10 to 11, because the pointer p still points to the first element of the array. The result produced by expressions * (p+0)

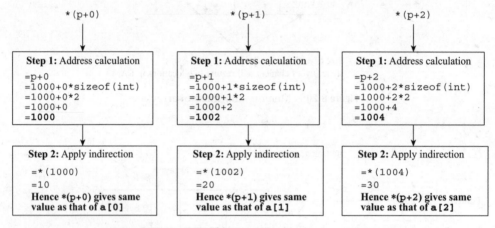

Figure 8.22: Accessing array elements using pointer p

NOTES

The Figure 8.22 proves that * (p+0) gives the same result as a[0], * (p+1) gives the same result as a[1] and * (p+2) gives the same result as a[2].

In general, * (p+i) will always give the same value as that of a[i] provided the pointer p stores the starting address of the array. Hence every element of the array can be accessed using a single pointer, provided that the pointer holds the base address of the array.

For example, the statement

printf("%d",a[i]);

is equivalent to

printf("%d",* (p+i));

Needless to say that, using the expression, (p+i) [without indirection operator] will give you the address of a[i] (&a[i]). The address of a[i] is typically needed when we use scanf() statement to accept the ith element of an array as input from the user

For example

scanf("%d",&a[i]);

can be rewritten as

scanf("%d",(p+i));

Note that, indirection operator * is not present with the expression (p+i) because call to scanf() function is always made by passing address of the variable as an argument to it.

and *(p+2) shown in Figure 8.22 can be understood using the same theory as explained for *(p+1).

As the pointer arithmetic already takes care of different sizes of data types while performing addition/subtraction operations with addresses, this theory of accessing elements of array using pointers can be applied to the arrays of any type including arrays of user-defined types. Pointer arithmetic in C/C++ is designed to save programmers efforts in worrying about the data type of the array while accessing the array elements using a single pointer.

According to Section 8.5.4; if name of the array is a it means that a is actually the pointer containing starting address of an array. Here, we have created another pointer p in which we are explicitly storing starting address of an array a. Is there any difference between pointers p and a. **?**

Yes, there is a difference between the two pointers. Pointer a is a constant pointer, whereas pointer p is not. Pointer p is explicitly created by the programmer and pointer a is created by compiler when an array named a is created. Since pointer p is owned by us, we can change p at runtime to point to any other value or even to any other array, but you cannot change the address inside pointer a in anyway because it is a constant pointer created by the compiler and it will continue pointing to the same array throughout the program execution.

8.6.1 Program to arrange n-numbers in ascending order using pointers: An example

As we have already implemented the solution for sorting the array of integers in Chapter 6 of this textbook, we will reuse the same solution to arrange numbers in ascending order by using **pointers**.

NOTES

If name of the array is a then &a[0] gives the starting address of an array. We also know that a in itself is a pointer which contains the starting address of an array. This means that you can use &a[0] and a interchangeably in the code. For example, if p is another pointer which is required to hold starting address of array a, you can do this using any one of the following statements

```
p=a;
```
OR
```
p=&a[0];
```

To perform sorting of elements in array a the code creates an integer type pointer p such that p holds the starting address of the array a using the following statements:

```
int *p;
p=&a[0];
```

The code given below is same as that of Chapter 6, except every access to element a[i] is now done by using an expression *(p+i).

Following substitutions are required to be applied on the solution discussed in Chapter 6, to solve the same program by using pointers:

1. Every occurrence of a[i] in the code should be replaced by *(p+i).
2. Every occurrence of &a[i] in the code should be replaced by (p+i).
3. Every occurrence of a[j] in the code should be replaced by *(p+j).

```
#include<stdio.h>
void main()
{
int a[100],temp,n,i,j;
int *p;
p=&a[0];
printf("Enter length of the array:");
scanf("%d",&n);
printf("Enter array elements\n");
      for(i=0;i<=n-1;i++)
      {
      scanf("%d", (p+i) ); /*Input element number i */
      }
      for(i=0;i<=n-2;i++)
      {
      for(j=i+1;j<=n-1;j++)
         {
             if(*(p+i) > *(p+j))
             {
         temp=*(p+i);  /*store value of a[i] in variable temp*/
                 *(p+i)=*(p+j);  /* store value of a[j] in a[i]*/
                 *(p+j)=temp;   /*store value of temp in a[j]*/
             }
         }
      }
printf("Ascending order is as below\n");
      for(i=0;i<=n-1;i++)
      {
      printf("%d\n",*(p+i)); //print a[i] using pointer p
      }

}
```

Output
```
Enter Length of the array:
5
Enter Array elements
30
```

```
10
20
6
50
Ascending order is as below
6
10
20
30
50
```

8.6.2 Program to check if the string is palindrome or not using pointers: An example

As we have already implemented the solution to check palindromes in Chapter 6 of this textbook, we will reuse the same solution to write a code to check palindromes using pointers.

As discussed in Example 6.5.3, we create two character arrays a and b such that the array a contains the original string and the array b contains its reverse. We then need to check if the original string is same as its reverse. Because there are two character type arrays, we will now need two character pointers say p and q such that the pointer p points to array a and pointer q points to array b as shown below:

```
/* Pointer p to point to array - a */
   char *p;
   p=&a[0];

/* Pointer q to point to array - b */
   char *q;
   q=&b[0];
```

The code given below is same as that of Chapter 6, with following substitutions applied, to solve the same program using pointers:

1. Every occurrence of a[i] in the code should be replaced by *(p+i).
2. Every occurrence of b[i] in the code should be replaced by *(q+i).
3. Every occurrence of b[j] in the code should be replaced by *(q+j).
4. Every occurrence of b[k] in the code should be replaced by *(q+k).

```
#include<stdio.h>
void main()
{
char a[100],b[100];
int i, len=0,last,k,flag=0;
```

```
char *p,*q;
p=&a[0];
q=&b[0];
printf("Enter a word:");
scanf("%s",a);
/*calculate the length of word in array -a*/
for(i=0;*(p+i)!='\0';i++) /*Execute the loop till a[i] is not null*/
    {
        len++;
    }
/*set the position of last character in array -a*/
last=len-1;
/*copy reverse of array -a in array -b*/
k=0;
for(i=last;i>=0;i--)
    {
        *(q+k)=*(p+i); /* Initialize b[k] to the value of a[i] */
        k++;
    }
/* Set the end of string marker for array -b*/
*(q+k)='\0';
/*check if the array-a is same as the reverse -b and set the flag
        if otherwise*/
for(i=0; i<=last;i++)
    {
        if(*(p+i)!=*(q+i))  /*check if a[i] is same as b[i]*/
            {
                    flag=1;
                    break;
            }
    }
    if(flag==0)
      {
      printf("Word is a Palindrome");
      }
      else
      {
      printf("Word is not a Palindrome");
      }
}
```

Output

```
Enter a word: MOM
Word is a Palindrome
```

8.7   Initialization of an Array: Revisited

Recall from Chapter 6, Section 6.2.1, we can directly initialize all the elements of an array at the time of creation using the following syntax

```
DataType arrayname={comma separated list of values};
```

An array name is actually a pointer which holds the starting address of an array. Hence when compiler comes across such a statement, it allocates an array space of the same size as that of the number of elements specified in the curly bracket, and stores the staring address in a constant pointer named as that of the "array name" provided by the programmer. For example, the statement

```
int a[]={10,20,30,40,50};
```

will allocate an array space to store 5 integer values and store the starting address of the array in a constant pointer named a as shown in Figure 8.23. Specifying the size of the array in this case is optional because, the right-hand side {10,20,30,40,50} itself instructs the compiler to create an array of size 5 to store the values specified in the curly bracket. Figure 8.23 assumes the base address of this array as 1000, which is stored inside the constant pointer a.

As a is a constant pointer, there is no way to change the address stored in a later in the program. This means that you will not be able to make a point to any other array. This also justifies why you cannot initialize an array after its creation. For example, the following statements will give an error

```
int a[5];
a={10,20,30,40,50}; /*ERROR: Cannot reinitialize a constant
    pointer */
```

because a is created as a constant pointer pointing to an array of 5 elements due to the first statement `int a[5];`. At this stage the array contains junk values as shown in Figure 8.24 and the constant pointer a holds the starting address of this array. Figure 8.24 assumes the base address of an array as 1000, which is stored inside the constant pointer a.

When you attempt to reinitialize an array with {10,20,30,40,50}, the compiler attempts to create another array with values specified in the curly bracket, obviously at some other location in memory. Remember {10,20,30,40,50} instructs the compiler to

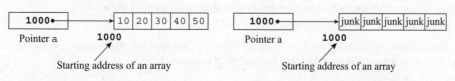

Figure 8.23:   Pointer pointing to an array with valid data values

Figure 8.24:   Pointer pointing to an array with junk values

create an array with specified values, as we mentioned before. As the new array will have a different address (let's say 2000), the statement,

```
a={10,20,30,40,50};
```

will attempt to modify the address in a constant pointer a to 2000, which is not allowed because the pointer is already initialized to an address 1000 (address of an array of junk values). Hence, this gives a compilation error as shown in Figure 8.25.

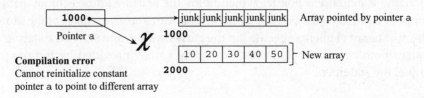

Figure 8.25: Compilation error on re-initialization of a

In a way, this is an advantage because it helps genuine programmers to avoid accidentally reinitializing an array pointer to some other location in memory, which may result in a complete loss of data which is already contained in the array. C/C++ says, if you need to store a different data set all together, create a new array instead of reusing an existing array pointer. The only way to initialize an array after its creation is by initializing one element at a time as seen in the statements below:

```
int a[5];
a[0]=10;
a[1]=20;
a[2]=30;
a[3]=40;
a[4]=50;
```

This works because it does not change the address in pointer a, but only stores values in locations of the array. The pointer continues to hold memory address 1000 (starting address of the array) but the individual array elements are now initialized with values as shown in Figure 8.26.

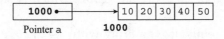

Figure 8.26: Initialization of array a

works well. Internally, the constant pointer a holds the starting address of the character array storing a string "ducks" as shown in Figure 8.27. Note that \0 will be automatically added by C/C++ to mark end of the string. Hence the memory allocated for a character array is always equal to length of the string+1 byte to store \0.

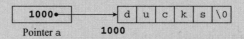

Figure 8.27: Character array

Following code will fail, because it applies string initialization to the array after its creation

```
char a[6]
a="ducks"; /*Error cannot apply string initialization after creation*/
```

Remember, the only option to initialize an array after its creation is to initialize it element by element as shown below. The initialization below will work because it does not attempt to change the address in pointer a, but only stores values in locations allocated for the array.

```
a[0]='d';
a[1]='u';
a[2]='c';
a[3]='k';
a[4]='s';
a[5]='\0';
```

8.7.1 Making re-initializations work with pointers

Why would you need to reinitialize the entire array in the program? Let us say, you have two different data sets (say Set1 = {10,20,30,40,50} and Set2 = {100,200,300,400,500}) and based on some condition at run time you need to decide which one to use. If a is created as an array of 5 elements, following piece of code which does direct initialization will not work.

```
int a[5];
if(condition)
{
a={10,20,30,40,50};
}
else
{
a={100,200,300,400,500};
}
```

The only way to make this code work is to apply element by element initialization in `if` and `else` blocks, because we need to initialize the array after its creation. This is because, a is created as a constant pointer internally. This code would have worked if a would not have been a constant pointer. We cannot change anything about pointer a because it is created internally by the compiler. As a workaround, we can create our own pointer which is not a constant pointer, and use it as an array. For example, we can create a pointer p as shown below.

```
int *p;   /*create a non-constant pointer*/
if(condition)
{
p=(int[5]){10,20,30,40,50};
}
else
{
p=(int[5]){100,200,300,400,500};
}
```

The statement,

```
p=(int[5]){10,20,30,40,50};
```

stores starting address of an array of size 5 in a pointer p as shown in the Figure 8.28.

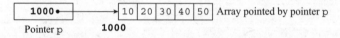

Figure 8.28:   Pointer pointing to an array of size 5

Note that, we have to apply type casting in this initialization because the `initializer{}` works only to initialize arrays and not pointers. The type cast `(int[5])` informs the compiler that the initializer type is an array of 5 integers. And we know that, when an array is initialized to the pointer, the pointer always stores the starting address of the array. Hence the whole statement works as if an array of size 5 is initialized to a pointer p.

As p points to the first element of the array, we can access any i^{th} element of the array as p[i] or *(p+i) as shown below:

```
for(i=0;i<=n-1;i++)
{
printf("%d\n",*(p+i)); /*print a[i] using pointer p*/
}
```

Similarly, the statement

```
p=(int[5]){100,200,300,400,500};
```

makes the pointer p point to a different data set.

NOTES

A string constant can be initialized to a character pointer without casting it to array type. This is because compiler anyway creates an array of characters to store a string. For example, the statement,
```
char *p="ducks";
```
makes pointer p point to a character array as shown in Figure 8.29.

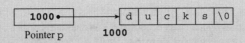

Figure 8.29: Pointer P pointing to a string

As p is not a constant pointer, it is possible to reinitialize it to another string. For example, the statement

```
p="pigs";
```

will make p to point to a different character array as shown in the Figure 8.30.

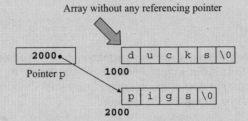

Figure 8.30: Pointer p pointing to a string

Remember, when you reinitialize the pointer the previous array to which it was pointing to is lost and there is no way to refer it back. In this case, since we have reinitialized the pointer to point to string "pigs" there is no way to refer to "ducks" unless some other pointer was made point to it before redirecting p to "pigs".

If you need to use the old string "ducks" even after p points to "pigs"; it is your responsibility to store the reference to "ducks" somewhere in the program before redirecting p. This can be achieved by creating another pointer say q and making it point to "ducks" before redirecting p to "pigs" as shown below:

```
char *p="ducks"; /*p points to "ducks"*/
char *q; /*create another pointer q*/
....
....
q=p; /*make q point to "ducks"*/
.....
.....
p="pigs"; /*Redirect p to "pigs" */
```

The statement,

```
q=p;
```

will copy the address stored in pointer p into pointer q, hence pointer q will point to the same memory location to which p points to. Before this statement, p was pointing to "ducks", hence q will also point to "ducks". The next statement,

```
p="pigs";
```

makes pointer p point to "pigs" as shown in Figure 8.31.

We know that strings can be printed directly on computer screen by using %s. This feature is preserved with character type pointers as well. The statement,

```
printf("%s",p);
```

will print "pigs" on the computer screen because pointer p points to "pigs". Do not confuse this statement here; for a

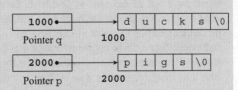

Figure 8.31: Pointers p and q

pointer of any other type (other than `char`) `p` represents address and `*p` represents a value. However `char` pointers are special pointers. Recall from Chapter 6, Section 6.3 an array of characters can be printed directly by using `%s` because it contains `\0` as an end of string marker. Similarly a pointer pointing to a string can also be printed directly using `%s`. Well, we know that array is also a pointer internally so printing an array using array name as we did in Chapter 6 or printing a string using a pointer name is indeed one and the same thing. Similarly, the statement,

```
printf("%s",q);
```

will print `"ducks"` on the computer screen.

NOTES

A pointer is just a variable which holds an address of some memory location. A pointer in itself cannot store data, hence you need to make sure that sufficient amount of data space is allocated and the pointer is made to point to it. When a pointer is initialized, compiler allocates the necessary memory which stores the data, so programmer need not worry about memory allocation. For example, the statement

```
char *p;
p="ducks";
```

will allocate data space of 6 bytes (5 bytes for characters + 1 byte for null character) and store the base address of the data space in the pointer `p`. However, if you do not initialize the pointer `p` and just declare it with a intention to accept a string as input from the user, the program will crash as shown below:

```
char *p;
printf("Enter a string");
scanf("%s",p); /*ERROR: No memory allocated for p*/
```

`scanf()` is a function which reads data from keyboard, however, its programmers responsibility to allocate necessary memory in RAM where the data read can be stored. In this case we have just created a pointer which is not pointing to any valid memory area as it contains junk address. Hence the input data from `scanf()` cannot be stored anywhere which makes it crash. To resolve this issue we must reserve some memory space to store the input data, one of the ways to do this is by creating an array as shown below. We obviously do not know what is the string in users mind, so we allocate the memory worth 100 characters with an assumption that user will not input a string whose length is greater than 100 (In fact 99, because 1 character needs to be reserved for `\0`)

```
char *p;
char a[100];
p=a; /*Store starting address of array a in p*/
printf("Enter a string");
scanf("%s",p); /*The input string will be stored in array a*/
```

The `scanf()` statement works well because we have ensured that the pointer `p` holds the starting address of an 100 byte space in memory before using it to accept a string.

We have intentionally taken an example of strings because C/C++ allows **direct input/output** operations with string arrays as explained in Chapter 6, Section 6.3. We can also perform direct input/output operations using a `char` type pointer which points to a string array, hence statements such as `scanf("%s",p);` and `printf("%s",p);` work well because `p` is a character pointer pointing to a character array. Remember, direct input/output can be performed using a user-defined pointer because the underlying array to which it points to allows it. Needless to say that you would not be able to perform direct input/output with pointers of any other type other than string. For example, if we initialize an integer pointer `z` as below:

```
int *z=(int[5]){10,20,30,40,50};
```

compiler will allocate the memory of 5 integers because we have initialized the pointer z to point to an array space of 5 integer values. But, if you need to print each data value pointed by z you must print it one element at a time as shown below:

```
for(i=0;i<=4;i++)
{
printf("%d",z[i]); /* or printf("%d",*(z+i)); */
}
```

Similarly, instead of initializing z to an array if you wish to accept the array values as input from the user you must follow the following two steps:

1. Allocate an array space and store its base address in pointer z

   ```
   int *z;
   int a[5];
   z=a; /*Store starting address of array a in z*/
   ```

2. Accept each element of an array as input from the user using executing scanf() in a loop as shown below:

   ```
   for(i=0;i<=4;i++)
   {
   scanf("%d",&z[i]); /* or scanf("%d", (z+i)); */
   }
   ```

Note that, call to scanf() is done by passing address of the element, hence we pass **&z[i]** or **(z+i)** for accepting i[th] element of the array as input from the user.

Important point to note here is that direct input/output operations are not possible with any other pointers accept char type pointers.

8.8 Self-addressability of Character Variables

If you try to print the address of a character you will actually get its value. Characters and Strings in C/C++ are said to be self-addressable.

Let c be a character variable with a value $, the statement

```
printf("%c",&c);
```

prints the value $ instead of printing memory address of the character variable. This proves that, C/C++ gives the value of character variable even when we try to get its address. The result of both the statements below is identical

```
printf("%c", c); /*prints value $ */
printf("%c",&c); /*prints value $ */
```

So, how can we print the address of the character variable? This can be done by changing the control string to %d rather than using %c. Hence the statement

```
printf("%d",&c); /*prints address of memory location where
    character is stored*/
```

will give a hint to the computer that the programmer asking for address of c and not the value of c. Hence this statement prints the address of variable c in memory. Do not confuse this statement with the statement below:

```
printf("%d", c); /*prints integer ASCII value of character*/
```

This statement does not use an & sign, so C/C++ will always give the value of variable c in this case. However, since we have used a control string %d, the ASCII value of $ will be printed on the screen instead of symbol $.

So in summary, using control string as %d and & operator with character variable will force C/C++ to print the address of a character variable.

This abrupt behaviour is only with character variables because they are self-addressable.

This also justifies why scanf() does not need an & symbol when inputting a string. If you are a C++ programmer and using cout statement you must read the question below:

I have created a variable a of type integer as below:

```
int a=10;
```

Now, the statement cout<<a; prints the value of variable a which is 10, whereas the statement cout<<&a; prints the address of the variable a.
However, if I create a variable c of type character,

```
char c='$';
```

then both the statements, cout<<c; and cout<<&c; print the value of variable c which is $. Why is the statement cout<<&c; printing the value of variable c instead of the address of the variable c **?**

This is because the operator << is overloaded for character type of variables in C++; to print the value of the variable instead of the address. Thus, both the statements cout<<c; and cout<<&c; print the value of the variable c. As a work around to print the address of the character variable, we can typecast the address of character memory location to a pointer of any other data type of C++. The below statement prints the address of the character c by typecasting it to an integer type of pointer(int*)

```
cout<<(int*)&c;
```

This aberrant behaviour with character pointers gives a privilege to the programmer to perform direct initialization of the string constants to a character type pointer. So, we can directly initialize a string value to the character type pointer, as shown below:

```
char* p="Hello";
```

Now the statement,

```
cout<<p;
```

will print the string Hello on the computer screen instead of printing the address which is stored inside the pointer. This is because the operator << is overloaded with character pointers to print all the characters of a string to which the pointer points (In this case C++ prints all the characters up to the NULL character of the string). This facilitates direct Input/output operations with *string constants* similar to other basic data types. Hence, we will also be able to take a string value as input from the user using a statement below:

```
cin>>p;
```

8.9 Array of Pointers

It is possible to create an array such that, each element of an array is a pointer. Every element of such an array can store the address of different variables thereby pointing to different data items. Below is the syntax to create an array of pointers:

```
Datatype *<array_name>[size];
```
For example, the statement,
```
int *p[3];
```

will create an array of pointers named as p of size 3. This array will contain three pointers p[0], p[1], and p[2]. And, because the array p is not yet initialized, each of the pointers p[0], p[1], and p[2] will contain junk addresses as shown in the Figure 8.32.

Let us now create three different integer variables a, b, and c with values 10, 20, and 30, respectively as shown in the Figure 8.33. We assume that the addresses of variables a, b, and c are 1000, 2000, and 3000, respectively.

```
int a=10,b=20,c=30;
```

We can now store address of each of these variables inside individual pointers present in array p. As a first step, let us store the address of variable a inside a pointer p[0] which can be done using the statement below:

```
p[0]=&a;
```

The Figure 8.34 now shows that p[0] contains 1000 which is the address of variable a. Note that the pointers p[1] and p[2] still contain junk values and they do not point to any meaningful location in the memory as shown in the Figure 8.34.

We can similarly store the addresses of variables b and c in the pointers p[1] and p[2] using statements below:

```
p[1]=&b;
p[2]=&c;
```

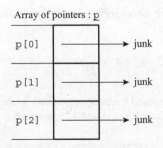

Figure 8.32: Array of pointers storing junk values

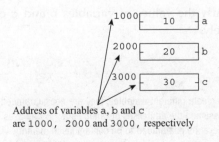

Figure 8.33: Storing variables a, b, and c in RAM

Address of variable <u>a</u> is stored in pointer p[0].
Hence p[0] points to variable <u>a</u>

Addresses of variables <u>a</u>, <u>b</u> and <u>c</u> are stored in
pointers p[0], p[1] and p[2], respectively.
Hence, pointer p[0] points to variable <u>a</u>
pointer p[1] points to variable <u>b</u> and
pointer p[2] points to variable <u>c</u>

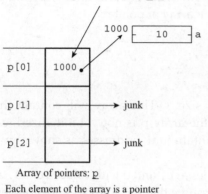

Array of pointers: <u>p</u>
Each element of the array is a pointer

Figure 8.34: p[0] pointing to variable a

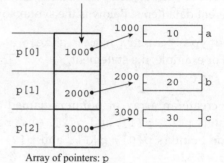

Array of pointers: <u>p</u>
Each element of the array is a pointer

Figure 8.35: Array of pointers storing addresses of three variables

The effect of these statements is illustrated in the Figure 8.35.

The table below gives the description of few **printf()** statements which can be of help to understand the concept of creating array of pointers.

Statement	Description
printf("%u",p[0]);	This statement prints the value stored inside the pointer p[0]. As shown in the Figure 8.35 the pointer p[0] contains the address of variable a. Hence, the statement printf("%u",p[0]) will print 1000 on the computer screen.
printf("%d",*p[0]);	This statement applies an indirection operator (*) to the pointer p[0]. The operator (*) directs the CPU to access the memory location using the address contained in the pointer and read the value stored inside that location. As pointer p[0] contains the address 1000, CPU will now fetch the value stored at location 1000 which is in reality the value of variable a as shown in the figure 8.35. Hence the statement printf("%d",*p[0]); will print the value of variable a thereby giving the output as 10 on the computer screen.

Similarly the values of variables b and c can be accessed using *p[1] and *p[2], respectively.

NOTES

When you create different variables, they are not guaranteed to be stored in contagious memory locations. Hence we have assumed the addresses of variables a, b and c as 1000, 2000 and 3000, respectively to show that they will never be guaranteed to be contagious in memory.

When we create an array, its elements will always be stored in contagious memory locations. Hence, each **pointer** in an **array of pointers** will be stored in **consecutive** memory locations.

By making each pointer in an array to point to one variable, we will be able to iterate through the values of three different variables in loop as shown below:

```
for(i=0;i<=2;i++)
{
printf("%d\n",*p[i]);
}
```

The given loop will print the values of three variables a, b and c because pointer p[0] points to a, p[1] points to b and p[2] points to c. Note that, using array of pointers, we have actually managed to iterate through the values of three values even if they are not stored in **consecutive** locations in memory.

8.9.1 Creating array of strings using 1-D array of character pointers

We know that the character type pointers can be initialized directly to a string value at any point in the program. We can use this feature provided by C/C++ to create an array of strings by creating 1-D array of character pointers and initializing each pointer to a string.

For example, consider the statement below which creates an 1-D array p of character pointers of size 3

```
char *p[3];
```

Hence the array p will contain three different pointers p[0], p[1], and p[2], each having an ability to point to a string. At this stage none of the pointers have been initialized.

We can initialize each of the individual pointers p[0], p[1], and p[2] to string values as shown below:

```
p[0]="ducks";
p[1]="pigs";
p[2]="dogs";
```

We know that string is internally assembled is an array of characters, so each of the pointer variables get initialized to respective string values as shown in the following Figure 8.36.

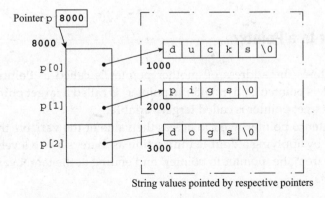

Figure 8.36: Array of character type pointers where each pointer points to a different string

Although the highlighted part in Figure 8.36 looks as if it is a matrix of characters it is not so. They are actually three different 1-D arrays of characters which are not contagious in memory. Internally, a 2-D array is also assembled using multiple 1-D arrays but in that case each of the 1-D arrays are stored in contiguous memory locations which is not the case here. Note that, the elements within a single 1-D array are always contiguous which means that individual characters within a string `"ducks"` will be stored contiguously in both the cases. But two strings `"ducks"` and `"pigs"` may not be contiguous in memory in this case but they are guaranteed to be contiguous when a 2-D array of characters is created.

Anyway, it isn't our requirement to store two different strings contiguously at least in this case. All we need is that, the characters within the same string must be stored contiguously, so the design shown in Figure 8.36 is a perfect for array of strings. We also know that the string can be printed directly using a pointer name, table below gives `printf()` statements to print each of the respective strings:

Statement	Output
`printf("%s",p[0]);`	ducks
`printf("%s",p[1]);`	pigs
`printf("%s",p[2]);`	dogs

Needless to say, you can also access the strings in a loop as if p is a 1-D array of strings. Hence the following loop will also print each of the individual strings and will have a same result as that of writing three different `printf()` statements

```
int i;
for(i=0;i<=2;i++)
{
printf("%s\n",p[i]);
}
```

This design of array of strings is internally used by C/C++ in the design of an array required to store command line arguments. You may revisit the explanation on how command line arguments are accessed using array of `char` pointers as given in Chapter 7, Section 7.12.

8.10   Pointer to a Pointer

A pointer that stores the address of another pointer is called a '**Pointer to a Pointer**'. A 'pointer' which is pointed by a 'pointer to pointer' is called a **target pointer** and the data item pointed by target pointer is called **target variable.**

Using a 'pointer to pointer' we can access the value of the variable that is pointed by a 'target pointer' by applying a **double indirection** as there is a two level chain created in memory starting from the 'pointer to pointer' and ending at the target variable.

The statements,

```
int a=10;
int *p=&a;
```

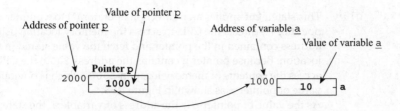

Figure 8.37: Pointer storing address of variable a

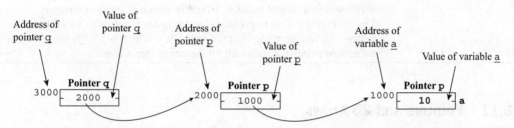

Figure 8.38: Pointer to pointer q storing address of pointer p

stores address of variable a in a pointer p.

The address of variable a is assumed as 1000 and address of the pointer p is assumed as 2000 in the Figure 8.37.

We can now create a pointer q such that, it stores the address of pointer p. Such a pointer q is called a 'pointer to a pointer' because it points to another pointer p. Below is the syntax for creating a 'pointer to a pointer':

```
Datatype **<Pointer_name>;
```

Since, pointer q is required to store the address of pointer p and also pointer p is of type integer the data type of q must also be integer. Hence, we create q as follows:

```
int **q;
```

The statement,

```
q=&p;
```

will store the address of pointer p inside the pointer q.

As the address of p is 2000 the value of pointer q will also be 2000 as shown in the Figure 8.38. Note that a value of 'pointer to a pointer' q stores the address of p which is a normal pointer.

The table below gives a description of few `printf()` statements which can be a help us understand the concept of 'pointers to pointers'.

Statement	Description
`printf("%u",q);`	This statement prints the value of pointer q. The pointer q stores 2000 which is address of pointer p as shown in the Figure 8.38. Hence, the statement prints 2000 on the computer screen.

`printf("%u",*q);`	This statement applies an indirection operator (*) to a pointer q. The operator (*) directs the CPU to access the memory location using the address contained in the pointer and fetch the value stored in that location. Because pointer q contains the address 2000, the CPU will access the contents of memory location 2000, which is obviously the value of pointer p as shown in Figure 8.38. As the value of pointer p is the address of variable a, the statement `printf("%u",*q);` prints **1000** on the computer screen.
`printf("%d",**q);`	This statement applies a 'double indirection' on pointer q. Hence the statement prints the value of the memory location whose address is contained in a 'target pointer' which is 'pointed' by the pointer q. The pointer q points to pointer p and pointer p points to variable a, hence `**q` will give the value of variable a which is 10. Therefore the statement prints the value **10** on the computer screen.

8.11   Pointers and 2D Arrays

We understand from Chapter 7 that a 2-D array is organized as a matrix of r-rows and c-columns. This section explains the procedure adopted by C/C++ in order to represent a 2-D matrix in computer memory

Compiler internally creates a 1-D 'array of pointers' with a size same as that of number of rows specified while creating a 2-D array. Every pointer present in this array points to one row of the 2-D matrix in memory.

There also exists a pointer that points to the 'array of pointers'. This will naturally be a 'pointer to a pointer' because it points to the 'array of pointers'. The 'pointer to pointer' will have a same name as that of the name of a 2-D array.

As an example, let us understand the creation of an integer type 2-D array with 3 rows and 4 columns shown below:

```
int a[3][4]={10,20,30,40,
             50,60,70,80,
             90,100,110,120
             };
```

We understand from Chapter 7 that this array is organized as a matrix shown in the Figure 8.39.

To create such a matrix in the computer memory compiler internally creates a 1-D array of pointers with a size three (because the array a has three rows in it.). The array of pointers created by the compiler is as shown in the Figure 8.40, where each element of the array points to one of the rows of the matrix. Also there is a 'pointer to pointer' that points to this array of pointers as shown. The name 'pointer to pointer' is a (same as the name given to the 2-D array). Figure 8.40 assumes that the starting address of an 'array of pointers' is 1000 (which is contained in 2-D pointer a). Considering that every pointer in the array is of 2 bytes the addresses of subsequent elements in the array can be derived as shown in Figure 8.40.

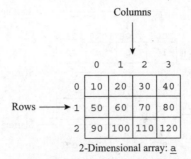

Figure 8.39: 2-D array matrix

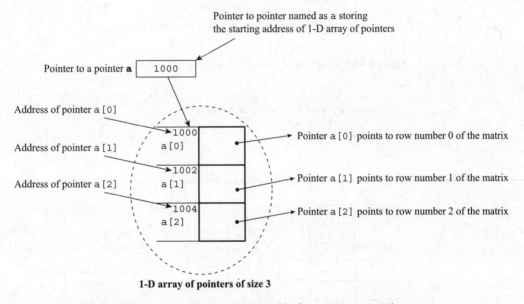

Figure 8.40: Array of pointers created before representing the matrix

Note that array elements are always stored at contiguous memory locations hence the first row will begin at an address 1006 (which is next address after 1004). Considering contiguous row allocations, the addresses of second and third row will be 1014 and 1022, respectively as shown in the Figure 8.41. (As the 2-D array is required to have four columns, each row of the 2-D array must store 4 integers). Figure 8.41 derives the address of each of the individual elements in the matrix. Note that the memory addresses of adjacent elements in the same row will differ by 2 because every integer will take two bytes in memory.

Putting all pieces together, the internal structure of a 2-D array a as shown in the Figure 8.42. The pointers a[0], a[1], and a[2] present in 'array of pointers' point to first, second, and third row of the matrix, respectively. Hence the pointer a[0] contains a value 1006 (address of the first row), pointer a[1] contains a value 1014 (address of the second row), and pointer a[2] contains a value 1022 (address of the third row) as shown in the Figure 8.42.

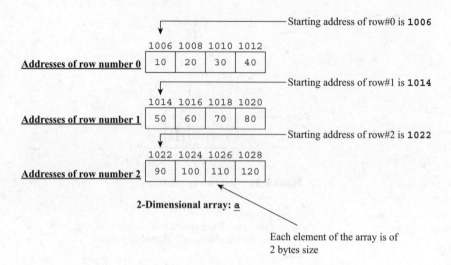

Figure 8.41: Address of individual elements in a matrix

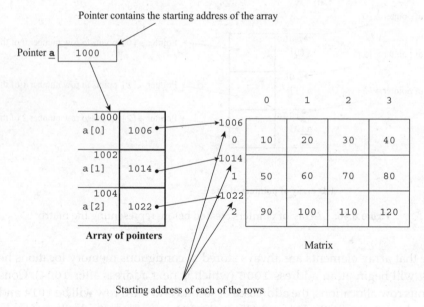

Figure 8.42: Storage of a 2-D array in computer memory

We can access all the elements of a 2-D array using a single pointer to a pointer. To illustrate this concept, we will create a 2-D pointer named as p

```
int **p;
```

The statement,

```
p=(int**)a;
```

will store the starting address of 2-D array in 2-D pointer p. Hence pointer p will contain 1000 which is same as the address contained in the 2-D pointer a as shown in Figure 8.43.

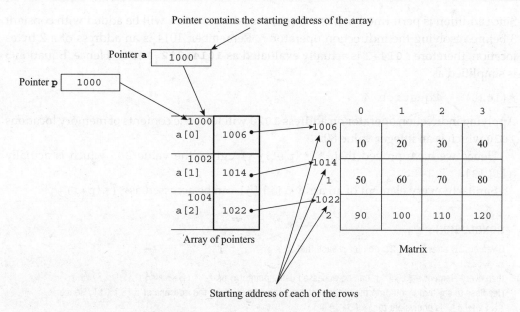

Figure 8.43: Pointer p pointing to a 2-D array

Note that we have performed type casting to convert the integer array type(int [] [])
to a integer pointer type(int**) in the initialization statement to avoid data type mismatch
error at the compilation stage. This type of casting was not needed when working with 1-D
arrays because compiler performs an implicit casting to pointer type, when a 1-D array
is initialized to a 1-D pointer which is not the case when working with 2-D arrays and
pointers. Hence, we have to explicitly cast to int** type when address of a 2-D array
needs to be stored in a 2-D pointer. After executing this statement, pointer p will also
contain 1000 which is the starting address of the 2-D array as shown in the Figure 8.43.

Any element of an array a[i][j] can be accessed using pointer p as *(*(p+i)+j).

Let us prove this with an example to access a element a[1][3] using an expression
((p+1)+3).

Substituting the value of p as 1000 in the expression *(*(p+1)+3) we have,

```
*(*(1000+1)+3) - Equation 1
```

Since parenthesis has a highest priority in this expression, the inner most parenthesis will
be evaluated first. This means that 1000+1 will be evaluated first, remember 1000 is an
address of a 2 bytes space in memory, therefore 1000+1 is evaluated as 1002. Hence the
expression is now simplified as,

```
*(*(1002)+3) - Equation 2
```

*(1002) needs to be evaluated before performing addition with constant 3. As seen from
Figure 8.43 the 1014 is stored at location 1002. Hence *(1002), evaluates to 1014 and the
expression is further simplified as below:

```
*(1014+3) - Equation 3
```

Since addition is performed in parenthesis, the address 1014 will be added with constant 3 before resolving the indirection operator *. Remember, 1014 is an address of a 2 bytes location, therefore 1014+3 is actually evaluated as **1014+3*2**=1020. Hence, Equation 3 is simplified as:

```
*(1020) - Equation 4
```

Applying indirection operator on address 1020 will fetch the contents of memory locations 1020 which is an integer value 80.

Hence we have proved that, * (* (p+1) +3)   gives the value 80   which is actually a[1][3].

Similarly, every element of an array a[i][j] can be accessed as * (* (p+i) +j).

CONCLUSION

Given an 2D array a and 2D pointer p such that ,
p = (int**) a;
then every element a[i][j] can be accessed using pointer p as * (* (p+i)+j)
Needless to say that if you drop the outermost * operator, you will get the **address of** a[i][j]. Hence
&a[i][j]   is equivalent to (* (p+i)+j)

8.11.1   Program to perform addition of 2 matrices using pointers: An example

As we have already implemented the solution to perform matrix operations in the Chapter 6, we will reuse the same solution to add the two matrices using **pointers**. As discussed in Chapter 6 we created three 2-D arrays a, b, and res, such that the result of addition of matrix a with matrix b is stored in matrix res. As there are three 2-D arrays we create three 'pointer to pointer' variables p, q, and r such that the pointer p points to matrix, pointer q points to matrix b, and pointer r points to matrix res as shown in the lines below:

```
/*Create three pointer to pointer variables*/
int **p,**q,**r;
/*make p,q, and r point to matrices a, b and "res" respectively*/
p=(int**)a;
q=(int**)b;
r=(int**)res;
```

The following code is same as that of Chapter 6, except every access to element a[i][j] is now done using an expression * (* (p+i) +j).

Following substitutions are required to be applied on the solution discussed in Chapter 6, to solve the same program using pointers:

1. Every occurrence of a[i][j] in the code should be replaced by * (* (p+i) +j)
2. Every occurrence of &a[i][j] in the code should be replaced by (* (p+i) +j)
3. Every occurrence of b[i][j] in the code should be replaced by * (* (q+i) +j)
4. Every occurrence of &b[i][j] in the code should be replaced by (* (q+i) +j)
5. Every occurrence of res[i][j] in the code should be replaced by * (* (r+i) +j)

```
#include<stdio.h>
void main()
{
int a[100][100],b[100][100],res[100][100];
int i,j,rows,cols;
printf("Enter the order of Matrices");
scanf("%d%d",&rows,&cols);
int **p,**q,**r;
p=(int**)a;
q=(int**)b;
r=(int**)res;
printf("Enter Matrix A\n");
for(i=0;i<rows;i++)
    {
      for(j=0;j<cols;j++)
      {
      scanf("%d",(*(p+i)+j)); /*Replace &a[i][j] by (*(p+i)+j)*/
      }
    }
printf("Enter Matrix B\n");
for(i=0;i<rows;i++)
    {
      for(j=0;j<cols;j++)
      {
      scanf("%d", (*(q+i)+j) ); /*Replace &b[i][j] by (*(q+i)+j)*/
      }
    }
printf("Result Matrix is\n");
for(i=0;i<rows;i++)
    {
      for(j=0;j<cols;j++)
      {
      /*apply substitution for arrays a,b and res*/
      *(*(r+i)+j)=*(*(p+i)+j) + *(*(q+i)+j);
      printf("%d",*(*(r+i)+j));
      /*Replace res[i][j] by *(*(r+i)+j)*/
      }
      printf("\n");
    }
}
```

Output

```
Enter the order of Matrices
2 2
```

```
Enter Matrix A
10 20
4  9
Enter Matrix B
5 10
12 1
Result Matrix is
15 20
16 10
```

8.12 void Pointers

The keyword void represents absence of data type, hence void type pointers can point to a variable of any type. void pointers are also called **universal pointers** because they have an ability to point to data values of every type.

Note that, we cannot directly apply an indirection operator to such pointers. This is because due to absence of data type CPU, will not be able to determine the number of memory locations required to be accessed in order to fetch the complete value of the variable whose address is contained in the pointer. Therefore we will always have to **cast** the address stored inside the void type pointer to a particular data type before applying an indirection operator to void pointers.

The code below creates two variables a and b of type int and float, respectively. The given program uses a void type pointer p to access the value of each of these variables. We have also created the pointers pint and pflt which are of types of int and float, respectively. The statement

```
p=&a;
```

will make the void type pointer p to point to floating point variable a. Note that, when we attempt to copy the address stored in pointer p to pointer pint, we have to do a type casting of a void pointer p to integer type as seen in the statement below

pint=(int*)p;

Similarly, the statement,

```
p=&b;
```

will make the void type pointer p to point to integer variable b. This time casting to float type pointer must be performed when, initializing the pointer p to pointer pflt as shown in the statement below

pflt=(float*)p;

We have accessed the values of variables a and b by applying indirection to pointers pint and pflt as shown in the code.

```
#include<stdio.h>
void main()
```

```
{
    int a=10;
    float b=32.5;
/*Create a void type pointer p*/
    void *p;
/*Create an integer type pointer "pint"*/
    int *pint;
/*Create a float type pointer "pflt"*/
    float *pflt;
/*Store the address of variable a in the pointer p*/
p=&a;
/*Copy the address inside p in pointer "pint"*/
pint=(int*)p;
/*Store the address of variable b in the pointer p*/
p=&b;
/*Copy the address inside p in pointer "pflt"*/
pflt=(float*)p;
printf("Value of variable a is %d\n", *pint);
printf("Value of variable b is %f\n", *pflt);
}
```

Output

```
Value of variable a is 10
value of variable b is 32.5
```

8.13 Pointer to a Function

Pointers in C/C++ can also point to a function which is defined in the program. This facilitates the programmer to call a particular function using a pointer. To make a pointer point to a function, type of the pointer must match with the prototype of the function.

Consider the given program, wherein we have created two functions add() and sub(). Both the functions take two integer values as an argument and return an integer as a result of execution. Since both of the function have a same prototype, it is possible to create a single pointer which has an ability to point to either of the functions. The statement

```
int (*pfunction)(int,int);
```

creates a pointer named pfunction that can point to any function taking two arguments of type int and returning a int value.

As the type of pointer pfunction exactly matches with the type of functions add() as well as sub(), the pointer can point to any of these functions. The statement,

```
pfunction=add;
```

makes the pointer pfunction to store the address of function add(). As pfunction points to add(), we can call the function add using the pointer pfunction. The statement

```
resA=(*pfunction)(a,b);
```

will call the function add() using the pointer pfunction by passing values of variables a and b as arguments and will store the result returned in resA. As the values of variables a and b are 10 and 20, respectively, the value of variable resA will be set to 30 after the execution of this statement.

Similarly, the statement,

```
pfunction=sub;
```

will make pointer pfunction to point to function sub(). Hence you can also call function sub() using the pointer pfunction using the statement below:

```
resB=(*pfunction)(a,b);
```

This will make the variable resB to store the value returned by the sub function.

The following is the full source code which shows calling of functions add() and sub() using a pointer pfunction

```
#include<stdio.h>
int add(int a, int b)
{
return (a+b);
}
int sub(int a, int b)
{
return (a-b);
}
void main()
{
int (*pfunction)(int,int);
int a=10,b=20,resA,resB;
/*store address of function "add" inside "pfunction"*/
pfunction=add;
/*call function "add" using "pfunction"*/
resA=(*pfunction)(a,b);
/*store address of function "sub" inside "pfunction"*/
pfunction=sub;
/*call function "sub" using "pfunction"*/
resB=(*pfunction)(a,b);
printf("Addition is %d\n",resA);
printf("Subtraction is %d\n", resB);
}
```

Output

```
Addition is 30
Subtraction is -10
```

8.14 Reference Variables (Only Available in C++ not in C)

This topic will slightly take you away from pointers, but this is a correct place to mention about it because reference variables in C++ provides somewhat similar features as that of pointers.

A reference variable in C++ is another name given to a variable. This means that we can give multiple names to the same memory location by creating multiple references to the same location. The following is the syntax for creating a reference variable in C++:

```
DataType& <anotherName>=<ActualName>;
```

As an example, let us consider a variable a with a value 10 as shown below:

```
int a=10;
```

The name of the variable is a and we assume the address of the variable as 9000 as shown in the Figure 8.44.

We can now give another name to a variable a by creating a reference to a variable a. Let us give another name to variable a as sample which can be done using the statement below:

```
int& sample=a;
```

Note that, int& indicates that the variable named sample is a reference variable of type integer. When a reference variable sample is initialized to a it indicates that variable sample is just another name to the variable a. As seen in the Figure 8.45 the variable a and sample will share a common memory space which is unlike pointers where a pointer consumes a separate memory to store the address of the variable to which it points to. It is important to understand that because the reference variable named as sample and the actual variable named as a share the same memory space the address

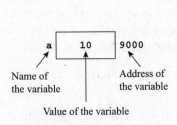

Figure 8.44: Creation of variable a in memory

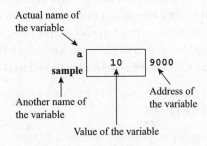

Figure 8.45: Giving another name to variable a

of the reference variable will be same as the address of the actual variable as shown in the Figure 8.45.

This means that the value 10 can now be accessed using any one of the two names (a or sample) in the code. Hence, the following two statements are exactly same and will give the identical result:

```
printf("%d",a);
printf("%d", sample);
```

Both of the above statements will print a value 10 which is the value stored in the memory location which has two names a and sample.

The table below gives a description of few printf() statements which can be a help to understand the concept of 'reference variables' in C++.

C++ statement	Description
printf("%d",a);	The statement prints the value of the variable a which is 10. Hence the output of the statement is 10 which is printed on the computer screen.
printf("%d",sample);	The statement prints the value of the variable sample on the computer screen. Variable sample is just another name to the variable a. Hence, this statement has a same effect as that of printing the value of a itself. Therefore the output of this statement will be 10.
printf("%u",&a);	The statement prints the address of variable a on the computer screen. We assume that the address of variable a is 9000, then the statement will print 9000 on the computer screen.
printf("%u",&sample);	The statement prints the address of variable sample on the computer screen. Variable sample is just another name to the variable a; hence the address of variable sample will be same as the address of the variable a as shown in the Figure 8.45. We assume that the address of variable a is 9000, then the statement will print 9000 on the computer screen.

Note that, as the reference variable and the actual variable share same memory, the address of the reference variable will be same as that of the address of the actual variable. Therefore, a reference variable is also called a **hidden pointer**.

Also, it is very important to note a reference variable that is created in the program must always be initialized to an actual name. This means that we cannot just declare a reference variable and keep it uninitialized. Therefore the following statement will be a compilation error as the reference sample is just declared without initializing it as some other variable

```
int& sample; /*ERROR,the reference variable sample is not
    initialized*/
```

Further, similar to pointers the data type of the 'reference variable' must always be same as the data type of the actual variable to which it refers to. This means that, a float type reference variable can refer only to float type variables whereas the int type reference

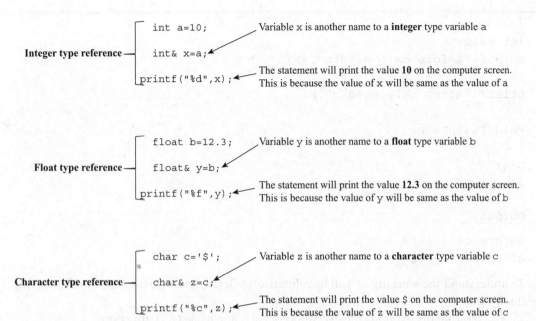

Figure 8.46: Creating reference variables x, y, and z

variable can only refer to int type variable and so on. Figure 8.46 shows the creation of three reference variables x, y, and z which refer to the actual variables a, b, and c which are of type int, float, and char, respectively. Note that, the value of variable a can now be accessed using two names a or x, similarly the value of variable b can be accessed using two names b or y in the code and the value of the variable c can also be accessed using two names c or z in the code as shown in the Figure 8.46.

8.14.1 Call by reference

When a function is called by passing the name of the actual parameters as argument instead of passing the values, the function call is then defined as a 'call by reference'. When a call to a function is made by reference the actual argument must be specified as the name of the variable whereas the formal argument is to be specified as a reference variable as seen in the code.

Let us consider the below code to understand the working of call by reference where we create two functions main() and f1(). The function main() has a local variable a whose name is passed to f1() at the time when function call is made. The formal argument of function f1() is a 'reference variable' that gives another name to the variable a defined in main() function. Hence function main() calls the function f1() using a mechanism called 'call by reference'.

```
#include<stdio.h>
void f1(int&);
void main()
```

```
{
int a=10;
printf("Before call a=%d\n",a);
f1(a);
printf("After call a=%d\n",a);
}
void f1(int& p)
{
p++;
}
```

Output

```
Before call a=10
After call a=11
```

To understand the working of 'call by reference' in detail, let us go through the above code line by line.

The table below explains the execution of each line in main() function.

C++ statement	Description
int a=10;	This statement creates a local variable a initialized to a value 10. Note that the variable a is declared inside main() function, so it is local to main and cannot be directly accessed by function f1().
printf("Before call a=%d\n",a);	This statement prints the value of variable a which is 10. Hence the following message is printed on the computer screen : Before call a=10
f1(a);	This statement is a function call to f1() by passing the 'name' of variable a as an argument. Because of the function call the control will now be transferred to the function definition by initializing the reference variable p with the actual argument a. Hence, the reference p refers to the same memory location as that of the actual argument a is shown in the Figure 8.47. The function definition now starts executing a statement p++. Since, p is just another name to the variable a, incrementing the value of the variable p will be same as actually incrementing the value of variable a. Hence, the value of variable p changes to 11 as shown in the Figure 8.48. This means that the value of variable a will also be 11, this is because the variables p and a share a same memory location whose address is 9000 as shown in the Figure 8.48.
printf("After call a=%d\n",a);	The statement prints the value of variable a after returning from the function f1(). Note that the function f1() has already changed the value of variable a using a reference variable. Hence, when the control returns to main() function the value of variable a will now be 11. Hence the following message is printed on the computer screen as a result of **printf()** statement: **After call a=11**

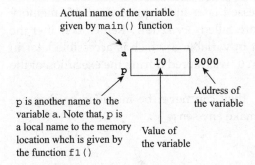

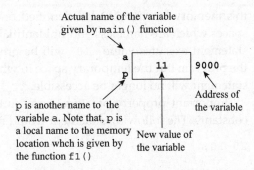

Figure 8.47: Call by reference

Figure 8.48: Execution of the statement p++

Hence, when a function is called by passing the name of the actual arguments, the 'called function' creates an additional reference to the variable created by 'calling function'. Hence, we can access the actual value of the variable in the 'calling' function using the formal argument (which is a reference variable) in called function.

> **NOTES**
>
> **Reference variable** is another name to a given variable.
>
> **Call by reference** provides similar results as that of **call by address**, without a need to create any physical pointer.

8.15 Lvalue and Rvalue

Any expression that we write in a program has two types of values

1. Lvalue
2. Rvalue

An expression in C/C++ is typically in a following format

```
Lvalue=Rvalue;
```

Lvalue is a value which can appear on the left-hand side of assignment operator in the expression, so it has to be a valid memory location which can be modified. Anything that is not Lvalue is called Rvalue. Hence Rvalue is a value that cannot appear on the left-hand side of assignment in the expression. For example, consider the following statement:

```
int a=10;
```

In this case, variable a actually represents a memory location which is to be written with a value 10. The value 10 present on right-hand side of assignment operator is a constant integer. This value is stored in temporary space for the time the statement is under execution. This temporary space is a part of literal pool and after the execution of the statement completes, the temporary space is deleted. Hence there is no way by which this memory location can be identified or accessed later in the program. Such memory spaces which are nameless and unidentifiable are called Rvalues. Remember, after the statement executes value 10 will be present in variable a which is accessible later in the program but the temporary space in which 10 was stored during the execution of the statement will no longer be accessible.

Important property of Rvalues is that, they can never be modified as they are constants. The following statement would not make any sense

```
20=10;
```

because 20 is a constant integer value and it cannot appear on the left-hand side of the assignment operator. Compiler gives following error if such statements are written in the program.

```
ERROR: Lvalue required.
```

This means that the value present on the left-hand side of the statement is not Lvalue but an Rvalue which cannot be modified.

8.15.1 Creating Lvalue'd function using reference variables (Possible only in C++ and not in C)

Lvalue'd function is a function which can appear as an Lvalue in the expression. Reference variables and pointers both can be used to create Lvalue'd function. In this section, we will implement an Lvalue'd function using reference variables. C programmers can skip this reading and directly read the note given at the end of this section which gives the implementation of Lvalue'd functions using pointers. This is because C does not support reference variables. If you are a C++ programmer, this section will explain you how to create an Lvalue'd function using reference variables.

Consider, the following code which creates a global variable a initialized with a value 10 and function f1() which increments the value of a and returns to function main().

```
#include<stdio.h>
int a=10;
int f1()
{
a++;
return a;
}
void main()
{
f1()=20;
printf("Value of a is %d",a);
}
```

The first statement in main(),

```
f1()=20;
```

attempts to call a function f1() as a Lvalue (The function call is placed on the left-hand side of assignment operator). As per the function definition of f1() it increments the value of a and returns the resultant value. Hence in this case, the function f1() returns 11. Remember, the function returns the value of a and not the memory location where a is stored. Hence the following statement, f1()=20 is decayed as:

```
11=20;
```

This statement does not make any sense because 11 is a constant whose value cannot be changed. Hence, the program crashes with a following error:

```
Lvalue required in the statement f1()=20;
```

If it is required to invoke the function on left-hand side of assignment the function must return the memory location which can be assigned a specific value. This means that the function must return the reference or address of the memory location rather than returning the value stored inside the location. We have changed the definition of function f1() to return a reference to a instead of value of a in the following code:

```
#include<stdio.h>
int a=10;
/*return reference to a*/
int& f1()
{
a++;
return a;
}
void main()
{
f1()=20;
printf("Value of a is %d",a);
}
```

This time the statement
```
f1()=20;
```

works perfectly fine because the function f1() decays to a reference variable which returns the memory location of variable a. Although a stores 11 at a point where f1() completes its execution, the statement f1()=20; will modify the value of variable a to 20.

Hence the statement,

```
printf("Value of a is %d",a);
```

in main() function will print the value of a as 20 on the computer screen.

NOTES

If it is required to invoke a function on left-hand side of assignment operator the function must return the memory location which can be assigned a specific value. In short, the function must return a Lvalue and not Rvalue.

NOTE FOR C PROGRAMMERS

`Lvalue'd` functions can also be implemented using pointers. Instead of returning a reference to the memory location the function can also return the address of the memory location which needs to be assigned with a value.

Remember the only requirement for a function to appear on left-hand side of assignment operator is that it should return a memory location which can be assigned with a value.

As seen in the code below, the function `f1()` returns address of `a`, so its return type is set as an integer type pointer. We know that if pointer `p` stores address of variable `a`, then `*p` can modify the value of `a`. Given that `f1()` decays into address of memory location, as per the principle of indirection `*f1()` will access the value stored in the memory location. Hence, the statement

```
*f1()=20;
```

initializes value of `a` to `20`. Although it is possible to create `Lvalue'd` functions using pointers, C++ programmers prefer to create them using reference variables because syntax to use reference variable is simple when compared to pointers. Remember reference variables are only supported by C++ and not by C. Hence, if you are C programmer, you will have to make use of pointers to create `Lvalue'd` functions as there is no way by which you can use references.

The following is the full source code to create `Lvalue'd` function using pointers. The following code will work in both C and C++ because it does not make use of reference variables.

```c
#include<stdio.h>
int a=10;
/*Function f1 returning a pointer */
int* f1()
{
a++;
return &a;
}
void main()
{
*f1()=20;
printf("Value of a is %d",a);
}
```

NOTES

When program throws an error as `Lvalue` required, it means that there is an illegal expression used on the left-hand side of assignment operator in at least one of the statements. Some more examples of this error are as given below.

Example 1

If `k` is an integer variable, the following statement will not work

```
k+1=50;
```

This is because `k+1` is an expression which returns a constant value. Let's say, the value of `k` is `289`, then `k+1` will return a constant value `290`. As `290` is a `Rvalue`, the statement gets decayed into

```
290=50;
```

which does not make any sense. Hence the program crashes throwing `Lvalue` required. To make this logic work, you must rewrite the statement as

```
k=50-1;
```

This will work perfectly fine because left-hand side of assignment is a simple variable. Hence the statement will set the value of `k` as `49`.

Example 2

This concept also justifies why all the elements of an array cannot be initialized after an array is created

```
char a[6]
a="ducks"; /*Error: Lvalue required*/
```

We know that a is a constant pointer, and constant variables cannot be initialized after they are created. Hence you will get this error even in the case when you are trying to modify a constant variable. Remember, the following statement which initializes the array at the time of creation just works fine

```
char a[6]="ducks";
```

So, it will be incorrect to say that a is not a Lvalue. Infact a represents a proper Lvalue in this case, so that it can be accurately initialized. a is called **unmodifiable Lvalue** because its value cannot be modified after its creation. The variable which is not a constant can be modified at any point in the program. Such Lvalues are called **modifiable** Lvalues.

Error Finding Exercise

Given below are some programs which may or may not contain errors. Correct the error(s) if exist in the code and determine the output.

Program 1

```
#include<stdio.h>
void main()
{
int *p;
float b=25.5;
p=&b;
printf("The value of b is %d\n",*p);
}
```

Program 2

```
#include<stdio.h>
void f1(int***);
void main()
{
int a=10;
int *p=&a;
int **q=&p;
f1(&q);
printf("Value of variable after the call is %d\n",a);
}
```

```
void f1(int ***x)
{
***x=*(*(*(x)))+10;
}
```

Program 3

```
#include<stdio.h>
void main()
{
int i;
char a[100][100];
*(a+0)="Sunday";
*(a+1)="Monday";
*(a+2)="Tuesday";
*(a+3)="Wednesday";
*(a+4)="Thursday";
*(a+5)="Friday";
*(a+6)="Saturday";
for(i=0;i<=6;i++)
printf("%s\n",*(a+i));
}
```

Program 4

```
#include<stdio.h>
int[] test();
void main()
{
int i;
int a[5];
a=test();
printf("The array elements are\n");
    for(i=0;i<5;i++)
    {
    printf("%d\n",a[i]);
    }
}
int[] test()
{
int p[]={10,20,30,40,50};
return p;
}
```

Program 5

```c
#include<stdio.h>
void main()
{
int a=10,b=20;
int *p,*q;
p=&a;
q=&b;
printf("%d\n",p*q);
printf("%d\n",*p**q);
printf("%d\n", (*p)*(*q) );
}
```

Program 6

```c
#include<stdio.h>
void main()
{
int a=10,b=20;
void *p,*q;
p=&a;
q=&b;
printf("%d\n",*p);
printf("%d\n",p);
printf("%d\n",*q);
printf("%d\n",p);
}
```

Program 7

```c
#include<stdio.h>
int multiply(int *a, int *b)
{
return (*a+*b);
}
void main()
{
void (*p)(int,int);
int result
p=multiply;
result=p(&10,&20);
printf("Result of multiplication is %d\n," result);
}
```

Program 8

```c
#include<stdio.h>
void main()
{
int *p;
int i;
        int a[]={10,20,30};
        int b[]={100,200,300};
        p=a;
        b=p;
        printf("The elements of array 'b' are\n");
        for(i=0;i<3;i++)
        {
        printf("%d\n",*(b+i));
        }
}
```

Quiz

1. Consider the following statements:

   ```c
   int a=10;
   int *p=&a;
   ```

   The statement:

   ```c
   *p=*p+1;
   ```

   Will have a following effect.
   (a) The statement will increment the address which is stored inside the pointer.
   (b) The statement will increment the value of variable a, so the new value of a will be 11.
   (c) The statement will change the address of pointer p in memory.
   (d) None of the above.

2. If p is a pointer of type float, then which of the following statements is correct?
   (a) A pointer can only point to floating point variables.
   (b) A pointer can point to float type as well as void type variables.
   (c) A float type pointer can point to all the variables whose size is less than or equal to 4 bytes example, int, char, float, short, etc.
   (d) The pointer can only point to 'float' and 'double' type of variables.

3. Which of the following statements is correct?
   (a) Call by value creates a duplication of data items required to be accessed by the 'called' function and the 'calling' function.
   (b) Call by address creates a duplication of data items required to be accessed by the 'called' function and the 'calling' function.

(c) Call by reference a duplication of data items required to be accessed by the 'called' function and the 'calling' function.

(d) None of the above.

4. Let us assume that p is a pointer of type integer which holds an address as 9000. What will be the address inside the pointer p after execution of the following statement:

```
p++;
```

(a) 9000

(b) 9001

(c) 9002

(d) 9003

5. Let us assume that q is a pointer of type double which holds an address as 8000. What will be the address inside the pointer q after execution of the following statement:

```
q=q+3
```

(a) 8000

(b) 8001

(c) 8036

(d) 8024

6. Which of the following function calls consume a least amount of data space:

(a) Call by value

(b) Call by address

(c) Call by reference

(d) All of the above function calls will require same amount of data space.

7. Consider the following code:

```
#include< stdio.h>
void f1(int);
void main()
{
int x=10;
f1(x);
printf("%d",x);
}
void f1(int x);
{
x=x+10;
}
```

8. What is the output of the program?

(a) 10

(b) 20

(c) This is a compilation error because x is created as a duplicate variable.

(d) This is a runtime error.

9. Consider the code below and select the correct answer:

```
int *P, i[3];
```

```
i[0]=3; i[1]=1; i[2]=2;
P=&i[1];
```

What is the value of expression *P++?
(a) 0
(b) 1
(c) 2
(d) None of the above

10. Consider the following code segment:

```
char a[20]
char *p="string"
int len=strlen(p); /*strlen(p) gives length of string p*/
for(i=0;i<len;i++)
a[i]=p[len-i];
printf("%s",a);
```

What is the output of the code?
(a) gnirts
(b) string
(c) gnirt
(d) Junk values are printed
(e) No output is printed
(f) None of the above.

11. Let us assume that the integer type pointer p points to a integer type variable named as a which has a value 10. Choose the correct answer considering the following two statements:
    (i) *p++
    (ii) (*p)++
(a) Both the statements (i) and (ii) will have a same effect which can change the value of variable a to 11.
(b) The statement (i) will change the value of variable a to 11 whereas the statement (ii) will change the address stored inside the pointer.
(c) The statement (i) will change the address stored inside the pointer whereas the statement (ii) will change the value of variable a to 11.
(d) The statement (ii) is a compilation error.

12. Consider the following statements:

```
int a[]={10,20,30,40};
int *p;
p=a;
printf("%d",*(p+5));
```

Choose the correct output.
(a) 30
(b) 40

    (c) Junk value

    (d) The statement p=a is a compilation error.

13. Which of the following statements are correct?

    (a) A void type pointer can point to variables of any type.

    (b) A void type pointer can only point to variables of type void.

    (c) The size of void type pointer is 0 bytes.

    (d) None of the above is true.

14. Consider the statement below and select a correct answer:

```
void (*p)(int,float);
```

    (a) The statement creates a pointer of type void which can point to integer or a float.

    (b) The statement is a compilation error.

    (c) The statement creates a pointer to a function which returns void and takes two arguments such that one argument if of type integer and the other is of type float.

    (d) The statement is a runtime error.

15. Which of the following statements are correct?

    (a) We can return multiple values from the 'called' function to the 'calling' function using pointers.

    (b) We can return only single value from the 'called' function to the 'calling' function using pointers.

    (c) We cannot use pointers along with the return statement.

    (d) None of the above is true.

Review Questions

1. What is a pointer? How will you declare and initialize a pointer?
2. Differentiate between Call by value and Call by address. Give examples.
3. Write a program to swap two integers using pointers. The program should have two different functions main() and swap() such that values of the variables in the main() function are exchanged by swap().
4. Write a program to calculate sum and average of n-numbers using pointers.
5. Write a program to arrange n-numbers in descending order using pointers.
6. How can you access the elements of 1-D and 2-D array using pointers? Give examples.
7. Write a program to perform multiplication of matrices using pointers.
8. Write a short note on void type pointers.
9. What is a pointer to a function? How will you declare and initialize a pointer to a function?
10. What is a pointer to a pointer? Explain with example.
11. Write a short note on pointer arithmetic's. Give examples.
12. Determine the output of the following code assuming the address of variable a in memory as 1000 (Output can be shown in decimal format). Specify errors if any.

```
int a=10;
int *p;
p=&a;
```

```
printf("%d\n", (*p)++);
printf("%d\n",*p++);
printf("%d\n",p--);
printf("%d\n",p++);
printf("%d\n",*p++);
```

Justify your answer.

13. Write a program to perform a string copy operation using pointers.
14. What do you mean by array of pointers? Explain with example.
15. Determine the output of following code assuming the addresses of variables a and b as 1000 and 2000 respectively (Output can be shown in decimal format). Also specify compilation or runtime errors (if any).

```
int a=50,b=75;
int *p,*q;
p=&a;
q=&b;
printf("%d\n",*p+10);
printf("%d\n",p+b);
printf("%d\n",(*p) +a);
printf("%d\n",*p +*p);
printf("%d\n",a+p+b);
printf("%d\n",q+p+b);
```

16. Write a program to find the smallest and largest number in an array using pointers.

Chapter

9 | Structures and Unions

9.1 Overview

Structure is a template used to create a user-defined data type. This means that, as we create the variables of built-in data types, such as `int`, `float`, and `double`, we can now, also create the variables of user-defined data types, provided that the template for this data type are defined by creating a structure in the program. Structure is a way to combine the logically related data elements into a single unit. Each of the data elements defined inside the structure, are called the members of a structure. The members defined inside the structure can be of a same or different data types. Hence, a structure can be defined as a template which is created for storing heterogeneous values in physically adjacent memory locations.

What is a "user-defined" data type? **?**

C/C++ has a built-in set of primitive data types like `int`, `float`, `char`, `double` etc, which we can be directly used in the program. We can create variables of **built-in types** and perform operations with the values stored in these variables. Along with using built-in data types, we can also create customized data types in a program. "User-defined data type" is a "customized" data type that the programmer can create as per the requirements to store data in computer memory.

Structures are used to create user-defined data types.

What is the need to create user-defined data types in the program? **?**

Let us assume that you need to store data about the vehicles assembled in an automobile industry. The relevant information that you wish to maintain for each vehicle is "colour", "no of seats", "type of fuel" and "mileage" of the vehicle. As and when a new car is assembled you will need to create 4 different variables to store its information in computer memory. Instead, it would be easy if the programmer has an ability to create a variable of type `Car` using the statement,

`Car c1;`

where c1 stores all the required information about the car in a real world. The variable c1 can internally store the 4 attributes "colour", "no of seats", "type of fuel" and "mileage" of the vehicle.

The requirement here is that, we need to create a variable of type `Car` just like we create variables of primitive types like `int`, `float`, etc. As the data type `Car` is not a built-in type of C/C++, we must create a template for Car before we create variables of its type. Creating the **template** for Car will make the compiler understand, what exactly does the programmer mean by creating variables of type Car. Such a template for the user-defined data type is defined using **structures**. In summary, we must define a structure for Car, in the program following which we can easily create variables of type Car. In this chapter, we will study how to create **user-defined types**.

What is the difference between a structure and array? ?

Unlike arrays, structure is a combination of heterogeneous types: which means that the member variables in a structure can have different data types. As discussed before, if we consider storing the information about the cars manufactured in an automobile industry, we would wish to store the "colour" which is a of type **string**, the "number of seats" which is of type **int**, the "mileage" which would be of type **float** and the type of fuel which is a **string** for every Car object.

This means that, storing information about a particular Car in a real world requires storing values having different data types. In actuality, Car in itself is a data type created as a composition of different members like "colour"(string), "no of seats"(int), "type of fuel"(string) and "mileage"(float); such a data type is called as **composite data type**. Structures in C/C++ are used to create composite data types. Another example of composite data type could be storing postal address which can be decomposed into different parts like flat number, building name, street name, city, zip code, etc.

Hence we could create a structure named as Address and create members as flat_number (int), building_name (string) street (string), city (string) and zip (string). After defining the structure, we can simply create a variable of type Address to store address of any person in computer memory as shown below:

```
Address a1;
```

This variable a1 will internally store all the members defined in the structure Address. This saves the programmers effort to redefine all the members required to store address each time a new address is to be created.

On the other hand, let us assume that we need to store telephone numbers of a particular person in computer memory. One person can obviously have multiple phone numbers and we need to store all of them. Such an attribute which can have multiple values is called as **multivalued attribute**. Although you can have multiple phone numbers, all of them will be indeed numeric. This means that all the values of a multi-valued attribute are always of a **same data type**. Hence in this case, you can create an array in a program named as telephoneNumber, which can store the telephone numbers. In this case, we have created an array because **it is a collection of values having same data type**.

One of the major difference between arrays and structures is that, **array is used to create an "multivalued data type" whereas a structure is used to create an "composite data type"**. A data type can be both, multivalued as well as composite, for example, if a person has multiple contact addresses you may be required to create an array of Address wherein each address value in itself is composite in nature.

In such a case, you can combine arrays and structures together by creating an **array of structures**. Creation of such complex data types is discussed later in this chapter, so don't worry about them right now.

9.2 Creating Structures

Figure 9.1 gives the syntax to define a structure. As seen, the keyword `struct` must be followed by the 'structure name' which defines a custom data type as a collection of heterogeneous members. Once the structure is defined, we can now create variables of type structure similar to how we create variables of any of the basic data types such as

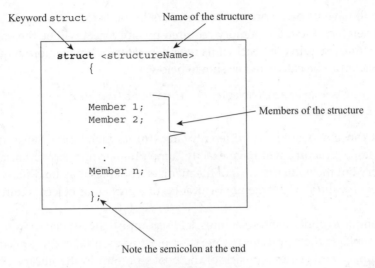

Keyword `struct`

Name of the structure

Members of the structure

Note the semicolon at the end

Figure 9.1: Syntax of a structure

`int`, `float`, and `char`. The variables which are of type defined by the structure are called as **objects** of the structure. The following is the syntax to create objects of a structure:

struct `<StructureName> <ObjectName>;`

We can create as many objects of the structure as required in the program. Note that, a structure is just a template for creating a 'user-defined data type', which means that, the memory for the member variables will not be allocated when a structure is defined, rather its actually allocated when the object of a structure is created. Every object of the structure will contain all the members defined by the structure in the memory that is allocated for that object. Further, each object of a structure will have different copy of the member variables in its memory. This means that, if we create two objects of a structure as o1 and o2 and if the structure contains n members as shown in the Figure 9.2, then each of

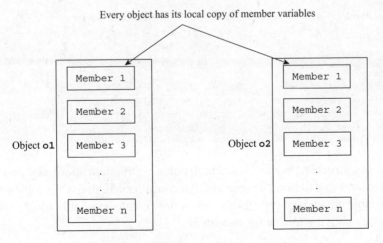

Every object has its local copy of member variables

Figure 9.2: Object memory for o1 and o2

the objects will have its own copy of the members in the object memory as shown in the Figure 9.2. Therefore, the total memory required by any object will be the addition of the amount of memory required by each of its members. Hence, the memory required for any structure object must be calculated as shown below:

```
sizeof(Object) = sizeof(member1) + sizeof(member2)··· +
    sizeof(memberN)
```

Every object can obviously store different values in its members. Hence, two different objects of a same structure will have exactly same number of member variables in their object memory but the values of each of the member variables may be different for each of them. The set of 'values' of the member variables of a particular object is called as a **'state'** of that object.

As an example to understand structures, let us assume that we need to store information about three **books** in the computer memory. Also, let us assume that we need to store id, title, author, and price for each of the books present in the library. Since this is a common requirement that, we need to store the members id, title, author, and price for each of the books, we can define a template for every book using a structure as shown below:

```
struct Book
{
int id;
char *title;
char *author;
float price;
};
```

What is the advantage that of creating Book as a structure? ?

This means that, we have created a "user-defined data type" named as Book. Hence, we will be able to create the variables of type Book just like we create the variables of built-in data types like int, float, char, etc. Following statement can now be used to create a variable b1 of type Book:

`struct Book b1;`

The variable b1 contains members id, title, author and price in its memory; thereby making it possible to store complete information about a particular book in b1. We can similarly, create multiple variables of type Book and each variable will contain all the members of the structure. This makes it possible to organize data about different books in the computer memory.

By defining a structure, we are not actually storing the data about any **book** in the real world, but we have just defined a template that compiler will use while allocating memory for every variable which is of type Book. Let us now create a variable b1 of type Book, this can be done by using the following statement:

`struct Book b1;`

The variable b1 is now called as an '**object**' of a structure Book. The object memory of b1 will contain members id, title, author and price as shown in the Figure 9.3. Note that, these members are present in the object memory of b1 because we have defined them inside the structure Book.

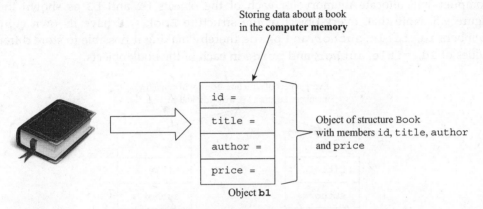

Figure 9.3: Object memory of b1

The total memory required for object b1 should be calculated as addition of the memory required by integer member id (which is 2 bytes), character pointer title (which is 2 bytes), character pointer author (which is 2 bytes) and float member price (which is 4 bytes). Therefore, the total memory required by each object of the structure will be **10** bytes as shown in the Figure 9.4. We assume title and author as near pointers and hence consider them of 2 byte each.

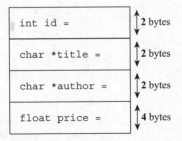

Total memory required for object b1 = **10 bytes**

Figure 9.4: Memory required for object b1

As we need to store data about three books, we create two more variables of type Book by using the following statement:

```
struct Book b2,b3;
```

Compiler will allocate memory for each of the objects b2 and b3 as shown in the Figure 9.5. Note that, every object of the structure Book will have its own copy of members id, title, author, and price thereby making it possible to store different values of id, title, author, and price in each of the book objects.

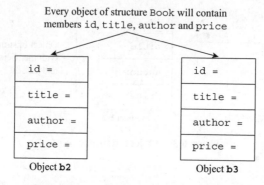

Figure 9.5: Structure of objects b2 and b3

NOTES

Each of the objects of the structure Book in computer memory represents one book in **real world** as shown in the Figure 9.6.

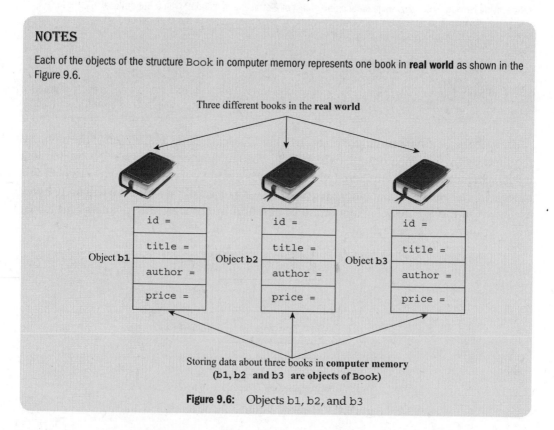

Figure 9.6: Objects b1, b2, and b3

We can access the attributes `id`, `title`, `author`, and `price` of each of the `Book` objects by using a **membership operator** ' . ' (DOT) using the following notation given below:

```
<ObjectName>.<memberName> = <value>;
```

For example, if the title of first Book is 'C++', second Book is 'Java', and the third Book is 'Fortran' then we can individually initialize the member variable `title` for each of the objects `b1`, `b2`, and `b3` as shown in the following:

```
b1.title="C++";
b2.title="Java";
b3.title="Fortran";
```

The state of the objects `b1`, `b2`, and `b3` after initializing the member `title` for each of them is as shown in Figure 9.7.

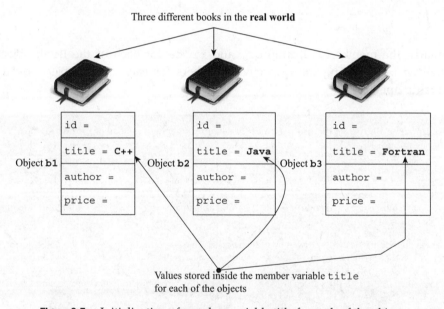

Figure 9.7: Initialization of member variable title for each of the objects

NOTES

In actuality `title` and `author` are **pointers** which points to the character array that store the string value. Hence the strings "C++", "Java" and "Fortran" are actually stored in the character array created **external to the object** as shown in the Figure 9.8. Hence the size of each book object remains 10 bytes immaterial of the number of characters in the string.

For simplicity, we show the values pointed by the pointer, directly within the object space in Figure 9.7 and later in this chapter. Remember, in actuality when a member is a pointer it stores address of a value which is actually present external to an object.

Recall from Chapter 8, Section 8.7, that creating a character pointer gives an additional flexibility of initializing it with string constant at any time in the program when compared to arrays. Hence we have created `title` and `author` as pointers rather than arrays.

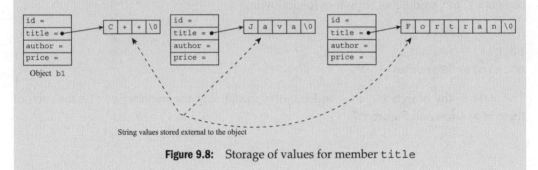

Figure 9.8: Storage of values for member `title`

Similarly, the members `id`, `author`, and `price` for each of the `Book` objects can be initialized by accessing the respective members for each of the objects by using a **membership operator '.'**

Can we initialize all the members of the object in a single statement, instead of initializing one member at a time? **?**

 Yes, we can initialize all the members of a particular object using a single statement. However, we can do so only at the time of creation of the object and no later than that. For example, we could have initialized the details of object b1 at the time of creating it, using the following statement:

```
struct Book b1 = {1,"C++","Kunal",900};
```

The values defined in the curly brackets will be assigned to a particular member of the object in the same order in which they are declared inside the structure. This means that the id of object b1 will be initialized as 1, the title will be initialized as "C++", author will be initialized as "Kunal" and the price will be initialized as 900. **The order in which the values are specified within the curly brackets must exactly match with the order in which the members are defined in the structure.**

I say it again, that such a initialization can only be applied at the time of creation of the object and not later than that. For example, the following code will not work because it first creates object b1 and then initializes all its members in the second statement

```
struct Book b1; /*Create object b1*/
b1 = {1, "C++","Kunal", 900}; /*Error - cannot initialize object b1*/
```

If you need to initialize members of an object after its creation, you have to initialize them one at a time as shown below:

```
b1.id=1
b1.title="C++";
b1.author="Kunal";
b1.price=900;
```

Can we initialize the members of the structure within the structure definition? **?**

📖 NO! This is because the memory for members is not allocated until an object of a structure is created. Therefore, you cannot initialize the members of the structure inside the structure definition because these members are not in the memory yet. For example, the following initialization will give an error:

```
struct Book
{
int id =2; /*ERROR.. members cannot be initialized inside the
            structure definition*/
....
.......
};
```

If you need to initialize any of the members, you must first create an object of the structure and then access the required members using a membership operator "." over an object, as discussed before.

9.2.1 Program to store the information about books in the computer memory: An example

For example, let us create a program that stores the data about three books in a computer memory and prints the information about each of the Book objects in a tabular format. As discussed in the previous section, let us store the following information about each book in the computer memory:

1. Identification number of the book in a library
2. Title of the book
3. Author of the book
4. Price of the book

We can create Book as a user-defined data type by defining a structure as given below:

```
struct Book
{
int id;
char title[100];
char author[100];
float price;
};
```

NOTES

In this case we have created members `title` and `author` as **arrays** rather than pointers. This is because we intend to accept this information as input from the user rather than directly initializing them as string constants. Recall from Chapter 8, Section 8.7 a pointer cannot be used to input a string or an array unless memory is allocated for the pointer. To avoid the complexities of dealing with pointers at this stage, we create `title` and `author` as an array of characters. This obviously means that the size of each `Book` object is going to increase because it has two character arrays of 100 bytes each, embedded within the object space, when compared to the previous design in Figure 9.8 where `title` and `author` were created as pointers pointing to the string external to the object space. The design shown in Figure 9.8 is better than what we are doing here because when `title` and `author` are pointers the external array is created of an exact size needed to store the data. Whereas in this case we unconditionally create an array with a capacity of 100 characters immaterial of the length of the input string. Although this is not an optimal design we will still create `title` and `author` as arrays to avoid complexities with pointers at the moment and focus on learning structures. We will discuss memory optimizations in Chapter 10, where we learn dynamic memory allocations. In this case, the total memory required for a single `Book` object is addition of memory required by integer member `id` (which is 2 bytes), character array `title` (which is 100 bytes), character array `author` (which is 100 bytes) and float member `price` (which is 4 bytes). Therefore, the total memory required by each object of the structure will be **206** bytes as shown in the Figure 9.9.

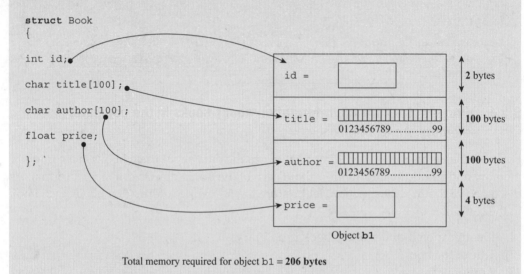

Total memory required for object b1 = **206 bytes**

Figure 9.9: Memory allocation of a structure object with arrays embedded within the object space

As we need to store the information about three books in computer memory, the following code creates three objects of a `Book` taking the details of each `Book` object as input from the user and printing them back on screen.

```
#include<stdio.h>
struct Book
{
int id;
char title[100];
char author[100];
float price;
};
void main()
{
struct Book b1,b2,b3;
```

```
printf("Enter the details of first Book\n");
scanf("%d%s%s%f",&b1.id,b1.title,b1.author,&b1.price);
printf("Enter the details of second Book\n");
scanf("%d%s%s%f",&b2.id,b2.title,b2.author,&b2.price);
printf("Enter the details of third Book\n");
scanf("%d%s%s%f",&b3.id,b3.title,b3.author,&b3.price);
printf("The Book details are\n");
printf("%d\t%s\t%s\t%f\n",b1.id,b1.title,b1.author,b1.price);
printf("%d\t%s\t%s\t%f\n",b2.id,b2.title,b2.author,b2.price);
printf("%d\t%s\t%s\t%f\n",b3.id,b3.title,b3.author,b3.price);
}
```

Output

```
Enter the details of first Book
1 C++ Kunal 800
Enter the details of second Book
2 Java Jack 900
Enter the details of third Book
3 Fortran Jill 400
The Book details are
1   C++       Kunal    800.000000
2   Java      Jack     900.000000
3   Fortran   Jill     400.000000
```

The first statement in `main()`,

```
struct Book b1,b2,b3;
```

creates 3 objects of a structure Book, each object will have members id, title, author, and price as shown in the Figure 9.10. Since these members are defined in the structure as seen in the code.

The statement,

```
scanf("%d%s%s%f",&b1.id,b1.title,b1.author,&b1.price);
```

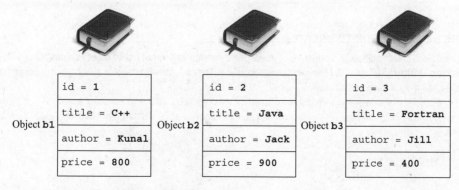

Figure 9.10: State of objects b1, b2 and b3

will take the values of id, title, author, and price of object b1 as input from the user. This is because, every member in the statement is accessed by applying a membership operator '.' over object b1.

CAUTION

Be careful when you specify & symbol in scanf() statement. The & symbol should be specified only for variables id and price and not for arrays title and author. This is because the array name in itself is a pointer storing starting address of an array. This is exactly in line with what we have discussed in Chapter 8, Section 8.7.1.

Similarly, the following statements

```
scanf("%d%s%s%f",&b2.id,b2.title,b2.author,&b2.price);

scanf("%d%s%s%f",&b3.id,b3.title,b3.author,&b3.price);
```

will accept the members of object b2 and b3 as input from the user, respectively. Let us assume that, the user inputs the id, title, author, and price for each of the Book objects as shown in the following table:

Object of structure book	Data entered by the user (id, title, author, and price)
b1	(1, "C++", "Kunal",800)
b2	(2, "Java", "Jack",900)
b3	(3, "Fortran", "Jill",400)

This means that the state of objects b1, b2, and b3 in the memory, will be as shown in the Figure 9.10.

The following **printf()** statements, print the member values of each of the Book objects on the screen, as seen in the output of the program:

```
printf("The Book details are\n");
printf("%d\t%s\t%s\t%f\n",b1.id,b1.title,b1.author,b1.price);
printf("%d\t%s\t%s\t%f\n",b2.id,b2.title,b2.author,b2.price);
printf("%d\t%s\t%s\t%f\n",b3.id,b3.title,b3.author,b3.price);
```

SHORTHAND NOTATION TO CREATE OBJECTS

It is possible to create objects of a structure by specifying a **comma separated list of object names** along with the **structure definition**. Figure 9.11 shows the syntax of creating multiple objects(obj1,obj2,...,objn) of a structure using a shorthand notation.

For example, in the given program instead of creating the objects b1, b2, and b3 using a statement struct Book b1,b2,b3; in main(); you can also create them as while defining the structure Book as shown below.

```
struct Book
{
int id;
```

```
char title[100];
char author[100];
float price;
}b1,b2,b3;
```

Remember, the objects b1, b2 and b3 will have same scope as that of the structure definition. In this case, since structure Book is defined globally the objects b1, b2 and b3 will also be created as global objects. On the other hand, if b1, b2 and b3 are created in main() using the statement

```
struct Book b1, b2, b3;
```

the objects will be local to main() function even if the structure Book is defined globally

```
struct <structureName>
    {


       Member 1;
       Member 2;

           .
           .
       Member n;

    }obj1,obj2,obj3...objn;
```

Objects of the structure

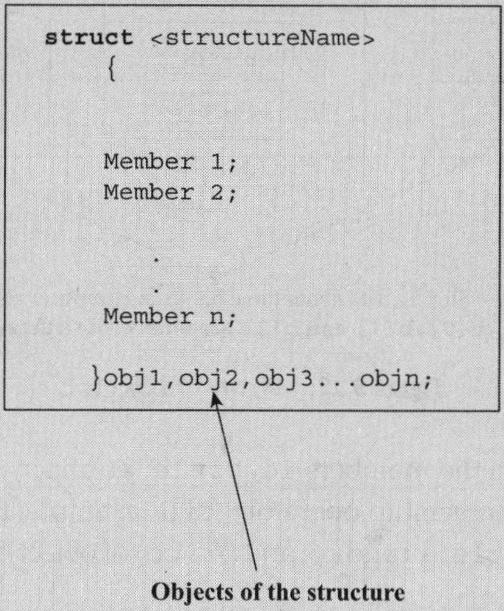

Figure 9.11: Syntax for creating objects of a structure using shorthand notation

9.3   Array of Structure Objects

It is possible to create an array such that each element of the array is an object of a structure. Let us consider the structure Book defined in Sections 9.2 with members id, title, author and price. We can create an array of Book objects named as b by using the following statement:

```
struct Book b[size];
```

The following statement will create an array b to store information about **three** books in the computer memory:

```
Book b[3];
```

Each element of the array b is an **object** of Book, because the data type of the array b is defined as Book. As the size of the array b is specified as 3 there will be three Book objects in an array b. The first Book object can be accessed as b[0], the second Book object can be accessed as b[1], and the third Book object can be accessed as b[2] as shown in the Figure 9.12.

Every element of the array represents one book in the **real world**

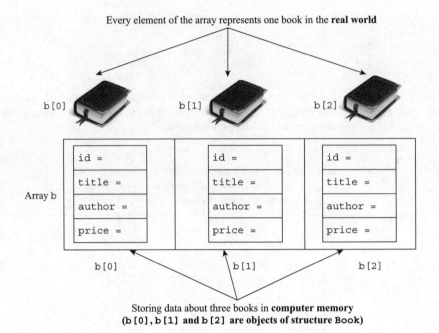

Storing data about three books in **computer memory**
(**b[0]**, **b[1]** and **b[2]** are objects of structure **Book**)

Figure 9.12: Array of objects b

We will be able to access the members id, title, author, and price for each of the Book objects by using a membership operator '.'. For example, the following statement will accept the members (id, title, author, and price) of object b[0] as input from the user:

```
scanf("%d%s%s%f",&b[0].id,b[0].title,b[0].author,&b[0].price);
```

Since we have only taken the members of b[0] as input, the state of array b assuming input data as (id=1, title="C++", author="Kunal", price=900) is as shown in the Figure 9.13.

Similarly, we can accept members of objects b[1] and b[2] as input from the user. Following for loop will accept the details for each of the Book objects b[0], b[1], and b[2] as input from the user because we have specified the range of loop variable i from 0 to 2.

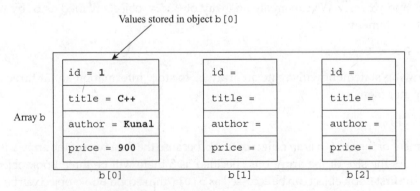

Figure 9.13: Initialization of object b[0]

```
for(i=0;i<=2;i++)
{
scanf("%d%s%s%f",&b[0].id,b[0].title,b[0].author,&b[0].price);
}
```

Figure 9.14 shows the final state of an array assuming sample input data.

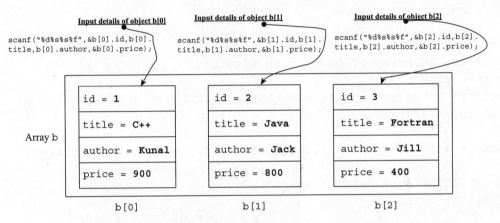

Figure 9.14: State of objects b[0], b[1], and b[2] after user input

In general, we can access a member of ith Book object in b by using the following statement:

```
b[i].<memberName>;
```

Following for loop will print the details of each of the Book objects on the computer screen:

```
for(i=0;i<=2;i++)
{
printf("%d\t%s\t%s\t%f\n", b[i].id, b[i].title, b[i].author, b[i].
    price);
}
```

When counter variable i takes a value 0, the **printf()** statement will print the id, title, author, and price of object b[0], whereas when the value of i is incremented to 1 the **printf()** statement will print the id, title, author, and price of object b[1] and so on. As the size of the array is 3, we terminate the for loop when the value of index variable i crosses 2. This is because the last Book object will be stored at position 2 as shown in the Figure 9.14. Therefore, the output of the given for loop will be as shown below:

```
1 C++       Kunal 900
2 Java      Jack  800
3 Fortran Jill   400
```

The following is the full source code which creates an array of type Book of size 3, accepts the details about each book as input from the user and prints them back on the computer screen.

```
#include<stdio.h>
struct Book
```

```
{
int id;
char title[100];
char author[100];
float price;
};
void main()
{
int i;
/*Create an array of books with size 3*/
struct Book b[3];
printf("Enter the id,title,author and price of 3 books\n");
for(i=0;i<=2;i++)
{
scanf("%d%s%s%f",&b[0].id,b[0].title,b[0].author,&b[0].price);
}
printf("The Book details are\n");
for(i=0;i<=2;i++)
{
printf("%d\t%s\t%s\t%f\n", b[i].id, b[i].title, b[i].author, b[i].
    price);
}
}
```

Output

```
Enter the id,title,author and price of 3 books
1 C++ Kunal 900
2 Java Jack 800
3 Fortran Jill 400
The Book details are
1 C++       Kunal   900.000000
2 Java      Jack    800.000000
3 Fortran   Jill    400.000000
```

INITIALIZATION OF ARRAY OF OBJECTS

Array of objects can be **initialized** directly at the time of creation as follows:

```
struct Book b[3] ={ {1,"C++","Kunal",900.00},
 {2,"Java","Jack",800.00},
 {3,"Fortran","Jill",400.00}};
```

The statement will create an array b and initialize its members as shown in the Figure 9.15.

Note that such an initialization can only be applied at the time of creation of an array and not later then that. For example, the following code will not work because it first creates an array b and then initializes all its objects in the second statement.

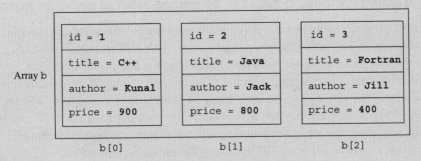

Figure 9.15: Elements of array b

```
struct Book b[3];
b ={ {1,"C++","Kunal",900.00},    /*ERROR : Cannot initialize array b*/
     {2,"Java","Jack",800.00},
     {3,"Fortran","Jill",400.00}};
```

If you need to initialize members of an array after its creation, you have to initialize them one at a time as shown below:

```
/*initialize id of b[0] */
b[0].id=1;

/*initialize title of b[0] */
b[0].title[0]='C';
b[0].title[1]='+';
b[0].title[2]='+';
b[0].title[3]='\0';

/*initialize author of b[0] */
b[0].author[0]='K';
b[0].author[1]='u';
b[0].author[2]='n';
b[0].author[3]='a';
b[0].author[4]='l';
b[0].author[5]='\0';

/*initialize price of b[0] */
b[0].price=900.00;
```

Similarly, members of object b[1] and b[2] can be initialized. Note that the arrays title and author are initialized one character at a time because string initialization can be applied to the array only at the time of creation and no later than that. Don't confuse this with what we have done in Section 9.2. We were able to use string initialization then, because the members title and author were created as pointers while defining the structure. The statements written for object b1 in Section 9.2,

```
b1.title="C++";
b2.author="Kunal";
```

work fine because both title and author were created as user-defined pointers. Similar statements cannot be written here, because we have created title and author as arrays (constant pointers) in this case.

9.3.1 Program to arrange n-books in ascending order of price: An example

Let us create a program to accept details of n different books as input from the user and to arrange the books in ascending order of their `price`. We will store the details of n-books entered by the user in an array of type `Book`. Therefore, the size of the array that we need to create must at least be n. Recall from Chapter 6, Section 6.2.2, we will not be able to actually specify the size of the array in terms of n because the value of variable n will be known at run time, whereas the compiler needs to allocate the memory for an array at the compile time. Hence, we create this program by assuming the maximum limit of value of n as 100. We create an array with a capacity 100 by using the following statement:

```
struct Book b[100];
```

This means that the array b can store at the most 100 objects inside it, and the elements of the array will therefore be indexed from 0 to 99 as shown in the Figure 9.16. Note that, all the elements of the array will have junk values unless we initialize the values explicitly.

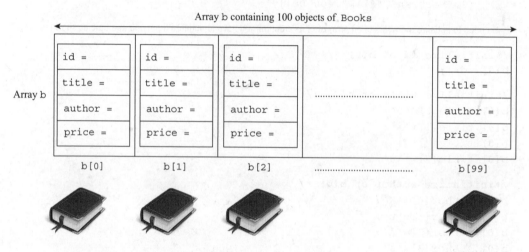

Figure 9.16: Array b of size 100

Although, we have created a space large enough to accommodate 100 `Book` objects, it does not mean that user should always store the details of 100 books in the memory. This is because, the user might actually require storing the details for different number of books each time the program is executed. Hence, before we start taking the actual array elements as input from the user, we will ask the user about the number of `Book` objects that the user wishes to store, to arrange the objects in ascending order of `price`. As seen in the code, we create a variable n as an integer variable, that will store the 'number of objects' that user will input, to store them in an array. Therefore, the first step of the program will now be to take the value of n as input as shown below:

```
int n;
printf("How many Books?\n");
scanf("%d",&n);
```

Once the value of variable n is known, we can then take only the required number of Book objects as input from the user and store them in first n-locations of the array, whereas the remaining part of the array can still continue to hold junk values. For example, if user inputs the value of variable n as 5, this means that the user wishes to store data about 5 books in the computer memory. Hence, we will now start taking the details of 5 books as input from the user, such that the details of the first Book object entered by the user are stored in b[0] (first location of the array), the details of the second Book object entered by the user are stored in b[1] and so on. Hence, the last Book object will be stored in b[4]. The remaining part of the array, which is the elements from position 5 to position 99 will still continue to hold junk values.

The id, title, author, and price of the n book objects to be stored as the first n-elements of the array can be taken as input from the user by using the following for loop:

```
for(i=0;i<=n-1;i++)
{
scanf("%d%s%s%f",&b[i].id,b[i].title,b[i].author,&b[i].price);
}
```

User may input the book details in any order of price and hence we now need to sort the input data in ascending order of price obtained by each book. Let us assume that the user inputs unordered data which is as follows:

Object of structure book	Data entered by the user (id, title, author, and price)
b[0]	(1, "C++", "Kunal",900)
b[1]	(2, "Java", "Jack",800)
b[2]	(3,"Fortran", "Jill",990)
b[3]	(4,"Basic","Tom",950)
b[4]	(5, "Cobol", "Jazz",400)

Figure 9.17 gives the set of for loops required to sort an array in ascending or descending order. These loops have been explained in detail in Chapter 6, Section 6.2.5 so we will not repeat that explanation here.

For simplifying the explanation, we will refer the element at lower index as a Book object above in the array and the element at higher index as a Book object below in the array.

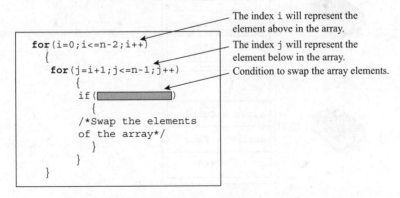

Figure 9.17: for loops required for sorting the array

This means that, element b[0] is present above b[1], element b[1] is present above b[2], element b[2] is present above b[3] and element b[3] is present above b[4] as seen from the Figure 9.18. The requirement of ascending order is that, the price of Book object above in the array must not be greater than the price of Book object below in the array. This means that any book b[i] must not have higher price when compared to b[j] if **i<j**. Hence, if we get a Book object b[i] whose price are greater than Book object b[j] then we swap the objects b[i] and b[j], so that the price of b[i] now becomes less than the price of b[j].

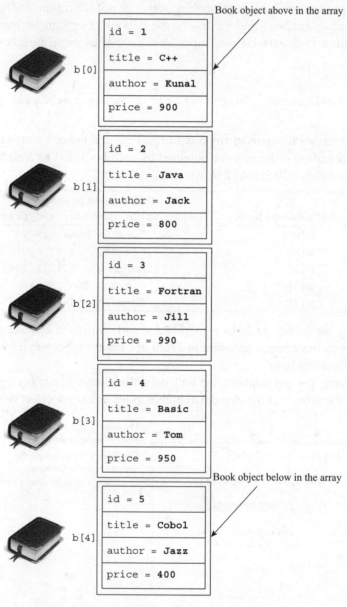

Book object above in the array

```
             id = 1
             title = C++
b[0]
             author = Kunal
             price = 900

             id = 2
             title = Java
b[1]
             author = Jack
             price = 800

             id = 3
             title = Fortran
b[2]
             author = Jill
             price = 990

             id = 4
             title = Basic
b[3]
             author = Tom
             price = 950
```

Book object below in the array

```
             id = 5
             title = Cobol
b[4]
             author = Jazz
             price = 400
```

Figure 9.18: Organization of book objects in an array

For example, if we consider the input data as shown in the Figure 9.18, we observe that the price of Book object stored at b[0] is greater than the price of a Book object stored at b[1] (as seen from the input data, the price of book on "C++" is 900 whereas the price of book on "Java" is 800). Hence, we need to swap the positions of books on "C++" and "Java" in the array as shown in the Figure 9.19.

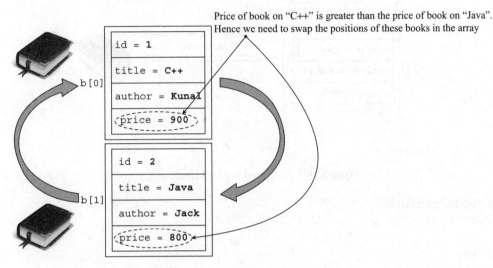

Price of book on "C++" is greater than the price of book on "Java". Hence we need to swap the positions of these books in the array

Figure 9.19: Swapping b[0] and b[1]

Note that, we have taken a decision to swap the position of books on "C++" and "Java" because the following condition is satisfied:

```
b[0].price > b [1].price
```

where, b[0].price represents the price of book on "C++" (which is 900) and b[1].price represents the price of book on "Java" (which is 800). It is very important to understand that, based on the attribute price we take a decision to change the order of occurrence of the Book objects in the array. This means that, we will take a decision about the positions of books on "C++" and "Java" in the array based on the price of each of these books and hence we swap these Book objects, to move the book on "Java" above in the array and the book on "C++" below in the array. The result of the 'swap' operation is as shown in the Figure 9.20.

In general, we will swap the Book objects b[i] and b[j] if the price of b[i] is greater than the price of b[j]. This means that, we will take a decision to swap b[i] and b[j] in the array if following condition is satisfied:

```
b[i].price > b[j].price
```

Given is the complete source code to arrange n-Books in the ascending order. After the books are sorted, we also print the resultant order of the books in the tabular format as seen in the code.

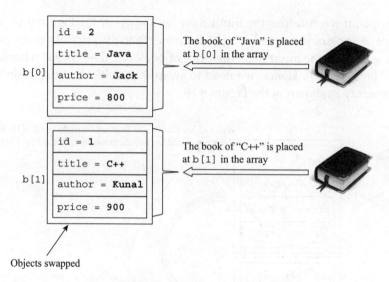

The book of "Java" is placed at b[0] in the array

The book of "C++" is placed at b[1] in the array

Objects swapped

Figure 9.20: Swapped books Kunal, Jack

```
#include<stdio.h>
struct Book
{
int id;
char title[100];
char author[100];
float price;
};
void main()
{
int n,i,j;
Book b[100];
Book t;
printf("How many Books?\n");
scanf("%d",&n);
printf("Enter the details of %d Books\n",n);
    for(i=0;i<=n-1;i++)
    {
    scanf("%d%s%s%f",&b[i].id,b[i].title,b[i].author,&b[i].price);
    }
    for(i=0;i<=n-2;i++)
    {
    for(j=i+1;j<=n-1;j++)
    {
      if(b[i].price>b[j].price)
        {
        t=b[i];
        b[i] =b[j];
        b[j]=t;
```

```
                }
            }
        }
printf("The Ascending order is \n");
    for(i=0;i<=n-1;i++)
    {
    printf("%d\t%s\t%s\t%f\n",b[i].id,b[i].title,b[i].author,b[i].
            price);
    }
}
```

Output

```
How many Books?
5
Enter the details of 5 Books
1 C++ Kunal 900
2 Java Jack 800
3 Fortran Jill 990
4 Basic Tom 950
5 Cobol Jazz 400
The Ascending order is
5   Cobol    Jazz    400.000000
2   Java     Jack    800.000000
1   C++      Kunal   900.000000
4   Basic    Tom     950.000000
3   Fortran  Jill    990.000000
```

How does the assignment operator work with structure objects? **?**

When we assign one structure object to another the assignment happens **member-by-member**. This means that the value of each member of the object on the right hand side of the assignment is assigned to the corresponding member of the object present on the left hand side of the operator. For example, if b1 and b2 are the objects of structure Book then the statement:

b1 = b2;

will copy every member of object b2 to corresponding member of object b1. This means, that the object b1 will now contain same values in all its members as stored in object b2. Assuming state of object b2 as (id=1, title= "C++", author="Kunal", price=900), the below figure shows the working of statement b1=b2;

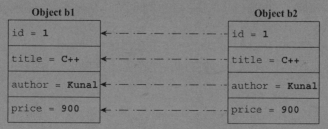

Working of statement b1=b2 if title and author are not created as pointers

In the program given in Section 9.3, we have used assignment operator with objects of Book while swapping them. This assignment actually happens member-by-member. We assume that title and author are created as arrays (which is true in the program given in Section 9.3) and hence their values are embedded within each of the objects.

Assignment operator must be used carefully when any of the members of an object is a pointer. For example, if we would have created title and author as pointers then the memory of object b2 is as shown in the below figure. The figure assumes the memory address of array storing title of the book as 1000 and the address of array storing author name as 2000. Note that the members title and author store the starting address of the array rather than direct string values.

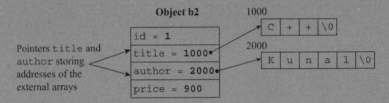

Memory for object b2 assuming title and author as pointers

In this case, the statement

```
b1 = b2;
```

will copy the values of variables id and salary as usual but copy the addresses stored within the pointers title and author instead of the values. Hence both the objects will share the same external arrays as shown in the below figure. This is because the address within the pointers was copied rather than the individual values of title and author.

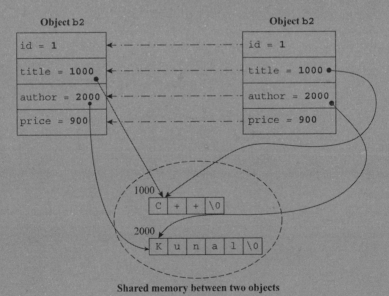

Shared memory between two objects

Shared memory storing title and author of book objects b1 and b2

Hence, any change made to title of book b1 will also get reflected in b2 and vice versa as both of them share the same space in memory where the actual value is stored. Similarly, any change made to the author array of b1 will get reflected in b2 and vice versa. It is programmers duty to remember this impact (if object has pointers as its members) when using assignment operator with objects. Necessary changes must be made in the program to copy the actual array contents rather than just the pointer addresses in this case. This can be done by creating a simple string copy function which copies all characters one-by-one from a source array to destination array instead of copying the pointer addresses.

9.4 Nesting of Structures

When a structure definition is included as a part of another structure definition then it is called as 'Nesting of Structures'. Figure 9.21 gives is the syntax to define a structure s2 as a part of a structure definition s1. In this case, the object of the inner structure (s2) must be created as a member of the outer structure (s1) as shown in the Figure 9.21.

As seen in the Figure 9.21, Member1 and Member2 are the direct members of the outer structure s1 along with the inner structure s2 whose object is also created as a part of the structure s1. This means that, object of the 'inner structure' will also be present in the object memory of the 'outer structure' along with Member1 and Member2 as shown in the Figure 9.22.

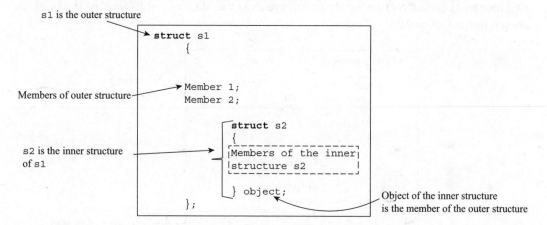

Figure 9.21: Syntax for nesting of structures

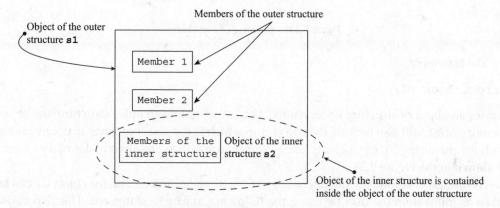

Figure 9.22: Object of the structure s1

As an example, let us enhance the structure Book to store the 'date of publishing' for each of the books along with the members id, title, author, and price. The attribute 'date of publishing' in itself is a composition of three integer values dd, mm, and yyyy. This means that, we should now create a structure Date with members dd, mm, and yyyy, so that its object can represent a particular date in the computer memory. The following is the definition of the structure Date containing fields dd, mm, and yyyy to represent the day, month, and year, parts of the date, respectively.

```
struct Date
{
int dd;
int mm;
int yyyy;
};
```

As the publishing date is required to be stored for each of the Book objects, we will define the structure Date inside the structure Book by creating the object of Date (named as **dop**) as a member of the structure Book. dop represents the 'date of publishing' of the book as shown in the Figure 9.23.

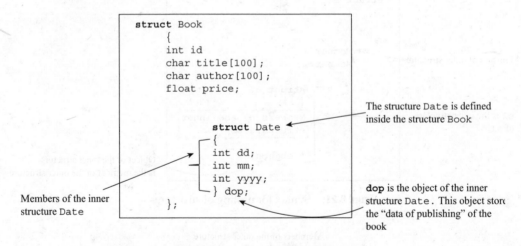

```
struct Book
    {
    int id
    char title[100];
    char author[100];
    float price;


            struct Date        ←  The structure Date is defined
             {                     inside the structure Book
             int dd;
             int mm;
             int yyyy;
             } dop;             dop is the object of the inner
                                structure Date. This object store
    };                          the "data of publishing" of the
                                book
```

Members of the inner structure Date

Figure 9.23: Nesting of structures

The statement,

```
struct Book b1;
```

creates an object of structure Book named as b1. As Book is an outer structure, the object memory of b1 will also include the object dop which is the object of inner structure, along with the members id, title, author, and price which are directly defined in Book, as shown in the Figure 9.24.

As discussed before, the members id, title, author, and price for object b1 can be taken as input from the user by using the following scanf() statement. This is because these members are directly defined in the outer structure as seen in the Figure 9.24.

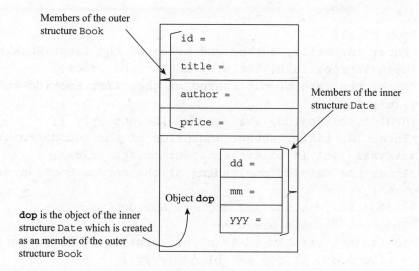

Figure 9.24: Object b1

```
scanf("%d%s%s%f",&b1.id,b1.title,b1.author,&b1.price);
```

To input the 'date of publishing' of object b1, we need to actually input the members of the inner structure Date. This can be done by using the object dop which is created as an object of structure Date. However, because the object dop is itself embedded inside the object memory of b1 we input the members dd, mm, and yyyy by using a membership operator as shown:

```
scanf("%d%d%d ",&b1.dop.dd, &b1.dop.mm, &b1.dop.yyyy);
```

The following is the full source code that creates two objects of the structure Book and takes the data about each book as input from the user. The code also prints the details of the two Book objects in tabular format on the computer screen.

```c
#include<stdio.h>
struct Book
{
int id;
char title[100];
char author[100];
float price;
    struct Date
    {
    int dd;
    int mm;
    int yyyy;
    } dop;
};
void main()
```

```
{
struct Book b1,b2;
printf("Enter id, title, author and price of the first Book\n");
scanf("%d%s%s%f",&b1.id,b1.title,b1.author,&b1.price);
printf("Enter the date of publishing of the first Book(dd mm
    yyyy)\n");
scanf("%d%d%d",&b1.dop.dd, &b1.dop.mm, &b1.dop.yyyy );
printf("Enter id, title, author and price of the second Book\n");
scanf("%d%s%s%f",&b2.id,b2.title,b2.author,&b2.price);
printf("Enter the date of publishing of the second Book(dd mm
    yyyy)\n");
scanf("%d%d%d",&b2.dop.dd, &b2.dop.mm, &b2.dop.yyyy );
printf("The Book details are\n");
printf("%d\t%s\t%s\t%f\t%d-%d-%d\n",b1.id,b1.title,b1.author,b1.
    price,b1.dop.dd, b1.dop.mm, b1.dop.yyyy);
printf("%d\t%s\t%s\t%f\t%d-%d-%d\n",b2.id,b2.title,b2.author,b2.
    price,b2.dop.dd, b2.dop.mm, b2.dop.yyyy);
}
```

Output

```
Enter id, title, author and price of the first Book
1 C++ Kunal 900
Enter the date of publishing of the first Book(dd mm yyyy)
1 10 1984
Enter id, title, author and price of the second Book
2 Java Jack 950
Enter the date of publishing of the second Book(dd mm yyyy)
12 6 2008
The Book details are
1       C++     Kunal   900.000000      1-10-1984
2       Java    Jack    950.000000      12-6-2008
```

9.5   Structures and Pointers

Let us consider a structure Book defined as below:

```
struct Book
{
int id;
char title[100];
char author[100];
float price;
};
```

We can also define pointers that can point to objects of a structure. Recall from Chapter 8 that, the data type of the pointer must be same as the data type of the object to which the pointer points to. As an example, let us create a pointer p to point to object of structure Book. As the pointer is required to point to Book object the data type of the pointer must also be Book as seen in the statement below:

```
struct Book *p;
```

Let us create two objects of structure Book as b1 and b2 by using the following statement:

```
struct Book b1, b2;
```

The objects b1 and b2 will be created in memory and we assume the address of object b1 as 8000 and the address of object b2 as 9000 which is shown in the Figure 9.25.

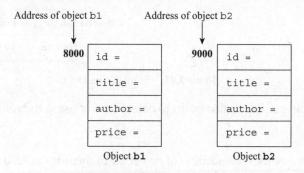

Figure 9.25: Objects b1 and b2

We can make a pointer p to point to any of these objects. This means that the pointer p can hold the address of object b1 or b2. Let us store the address of object b1 inside a pointer p, which can be done by using the following statement:

```
p=&b1;
```

Hence, the pointer p will point to object b1 as shown in the Figure 9.26. The figure assumes that the address of object b1 in memory is 8000 which is now present in pointer p.

We can access the members of object b1 by using a pointer p with an 'arrow' operator ->. The syntax to access member of an object using a pointer which points to it, is as shown below:

```
Pointer->Member;
```

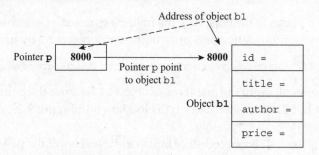

Figure 9.26: Pointer p pointing to object b1

This means that, the following `scanf()` statement can be used to input the members `id`, `title`, `author`, and `price` of the `Book` object `b1` by using the pointer `p`:

```
scanf("%d%s%s%f",&p->id,p->title,p->author,&p->price);
```

The above statement will input the members of object `b1` because the pointer `p` is currently pointing to object `b1`. The state of object `b1` is as shown in Figure 9.27, assuming sample input values.

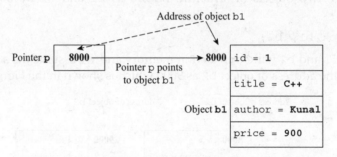

Figure 9.27: State of object `b1`

The pointer `p` can similarly, also point to object `b2` by using the following statement:

```
p=&b2;
```

The Figure 9.28 assumes that the address of object `b2` in memory is 9000 and which is now present in pointer `p`.

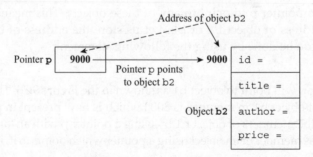

Figure 9.28: Pointer p pointing to object b2

As the pointer `p` points to the object `b2`, the following `scanf()` statement can be used to input the members `id`, `title`, `author`, and `price` of the `Book` object `b2` by using the pointer `p`:

```
scanf("%d%s%s%f",&p->id,p->title,p->author,&p->price);
```

The above statement will input the members of object `b2` because the pointer `p` is currently pointing to object `b2`. The state of object `b2` is as shown in Figure 9.29, assuming sample input values.

The following is the full source code that inputs the members of the two objects and prints them by using a single pointer `p`. It is important to understand that, at a time, the pointer `p` can only point to one of the objects, hence we should make sure that the details of object `b1` are printed on the screen before we make the pointer `p` point to object `b2`, as seen in the code below:

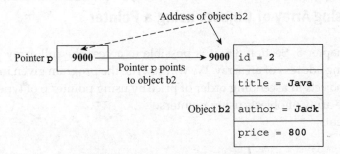

Figure 9.29: Pointer p pointing to object b2

```c
#include<stdio.h>
struct Book
{
int id;
char title[100];
char *author[100];
float price;
};
void main()
{
Book b1, b2;
/*Pointer p of type Book*/
Book *p;
/*p points to the first object b1*/
p=&b1;
printf("Enter id, title, author and price of the first Book\n");
scanf("%d%s%s%f",&p->id,p->title,p->author,&p->price);
printf("The details of the first book are\n");
printf("%d\t%s\t%s\t%f\n",p->id,p->title,p->author,p->price);
/*p points to the second object b2*/
p=&b2;
printf("Enter id, title, author and price of the first Book\n");
scanf("%d%s%s%f",&p->id,p->title,p->author,&p->price);
printf("The details of the first book are\n");
printf("%d\t%s\t%s\t%f\n",p->id,p->title,p->author,p->price);
}
```

Output

```
Enter id, title, author and price of the first Book
1 C++ Kunal 900
The details of the first book are
1       C++     Kunal   900.000000
Enter id, title, author and price of the first Book
2 Java Jack 800
The details of the first book are
2       Java    Jack    800.000000
```

9.6 Accessing Array of Objects using a Pointer

Recall from Chapter 8, Section 8.6, it is possible to access the full array using a pointer holds the starting address of an array. We will rewrite the program given in Section 9.3.1 to arrange Book objects in ascending order of price by using pointer p of type Book, to show accessing of the array of objects using pointers.

The statements,

```
struct Book *p;
p=&b[0];
```

create a Book type pointer named as p and store the starting address of array b in p. This means following two things, as per our discussion in Chapter 8, Section 8.6

1. Every object b[i] in an array can be accessed using a pointer as *(p+i)
2. Address of an object b[i] can be obtained by an expression (p+i)

We know from Section 9.5 that, the syntax to access member of an object using a pointer which points to it, is as shown in the following:

```
Pointer->Member;
```

Note that the left-hand side of the -> operator is a pointer name without a * operator. This means that the left-hand side of an arrow operator must be an address of the object whose member is required to be accessed using the pointer. Therefore, to access the members of object b[i] using a pointer, you will need the address of object b[i], which is (p+i). Hence, the members id, title, author, and price of object b[i] can be accessed by using pointer p as:

```
(p+i)->id
(p+i)->title
(p+i)->author
(p+i)->price
```

If you need to obtain the address of any of the members, you can get it by applying an & operator to the expression which accesses the member. For example, address of member id of object b[i] by using pointer p can be obtained as:

```
&((p+i)->id)
```

You can also rewrite the statement by avoiding the outer parenthesis because the priority of -> is anyway greater than the priority of &, but we have added them to make the expression more readable. Technically, this expression can also be written as:

```
&(p+i)->id
```

The following for loop, inputs the details of n Book objects in array b:

```
for(i=0;i<=n-1;i++)
```

```
{
scanf("%d%s%s%f",&((p+i)->id),(p+i)->title,(p+i)->
author,&((p+i)->price));
}
```

When compared to Section 9.3.1, we have applied following replacements to the `scanf()` statement:

1. `&b[i].id` is replaced with `&((p+i)->id)` and `&b[i].price` is replaced with `&((p+i)->price)`

2. `b[i].title` is replaced with `(p+i)->title` and `b[i].author` is replaced with `(p+i)->author`

Now, let's focus on the sorting logic. The `if` block in Section 9.3.1, has an condition written as follows:

`b[i].price>b[j].price`

We have already mentioned that any member can be accessed using a pointer and `->` operator by putting the address of relevant object on the left of `->`. Hence, we rewrite this condition as follows:

`(p+i)->price > (p+j)->price`

Also, as mentioned in the beginning of this section, the object `b[i]` can be accessed as `*(p+i)` and hence swapping logic in Section 9.3.1 can be rewritten by using pointer `p` as in the following:

```
t=*(p+i); /* Equivalent to t=b[i]*/
*(p+i) =*(p+j); /* Equivalent to b[i]=b[j]*/
*(p+j)=t; /* Equivalent to b[j]=t*/
```

The following is the full source code which sorts the `Book` objects in ascending order of price using pointers:

```
#include<stdio.h>
struct Book
{
int id;
char title[100];
char author[100];
float price;
};
void main()
{
int n,i,j;
struct Book b[100];
```

```
struct Book t;
/*Create a pointer of type Book*/
struct Book *p;
/*Store the starting address of array b in pointer p*/
p=&b[0]; /* or p=b */
printf("How many Books?\n");
scanf("%d",&n);
printf("Enter the details of %d Books\n",n);
    for(i=0;i<=n-1;i++)
    {
    scanf("%d%s%s%f",&((p+i)->id),(p+i)->title,(p+i)->
    author,&((p+i)->price));
    }
    for(i=0;i<=n-2;i++)
    {
       for(j=i+1;j<=n-1;j++)
          {
              if((p+i)->price>(p+j)->price)
                 {
                 t=*(p+i);
                 *(p+i) =*(p+j);
                 *(p+j)=t;
                 }
          }
    }
printf("The Ascending order is \n");
    for(i=0;i<=n-1;i++)
    {
printf("%d\t%s\t%s\t%f\n",(p+i)->id,(p+i)->title,(p+i)->
    author,(p+i)->price);
    }
}
```

Output

```
How many Books?
3
Enter the details of 3 Books
1 C++ Kunal 900
2 Java Jack 800
3 Cobol John 200
The Ascending order is
3       Cobol   John    200.000000
2       Java    Jack    800.000000
1       C++     Kunal   900.000000
```

9.7 Passing Object as an Argument to a Function

Similar to any other variable, we can also pass the structure variable as an argument to the function. The following is the code that defines a function `display()`, to print the details of each of the `Book` object passed to it as an argument.

```
#include<stdio.h>
struct Book
{
int id;
char title[100];
char author[100];
float price;
};
void display(Book t)
{
printf("%d\t%s\t%s\t%f\n",t.id,t.title,t.author,t.price);
}
void main()
{
struct Book b1,b2;
printf("Enter id, title, author and price of the first Book\n");
scanf("%d%s%s%f",&b1.id,b1.title,b1.author,&b1.price);
printf("Enter id, title, author and price of the second Book\n");
scanf("%d%s%s%f",&b2.id,b2.title,b2.author,&b2.price);
printf("The Book details are\n");
display(b1);
display(b2);
}
```

Output

```
Enter id, title, author and price of the first Book
1 C++ Kunal 900
Enter id, title, author and price of the second Book
2 Java Jack 800
The Book details are
1       C++       Kunal     900.000000
2       Java      Jack      800.000000
```

The statement,

```
display(b1);
```

invokes a function `display()` by passing the object b1 as an argument to it. Thus, the actual argument b1 is initialized to a formal argument t as shown in Figure 9.30. Hence the members of object b1 can be accessed by using object t in the `display()` function. The statement:

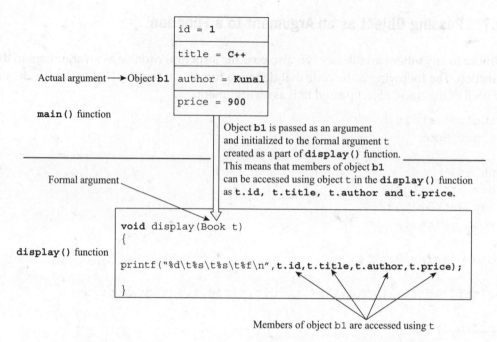

Figure 9.30: Calling display() function by passing the object b1

```
printf("%d\t%s\t%s\t%f\n",t.id,t.title,t.author,t.price);
```

written inside the display() function will actually print the member values of object b1, because it is the object which is passed as an argument to display().

Similarly, the function call,

```
display(b2);
```

calls the function display() by passing the object b2 as an argument to it. Thus, the actual argument b2 is now initialize to a formal argument t. Hence the printf() statement inside the function this time prints the members of object b2 on the computer screen.

NOTES

In the given program, we have passed object by value. When an object is relatively large in size, passing an object by reference is always a better option than passing it by value, unless absolutely necessary for the program logic to pass it by value. This is because call by value creates another copy of the same object which results into considerable utilization of memory as well as time during the program execution.

Instead of creating duplicate objects, you can pass an object by reference by creating the formal argument t as a reference of type Book rather than object of type Book as shown below

```
void display(Book& t)  ←──────────────  t is a reference variable which refers to
{                                          the Book object passed by the caller

printf("%d\t%s\t%s\t%f\n",t.id,t.title,t.author,t.price);
}
```

Remember, call by reference is only supported by C++ compilers if you are working with C compilers you can alternately use call by address by creating t as a pointer of type Book rather than reference of type Book.

9.8 Difference between Structure and Union

Union is also a template used for creating a 'user-defined data type' like a structure with only difference that union facilitates the programmer to create members that share a common memory space unlike structures wherein each of the members are stored in a separate memory space. The syntax of defining a union is exactly similar to that of defining a structure except the keyword `struct` is replaced by `union` as shown in the Figure 9.31.

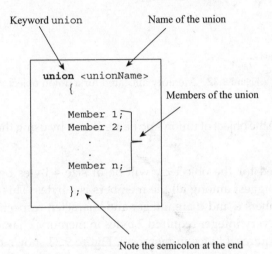

Figure 9.31: Syntax for creating an union

As unions facilitate sharing of memory among its members, the memory allocated for a union object will be exactly same as the memory required by the member of the biggest size defined in the union. Hence, the amount of memory for a union object is calculated as below:

```
sizeof(UnionObject) = Max (sizeof(member1), sizeof(member2)............
   sizeof(memberN))
```

where union has n members defined as shown in the Figure 9.31.

This means that, we will not be able to simultaneously access and store the values of two different member variables defined inside the union. This is because, the value stored for a particular member would overwrite the value of some other member that was previously stored in the memory of the union object.

As an example, let us create a union named as Abc with members a, b, and c of type integer, float and character, respectively (Figure 9.31). The definition of the union is as in the following:

```
union Abc
{
int a;
float b;
char c;
};
```

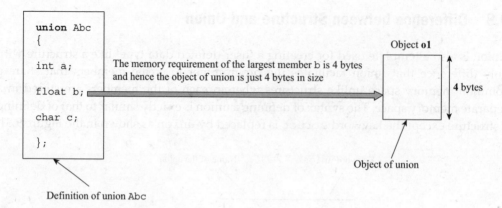

Figure 9.32   Memory allocated for a union object

We can now create the object of union Abc named as o1 by using the following statement:

Abc o1;

The memory allocated for the object o1 will be of size 4 bytes because the size of the member b which is biggest among all the members is 4 bytes. This is because member b is float whereas members a and c are integer and character, respectively. (As we recollect from Chapter 2 that every integer required 2 bytes in memory, character requires 1 byte in memory and float requires 4 bytes in memory). Figure 9.33 shows the memory allocated for a union object.

We can now initialize and store the value of any one member at time in the object memory. Let us initialize the value of integer member a with 10 as shown in the following statement:

o1.a=10;

As the member a is of type integer, it will occupy the first 2 bytes in the total object memory of 4 bytes which is allocated for object o1 as shown in the Figure 9.33.

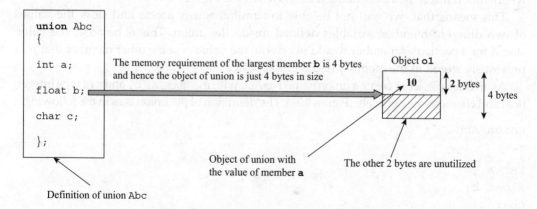

Figure 9.33:   Initialization of member variable a

Now, if we initialize the value of member b of an object o1 then the value of member a which is already contained in the memory will be overwritten. This means that, we must be sure that, we no more need the value stored for the previous member when we initialize a value for the new member of the union. To understand this constraint, let us store a value of 25.9 inside a union object o1 by initializing the floating point member b using the following statement:

```
o1.b=25.9;
```

This means that, the value of member a which was stored before in the memory will be overwritten, thereby storing the value of member b in the object memory as shown in the Figure 9.34.

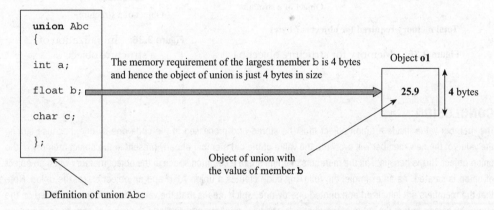

Figure 9.34: Storing value of member b

Similarly, initializing the value of character c for object o1 would overwrite the existing value of float b stored in the object memory. This means that, unions will have a limitation that the values for all the members cannot be stored simultaneously inside the object memory of union due to the memory constraint.

Further, if Abc would have been a structure, then all the members can be stored simultaneously in the object memory of a structure because the total memory allocated for a structure is the addition of the memory required by each of its members. Hence, each member of the structure has an independent separate space assigned in the object memory of the structure object which is as calculated given below:

```
sizeof(StructureObject) = sizeof(member1) + sizeof(member2)... +
    sizeof(memberN)
```

Therefore, if Abc would have been a structure and then the memory allocated for the structure object o1 is as shown in the Figure 9.35.

Hence, we can now initialize and store all the members of the structure simultaneously in the memory, using the following statements:

```
o1.a=10;
o1.b=25.9;
o1.c='$';
```

The initialization of the structure object o1 is as shown in the Figure 9.36.

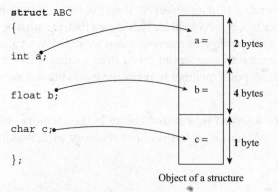

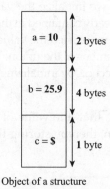

Object of a structure

Total memory required for object = 7 bytes

Figure 9.35: Memory for structure object o1

Object of a structure

Figure 9.36: Initialization of a structure object

CONCLUSION

The member value inside a union object must be stored and processed in the code one-by-one, because storing the value of the new member will overwrite the value of the old member already present in the object memory of the union object. This is because, all the members of union share a common space in the object memory when an object of union is created. As an example, the following code creates a union Abc and an object o1 of the union. Note that the members are initialized and printed one-by-one, which means that, the value of member a is printed on the computer screen before the value of member b is actually initialized and similarly, the value of member b is printed on the screen before the value of member c is initialized.

```c
#include<stdio.h>
union Abc
{
int a;
float b;
char c;
};
void main()
{
Abc o1;
o1.a=10;
printf("The value of member a is %d\n",o1.a);
o1.b=25.9;
printf("The value of member b is %f\n",o1.b);
o1.c='$';
printf("The value of member c is %c\n",o1.c);
}
```

Output

```
The value of member a is 10
The value of member b is 25.900000
The value of member c is $
```

Solved Example 9.1

Write a program to create a structure `Employee` with three members `name`, `gender`, and `salary`. Store the details about n-Employee objects in computer memory. Also determine the following information:

1. List of all the MALE Employees in ascending order of salary.
2. List of all the FEMALE Employees in ascending order of salary.
3. Calculate the PERCENTAGE of female Employees in the organization.

```c
#include<stdio.h>
struct Employee
{
char name[100];
char gender;
int salary;
};
void main()
{
struct Employee e[100];
struct Employee t;
int n,i,j, count_male=0,count_female=0;
float female_ratio;
printf("Enter the total number of objects to be stored in the
    array\n");
scanf("%d",&n);
printf("Enter the name, gender and salary of %d employees\n",n);
    for(i=0;i<=n-1;i++)
    {
    printf("Enter the name, gender and salary of Employee
    %d\n",i);
    scanf("%s %c %d",e[i].name,&e[i].gender,&e[i].salary);
    }
for(i=0;i<=n-2;i++)
{
    for(j=i+1;j<=n-1;j++)
      {
          if(e[i].salary<e[j].salary)
```

```
            {
            t=e[i];
            e[i] =e[j];
            e[j]=t;
            }
        }
}
printf("List of Male Employees is as below\n");
for(i=0;i<=n-1;i++)
{
    if(e[i].gender=='m')
        {
printf("%s\t%c\t%d\n",e[i].name,e[i].gender,e[i].salary);
count_male++;
        }
}
printf("List of Female Employees is as below\n");
for(i=0;i<=n-1;i++)
{
    if(e[i].gender=='f')
        {
printf("%s\t%c\t%d\n",e[i].name,e[i].gender,e[i].salary);
count_female++;
        }
}
female_ratio = (float)count_female/(count_male+count_female);
printf("The percentage of female employees is
    %f\n",female_ratio*100);
}
```

Output

```
Enter the total number of objects to be stored in the array
5
Enter the name, gender and salary of 5 employees
Enter the name, gender and salary of Employee 0
John m 4000
Enter the name, gender and salary of Employee 1
Jack m 8000
Enter the name, gender and salary of Employee 2
Tina f 7500
Enter the name, gender and salary of Employee 3
Jazz f 9000
Enter the name, gender and salary of Employee 4
Jill m 5000
```

```
List of Male Employees is as below
Jack     m       8000
Jill     m       5000
John     m       4000
List of Female Employees is as below
Jazz     f       9000
Tina     f       7500
The percentage of female employees is 40.000001
```

Solved Example 9.2

Write a program to store information about n students in the computer memory. Following information is required to be stored for each student:

1. Name of the student
2. Marks obtained by the student
3. Date of birth of the student
4. Roll number of the student

Generate following data as an output of the program

1. List of students sorted as per AGE in descending order
2. List of students sorted as per MARKS in ascending order
3. List of students sorted as per NAME in ascending order

```c
#include<stdio.h>
#include<string.h>
struct Date
{
int dd;
int mm;
int yyyy;
};
struct Student
{
char name[100];
int marks;
int roll_no;
Date dob;
};
/* We define a function isGreater to compare two date of births*/
int isGreater(Date d1,Date d2);
void display(Student[],int);
void main()
```

```
{
Student s[100];
int n,i,j;
    Student t;
printf("Enter the total number of objects to be stored in the
    array\n");
scanf("%d",&n);
printf("Enter the details %d students\n",n);
for(i=0;i<=n-1;i++)
{
printf("******************Input Student Object********************
    ********\n");
printf("Enter name, marks and roll_no of the student\n");
scanf("%s%d%d",s[i].name,&s[i]. marks,&s[i].roll_no);
printf("Enter date of birth of %s (in format dd mm yyyy separated
    by space)\n",s[i].name);
scanf("%d%d%d",&s[i].dob.dd,&s[i].dob.mm,&s[i].dob.yyyy);
}
printf("***********LIST OF STUDENTS IN DESCENDING ORDER OF
    AGE*********\n");
for(i=0;i<=n-2;i++)
{
    for(j=i+1;j<=n-1;j++)
      {
          if(isGreater(s[i].dob,s[j].dob))
              {
              t=s[i];
              s[i] =s[j];
              s[j]=t;
              }
      }
}
display(s,n);
printf("***********LIST OF STUDENTS IN ASCENDING ORDER OF
    MARKS*********\n");
for(i=0;i<=n-2;i++)
{
    for(j=i+1;j<=n-1;j++)
      {
          if(s[i].marks>s[j].marks)
              {
              t=s[i];
              s[i] =s[j];
              s[j]=t;
```

```
            }
        }
}
display(s,n);
printf("**********LIST OF STUDENTS IN ASCENDING ORDER OF
    NAME*********\n");
for(i=0;i<=n-2;i++)
{
    for(j=i+1;j<=n-1;j++)
        {
            if(strcmp(s[i].name,s[j].name)>0)
                {
                t=s[i];
                s[i] =s[j];
                s[j]=t;
                }
        }
}
display(s,n);
}
int isGreater(Date d1,Date d2)
{
    if(d1.yyyy>d2.yyyy)
    {
    return 1;
    }
    else if(d1.yyyy<d2.yyyy)
    {
    return 0;
    }
    else
    {
      if(d1.mm>d2.mm)
      {
      return 1;
      }
      else if(d1.mm<d2.mm)
      {
      return 0;
      }
      else
      {
          if(d1.dd>d2.dd)
          {
```

```
            return 1;
            }
        else if(d1.dd<d2.dd)
            {
            return 0;
            }
        }
    }
return 0;
}
void display(Student s[],int n)
{
    int i;
    for(i=0;i<=n-1;i++)
    {
    printf("%s\t%d\t%d\t%d-%d-%d\n",s[i].name,s[i].marks,s[i].
    roll_no,s[i].dob.dd,s[i].dob.mm,s[i].dob.yyyy);
    }
}
```

Output

```
Enter the total number of objects to be stored in the array
4
Enter the details 4 students
******************Input Student Object***************************
Enter name, marks and roll_no of the student
John 90 1
Enter date of birth of John (in format dd mm yyyy separated by space)
1 2 1976
******************Input Student Object***************************
Enter name, marks and roll_no of the student
Jack 50 2
Enter date of birth of Jack (in format dd mm yyyy separated by space)
12 4 2000
******************Input Student Object***************************
Enter name, marks and roll_no of the student
Jill 60 3
Enter date of birth of Jill (in format dd mm yyyy separated by space)
11 6 1999
******************Input Student Object***************************
Enter name, marks and roll_no of the student
Tina 55 4
Enter date of birth of Tina (in format dd mm yyyy separated by space)
9 5 2002
```

```
***********LIST OF STUDENTS IN DESCENDING ORDER OF AGE*********
John      90      1       1-2-1976
Jill      60      3       11-6-1999
Jack      50      2       12-4-2000
Tina      55      4       9-5-2002
***********LIST OF STUDENTS IN ASCENDING ORDER OF MARKS*********
Jack      50      2       12-4-2000
Tina      55      4       9-5-2002
Jill      60      3       11-6-1999
John      90      1       1-2-1976
***********LIST OF STUDENTS IN ASCENDING ORDER OF NAME*********
Jack      50      2       12-4-2000
Jill      60      3       11-6-1999
John      90      1       1-2-1976
Tina      55      4       9-5-2002
```

Solved Example 9.3

Write a program to create a structure `Employee` with three members `name`, `designation` and `salary`. Store the details about n-Employee objects in computer memory. Print the details of the employee with the highest salary.

```c
#include<stdio.h>
struct Employee
{
char name[100];
char designation[100];
int salary;
};
void main()
{
Employee e[100];
Employee  t;
int n,i,j,max;
printf("Enter the total number of objects to be stored in the
    array\n");
scanf("%d",&n);
printf("Enter the name, designation and salary of each of the
    employees\n");
for(i=0;i<=n-1;i++)
{
scanf("%s%s%d",e[i].name,e[i].designation,&e[i].salary);
}
```

```
max=e[0].salary;
t=e[0];
for(i=1;i<=n-1;i++)
{
    if(e[i].salary>max)
    {
    max=e[i].salary;
    t=e[i];
    }
}
printf("The details of the Employee with highest salary are: \n");
printf("%s\t%s\t%d\n",t.name,t.designation,t.salary);
}
```

Output

```
Enter the total number of objects to be stored in the array
3
Enter the name, designation and salary of each of the employees
John Trainee 4000
Jack Director 25000
Jill Manager 15000
The details of the Employee with highest salary are:
Jack     Director        25000
```

Error Finding Exercise

Given are some programs which may or may not contain errors. Correct the error if exist in the code and determine the output.

Program 1

```
#include<stdio.h>
struct Student
{
int roll_no;
char name[100];
};
void main()
{
Student s1;
printf("Enter the data about a student\n");
scanf("%s",s1);
printf("The student details are"<<endl;
```

```
printf("%s",s1);
}
```

Program 2

```c
#include<stdio.h>
struct Car
{
int id;
char name[]="MyCar";
};
void main()
{
Car c1;
printf("Enter the data about a Car\n");
scanf("%d %s",c1.id,c1.name);
printf("The data about a Car is\n");
printf("%d %s",c1.id,c1.name);
}
```

Program 3

```c
#include<stdio.h>
struct Number
{
int a,b;
int c=a+b;
};
void main()
{
Number n1;
printf("Enter the data for the object n1\n");
scanf("%d %d",&n1.a,&n1.b);
printf("The result of addition is %d\n", n1.c);
}
```

Program 4

```c
#include<stdio.h>
struct DATA
{
int a;
};
void main()
```

```
{
DATA d1,d2,d3;
printf("Enter two numbers\n");
scanf("%d %d",&d1.a,&d2.a);
d3=d1+d2;
printf("The result of addition is %d\n", d3.a);
}
```

Program 5

```
/*Assume sample input values to justify your answer*/
    #include<stdio.h>
    struct DATA
    {
    int a;
    };
    void main()
    {
    DATA d1,d2;
    printf("Enter two numbers\n");
    scanf("%d %d",&d1.a,&d2.a);
      if(d1==d2)
      {
      printf("Two objects are same");
      }
      else
      {
      printf("Two objects are different");
      }
    }
```

Quiz

1. Consider a structure Abc defined as below:
   ```
   struct Abc
   {
   int a;
   char b;
   float c;
   };
   ```

   The size of each object of a structure Abc will be:
   (a) 2 bytes   (b) 1 byte   (c) 4 bytes   (d) 7 bytes

2. Which of the following statement is correct?
   (a) Memory for each of the members of a structure is allocated when a structure is defined.
   (b) Memory for each of the members of a structure is allocated when an object of a structure is created.
   (c) Memory for each of the members of a structure is allocated when the members are initialized to some value.
   (d) None of the above statement is true.

3. Consider the union DATA defined as below:

```
union DATA
{
int a[100];
char b;
float c;
};
```

   The size of each object of the union DATA will be:
   (a) 100 bytes   (c) 1 bytes   (e) 2 bytes
   (b) 200 bytes   (d) 4 bytes

4. If a structure and a union have an identical definition, and if s1 is an object of a structure and u1 is an object of a union then:
   (a) `sizeof(s1)>sizeof(u1)`   (d) `sizeof(s1)<=sizeof(u1)`
   (b) `sizeof(s1)<sizeof(u1)`   (e) `sizeof(s1)!=sizeof(u1)`
   (c) `sizeof(s1)>=sizeof(u1)`

5. Which of the following statement is correct?
   (a) C/C++ does not support forward referencing, this mean that a structure should always be defined before the object of a structure is created.
   (b) A structure definition cannot be included inside a function.
   (c) A structure object cannot be created as a global variable.
   (d) A structure object cannot be passed as an argument to the function.
   (e) None of the above.

6. Consider the following structure definition:

```
struct Employee
{
int id;
char name[100];
Employee e[100];
};
```

   Which of the following statement is correct?
   (a) This is a compilation error because the array of Employee (which is named as e) cannot be a member of the structure Employee itself.
   (b) The structure definition is correct because C/C++ supports nesting of structure objects.
   (c) This is a runtime error.
   (d) Both A and C are true.

Review Questions

1. Write a short note on structures. Explain the syntax for creating structures with an example.
2. Write a program for storing data about n-Accounts in the computer memory. For each account store the customer name, balance and the account type in the system. Ensure that account type can be set to "saving" or "current" only.
3. Write a program to store information about Insurance policies in the computer memory, for each of the policy store the following information:
   (a) Type of the policy (Life insurance, travel insurance, etc.)
   (b) Annual premium of the policy
   (c) Grade of the policy
   (d) Name of the policy holder
   Grade of the policy must be set to "Gold" if premium is greater than 10,000, should be set to "Platinum" if the premium is greater than 20,000. For any premium which is less than or equal to 10,000 the grade of the policy must be set to "Silver".
   Store the details about n-Policies in the memory and generate the following lists:
   1. List of all the Silver policies in ascending order of premium.
   2. List of all the Gold policies in ascending order of premium.
   3. List of all the Platinum policies in ascending order of premium.
4. Write a function `average()` to find the average salary of the Employees stored in the system. The function must take array of structure objects as a parameter and return a floating point value which is the average of all the salaries of the `Employee` objects stored in the array.
5. Explain the process to access the members of a structure object using a pointer with an appropriate example.
6. Explain the similarities and differences between structures and unions with an example.
7. Write a program to store the definition of a cube in a computer memory. A cube is to be defined as a collection of 3 dimensional points in the Cartesian co-ordinate system. For each of the three dimensional points store x, y and z coordinate values.
8. What do you mean by 'user-defined data type'. Explain the advantages of creating a 'user-defined data type' in a program.

Dynamic Memory Allocation in C++

10.1 Overview

The memory that is allocated at the time of compilation of a program is called as **static memory**. The compiler allocates the memory for all the variables, arrays, and objects created by the programmer, hence the memory allocation is by default **static** in C++. One of the major limitations of the static memory allocation is that, the amount of memory required by the program must be exactly known at the time of compilation, to avoid **over allocation** or **under allocation** of the required space. However, in many cases the programmer might not know the exact amount of memory to be allocated for implementing the functionality. Hence, in the case of **static memory allocation** the programmer might **overestimate** the actual amount of memory required by the program at run time. Therefore, the programmer may end up allocating the memory which is much higher than the actual amount of memory required when the program runs. This will result into large wastage of storage space in the primary memory of the computer system. On the other hand, it is also possible that the programmer **underestimates** the amount of memory required by the program at run time, then the program may crash at run time because of lack of storage space allocated by the programmer in the primary memory, thereby resulting into an 'out of memory' error.

As an example to understand **static memory** allocation, let us create an array of size 3 by using the following statement:

```
float a[3];
```

As each floating point element requires 4 bytes in memory, compiler will allocate the memory for array a as $4 \times 3 = 12$ bytes. Recall that, we cannot create an array by indirectly specifying the size of array in terms of another variable. For instance, let us create a variable n initialized to a value 3 and then create an array a with the size of array specified in terms of n as follows:

```
int n=3;

float a[n]; /*ERROR: value of n is not known at the time of
    compilation*/
```

Logically, the statements float a[3]; and float a[n]; will have a same meaning because the value of variable n is initialized as 3. However, the later statement will not compile because the value of variable n will be initialized only when the program starts running and whereas the compiler allocates the memory for the array at the time of compilation. This means that the exact size of the array a will not be known at the time of compilation of the statement float a[n]; as the value of n is not known at the time of compilation.

However, if it is the case that, the value of variable n which represents the size of the array is to be actually calculated at runtime, it is the genuine requirement that the size of the array a is to be specified in terms of a variable n. As this is not possible, the programmer may overestimate the value of variable n, thereby declaring the array by assuming some maximum limit of variable n, say 100 using a following statement:

float a[100];

This means that the array a can store at the most 100 floating point values inside it and the elements of the array will therefore be indexed from 0 to 99 as shown in the Figure 10.1.

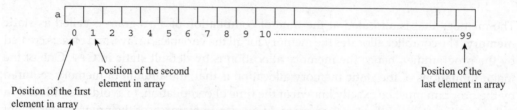

Figure 10.1: Array of size 100

Now, if the actual size of the array required is much lesser than 100, say the size of the array(n) which is calculated at runtime is just 4, then this means that only first 4 locations of the array will store valid data values and the remaining part of the memory will be unutilized as shown in the Figure 10.2.

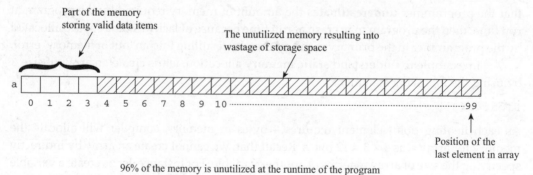

96% of the memory is unutilized at the runtime of the program

Figure 10.2: Unutilized memory space in array

Hence, wastage of storage space is one of the major drawbacks of **static** memory allocation.

On the other hand it may be a possibility that the programmer **underestimates** the actual size of the array required at the run time of the program. This may be the case when the required size of the array calculated at run time is greater than 100. This means that, we realize at **run time** that the number of data items to be stored in the array is greater than 100, however we have allocated a space only for 100 elements in the memory while declaring array a. Hence the program may malfunction thereby going 'out of memory' while storing the data elements into the array.

These drawbacks of static memory allocation can be avoided by allocating the memory at run time of the program when the exact amount of the memory required is precisely determined. The memory that is allocated at the run time of the program is called as **dynamic memory**. In this chapter, we discuss the details of **'dynamic memory allocation'** supported in C++.

NOTES

This chapter discusses dynamic memory allocation in C++ style and the programs written in this chapter will not compile with C compilers. Although, C supports dynamic memory allocation we do not discuss conventional C style syntax in this chapter as it is too complex compared to what C++ offers. Hence, you must have a C++ compiler to execute programs given in this chapter and the chapters ahead. We have used `cout` instead of `printf()` statement in all the programs from this chapter onwards, because the programs are no more generic from now on. Reason we have used `printf()`/`scanf()` functions in most of the other programs from Chapters 1 to 9 is that `printf()`/`scanf()` are supported by C as well as C++. Hence most of the programs from Chapters 1 to 9 can work on C as well as C++ compilers unless mentioned otherwise. However, programs from this chapter onwards are exclusive to C++, so you will find that we have used `cout`/`cin` statements instead of `printf()`/`scanf()` statements in the programs ahead. This also eliminates complexities associated with control strings while discussing complex topics as `cout`/`cin` do not need control strings.

10.2 Dynamic Memory Management in C++

C++ supports operators `new` and `delete` for supporting dynamic memory management. The operator `new` is used to allocate the memory at the run time whereas the operator `delete` is used to free the memory that is allocated dynamically. Note that all the dynamic memory objects are allocated in a part of RAM called heap. Also, it is important to note that the memory that is allocated at the runtime of the program will be unnamed unlike the static memory where each object allocated has a name in memory. Hence, the dynamic memory allocated can only be accessed by creating a pointer of a specific type that points to the allocated memory. The operators `new` and `delete` can work with the primitive data types, array types as well as object types in C++. This means that we must also create the pointers of the respective types if we want to perform dynamic allocations for these types. The pointers can point to the memory allocated in heap and we can therefore access the unnamed memory by using a pointer. Let us discuss the usage of the operators `new` and `delete` for each of these types:

Why do we say that dynamic memory is unnamed?   **?**

This means that a memory that is allocated dynamically using a keyword new will not have any name unlike the static memory. For example, let us consider the below C++ statement:

`int a=10;`

Here, compiler allocates a static memory of 2 bytes named as a and stores a value 10 in that memory. Note that, every variable in C++ must have a name. Hence, we say that static memory is always a named memory location. However, in case of dynamic memory allocation, the memory allocated will not have any name and hence we will need to create a pointer that points to the dynamically allocated memory. Therefore, we can access the dynamically allocated memory only using a pointer.

10.2.1 Allocating dynamic memory for primitive types

As discussed before, the operator new is used to allocate memory at the run time of the program. The following is the syntax for using operator new in the code:

```
pointer=new <dataType>;
```

The operator new will allocate the required memory for the data type specified, in the heap space. The address of the memory allocated will be returned in the pointer, hence the programmer can now access the value of the memory location by using a pointer. For example, given that p is an integer type pointer than the following statement will allocate the memory of 2 bytes for storing an integer value at run time.

```
p=new int;
```

Assuming the starting address of the newly allocated integer as 1000, the pointer p will point to the newly allocated memory as shown in the Figure 10.3.

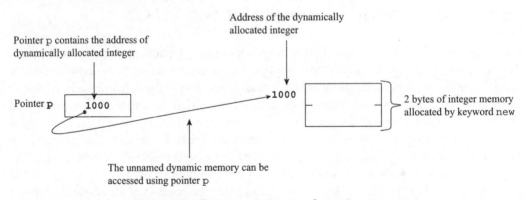

Figure 10.3: Pointer pointing to a dynamic memory

This means that we can now access the memory allocated by applying an indirection operator (*) over the pointer p. Therefore, the following statement will store the integer value 10 inside the memory space allocated by the operator new as shown in the Figure 10.4.

```
*p=10;
```

The operator new can be similarly used to allocate dynamic memory for other primitive data types as shown in the Figure 10.5. Recall the data type of the pointer must be same as the data type of the memory that is allocated by using the operator new. For example, if the operator new allocates the memory of type double then the data type of the pointer which points to the allocated memory must also be double as shown in the Figure 10.5.

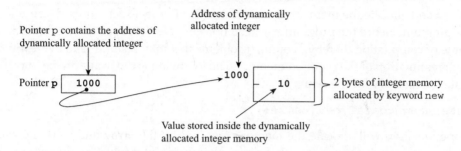

Figure 10.4: Pointer pointing to a dynamic memory

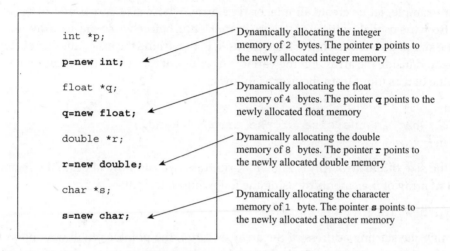

Figure 10.5: Usage of operator new

The following is an example that allocates one variable of type integer at runtime by using an operator new.

```
#include<iostream.h>
void main()
{
int *p;
/*pointer p points to a dynamically allocated memory*/
p=new int;
*p=10;
cout<<"The value stored inside the dynamic memory is " <<*p;
}
```

Output

```
The value stored inside the dynamic memory is 10
```

10.2.2   Allocating dynamic memory for array types

The operator new can also be used to allocate the memory required for an array at run time. The advantage of this is that, we can now calculate the amount of the memory required for the array and allocate the memory for an array only after its exact required size is known in the program. Hence the programmer need not estimate the required size of the array at the time of compilation thereby avoiding problems that may result due to **overestimation** or **underestimation** of the required memory. The following is the usage of operator new to allocate the memory for the array:

```
pointer=new <dataType>[<size>];
```

The operator new will allocate the memory required by the array and store the starting address of an array in the pointer. This means that the pointer will now point to the array that is allocated dynamically.

For example, let us create an integer type array whose size is required to be taken as input from the user at runtime of the program. Hence, before we create an array, let us first take the size of the array as input from the user, to determine the exact number of elements to be stored inside the array. Let the variable n represent the size of the array, then we take the value of n as input from the user as follows:

```
int n;
cout<<"What is the size of the array?"<<endl;
cin>>n;
```

Once the size of the array (n) is known at run time we can now allocate the memory to create an array of n-elements by using the following statement:

```
int *p=new int[n];
```

Assuming the starting address of the array as 1000, the pointer p will now point to the array of n-elements as shown in the Figure 10.6. The figure assumes value of variable n as 3 hence the array of 3 elements will be created in memory as shown.

Note that, the array allocated in dynamic fashion will be unnamed in the memory, hence each element of the array can only be accessed by using a pointer p. Recall from the Chapter 8 that the every element of the array can be accessed by using a pointer, if the pointer points to the starting address of the array in memory. This means that we can now access every i^{th} element of the array by using an expression *(p+i) as seen in the given code.

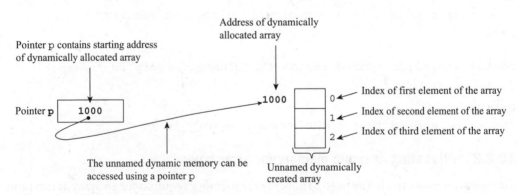

Figure 10.6: Pointer pointing at the array

The following is an example that creates an array in dynamic fashion and initializes each of the elements of that array.

```cpp
#include<iostream.h>
void main()
{
int *p;
int n,i;
cout<<"What is the size of the array?"<<endl;
cin>>n;
/*pointer p points to a dynamically allocated array*/
p=new int[n];
cout<<"Enter the "<<n<<" values to be stored inside the
    array"<<endl;
    for(i=0;i<=n-1;i++)
    {
    cin>>*(p+i);
    }
cout<<"The array elements are"<<endl;
    for(i=0;i<=n-1;i++)
    {
    cout<<*(p+i)<<endl;
    }
}
```

The first statement in `main ()` function creates a pointer p so that it can later point to the array of integers to be created dynamically. Further, we also take the variable n as input from the user, to determine the exact size of the array which is required to be created. Once the value of variable n is known, we are ready to create an array of n-elements as follows:

```cpp
p=new int[n];
```

The above statement will create an array of integers with a size n at run time and store the starting address of the array inside the pointer p. Hence, the pointer p will now start pointing to the first location of the array. Let us assume that the user enters the value of variable n as 3, then the statement will create an array of 3 elements in the memory as shown in the Figure 10.7. The figure assumes that the starting address of the array in memory is 1000. Further, every ith element of the array can now be accessed by using an expression * (p+i), as discussed in Chapter 8 of this textbook. This means that, we can

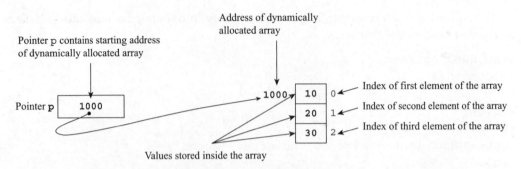

Figure 10.7: Pointer pointing to the array

now access the element at index 0 inside the array by using the expression *(p+0), the element at index 1 of the array using the expression *(p+1) and the element at index 2 of the array by using the expression *(p+2). Therefore, the following for loop takes every element of the array pointed by pointer p as input from the user.

```
for(i=0;i<=n-1;i++)
{
cin>>*(p+i);
}
```

Let us assume that the user enters the three values as 10, 20, and 30. Hence the value 10 will now be stored at position 0 of the array, value 20 will be stored at position 1 of the array and value 30 will be stored at the position 2 in the array as shown in the Figure 10.7.

Similarly, the next for loop prints all the elements of the array on the computer screen as seen in the code.

10.2.3 C++ program to arrange n-numbers in ascending order with dynamic memory allocation to store data elements: An example

As we have already implemented the solution for sorting integers in the Chapter 6, we will reuse the same solution to arrange numbers in ascending order by using **pointers and dynamic memory allocation**.

To sort of elements of array the code creates an integer type pointer p, so that p can hold the starting address of the array that we will be creating by using operator new:

```
int *p;
```

Further, as seen from the code, we also take the variable n as input from the user to determine the exact size of the array which is required to be created. Once the value of variable n is known, we can now create an array of n-elements as follows:

```
p=new int[n];
```

The above statement will create an array of integers with a size n in the computer memory and store the starting address of the array inside the pointer p. Hence, the pointer p will now start pointing to the first location of the array. The following code is same as that of Chapter 6, except every access to the ith element of the array is now done by using an expression $*(p+i)$. Remember, the dynamically created array in the given code is unnamed, so every element of the array can only be accessed by using a pointer as shown in the program. Therefore, following changes are required to be applied on the solution discussed in Chapter 6, to solve the same program by using pointers and dynamic memory allocation:

1. Create an array of integers by using operator new for dynamic memory allocation.
2. Note that the array created is unnamed so, every access to the ith element of the array should be done by using an expression $*(p+i)$ and every access to the jth element of the array should be done by using an expression $*(p+j)$.

The following is the full source code to arrange the n-numbers in ascending order by using dynamic memory allocation:

```cpp
#include<iostream.h>
void main()
{
int temp,n,i,j;
int *p;
cout<<"Enter length of the array";
cin>>n;
/*pointer p points to a dynamically allocated memory*/
p=new int[n];
cout<<"Enter array elements";
    for(i=0;i<=n-1;i++)
    {
    cin>>*(p+i); //Input each element of the array
    }
    for(i=0;i<=n-2;i++)
    {
      for(j=i+1;j<=n-1;j++)
      {
        if(*(p+i) > *(p+j))
        {
        temp=*(p+i);    //swap operation
        *(p+i)=*(p+j);
        *(p+j)=temp;
        }
      }
    }
cout<<"Ascending order is as below"<<endl;
    for(i=0;i<=n-1;i++)
    {
    cout<<*(p+i)<<endl; /*print each element of the array using
    pointer p*/
    }
}
```

Output

```
Enter Length of the array
5
Enter Array elements
30
10
20
6
50
Ascending order is as below
6
10
20
30
50
```

10.2.4 Allocating dynamic memory for object types

We can also create an object of a structure at runtime of the program by using a keyword new. The following is the syntax of creating a structure object dynamically in the program

```
pointer=new <StructureName>;
```

The statement will create an object of structure at run time and store the address of the object inside a pointer. Hence, the pointer will now start pointing to the structure object created in the heap. Also, as discussed in Chapter 9 of this textbook, we can access the members of the structure object by using an 'arrow operator' with the help of pointer. Remember, the type of the pointer must be same as that of the type defined by the structure, to make the pointer point to a structure object.

As an example, let us create a structure Employee with members id, name, and salary as follows:

```
struct Employee
{
int id;
char *name;
int salary;
};
```

We can now create an object of the structure Employee at run time by using the operator new. As this object is dynamically created it will be unnamed in the memory. Therefore, we create a pointer p as follows, such that the pointer can point to the object of structure Employee created at run time in the program.

```
Employee *p;
```

We now create an object of Employee by using the following statement:

```
p=new Employee;
```

Let the address of the newly created `Employee` object be `8000`, this means that the address `8000` will now be stored inside the pointer `p`, as shown in the Figure 10.8.

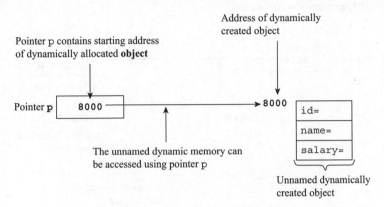

Figure 10.8: Pointer pointing to an object

We can now access the members of the `Employee` object by using the pointer p with an 'arrow operator' as shown in the following statements:

```
p->id=10;
p->name="John";
p->salary=5000;
```

The above statements will initialize the values `10`, `John` and `5000` to the members `id`, `name`, and `salary` of the `Employee` object, respectively. The initialization of the members is as shown in the Figure 10.9.

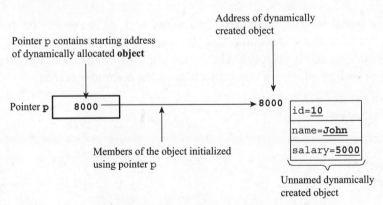

Figure 10.9: Initialization of the members

The following is the full C++ code that creates two objects of a structure `Employee` at the run time of the program. The program also initializes and prints all the members of these objects. The code creates two pointers of type `Employee` as p and q respectively such that each of the pointer points to one of the dynamically created objects as shown in the Figure 10.10.

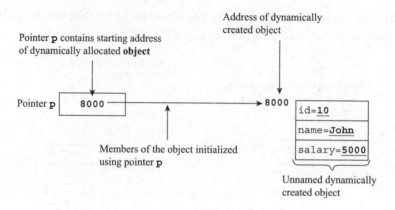

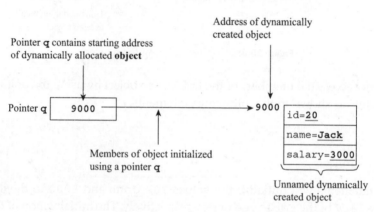

Figure 10.10: Initialization of the dynamically created objects

The code initializes the members (id, name, and salary) of the first object as (10, "John", 5000) and the members of the second object as (20, "Jack", 3000) by using the pointers p and q, respectively. Following the initialization, the program prints the data about each employee in tabular format on the computer screen.

```
#include<iostream.h>
struct Employee
{
int id;
char *name;
int salary;
};
void main()
{
Employee *p,*q;
/*pointer p and q point to dynamically allocated objects of
    Employee*/
p=new Employee;
q=new Employee;
```

```
/*Initialize the members of the Employee object pointed by the
    pointer p */
p->id=10;
p->name="John";
p->salary=5000;
/*Initialize the members of the Employee object pointed by the
    pointer q */
q->id=20;
q->name="Jack";
q->salary=3000;
cout<<"Employee Details are:"<<endl;
cout<< p->id<<"   "<<p->name<<"   "<<p->salary<<endl;
cout<< q->id<<"   "<<q->name<<"   "<<q->salary<<endl;
}
```

10.3   Linked List

One of the limitations of storing the data elements using an array is that the size of the array must be specified at the time of creating it. Also, the size of the array once decided at the time of creation cannot be later changed in the program. Hence, an array is a data structure of a fixed size which cannot 'grow' or 'shrink' at run time after its creation. For example, if we create an array a of say 5 elements, the capacity of the array becomes 5, then the array can store a maximum of 5 elements inside it. Note that, the size of the array is now constant, so we will not be able to 'grow' or 'shrink' the array in the program as per the requirements. Therefore, if there is a requirement to store 6 elements in the array at **run time** then fulfilling such a requirement will not be possible because the capacity of the array is exactly to store 5 elements.

This problem with arrays can be solved by creating a new data structure called **linked list**. It is a data structure which is created as a collection of nodes such that the new nodes can be added to the linked list or existing nodes can be removed from the linked list at runtime of the program. This means that the number of nodes in the linked list can be changed at runtime as per the requirement of the incoming data. As the linked list is a chain of nodes which can 'grow' or 'shrink' at runtime of the program, it avoids the drawback with arrays because no maximum bound or capacity associated with linked list unlike arrays where the maximum capacity of the array must be given at the time of creating it.

What is the advantage of linked list?   **?**

The main advantage of linked list is that we need not specify the size of linked list at the time of creating it. The size of the linked list can grow or shrink as and when we add or delete elements. Hence, the programmer need not estimate the amount of memory required for storing the data at compile time or even at run time because there is no maximum size or capacity associated with a linked list. We can keep on adding or deleting elements in the linked list at run time of the program as and when needed.

10.3.1 Structure of a node in a linked list

Every node of a linked list consists of two parts in it. The first part of the node stores the data value to be stored in the list and the second part of the node is a pointer that points to the next node thereby creating a chain of nodes. Figure 10.11 shows the structure of a single node in a linked list:

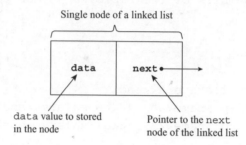

Figure 10.11: Structure of a node in a linked list

The data element to be stored in a node can be a primitive or of an object type. For simplicity of programming we assume an integer data to be stored inside a linked list. Along with the data to be stored, each node also has a pointer that points to the next Node object as shown in the Figure 10.12. Hence we can consider that each node should have following two members:

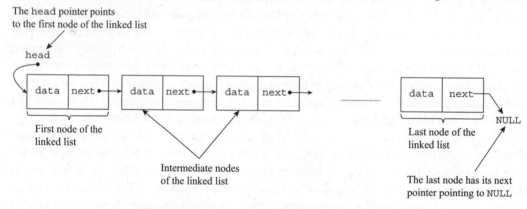

Figure 10.12: Basic representation of a linked list

1. **data**: A integer data value
2. **next**: A pointer to a next node present in the linked list. The pointer next will contain NULL for a last node of the linked list.

Since storing the members data and next is a common requirement of each of the node objects to be created in a linked list, we can now create a structure Node which defines the properties of each of the node objects as follows:

```
struct Node
{
int data;
Node *next;
};
```

Note that the data type of the pointer next is Node itself, because the pointer next should point to the next node in the linked list which will also be the object of the structure Node. Hence a structure Node is called as a **self-referential structure**, because it contains a pointer as a member that can point to other object of the same structure. We can now create objects of Node at run time by using a keyword new, hence the number of nodes present in the linked list can now be easily changed at runtime of the program.

Why have we created Node as a structure? ?

Recall from Chapter 9 that a structure is a template for all its objects. This means that, every object of the structure will contain all the members defined in the structure. In this case, we need every node to contain integer data and a pointer next, hence we have created a structure Node that defines data and next as its members. Therefore, every object of the structure Node will contain the members data and next hence one object of structure represents one node in the linked list. In the later sections we will learn to create the structure objects dynamically as and when we need to add a new node to the list.

10.3.2   Creating a first node in a linked list

Every linked list must have a header pointer that points to the first node of the linked list. Let us create this pointer with a name as head by using the following statement:

```
Node *head=NULL;
```

Note that the linked list will initially be empty without any nodes in it. Hence, the initial value of the pointer head is set to NULL indicating that there are no nodes in the linked list as shown in the Figure 10.13.

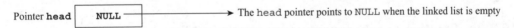

Pointer **head** | NULL ⟶ The head pointer points to NULL when the linked list is empty

Figure 10.13:   Empty linked list

Let us assume that we now need to store the first value (say 10) inside the linked list. So as to store this data element we need to create a node in a linked list at runtime by using a keyword new as follows. Also, as this is the first node of the linked list, we must make the pointer head to point to this node as shown in the below statement:

```
head=new Node;
```

Hence, the pointer head now points to a newly created node as shown in the Figure 10.14. This means that, if the address of the newly created node is 1000 then the pointer head will now store 1000 as shown in the Figure 10.14.

Once the node is created, we can now initialize the member variables of that node object. As the data to be stored in the node is 10, we initialize the member data by using

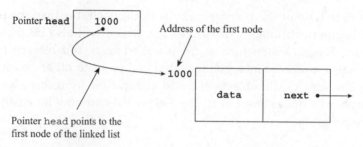

Figure 10.14:   Pointer head pointing to a first node

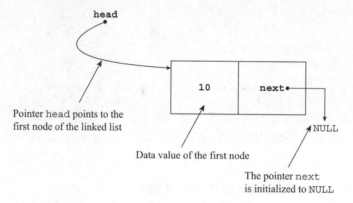

Figure 10.15:   Initialization of first node in a linked list

the pointer head to store 10 as follows. Also, as the list currently contains only a single node the next pointer of the node is set to NULL indicating that there are no further nodes in the linked list. The effect of the following statements is as shown in the Figure 10.15.

```
head->data=10;
```

```
head->next=NULL;
```

10.3.3   Creation of subsequent nodes in a linked list

To understand the process to insert subsequent nodes in the linked list, let us assume that the following linked list is already created with three nodes in it. As seen, the pointer head points to the first node and the next pointer of each of the nodes points to the node present to the right of that node. That is, the next pointer of the node that contains data as 10 points to the node with data value as 20, similarly the next pointer of the node that contains data as 20 points to the node with data value as 30 and so on. Also, the next pointer of the last node points to NULL indicating the end of the linked list as shown in the Figure 10.16.

To understand the process of inserting a node into a linked list, let us now try to insert a fourth node at the end of the existing linked list shown in the Figure 10.17. Let the data value of the fourth node to be inserted be 40. Hence, we now create a new node in the computer memory using a temporary pointer d as follows. We will also set the data value

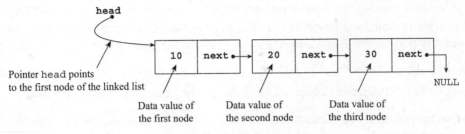

Figure 10.16: Existing linked list

of the new node to 40 and the next value of the new node to NULL as this is now going to be the new last node of the linked list

```
Node *d=new Node;
d->data=40;
d->next=NULL;
```

Note that the new node is now pointed by the pointer d and is not yet linked with the existing linked list which is pointed by head as shown in the Figure 10.17.

To attach the new node pointed by d at the end of the linked list pointed by head, we need to obviously reach the last node of the linked list that is pointer by head. Once we reach the last node we can make the next pointer of the last node to point to the node object pointed by d, thereby attaching the new node at the end of the linked list. Also, it is important to understand that this is a singly linked list, which means that we can move only in one direction from header node to the last node. This also means that, we will not be able to directly reach any node without visiting all the nodes previous to it. Therefore, if we need to search for a last node in an existing linked list, we must start the searching process from the header node and end the search once we find a node whose next is NULL.

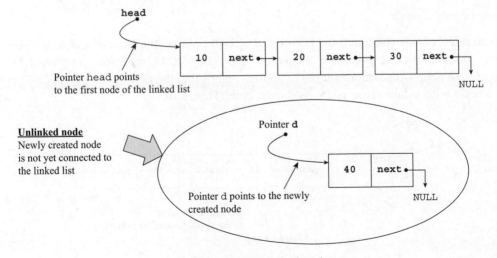

Figure 10.17: Unlinked node

This is because a node with a next pointer as NULL is always a last node in the linked list. So as to start the searching process to reach the last node, let us create a pointer temp which will initially point to the head node by using the following statements:

```
Node *temp;
temp=head; /*Pointer temp will now point to the first node*/
```

Note that the pointer temp is initialized to a pointer head, this means that the address inside the pointer head will now be copied inside the pointer temp, so the pointer temp will now point to the same object to which the pointer head points, as shown in the Figure 10.18.

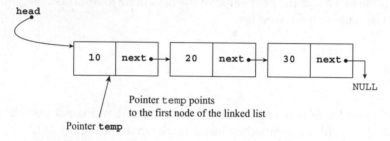

Figure 10.18: Pointer temp pointing to the first node

As discussed before, we now need to take the pointer temp to point to the last node, hence our job is to move the pointer temp ahead in the linked list if the current node to which temp points to is not the last node. We can determine if the current node is a last node or not by looking at the value present in the pointer next of the current node. Recall that, the last node is such a node which has its pointer next set to **NULL**. The pointer temp currently points to a node with a data value as 10 and as seen the value of **temp->next** (next of the node pointed by temp) **is not** NULL, then we move the pointer temp ahead in the linked list by using the statement as follows:

```
temp=temp->next;
```

As an effect of this statement the pointer temp will point to the same object to which the next pointer of temp points to. As seen in the Figure 10.18, the next pointer of temp points to a node with a data value as 20, which means that the pointer temp will also point to a node with a data value as 20, as shown in the Figure 10.19.

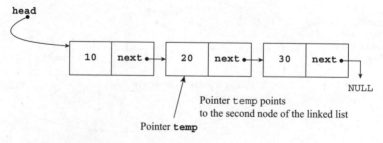

Figure 10.19: Pointer temp moves ahead in the list

We again check if the current node is a last node by looking at the next value of the current node. The next value of the node to which temp currently points (temp->next) is also not NULL, and hence this indicates that a node with a data value 20 is also not a last node. Therefore, we move the pointer temp ahead in the linked list by using the following statement:

```
temp=temp->next;
```

Therefore, the pointer temp will now point to a node with a data value as 30 as shown in the Figure 10.20.

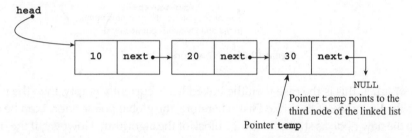

Figure 10.20: Pointer temp pointing to a node with data value 30

As seen from the Figure 10.20, the pointer temp now points to the last node, then the next value of temp (temp->next) is now NULL. Therefore, it will not move the pointer temp ahead in the list because we have now searched the last node of the linked list.

In summary, thus to make the pointer temp to point to the last to the last node we must start the pointer temp from the first node and move the pointer temp ahead in the list until temp->next!=NULL.

Hence, the following while loop can be used to make the pointer temp to point to the last node after its execution:

```
while(temp->next!=NULL)
{
temp=temp -> next;
}
```

We can now make the next of the last node to point to the unlinked node d by using the following statement.

```
temp->next=d;
```

Hence, the next value of the last node will now point to the object which is pointed by the pointer d as shown in the Figure 10.21, thereby attaching a new node at the end of the linked list.

The following is the complete code for the insert() function that is used to insert a new node at the end of the linked list. The function takes one argument of type integer(x) which is the data value of the new node to be inserted in the list. The insert() function first checks

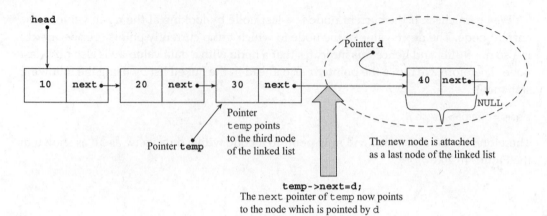

Figure 10.21: New node attached

if head ==NULL, if this is the case then the linked list is currently empty, then the node to be inserted is the first node of the linked list. Therefore, the global pointer head can be modified to point to the new node as shown in the if block of the algorithm. However, if the node to be inserted is not the first node then the control of execution will be transferred inside the else block which will first find the last node of the list using a while loop as discussed before and then attach the new node d at the end of the existing linked list as seen in the code.

```
void insert(int x)
{
     if(head==NULL)
     {
/*Node to be inserted is the first node*/
     head=new Node;
     head->data=x;
     head->next=NULL;
     }
     else
     {
/*Node to be inserted is the subsequent node*/
     Node *d=new Node;
     d->data=x;
     d->next=NULL;
     Node *temp;
     temp=head;
        while(temp->next!=NULL)
        {
        temp=temp -> next;
        }
     temp->next=d;
     }
}
```

10.3.4 Traversing a linked list

The process of visiting each and every node of the linked list is called as traversing the linked list. As a proof of traversing, we will print the data value of each node in the linked list staring from the header node. Let us again assume a linked list with three nodes created as shown in the Figure 10.22 to understand the traversal process.

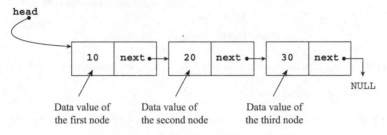

Figure 10.22   Linked list with three nodes

To start the traversing process, let us create a pointer temp that will initially point to the head node by using the following statement:

```
Node *temp;
temp=head; /*Pointer temp will now point to the first node*/
```

Note that the pointer temp is initialized to a pointer head, this means that the pointer temp will now point to the same object to which the pointer head points as shown in the Figure 10.23.

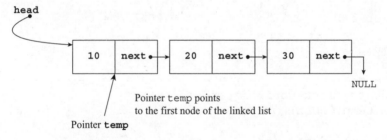

Figure 10.23   Pointer temp points to the first node

As the temp points to the first node, we can now print the data value stored inside the first node using the following **cout** statement:

```
cout<<temp->data<<endl;
```

The above statement will print the value **10** because the data value of the node pointed by the pointer temp is 10 as seen in the Figure 10.23. So as to now print the value of the next node, we can take the pointer temp ahead using the following statement:

```
temp=temp->next;
```

As an effect of this statement the pointer temp will point to the same object to which the next pointer of temp points to. As seen in the Figure 10.23, the next pointer of temp points to a node with a data value as 20, which means that the pointer temp will also point to a node with a data value as 20 as shown in the Figure 10.24.

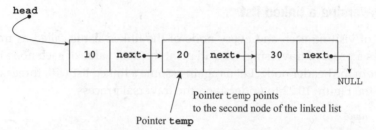

Figure 10.24: temp moves ahead

As the pointer temp now points to a next node we can again execute the statement:

```
cout<<temp->data<<endl;
```

which will print the value **20** because the data value of the node pointed by the pointer temp is, this time, 20 as seen in the Figure 10.24. So, the process of printing node values can continue until the time pointer temp goes out of the linked list. Hence the following while loop can be used to traverse through a complete linked list. Note that, while loop terminates when temp=NULL which indicates that the pointer has crossed the last node of the linked list. Do not confuse between the two conditions, temp->next=NULL means temp points to the last node of the linked list whereas temp=NULL means temp has crossed the last node of the linked list. Here, we are traversing and printing data values stored in the linked list and we also need to print the data value of the last node. Therefore the while loop should keep running if condition temp!=NULL is true

```
void traverse()
{
Node *temp;
temp=head;
cout<<"The elements of the linked list are as below:"<<endl;
/*Traverse the list until it ends*/
    while(temp!=NULL)
    {
    cout<<temp->data<<endl;
    temp=temp -> next;
    }
}
```

10.3.5   Searching an element in a linked list

Let us now write a function find() that searches the presence of a particular data value in a linked list. The function will take an integer argument(x), and search the presence of value x starting from the first node in the linked list. As shown in the code given below, the pointer temp is initialized to the first node of the linked list and the traversal loop terminates if any one of the following condition is satisfied:

1. **Element x is found in the linked list:** We need not traverse ahead in the list if the data element x we are searching for is found in the list. This means that, we should

continue with the search loop until the data value of the node pointed by `temp` is not equal to x. If the `while` loop terminates because the data value of the node pointed by `temp` is equal to x it means that the node we are searching for is found in the linked list. Therefore, we print the message as "Element found" on the computer screen as shown in the code. This means that, the `while` loop should continue traversing until the time following condition is true:

```
temp->data!=x
```

2. **End of the linked list reached:** If this is the case then the value of the pointer `temp` will become NULL and the `while` loop will terminate as the condition `temp!=NULL` is now false. If the `while` loop terminates because of this condition, it indicates that the pointer `temp` has crossed the last node of the linked list but has still not found the data element x. Hence it indicates that the data element x is not present in the linked list. Therefore, we print the message as 'Node Not Found' on the computer screen, if the traversal loop terminates because of the fact that `temp` goes NULL. This means that the `while` loop should also continue traversing until the time following condition is true:

```
temp!=NULL
```

The following is the algorithm for the `find()` function. At the end of the `while loop`, we check the exact reason as to why did the loop terminate. At this stage we come to know whether the `while loop` terminated because of point 1 or 2 described above. If `temp==NULL` is true after the `while loop` completes then it means for sure that temp has crossed the linked list which means that the loop terminated because of point 2 mentioned above. Hence, we are certain that the node which we are searching for is not present in the linked list as indicated in the `if` block after the `while loop`. However, if `temp==NULL` is false at the end of `while loop`, the control will be transferred to else block. This indeed means that the `while loop` terminated before end of list was reached and hence we are certain that the node we are searching for is found in the list because there was no reason left for `while loop` to terminate otherwise. This is as seen in the else block in the code.

```
void find(int x)
{
Node *temp;
temp=head;
/*Traverse the list until the node is not found and end of the
    list is not reached*/
    while(temp!=NULL && temp->data!=x)
    {
    temp=temp -> next;
    }
if(temp==NULL)
{
/*Node not found*/
cout<<"Node not found"<<endl;
}
else
```

```
{
/*Node found*/
cout<<"Element found"<<endl;
}
}
```

10.3.6   Deleting an element from the linked list

To understand the algorithm for deleting a node from the existing linked list, let us consider a following linked list created with four nodes as shown in the Figure 10.25.

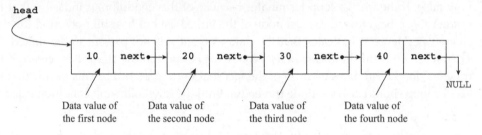

Figure 10.25:   Linked list with four nodes

Let us understand the process to delete a node with a data value 30 from the linked list shown in the Figure 10.25.

If x is the node to be deleted then we can search the node with a data value x using the following while loop which is discussed when writing the find() function in the previous section.

```
Node *temp;
temp=head;
    while(temp!=NULL && temp->data!=x)
    {
    temp=temp->next;
    }
```

In this case the data value of node to be deleted x is 30. Therefore, the above while loop will make the pointer temp to point to a node be deleted after the loop completes its execution as shown in the Figure 10.26.

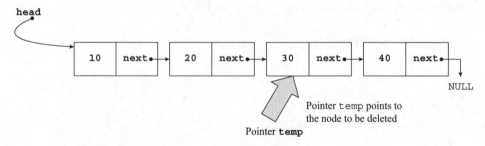

Figure 10.26:   The pointer temp points to the node to be deleted

Even if we have found the node to be deleted and the pointer temp points to it, we will not be able to delete this node from the linked list using the pointer temp alone. This is because the requirement of deletion is that the next pointer of the 'previous node' of the 'node to be deleted' must point to the 'next node' of the 'node to be deleted' thereby removing all the references to the 'node to be deleted' from the linked list. This means that, to delete a node with a data value as 30, we should make the next of 20 to point to 40, this is because 20 is the previous node to 30 and 40 is the next node to 30. Hence, all the references to node 30 will now be removed from the linked list as shown in the Figure 10.27, thereby removing a node with data as 30 from the list.

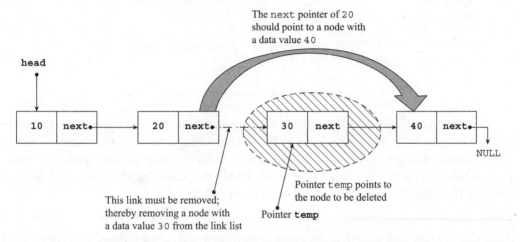

Figure 10.27 Removing the references of the node to be deleted

To set the next pointer of the 'previous node' of the 'node to be deleted' we would need one more pointer that always points to the 'previous node' of the 'node to be deleted'. Let us name this pointer as prev. The job of pointer prev is to always point to the previous node of the node to which temp points to. This means that, initially when the pointer temp points to the first node the pointer prev should point to NULL, as there is no node previous to the 'first node'. Hence the initial value of the pointer prev is set to NULL as shown in the following statement:

```
Node *prev=NULL;
```

Also, each time we make the pointer temp to move to the next node we will store the old value of the pointer temp inside the pointer prev as shown in the following statements. This will ensure that the pointer prev is always pointing to one node previous to pointer temp.

```
while(temp!=NULL && temp->data!=x)
{
        prev=temp;        /*store the old value of temp in prev*/
        temp=temp->next;  /*move temp ahead*/
}
```

Hence, when the pointer temp stops at a node with a data value 30, the pointer prev will point to a node with a data value 20 as shown in the Figure 10.28. This is because a node with a data value 20 is previous to a node with a data value 30.

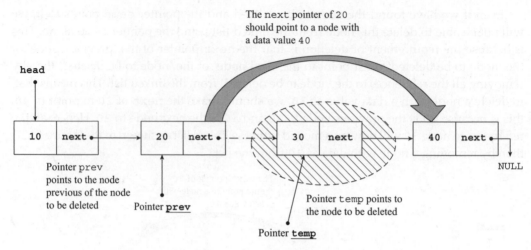

Figure 10.28: Pointers `prev` and `temp`

To make the next of 20 to point to 40, we need to set the next pointer of the node pointed by prev to point to the 'next node' of temp. This is because the next pointer of prev refers to the next value of node with data value as 20 and the next pointer of node temp refers to a node with data value as 40. Hence the following statement will remove node 30 from the linked list as shown in the Figure 10.29.

```
prev->next=temp->next;
```

Also, note that the first node has no node previous to it and hence if the node to be deleted is the first node then we will need to modify the head pointer so that the head points to the second node in the linked list, which means that the first node is deleted from the list. Hence we will not execute the above statement if the node to be deleted is the first node (temp==head) as the first node has its prev pointing to NULL.

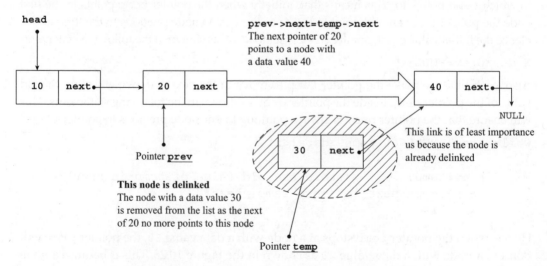

Figure 10.29: Deletion of node with a data value as 30

Therefore, following block must be executed to modify the header of the linked list if the node to be deleted is the first node of the list:

```
if(temp==head)
    {
    head=head->next;
    }
```

The following is the complete algorithm to delete a node with a value x from the linked list

```
void remove(int x)
{
    Node *temp;
    temp=head;
    Node *prev=NULL;
    while(temp!=NULL && temp->data!=x)
    {
      prev=temp;          /*store the old value of temp in prev*/
      temp=temp->next;   /*move temp ahead*/
    }
    if(temp==head)
    {
    /*Node to be deleted is the first node*/
    head=head->next;
    }
    else
    {
    /*Node to be deleted is not the first node*/
    prev->next=temp->next;
    }
}
```

> **What is the meaning of deleting a node from the linked list? Do we free up the memory allocated to that node or we just delink the node from the list?** ❓
>
> 📖 The delete algorithm we have written just delinks the node from the linked list. We have currently not written an explicit delete statement because we have created the complete linked list in RAM and its anyway not persistent. When we delink a node from the list, that particular node will not be considered as a part of the linked list when we perform any further operations on the list. Hence delinking the node is equivalent to deleting it from the linked list. However, it is always a good practice to timely **free up** the **unused** memory occupied by the program, this can be done using the **delete** keyword in C++. We discus the keyword delete later in this chapter.

10.3.7 Creation and manipulation of the linked list

The complete source code to create a linked list is as given below. The main program is menu driven where a user will be given the following options to perform operations on the linked list.

1. Insertion of a node in a linked list
2. Traversing a linked list
3. Searching an element from the linked list
4. Deletion of a node from a linked list
5. Exit

The user can enter an appropriate menu option to perform a specific operation on the linked list at each iteration of the do-while loop which implements a menu driven program.

```cpp
#include<iostream.h>
struct Node
{
int data;
Node *next;
};
/*Creation of a global pointer head*/
Node *head;
void insert(int x)
{
    if(head ==NULL)
    {
/*Node to be inserted is the first node*/
    head=new Node;
    head->data=x;
    head->next=NULL;
    }
    else
    {
/*Node to be inserted is the subsequent node*/
    Node *d = new Node;
    d->data=x;
    d->next=NULL;
    Node *temp;
    temp=head;
      while(temp->next!=NULL)
      {
      temp=temp -> next;
      }
    temp->next=d;
    }
}
void traverse()
{
Node *temp;
temp=head;
```

```
cout<<"The elements of the linked list are as below:"<<endl;
/*Traverse the list until it ends*/
    while(temp!=NULL)
    {
    cout<<temp->data<<endl;
    temp=temp -> next;
    }
}
void find(int x)
{
Node *temp;
temp=head;
/*Traverse the list until the node is not found and end of the
    list is not reached*/
    while(temp!=NULL && temp->data!=x)
    {
    temp=temp -> next;
    }
if(temp==NULL)
{
/*Node not found*/
cout<<"Node not found"<<endl;
}
else
{
/*Node found*/
cout<<"Element found"<<endl;
}
}
void remove(int x)
{
    Node *temp;
    temp=head;
    Node *prev=NULL;
    while(temp!=NULL && temp->data!=x)
    {
      prev=temp;         /*store the old value of temp in prev*/
      temp=temp->next;   /*move temp ahead*/
    }
    if(temp==head)
    {
    /*Node to be deleted is the first node*/
    head=head->next;
    }
```

```
    else
    {
    /*Node to be deleted is not the first node*/
    prev->next=temp->next;
    }
}
void main()
{
char answer;
int choice,x;
cout<<"Please select of of the following choices:"<<endl;
cout<<"1.Insert a node"<<endl;
cout<<"2.Traverse the list"<<endl;
cout<<"3.Find a node"<<endl;
cout<<"4.Delete a node"<<endl;
do
{
cout<<"Enter your choice"<<endl;
cin>>choice;
    switch(choice)
    {
    case 1: cout<<"Enter the data value to be inserted"<<endl;
            cin>>x;
            insert(x);
            break;
    case 2: traverse();
            break;
    case 3: cout<<"Enter the data value to be searched in the
                    list"<<endl;
            cin>>x;
            find(x);
            break;
    case 4: cout<<"Enter the data value to be deleted from the
                    list"<<endl;
            cin>>x;
            remove(x);
            break;
    default: cout<<"Invalid option selected"<<endl;
    }
cout<<"Do you want to continue(Y/N)?"<<endl;
cin>>answer;
} while(answer=='y');
}
```

10.4 `delete` Keyword in C++

The keyword `delete` is used to free the memory that is allocated dynamically. It is always a good programming practice free up the resources that are occupied by the program before the execution of the code completes. This helps in optimum utilization of the available heap space. The following is the syntax of using `delete` keyword:

```
delete <pointer>;
```

When a keyword `delete` is followed by the name of the pointer, system will free up the memory pointed by the pointer.

For example, let us create an integer memory of 2 bytes dynamically and store its address in a pointer p, which can be done by using the following statement:

```
int *p=new int;
```

After performing the operations with the memory, we can free the memory pointed by the pointer p by using the following statement:

```
delete p;
```

If the pointer p points to an array that is created dynamically then the `delete` statement to free the complete array space pointed by the pointer must be written as below:

```
delete [] p;
```

Error Finding Exercise

Given below are some programs which may or may not contain errors. Correct the error(s) if exist in the code and determine the output.

Program 1

```cpp
#include<iostream.h>
void display(int *p=new int[5])
{
for(int i=0;i<5;i++)
    {
    cout<<*(p+i)<<endl;
    }
}
void main()
{
int a[]={10,20,30,40,50};
cout<<"The array elements are"<<endl;
display(a);
}
```

Program 2

```cpp
#include<iostream.h>
void main()
{
int a;
a=10;
cout<<"Enter a number"<<endl;
cin>>a;
delete a;
cout<<"The value of variable 'a' is"<<a<<endl;
}
```

Program 3

Modify the following function to traverse a linked list starting from head in reverse direction. Assume pointer head is globally defined.

```cpp
void traverse()
{
Node *temp;
temp=head;
cout<<"The elements of the linked list are as below:"<<endl;
    while(temp!=NULL)
    {
    cout<<temp->data<<endl;
    temp=temp -> next;
    }
}
```

Program 4

Given below is the function that can be used to insert elements into a singly linked list starting from head. Assuming that head is a globally defined pointer, modify the following code to insert elements in ascending order.

```cpp
void insert(int x)
{
    if(head ==NULL)
    {
/*Node to be inserted is the first node*/
    head=new Node;
    head->data=x;
    head->next=NULL;
    }
    else
    {
```

```
/*Node to be inserted is the subsequent node*/
    Node *d=new Node;
    d->data=x;
    d->next=NULL;
    Node *temp;
    temp=head;
        while(temp->next!=NULL)
        {
        temp=temp -> next;
        }
    temp->next=d;
    }
}
```

Quiz

1. The memory that is allocated at the time of compilation is called as:
   (a) Dynamic memory
   (b) Static memory
   (c) Early memory
   (d) Late memory
2. Choose the correct statement.
   (a) Every static memory location is always unnamed.
   (b) Every dynamic memory location is always unnamed.
   (c) In some case, we can give name to the dynamic memory location that is allocated using a keyword new.
   (d) None of the above is true.
3. Which of the following statement(s) is/are true?
   (a) Linked list is a data structure of a fixed size.
   (b) The nodes of a linked list are allocated at runtime on demand basis.
   (c) Linked list has lesser flexibility when compared to arrays.
   (d) The data type of the value to be stored in the linked list is always integer.
4. Consider the following statement and select a correct answer.

   `int *p=new int[5];`

   (a) The statement creates 5 pointers of type integer.
   (b) The statement creates an integer array of 5 elements at compile time.
   (c) The statement creates an integer array of 5 elements at run time.
   (d) None of the above is true.
5. Which of the following statement(s) is/are correct?
   (a) The dynamic array always has a fixed size.
   (b) The dynamic array is the array that is created at run time of the program.
   (c) Array that is created dynamically is a collection of heterogeneous elements.
   (d) None of the above is true.
6. We can create a reference variable to refer to a dynamically allocated memory location.
   (a) True
   (b) False

7. If the following statement is used to allocate a 2D array dynamically,

   ```
   p=new int[4][3];
   ```

   then, which of the following is true?
   (a) Variable p must be of type int*
   (b) Variable p must be of type int
   (c) Variable p must be of type int**
   (d) None of the above is true

8. Which of the following cannot be allocated dynamically?
   (a) Memory for a pointer   **(d)** Memory for a primitive variable
   (b) Memory for a structure object   **(e)** Memory for a function
   (c) Memory for an array

9. Consider a structure Node which contains a pointer that can point to its own object.

   ```
   struct Node
   {
   int data;
   Node *next;
   };
   ```

   Choose the correct statement.
   (a) Structure Node implements a concept of Nesting of structures.
   (b) Structure Node is called as a recursive structure.
   (c) Structure Node is a self-referential structure.
   (d) None of the above is true.

Review Questions

1. What are the drawbacks of static memory allocation? How will you solve them?
2. Explain the keywords new and delete in C++ with examples.
3. Write a C++ program to find sum and average on n-numbers by creating an array of n elements. Use dynamic memory allocation.
4. Write a C++ program to arrange n-students in ascending order of marks. For each student object store roll_number, name, and marks. Use dynamic memory allocation to create an array of students.
5. Write a C++ program to create, insert and delete elements from a linked list.
6. Write a function sort() to sort linked list that stores integers in ascending order.
7. Write a function reverse() to find reverse of the existing linked list.
8. Write a C++ program to perform concatenation of two linked list objects l1 and l2. Print the resultant linked list l3 by traversing it.
9. Explain the use of delete keyword in C++ with example.

PART-II

Object Oriented Programming

Chapter

11 | Classes and Objects

11.1 Overview

Class is a template that wraps data (variables) and related functions together into a single capsule as shown in the Figure 11.1. This process of wrapping data and related functions together is called **encapsulation**. Class in C++ is used to create a **user-defined data type.** Similar to how we create the variables of built-in data types such as int, float, double, etc.; we can also create the variables of user-defined data types if the template for the data type is defined by writing a class in the C++ program. This process to create variables of 'type' defined by the class is called **instantiation**. Every variable which is of a 'type' defined by the class is called an **object** of that class. An object preserves all the properties of the class for which it is instantiated. Hence, the class is a **'schema'** for all its objects, and an object is defined as an **'instance'** or a **'snapshot'** of the class.

Let us consider a scenario in which we want to perform addition of two integer variables a and b and store the result in a variable c. Hence, we declare three integer variables as shown below:

```
int a,b,c;
```

We can create variables of type integer because int is a basic and built-in data type, which is directly recognized by C++.

At times, it may be required to create a **'user-defined data type'** in the program rather than making use of built-in types supported by the language. For example, let us assume

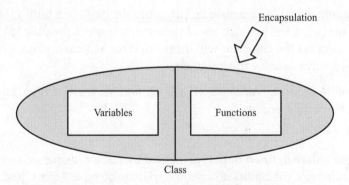

Figure 11.1: Combination of variables and functions

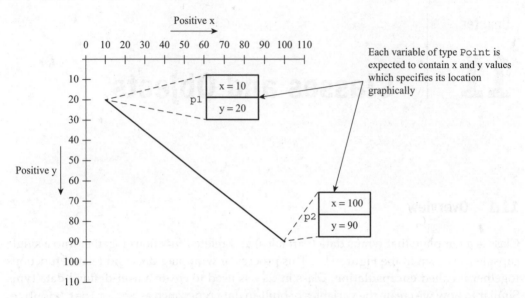

Figure 11.2: Creating line from p1 to p2

that we want to write a C++ program to calculate the slope of a line. To calculate the slope, we must store the start point (x1, y1) from where the line begins and end point (x2, y2) where the line ends. Instead of creating 4 different variables, x1, y1, x2 and y2, it would be convenient to work if we could just create two points p1 and p2 such that each point is packaged with x and y coordinates. It would have been very easy if C++ could have offered a data type named as Point, just like it offers other built-in data types such as int, float, char etc. Then, each variable of type Point has x and y values to specify the location of the point graphically. If this approach would have been supported, we could have created two variables of type Point, named as p1 and p2 such that the line starts at point p1 and ends at a point p2 as shown in the Figure 11.2. As seen, our expectation will be that, each Point type variable will have its own x and y coordinates. However, the statement

```
Point p1,p2;
```

will not be recognized by C++ because Point is not the basic or a built-in data type of the language such as int, float, char etc. In summary, it is not possible to create variables of type Point, because the compiler will throw an error as Point cannot be recognized.

There are two ways to solve this problem.

Option 1: Create 4 separate variables x1, y1, x2, and y2 each of type int rather than creating variables of type Point.

OR

Option 2: Create a **user-defined data type** named as Point, using a class in C++. This will give programmers the ability to create variables of type Point just like we create variables of any other basic types such as int, float, char etc.

There are a multiple advantages of working with classes which we will discuss in this chapter and the chapters ahead. Hence, for now, we will proceed with option 2 as a first step in learning object oriented programming (OOP).

We mentioned before that, `class` in C++ is used to create a 'user-defined data type' and hence we can now create a class `Point` as shown in the Figure 11.3. Once the template for `Point` is defined by the class, we will be able to create variables of type `Point` just like we create variables of any other data type as shown in the Figure 11.3.

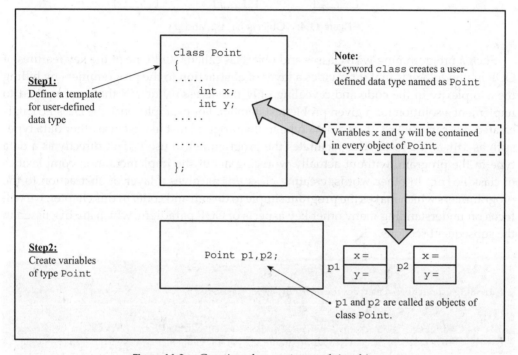

Figure 11.3:   Creating class `Point` and its objects

The variables p1 and p2 of type `Point` are called **objects** of class `Point`. Objects will preserve all the properties defined by the class `Point`. This means that all the member variables defined in class `Point` will be incorporated by every object of `Point`. Each point object requires a variable x that stores x-coordinate value of the point and a variable y that stores y-coordinate value of the point. Since the members x and y are the properties required to be stored for every point, we can define a template that will contain these members by creating a class named as `Point`. Once the class is defined, we can create any number of **objects** of that class. For example, we can create three variables (objects) of type `Point` using a C++ statement below:

```
Point p1,p2,p3;
```

Note that every object of class `Point` will contain all the member variables defined by the class `Point`. This means that, each of the objects p1, p2, and p3 will have members x and y to represent x and y coordinate values of a particular point as shown in the Figure 11.4.

Every object of class Point will contain x value and a y value

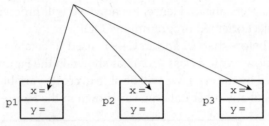

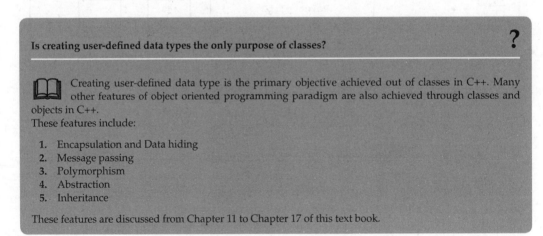

Figure 11.4: Objects p1, p2, and p3

Such a programming with classes and objects is called OOP. One of the key features of OOP methodology is that it provides a layer of **abstraction** to the programmers by hiding the complexity in the code and revealing only the necessary details that are required to implement a solution for a given problem statement. For example, once the class Point is created, we can use Point as a data type in the program just like we use other data types such as int and float. This facilitates the programmer to use Point directly as a data type in the program, without actually worrying about the implementation complexities of class Point. In other words, creating class Point gives a layer of abstraction to the programmers which makes the program simple to design and code. In this chapter, we will focus on understanding many other key aspects of OOP paradigm, which are discussed in the subsequent sections.

Is creating user-defined data types the only purpose of classes? ?

Creating user-defined data type is the primary objective achieved out of classes in C++. Many other features of object oriented programming paradigm are also achieved through classes and objects in C++.

These features include:

1. Encapsulation and Data hiding
2. Message passing
3. Polymorphism
4. Abstraction
5. Inheritance

These features are discussed from Chapter 11 to Chapter 17 of this text book.

NOTES

◆ Programming with classes and objects is called as **object oriented programming** (often abbreviated as OOP). In this chapter, we will study basic properties of Object oriented programming paradigm which are supported by C++.
◆ Class is a **schema** and abject is an **instance** of it. Class provides **generic template** for its objects.
◆ Process of creating objects of a class is called as **instantiation**. You can have as many objects of class as you want.
◆ A class wraps data and related functions together, this is called as **encapsulation**.

- Process of hiding the complexities and only revealing necessary details required to implement a particular solution is called as **abstraction**.
- Apart from instantiation, encapsulation and abstraction; C++ also provides other object oriented features like polymorphism, data hiding, message passing, inheritance, etc. These features are discussed one by one in the later chapters of this text book.

11.2 Creating Classes

A class is a template that wraps variables and function into a single unit. The Figure 11.5 shows the syntax for creating a class in C++. Keyword **class** must be followed by the class name which is used to create objects of a class. Body of the class can contain member variables as well as member functions, and the class definition should end with a semicolon as shown in the Figure 11.5.

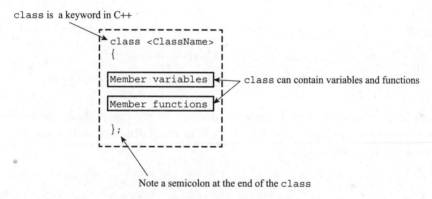

Figure 11.5: Syntax for creating a class

For example, let us create a class Employee to store the following information about each employee in the firm:

- Name of the employee
- Salary of the employee
- Identification number of the employee

We create a class with member variables id, name and salary as shown in the Figure 11.6. A class can also contain member functions so as to perform operations on these variables. To show the inclusion of member functions in the class, we have written two member functions **input()** and **output()** such that the function input() takes the values of id, name and salary as input from the user and the function output prints the details of id, name and salary of a particular employee.

NOTES

- Variables defined in the class are called as **Member variables** or **Instance variables**.
- Functions defined in the class are called as **Member functions** or **Methods** or **Operations** of that class.

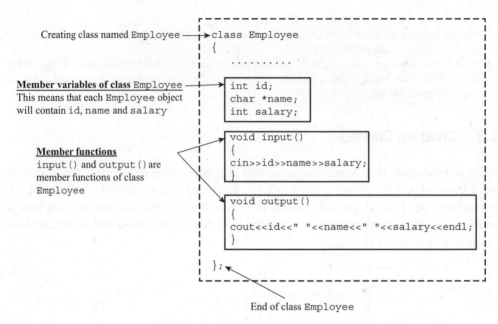

Figure 11.6: Creating a class named as `Employee`

Access to every member or a member function of the class can be controlled using different **access specifiers** available in C++. Details about different access specifiers in C++ are discussed in the Section 11.4.

NOTES

We will be using object oriented input and output streams **cin** and **cout** instead of **printf()** and **scanf()** functions. The usage of these streams is discussed in Chapter 2, Section 2.7 of this text book. Recall, as we discussed in Chapter 2, the objects **cin** an **cout** provide us with a layer of **abstraction**, as we do not have to worry about the data type of the value that is to be taken as input or generated as output.

The comparison of **printf()/scanf()** functions with **cin/cout** objects is given in Chapter 2. The objects cin/cout do not need any **control string** unlike **printf()/scanf()**. This makes **cin/cout simple** to use in the programs compared to **printf()/scanf()**. In other words, **cin/cout** objects provide a layer of **abstraction** to the programmer in a way that the format and syntax of the statements using **cin/cout** do not change with the type of data to be inputted or outputted. However, while using printf() and scanf() functions, the programmer has to worry about the specific data type to be inputted or outputted and use a correct control sting for that data type, like **%d** for integer, **%f** for float **%s** for string etc.

As noted in Chapter 2, **cin** and **cout** are built-in objects of class **istream** and **ostream** respectively and are declared in a header file **iostream.h**. Hence, we will be including the header fie **iostream.h** whenever we make use of **cin** and **cout** objects in the code.

11.3 Creating Objects of a Class

We can create variables which are of the type defined by the class. These variables are called objects of the class. An object preserves all the properties defined by the class, such that each object of a class will contain all the member variables present in the class definition[1]. Given below is the syntax to create objects of a class:

```
<ClassName> objectName;
```

For example, we can create three objects of a class `Employee` which is defined in Figure 11.6, using the following statement:

```
Employee e1,e2,e3;
```

The variables e1, e2, and e3 have a data type as `Employee`, and hence they are called objects of class `Employee`. Each of these objects will have members id, name, and salary as shown in the Figure 11.7, and this is because these are the members defined in class `Employee`.

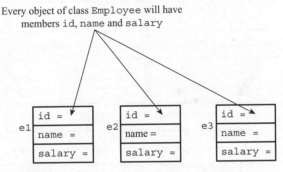

Figure 11.7:   Members of objects e1, e2 and e3

The members of the class are contained in the object memory of each of the objects, and they will store junk values unless they are initialized. The class `Employee` also contains two member functions **input()** and **output()** so as to operate on the member variables of each of the objects.

NOTES

Although, it would be simpler to imagine that the member functions are stored inside each of the individual objects, it would result in duplication of code in each of the objects if this is the case. Hence, member functions are stored in memory area **shared by all objects** of a class as shown in Figure 11.8. This memory is allocated when the class definition is loaded in RAM.

NOTES

When you use the `sizeof` operator with objects, it will give you the sum of sizes (in bytes) of all the member variables of the object. Member functions are not considered in the object memory of any object because they are stored in a different space in memory as mentioned before. For example, `sizeof(e1)` will give be calculated as

---

[1] Static members of a class are the exceptions to this rule because they are not the part of object memory. Static members and member functions are discussed in Chapter 12.

```
sizeof(id) +sizeof(name)+sizeof(salary)
= 2 Bytes+ 2 Bytes +2 Bytes
= 6 Bytes
```

Hence, you can say that every object of `Employee` is of 6 bytes in size because it will have 3 members (`id`, `name` and `salary`) of 2 bytes each. We have considered `name` as 2 bytes because every near pointer in C++ is of 2 bytes in size (assuming 16 bit compiler).

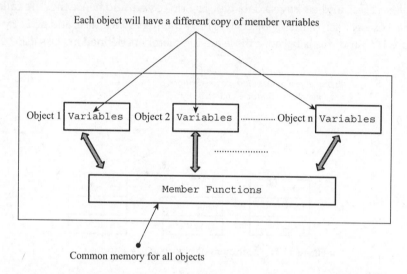

Figure 11.8: Objects share a common memory for member functions

Every object that we create in the program actually simulates one object in a real world. This means that the objects e1, e2, and e3 would actually represent the data about three different employees in the real word. The members of each of the objects can be accessed using a membership operator '.'. For example, if the names of the three employees are "John", "Jack", and "Jill", then we can individually initialize a member variable name for each of the objects e1, e2, and e3 as shown below:

```
e1.name="John";
e2.name="Jack";
e3.name="Jill";
```

This means that the variable name inside object e1 is initialized to store a string constant "John", variable name inside object e2 is initialized to store a string constant "Jack" and variable name inside object e3 is initialized to store a string constant "Jill" as shown in the Figure 11.9.

Similarly, the id and salary of each of the employees can be initialized by accessing the respective members inside each of these objects.

Similar to member variables, we can also invoke the member functions of a class using individual objects by applying a membership operator '.' It is important to understand that

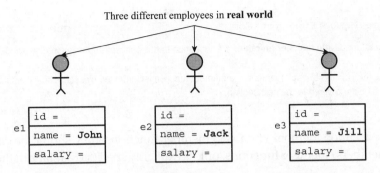

Figure 11.9: Initialization of member variable name for each of the objects

when we invoke a member function of a class using a particular object, the members of that object can be directly accessed inside the member function. For example, the member function input () can be invoked using object e1 by using the following statement:

```
e1.input();
```

The statement will transfer the control of execution inside the member function input (), using object e1. Hence, the statement

cin>>id>>name>>salary;

written inside input () will execute on behalf of object e1, thereby taking to members id, name, and salary of object e1 as input from the user.

Similarly, the statements, e2.input () and e3.input () will take the members of objects e2 and e3 as input from the user, respectively.

Also, we can invoke a member function **output ()** to print the details of each of the employee using the statements:

```
e1.output(); //will print the details of employee e1
e2.output(); //will print the details of employee e2
e3.output(); //will print the details of employee e3
```

Although, we have accessed all the members and the member functions of the class Employee using each of the objects e1, e2 and e3; the access to every member or a member function of the class should be controlled by different access specifiers to correctly implement principles of object orientation. The details of different access specifiers in C++ are discussed in the Section 11.4.

NOTES

Members and member functions of a class should be accessed using **object** of the class followed by a **membership operator** DOT(.). The syntax to access member variable using an object is as given below

```
ObjectName.MemberVariableName
```

The syntax to invoke a member function using an object is as given below

```
ObjectName.MemberFunction(Comma separated list of arguments);
```

Static members and **Static member functions** are exception to this concept and they are discussed in Chapter 12 of this text book.

Also, note that, access to each member or a member function is controlled by access specifiers in C++. **Access specifiers** in C++ are covered in the next section.

When we mention member variables/member functions, they should be considered as non-static members/member functions, unless explicitly specified as static in the statement.

11.4 Access Specifiers in C++

Access to each of the member variables and member functions of the class can be controlled using the following keywords:

- private
- public
- protected

In this section, we will discuss each of these access specifiers in detail.

11.4.1 private access

A private member or a member function can only be accessed inside a class in which the member is defined. This means that, when a **member variable** is defined as private, its value cannot be accessed from any place outside class, and when a **member function** is defined as private, it cannot be invoked from any place outside class.

All members/member functions of the class are by default private, you can also use the keyword private to explicitly mention private members. Figure 11.10 gives the syntax

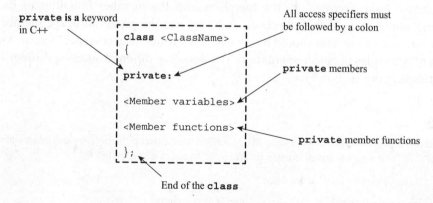

Figure 11.10: Syntax for creating private members

for using a private keyword in C++. Note that all the members and member functions declared after the keyword **private:** will be marked as private members, and hence they cannot be accessed from anyplace outside the class.

For example, consider a class Employee with all the members and member functions written under private: as shown in the Figure 11.11. This means that accessing any function or a variable of class Employee from the outside world will give an **error**. In the Figure 11.11, we create e1 as an object of class Employee as seen in the first line of main() function; however, we cannot access any member variable or any member function using object e1 because all of them are made private. Therefore, classes which have all the members and member functions as private are of **no use** to the programmer because such classes cannot communicate with the outside world at all. Figure 11.11 shows the statements that will cause compilation errors if we attempt to access private members outside class.

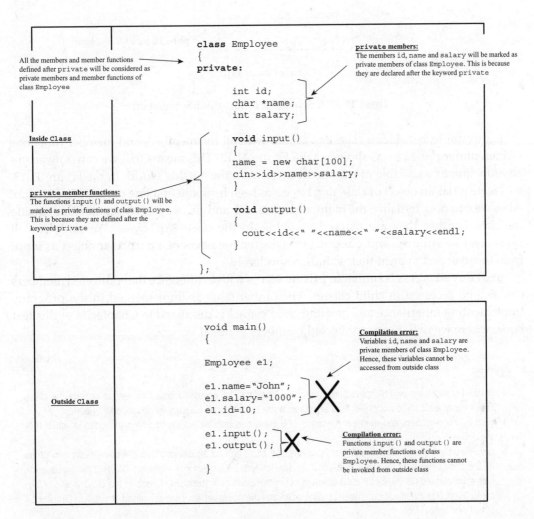

Figure 11.11: Making members and member functions of class Employee as private

11.4.2 `public` **access**

The public members and member functions of the class can be accessed from any place in the program (they can be accessed from any place inside or outside the class). Figure 11.12 gives the syntax for using a `public` keyword. Note that all the members and member functions written after the keyword **public:** will be marked as public members, and hence they can now be accessed from anyplace in the program.

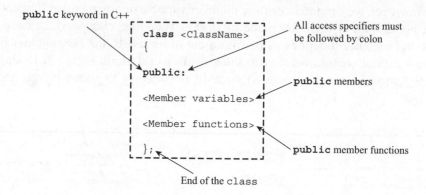

Figure 11.12: Syntax for creating public members

For example, consider a class `Employee` with all the members and member functions written under `public:` as shown in the Figure 11.13. This means that we can now access any function or a variable of class `Employee` from the outside world. In the Figure 11.13, we create `e1` as an object of class `Employee` as seen from the first line of `main()` function. Also, we can now initialize the members `name`, `id`, and `salary` of object `e1` from outside the class because they are marked as public in the class `Employee`. We can also call functions like `input()` and `output()` to take the members of a particular object as input from the user and to print their values, respectively.

protected access is similar to private access with a difference that protected members can also be accessed in child classes when inheritance is implemented in the program. Implementing inheritance and creating child classes is discussed in Chapter 14 of this text book, where we will discuss protected members in detail.

NOTES

♦ `public` members and member functions of the class can be accessed inside as well as outside the class. These members can be accessed from anyplace in the program and hence they are called as public.

♦ `private` members and member functions of a class can only be accessed within the class in which they are defined.

♦ `protected` members and member functions of a class can be accessed within the same class and within all the child classes of the class in which they are defined. `protected` members **CANNOT** be accessed in non-child classes OR in any function which is not in the class or in the child classes of the class in which they are defined. Don't worry about understanding protected members yet, they are discussed in detail in Chapter 14 of this text book.

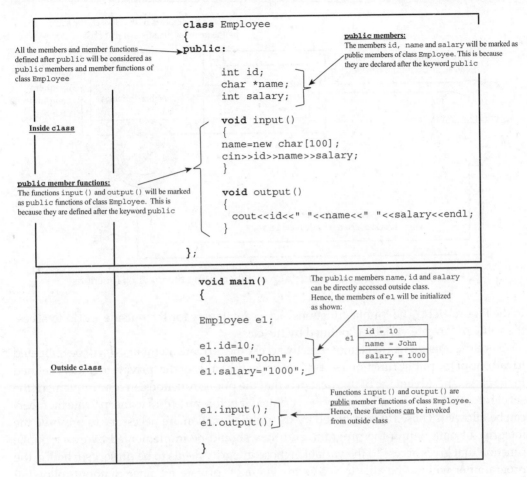

Figure 11.13: Making members and member functions of class Employee as public

11.5 Data Hiding and Encapsulation

We understand from Section 11.4 that the private member of the class cannot be accessed from the outside world. Hence, we say that the private members are hidden from the outside world. Therefore, making a member variable of a class as `private` implements **data hiding** in the program.

A class with all its members as private is of no use to the programmer because it cannot interact with the external world at all, and there is no way to set or get the values of the members declared inside the class. Therefore, we usually create 'public functions' inside the class for the outside world to access 'private members' with certain regulations imposed by public functions. 'Public functions' are inside the class and hence they can access the 'private members' defined in the class, and since these functions are public, they can be called by the outside world. Therefore, using this design the **outside world** can access the value of 'private members' through respective 'public functions' as shown

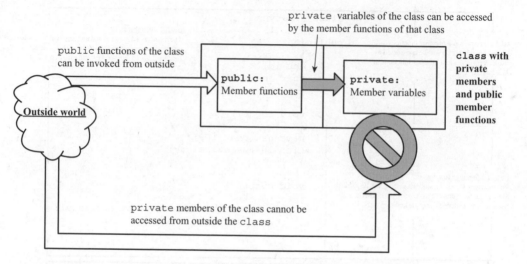

Figure 11.14: Accessing the `private` members using the `public` functions

in the Figure 11.14. The 'public functions' act as a **gateway** for the outside world to access the value of 'private variables' defined by the class.

Since the outside world cannot directly access the 'private member', it will be obligated to call one of the public functions so as to set or get the value of the 'private member' defined in the class. The advantage of this design is that the public function can now implement the set of rules that are to be followed by every outsider before an access to the 'private member' can be allowed. These rules imposed by the public function are necessary to preserve the integrity of data within the program, and they should be implemented by every public function that gives access to the variable whose integrity needs to be preserved; hence, the programmer will not be able to access the value of 'private member' without following the rules defined by the 'public function'. Such a combination of a 'private variable' with a 'public function' is called **encapsulation**. The key principle of encapsulation is to provide security to a 'private variable' by assuring that every access to 'private variable' is passed through a set of rules that are defined by the 'public function'.

To understand the need of preserving data integrity rules, let us consider a class Employee with **public** members: name, id, and salary. As the members of class Employee are public, they can now be directly accessed from the outside world (without any need of a function) as shown in the Figure 11.15. Hence, we create an object e1 of class Employee and initialize the name, salary, and id of the object e1 as shown in the Figure 11.15.

In this way, we have managed to set the salary of an employee named "John" as a negative number, which is logically an incorrect value for salary, because you cannot pay the firm while you are working for the firm. However, C++ will still allow setting the value of −1000 to a variable salary because variable salary of type **int** allows positive as well as negative numbers to be stored in the variable. Hence, the statement executes successfully leaving the data about a real world object in an **inconsistent state** as shown in the Figure 11.15. Although, this might be a silly typing mistake of the programmer that sets the value of the variable salary as negative but it still leaves the results of the program in

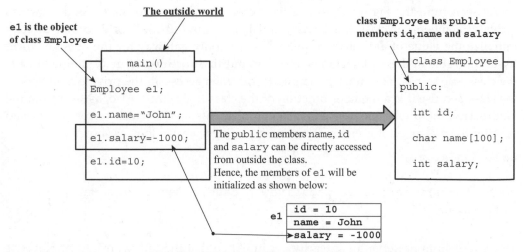

Figure 11.15: Setting salary of object e1 as a negative number

a very much **inconsistent** state. The aim of data hiding is to protect genuine programmers from committing such accidental mistakes, thus avoiding inconsistency in the data which is stored for a real world object.

As a solution, we can make the variable salary as a 'private variable' of class Employee and create 'public function' to set the value of salary from the outside world. The 'public function' can implement a check on the value of salary and put an alert to the programmer if the value of variable salary is set as a negative value. This will facilitate the programmer to correct the mistake and re-enter the value of variable salary as shown in the Figure 11.16.

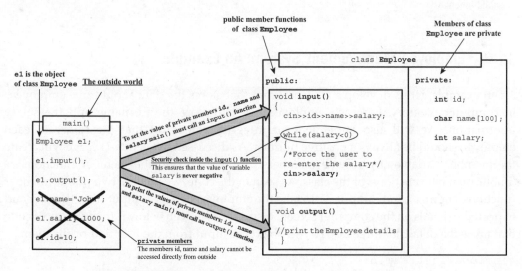

Figure 11.16: Making variables as private and functions as public

As seen from the Figure 11.16, we have created members id, name, and salary as 'private members' of class Employee, and hence, the outside world cannot directly initialize the value of any of these members. The only **gateway** for the outside world to set the value of these members is to call an **public function** input() defined inside the class Employee. The function input() can then access all the private members of the class because it is a member function of the class Employee. Also, as seen from the Figure 11.6, the public function input() implements a rule which forces the user to re-enter the salary if it is entered as negative using a while loop as shown below:

```
while(salary<0)
{
cout<<"Salary cannot be negative, please re-enter its value";
cin>>salary;
}
```

This will help to preserve the integrity constraint so that the salary for any employee is always a positive number. This is because programmer cannot directly initialize the value of variable salary as a negative number from the outside world as all the accesses to members of class Employee are restricted from outside. Also, the function input() is the only way to set the salary of any Employee and to implement the required check on salary, thereby assuring that the salary is never negative. Similar rules can be implemented using other variables of the class as per the requirement of the program.

Hence, we say that encapsulation gives security to a 'private variable' by controlling its access through a 'public function'.

CONCLUSION

Any object oriented program must provide **security** to its data variables using **encapsulation** and **data hiding**. Hence in the programs going forward, we will make the member variables of the class as **private** and the member functions as **public**, such that the value of the **private variables** can only be accessed using a certain set of the **public functions**.

11.6 Employee Management System: An Example

As an example, let us develop a C++ program that stores the data about three employees in computer memory. For each employee, we will store the id, name and the salary information. We will also implement an **integrity constraint** that the salary of each employee should be always a positive number. As discussed in Section 11.5, we will create the member variables as 'private members' of the class and the member functions as 'public member functions' of the class. As seen in the code, we include two public member functions input() and output() to take the employee details as input from the user and to print the details on the computer screen, respectively. Given below is the full source code that takes the details of three Employee objects as input from the user and prints them:

```
#include<iostream.h>
class Employee
```

```cpp
{
private:
    int id;
    char name[100];
    int salary;
public:
void input()
{
cin>>id>>name>>salary;
    while(salary<0)
    {
    cout<<"Salary cannot be negative, please re-enter its value";
    cin>>salary;
    }
}
void output()
{
cout<<id<<"    "<<name<<"   "<<salary<<endl;
}
};
void main()
{
Employee e1,e2,e3;
cout<<"Enter the details of first employee"<<endl;
e1.input();
cout<<"Enter the details of second employee"<<endl;
e2.input();
cout<<"Enter the details of third employee"<<endl;
e3.input();
cout<<"The Employee details are"<<endl;
e1.output();
e2.output();
e3.output();
}
```

Output:
```
Enter the details of first employee
1 John 1000
Enter the details of second employee
2 Jack 5000
Enter the details of third employee
3 Jill 3000
The Employee details are
1 John 1000
2 Jack 5000
3 Jill 3000
```

Note that in the public member function `input()` there is a security check to ensure that the value of the `salary` for any of the employee objects is never initialized as negative value.

The execution of the code will always start from `main()` function; let us understand the code starting from the first line of `main()` function.

The statement

```
Employee e1,e2,e3;
```

creates three objects of class `Employee` as shown in the Figure 11.17a. Each object of class `Employee` has members `id`, `name`, and `salary` because these variables are defined in the class `Employee`. Initially, all the members will contain junk values.

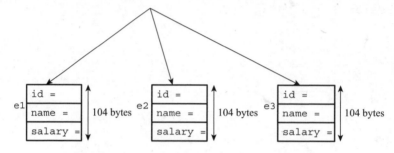

The members of each object (`id`, `name` and `salary`) will intially store junk values

Figure 11.17a: State of objects e1, e2, and e3

This time we have created name as an array of characters (of size 100) instead of creating it as a pointer. This means that 100 bytes will be allocated for storing name in each object. Also members `id` and `salary` will take 2 bytes each. Hence the total size of each object will be **104 bytes**. If name would have been a pointer (like in Figure 11.13), only the address of the memory location where name is stored would have been the part of the object. Since, every near pointer is of 2 bytes in size, total size of `Employee` object would have been 6 bytes as calculated in Section 11.3. However, in this case, we have created name as a direct array of size 100, and hence all the 100 bytes are occupied by the space, which is reserved for the object, thereby making the size of the object as 104 bytes as shown in the Figure 11.7b. We have compared both the implementations in Chapter 8 of this text book. In this example, we use the array implementation for simplicity and improving the readability of the program. Because our focus here is to understand classes and objects and not to worry much about pointers and dynamic memory allocations.

The statement

```
e1.input();
```

will invoke the function **input()** using object e1. As the member function `input()` is defined inside the class `Employee`, the statement actually transfers the control of execution inside the class, and hence, we can access the 'private members' of the class inside the member function `input()`. Also, calling the member function `input()` will execute the following statement:

```
cin>>id>>name>>salary;
```

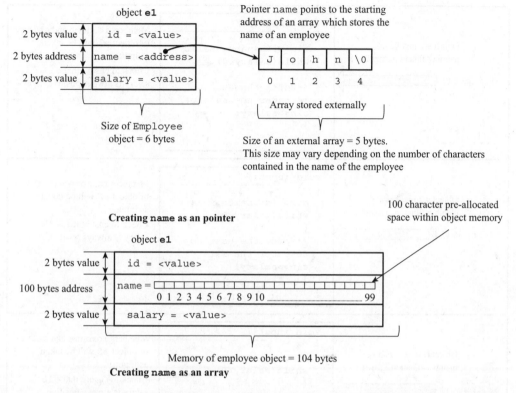

Figure 11.17b: Size of `Employee` object when name is an array v/s when name is created as a pointer

This means that the id, name, and salary values of object e1 will be taken as input from the user because the member function input () is invoked using the object e1. Note that the members of the object e1 can be directly accessed inside the member function input () because it is the object that invoked the function. Similarly, the statements **e2.input();** and **e3.input();** will take id, name, and salary values of objects e2 and e3 as input from the user. The process of accessing the members of respective objects is as shown in the Figure 11.18.

Let us assume that the user enters the id, name, and salary of each of the Employee objects as shown in the table below:

Object of class Employee	Data entered by the user (id, name, salary)
e1	(1, "John", 1000)
e2	(2, "Jack", 5000)
e3	(3, "Jill", 3000)

This means that the state of objects e1, e2 and e3 in the computer memory will be as shown in the Figure 11.19.

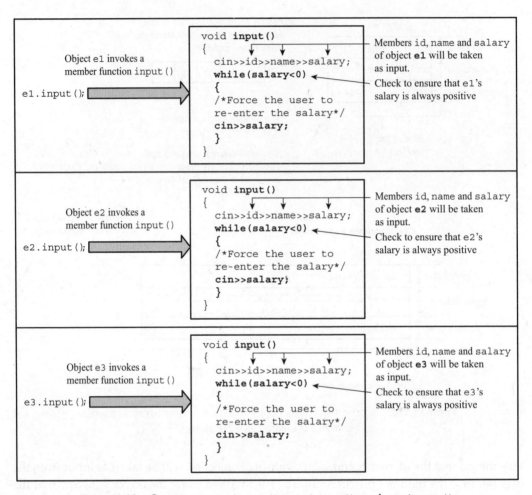

Figure 11.18:   Statements e1.input(), e2.input(), and e3.input()

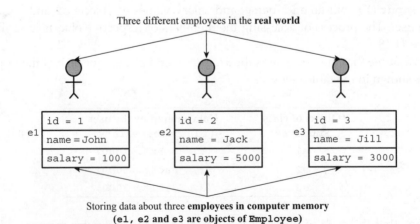

Three different employees in the **real world**

Storing data about three **employees in computer memory**
(e1, e2 and e3 are objects of Employee)

Figure 11.19:   State of objects e1, e2, and e3

Similarly, the statements

```
e1.output();
e2.output();
e3.output();
```

will execute a **cout** statement and will print the details of each employee as seen in the code.

Can assignment operator be used with objects? For example, can we write a statement e1=e2; in the code?

Yes. Assignment operator can be used with objects. If you write a statement

```
e1=e2;
```

all the values of members of object e2 will be copied to corresponding members of object e1. Hence the statement will modify object e1 and set its member values same as that of object e2 as shown below:

This is possible because the **assignment operator function** is overloaded in every class by the compiler. We will learn **operator overloading** in Chapter 13, but remember for now that **assignment operator function** is a function which does a member by member copy when used with objects and is by default provided by the compiler with every class you create.

What is the difference between a structure and a class?

In C++, you can use structure or a class interchangeably. Like class, we can also have members and member functions in structure. This means that everything that you can achieve using classes can also be achieved using structures. The only difference is that, by default all the members and member functions of a structure are **public** in nature; whereas the members and member functions within the class are by default **private** unless you explicitly make them public. You can also use access specifiers private, public and protected within structures just like we have used them inside classes. Hence any program that we have written using a class will also execute by replacing the keyword class with the keyword struct. For example, instead of creating a class Employee, you could have also created a structure Employee, keeping everything else same. The program will still execute with the same main() function because we have made the members inside structure as private and member functions as public (same as what we had done with a class)

```
struct Employee
{
private:
        int id;
        char name[100];
        int salary;
public:
    void input()
    {
    cin>>id>>name>>salary;
        while (salary<0)
```

```
    {
    cout<<"salary cannot be negative,please re-enter its value";
    cin>>salary;
    }
    }
    void output()
    {
    cout<<id<<" "<<name<<" "<<salary<<endl;
    }
};
```

However, a class is a defined entity in object oriented programming paradigm, used to wrap members and member functions. Hence, it is a standard programming practice to use classes in the program rather than structures when implementing any of the object oriented principles. We have started implementing principles of object orientation from this chapter; hence we will be working with classes going forward instead of structures. Structures are typically used to combine variables only, as we did with a variety of examples in Chapter 9; whereas classes are typically used when we want to combine variables as well as functions together.

11.7 Account Management System: An Example

As an example, let us develop a program to store data about different bank accounts in computer memory. For each account, we will store the following details:

- Account number
- Name of the customer holding the account
- Balance in the account

As each account object is required to store the above information, we create a class Account defining 'private members' as acc_no, name, and balance as seen in the code. Further, we will support following operations on every account:

- Opening an account
- Withdraw a specific amount from the account
- Deposit a specific amount in the account
- Balance enquiry

As an integrity constraint, we will ensure that the minimum balance of Rs. 500 is always maintained in each of the bank accounts. This means that the condition to ensure minimum balance of Rs. 500 must be checked at two places: first, while opening the account where we set the initial balance, and second, when we attempt to withdraw money from the account, to ensure that the customer should not withdraw any amount which will make the balance fall below 500. As seen in the code, the function input() can be used to **open an account** in a bank where we take the acc_no, name, and balance of that account as input from the user. Hence, to ensure that the minimum balance is always 500, the while loop will force the user to re-enter the value of variable balance if it is less than 500.

```
while(bal<500)
{
```

```
cout<<"Balance cannot be less than 500, please re-enter its
    value";
cin>>bal;
}
```

This will always ensure that the initial opening balance is always ≥500 in each of the accounts. The member function **withdraw()** will be used to withdraw a specific amount from a particular account. Note that before allowing the withdraw operation to succeed, the `if` statement will check if the 'minimum balance of 500 is maintained in the account' even after the withdraw transaction. If this is not the case, then the withdraw operation will print a message "Insufficient funds" on the computer screen.

The function **deposit()** is used to deposit money in the account. In an ideal case, this should not violate any integrity constraint because the function **deposit()** will aim to increase the balance in the account by adding the `amount` value passed to it. However, if the user passes a negative value to deposit function in order to hack the code, then the deposit operation would be converted into a withdraw operation. Hence, we apply a security check in the function `deposit()` that the amount passed as an argument to it should always be **positive**. The deposit operation will print a message 'Illegal operation' if a negative value of amount is passed to it.

Finally, the function `output()` can serve as an implementation of the functionality 'Balance Enquiry' because it prints all the details of the particular account on the computer screen.

Given below is the source code that stores the details of two account objects `a1` and `a2` in computer memory and invokes the respective functions.

```
#include<iostream.h>
class Account
{
private:
int acc_no;
char name[100];
float bal;
public:
    void input()
    {
    cin>>acc_no>>name>>bal;
       while(bal<500)
       {
    cout<<"Balance cannot be less than 500, please re-enter its
           value";
       cin>>bal;
       }
    }
    void withdraw(float amount)
```

```
    {
      if(bal-amount>=500)
      {
      bal = bal - amount;
      cout<<"New Balance is "<<bal<<endl;
      }
      else
      {
      cout<<"Insufficient funds" <<endl;
      }
    }
    void deposit(float amount)
    {
      if(amount<0)
      {
      cout<<"Amount to deposit cannot be negative"<<endl;
      }
      else
      {
      bal-bal-amount;
      cout<<"New Balance is "<<bal<<endl;
      }
    }
    void output()
    {
    cout<<acc_no<<"  "<<name<<"  "<<bal<<endl;
    }
};
void main()
{
Account a1,a2;
cout<<"Enter the details of first account"<<endl;
a1.input();
cout<<"Enter the details of second account"<<endl;
a2.input();
cout<<"Withdraw Rs 4200 from John's account"<<endl;
a1.withdraw(4200);
cout<<"Deposit Rs 2000 in Jack's account"<<endl;
a2.deposit(2000);
cout<<"The account details are"<<endl;
a1.output();
a2.output();
}
```

Output
```
Enter the details of first account
1 John 5000
Enter the details of second account
2 Jack 3000
Withdraw Rs 4200 from John's account
New Balance is 800
Deposit Rs 2000 in Jack's account
New Balance is 5000
The account details are

1 John 800
2 Jack 5000
```

Let us understand the program from the first line of main function.

The statement

```
Account a1,a2;
```

creates two objects of class account as shown in the Figure 11.20. The members of each of the objects will have junk values initially till the time valid values are set.

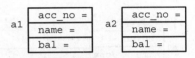

Figure 11.20: State of account objects a1 and a2

The statement

```
a1.input();
```

will invoke the `input()` function over object a1, and hence it will take the acc_no, name and balance of object a1 as input from the user. Similarly, the statement **a2.input();** will take the acc_no, name and balance of object a2 as input from the user. Let us assume that the user enters the following values for Account objects a1 and a2 as tabulated:

Object of class Account	Data entered by the user (id, name, balance)
a1	(1, "John", 5000)
a2	(2, "Jack", 3000)

This means that the state of Account objects a1 and a2 is as shown in the Figure 11.21.

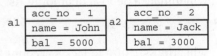

Figure 11.21: State of Account objects a1 and a2

When we compare this memory representation with the real world, we understand that there are two different accounts in a bank. One of the accounts is of a customer "John" and other account is of a customer "Jack". Figure 11.21 shows that the data about two accounts is very well organized in computer memory by creating objects of class Account, and hence we say that OOP is a programming that correctly simulates **'real world'**.

The next statement

```
a1.withdraw(4200);
```

implies that we attempt to withdraw Rs. 4200 from the account `a1` which means that John has initiated a withdrawal of amount 4200 from his account. The `withdraw()` function will now start executing as shown in the Figure 11.22. Note that any access to variable `bal` in `withdraw()` function will refer to the balance of object `a1` because it is the object that invoked the function. Hence, the following statement will modify the value of `bal` for object `a1` by reducing the balance by the amount to be withdrawn from account:

```
bal = bal - amount;
```

Hence, the new balance of "John" is now Rs. 800 as shown in the Figure 11.22.

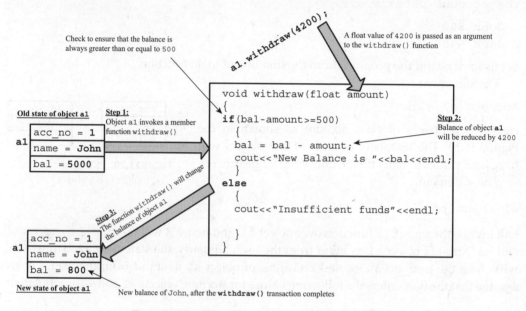

Figure 11.22: Execution of `a1.withdraw(4200)`

Similarly, the statement

```
a2.deposit(2000);
```

will initiate a deposit of amount Rs. 2000 in Jack's account. Hence, the statement

```
bal = bal + amount;
```

will add Rs. 2000 to Jack's account thereby storing the new balance in object a2 as 5000 as shown in the Figure 11.23.

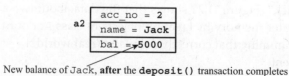

New balance of Jack, **after** the **deposit()** transaction completes

Figure 11.23: State of object a2

The last statements a1.output() and a2.output() print the complete details of Account objects a1 and a2 as seen in the code.

NOTES

A member function of a class is always invoked using an object of that class. Invoking a member function using an object is referred as **passing a message** to the object. One of the examples of message passing could be,

```
a1.withdraw(4200);
```

This means that, we are passing a message to a Account object a1 to reduce its balance by 4200. Passing a message to a object may or may not change its state, although in this specific case it has changed the state of object.

11.8 Calculating Slope of the Line: An Example

As an example, let us develop a program to calculate the slope of a line defined from point p1(x, y) to point p2(x, y).Clearly, each point object must store x value and y value and hence we create a class Point with private members x and y as seen in the code. Also, we will need following member functions in class Point:

- **input()**: To take x and y values of each point as input from the user.
- **output()**: To print the x and y values of each point on the computer screen
- **slope()**: To calculate the slope of the line defined between two point objects

The functions input() and output() will be similar to the one designed with earlier examples. Hence, we start explanation of this example by describing the logic used to calculate the slope. The slope (represented by s) of a line from (x1, y1) to (x2, y2) is defined as

```
s = (y2-y1)/(x2-x1)
```

In this case, as the line is defined between two Point objects p1 and p2, the equation for slope can be re-written as follows:

```
s =(p2.y-p1.y)/(p2.x-p1.x);
```

Since calculating the slope needs access to private members x and y, we create a function slope() as a member function of the class Point as seen in the code.

As slope() is a member function, it must be invoked using object of a class. This means that the member function slope() must be invoked using object p1 or using object p2. If we invoke the member function slope() using object p1, the values of members x and y for object p1 can be directly accessed inside the function as shown in the Figure 11.24a.

As noted, the x and y coordinate values of the end point p2 will also be required inside the slope() function to calculate the slope of the line. Since the function is invoked using object p1; p2's members cannot be directly accessed inside it. To solve this problem, we will have to pass object p2 as an argument to the function so that the complete object p2 will now be available in the formal argument t as shown in

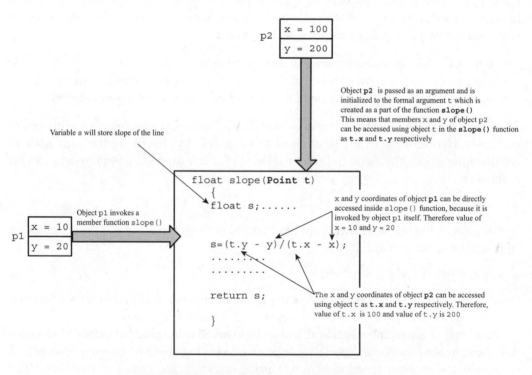

Figure 11.24a: Direct access to p1's x and y values inside function slope()

Figure 11.24b: Invoking the slope() function

the Figure 11.24b. Note that t is also the object of class Point like p2, and hence the member values x and y of object t will carry the same values as that of x and y of object p2. This is because object t is a formal argument and object p2 is the actual argument passed to the `slope()` function. Hence, a call to the `slope()` function must be made as

```
s= p1.slope(p2);
```

The member function `slope()` is invoked by object p1, and object p2 is passed as an argument to it. This means that x and y values of p1 can be directly accessed inside the function, whereas the x and y values of p2 must be accessed using object t as **t.x** and **t.y**, respectively, as shown in the Figure 11.24b.

The function `slope()` now evaluates the slope of the line defined between two `Point` objects and returns the calculated slope (a float value) back to the calling function. Given below is the complete source code to calculate the slope of the line.

```cpp
#include<iostream.h>
class Point
{
private:
int x;
int y;
public:
    void input()
    {
    cin>>x>>y;
    }
    void output()
    {
    cout<<x<<"    "<<y<<endl;
    }
    float slope(Point t)
    {
    float s;
    if(t.x-x!=0)
    {
    s=(float)(t.y-y)/(t.x-x);
    return s;
    }
    else
    {
    cout<<"Slope is undefined, printing a dummy value as 0"<<endl;
    return 0;
    }
    }
};
```

```
void main()
{
float s;
Point p1,p2;
cout<<"Enter the start point of the line"<<endl;
p1.input();
cout<<"Enter the end point of the line"<<endl;
p2.input();
s=p1.slope(p2);
cout<<"Slope of the line is "<<s;
}
```

Output:

```
Enter the start point of the line
10 43
Enter the end point of the line
34 45
Slope of the line is 0.083333
```

Let us understand the code from the first line of the main function.

The statement

```
Point p1,p2;
```

creates two objects of class `Point` as shown in the Figure 11.25. Following this we take the x and y values of each of the `Point` objects as input from the user by invoking the input () function over each of the objects as shown:

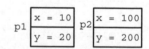

Figure 11.25: State of Point objects p1 and p2

```
p1.input();
p2.input();
```

Let us assume that the user enters the following values for `Point` objects p1 and p2 as tabulated:

Object of class Point	Data entered by the user (x,y)
p1	(10, 20)
p2	(100, 200)

This means that the state of `Point` objects p1 and p2 is as shown in the Figure 11.25.

The next statement

```
s=p1.slope(p2);
```

invokes the member function slope using object p1 and passing p2 as an argument. Hence the variable s now stores the slope of the line returned by the member function `slope()`. Following this we print the result s on the computer screen as seen in the code.

NOTES

The statement

```
s=p1.slope(p2);
```

invokes member function `slope()` using object p1 and passes object p2 as an argument to the function. The member function slope creates another object named as t as a formal argument and hence p2's members x and y can be accessed using object t as t.x and t.y respectively. It is important to understand that p2 and t are two different objects in memory but the member values of object p2 will be same as that of the member values of object t because p2 is a actual argument and t is the formal argument.

Instead of creating p2 and t as two different objects you can also pass **object by reference**. Passing object p2 by reference is possible by creating the formal argument t as a reference of type Point rather than an object of type Point as shown below

```
float slope(Point& t)          t a reference variable of type Point
{                              which will refer to the actual argument p2
float s;
      if(t.x-x!=0)
      {
      s=(float)(t.y-y)/(t.x-x);
      return s;
      }
      else
      {
      cout<<"Slope is undefined, printing a dummy value as 0"<<endl;
      return 0;
      }
}
```

Rest of the logic used in the `slope()` function is exactly same as what is given in the program. When object is relatively large in size, passing objects by reference is always a better option instead of passing them by value. This is because call by value, (unlike call by reference or call by address) creates two different copies of the same object which may result into a considerable utilization of storage space during program execution.

11.9   Addition of Complex Numbers: An Example

Just like each Point object is defined by specifying its x value and y value, every complex number also is defined by specifying its real part and imaginary part. Hence, we create two private variables real and img as members of class Complex as seen from the code.

Further, we need following member functions in class Complex:

- **input()**: To take real and img values of each Complex object as input from the user.
- **output()**: To print the real and img values of each Complex object on the computer screen.
- **add()**: To perform the addition of two Complex objects and return the result of addition.

The functions input() and output() will be similar to the one designed with previous examples. Hence, we start the explanation of this example from the member function add().

If C1 and C2 are two objects of class Complex and if we need to store the result of addition of C1 and C2 in another complex number C3, then the value of C3's real part is to be obtained as addition of C1's real part and C2's real part, whereas the value of C3's imaginary part is to be obtained as addition of C1's imaginary part and C2's imaginary part. In the absence of data hiding, this can be achieved using following C++ statements:

```
C3.real=C1.real+C2.real;
C3.img=C1.img+C2.img;
```

However, we understand that the members real and img are private members of class Complex, and hence we must write a member function inside a class to perform addition of Complex objects. Let us name this member function as add().

Recall that a member function of the class is always invoked using the object of that class. This means that the member function add() must be invoked using object C1 or using object C2. If we invoke the member function **add()** using object C1, then the values of members real and img for object C1 can be directly accessed inside the add() function as shown in the Figure 11.26.

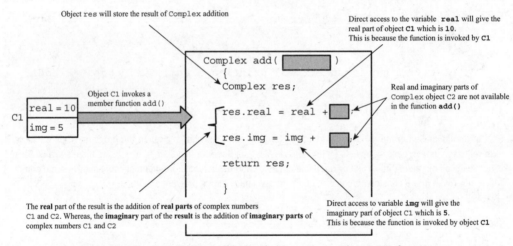

Figure 11.26: Accessing members of object C1 inside add() function

As noted, the real and img values of the complex object C2 will also be required inside the **add()** function to calculate the result of addition of two complex numbers. Hence, we apply a similar logic as discussed with the example to calculate the slope and pass C2 as an argument to function add(). Therefore, we make a call to function add() as shown below:

```
C3= C1.add(C2);
```

The member function add() is invoked by object C1 and passing C2 as an argument. This means that real and img values of C1 can be directly accessed inside the add() function, whereas the real and img values of C2 must be accessed using object t as **t.real** and **t.img**, respectively. This is because t is a formal argument corresponding to the actual argument C2 as shown in the Figure 11.27.

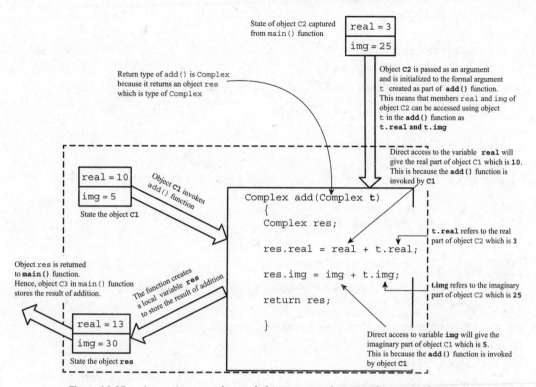

State of object C2 captured from main() function

real = 3
img = 25

Object **C2** is passed as an argument and is initialized to the formal argument t created as part of **add()** function. This means that members real and img of object C2 can be accessed using object t in the **add()** function as **t.real and t.img**

Return type of add() is Complex because it returns an object res which is type of Complex

Direct access to the variable **real** will give the real part of object C1 which is **10**. This is because the **add()** function is invoked by **C1**

real = 10
img = 5

State the object **C1**

Object **C1** invokes add() function

```
Complex add(Complex t)
{
    Complex res;

    res.real = real + t.real;

    res.img = img + t.img;

    return res;

}
```

t.real refers to the real part of object C2 which is **3**

t.img refers to the imaginary part of object C2 which is **25**

Object res is returned to **main()** function. Hence, object C3 in main() function stores the result of addition.

The function creates a local variable **res** to store the result of addition

real = 13
img = 30

State the object **res**

Direct access to variable **img** will give the imaginary part of object C1 which is **5**. This is because the **add()** function is invoked by object **C1**

Figure 11.27: Accessing members of objects C1 and C2 inside add() function

Also, we need to store the result of addition in the Complex object C3. However, the object C3 will not be accessible inside the add() function because its scope is limited to main(). Hence, we create a temporary object res, which stores the result of addition of the two complex numbers in add() function. The object res is later returned to the calling function and initialized to object C3 as shown in the Figure 11.27. Hence, the result of addition will be available in C3 after add() completes its execution.

The following is the complete source code to perform the addition of complex numbers:

```
#include<iostream.h>
class Complex
{
private:
    int real;
    int img;
public:
  void input()
    {
    cin>>real>>img;
    }
```

```
   Complex add(Complex t)
     {
       Complex res;
       res.real=real+t.real;
       res.img =img +t.img;
       return res;
     }
     void output()
     {
     cout<<"Real part is "<<real<<"Img part is "<<img;
     }
};
void main()
{
Complex C1,C2,C3;
cout<<"Enter first Complex  number"<<endl;
C1.input();
cout<<"Enter second Complex number"<<endl;
C2.input();
C3 = C1.add(C2);
cout<<"Result Complex number is"<<endl;
C3.output();
}
```

Output:

```
Enter first Complex number
10 5
Enter second Complex number
3 25
Result Complex number is
Real part is 13 Img part is 30
```

Let us understand the code from the first line of the main() function. The statement

```
Complex C1,C2,C3;
```

creates three objects of class Complex. Following this we take the real and img values of two complex numbers C1 and C2 as input from the user by invoking the input() function over each of the objects as shown below:

```
C1.input();
C2.input();
```

Let us assume that the user enters the following values for Complex objects C1 and C2 as tabulated:

Object of class Complex	Data entered by the user (real, img)
C1	(10, 5)
C2	(3, 25)

This means that the state of Complex objects C1 and C2 is as shown in the Figure 11.28.

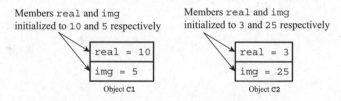

Figure 11.28: State of Complex objects C1 and C2

The next statement

```
C3=C1.add(C2);
```

invokes the member function add() using object C1 and passing C2 as an argument. The result of addition will be returned and stored in the object C3 after the execution of add() completes. We can now print the result of complex addition by printing the value of members real and img for object C3. This can be done by invoking the function output() using object C3 as done in the last line of main() function.

11.10 Addition of Points in Cartesian Coordinate System: An Example

Just like every complex number has two parts real and imaginary, every two-dimensional point is defined using x and y coordinates. Hence, we can add two points in Cartesian coordinate system in the same way as we performed addition of complex numbers in the previous section.

Given below is the full source code to perform addition of Point objects:

```
#include<iostream.h>
class Point
{
private:
int x;
int y;
public:
void input()
{
```

```
cin>>x>>y;
}
void output()
{
cout<<x<<"    "<<y<<endl;
}
Point add(Point t)
    {
Point res;
res.x=x+t.x;
res.y=y+t.y;
return res;
    }
};
void main()
{
Point p1,p2,p3;
cout<<"Enter first point"<<endl;
p1.input();
cout<<"Enter second point"<<endl;
p2.input();
p3 =p1.add(p2);
cout<<"Resultant point is"<<endl;
p3.output();
}
Enter first point
10 20
Enter second point
5 15
Resultant point is
15    35
```

The program creates three point objects p1, p2, and p3. The x and y coordinate values for objects p1 and p2 are taken as input from the user.

Let us assume that the user inputs the following values for Point objects p1 and p2:

Object of class Point	Data entered by the user (x, y)
p1	(10, 20)
p2	(5, 15)

The statement

```
p3 =p1.add(p2);
```

will invoke the function add() using object p1 and pass object p2 as an argument. The statement performs addition of point object p1 and p2 and store the result of addition in object p3. Hence x and y values of object p3 will be 15 and 35, respectively.

Finally, we print the result on the computer screen by invoking output() function over p3.

Is it possible to add more than two Point objects in a single statement? ?

Yes. As each add() function returns a Point object, it is possible to cascade the function calls to add(). Let us assume that we need to perform addition of 5 Point objects p1, p2, p3, p4, p5 and store the result in object p6. It is possible to perform the complete addition using a single statement by cascading function calls to add() as shown below

```
p6=p1.add(p2).add(p3).add(p4).add(p5);
```

The function calls will be resolved from left to right and hence the first invocation of add() will return a temporary Point object which gives the result of addition of p1 and p2. The second add() function is invoked using this temporary object and by passing p3 as an argument to it. In summary, the object representing the result of previous addition is used to invoke the next add() function; hence p6 will contain the result of addition of all point objects p1 to p5. **Remember, cascading function calls to add() is possible because add() returns an object of class Point.**

11.11 Array of Objects

Just like any other array, we can also create an array of objects in C++. Given below is the syntax to create an array of class objects:

```
ClassName ArrayName[size];
```

As an example to create array of objects, let us consider the class Employee defined in Section 11.6 with private members id, name, and salary and public functions input() and output(). The below C++ statement creates an array of Employee objects named as e with a size of 3.

```
Employee e[3];
```

Note that each element of the array e will be an object of class Employee because the data type of the full array is Employee. As the size of the array e is specified as 3, the first Employee object can be accessed as e[0], the second Employee object can be accessed as e[1] and the last Employee object can be accessed as e[2] as shown in the Figure 11.29.

Each element of the array e[0], e[1], and e[2] are actually separate objects of class Employee. Therefore each element of the array contains members id, name, and salary as shown in the Figure 11.29. This also means that we can invoke the member functions input() and output() using each of the objects. For example, the statement

```
e[0].input();
```

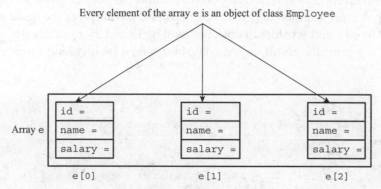

Figure 11.29: Array of objects e

will invoke the member function input() using object e[0], and hence, the **cin** statement written inside the input function will execute and take the id, name, and salary of employee e[0] as input from the user.

Similarly, the statements

```
e[1].input();
```

and

```
e[2].input();
```

will invoke the member function input() using objects e[1] and e[2], respectively, to take the member values of each of the objects as input from the user. Let us assume that the user inputs the id, name, and salary of each of the employee objects as shown in the table below:

Invocation of input() function	Data entered by the user (id, name, salary)
e[0].input();	(1,"John",1000)
e[1].input();	(2,"Jack",5000)
e[2].input();	(3,"Jill",3000)

This means that the state of array e in the computer memory will be as shown in the Figure 11.30.

Similarly, the statements

```
e[0].output();
e[1].output();
e[2].output();
```

will invoke a output() function and execute a **cout** statement which will print the member values of each of the respective Employee objects.

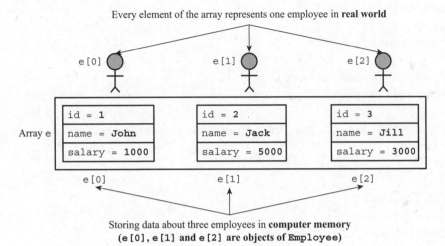

Storing data about three employees in **computer memory**
(e[0], e[1] and e[2] are objects of Employee)

Figure 11.30:   State of the array e

11.12 Employee Management System: Revisited

Let us develop a C++ program to store the details of n employees in a computer memory. As the value of n is not known at the time of compilation, we will create an array e of size 100, assuming that the maximum number of employees will always be ≤100. The below statement will create an array e of type Employee with a size as 100:

```
Employee e[100];
```

As seen later in the code, the program also takes the value of variable n as input from the user to determine the actual number of employees to be stored in the computer memory. Recall from Section 11.11 that each element e[i] of the array e is actually the object of class Employee, hence we can invoke the function input() over each of the object e[i] to accept members id, name, and salary of e[i] as input from the user. Similarly, we can invoke the function output() over each of the object e[i] to print the members id, name, and salary of e[i]. In the program, we have used a simple for loop to iterate over the array e. As there are a total of n objects in the array, the value index i will range from 0 to n–1 as seen in the code.

In the following code, we first accept the data about all the employees as input from the user by invoking the input() function for each of the Employee objects in the for loop and then print the members of each of the Employee objects using another for loop as shown.

```
#include<iostream.h>
class Employee
{
private:
    int id;
    char name[100];
```

```
        int salary;
public:
    void input()
    {
    cin>>id>>name>>salary;
    while(salary<0)
    {
    cout<<"Salary cannot be negative, please re-enter its value";
    cin>>salary;
    }
    }
    void output()
    {
    cout<<id<<"    "<<name<<"    "<<salary<<endl;
    }
};
void main()
{
Employee e[100];
int i,n;
cout<<"Enter the total number of employees"<<endl;
cin>>n;
    for(i=0;i<=n-1;i++)
    {
    cout<<"Enter the details of Employee Number "<<i+1<<endl;
    e[i].input();
    }
cout<<"Employee details are"<<endl;
    for(i=0;i<=n-1;i++)
    {
    e[i].output();
    }
}
```

Output:

```
Enter the total number of employees
2
Enter the details of Employee Number 1
1 John 2000
Enter the details of Employee Number 2
2 Jack 3000
Employee details are
1 John 2000
2 Jack 3000
```

11.13   `friend` Functions

Until this point, we learned that the private members of a class can only be accessed inside the class. Creating a friend function is an exception to this statement because a friend function is always present outside the class but can still access the private members of that class.

To create a friend function, a class must prototype that function using a keyword `friend` as shown in the Figure 11.31. Here, we create function `f1()` as a friend of class `Pqr` by prototyping the function `f1()` inside the class `Pqr`. The complete function definition of a friend function is always present outside the class because a friend function is not the member of a class. (As seen from Figure 11.31, the function `f1()` is just prototyped in class `Pqr` but is defined outside the class.) Therefore, a friend function is never invoked using object of a class like member functions. The friend function must be invoked directly just like any other non-member function.

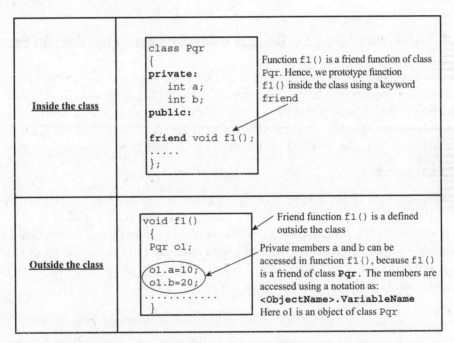

Figure 11.31:   Accessing members of a class using friend function

Since friend function is not invoked using any of the objects, the member variables cannot be directly accessed from the friend function. Rather the members of the object should be accessed by explicitly giving the object name followed by membership operator to determine the exact object whose member is to be accessed.

`<objectName>.VariableName`

Similarly, if a friend function needs to call any member function from its definition, you must explicitly specify the name of the object using which the member function needs to be invoked. Hence, the syntax to invoke the member function from the friend function is as follows:

```
<objectName>.MemberFunctionName(argument List);
```

You can also access the members and member functions of a class from friend function by creating a pointer to object. Creation and usage of pointers with class objects is discussed in section 11.15. For now, we will use the notation to access members using object name as seen in the Figure 11.31.

NOTES

friend function is defined outside class but it can still access private members and private member functions of the class.

11.14 Addition of `Point` Objects using `friend` Function: An Example

As an example, let us perform addition of `Point` objects using a friend function `add()`. The complete program is same as discussed in Section 11.11 with an only difference that the function `add()` is now created as a friend function of class `Point` as seen in the code.

Since the function `add()` is created as a friend function, we do not need an object to invoke it. Hence, we have invoked the function `add()` using the following statement:

```
p3 = add(p1,p2);
```

The members of no object can be directly accessed inside the function `add()` because it is not invoked using any of the objects. Hence, we pass both the objects p1 and p2 as an argument to the function such that the actual argument p1 gets initialized to the formal object t and the actual argument p2 gets initialized to the formal object p as seen in the code. This means that, members of object p1 and p2 can be accessed using formal arguments t and p, respectively, as shown in the Figure 11.32.

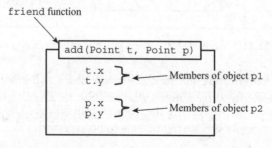

Figure 11.32: Addition of `Point` objects using `friend` function

The following is the full source code to perform addition of `Point` objects using friend function `add()`:

```
#include<iostream.h>
class Point
{
private:
int x;
int y;
public:
    void input()
    {
    cin>>x>>y;
    }
    void output()
    {
    cout<<x<<"    "<<y<<endl;
    }
/*Declare the function add() as a friend of class Point*/
friend Point add(Point,Point);
};
Point add(Point t,Point p)
{
Point res;
res.x=t.x+p.x;
res.y =t.y +p.y;
return res;
}
void main()
{
Point p1,p2,p3;
cout<<"Enter first point"<<endl;
p1.input();
cout<<"Enter second point"<<endl;
p2.input();
p3 =add(p1,p2);
cout<<"Resultant point is"<<endl;
p3.output();
}
```

Output

```
Enter first point
10 20
Enter second point
5 15
Resultant point is
15    35
```

> **NOTES**
>
> The function add() can directly access private members x and y of class Point, because it is created as a friend of class Point. The following statement in Point class, declares add() as a friend function of class Point
> `friend Point add(Point,Point);`

11.14.1 `friend` class

A class can be made a friend of another class. If class C1 is made a friend of class C2, it means that all the member functions of class C1 can access the private members of class C2. To make C1 a friend of C2, we must declare prototype the class C1 using a friend keyword when defining class C2 as follows:

```
class C2
{
/*members and member functions of class C2*/
friend class C1; // Declares C1 as a friend of C2
};
```

class C1 should be defined as usual with no change in syntax as shown below:

```
class C1
{
/*members and member functions of class C1*/
};
```

You can now access all the private members of class C2 inside any of the member functions within class C1 because when C1 is declared as a friend of class C2, all the member functions of class C1 will be considered as friend functions of class C2.

As an example, let us create a class named as Data and create a class named as Result as a friend of class Data.

As seen from the Figure 11.33, class Data has two integer type members a and b with an input() function to take the value of these members as input from the user. Class Result has three members res_add, res_sub, and res_mul that are responsible to store the result of addition, subtraction, and multiplication of members a and b, respectively. As shown in the Figure 11.33, the statement written in class Data,

```
friend class Result;
```

makes Result as a friend of class Data. This means that all the member functions within class Result can access the private members of class Data. Hence, we can access members a and b of class Data in the member functions add(), sub(), and mul() directly as shown in the Figure 11.33. Note that each of the functions add(), sub(), and mul() take an object of class Data as an argument and performs addition, subtraction, and multiplication (of members a and b of class Data), respectively.

In the program main(), creates two objects named as d1 and r1 of class Data and class Result, respectively. The statement

```
d1.input();
```

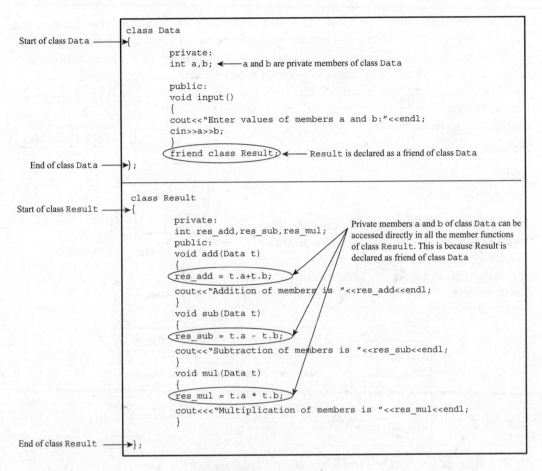

Figure 11.33: `friend` classes

invokes a public member function `input()` of class `Data` to take the values of members `a` and `b` as input from the user. We assume that the user inputs the value of member `a` as `10` and `b` as `20`, hence the state of object `d1` is as shown in Figure 11.34a.

Since the object `d1` is a local variable of `main()` function, we have passed this object as an argument to function `add()`, `sub()`, and `mul()` so that these functions can access the members of object `d1`. The statement

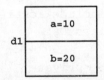

Figure 11.34a: State of object `d1`

```
r1.add(d1);
```

written inside `main()` function invokes the function `add()` by passing `d1` as an argument. The formal argument in function `add()` is named as `t`, and hence, members `a` and `b` of object `d1` can be accessed using object `t` inside `add()` function.

The following statement in `add` function

```
res_add = t.a+t.b;
```

will perform the addition of members a and b of object d1 and store the result in the variable res_add(), which is the private member of object r1. Note that, although a and b are private members of class Data, they can be accessed directly within the function add() because Result is declared as a **friend class of** Data.

Hence, after execution of add() function, the state of object r1 will be as shown in Figure 11.34b:

Similarly, the statements

r1.sub(d1);

and

r1.mul(d1);

will perform subtraction and multiplication of members a and b by passing object d1 as an argument to functions sub() and mul(), respectively. Hence, the final state of object r1 after execution of the functions add(), sub(), and mul() is as shown in the Figure 11.34c.

Figure 11.34b: State of object r1

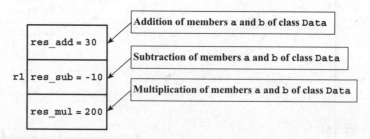

Figure 11.34c: Object r1 after execution of functions add(), sub(), and mul()

The following is the full source code to attain the mentioned results:

```cpp
#include<iostream.h>
class Data
{
    private:
    int a,b;
    public:
    void input()
    {
      cout<<"Enter values of members a and b:"<<endl;
      cin>>a>>b;
    }
    friend class Result;
};
class Result
```

```
{
    private:
    int res_add,res_sub,res_mul;
    public:
    void add(Data t)
    {
      res_add = t.a+t.b;
      cout<<"Addition of members is "<<res_add<<endl;
    }
    void sub(Data t)
    {
      res_sub = t.a - t.b;
      cout<<"Subtraction of members is "<<res_sub<<endl;
    }
    void mul(Data t)
    {
      res_mul = t.a * t.b;
      cout<<"Multiplication of members is "<<res_mul<<endl;
    }
};
void main()
{
    Data d1;
    Result r1;
    /*Take members a and b as input from the user*/
    d1.input();
    /*Perform addition of members of object d1, using an object of
    class Result*/
    r1.add(d1);
/*Perform subtraction of members of object d1, using an object of
    class Result*/
    r1.sub(d1);
/*Perform multiplication of members of object d1, using an object
    of class Result*/
    r1.mul(d1);
}
```

Output

```
Enter values of members a and b:
10 20
```

```
Addition of members is 30
Subtraction of members is -10
Multiplication of members is 200
```

> **Is friendship among classes transitive in nature? For example, if class C is a friend of class B and class B is a friend of class A, then can we say that class C is a friend of class A?**　**?**

NO! Friendships are not at all transitive in nature. If class C is a friend of class B, it can access the private variables and functions of class B, but it will not be able to access private variables and functions of class A even if class B is a friend of class A. If you want class C to access the private members of class A, then class C must be declared as a friend class of A as well. The keyword friend in C++ very much simulates how friendship works in real world. If you have two friends say Peter and John, it does not mean that Peter and John are also friends of each other, it just means that you know both of them. It is very much possible that Peter and John may not recognize each other at all.

NOTES

The principle of **data hiding** says that, private members should not be accessible at anyplace outside class. The keyword **friend** in a way, **violates** the principle of data hiding because it makes private members of a particular class accessible to **friends of the class**. Hence, concept of friend functions or friend classes must be used with an extra caution in the programs so as to ensure that the integrity of the data is not violated. It is a good programming practice to avoid usage of friend classes and friend functions as much as possible and tune the encapsulation itself such that it provides necessary public methods which can provide a gateway to access private members of the class.

11.15　Pointer to Objects

We can define pointers that can point to objects of a class. Recall from Chapter 8 that the data type of the pointer must be same as the data type of the object to which the pointer points to. (We will discuss an exception to this rule in Chapter 14.)

As an example, let us create a pointer p to point to object of class Employee. As the pointer is required to point to Employee object, the data type of the pointer must also be Employee as shown below:

```
Employee *p;
```

Let us now create two objects of class Employee named as e1 and e2, using the following C++ statement:

```
Employee e1, e2;
```

This means that the objects e1 and e2 will be created in RAM, and we assume the address of object e1 as 8000 and address of object e2 as 9000 as shown in the Figure 11.35.

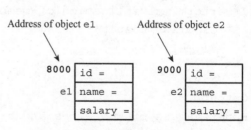

Figure 11.35: Objects e1 and e2

Once the objects are created in memory, we can make a pointer p to point to any of the objects. This means that the pointer p can hold the address of object e1 or e2. Let us store the address of object e1 inside a pointer p, which can be done using the following statement:

```
p=&e1;
```

The pointer p will now point to object e1 as shown in the Figure 11.36.

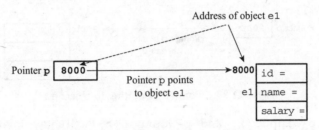

Figure 11.36: Pointer p pointing to object e1

We can now invoke the member functions of object e1 using a pointer p with an arrow operator ->.

This means that the statement

```
p->input();
```

will invoke the member function input() for object e1 because the pointer p points to object e1 as shown in the Figure 11.36. Therefore, the statement p->input(); will take the members id, name and salary of Employee object e1 as input from the user. If the user enters the id of e1 as 1, name of e1 as John, and the salary of e1 as 5000, then the state of object e1 is changed as shown in the Figure 11.37.

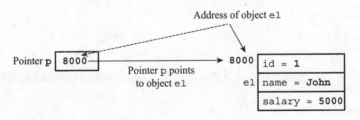

Figure 11.37: State of object e1

Similarly, the statement

```
p->output();
```

will invoke the member function output() for object e1 because the pointer p still points to object e1 as shown in the Figure 11.36. Therefore, the statement p->output(); will print the members id, name and salary of employee object e1 on the computer screen.

The pointer p can similarly also point to object e2 using the statement

```
p=&e2;
```

as shown in the Figure 11.38.

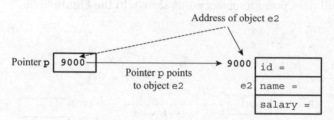

Figure 11.38: Pointer p pointing to object e2

The statements p->input(); and p->output(); will now invoke the member functions input() and output() for object e2. Given is the source code that demonstrates usage of pointers with objects of class Employee.

```cpp
#include<iostream.h>
class Employee
{
private:
    int id;
    char name[100];
    int salary;
public:
void input()
{
cin>>id>>name>>salary;
    while(salary<0)
    {
    cout<<"Salary cannot be negative, please re-enter its value";
    cin>>salary;
    }
}
void output()
{
cout<<id<<"    "<<name<<"    "<<salary<<endl;
}
};
void main()
{
```

```
Employee e1,e2;
Employee *p;
//make pointer p point to object e1
p=&e1;
cout<<"Enter the details of first employee"<<endl;
p->input();
cout<<"The details of first employee are"<<endl;
p->output();
//make pointer p point to object e2
p=&e2;
cout<<"Enter the details of second employee"<<endl;
p->input();
cout<<"The details of second employee are"<<endl;
p->output();
}
```

Output:

```
Enter the details of first employee
1 John 5000
The details of first employee are
1 John 5000
Enter the details of second employee
2 Jack 3000
The details of second employee are
2 Jack 3000
```

NOTES

When passing object as an argument to the function, we can pass the object by address in a similar manner as we explained **call by address** for primitive types in Chapter 8 of this text book.

To pass objects by address the actual argument specified during the function call should be address of the object and the formal argument in the function definition should be a **pointer** of type class.

For example, consider the program to calculate slope of a line given in Section 11.8, which invokes the member function `slope()` using object `p1` by passing `p2` as an argument as shown below

```
s=p1.slope(p2);
```

We have used normal call by value in the program given in Section 11.8. Instead of passing `p2` by value, you could pass address of object `p2` in the function call as show below

```
s=p1.slope(&p2);
```

Note that the formal argument is **&p2** which means address of object `p2` is passed to the function `slope()` rather than passing the full object. Hence the member function `slope()` in class `Point` must accept the address by declaring the formal argument as a pointer of type `Point` as shown below. As seen the formal argument of the function is a pointer named as `ptr` which will contain the address of object p2 (which is the actual argument). Hence the x and y coordinate values of object p2 can be accessed as `ptr->x` and `ptr->y` respectively

```
float slope(Point* ptr)
{
    float s;
    if(ptr->x-x!=0)
    {
    s=(float)(ptr->y-y)/(ptr->x-x);
    return s;
    }
    else
    {
    cout<<"Slope is undefined, printing a dummy value as 0"<<endl;
    return 0;
    }
}
```

If you compare this function with the one given in Section 11.8, you will see that every occurrence of t . x is replaced by `ptr->x` and t . y is replaced by `ptr->y` because the formal argument which was object t in Section 11.8 is replaced by pointer `ptr`. When object is relatively large in size, passing objects by address or by reference is always a better option instead of passing them by value. This is because call by value (unlike call by address or call by reference) creates two different copies of the same object which may result into a heavy utilization of storage space during program execution.

11.16 Binding of Pointers with Individual Members of the Class

In the previous section, we have created a pointer to object and accessed individual members/member functions. Instead of creating a pointer to the full object, you can also create a pointer to a specific member or a member function of the class. Creating a pointer to a specific member is a three-step process.

Step 1: Declare a pointer to a member of a class

If the name of the class is A and the data type of the member for which a pointer needs to be created is B, then the syntax to declare a pointer named as `ptr`, which will have an ability to point to member of class A having a data type B is as given below:

`B A::*ptr;`

You can also declare a pointer that has the ability to point to a member function of a class. If the member function of class A has a return type R, then following syntax can be used to declare a pointer named as `pftr` that has the ability to point to the member function.

`R (A::*pftr)(comma separated list of data types of the arguments);`

Note that, at this stage, the pointer is not pointing to any member. We have just declared a pointer that has the ability to point to a particular member or a member function.

Step 2: Bind the pointer to a specific member of a class

After the pointer is declared, you must bind the pointer to a specific member. If delta is a member variable within class A and has a data type as B, you can bind the pointer ptr we created in step 1 to the member delta using the following syntax:

```
ptr = &A::delta;
```

&A::delta in the above statement should be read as address of member delta declared in class A. At this stage, the pointer named as ptr is attached to member delta of class A, which means that you can use pointer named ptr with any of the objects of the class to access the member delta of a particular object. For example, if you use the pointer ptr with object o1, system will access member delta of o1. Similarly, if ptr is used with another object o2, system will access the member delta of object o2. The syntax to use a pointer with a particular object is given in step 3.

Similar to pointer to member variables, you must also bind pointer to member functions before they can be used with any specific object to invoke the member function of that object. Let us assume that f1() is the member function of class A taking 2 arguments of data types d1 and d2, and having a return type as R. In this case, we can create the pointer pftr and bind it to member function f1() using the following syntax:

```
/*create the pointer named pftr to point to a member function of
    class A*/
R (A::*pftr)(d1,d2);
/*Bind the pointer with member function f1*/
pftr = &A::f1;
```

Note that, at this stage, we have not accessed any member or a member function using a pointer but we have just attached the pointer to a member/member function. To access any non-static member or a member function of a class, you will always need an object of the class.

Step 3: Access the member using object of class and a bindable pointer

After the pointer is attached to a specific member, you can use it with any object. For example, let us assume that o1 and o2 are two objects of class A, then the statement

```
o1.*ptr = 10;
```

will set the value of member delta of object o1 to 10. This is because ptr is attached to delta. Similarly, the statement

```
o2.*ptr=55;
```

will set the value of member delta of object o2 to 55.

You can also invoke a member function f1() with any of the objects and using a pointer to a member function named as pftr, which we have created in step 2.

The statement

```
x = (o1.*pftr)(v1,v2);
```

will invoke the function f1() using object o1 because pftr is attached to function f1() as per step 2. We assume that v1 and v2 are the values of data types d1 and d2, respectively, and the data type of variable x is R. Similarly, the statement

```
x = (o2.*pftr)(v1,v2);
```

will invoke function f1() for object o2 by passing v1 and v2 as arguments and will store return value in x.

To illustrate the concept of binding pointers with members of the class, we create a simple class named as Data. The class has private members a, b and resultA and a public member named as resultS. The class has public function input to take the value of variables a and b as input from the user. The function operate() stores the result of addition of members a and b in variable resultA and result of subtraction of a and b in variable resultS. The operate() function returns the value of resultA, which is the result of addition. Notice that, there is no need to return the value of resultS from operate() function because it is anyway a public member of class Data. We will now access all the public members of class Data using the concept of bindable pointers in main() function. Note that, you will not be able to bind the pointers you create in main() function to private members of class Data because private members are not accessible at anyplace outside class. Bindable pointers will not breach the security of data which is provided by access specifiers of C++ in any manner.

```
#include<iostream.h>
class Data
{
    private:
        int a,b;
        int resultA;
    public:
        int resultS;
        void input()
        {
                cout<<"Enter values of members a and b:"<<endl;
                cin>>a>>b;
        }
        int operate()
        {
                resultA = a+b;
                resultS=a-b;
                return resultA;
        }
```

```
      float sumOfProd(float k1,float k2)
      {
      return a*k1+b*k2;
      }
};
void main()
{
/*Create 2 objects of class Data*/
Data o1,o2;
/*Create required pointers*/
int Data::*ptr;
void (Data::*pvftr)();
int (Data::*piftr)();
/*Bind pointers to individual members*/
ptr =&Data::resultS;
pvftr = &Data::input;
piftr = &Data::operate;
cout<<"**********Object o1**********"<<endl;
/*call function input for object o1*/
(o1.*pvftr)();
/*call function operate for object o1*/
int x= (o1.*piftr)();
cout<<"Addition is "<<x<<endl;
cout<<"Subtraction is "<<o1.*ptr<<endl;
/*Calling functions with arguments using bindable pointer*/
/*Step 1: Declare a pointer*/
float (Data::*pfmul)(float,float);
/*Step 2: Bind the pointer to sumOfProd function*/
pfmul = &Data::sumOfProd;
/*Step 3: invoke function sumOfProd using object o1*/
float res = (o1.*pfmul)(10.5,5.5);
cout<<"Sum of Products is "<<res<<endl;
cout<<"**********Object o2**********"<<endl;
/*call function input for object o2*/
(o2.*pvftr)();
/*call function operate for object o2*/
int y =(o2.*piftr)();
cout<<"Addition is "<<y<<endl;
cout<<"Subtraction is "<<o2.*ptr<<endl;
/*Call Multiply function for object o2*/
res = (o1.*pfmul)(50.5,8.5);
cout<<"Sum of Products is "<<res<<endl;
}
```

```
***********Object o1**********
Enter values of members a and b:
10 20
Addition is 30
Subtraction is -10
Sum of Products is 215
***********Object o2**********
Enter values of members a and b:
100 200
Addition is 300
Subtraction is -100
Sum of Products is 675
```

The statement

```
int Data::*ptr;
```

creates a pointer named as `ptr`, which has the ability to point to any member of type integer of class `Data`.

The statements

```
void (Data::*pvftr)();
int (Data::*piftr)();
```

create two pointers named as `pvftr` and `piftr`, which have the ability to point to any member functions of class `Data`. The pointer `pvftr` can point to any member function of class `Data` that takes no arguments and returns `void`. Whereas, `piftr` can point to any member function of class `Data` that takes no arguments but returns an integer.

The statements

```
ptr = &Data::resultS;
pvftr = &Data::input;
piftr = &Data::operate;
```

bind the pointer `ptr` with the member `resultS`, pointer `pvftr` with the member function `input()`, and `piftr` with the member function `operate()`.

Since we have created two objects o1 and o2 of class `Data`, you can use these pointers with any of the objects to access the member or a member function of that object.

The statement

```
(o1.*pvftr)();
```

will invoke the member function `input()` for object o1 because pointer `pvftr` is attached to `input()` function of class `Data`.

Similarly, the statement

```
int x= (o1.*piftr)();
```

will invoke the member function operate() for object o1 because pointer piftr is attached to operate() function of class Data. The resultant value returned by the operate() function will be stored in variable x. Hence, variable x will contain the result of addition of members a and b of object o1.

Since the pointer ptr is attached to the member resultS, we can access the member resultS of object o1 using pointer ptr as follows:

```
o1.*ptr
```

Hence, the statement

```
cout<<"Subtraction is "<<o1.*ptr<<endl;
```

will print the value of variable resultS of object o1.

To show how to call a function with parameters using bindable pointers, we have created a function named as sumOfProd() which accepts two floating point values k1 and k2, multiplies member a with k1 and member b with k2 and returns the sum of products. This is invoked by creating a pointer named as pfmul in the code as follows:

```
/*Step 1: Declare a pointer which can point to a function that
    takes two floating point numbers and returns a float*/
float (Data::*pfmul)(float,float);
/*Step 2: Bind the pointer to sumOfProd function*/
pfmul = &Data::sumOfProd;
/*Step 3: Invoke function sumOfProd using object o1 by passing two
    constants to it 10.5 and 5.5*/
float res = (o1.*pfmul)(10.5,5.5);
cout<<"Sum of Products is "<<res<<endl;
```

The variable res will contain the following sum for object o1:

```
a*10.5+b*5.5
```

Assuming the value of a as 10 and b as 20 for object o1, the value of variable res will be **215.00,** which is printed on the computer screen by the cout statement.

We have mirrored similar statements for object o2 and invoked functions input() and operate() using the same pointers pvftr and piftr, respectively. We have again used the pointer ptr to print the result of subtraction for object o2.

11.17 this Pointer

this is a built-in pointer in C++ that points to the object using which the function is invoked. The keyword this is generally used inside the body of the member function to determine which object has invoked the function. We know that a class can have multiple objects, and a member function can be invoked using any one of the objects of the class. You may come across a situation wherein you have already entered into the function and need to determine the exact object that invoked the function within the function body.

This is a very realistic situation in designing C++ projects; imagine that you are writing just one class, and the caller code (the part of the program that calls functions of your class) is designed by someone else. Also, you do not have access to view the caller code, and while designing one of the member functions in your class, you need to refer to the object that invokes the function. Under such circumstances, you can use keyword this in your code because this by default points to the object that invoked the function.

The pointer this is generally used inside the body of a member function or inside the body of the constructor to get the object reference of the invoking object. As this is a pointer, we must use arrow operator (->) when accessing the members of the object using this keyword. The syntax to access any member variable of the invoking object using this keyword is as follows:

```
this->MemberName;
```

You can also, invoke another member function inside a body of particular member function over the same object using this keyword. The syntax to invoke a member function using this is as follows:

```
this->MemberFunctionName(comma separated list of arguments);
```

As an example to understand the syntax of this keyword, we create a class Abc with a single integer member variable a and input() and output() functions to take the value of a as input from the user and print it on the computer screen, respectively.

The member function input() of class Abc is defined as

```
void input()
{
cin>>this->a;
}
```

Note the presence of arrow operator -> inside() the input() function, which is used to access the member a of the invoking object.

Let O1 and O2 be two different objects of class Abc. The pointer **this** will always refer to the object that has invoked the member function of the class. This means that when the object O1 invokes the member function input(), this->a means member a of object O1, and hence, the statement

```
cin>>this->a;
```

will accept the value of member a of object O1 as input from the user.

Similarly, when the object O2 invokes the member function input(), this->a means member a of object O2 and hence the statement

```
cin>>this->a;
```

will accept the value of member a of object O2 as input from the user.

In this case, there is really no need to write this->a in the body of the function because the statement **cin>>a;** without the presence of this keyword inside the input() function just works fine. Hence the following input() function is equivalent to what is defined previously

```
void input()
{
cin>>a;
}
```

This is because any direct access of member a inside input () function will mean that we are accessing member a of the invoking object by default. This means that when input() is invoked using object O1, the statement

```
cin>>a;
```

will by default take member a of object O1 as input from the user, and when input() is invoked using object O2, the same statement

```
cin>>a;
```

will take member a of object O2 as input from the user. Hence in this case, there is no particular need to use the this keyword. But, anyway using this keyword just works fine. Similarly, we have used this keyword in the output () function to print the value of the member a on the computer screen as seen from the code.

The following is the full source code that shows the usage of **this** keyword in C++ by creating two objects O1 and O2 of the class Abc

```
#include<iostream.h>
class Abc
{
    private:
      int a;
    public:
    void input()
    {
    cin>>this->a;
    }
    void output()
    {
    cout<<"Value is "<<this->a<<endl;
    }
};
void main()
{
Abc O1,O2;
cout<<"Enter the value of O1's member"<<endl;
O1.input();
O1.output();
cout<<"Enter the value of O2's member"<<endl;
O2.input();
```

```
O2.output();
}
```

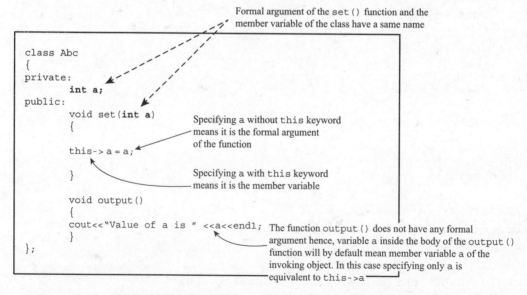

Turbo C++ IDE
```
Enter the value of O1's member
10
Value is 10
Enter the value of O2's member
20
Value is 20
```

11.18 Resolving Ambiguity using `this` Pointer

`this` keyword can be used to resolve the ambiguity that may occur when the formal argument of the member function has the same name as that of the member variable defined in the class.

For example, consider a class `Abc` with public functions `set()` and `output()` and a private member variable named a, as shown in the Figure 11.39. The function `set()` takes a formal argument which is also named as a. Hence, compiler will not be able to differentiate between an access made to the member variable a and the access made to the formal argument a within the scope of `set()` function. This ambiguity can be resolved using a `this` pointer in C++. When a variable is referred using a `this` pointer, it will be considered as an access the value of the member variable of the object, whereas if the variable is referred without using a `this` pointer it will be considered as access the formal argument of the function.

Formal argument of the `set()` function and the member variable of the class have a same name

```
class Abc
{
private:
        int a;
public:
        void set(int a)
        {

        this-> a = a;

        }
        void output()
        {
        cout<<"Value of a is " <<a<<endl;
        }
};
```

Specifying a without `this` keyword means it is the formal argument of the function

Specifying a with `this` keyword means it is the member variable

The function `output()` does not have any formal argument hence, variable a inside the body of the `output()` function will by default mean member variable a of the invoking object. In this case specifying only a is equivalent to `this->a`

Figure 11.39: Resolving ambiguity using `this` keyword

The statement

```
this->a=a;
```

will initialize the value of member variable a with the value passed to the formal argument of set () function (which is also named as a).

The following is the full source code that shows the ambiguity resolution within the set () function, using this pointer.

```
#include<iostream.h>
class Abc
{
private:
    int a;
public:
    void set(int a)
    {
    this->a=a;
    }
    void output()
    {
    cout<<"Value of a is "<<a<<endl;
    }
};
void main()
{
    Abc o1,o2;
    o1.set(10);
    o2.set(20);
    o1.output();
    o2.output();
}
```

NOTES

this is built-in pointer in C++ which points to the objects that invoked the member function. When used within the scope of member function this keyword generally is used to resolve ambiguity that may occur if the formal argument of the member function has the same name as that of the member variable defined in the class.

11.19 Cloning Objects using `this` Pointer: An Example

As another example of `this` keyword, we will create a member function `clone()` to create a copy of the invoking object. Consider class `Data` which has one private member named as a and public functions `set()` , `clone()`, and `output()`. The function `set()` is used to initialize the value of a and output() prints the value of member a on computer screen.

The function `clone()` is defined such that it returns the object that invoked it to the caller.

```
Data clone()
    {
    return *this;
    }
```

The statement

```
return *this;
```

returns the object that is pointed by the `this` pointer (which is the invoking object itself). Note that, we have applied an indirection operator * to the `this` pointer so as to ensure that the target object is returned and not the memory address. Hence, the statement

```
o2=o1.clone();
```

will create a copy of object o1 in object o2. In other words, object o2 will be created as a cloned version of object o1, and hence, all the members of object o2 will have same value as that of members of object o1. In this case, there is only one member variable defined in the class named as a hence value of member a of object o2 will also be set to 10.

We have also illustrated another way to clone the objects using the statement

```
o3=o2;
```

which is an alternative to `clone()` function designed by us. This statement will also do a member by member copy by using an assignment operator function. However, if we need to customize the cloning process, it will be absolutely necessary to create a custom function rather than using the built-in assignment operator. For example, consider the following definition of `clone()` function, which squares the value of member a of the invoking object before cloning it

```
Data clone()
    {
    a=a*a;
    return *this;
    }
```

The following is the full source code defining a simple `clone()` function to create copy of object using `this` keyword:

```cpp
#include<iostream.h>
class Data
{
    private:
      int a;
    public:
    void set(int t)
    {
      a=t;
    }
    Data clone()
    {
    return *this;
    }

    void output()
    {
      cout<<"a="<<a<<endl;
    }
};
void main()
{
Data o1,o2,o3;
o1.set(10);
o2=o1.clone();
cout<<"******o1*********"<<endl;
o1.output();
cout<<"******o2*********"<<endl;
o2.output();
o3=o2; //another way to clone objects
cout<<"******o3*********"<<endl;
o3.output();
}
```

Output

```
******o1*********
a=10
******o2*********
a=10
******o3*********
a=10
```

NOTES

`this` pointer holds the address of the object which invoked the member function. Hence if we use pointer `this` without indirection operator, it will give the starting address of the memory location where object is stored. From the function `clone()`, we need to return the target object and not the address; hence we have applied an indirection operator * with `this` pointer as highlighted below

```
return *this;
```

11.20 Dynamic Memory Allocation of Objects

We have learned the advantages of dynamic memory allocation in Chapter 10 of this text book. Just like you can use operator `new` for dynamic memory allocation of basic data types and structure objects, you can also use operator new to create an object of a class dynamically. Recall from Chapter 10 that dynamic memory is always unnamed; hence, we need a pointer to access it. The following is the syntax for dynamically creating an object of a class in the program:

```
pointer = new <ClassName>;
```

The statement will create an object of a class at run time and store the address of the object inside a pointer. Hence, the pointer will now start pointing to the object created in the heap. Similar to structures, we can access the members of the class object using an 'arrow operator' with the help of pointer. Note that the type of the pointer must be same as that of the 'type' defined by the class to make the pointer point to a class object.

As an example, let us create a class `Employee` with private members `id`, `name`, and `salary` and public functions `input()` and `output()` as shown below:

```cpp
class Employee
{
private:
    int id;
    char name[100];
    int salary;
public:
    void input()
    {
    cin>>id>>name>>salary;
    }
    void output()
    {
    cout<<id<<"    "<<name<<"    "<<salary<<endl;
    }
};
```

We can now create an object of the class Employee at run time, using the operator new. As this object is dynamically created, it will be unnamed in the memory. Therefore, we create a pointer p as shown below, such that the pointer can point to the object of Employee created at 'run time' in the program.

```
Employee *p;
```

We now create an object of Employee using the following statement:

```
p= new Employee;
```

Let the address of the newly created Employee object be 8000; this means that the address 8000 will now be stored inside the pointer p. And hence, it will be correct to say that the pointer p points to the object of Employee as shown in the Figure 11.40. Note that the object of the class contains all the members of class Employee, and as we discussed in Section 11.3, all the objects of the class will share the common memory of storing member functions defined by the class. But just like you can invoke member functions of a class using any object of the class, you can also invoke member functions using pointer to a object.

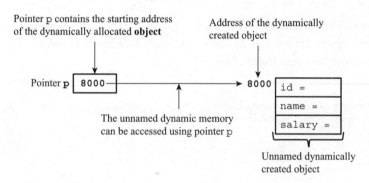

Figure 11.40: Pointer pointing to an object

The statement

```
p->input();
```

will invoke member function input () using pointer p. Assuming that the user inputs the values of id, name, and salary as 10, "John", and 5000, respectively, the members of the object pointed by p will be initialized as shown in the Figure 11.41. Similarly, the statement

```
p->output();
```

will invoke output () function using pointer p, which will print the values of members (id, name, and salary) of object pointed by p. You will not be able to directly access members id, name, and salary using pointer p because they are the private members of class Employee, and they cannot be accessed outside the class. Hence, the following statements will give an error:

```
p->id=10; //ERROR - id is a private member of class Employee
```

```
p->name="John"; //ERROR - name is a private member of class
    Employee
p->salary=5000; /*ERROR - salary is a private member of class
    Employee*/
```

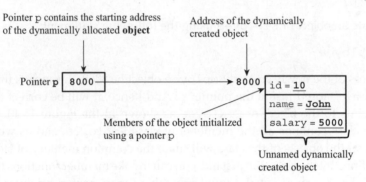

Figure 11.41: Initialization of the members

The initialization statements would work if id, name, and salary are created as public members. Remember, the idea of dynamic memory allocation is not to violate the access rules imposed by access specifiers of C++.

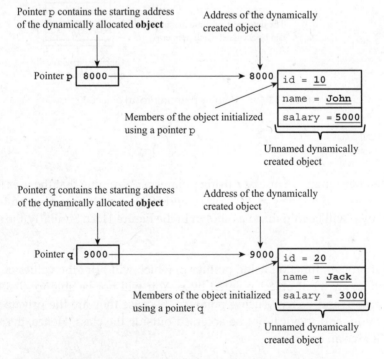

Figure 11.42: Initialization of the dynamically created objects

The following is the full C++ code that creates two objects of a class Employee at the run time of the program. The code creates two pointers of type Employee as p and q, respectively, such that each of the pointer points to one of the dynamically created objects as shown in the Figure 11.42.

The program invokes input () functions using pointer p as well as pointer q, using the following statements.

```
p->input();
q->input();
```

Assuming that the user enters the data as shown in the table below, the members of the objects pointer by pointers p and q will be initialized as shown in the Figure 11.42.

Invocation of input function	Data entered by the user (id, name, salary)
p->input();	(10,"John",5000)
q->input();	(20,"Jack",3000)

The statements

```
p->output();
q->output();
```

invoke the output () function using pointers p and q, to print the value of the respective members.

```
#include<iostream.h>
class Employee
{
private:
    int id;
    char name[100];
    int salary;
public:
    void input()
    {
    cin>>id>>name>>salary;
    }
     void output()
    {
    cout<<id<<"    "<<name<<"    "<<salary<<endl;
    }
};
void main()
{
Employee *p,*q;
```

```
/*pointer p and q point to dynamically allocated objects of
    Employee*/
p= new Employee;
q= new Employee;
/*Input the members of the Employee object pointed by the pointer
    p*/
cout<<"Enter the value of id , name and salary for object pointed
    by p"<<endl;
p->input();
/*Input the members of the Employee object pointed by the pointer
    q*/
cout<<"Enter the value of id , name and salary for object pointed
    by q"<<endl;
q->input();
/*Print the members of the Employee object pointed by the pointers
    p and q*/
cout<<"Employee Details are:"<<endl;
p->output();
q->output();
}
```

Output

```
Enter the value of id, name and salary for  object pointed by p
10 John 5000
Enter the value of id, name and salary for  object pointed by q
20 Jack 3000
Employee Details are:
10    John   5000
20    Jack   3000
```

11.21   Linked List to Maintain Data about Employees

We have implemented linked list that can store integer data in Chapter 10, using dynamic memory allocation of structure objects. We have also specified the advantages of linked list over arrays in Chapter 10. Now that we understand dynamic memory allocation for class objects, we will upgrade our code in Section 11.12 that creates array of Employee objects by creating a linked list that can store data about employees instead of creating an array of objects.

The full source code to store employee data by creating a linked list is given with following functions in class Node:

void insert(Employee x)

This function is used to insert the Employee object x into the linked list.

void traverse()

This function is used to print the data about all the employees present in the linked list by iterating through the list.

void remove(int id)

This function is used to delete the `Employee` node from the linked list, whose id matches with the integer argument passed to the function.

These functions are implemented with a similar logic as described in Chapter 10, with the only difference being that the data in the linked list of type `Employee` rather than in `int`.

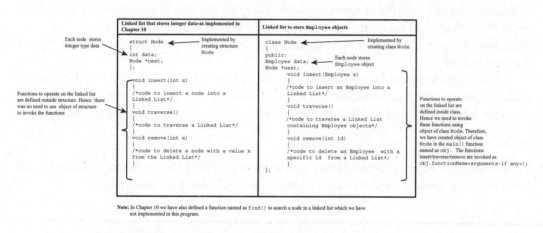

Note: In Chapter 10 we have also defined a function named as `find()` to search a node in a linked list which we have not implemented in this program.

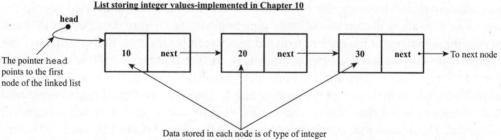

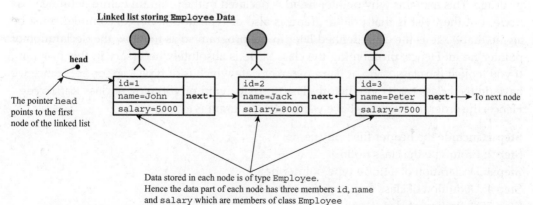

Figure 11.43: Comparison of linked list of integers with linked list of `Employee` objects

Recall from Chapter 10 that the structure Node had two members' data and next as shown in the Figure 11.43. The data type of member data was integer because the linked list implemented in Chapter 10 is required to store integers. In this section, we have created a class Node with two members data and next. This time, the data type of data is Employee because we intend to store Employee objects in the linked list rather than just integers, as shown in the Figure 11.43.

Since Employee is a user-defined type, we have created a class Employee with private members id, name, and salary and public member functions input(), output(), and getId(). The function input is used to read the values of members id, name, and salary as input from the user, whereas the function output() is used to print the value of all members on the computer screen. The function getId() returns only the value of member id to its caller, and we will discuss the significance of this function shortly.

As we know from the implementation given in Chapter 10, creation of linked list needs a global pointer head to be created which can be accessed throughout the code. For consistency, we will create a similar global pointer head in the given program using the statement

```
Node *head;
```

However, class Node is defined later in the program (after the declaration statement of head pointer), hence we must prototype the class Node using the statement

```
class Node;
```

This statement makes the compiler aware that class named as Node is defined later in the program so as to allow declaration of Node type pointer head before class Node is defined. You may think that one of the options to avoid prototyping of the class Node, is to move the complete definition of class Node before creating Node type pointer head. This would cause other problems because there are functions like insert(), traverse(), and remove() in class Node, which make use of the pointer head. Hence pointer head must be declared before definition of the class Node because C++ does not support forward referencing of variables. This means that every variable used in the program must be declared before its usage. This explains why pointer head is declared in the program before defining class Node, but the twist is that pointer head is also of type Node. Hence, compiler must be aware that Node is the class defined later in the program so as to allow the declaration of pointer head. Hence, prototyping the class Node is absolutely necessary in this program. If you look at the class Node, it has a member data which is of type Employee. Hence we have defined class Employee before class Node to avoid prototyping of class Employee. Hence, the order in which we have written the program is as follows:

Step 1: Include the header file iostream.h
Step 2: Prototype the class Node
Step 3: Declaration of a Node type pointer head
Step 4: Definition of class Employee
Step 5: Definition of class Node
Step 6: Definition of main() function which runs the program

Now that we have understood the layout of the program we will highlight a certain differences in the linked list implementation to store `Employee` objects when compared with the linked list defined in Chapter 10 to store integer data values.

void insert(Employee x)

This is a member function of class `Node` to insert data into a linked list. Note that the function takes the argument of type `Employee` because it is required to insert the object x as the `data` of the node that it inserts into the list. Rest of the implementation of insert function is exactly identical to what is given in Chapter 10. If the node to be inserted is the first node, the following statement in the `if` block

head->data=x;

will copy all the members of object x to object `data` which is contained in the `Node` pointed by `head`. This is possible because we know that when assignment operator of C++ is used with objects, it will copy the value of members of object on the right-hand side of assignment to the object on the left-hand side. In other words, the object `data` will be an exact clone of object x, and hence it is as good as storing object x as the data the node which is pointed by `head`. Similarly, if the node to be inserted is not the first node, the highlighted statement in `else` block will set the `data` of the temporary node d correctly to as members of x

```
Node *d = new Node;
d->data=x;
d->next=NULL;
```

Hence, when node d is linked to the linked list, data about employee x will be inserted in the list

void traverse()

This function is used to print the data about all the Employees present in the linked list by iterating through the list. The implementation of this function is similar to what is implemented in Chapter 10, with the difference being that when we print the data in each node, we use the statement

```
temp->data.output();
```

This is because temp is a pointer that iterates through each node if the linked list. The `data` of each node is actually an object of class `Employee` and it is not a primitive type. Hence, `temp->data` will always be an `Employee` object irrespective to which node of the list pointer `temp` points to. Hence, you can invoke any `public` member functions of class `Employee` using `temp->data`. Therefore, we invoke the `output()` member function to print the members `id`, `name`, and `salary` of the object `temp->data` as shown in the Figure 11.44. Since pointer temp iterates through all the objects of the linked list, the function `traverse()` will print the members `id`, `name`, and `salary` of all the objects.

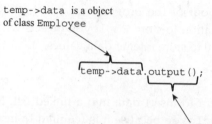

output () is a member function of class Employee and hence
it is invoked using an object of class Employee which is pointed by temp

Figure 11. 44: Invoking member function output ()

void remove(int id)

This function is used to delete the Employee node from the linked list, whose id matches with the integer argument passed to the function. The implementation of this function is similar to what is implemented in Chapter 10, with the difference being that before deleting any particular node, we check if the id value of the Employee object contained in that node is same as that of the id value passed as an argument. We already know that since pointer temp iterates through all the nodes of the linked list, the expression temp->data will always represent an Employee object. We cannot access the member id directly using object temp->data because id is a private member of class Employee. The following expression will give an error:

```
temp->data.id; //Error - id is a private member of class Employee
```

Hence, we have written a public function named as getId() in class Employee, which simply returns the value of member id of the invoking object to the caller. getId() is a simple member function of class Employee that is defined as follows:

```
int getId()
    {
        return id;
    }
```

Since getId() is a public member function, you can call it using an object even from outside class. Hence, the expression

```
temp->data.getId()
```

is used to obtain the id value of the Employee object stored in the node pointed by temp. The requirement of remove() function is that the while loop should run till the time employee with a matching id is not found; hence, one of the terminating conditions added to the while loop is as follows:

```
temp->data.getId()!=id
```

The conditions of the while loop in the remove() function are described in Figure 11.45.

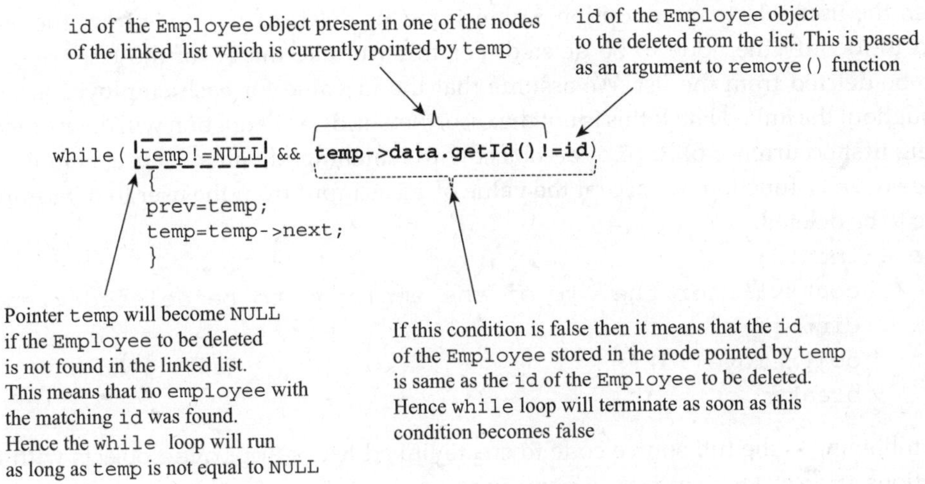

id of the Employee object present in one of the nodes of the linked list which is currently pointed by temp

id of the Employee object to the deleted from the list. This is passed as an argument to remove() function

```
while( temp!=NULL && temp->data.getId()!=id)
     {
     prev=temp;
     temp=temp->next;
     }
```

Pointer temp will become NULL if the Employee to be deleted is not found in the linked list. This means that no employee with the matching id was found. Hence the while loop will run as long as temp is not equal to NULL

If this condition is false then it means that the id of the Employee stored in the node pointed by temp is same as the id of the Employee to be deleted. Hence while loop will terminate as soon as this condition becomes false

Figure 11.45: while loop of remove() function

At last, we have written a main() function in the program that displays a menu for insertion, traversal, and deletion of node in the linked list and continues operations in do-while loop. Functions insert(), traverse(), and delete() are present in class Node, and hence, they can be called only using an object of class Node. Therefore, the main() function creates an object of class Node named as obj using the statement below:

```
Node obj;
```

When user selects menu option 1, which means insertion of a new node to the list, the control is transferred to the case 1 of the switch block. The insert function requires object of Employee class as an argument, which is inserted into the linked list. Hence, before calling insert() function, we first create an object of class Employee (named as e1) and take its members as input from the user by calling the input function. After the user inputs the values of id, name, and salary, the object is passed as an argument to the insert() function as shown in the piece of code below:

```
case 1: cout<<"Enter the data value to be inserted"<<endl;
        Employee e1;
        e1.input();
        obj.insert(e1);
        break;
```

When the user selects menu option 2, which means traversal of the list, we just need to print the contents of the list. Hence, we directly call the traverse function that iterates over the list in the case 2 of the switch block

```
case 2: obj.traverse();
        break;
```

When the user selects menu option 3, which means deletion of a node from the list, we need to identify the node to be deleted. For this we take the id of the Employee that is to be deleted from the list. We assume that the id value for each employee is unique throughout the linked list. If this is not the case, the remove() function will delete the node giving first occurrence of Employee object with matching id value. Hence, before calling the remove() function, we accept the value of id as input from the user to determine the node to be deleted.

```
case 3:int id;
        cout<<"Enter the  ID of the employee to be deleted"<<endl;
        cin>>id;
        obj.remove(id);
        break;
```

The following is the full source code to create linked list of Employee objects with three functions insert(), traverse() and remove():

```
#include<iostream.h>
class Node;/*Prototype the class Node*/
/*Creation of a global pointer head*/
Node *head;
class Employee
{
private:
    int id;
    char name[100];
    int salary;
public:
    void input()
    {
    cout<<"Enter ID,Name and Salary"<<endl;
    cin>>id>>name>>salary;
    }
      void output()
    {
    cout<<"id="<<id<<"Name="<<name<<"Salary="<<salary<<endl;
    }
    int getId()
    {
        return id;
    }
};
class Node
{
public:
Employee data;
```

```
Node *next;
      void insert(Employee x)
      {
          if(head ==NULL)
          {
          /*Node to be inserted is the first node*/
          head= new Node;
          head->data=x;
          head->next=NULL;
          }
          else
          {
          /*Node to be inserted is the subsequent node*/
          Node *d = new Node;
          d->data=x;
          d->next=NULL;
                  Node *temp;
        temp=head;
                     while(temp->next!=NULL)
                     {
                     temp = temp -> next;
                     }
          temp->next=d;
          }
      }
      void traverse()
      {
      Node *temp;
      temp=head;
      cout<<"The elements of the linked list are as below:"<<endl;
      /*Traverse the list until it ends*/
                  while(temp!=NULL)
                  {
                  temp->data.output();
                  temp = temp -> next;
                  }
      }
      void remove(int id)
      {
      Node *temp;
      temp=head;
      Node *prev=NULL;
```

```
                        while(temp!=NULL && temp->data.getId()!=id)
                        {
                        prev=temp;          /*store the old value of temp in
        prev*/
                        temp=temp->next;    /*move temp ahead*/
                        }
                        if(temp==NULL)
                        {
                        cout<<"Employee with id="<<id<<"does not exists
        in the list"<<endl;
                        }
                        else
                        {
                          if(temp==head)
                          {
                          /*Node to be deleted is the first node*/
                          head=head->next;
                          }
                          else
                          {
                          /*Node to be deleted is not  the first node*/
                          prev->next=temp->next;
                          }
                        cout<<"Employee Deleted"<<endl;
                        }
            }
};
void main()
{
Node obj;
int answer =1;
int choice,x;
cout<<"Please select one of the following choices:"<<endl;
cout<<"1.Insert a node"<<endl;
cout<<"2.Traverse the list"<<endl;
cout<<"3.Delete a node"<<endl;
do
{
cout<<"Enter your choice"<<endl;
cin>>choice;
      switch(choice)
      {
```

```
     case 1: cout<<"Enter the data value to be inserted"<<endl;
             Employee e1;
             e1.input();
             obj.insert(e1);
             break;
     case 2:obj.traverse();
             break;
     case 3:int id;
                  cout<<"Enter the  ID of the employee to be
        deleted"<<endl;
                  cin>>id;
                  obj.remove(id);
                     break;
     default: cout<<"Invalid option selected"<<endl;
     }
cout<<"Do you want to continue(Enter 1 is yes 0 if No)?"<<endl;
cin>>answer;
} while(answer==1);
}
```

11.22   Composition and Aggregation between Classes

Given two classes C1 and C2 such that object of C1 is a part of object of C2; and if object of C1 is automatically destroyed when object of C2 is destroyed, then the relationship between C1 and C2 is called composition. However, if the design is such that the object of C1 can be independently retained in memory even after object of C2 is destroyed, then the relationship between C1 and C2 is called aggregation. Composition between classes is also called HAS-A relationship or containership because one object is contained inside another.

   We will show the implementation of composition between classes first and later suggest modifications to change the relationship into aggregation. For example, let us assume that we need to store a detailed mark sheet for each student along with the roll number, name, and the total marks. The mark sheet is required to contain the marks of three subjects and let us name them as m1, m2, and m3.

   For every Student object, we are required to store the following information:

1. Roll number of a student
2. Name of the student
3. Total of the marks
4. Mark sheet giving the marks of individual subjects

The mark sheet of the student is itself a composite attribute that is required to contain the marks of each of the three subjects. Hence, every mark sheet must contain three members m1, m2, and m3 as shown in Figure 11.46.

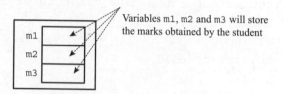

Figure 11.46: Members of `MarkSheet`

The data requirement is that every student has one mark sheet giving the marks obtained by the student in each of the subjects. To solve this problem, we create a class named as `MarkSheet` with three members `m1`, `m2`, and `m3`. With this approach, each object of class `MarkSheet` will represent one mark sheet in the real world. When we define class `Student`, we can define object of class `MarkSheet` as a member of class `Student` along with other members `roll_no`, `name`, and `total`. So every object of class `Student` will have object of class `MarkSheet` as a part of it as shown in Figure 11.47. This relationship between a `Student` object and a `MarkSheet` object is called **containership or composition**.

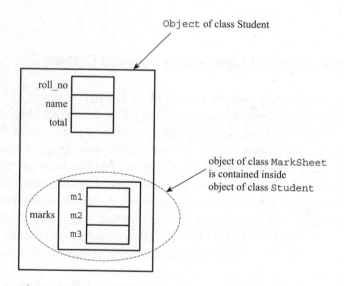

Figure 11.47: Composition of objects

It is clear that the object of class `MarkSheet` is a sub part of the `Student` object, and hence, if the `Student` object is destroyed, the corresponding `MarkSheet` object will also be destroyed. Hence, this is composition, and not aggregation, between classes. Composition between classes is represented by an association link with a filled diamond on the whole part as shown in Figure 11.48. This notation is called a UML notation used to model class diagrams in large projects.

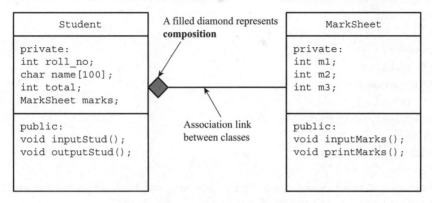

Figure 11.48: Notation of composition

NOTES

UML stands for unfilled modelling language. It is a language which gives set of notations to represent relationships between classes. Scope of UML is not just modelling of classes; it has many modelling notations which cover the complete software development lifecycle right from requirement gathering to maintenance of the developed system. Figures drawn with UML notations simplify the studies required in **object oriented analysis and design** paradigms. The detailed study of UML is out of scope of this text book but we have mentioned about it here because we have used one of the UML notations in Figure 11.48.

The following is the full source code, which shows the creation of composition between classes Student and MarkSheet:

```
#include<iostream.h>
class MarkSheet
{
    private:
    int m1,m2,m3;
    public:
    void inputMarks()
    {
    cout<<"Enter Marks m1,m2 and m3"<<endl;
    cin>>m1>>m2>>m3;
    }
    void printMarks()
    {
    cout<<"::::::Marks obtained in individual subjects
    are::::::"<<endl;
    cout<<"m1="<<m1<<"m2="<<m2<<"m3="<<m3<<endl;
    }
    friend class Student;
};
```

```
class Student
{
    private:
    int roll_no;
    char name[100];
    int total;
    MarkSheet marks;
    public:
    void inputStud()
    {
      cout<<"Enter Name and Roll Number of the student"<<endl;
      cin>>name>>roll_no;
      /*Also input individual marks*/
      marks.inputMarks();
    }

    void outputStud()
    {
      cout<<"*****************************************"<<endl;
      /*Calculate Total marks*/
      total =marks.m1+marks.m2+marks.m3;
      cout<<"Student details are"<<endl;
cout<<"Roll Number="<<roll_no<<"| Name="<<name<<"| Total="
    <<total<<endl;
/*print individual marks using MarkSheet object*/
      marks.printMarks();
      cout<<"*****************************************"<<endl;
    }
};
void main()
{

    Student s1,s2;
    s1.inputStud();
    s2.inputStud();
    s1.outputStud();
    s2.outputStud();
}
```

Output

```
Enter Name and Roll Number of the student
John 10
Enter Marks m1,m2 and m3
90 85 34
Enter Name and Roll Number of the student
```

```
Jill 20
Enter Marks m1,m2 and m3
89 66 55
*****************************************
Student details are
Roll Number=10 | Name=John |Total=209
::::::Marks obtained in individual subjects are::::::
m1=90   m2=85   m3=34
*****************************************
*****************************************
Student details are
Roll Number=20 | Name=Jill |Total= 210
::::::Marks obtained in individual subjects are::::::
m1=89   m2=66   m3=55
*****************************************
```

The first statement in `main()`

```
Student s1,s2;
```

creates two objects of class `Student` named as `s1` and `s2`. Each object will have an object of class `MarkSheet` named as `marks` embedded in its memory.

The statement

```
s1.inputStud();
```

invokes the `inputStud()` function over object `s1` which accepts the `roll_no` and name of `s1` as input from the user. The execution of this statement is as shown in Figure 11.49. It also invokes `inputMarks()` internally using the object `marks` as shown below

```
marks.inputMarks();
```

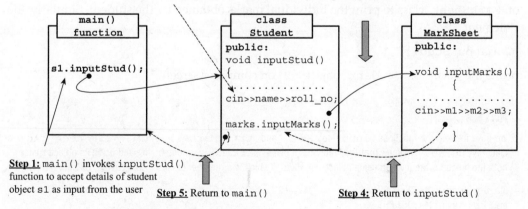

Figure 11.49: Execution of `s1.inputStud();`

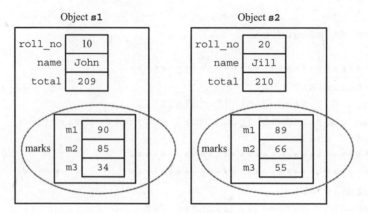

Figure 11.50: Objects s1 and s2

Remember, we are in a scope of object s1, and hence, the members m1, m2, and m3 of the mark sheet of student object s1 will be taken as input from the user due to this statement.

Similarly, the statement

```
s2.inputStud();
```

will accept roll_no, name and marks of object s2 as input from the user. Assuming the sample input values, state of objects s1 and s2 is as show in Figure 11.50.

The statement

```
s1.outputStud();
```

invokes outputStud() method to print the details of student s1 on computer screen. Before printing the data, it calculates total marks of the student, using the statement

```
total =marks.m1+marks.m2+marks.m3;
```

Note that, we have directly accessed private members m1, m2 and m3 of class MarkSheet in the scope of method outputStud(). This is possible because we have created class Student as a friend class of class MarkSheet as seen in the code. The function prints the value of members roll_no, name, and total and also invokes printMarks() of MarkSheet class to print the individual marks obtained by the student. Similarly, the statement

```
s2.outputStud();
```

prints the details of Student object s2 on computer screen

NOTES

We have invoked the functions inputMarks() and printMarks() of class MarkSheet from class Student. We know that the functions of class MarkSheet must be invoked using its object. Hence both the functions are invoked using object marks (which is a member of class Student) as shown below

```
marks.inputMarks();
marks.printMarks();
```

11.23   Converting the Relationship to Aggregation

To create an aggregation between class Student and MarkSheet, the requirement is that the object of MarkSheet must not be destroyed even if the Student object goes out of scope. To attain this result, the MarkSheet object must be stored external to Student object and should not be embedded within the Student object. This can be achieved by creating a pointer in the Student object that points externally as shown in Figure 11.51.

marks is created as a pointer of type MarkSheet rather than its direct object. The pointer marks points to the externally present Marksheet object, and hence the MarkSheet object can still be retained in the memory even if the Student object goes out of scope. The relationship of aggregation between Student and MarkSheet classes is represented using an UML notation shown in Figure 11.52. Notice that the notation of aggregation is very much similar as that of the notation of composition with the only difference that the diamond is **not filled**. Remember, a filled diamond represents composition, whereas an unfilled diamond represents aggregation between the classes.

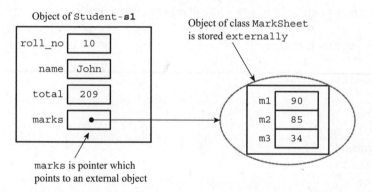

Figure 11.51:   Objects of class Student and MarkSheet linked using a pointer

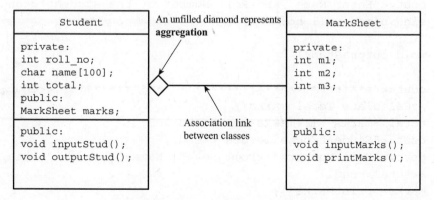

Figure 11.52:   UML notation of aggregation

The following is the full source code, which creates aggregation between classes
`Student` and `MarkSheet`:

```cpp
#include<iostream.h>
class MarkSheet
{
    private:
    int m1,m2,m3;
    public:
    void inputMarks()
    {
    cout<<"Enter Marks m1,m2 and m3"<<endl;
    cin>>m1>>m2>>m3;
    }
    void printMarks()
    {
    cout<<"::::::Marks obtained in individual subjects
          are:::::"<<endl;
    cout<<"m1="<<m1<<"m2="<<m2<<"m3="<<m3<<endl;
    }
    friend class Student;
};
class Student
{
    private:
    int roll_no;
    char name[100];
    int total;
    public:
    MarkSheet *marks;
    void inputStud()
    {
      cout<<"Enter Name  and Roll Number of the student"<<endl;
      cin>>name>>roll_no;
    }
    void outputStud()
    {
    cout<<"*****************************************"<<endl;
    /*Calculate Total marks*/
    total =marks->m1+marks->m2+marks->m3;
    cout<<"Student details are"<<endl;
    cout<<"Roll Number="<<roll_no<<"| Name="<<name<<"|Total="
    <<total<<endl;
    marks->printMarks();
    cout<<"*****************************************"<<endl;
```

```
        }
    };
    void main()
    {
        /*Single Object of class MarkSheet*/
        MarkSheet info;
        { /*OPEN a new Scope*/
          Student s1;
        /*Input roll_no and name  of s1*/
        s1.inputStud();
        /*Input marks to be populated in marksheet*/
        info.inputMarks();
        /*Relate s1 with MarkSheet object*/
        s1.marks =&info;
        /*Print full data about s1*/
        s1.outputStud();
      } /*object s1 goes out of scope*/
        {/*OPEN a new Scope*/
        Student s2;
    /*Input roll_no and name  of s2*/
        s2.inputStud();
    /*Change the state of object of class MarkSheet by again inputting
        its details*/
        info.inputMarks();
        /*Relate s2 with Marksheet object*/
        s2.marks =&info;
    /*Print full data about s2*/
        s2.outputStud();
      } /*object s2 goes out of scope*/
    }
```

Output

```
Enter Name and Roll Number of the student
John 10
Enter Marks m1,m2 and m3
90 85 34
****************************************
Student details are
Roll Number=10 | Name=John |Total= 209
::::::Marks obtained in individual subjects are:::::
m1=90  m2=85  m3=34
****************************************
Enter Name  and Roll Number of the student
Jill 20
```

```
Enter Marks m1,m2 and m3
89 66 55
******************************************
Student details are
Roll Number=20 | Name=Jill |Total= 210
::::::Marks obtained in individual subjects are:::::
m1=89   m2=66   m3=55
******************************************
```

The object of class MarkSheet named as info is created in the scope of main() function using the following statement:

MarkSheet info;

The main() function opens a new scope in which a Student object s1 is created. The statement

s1.inputStud();

inputs roll_no and name of object s1. And the statement

info.inputMarks();

inputs values m1, m2, and m3 of object info. Let us assume that the user inputs the values as m1=90, m2=85, m3=34, which represent the marks obtained by student s1. We link the object info with the Student object s1 by storing the address of info in the pointer marks, using the statement below:

s1.marks=&info;

Note that the pointer marks can be directly accessed from main() function because it is created as a public member in class Student. The member marks of s1 points to info, indicating that the individual marks m1, m2, and m3 of student s1.

The statement

s1.outputStud();

prints the data about s1 on the computer screen. The working of function outputStud() is same as explained before with the only difference being that marks is a pointer and hence its members are accessed using an -> operator. The following statement calculates the total of m1, m2 and m3; and stores the result in member total of object s1

total =marks->m1+marks->m2+marks->m3;

Clearly, the MarkSheet object is stored external to the Student object. Hence the MarkSheet object will remain in memory even if the Student object goes out of scope. By this way, we have implemented aggregation between classes Student and MarkSheet.

We have intentionally created two different inner scopes in main() function to show the principle of aggregation.

When the first inner scope ends, object s1 goes out of scope but the object info still remains in memory. The main() function opens another scope and creates Student object s2. The roll_no and name of s2 are taken as input from the user by invoking the function `inputStud();`. We reuse the same object `info` to store the marks `m1`, `m2`, and `m3` for object `s2`. Note that, at this stage info already contains the values of `m1`, `m2`, and `m3`, which were actually entered for Student object `s1`. Hence, we again invoke the function `inputMarks();` which will accept fresh values of `m1`, `m2`, and `m3` as input from the user using the statement below. These values will represent the marks obtained by Student object `s2`.

`info.inputMarks();`

Let us assume that the user inputs the values as `m1=89`, `m2=66`, `m3=55` which represent the marks obtained by Student `s2`. The object `info` is actually same in memory, but it has changed the values of its members.

> **NOTES**
>
> The value of the members of an object is called the **state of the object.** `info` was previously storing marks obtained by `Student` object `s1`, but it now stores the marks obtained by another `Student` object `s2`, thereby changing its state as shown in Figure 11.53.

The statement

`s2.marks =&info;`

makes the pointer `marks` of object `s2` to point to `info` because the object `info` now stores the marks obtained by `s2` as shown in Figure 11.54.

Other details of `s2` are accepted as input and printed on the screen similar to that of `s1`.

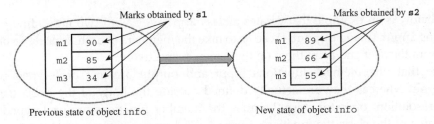

Figure 11.53: Change of state of object `info`

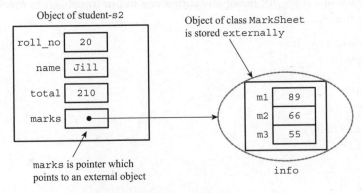

Figure 11.54: Objects `s2` and `info`

11.24 Defining the Member Functions Outside Class using Scope Resolution Operator

Whenever a member function is defined inside the class, by default, it is considered as an 'inline' member function. So to make a member function as non-inline member function, we will have to define the member function of the class outside the body of the class.

C++ supports definition of member functions outside class using a 'scope resolution operator' [::].

Note that, even if the function is defined outside class, it will still be considered as a member function of a class because the 'scope resolution' operator informs the C++ compiler that the function is actually present in the scope of the class. This means that the 'scope resolution' operator facilitates the programmer to define the member functions of the class outside the body of the class. Further, C++ makes it mandatory to prototype such functions within the body of the class, so that it can differentiate between `private` and `public` member functions of that class. Hence, if we prototype a member function in the 'private area' of the class, then C++ considers it is `private` member function of the class, and if we prototype the member function in the 'public area' of the class, then C++ considers it as `public` member function of the class. The key point to remember is that we must always prototype all the functions that are required to be the member functions of the class but are defined outside the body of the class using a 'scope resolution' operator.

To create a member function that is non-inline, we must perform following steps:

1. Prototype the function inside the body of the class
2. Define the function outside the class using a "scope resolution" operator

Given below is an example that creates a class `Employee` with two non-inline member functions `input()` and `output()`, so as to take the members of each `Employee` object as input from the user and print them on the screen, respectively.

Note that, the member functions input and output are just prototyped in class `Employee`, whereas they are actually defined outside the body of the class, using the 'scope resolution' operator. Also, because the member functions are prototyped in the public area of the class, the functions `input()` and `output()` are considered as public member functions of the class `Employee`. Also, as seen in the code, creating a member function as non-inline does not make any difference in our approach to invoke a member function using the object of the class.

```
#include<iostream.h>
class Employee
{
private:
    int id;
    char name[100];
    int salary;
public:
void input();
```

```cpp
void output();
};
void Employee::input()
{
cin>>id>>name>>salary;
    while(salary<0)
    {
    cout<<"Salary cannot be negative, please re-enter its value";
    cin>>salary;
    }
}
void Employee::output()
{
cout<<id<<"   "<<name<<"   "<<salary<<endl;
}
Employee e1,e2;
cout<<"Enter the details of first employee"<<endl;
e1.input();
cout<<"Enter the details of second employee"<<endl;
e2.input();
cout<<"The details of first employee are"<<endl;
e1.output();
cout<<"The details of second employee are"<<endl;
e2.output();
}
```

Output:

```
Enter the details of first employee
1 John 5000
The details of first employee are
1 John 5000
Enter the details of second employee
2 Jack 3000
The details of second employee are
2 Jack 3000
```

NOTES

When the complete definition of the member function is inside the class, then it is by default considered as **inline function** by the C++ compiler.

When a member function of a particular class is defined outside the class using **scope resolution operator**, the member function will **NOT** be considered as inline function.

Having said that, you can always add keyword `inline` to explicitly force C++ to make a particular function inline, even if it is defined outside class.

For example, let us assume ABC is a class defined as follows

```
class ABC
{
void f1(); /*f1() is a member function of class ABC to be defined outside*/
};
```

If you want to create function f1() as inline function and also define it outside the class using scope resolution operator, then you must explicitly add an keyword inline when defining function f1() as shown below

```
inline void ABC::f1()
{
/*body of function f1()*/
}
```

Difference between inline and non inline functions is explained in Chapter 7 of this text book.

11.25   Function Overloading and Compile Time Binding

When a function is called by the programmer, C++ compiler correctly identifies which function to call based on the **signature of the function**. The function signature of any function includes the following:

1. Name of the function
2. Number of arguments the function takes
3. Data type of each of the arguments
4. Order in which arguments are passed to the function

Note that return type of the function is not included in its signature. This means that two functions with same signature cannot exist in the program even if their return types are different.

NOTES

Two functions with the same signature cannot coexist in the same program. Given below are some example prototypes showing valid/invalid coexistence of the functions.

Example 1:

```
void area(int,int);
int area(int,int);
```

Both the functions have same name, and both of them take two arguments of type integer. Hence, it is not possible for these two functions to coexist in the program because their signatures are exactly the same. It does not matter whether the return type of the function is same or different; the thumb rule is that two functions with same signature cannot be created in the program. Hence, this combination of area() functions gives a **compilation error.**

Example 2:

```
void area(int,int);
void area(int,float);
```

This is a valid combination of functions that can coexists in the program because the data type of one argument is different in both of the functions. The first function takes both the arguments of type int, whereas the second function takes one argument of type int and the other of type float. Hence, these two functions with same name can exists in the same program because their signature is different.

Example 3:

```
void area(int,float);
void area(float,int);
```

This is a valid combination of functions that can coexists in the program because the order of arguments is different in first and second area() functions. Hence, the two functions have a different function signature even if their names are same.

Example 4:

```
float f1(int,int);
float f2(int,int);
```

This is a valid combination of functions which can coexists in the program because the names of two functions are different. The name of the first function is f1() and second function is f2(). In this case, it does not matter whether the arguments are same or different.

When a function with same name is defined multiple times in the program with different signatures, then the function name is said to be **overloaded**. For example, let us consider the code below which has two functions with the same name **area()**. Even if the name of the two functions is same, the arguments that each of the **area()** function takes is different. One of the area() function takes a single argument of type float, whereas the other area function takes two arguments of type integer, and hence, they have a different signature and can be safely written in the same program. If we observe the set of operations in each of the functions, we see that the area() function that takes only one argument actually calculates the area of circle by considering the argument passed to it as a radius value. Also, the area function that takes two arguments actually calculates the area of rectangle by considering the arguments passed to it as a length and breadth values, respectively.

DEFINITION

When a function with same name is defined multiple times in the program with different signatures, then the function name is said to be **overloaded**.

```
#include<iostream.h>
void area(float r)
{
float area= 3.14*r*r;
cout<<"Area of circle is "<<area<<endl;
}
void area(int l,int b)
{
int area=l*b;
```

```
cout<<"Area of rectangle is "<<area<<endl;
}
void main()
{
area(12.5);
area(10,2);
}
```

Output

```
Area of the circle is 490.625
Area of the rectangle is 20
```

As seen from the code the main program calls two different functions, the first call is

```
area(12.5);
```

wherein a single argument is passed to the function during the function call. Hence, the compiler calls the function area that takes one argument of type float, thereby considering 12.5 as a radius of the circle and hence the output of the statement is as follows:

```
Area of the circle is 490.625
```

The second call to function area from main is

```
area(10,2);
```

wherein two arguments are passed to the function area during the function call. Hence, the compiler, this time, calls the function area that takes two arguments of type int, thereby considering values 10 and 2 as length and breadth of a rectangle, respectively, and hence the output of the statement is as follows:

```
Area of the rectangle is 20
```

Although there are two function with same name in the program, the compiler determines the correct function to call based on the function signature. This process is called **compile time binding**. Binding is actually a process to attach a 'function call' with a 'function definition', in this case binding is performed by the compiler and hence it is called **compile time binding** or **Early binding or static binding**. The function name area() takes two forms: one form is to calculate the area of circle, whereas the other is to calculate the area of rectangle. The ability of a single name to take multiple forms is called polymorphism, and because this polymorphism is implemented using compile time binding, it is called **compile time polymorphism**.

What is Binding?   **?**

 Binding is a process to attach a function call with a function definition. Compiler creates a link between a "call" to a function and the "definition" of the function so as to correctly determine which function block to execute when a function is called. Hence the correct function definitions are executed for each of the function calls made in the program. This binding is performed at compile time (even before the program starts running) based on the function signature. When the CPU runs the program its just the matter of transferring control to the correct function body and executing it in response to a function call. There is hardly anything to do at runtime because the correct function to be invoked for each of the function calls is being already identified by the compiler beforehand (at compile time). Hence this type of binding is called as **early binding or static binding or compile time binding**.

Why Compile time binding is called as "Early" Binding? Is there any other type of binding as well? ❓

Yes, there are two types of bindings to handle function calls

1. Early binding.
2. Late Binding.

In case of late binding the function calls are not resolved by the compiler but the decision about which function to call is taken by the C++ runtime environment when the program actually starts running. Hence Late Binding is also called as **runtime binding or dynamic binding**. C++ supports late binding only for **virtual functions** which will be discussed Chapter 14. Don't worry about virtual functions right now as it is a big topic in itself which is discussed in detail in Chapter 14.

11.26   Local Classes

It is possible to define a class within a function. Such a class can only be accessed within the scope of the function and nowhere else. This is called a local class. For example, consider a function add() which creates a class Number to perform addition of two integers. Observe that class Number is defined within the body of function add(), and hence the class cannot be accessed outside the scope of add()

```cpp
# include <iostream.h>
void add()
{
    class Number /*Class Defined inside function add()*/
      {
      private:
      int a,b;
      public:
            void input()
            {
                    cout<<"Enter 2 numbers"<<endl;
                    cin>>a>>b;
            }
            int getA()
            {
                    return a;
```

```
            }
            int getB()
            {
                    return b;
            }
    };/*End of class Definition*/
    Number o1;
    int res;
    o1.input();
    res = o1.getA()+o1.getB();
    cout<<"Result of Addition is"<<res<<endl;
}/*End of function add()*/
void main()
{
    add();
}/*End of function main()*/
```

Output

```
Enter 2 numbers
10 20
Result of Addition is 30
```

The function definition of add() creates a class Number with two private members a and b. As always the case, the members of Number cannot be accessed outside the class Number. The function add() creates an object of class Number as

```
Number o1;
```

This is possible within add() because Number is defined within add(). If main() attempts to create an object of Number, it will cause an error. This is because Number is not accessible anywhere else outside the scope of add().

The statement inside add() function

```
o1.input();
```

inputs the values of members a and b for object o1. The values of a and b are added and stored in the local variable res by statement

```
res = o1.getA()+o1.getB();
```

Note that we have created functions getA() and getB() to access the values of a and b because they are private members of class Number and cannot be accessed at anyplace outside class Number.

NOTES

You cannot use scope resolution operator to define the member functions of local class outside the class. All of the member functions of the local class must be defined within the class itself as we have done in this example.

11.27 Nested Classes

It is possible to define a class inside another class. This design is called nesting of classes. For example, consider the following code:

```
# include <iostream.h>
class Number
{
      public:
      int a,b;
            class Floats /*inner class*/
            {
                  private:
                  float x,y;
                  public:
                  void input()
                  {
                        cout<<"Enter two floats"<<endl;
                        cin>>x>>y;
                  }
                  float getX()
                  {
                        return x;
                  }
                  float getY()
                  {
                        return y;
                  }
                  void addAll(Number t)
                  {
                        float res=t.a+t.b+x+y;
                        cout<<"Inner Result is "<<res<<endl;
                  }
            };/*End of class Floats*/
    public:
      Floats p1;
    void input()
    {
    cout<<"Enter two integers"<<endl;
    cin>>a>>b;
    }
    void addAll()
    {
    float res;
```

```
    p1.input();
    res=a+b+p1.getX()+p1.getY();
    cout<<"Outer Result is "<<res<<endl;
    }
};/*End of class Definition*/
void main()
{
Number o1;
/*Invoke functions of outer class*/
o1.input();
o1.addAll();
/*Function of inner class*/
o1.p1.addAll(o1);
}/*End of function main()*/
```

Class Number has an inner class named as Floats. Although Floats is defined within Number, it cannot access private members of class Number. Likewise, Number cannot access private members of Floats.

In the main() function, we have created an object of class Number

```
Number o1;
```

The statement

```
o1.input();
```

invokes the input() function defined in class Number(outer class), which accepts the values of members a and b as input from the user. The next statement

```
o1.addAll();
```

invokes addAll() defined in class Number(outer class). If you see the function definition of addAll(), it has a statement

```
p1.input();
```

where, p1 is the object of inner class created within outer class. Hence, this statement will invoke the function input() of class Floats(inner class) to input the values of members x and y for object p1.

The statement

```
res=a+b+p1.getX()+p1.getY();
```

calculates the result by adding all the values. Note that a and b are accessed directly because we are in the scope of outer class. Whereas, x and y are accessed by invoking public functions getX() and getY() over object p1.This is because x and y are private members of inner class, and they cannot be directly accessed outside the scope of inner class. The public functions getX() and getY() make it possible to get the values of variables x and y in the scope of outer class.

As object p1 is a public member of class `Number`, it can be accessed directly by `main()` function. Hence `main()` function can directly call a public function of inner class using the statement below:

```
o1.p1.addAll(o1);
```

This will invoke the function `addAll()` of class `Floats` by passing the object o1 (outer object) as a parameter.

NOTES

If inner class is created and marked as public, then it is possible to create an object of inner class in `main()` function. If we write following statement in `main()`

```
Number::Floats o2;
```

it will create object of inner class `Floats`. Using object o2, you can access public members and member functions of inner class. Note that you will not be able to invoke any member or member function of outer class using object o2. The statement

```
o2.input();
```

will invoke `input()` inside class `Floats`. And the statement

```
o2.addAll(o1);
```

will invoke `addAll()` inside class `Floats` by passing o1 as a parameter.

Needless to say, it will not be possible to write following statement in `main()` if inner class `Floats` is created in the `private` area of outer class `Number`

```
Number::Floats o2;
```

Solved Example 11.1

A hospital wishes to maintain database of all the doctors and the patients in the hospital. For each doctor, the hospital is required to store the following information:

1. Name of the doctor
2. ID of the doctor
3. Telephone number of the doctor

Also, for each patient, the hospital is required to maintain the following information:

1. Name of the patient
2. Ward number in which the patient is admitted
3. Fees charged to the patient
4. ID of the doctor who is treating the patient

Write a C++ program that will create necessary classes to store this data.

```
#include<iostream.h>
class Doctor
{
private:
    char name[100];
    int id;
    unsigned long int tel_no;
public:
    void input()
    {
cout<<"Enter Name, ID and telephone Number of the Doctor"<<endl;
    cin>>name>>id>>tel_no;
    }
    void output()
    {
    cout<<"Name:"<<name<<"ID:"<<id<<"Tel No:"<<tel_no<<endl;
    }
};
class Patient
{
private:
    char name[100];
    int ward_no;
    float fees;
    int doctor_id;
public:
    void input()
    {
    cout<<"Enter Name, Ward_no,fees and doctor_id for the patient"
    <<endl;
    cin>>name>>ward_no>>fees>>doctor_id;
    }
    void output()
    {
    cout<<"Name:"<<name<<"Ward No:"<<ward_
    no<<"Fees:"<<fees<<"Doctor ID:"<<doctor_id<<endl;
    }
};
class Hospital
{
private:
```

```cpp
Doctor d[100];
Patient p[100];
int no_of_docs;
int no_of_pats;
public:
void input()
{
int i;
cout<<"Enter the number of doctors in the Hospital"<<endl;
cin>>no_of_docs;
cout<<"***Enter the details of each Doctor*******"<<endl;
    for(i=0;i<=no_of_docs-1;i++)
    {
    cout<<"********INPUT Doctor******"<<i+1<<endl;
    d[i].input();
    }
cout<<"Enter the number of patients in the Hospital"<<endl;
cin>>no_of_pats;
cout<<"***Enter the details of each Patient*******"<<endl;
    for(i=0;i<=no_of_pats-1;i++)
    {
    cout<<"********INPUT Patient******"<<i+1<<endl;
    p[i].input();
    }
}
void output()
{
int i;
cout<<"***DOCTOR DETAILS*******"<<endl;
    for(i=0;i<=no_of_docs-1;i++)
    {
    d[i].output();
    }
cout<<"***PATIENT DETAILS*******"<<endl;
    for(i=0;i<=no_of_pats-1;i++)
    {
    p[i].output();
    }
}
};
void main()
```

```
{
Hospital h1;
cout<<"**********HOSPITAL h1**********"<<endl;
h1.input();
h1.output();
}
```

NOTES

We have created 100 objects of class Patient and Doctor within the body of class Hospital. This means that any object of class Hospital will contain objects of class Patient as well as Doctor. In other words, doctors and patients are a **part of** hospital such that Hospital is a **whole part** and Doctor and Patient objects are **subparts** of it. Such a relationship between classes is called **composition**. Composition is also called as **HAS-A** relationship between classes. It goes inline with pure English where we say hospital **HAS** patients and doctors.

SCRATCH PAD

- As seen, we have created three different classes so as to solve a given problem.

  1. **Patient:** Each object of a class Patient represents the data about one patient admitted in the hospital. Hence, the members of class Patient are name, ward_no, fees and doctor_id, so as to store the relevant information about each patient in the memory.

  2. **Doctor:** Each object of a class Doctor represents the data about one doctor working with the hospital. Hence, the members of class Doctor are name, id, tel_no so as to store the relevant information about each doctor in the memory.

  3. **Hospital:** A Hospital object is to be represented as a collection of doctors and patients. Hence we create two different array of objects in class Hospital. The first member of class Hospital is the array of Patient objects named as p, such that each element of the array p represents the data about

one patient admitted in the hospital. Whereas, the second member of class `Hospital` is the array of `Doctor` objects named as `d`, such that each element of the array `d` represents the data about one doctor working with the hospital.

```
class Hospital
{
private:
        Doctor d[100];
        Patient p[100];
        .
        .
        .

};
```

Class `Hospital` also defines member functions `input()` and `output()` to input/output the list of doctors and patients in the hospital as shown in the code.

Solved Example 11.2

A Library wishes to maintain database of its customers. Also, the library has a rule that each customer can borrow a maximum of two books at a time. For each customer, the library database must store the following information:

1. Name of the customer
2. Complete details of all the books issued to the customer
3. ID and telephone number of the customer

Also, the library is required to maintain the following information about each book that is issued to the customer:

1. Title of the book
2. Author of the book
3. ID of the book

The program should read the data about two customers and print the customer details on the screen. Further, a customer can invoke a function `issue()` to borrow a book from the library.

```
#include<iostream.h>
class Book
{
private:
int book_id;
char title[100];
char author[100];
```

```cpp
public:
void input()
{
cin>>book_id>>title>>author;
}
void output()
{
cout<<"Book ID is:"<<book_id<<"Title is:"<<title<<"Author
    is:"<<author<<endl;
}
void setId(int id)
{
book_id=id;
}
int getId()
{
return book_id;
}
};
class Customer
{
private:
int customer_id;
char name[100];
unsigned long int tel_no;
int books_issued;
Book b[2];
public:
    void input()
    {
    cin>>customer_id>>name>>tel_no;
    books_issued=0;
    }
    void issue()
    {
       if(books_issued==2)
            {
            cout<<"Cannot issue more books"<<endl;
            }
       else
            {
cout<<"Enter the ID,title and author of the books to be
    issued"<<endl;
```

```
                b[books_issued].input();
                books_issued++;
                }
        }
    void return_book()
    {
    int id,i;
    cout<<"Enter the book ID of the book to be returned"<<endl;
    cin>>id;
    /*we set the ID of the book as -1 once the book is returned*/
        for(i=0;i<books_issued;i++)
        {
                if(b[i].getId()==id)
                    {
                    b[i].setId(-1);
                    books_issued--;
                    return;
                    }
        }
        cout<<"The Book with ID"<<id<<"is not issued by the
    customer"<<endl;
    }
    void output()
    {
    cout<<"the ID name and tel_no of the customer is"<<endl;
    cout<<customer_id<<"  "<<name<<"     "<<tel_no<<endl;
    cout<<"The number of books issued by the customer
    are:"<<books_issued<<endl;
        int i;
        for(i=0;i<books_issued;i++)
        {
                if(b[i].getId()!=-1)
                {
                b[i].output();
                }
        }
    }
};
void main()
{
Customer c1,c2;
```

```
cout<<"Enter the ID,name and tel_no of first customer"<<endl;
c1.input();
cout<<"Enter the ID, name and tel_no of second customer"<<endl;
c2.input();
cout<<"********C1 calls issue**********"<<endl;
c1.issue();
cout<<"********C1 calls issue**********"<<endl;
c1.issue();
cout<<"*******C1 returns a book*********"<<endl;
c1.return_book();
cout<<"**********C2 calls issue**********"<<endl;
c2.issue();
cout<<"*********Customer C1***********"<<endl;
c1.output();
cout<<"*********Customer C2***********"<<endl;
c2.output();
}
```

EXERCISE

Trace the output of this program assuming input data of your choice.

SCRATCH PAD

- As we need to store the data about books and customers in a library we create the following two classes so as to solve a given problem statement.
    1. Book
    2. Customer

Book: The class Book defines the data elements that are to be stored for each book in a real world. Hence, we create members of class Book as book_id, title, author. The class also defines the member functions input() and output() so as to read and print the details of each Book object.

Customer: Each object of class Customer represents one customer of the library in a real world. Hence, we define members customer_id, name and tel_no inside class Customer so as to store the relevant information about each customer in the computer memory. Further, it is a rule that each customer can at the most issue two books at a time. Hence, we create an array of class Book inside class Customer so as to represent the data about books that are issued by the customer.

```
Book b[2];
```

However, not every customer will always issue 2 books from the library. Hence we have also created a variable books_issued which represents the count of number of books issued by a particular customer. We invoke a function issue() if the customer wants to issue a book from the library and we invoke a function return_book()

if the customer wants to return a book to the library. Hence the function `issue()` increments the value of variable `books_issued` whereas the function `return_book()` decrements the value of variable `books_issued` as seen in the code.

The **integrity constraint** of the organization is that each customer of the library can at the most issue two books at a time; we have made a security check in the function `issue()` of class library such that the book is issued to the customer only if the count of number of books issued is less than 2.

Solved Example 11.3

Create a class to represent a dimension of a line segment that is specified in terms of centimetres and millimetres. The program should read the dimensions of two line segments and calculate a resultant dimension, which is the addition of two dimensions. For example, if the two dimensions are

```
d1= 10 cm and 5 mm
d2 = 15 cm 7 mm,
```

then the resultant dimension should be calculated as: 26 cm and 2 mm.

```cpp
#include<iostream.h>
class Dimension
{
private:
    int CM;
    int MM;
public:
void input()
{
cout<<"Enter centimetres and millimetres for the object"<<endl;
cin>>CM>>MM;
}
void output()
{
cout<<CM<<" centimetres and "<<MM<<" millimetres"<<endl;
}
Dimension add(Dimension t)
{
Dimension res;
res.CM = CM+t.CM;
res.MM = MM+t.MM;
```

```
    while(res.MM>=10)
    {
    res.MM=res.MM-10;
    res.CM++;
    }
return res;
}
};
void main()
{
Dimension d1,d2,d3;
cout<<"*************d1**********"<<endl;
d1.input();
cout<<"*************d2**********"<<endl;
d2.input();
d3=d1.add(d2);
cout<<"The result of addition is"<<endl;
d3.output();
}
```

Turbo C++ IDE

```
*************d1**********
Enter centimetres and millimetres for the object
10 5
*************d2**********
Enter centimetres and millimetres for the object
15 7
The result of addition is
26 centimetres and 2 millimetres
```

SCRATCH PAD

- The program is very similar to the code for addition of complex numbers as we have written before in this chapter. Just like every complex number has 2 parts real and imaginary, every Dimension object is also specified in two parts **centimeters** and **millimeters**. Hence, we have created a class Dimension with two members CM and MM to represent the centimeter and the millimeter value respectively.
- The statement,

    ```
    d3=d1.add(d2);
    ```

invokes a function add() using the object d1 and passes the object d2 as an argument. Hence, we can now calculate the centimeter and millimeter value of the result object as addition of centimeters and millimeters values of objects d1 and d2 using the statements below:

```
res.CM = CM+t.CM;
res.MM = MM+t.MM;
```

Also, it may happen that we get the value of millimeters greater than 10 as a result of addition. We will then convert the millimeter part into centimeter using the following while loop.

```
while(res.MM>=10)
{
res.MM=res.MM-10;
res.CM++;
}
```

For example, if the result of addition is 25 cm and 12 mm then the `while` loop converts the result into 26 cm and 2 mm by reducing a value 10 from the millimeter part of the result and adding 1 to the centimeter part of the result object.

Solved Example 11.4

Write a class to represent a vector (a series of floating point values). Include the following functions in the class:

1. A member function to input the elements of the vector
2. A member function to modify the value of the given element
3. A member function to display the vector as a comma separated list
4. A member function to find the scalar product of two vectors

Also create a friend function that performs multiplication of a scalar value with the vector.

```
#include<iostream.h>

class Vector
{
private:
float v[100];
int size;
public:
  void input ()
  {
int i;
cout<<"Enter the size of the vector";
cin>>size;
cout<<"Enter the elements of the vector"<<endl;
    for(i=0;i<size;i++)
    {
    cin>>v[i];
    }
  }
  void output()
  {
```

```
    int i;
    cout<<"The elements of the vector are"<<endl;
    for(i=0;i<size;i++)
    {
    if(i!=size-1)
    {
    cout<<v[i]<<",";
    }
    else
    {
    cout<<v[i]<<endl;
    }
    }
    }
    void edit(int element, int pos)
    {
    if(pos<size && pos>0)
    {
    v[pos]=element;
    }
    else
    {
cout<<"The position specified is not in bounds of the
    vector"<<endl;
    }
    }
    float product(Vector t)
    {
    int i;
    float scalar_prod=0;
    for(i=0;i<=size-1;i++)
    {
    scalar_prod = scalar_prod+v[i]*t.v[i];
    }
    return scalar_prod;
    }
friend Vector multiply(float, Vector);
};
Vector multiply(float element, Vector t)
{
int i;
Vector res;
    for(i=0;i<=t.size-1;i++)
    {
```

```
        res.v[i]= t.v[i]*element;
        }
return res;
}
void main()
{
Vector v1,v2,v3;
float scalar_product,q,element;
int position;
cout<<"Enter a vector"<<endl;
v1.input();
cout<<"Enter another vector"<<endl;
v2.input();
scalar_product = v1.product(v2);
cout<<"Scalar product of two vectors is"<< scalar_product<<endl;
cout<<"Enter a scalar quantity to be multiplied with the first
    vector"<<endl;
cin>>q;
v3= multiply(q,v1);
cout<<"************Result of scalar multiplication********"
    <<endl;
v3.output();
cout<<"Enter the element and the position of vector to be
    edited"<<endl;
cin>>element>>position;
v1.edit(element,position);
cout<<"********* state of vector after editing the element******"
    <<endl;
v1.output();
}
```

```
Turbo C++ IDE

*******Enter a vector***********
Enter the size of the vector 4
Enter the elements of the vector
10 20 30 40
***********Enter another vector********
Enter the size of the vector 4
Enter the elements of the vector
12 3 45 9
Scalar product of two vectors is 1890
Enter a scalar quantity to be multiplied with the first vector
2
************Result of scalar multiplication*********
The elements of the vector are
20,40,60,80
Enter the element and the position of vector to be edited
90 2
********* state of vector after editing the element******
The elements of the vector are
10,20,90,40
```

SCRATCH PAD

We create a class `Vector` which defines a floating point array `v` so as to store the series of floating point numbers. Along with the functions `input()` and `output()` so as to read and print the elements of the vector, the class also defines following additional functions:

1. **`float product(Vector):`** The function returns a floating point value which represents the scalar product of two vectors. As seen in the code, we invoke the function `product()` using following statement:

   ```
   scalar_product = v1.product(v2);
   ```

   This means that, we invoke a function using object `v1` and pass `v2` as an argument to the function. Also, the function `product()` defines a formal argument named as `t` which is initialized to the actual argument `v2`. Therefore, the ith element of the array `v` of object `v2` can be accessed using object `t` as **`t.v[i]`** whereas, the ith element of the array `v` of object `v1` can be directly accessed as `v[i]`. Hence, executing the below statement for all the vector elements in the `product()` function will calculate the value of scalar product:

   ```
   scalar_prod = scalar_prod+ v[i]*t.v[i];
   ```

2. **`friend Vector multiply(float,Vector):`** The function `multiply()` is used to multiply a vector with a scalar quantity. The function is required to multiply a scalar quantity (named as `element`) with every element of the vector (named as `v`), by executing the following statement in loop.

   ```
   res.v[i] = t.v[i]*element;
   ```

   The vector inside object `res` represents a resultant vector which will be returned to the calling function. Note that the function `multiply()` is a **friend function** and hence we invoke the function as shown below:

   ```
   v3 = multiply(q,v1);
   ```

   The object `v3` now represents a resultant vector which is the multiplication of static quantity `q` and a vector `v1`.

3. **`void edit(int, int):`** The function is used to modify a element at a particular position in the vector. For example, the following statement,

   ```
   v1.edit(90,2);
   ```

   will set the value 90 at the position 2 of the vector. Obviously, the previous value at the position 2 will be overwritten.

Solved Example 11.5

Write a C++ program to create a class `Matrix` and define following operations on the matrix objects:

1. Operation to perform addition of two `Matrix` objects
2. Operation to perform subtraction of two `Matrix` objects
3. Operation to perform multiplication of two `Matrix` objects

```cpp
#include<iostream.h>
class Matrix
{
private:
int mat[100][100];
```

```
int rows;
int cols;
public:
void input()
{
int i,j;
    cout<<"Enter the order of the matrix";
     cin>>rows>>cols;
    cout<<"Enter the Matrix elements"<<endl;
     for(i=0;i<=rows-1;i++)
     {
      for(j=0;j<=cols-1;j++)
      {
      cin>>mat[i][j];
      }
     }
}
void output()
{
int i,j;
cout<<"The matrix elements are"<<endl;
    for(i=0;i<=rows-1;i++)
     {
       for(j=0;j<=cols-1;j++)
       {
       cout<<mat[i][j]<<" ";
       }
       cout<<endl;
     }
}
Matrix add(Matrix t)
{
int i,j;
Matrix res;
res.rows=rows;
res.cols=cols;
    if(rows==t.rows && cols==t.cols)
    {
    for(i=0;i<=rows-1;i++)
     {
     for(j=0;j<=cols-1;j++)
      {
       res.mat[i][j]=mat[i][j]+t.mat[i][j];
      }
```

```
    }
    }
    else
    {
    cout<<"Addition is not possible"<<endl;
    }
return res;
}
Matrix sub(Matrix t)
{
int i,j;
Matrix res;
res.rows=rows;
res.cols=cols;
    if(rows==t.rows && cols==t.cols)
    {
    for(i=0;i<=rows-1;i++)
     {
     for(j=0;j<=cols-1;j++)
      {
        res.mat[i][j]=mat[i][j]-t.mat[i][j];
      }
     }
    }
    else
    {
    cout<<"Subtraction is not possible"<<endl;
    }
return res;
}
Matrix multiply(Matrix t)
{
int i,j,k;
Matrix res;
if(cols==t.rows)
{
res.rows=rows;
res.cols=t.cols;
    for(i=0;i<=rows-1;i++)
      {
            for(j=0;j<=t.cols-1;j++)
            {
                res.mat[i][j]=0;
                    for(k=0;k<=cols-1;k++)
```

```
                          {
                res.mat[i][j]+= mat[i][k]*t.mat[k][j];
                          }
                }
            cout<<endl;
        }
    }
else
{
cout<<"Multiplication is not possible";
}
    return res;
    }/*End of function*/
};
void main()
{
Matrix m1,m2,m3,m4,m5;
cout<<"*********Matrix m1*********"<<endl;
m1.input();
cout<<"*********Matrix m2*********"<<endl;
m2.input();
m3=m1.add(m2);
m4=m1.sub(m2);
m5=m1.multiply(m2);
cout<<"Addition of two matrices is"<<endl;
m3.output();
cout<<"Subtraction of two matrices is"<<endl;
m4.output();
cout<<"Multiplication of two matrices is"<<endl;
m5.output();
}
```

Error Finding Exercise

The following are some programs which may or may not contain errors. Correct the errors if they exist in the code and determine the output.

Program 1

```
#include<iostream.h>
class DATA
{
private:
    int a;
```

```
    int b;
    void input()
    {
    cin>>a>>b;
    }
    void output()
    {
    cout<<a<<b;
    }
};
void main()
{
DATA o1,o2;
o1.a=10;
o1.b=20;
o2.input();
o1.output();
o2.output();
}
```

Program 2

```
#include<iostream.h>
void main()
{
 DATA d1,d2;
 d1.inpput();
 d1.output(t1);
 d2.inpput();
 d2.output(t1);
}
class DATA
{
private:
int x;
int y;
public:
    void input()
    {
    cin>>x>>y;
    }
    void output()
    {
    cout<<x<<"   "<<y;
    }
};
```

Program 3

```
#include<iostream.h>
class Student
{
private:
int roll_no;
char name[100];
public:
    void input()
    {
    cin>>roll_no>>name;
    }
    void output()
    {
    cout<<roll_no<<"   "<<name<<endl;
    }
};
void main()
{
Student s1;
Student.input()
Student.output();
Student s2,s3;
s2.output();
s3.output();
}
```

Program 4

```
#include<iostream.h>
class NUMBER
{
private:
int x;
int f;
public:
    void input()
    {
    cout<<"Enter x";
    cin>>x;
    }
    f=1;
    while(x>0)
    {
    f=f*x;
```

```
    x--;
    }
    void output()
    {
    cout<<"Factorial of the number is" <<f<<endl;
    }
};
void main()
{
NUMBER n1;
NUMBER n2;
n1.input();
n2.input();
n1.output();
n2.output();
}
```

Program 5

```
#include<iostream.h>
class FLOAT
{
private:
int a;
public:
    void set_data(int x)
    {
    a=x;
    }
friend void increment();
    void output()
    {
    cout<<"a="<<a<<endl;
    }
};
void increment()
{
a++;
}
void main()
{
FLOAT o1,o2;
o1.set_data(10);
```

```
o2.set_data(20);
o1.increment();
o2.increment();
o1.output();
o2.output();
}
```

Program 6

```
#include<iostream.h>
class Course
{
private:
char name[100];
float fees;
public:
    void input()
    {
    cin>>name>>fees;
    }
    void output()
    {
    cout<<"name="<<name<<"fees="<<fees<<endl;
    }
};
void main()
{
Course c1;
Course *p;
p.input();
p.output();
Course *q;
q.input();
q.output();
}
```

1. Which of the following is not a feature of OOP paradigm?
   (a) Encapsulation
   (b) Data hiding
   (c) Security
   (d) Modularity

2. Which of the following statement(s) is true?
   (a) Structure does not support encapsulation, whereas class supports encapsulation.
   (b) All members of the structure are by default private, whereas all the members of the class are by default public.
   (c) All members of a structure are by default public, whereas all the members of the class are by default private.
   (d) There is no difference between a structure and a class.
3. The primary use of friend functions is
   (a) to implement data hiding
   (b) to implement polymorphism
   (c) to access private members of the class outside the scope of the class
   (d) to implement encapsulation
4. Memory for the member variables of a class is allocated when
   (a) object of a class is created
   (b) class is defined
   (c) a pointer to a class is created
   (d) the member variable is initialized to a particular value
5. Following operator can be used to access the members of the class using a pointer
   (a) Membership operator (.)   (c) Address operator (&)
   (b) Arrow operator (->)   (d) None of the above
6. Advantage of data hiding and encapsulation is that
   (a) they hide the programmers from the complexity of the code
   (b) they help in reusability of the code
   (c) they give security to the private variables of the class
   (d) they reduce the lines of code of a program
7. When a member function of a class is invoked using an object, then it is called
   (a) Abstraction   (c) Polymorphism
   (b) Message passing   (d) Inheritance
8. Object is by default passed to a function using
   (a) Call by value   (d) Object cannot be passed as an argument to a function
   (b) Call by reference
   (c) Call by address

Review Questions

1. What is the need for Object oriented programming? Explain with examples.
2. Write a short note on classes and objects in C++.
3. Write a C++ program to create a class named `Student` with members as `roll_number`, `names`, and `marks`. Store data about *n* number of students in computer memory and arrange the *n*-students in ascending order of marks.
4. Write a C++ program to create a class `Polar` with two members radius and angle. Write a function `add()` to perform addition of `Polar` objects.

5. Write a C++ program to create a class `Date` with members dd, mm, and yyyy. Create a member function `diff()` to find the number of days between two dates. Also consider a case of leap year, while finding the difference between two `Date` objects.

6. Explain the usage of pointers with objects. Also explain the process to invoke a member function of a class using pointers with an example.

7. What is the advantage of creating an array of objects? How it is different when compared with an array of basic types?

8. Write a short note on friend functions. Give one example of friend function in C++. What is the drawback of friend functions?

9. What is encapsulation and data hiding? Explain with example.

10. Write a C++ program to overload function `root()` to return the square root of integer, float, and long data types. Also write the output of the program.

Chapter

12

Constructors and Destructors

12.1 Overview

We know that a class in C++ is a user-defined data type which combines members and member functions into a single unit. Recall from Chapter 11, data hiding and encapsulation are the key features of object oriented programming paradigm. Hence, it is recommended to create variables inside the class as `private` and the function defined inside the class as `public`, such that the value of private variables which are defined inside the class can only be accessed through public functions of that class. This feature provides security to the `private` members of the class as they can only be accessed using the public functions defined by the class.

Further, as we give initial values to the variables of basic types, we may also be required to give initial values to the member variables of each of the objects created in the program. For example, let us consider a class `ShoppingCart` whose object can store list of items purchased by the customer in an online shopping system. As seen in the Figure 12.1,

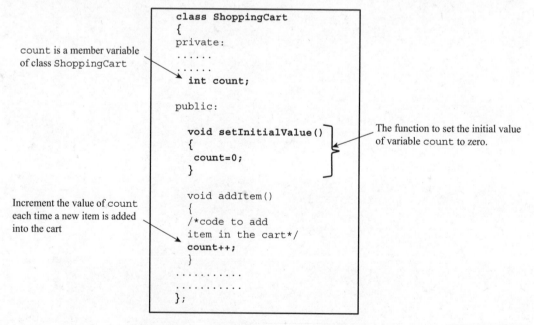

Figure 12.1: Pseudo code for class ShoppingCart

we create a variable count inside the class ShoppingCart which represents the count of items to be purchased by the customer. Hence, the initial value of variable count, which represents the number of items in the cart must be set to zero each time when a new cart is created. Obviously, as and when an item is added into the cart, the value of variable count must be incremented to represent the number of items in the cart at any point of time. Hence, we have included a function addItem(), which increments the value of count when an item is added to the cart, as shown in the Figure 12.1. Further, we have also written a function setInitialValue() that sets the initial value of the variable count as zero, which represents an empty cart.

Hence, it is the responsibility of the programmer to invoke the function setInitialValue() to set the initial value of the variable count to zero each time a new ShoppingCart object is created. This means that creating a ShoppingCart object would require the following two statements to be written in the program to allow the complete program to function accurately:

```
ShoppingCart c1;
c1.setInitialValue();
```

The first statement above, creates an object of class ShoppingCart named as c1, and the second statement invokes a member function setInitialValue(), which sets the initial value of the variable count to zero. Similarly, if we create *n*-objects of the class ShoppingCart as $c_1, c_2 \dots c_n$, it will now be the responsibility of the programmer to invoke the function setInitialValue() for each of the objects c_1 to c_n as shown in the Figure 12.2. This is because, every new cart created by the customer must be initially kept as empty in the program.

Therefore, as seen from the Figure 12.2, we need to repeatedly invoke the same function for each of the objects of class ShoppingCart. This is because, every object of the class ShoppingCart has a common requirement to set the initial value of the member count as zero. This can be an extra overhead on the programmer when there are a large number of ShoppingCart objects to be created in the program. The overhead of such repetitive function calls to set the initial values of each of the objects can be avoided using 'constructors' in C++.

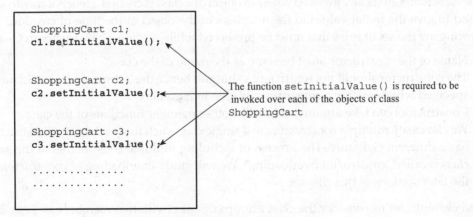

Figure 12.2: Creating multiple objects of class ShoppingCart

Constructor is a member function of a class that is automatically invoked by the compiler when an object of the class is created by the programmer. Therefore, we can write a code to set the initial values of all the members inside the constructor. As the constructor is always 'called' for every object when an object is created, the initial values of the members of object can be set at the time of creation itself. In this chapter, we study the details of working and usage of constructors in a C++ program.

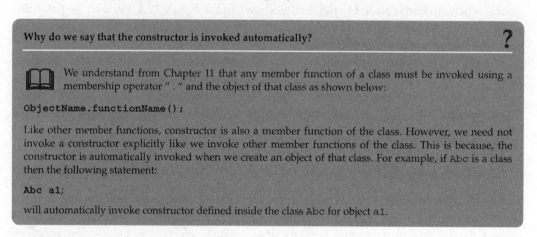

Why do we say that the constructor is invoked automatically? ?

We understand from Chapter 11 that any member function of a class must be invoked using a membership operator " . " and the object of that class as shown below:

`ObjectName.functionName();`

Like other member functions, constructor is also a member function of the class. However, we need not invoke a constructor explicitly like we invoke other member functions of the class. This is because, the constructor is automatically invoked when we create an object of that class. For example, if Abc is a class then the following statement:

`Abc a1;`

will automatically invoke constructor defined inside the class Abc for object a1.

12.2 Creating Constructors

The following is the syntax for creating constructors in C++:

```
ClassName(<arguments>)
{
/* constructor body*/
}
```

A constructor must always be written as a member function of a class. A constructor defined in the class is automatically invoked when an object of a class is created. Hence, a constructor is used to give the initial values to the members of the object at the time of creation. The following are the set of rules that must be preserved while writing a constructor in C++:

1. Name of the constructor must be same as the name of the class.
2. The constructor should not return any value and hence the 'return type' should not be specified while creating a constructor as seen in its syntax.
3. Constructors can take arguments just like other member functions of the class.
4. We can create multiple constructors in a single class such that each of the constructors has a different signature. The process of including multiple constructors in the same class is called 'constructor overloading'. We will study overloading of constructors in the later sections of this chapter.

As an example, let us consider the class ShoppingCart with two members as list and count, where count is a member that represents the number of items which are added in

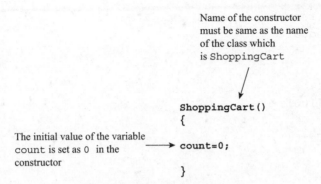

Name of the constructor
must be same as the name
of the class which
is ShoppingCart

```
ShoppingCart()
{
count=0;
}
```

The initial value of the variable
count is set as 0 in the
constructor

Figure 12.3: Default constructor

the shopping cart by the customer at any point of time, and list represents the actual list of items selected by the user while shopping online. Let us assume that at the most a user can shop 100 items in a single transaction, and hence we have created an integer array named as list with a size of 100 as seen in the code. Further, we have included a constructor to set the initial value of variable count as 0, this means that initially the number of items in the cart will always be set as zero for each of the new carts that are created when the user logs on to the online shopping web page. The constructor ShoppingCart() does not take any parameters as shown in the Figure 12.3. Such a constructor that does not take any parameters is called as a **default constructor**.

Note that the constructor will be automatically invoked when an object of class ShoppingCart is created. Hence, the initial value of the number of items in the cart will always be zero. Further, each time we invoke a function addItem(), the 'item id' of the selected item will be taken as input from the user, thereby adding it to the list of items in the shopping cart as seen in the Figure 12.4. Also, the function addItem() will increment the value of the variable count each time a new item is added to the list as shown in the Figure 12.4.

The following is the full source code for storing the details of ShoppingCart to understand the working of constructors in C++.

```
void addItem()
{
int id;
cout<<"Enter the Item identification of the item to be added"<<endl;
cin>>id;

list[count]=id;

count++;
}
```

Insert an element into the list
of selected items

Increment the value of variable count
each time an item is added to the list

Figure 12.4: Function definition of addItem()

```cpp
#include<iostream.h>
class ShoppingCart
{
private:
    int count;
    int list[100];
  public:
    ShoppingCart()
    {
    count=0;
    }
        void addItem()
        {
        int id;
        cout<<"Enter the Item identification of the item to be
        added"<<endl;
        cin>>id;
        list[count]=id;
        count++;
        }
    void display()
    {
    int i;
    cout<<"The items in the list are"<<endl;
    for(i=0;i<count;i++)
        {
        cout<<list[i]<<endl;
        }
    }
};
void main()
{
ShoppingCart c1;
ShoppingCart c2;
c1.addItem();
c1.addItem();
c1.addItem();
c2.addItem();
c2.addItem();
cout<<"------------Cart C1-----------------"<<endl;
c1.display();
cout<<"------------Cart C2-----------------"<<endl;
c2.display();
}
```

```
Turbo C++ IDE                                                    _  □  X
Enter the Item identification of the item to be added
45
Enter the Item identification of the item to be added
46
Enter the Item identification of the item to be added
47
Enter the Item identification of the item to be added
55
Enter the Item identification of the item to be added
56
------------Cart C1------------
The items in the list are
45
46
47
------------Cart C2------------
The items in the list are
55
56
```

Let us understand the working of the given code from the first line of the main() function. The statement

```
ShoppingCart c1;
```

creates an object of class ShoppingCart which is named as c1. Note that whenever an object is created, the constructor of the class is automatically invoked by the compiler. Hence, the member count of the object c1 will be initialized to 0 as shown in the Figure 12.5. The integer array which is named as list is not initialized by the constructor because it is required to be initialized at runtime, depending on the items selected by the customer while shopping online.

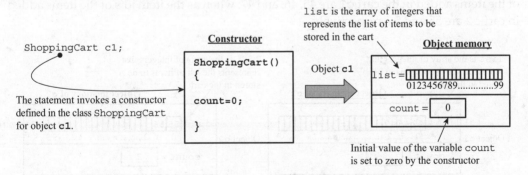

Figure 12.5: State of object c1

Similarly, the statement

```
ShoppingCart c2;
```

creates another object of class ShoppingCart which will again invoke a constructor for creating object c2. Hence, the member count for object c2 will also be set to zero by the **constructor** written inside the class, as seen in the Figure 12.6.

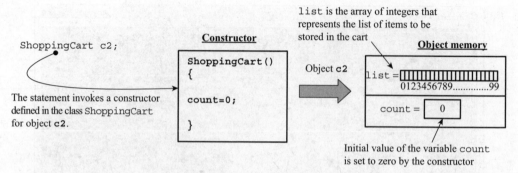

Figure 12.6: State of object c2

Further, we have invoked the function addItem() three times using object c1 and two times using object c2 as shown below:

```
c1.addItem();
c1.addItem();
c1.addItem();
c2.addItem();
c2.addItem();
```

This means that three items are added in cart c1, whereas two items are added in the cart c2 by the user of the online shopping system. Hence, the value of the member count for object c1 will be set to 3, and the value of the member count for object c2 will be set to 2 as shown in the Figure 12.7. This is because the function addItem() increments the value of variable count each time it is invoked. The Figure 12.7 assumes that the actual item id's of the items added in the cart c1 are 45, 46, and 47, whereas the item id's of the items added in cart c2 are 55 and 56, respectively.

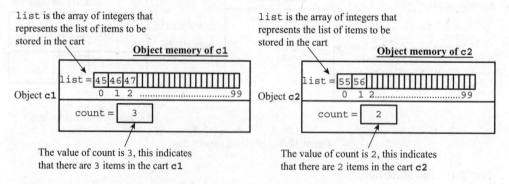

Figure 12.7: State of objects c1 and c2

Further, we invoke a function display() that prints the members list and count for each of the objects as seen at the end of the main() function. This prints the list of items in each of the carts on the computer screen as an output of the given program.

What happens if the class does not have any constructor?   ?

If we do not create a constructor in the class, compiler provides a default constructor with every class. The constructor provided by the compiler does not take any arguments. Hence, if we do not define a constructor in class `ShoppingCart` then the statement:

```
ShoppingCart c1;
```

will invoke the constructor provided by the compiler, so as to create the object `c1`. Obviously, in this case initial value to the members of the object will not be given automatically. Rather, it will be the responsibility of the programmer to create a separate member function to give initial values to the members of the object. This member function must be invoked explicitly in the program to initialize the members of the object as discussed in the Section 12.1.

12.3   Constructor Overloading

We understand from the previous section that the constructor should always be written as a member function of a class. Further, it is important to note that, we can also include multiple constructors in the same class. When a class contains multiple constructors defined inside it, such that each constructor has a different signature, then it is called constructor overloading. In case of constructor overloading, the compiler correctly determines which

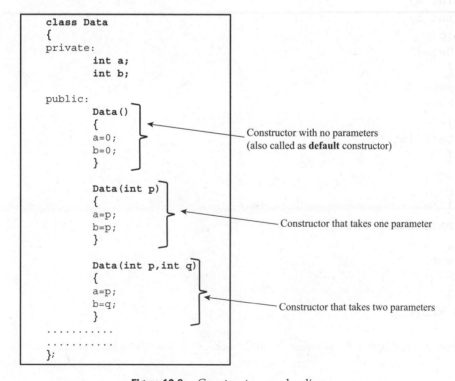

Figure 12.8:   Constructor overloading

constructor is to be invoked based on the 'constructor signature', which includes the following specifications about the constructor:

1. Number of arguments the constructor takes as parameters
2. Data type of the arguments
3. Order of the arguments

As an example, let us consider the class Data with members a and b of type integer as seen in the code. The class defines three constructors inside it, such that the first constructor does not take any arguments and initializes the values of members a and b with 0 and 10, respectively. The second constructor takes only one parameter and initializes both the members a and b with the same value, which is passed to it as an argument. Whereas, the third constructor takes two parameters such that the first parameter passed to it is initialized to the member a and the second parameter passed to it will be initialized to member b as shown in the Figure 12.8.

The class Data also contains a function add() that prints the result of addition of the values of members a and b on the computer screen. The following is the full source code that creates three objects of class Data and invokes the function add() for each of these objects.

```cpp
#include<iostream.h>
class Data
{
private:
    int a;
    int b;
public:
    Data()
    {
    a=0;
    b=10;
    }
    Data(int p)
    {
    a=p;
    b=p;
    }
    Data(int p,int q)
    {
    a=p;
    b=q;
    }
void add()
{
cout<<"Addition of "<<a<< " and"<<b<< " is "<<a+b<<endl;
}
};
```

```
void main()
{
Data d1(100,200);
Data d2(50);
Data d3;
cout<<"---------------d1------------"<<endl;
d1.add();
cout<<"---------------d2------------"<<endl;
d2.add();
cout<<"---------------d3------------"<<endl;
d3.add();
}
```

Output

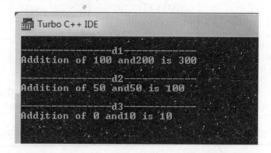

Let us understand the code from the first line of `main()` function.
   The statement

```
Data d1(100,200);
```

creates an object of class `Data` named as d1. Note that we have also passed the values of the members of the object d1 at the time of its creation. Hence, the statement will invoke a constructor of class `Data` that takes two arguments. This is because we have specified two values in the parenthesis while creating the object d1. The integer constants 100 and 200 will be passed as actual arguments to the constructor, thereby initializing the formal arguments p and q with 100 and 200, respectively. This means that the members a and b of object d1 will be initialized to values 100 and 200, respectively, by the constructor with two arguments as shown in the Figure 12.9.
   The next statement

```
Data d2(50);
```

creates an object of class `Data` named as d2. Note that, this time, we have passed only one value in the parenthesis at the time of creation of object d2. Hence, the statement will invoke a constructor of class `Data` that takes only one argument, thereby initializing the value of member a as well as b to 50 as shown in the Figure 12.10. As seen, the actual argument 50 is initialized to the formal argument p of the constructor, thereby initializing the value 50 to both the members a and b of object d2 as shown in the Figure 12.10.

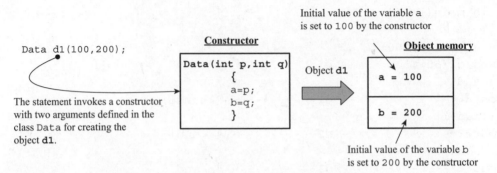

Figure 12.9: Calling constructor with two arguments

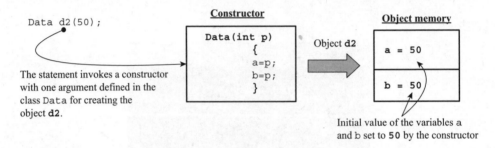

Figure 12.10: Calling constructor with one argument

The next statement

```
Data d3;
```

creates another object of class Data which is named d3. As we have not passed any values at the time of creating object d3, the compiler will bind the statement to invoke a constructor that does not take any arguments as shown in the Figure 12.11. Hence, the members a and b of object d3 will be initialized to values 0 and 10, respectively, by the default constructor as shown in the Figure 12.11.

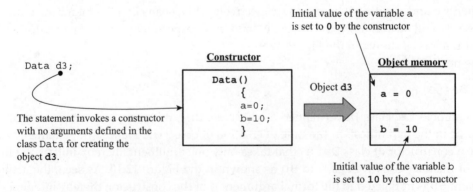

Figure 12.11: Calling constructor with no arguments

Further, the statement

```
d1.add();
```

will invoke the member function add() using object d1, which will perform the addition of members a and b of object d1. Hence, the statement will print the result of addition as 300 as the value of members a and b of object d1 are 100 and 200, respectively.

Similarly, the statements d2.add(); and d3.add(); will print the addition of values of the members a and b of object d2 and d3, respectively. The statement d2.add(); will print the addition as **100** because the value of a is 50 and b is also 50 for object d2. The statement d3.add(); will print the addition as **10** because the value of a is 0 and b is 10 for object d3.

NOTES

C++ also supports an alternate syntax to initialize members using constructors. This syntax allows the programmer to initialize the members of the object on the first line of constructor declaration itself. The following is an alternative syntax to initialize members of object using constructors.

```
Constructor(parameter1,parameter2,......parameterN)  :
Member1(Value1),Member2(Value2).....MemberN(ValueN)

{
/*Body of constructor*/
}
```

Note the presence of : operator after which the member initialization begins.
For example, the default constructor

```
    Data()
    {
    a=0;
    b=10;
    }
```

can also be written as

```
Data():a(0),b(10)
    {
    }
```

Note that the body of the constructor is empty but the constructor is declared as

```
Data():a(0),b(10)
```

which means that value of member a is initialized to zero and value of member b is initialized to 10. Similarly, the constructors with parameters can be rewritten as shown below.

```
class Data
{
private:
    int a;
    int b;
```

```
public:
    Data():a(0),b(10)
    {
/*Initialize a to 0 and b to 10*/
    }
    Data(int p):a(p),b(p)
    {
/*Initialize a to value of p and b also to  value of  p*/
    }
    Data(int p,int q):a(p),b(q)
    {
/*Initialize a to value of p and b  to value of q*/
    }
    void add()
    {
    cout<<"Addition of " <<a<< " and " <<b<< " is " <<a+b<<endl;
    }
};
void main()
{
Data d1(100,200);
Data d2(50);
Data d3;
cout<<"---------------d1------------"<<endl;
d1.add();
cout<<"---------------d2------------"<<endl;
d2.add();
cout<<"---------------d3------------"<<endl;
d3.add();
}
```

Needless to mention that the order in which parameters are specified to the constructor is independent to the order in which the object members are initialized. The constructor given below initializes member a of the object to value of p and member b of the object to value of q.

```
Data(int p,int q):a(p),b(q)
    {
/*Initialize a to value of p and b  to value of q*/
    }
```

Whereas, if we rewrite the constructor as
```
Data(int p,int q):b(p),a(q)
    {
/*Initialize b to value of p and a  to value of q*/
    }
```

it will initialize the value of p to member b and value of q to member a.

12.4 Program to Perform Addition of `Point` Objects using Constructors: An Example

As an example, let us design a C++ program to create a class `Point` and to perform addition of points in Cartesian coordinates. The code is exactly similar to the program as already discussed in Chapter 11, with the only difference being that the members of the `Point` objects are initialized using constructors instead of the function `input()` as seen in the code.

We create class `Point` with two members x and y to represent the x and y values of each of the points. Further, we have included two constructors in the class `Point` as shown in the Figure 12.12, such that one of the constructors take two parameters which will initialize the members x and y with the values passed to it as arguments. The other constructor is a default constructor that does not take any parameters and has an empty body that facilitates the creation of a `Point` object without initializing its members.

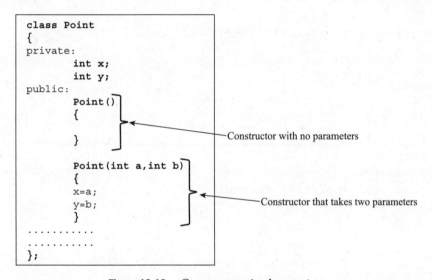

Figure 12.12: Constructors in class `Point`

The full source code to perform addition of `Point` objects is as given below. The program creates three objects of class `Point` as P1, P2 and P3 such that the result of addition of the objects P1 and P2 is stored in P3.

```
#include<iostream.h>
class Point
{
private:
    int x;
    int y;
public:
  Point()
        {
```

```
        }
  Point(int a,int b)
     {
     x=a;
     y=b;
     }
  Point add(Point t)
     {
     Point res;
     res.x=x+t.x;
     res.y =y +t.y;
     return res;
     }
  void output()
  {
  cout<<"("<<x<<","<<y<<")"<<endl;
  }
};
void main()
{
Point P1(5,10);
Point P2(15,20);
Point P3;
P3 = P1.add(P2);
cout<<"Resultant point is "<<endl;
P3.output();
}
```

Output

```
Resultant point is

(20,30)
```

Let us understand the code from the first line of `main()` function.

The statement

```
Point P1(5,10);
```

creates an object of class `Point`, which is named as `P1`. Note that we have also passed the values of the members of the object `P1` at the time of creating it. Hence, the statement will invoke a constructor of class `Point` that takes two arguments. This is because we have specified two values in the parenthesis while creating the object `P1`. The integer constants 5 and 10 will be passed as actual arguments to the constructor, thereby initializing the formal arguments a and b with 5 and 10, respectively. This means that the members x and y of object `P1` will be initialized to values 5 and 10, respectively, by the constructor with two parameters as shown in the Figure 12.13.

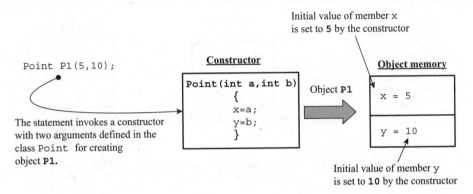

Figure 12.13: Constructor with two arguments invoked for P1

Similarly, the statement

```
Point P2(15,20);
```

will invoke a constructor with two arguments for object P2, thereby initializing the members x and y of object P2 as 15 and 20, respectively, as shown in the Figure 12.14.

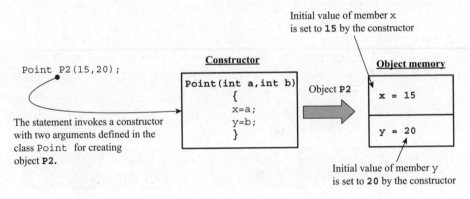

Figure 12.14: Constructor with two arguments invoked for P2

Further, the statement

```
Point P3;
```

will invoke a constructor with no arguments as we have not passed any value at the time of creating object P3. Hence, the members x and y of object P3 will not be initialized and will hold junk values as shown in the Figure 12.15. This is because we have kept the default constructor as empty in the program.

Note that we have kept the constructor as empty because the members of object P3 should be actually initialized by the object returned from the add () function that represents the result of addition of two points, as seen in the code. Hence, we now perform addition of two Point objects P1 and P2, thereby storing the result in P3, and print the x and y values

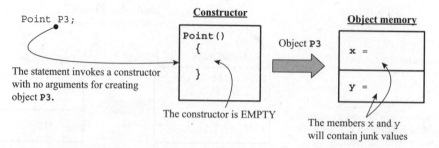

Figure 12.15: Constructor with two arguments invoked for P3

of P3, as seen in the code. The complete process to perform addition of `Point` objects is exactly same as discussed in Chapter 11. Therefore, x value of P3 will be 20 and y value of P3 will be set to 30 after the execution of the `add()` function as shown in the Figure 12.16.

x = 5		x = 15		x = 20
y = 10	+	y = 20	=	y = 30
Object **P1**		Object **P2**		Object **P3**

Figure 12.16: Addition of objects P1 and P2 performed by function `add()`

What is the significance of a empty constructor that takes no parameters inside class Point? **?**

📖 When we do not write a constructor in the class, compiler still provides a default constructor with every class, so as to create objects of that class. The constructor provided by the compiler does not take any arguments. However, compiler will not provide any default constructor to the class, if the programmer defines a constructor with parameters. In this case, we have created a constructor with parameters inside class `Point` and hence compiler will not provide any default constructor to class `Point`. This means that statement:

`Point P3;`

will not work because, in this case a default constructor is to be invoked for creating object P3. Hence, we have created a empty constructor without any parameters so as to allow the creation of the objects of class `Point` without passing any parameters. Therefore, we can now create object **P3** successfully.

12.5   Constructor with Default Arguments

You can specify default values to the parameters of the constructor. The rules for creating constructors with default arguments as same as that of creating functions with default arguments as specified in Chapter 7, Section 7.11. For example, consider a `Point` constructor as written below

```
Point(int a,int b=20)
    {
    x=a;
    y=b;
    }
```

This constructor has two parameters a and b. The value of parameter b is defaulted to 20, which means that if the value of b is not passed by the caller it will be considered as 20. In summary, the constructor is coded such that it is mandatory to pass the value of first parameter, whereas specifying the value of second parameter is optional. The statement

```
Point p1(10);
```

will initialize first parameter of the constructor to 10, whereas the default value is used for second parameter. Hence, this statement will create an object p1 with x value initialized as 10 and y value initialized as 20. However, you could also create point object as

```
Point p2(100,200);
```

While creating p2, we have specified both the values. Hence, it also calls the same constructor, with the only difference being the default value of parameter b will not be used this time. This statement creates a point object p2 with value of x as 100 and value of y as 200.

12.6   Cloning Objects using Constructor/Copy Constructor

A constructor that takes the reference to the object of the same class as an argument to copy the values of the member variables of one object into another object is called 'copy constructor'. For example, let us create a class Data with members a and b of type integer and float, respectively. We have written three constructors in class Data as shown in the Figure 12.17.

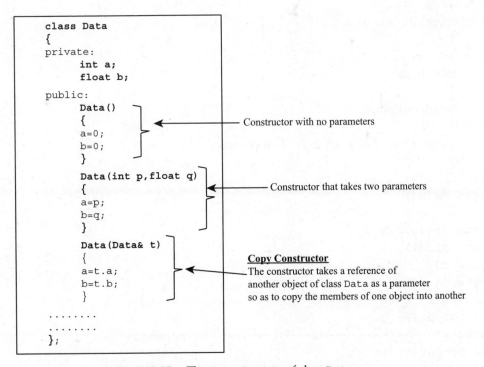

Figure 12.17:   Three constructors of class Data

The first constructor is the constructor without parameters, and the second constructor is the constructor with two parameters as shown in the Figure 12.17. The third constructor takes the reference to another object of class Data as an argument, thereby copying the member values of some other object into the object that is to be created by the constructor.

The following is the source code that illustrates the usage of copy constructor.

```cpp
#include<iostream.h>
class Data
{
private:
int a;
float b;
public:
    Data()
    {
    a=0;
    b=0;
    }
    Data(int p,float q)
    {
    a=p;
    b=q;
    }
    Data(Data& t)
    {
    a=t.a;
    b=t.b;
    }
    void output()
    {
    cout<<"a= "<<a<<" b= "<<b<<endl;
    }
};
void main()
{
Data d1(10,2.5);
Data d2(d1);
Data d3;
Data d4(d3);
cout<<"--------------d1----------------"<<endl;
d1.output();
cout<<"--------------d2----------------"<<endl;
d2.output();
cout<<"--------------d3----------------"<<endl;
```

```
d3.output();
cout<<"--------------d4---------------"<<endl;
d4.output();
}
```

Output

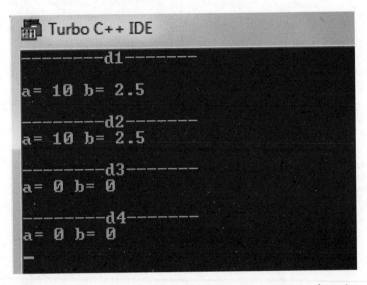

Let us trace the output of the code from the first line of the `main()` function.

The statement

```
Data d1(10,2.5);
```

creates an object d1 of class `Data` by invoking the constructor with two arguments, thereby initializing the members a and b to 10 and 2.5, respectively, as shown in the Figure 12.18.

The next statement

```
Data d2(d1);
```

a=10
b=2.5

Object **d1**

Figure 12.18: State of object d1

creates the object d2 of class `Data` by invoking a 'copy constructor' with passing the object d1 as an argument to the constructor. As seen, the object d1 as passed by reference, therefore the reference variable t (which is created as a formal argument to the constructor) now represents another name to the actual argument d1. Hence, we can now access the value of the member a of object d1 as t.a and the value of the member b of object d1 as **t.b**. This is because the reference t is just another name to object d1. Also, it is important to understand that the copy constructor is invoked by the object d2, and hence the members a and b of object d2 can be directly accessed inside the copy constructor as seen in the Figure 12.19. Therefore, the copy constructor will copy the members of object d1 into object d2, using a reference variable t as shown in the Figure 12.19. Hence, the values of the members a and b of the object d2 will also be 10 and 2.5 respectively, which are exactly same as that of the object d1.

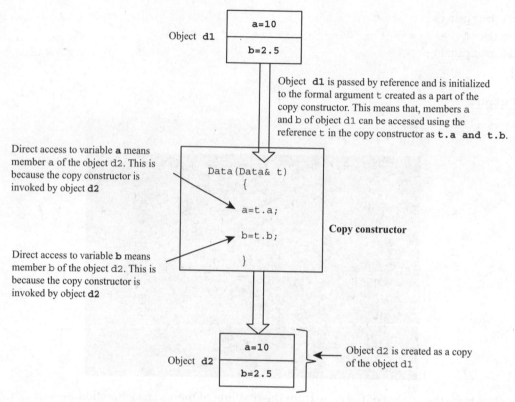

Figure 12.19: Invoking the copy constructor for object d2

The statement

```
Data d3;
```

creates an object d3 of class Data by invoking the constructor with no arguments, thereby initializing the members a and b to 0 as shown in the Figure 12.20.

Similarly, the next statement

```
Data d4(d3);
```

creates the object d4 of class Data by invoking a 'copy constructor' with passing the object d3 as an argument to the constructor. Hence, the members of object d4 will store the same values as that of object d3 as show in the Figure 12.21.

a=0
b=0

Object **d3**

Figure 12.20: State of object d3

Further, we invoke the output functions of each of the objects to print the values of the respective members a and b on the computer screen as seen from the code.

Although, we understand that the copy constructor copies the members of one object into another, it is still important to note that the copy constructors can only be invoked at the time of declaration of object and no time later in the program. To understand the

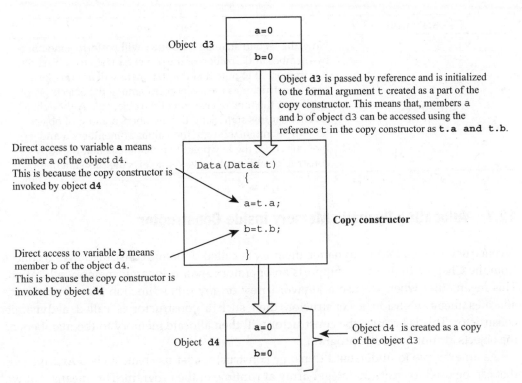

Figure 12.21: Invoking the copy constructor for object d4

usage of copy constructors, let us understand the description of three C++ statements tabulated below:

C++ Statement	Description
Data d2(d1);	The statement will invoke a copy constructor defined inside class Data. Hence, the member values of the object d1 will be copied into object d2 by the copy constructor defined in class Data.
Data d2=d1;	As seen, we have applied an initialization operator with the objects d2 and d1 at the time of creating the object d2. As the assignment is performed at the time of creation of the object d2, this statement is exactly same as that of the previous statement **Data d2(d1);**. Hence, the statement Data d2=d1; will invoke a copy constructor for object d2 by passing object d1 as an argument. Hence, the member values of the object d1 will be copied into object d2 by the copy constructor defined in class Data.
Data d3; d3=d2;	The first statement creates an object d3 of class Data, thereby invoking a default constructor for d3. This is because we have not passed any parameters while creating the object d3. Hence, the members a and b of object d3 will be set to **zero** by the default constructor.

C++ Statement	Description
	Now, the second statement **d3=d2;** will perform a member-by-member initialization of the object d3 from the object d2. It is important to note that the statement will not invoke a copy constructor as the assignment among the objects is not applied at the time of creation of the object d3. Although, as an effect of this statement, the members a and b of object d3 will be initialized with the values of members a and b of object d1, the key point to note here is that the copy constructor will not be invoked to execute this statement.

12.7 Allocating Dynamic Memory Inside Constructor

A constructor that allocates dynamic memory is called dynamic constructor. We recollect from the Chapter 10 that C++ supports an operator new for dynamic memory allocation. This means that when we use a keyword new or any other function that dynamically allocates memory inside a constructor, then such a constructor is called a dynamic constructor. This is because the constructor will then allocate memory to the members of the objects at runtime of the program.

As an example to understand dynamic constructors, let us create a class ArrayList that can be used to create an integer array at runtime of the program. This means that we will create a constructor in the class ArrayList, which will dynamically create an array of the required size. Hence, the programmer can pass the capacity of the array list to be created as an argument to the constructor following which the constructor can create an array using the new operator as seen in the code.

Also, we will create following functions to perform operations with the array list.

1. **void add(int);** The function add() will insert an integer element into the array list which is passed to it as an argument.
2. **int getCapacity():** The function returns the maximum capacity of the array list.
3. **void display():** The function can be used to print all the elements of the ArrayList on the computer screen.

Also, we will create a **copy constructor** to perform copy operation from one ArrayList object to another. For example, the following statement:

```
ArrayList L2(L1);
```

will create an array list named as L2, which is the exact copy of the existing array list L1.

Along with the above member functions, the class ArrayList also contains the following members as listed below:

1. **Integer type pointer p:** The pointer p points to the dynamically created array to which the programmer can add elements.
2. **Integer variable count:** The variable count represents the total number of elements currently stored in the array list. The initial value of the variable count will be set

to zero by the constructor. Also, this means that we must increment the value of the variable count each time we add an element into the array list so that the variable count represents the number of active elements stored in the list at any point of time.

3. **Integer variable size:** The variable size represents the maximum capacity of the array list, which should be specified at the time of creating the list. Hence, the array list will be considered as full if the value of variable count is same as the value of size.

To create an array list of size 5, the programmer can write a statement as shown below:

```
ArrayList L1(5);
```

In this case, L1 will be created as an object of class ArrayList, which has a capacity to store 5 integer values in it. Hence, we define a constructor with one argument that dynamically creates an array of integers and stores the starting address of the array in the pointer p as shown in the Figure 12.22. Note that the constructor takes one argument as a variable n, which represents the capacity of the array list that programmer wishes to create. The constructor then allocates memory for 5 integer values, and hence the pointer p points to the dynamic array of size 5 using the following statement:

```
p = new int[n];
```

As the constructor allocates dynamic memory, it is called dynamic constructor. Further, the constructor also initializes the member size to the value of n because the maximum capacity of the array list is required to be n. Also, the constructor initializes the value of the variable count to 0 representing that the array list is initially empty.

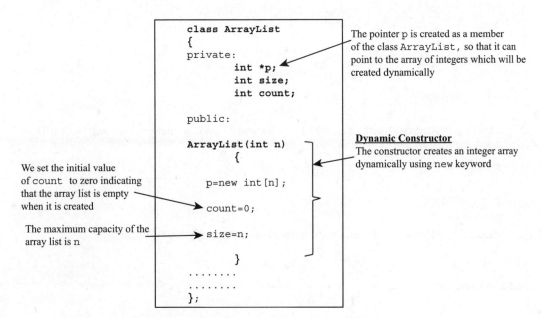

Figure 12.22:   Allocating dynamic memory inside constructor

The following is the full source code for creation and manipulation of `ArrayList`.

```cpp
#include<iostream.h>
class ArrayList
{
private:
    int *p;
    int size;
    int count;
public:
ArrayList(int n)
    {
    p = new int[n];
    count=0;
    size =n;
    }
ArrayList(ArrayList & t)
    {
int i;
p = new int[t.size];
count = t.count;
size =t.size;
/*copy the elements of the array*/
for(i=0;i<count;i++)
    {
    p[i] =t.p[i];
    }
}
void add(int k)
{
    if(count==size)
    {
    cout<< "Array List is Full , cannot add a new element"<<endl;
    }
    else
    {
    p[count]=k;
    count++;
    cout<< "Element "<<k<< " added successfully"<<endl;
    }
}
void display()
{
int i;
```

```
cout<< " Elements in the array list are"<<endl;
    for(i=0;i<count;i++)
    {
    cout<<p[i]<<endl;
    }
}
};
void main()
{
ArrayList L1(5);
L1.add(10);
L1.add(20);
L1.add(30);
  ArrayList L2(L1);
cout<< "------------- L1 ---------------"<<endl;
L1.display();
cout<< "------------ L2 ---------------"<<endl;
L2.display();
}
```

As the execution of the code will always start from the main() function, let us understand the code from the first line of the main() function.

The statement

```
ArrayList L1(5);
```

creates an array list object named as L1 with a capacity of 5 using a dynamic constructor that makes the pointer p point to an array of size 5 as shown in the Figure 12.23. Also, the member size is set as 5 and the member count is set as 0 by the constructor.

Further, the function add() inserts an integer element specified to it as an argument into the ArrayList object. Hence, the following function calls will insert the values 10, 20, and 30 into the object L1 as shown in the Figure 12.24.

```
L1.add(10);
L1.add(20);
L1.add(30);
```

Also, each time we add the element into the array list, the value of the variable count will get incremented. Hence, the value of variable count will set as 3 for the object L1 as the number of elements present inside L1 is 3 as shown in the Figure 12.24.

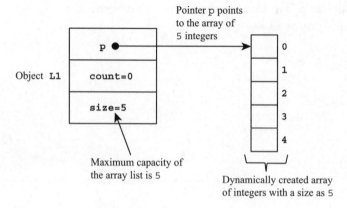

Figure 12.23: Creation of L1

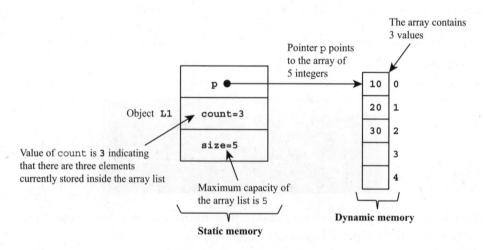

Figure 12.24: State of list L1

The statement

```
ArrayList L2(L1);
```

will invoke a copy constructor, which creates a copy of list L1 into another list L2. Along with the data stored inside the list L1, the variables count and size of object L1 must also be copied into object L2 by the copy constructor as seen in the code. This means that we must create the object L2 as an exact image of object L1. Also, it is important to recollect that the copy constructor takes an 'object reference' as an argument. This means that the actual argument L1 will be passed as a reference and will be assigned to a formal argument t, which is created as a part of defining the copy constructor. Hence, the members of object L1 can be accessed using object t inside the copy constructor as shown in the Figure 12.25. Whereas, the members of the object L2 can be directly accessed inside the copy constructor as the constructor is invoked by the object L2 itself.

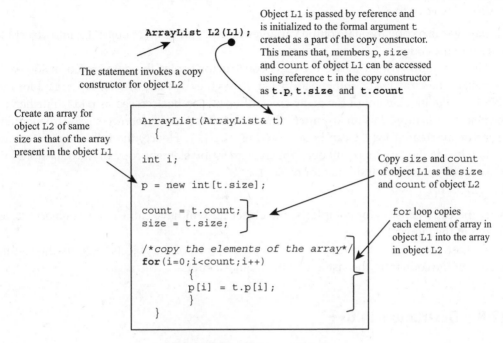

Object L1 is passed by reference and is initialized to the formal argument t created as a part of the copy constructor. This means that, members p, size and count of object L1 can be accessed using reference t in the copy constructor as **t.p**, **t.size** and **t.count**

`ArrayList L2(L1);`

The statement invokes a copy constructor for object L2

Create an array for object L2 of same size as that of the array present in the object L1

```
ArrayList(ArrayList& t)
    {

    int i;

    p = new int[t.size];

    count = t.count;
    size = t.size;

    /*copy the elements of the array*/
    for(i=0;i<count;i++)
            {
            p[i] = t.p[i];
            }
    }
```

Copy size and count of object L1 as the size and count of object L2

for loop copies each element of array in object L1 into the array in object L2

Figure 12.25: Copy constructor

The copy constructor first allocates the memory by creating a dynamic array to which the pointer p of the object L2 points to, as shown in the Figure 12.25. Note that as we are performing a copy operation from object L1 to object L2, the dynamic array created for object L2 should be of the same size as that of the object L1. We can access the maximum capacity of the object L1 as **t.size** inside the copy constructor; hence, we create the dynamic array for list L2 of same size as that of L1, using the following statement:

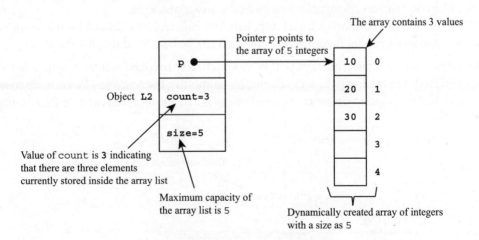

The array contains 3 values

Pointer p points to the array of 5 integers

Value of count is **3** indicating that there are three elements currently stored inside the array list

Maximum capacity of the array list is 5

Dynamically created array of integers with a size as 5

Object L2 is created as a copy of L1

Figure 12.26: State of the object L2

```
p=new int[t.size];
```

Further, we also copy the state of the variables count and size of object L1 into object L2 as seen in the code.

The for loop written inside the copy constructor copies the data stored inside each element of the array list L1 into the array list L2. As the copy constructor is invoked for the object L2, the ith element of the array created for L2 can be accessed as **p[i]**. Further, as the object L1 is passed as an argument that is initialized to a reference t, the ith element of the array created for L1 can be accessed as **t.p[i]**. Hence, the following statement written inside the for loop will perform an element-by element copy of the data stored in array for object L1 into the array for object L2 .

```
p[i]=t.p[i];
```

After the copy constructor completes, the object L2 will have same state as object L1, as shown in the Figure 12.26.

Further, we call the display() function using each of the objects to verify the results as seen in the code from the last line of the main function.

12.8   Destructors in C++

The destructor is a member function of the class, which is automatically invoked just before any of the objects of that class go out of scope. Hence, we can write destructors in the program to free up the resources that are held by the object before a particular object goes out of scope. The following are the rules to create destructors in C++:

1. The name of the destructor must be same as the name of the class with a tilde (symbol ~) prefixed at its name. Figure 12.27 shows the syntax for creating destructors in C++.
2. Unlike constructors, destructors cannot return a value. Hence the 'return type' should not be specified while creating a destructor as shown in the Figure 12.27.
3. Unlike constructors, destructors cannot take any arguments.
4. Destructors can be made virtual, whereas the constructors cannot be made virtual. The concept of virtual functions is explained in Chapter 14 of this text book.

A destructor is a member function that is automatically invoked when an object is to be destroyed from the memory. As an example, let us modify the ArrayList code discussed in Section 12.7 to include a destructor. Given below is a destructor that can free the resources

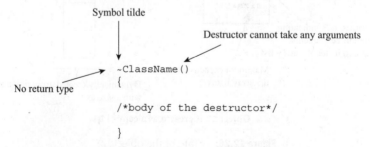

Figure 12.27:   Syntax for creating destructors

of objects of the `ArrayList` object before the object goes out of scope.

```
~ArrayList()
{
delete [] p;
cout<<"Array List Deleted"<<endl;
}
```

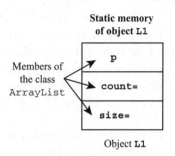

Figure 12.28: Memory allocated for object L1

As discussed from the Section 12.7, the memory for the object L1, which is the object of the class `ArrayList`, will be allocated by the compiler as shown in Figure 12.28:

Further, the keyword `new` allocates a dynamic memory at the time of creating the object L1 using a dynamic **constructor**. The dynamic memory allocated is pointed by the pointer p, which is the member of the object L1 as shown in the Figure 12.29.

When the object goes out of scope, which is when the `main()` function completes its execution, the static memory for the object L1 will be destroyed; however, it is possible that the dynamic memory allocated for the

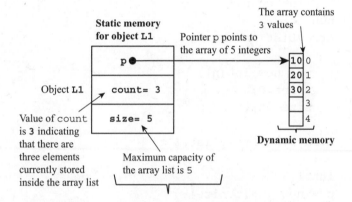

Figure 12.29: Dynamic memory allocated for object L1

array is still present in the heap space. Note that the dynamic memory is actually allocated by the programmer at runtime of the program, and hence the system will not be able to delete it automatically even if the object L1 goes out of scope. Therefore, the dynamic array created would unnecessarily occupy the heap space as shown in the Figure 12.30.

Hence, it is a good programming practice to delete all the resources held by the object before the object goes out of scope. To do this job, we can write destructor as a member function in the class. Note that we need not worry about calling a destructor explicitly; this is because C++ will automatically call it before a particular object goes out of scope. Hence, when we write the statement

```
delete [] p;
```

inside the destructor, we are sure that the dynamic array created for a particular object will always get deleted before that object is destroyed. Therefore, this will help in optimum utilization of the available heap space.

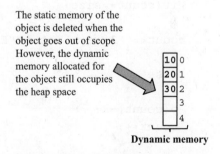

Figure 12.30: Deletion of object L1

Given below is the full source code to create an `ArrayList`, including a destructor in the class `ArrayList`.

As seen in the output of the program, the destructor will be called two times at the end of `main()` function: first, when the object L1 goes out of scope and second, when the object L2 goes out of scope. Therefore, the dynamic memory allocated for both the objects L1 and L2 will be deleted by the destructor just before the objects L1 and L2 are destroyed.

```cpp
#include<iostream.h>
class ArrayList
{
private:
    int *p;
    int size;
    int count;
public:
ArrayList(int n)
    {
    p = new int[n];
    count=0;
    size =n;
    }
ArrayList(ArrayList & t)
    {
int i;
p = new int[t.size];
count = t.count;
size =t.size;
/*copy the elements of the array*/
for(i=0;i<count;i++)
    {
    p[i] =t.p[i];
    }
}
void add(int k)
{
    if(count==size)
    {
    cout<< "Array List is Full , cannot add a new element"<<endl;
    }
    else
    {
    p[count]=k;
    count++;
```

```
        cout<< "Element "<<k<< " added successfully"<<endl;
        }
}
void display()
{
int i;
cout<< " Elements in the array list are"<<endl;
    for(i=0;i<count;i++)
    {
    cout<<p[i]<<endl;
    }
}
~ArrayList()
{
delete [] p;
cout<<"Array List Deleted"<<endl;
}
};
void main()
{
ArrayList L1(5);
L1.add(10);
L1.add(20);
L1.add(30);
   ArrayList L2(L1);
cout<< "---------------- L1 ----------------"<<endl;
L1.display();
cout<< "----------------- L2 ----------------"<<endl;
L2.display();
}
```

Output

12.9 Static Members and Static Member Functions

We understand from Chapter 11 of this text book that the object memory of the object will always contain all the members and member functions that are defined inside the class. Hence, we can access every member of a class by applying a membership operator over a particular object. However, the static members and member functions are exceptions to this rule.

Static members defined inside the class are member variables associated with the class but not with the object. This means that static members and member functions created in the class will not be present as a part of object memory of any of the objects of that class. Rather, all the objects of a class will share a common copy of static members and member functions.

As the static members are not part of the object memory, they must be always defined outside the class using the syntax as shown below:

```
<DataType> <Classname>::<variableName>;
```

Along with defining the variable outside the class, we must also declare a static variable inside the class using a keyword static with a syntax as shown below:

```
static <DataType> <variableName>;
```

For example, if we want to create a variable c as a static variable of class Data, then we must defined variable c outside the class Data as shown below:

```
int Data::c;
```

The default value of the static variables is always zero. We can also give some other value to a static variable at the time of defining it in the program. The following statement gives an initial value of 25 to a static variable c, which is a member of class Data:

```
int Data::c = 25;
```

Further, it is important to note that, along with defining the static variable outside class, we must also declare the static variable c inside class Data using a keyword **static** as shown in the Figure 12.31.

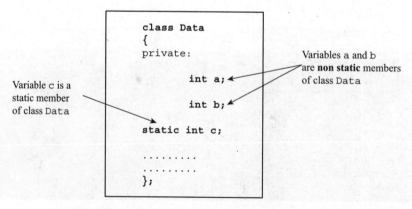

Figure 12.31: Declaring static variable inside the class Data

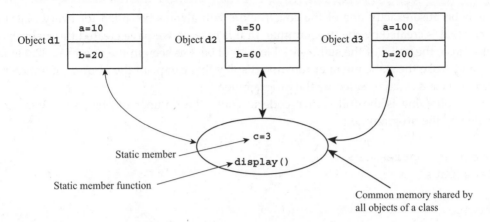

Figure 12.32: Shared memory for static members

Similar to static members, the static member functions are the member functions that are associated with the class but not with the object. To create a member function as `static`, we must add a keyword **static** at the time of defining the function in the class. The Figure 12.32 shows shared memory for `static` function `display()` inside class `Data` that prints the value of static variable c. Note that the static member function can only access static members of the class. Also, as the `static` member functions are not the parts of 'object memory', we must not invoke the static member function using an object of a class, which is unlike other member functions. Hence, we invoke a static member function using a class name followed by a scope resolution operator using the syntax shown below:

```
<Classname>::functionName();
```

This means that we should call the static function `display()` defined inside class `Data` using the following syntax:

```
Data::display();
```

As seen in the source code given below, we create a class `Data` with members a and b along with the two constructors. The first constructor is one without parameters, and the second is one that takes two parameters. Also, we have created a function `output()` so as to print the values of the members a and b for each of the objects of class `Data`. We create three objects of class `Data`, which are named as d1, d2, and d3 as shown in the Figure 12.32.

Further, we have also created a static member c with a default value as 0 and a static member function `display()` that prints the value of the variable c. Note that the static member c and the static member function `display()` will be shared by all the objects d1, d2, and d3. This is because a common copy of the static members is maintained by C++ for all the objects of a class.

In each of the constructors, we increment the value of the static variable c as seen in the code. Hence, the static variable is guaranteed to be incremented each time when an object of class `Data` is created. Therefore, it will be appropriate to say that the variable c will represent the count of the number of the objects of class `Data` created in the memory.

This is because exactly one of the constructors will always be called for every object of Data that is created by the programmer. In this case, as we have created three objects of class Data, the value of the static variable c will be 3 as seen in the Figure 12.32. Hence, we can invoke the static member function display that can print the count of number of objects of class Data created by the programmer.

The following is the full source code to count the number of objects of class Data created by the programmer:

```cpp
#include<iostream.h>
class Data
{
private:
    int a;
    int b;
static int c;
public:
    Data()
    {
    a=10;
    b=20;
    c++;
    }
    Data(int p,int q)
    {
    a=p;
    b=q;
    c++;
    }
    void output()
    {
    cout<<"Members of the object are"<<endl;
    cout<<"a="<<a<<"b="<<b<<endl;
    }
    static void display()
    {
    cout<<"The number of objects of class Data are "<<c<<endl;
    }
};
int Data::c;
void main()
{
Data d1;
Data d2(50,60);
Data d3(100,200);
```

```
Data::display();
}
```

Output

The number of objects of class Data are 3

Solved Example 12.1

Write a C++ program to generate the Fibonacci series using constructor function.

```
#include<iostream.h>
class Fibo
{
private:
    int limit;
public:
    Fibo(int n)
    {
    limit=n;
    int i=0;
    int f1=0,f2=1,f3;
    /*First two numbers are 0 and 1*/
    cout<<f1<<"  "<<f2<<"  ";
      while(i<=limit-2)
      {
      f3=f1+f2;
      cout<<f3<<"   ";
      f1=f2;
      f2=f3;
      i++;
      }
    }
};
void main()
{
cout<<"*************FIBONACCI series of length
    5***********"<<endl;
Fibo o1(5);
cout<<endl<<endl;
cout<<"*************FIBONACCI series of length
    10***********"<<endl;
Fibo o2(10);
}
```

Output

```
Turbo C++ IDE
****************FIBONACII series of length 5***********
0  1  1  2  3  5

****************FIBONACII series of length 10**********
0  1  1  2  3  5  8  13  21  34  55
```

SCRATCH PAD

We have written the program to calculate Fibonacci series inside a constructor with one argument. Hence the process to create Fibonacci series will start as we create an object of class `Fibo`.

For example, the statement,

`Fibo o1(5);`

creates a object of class `Fibo` named as o1 and prints the first 5 numbers in the Fibonacci series. This is because, we have passed the value of `limit` as 5 to the constructor with one argument. Similarly, the statement,

`Fibo o2(10);`

creates a object of class `Fibo` named as o2 and prints the first 10 numbers in the Fibonacci series. This is because, we have passed the value of `limit` as 10 to the constructor with one argument inside class `Fibo`.

Solved Example 12.2

Create a class to represent a rectangle. Store the length and breadth for each of the `Rectangle` objects. Also, create a member function `area()` that can calculate the area of a particular `Rectangle` object. Initialize the length and breadth of each of the `Rectangle` objects using constructors.

```cpp
#include<iostream.h>
class Rectangle
{
private:
int length;
int breadth;
public:
    Rectangle()
    {
    /*default values of length and breadth*/
    length=5;
    breadth=5;
    }
    Rectangle(int p,int q)
```

```
    {
    length=p;
    breadth=q;
    }
    void area()
    {
    int a;
    a= length*breadth;
    cout<<"Area of the rectangle is "<<a<<endl;
    }
};
void main()
{
cout<<"**********object r1**********"<<endl;
Rectangle r1;
r1.area();
cout<<"**********object r2**********"<<endl;
Rectangle r2(10,3);
r2.area();
}
```

Output

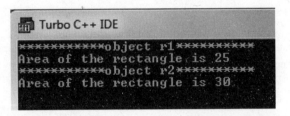

SCRATCH PAD

As, we have created class `Rectangle` with members `length` and `breadth` each object of class `Rectangle` actually represents one rectangle in real world. Further we have included a default as well as a parameterized constructor inside the class `Rectangle` to initialize its length and breath.

Hence, the statement,

`Rectangle r1;`

creates an object of class `Rectangle` named as `r1` and also invokes a default constructor thereby initializing the `length` and the `breadth` values of `r1` to 5.

Similarly, the statement,

`Rectangle r2(10,3);`

creates an object of class `Rectangle` which is named as `r2` and also invokes a **parameterized constructor** with two arguments, thereby initializing the `length` of the rectangle `r2` as 10 and the `breath` as 3.

Further, the function `area()` is invoked or each of the `Rectangle` objects so as to calculate the area and print it on the computer screen.

Solved Example 12.3

Write a C++ program to calculate the volume of cube, cylinder, and cone using overloaded constructor functions.

```cpp
#include<iostream.h>
class Volume
{
private:
    float side;
    float radius;
    float height;
public:
    Volume(float s)
    {
    side=s;
    float volume= side*side*side;
      cout<<"Volume of the Cube is "<<volume<<endl;
      }
Volume(float r,float h)
    {
    radius = r;
    height =h;
    float volume= 0.3333*3.14*radius*radius*height;
    cout<<"Volume of the Cone is "<<volume<<endl;
    }
Volume(float r,float h,int dummy)
    {
    radius = r;
    height =h;
    float volume= 3.14*radius*radius*height;
    cout<<"Volume of the Cylinder is "<<volume<<endl;
    }
};
void main()
{
cout<<"**********CUBE**********"<<endl;
Volume cube(10);
cout<<"**********CONE**********"<<endl;
Volume cone(120,8);
cout<<"**********CYLINDER**********"<<endl;
Volume cyl(12,3,0);
}
```

Output

```
**********CUBE**********
Volume of the Cube is 1000

**********CONE**********
Volume of the Cone is 120564

**********CYLINDER**********
Volume of the Cylinder is 1356.48
```

Error Finding Exercise

Given below are some programs which may or may not contain errors. Correct the error(s) if exist in the code and determine the output.

Program 1

```cpp
#include<iostream.h>
class NUMBER
{
private:
    int a;
    int b;
NUMBER()
    {
    a=0;
    b=0;
    }
NUMBER(int p,int q)
    {
    a=p;
    b=q;
    }
    void output()
    {
    cout<<"Values of variables are "<<endl;
    cout<<a<<" "<<b;
    }
};
void main()
{
NUMBER n1,n2(1,20);
n1.output();
n2.output();
}
```

Program 2

```
#include<iostream.h>
class MyClass
{
private:
    int a;
    int b;
    int c;
public:
MyClass(int p,int q,int r)
    {
    a=p;
    b=q;
    c=r;
    }
    void output()
    {
    cout<<"Values of variables are "<<endl;
    cout<<a<<" "<<b <<" "<<c<<endl;
    }
};
void main()
{
MyClass m1;
MyClass m2(10,20,30),m3(10);
m1.output();
m2.output();
m3.output();
}
```

Program 3

```
#include<iostream.h>
class Test
{
float a;
int b;
public:
    Test(int p,int q)
    {
    a=p;
    b=q;
    }
    Test(Test obj)
```

```
    {
    a=obj.a;
    b=obj.b;
    }
    void output()
    {
    cout<<"a="<<a<<"  b="<<b;
    }
};
void main()
{
Test o1(10,20)  , o2(45,55);
Test o3(o1);
Test o4(o2);
o1.output();
o2.output();
o3.output();
o4.output();
}
```

Program 4

```
#include<iostream.h>
class DATA
{
float a;
int b;
public:
    DATA()
    {
    DATA(0,-10);
    }
    DATA(int p,int q)
    {
    a=p;
    b=q;
    }
    void output()
    {
    cout<<"a="<<a<<"  b="<<b;
    }
};
void main()
{
```

```
DATA d1(10,20);
DATA d2;
d1.output();
d2.output();
}
```

Program 5

```
#include<iostream.h>
class DATA
{
float a;
int b;
public:
    DATA()
    {
    a=0;
    b=-2;
    }
    DATA(int p,int q)
    {
    a=p;
    b=q;
    }
    void output()
    {
    cout<<"a="<<a<<"  b="<<b;
    }
};
void main()
{
DATA d1(10,20);
DATA d2;
d2(35,40)
Data d3(900,800);
d3(500,560);
d1.output();
d2.output();
d3.output();
}
```

Program 6

```
#include<iostream.h>
class Test
```

```
{
private:
int a;
int b,c;
public:
    void input()
    {
    cin>>a>>b>>c;
    }
    static void output()
    {
    cout<<"Values of variables are "<<endl;
    cout<<a<<" "<<b<<"   "<<c;
    }
};
void main()
{
 Test t1;
 t1.input();
 t1.output();
}
```

Program 7

```
#include<iostream.h>
class DATA
{
private:
int x;
int y;
    static void set_data(DATA t1)
    {
    x=t1.x;
    y=t1.y;
    }
public:
    void output()
    {
    cout<<"Values of variables are "<<endl;
    cout<<x<<"   "<<y;
    }
};
void main()
{
```

```
DATA d1;
DATA::set_data (10,20);
d1.output(t1);
}
```

Program 8

```
#include<iostream.h>
class Test
{
private:
int a;
int b,c;
public:
    Test(int x,int y,int z)
    {
    a=x;
    b=y;
    c=z;
    }
    void set_data(int p,int q,int r)
    {
    Test(p,q,r);
    }
    static void output()
    {
    cout<<"Values of variables are "<<endl;
    cout<<a<<" "<<b<<" "<<c;
    }
};
void main()
{
 Test t1;
 Test t2;
t2(500,600,700);
 t1.set_data(40.50,70);
 t1.output();
}
```

Quiz

1. Constructors are used for the following:
   (a) To create an object of the class.
   (b) To initialize the members of the objects

(c) To delete the unrequired resources, which are locked by the objects

(d) To implement abstraction

2. When a class contains multiple constructors inside it, then it is called
    (a) Data hiding
    (b) Constructor overloading
    (c) Method overriding
    (d) Multiple inheritance

3. Which of the following statement(s) is true?
    (a) Every class in C++ must have at least one constructor.
    (b) If we do not define any constructor in the class, then the compiler provides every class with a default constructor.
    (c) Constructors can be created as virtual.
    (d) None of the above statements are true.

4. Dynamic constructor is a constructor that
    (a) creates an object of a class at the time of compilation
    (b) destroys the object of a class at runtime
    (c) allocates the memory for the members of the object at runtime
    (d) performs initialization of the members of the object at runtime

5. Copy constructor is a constructor that
    (a) takes a reference to the object of the same class as an argument
    (b) takes no arguments
    (c) we cannot comment on the arguments of the copy constructor

6. Which of the following statement(s) is true?
    (a) Static members and member functions are the part of object memory of the class.
    (b) All objects share a common copy of static members and member functions.
    (c) Static members cannot be created as private members of a class.
    (d) Constructor of a class can be created as static.

7. Constructor of a class can be created as a
    (a) friend of the class
    (b) non-static member of the class
    (c) static member of the class
    (d) virtual function inside the class

8. Assuming the name of the class as X, which of the following is/are correct constructor(s) defined inside the class X
    (a) ```
void X()
{
/*initialization statements*/
}
```
    (b) ```
X()
{
int o1;
/*initialization statements*/
return o1;
}
```
    (c) ```
X()
{
/*initialization statements*/
}
```
    (d) All of the above.
```

9. Which of the following statements are correct?
   (a) Destructors in C++ are used to create an object of a class.
   (b) Destructors in C++ are used to destroy the object of a class.
   (c) Destructors in C++ are used free up the used resources before the object is destroyed from the memory.
   (d) None of the above statements are correct.

Review Questions

1. Write a short note on constructors in C++. Give one example of code that uses a constructor.
2. What are different types of constructors that can be written in a C++ program? Give an example of each of the types using a sample code.
3. What is a difference between a constructor and a destructor? Also explain the applications of destructors in a C++ program.
4. Write a C++ program for creation and manipulation of a linked list using constructors.
5. Write a C++ program to perform addition of matrices by creating a class `Matrix`. The class `Matrix` must include default and parameterized constructors.
6. Write a short note on dynamic constructors in C++. Explain the use of creating dynamic constructors in a C++ program.
7. Write a short note on static members and static member functions. Write a C++ program to show the usage of static members of the class.

Chapter

13 | Operator Overloading

13.1 Overview

All the operators in C++ are designed to operate with the basic data types only. For example, an arithmetic operator + can be used to perform addition of integers, floats, doubles etc. but cannot be used to perform addition of **user-defined objects**. Let's say if we create a class `Point` to represent points in Cartesian coordinate system, we are not able to perform addition of two `Point` objects using operator + like we do it for primitive types. Recall from Chapter 11 section 11.10 that addition of `Point` objects P1 and P2 is performed using a function `add()` defined inside the class. We performed the addition of two points P1 and P2 by making a call to `add()` as follows:

```
P3=P1.add(P2);
```

The function is invoked by P1 passing P2 is passed as an argument, the result of addition is stored in object P3 , which gives the x and y coordinate values of the resultant point. The addition of `Point` objects is performed using a member function `add()`, merely because the arithmetic operator + cannot be used to perform addition of user-defined objects. The basic principle of operator overloading is to extend the capability of C++ operators in order to use them with user-defined types in the same way and with the same syntax as with basic types. When we say that classes are used to create user-defined data types, it is a fair expectation that the operation with user-defined objects should be performed in the same way as they are performed with primitive types.

If we overload operator + in class `Point`, we will be able to perform addition of `Point` objects as follows:

```
P3=P1+P2;
```

Making use of operator + to add `Point` objects makes the statement very easy to read and understand when compared to the former statement. Operator overloading is essentially used by the programmers to create programs with a **friendly syntax**. Clearly it is not a necessity, but it provides great luxury to the programmers to read and maintain the program. Even without overloading an operator, you can still perform addition of `Point` objects using the statement P3=P1.add(P2); however P3=P1+P2; is much programmer friendly when compared to P3=P1.add(P2);

NOTES

When an operator is **overloaded**, it can take **multiple forms** and its behaviour will be dependent upon the context in which the operator is used. For example, if a and b are variables of type integer, the expression a+b will perform addition of two **integer values**. On the other hand, if a and b are objects of type Point then the same expression a+b will perform addition of **Point objects** (Assuming the operator + is overloaded for class Point)

C++ compiler can correctly identify which definition of the operator must be used depending on the **data types of the operands** used in the expression. Out of the multiple forms an operator takes, compiler correctly identifies and **binds** one of the forms for each occurrence of the operator in the program. This is called as **compile time binding** and the ability of the compiler to assign multiple forms to a single operator is called as **compile time polymorphism**. We will discuss more on compile time binding and polymorphism in the later sections of this chapter, so don't think much about it right now.

Is creating programs with friendly syntax the only reason to overload any operator?　　　**?**

Creating programs with friendly syntax is one of the major reasons to overload any operator; but note that when an operator is overload compiler also borrows all its properties like precedence, associativity etc. from its basic definition and applies them in the same way to the user-defined types. For example, when you overload operators +, - and * for objects of class Point, it means that you can use them in the way for Point objects as you could use them for primitive types. So, if P1, P2 ... P10 are different Point objects you could create an mixed arithmetic expression to perform various operations as shown below

```
P10 = P1+P2*(P3+P4)-P5*P6+(P7-P8-P9);
```

The statement will execute using the same priority and associativity rules as they were when using these operators for basic data types. Establishing these results by creating different user-defined functions for addition, subtraction and multiplication would be possible but syntactically cumbersome, making the program difficult to create and maintain. Although we say that operator overloading is just a luxury to create programs with better syntax, there are some situations (like this one), where the programmers can't avoid using it.

13.2　Overloading Operators

If we need to use a particular operator with objects, we must define an **operator function** to describe the behaviour of that operator when used with objects of a class. C++ supports a keyword operator, which is used to create an operator function. Figure 13.1 gives the syntax for creating an operator function. The operator symbol that is followed by the keyword operator will be overloaded and can be used with the objects of the class.

```
<returnType> operator<Operator Symbol>(<arguments>)
{
    ....function body
}
```

Figure 13.1:　Syntax of creating an operator function

What are the operations that should be performed in the operator function? **?**

We know that a class is used to create an user-defined data type. Although, operator function facilitates the programmer to use an operator with objects of the class, the C++ compiler will not be in a position to know the set of operations that are to be performed when the operator is actually used with objects. For example, if P1 and P2 are objects of class Point and when we use operator + with P1 and P2 we should not expect the compiler to be aware of how two points must be really added. Hence the operator function must define set of operations in its definition which will inform the compiler that when two points are added the addition of their individual x coordinates gives the x coordinate of the result and the addition of their individual y coordinates gives the y coordinate of the result. This means that the operator function explains the process(or **behaviour**) of the operator when used with user-defined types.

When is the operator function executed? Do we call the operator function explicitly like other functions in C++? **?**

We do not call the operator function explicitly. The operator function is internally invoked by the compiler when we use an operator along with the objects of the class. This makes C++ understand the exact operations to be followed when an operator is used with objects of the class.

Every C++ operator has an associated syntax as well as semantics. The **syntax of an operator** refers to the rules of using the operator which are defined by the grammar of the language, whereas **semantics of an operator** refers to the meaning of the operator describing the actual operation it performs. For instance, if we consider an operator +, the meaning or **semantic** for the operator is addition and the **syntax** to perform binary addition is as follows:

```
<ResultVariable> = <Operand1> + <Operand2>;
```

Operator overloading allows the programmer to enhance the semantics–or even change them–of the operator when redefining its behaviour for user-defined types. But programmer can in no way attempt to change the syntax to be followed to use the operator. This means that operator should be used with user-defined types with the same syntax as with basic types, even if it is overloaded. In fact, this is the reason why you would want to overload any operator.

Although, operator overloading technically allows you to drastically change the meaning/ semantic of the operator for user-defined types, it is not recommended that you do so. For example, if we overload operator +, for using it with objects of class Point, then we may create the operator function as a member function of class Point as shown in Figure 13.2.

We should now be able to use operator + along with objects of class Point as shown below:

```
<ResultObject> = <PointObject1> + <PointObject2>;
```

Let us assume that the function body of the **operator**+ is written by the programmer such that the operator function performs **multiplication** instead of actually performing the **addition**. This means that the meaning or semantics of operator + is now changed to **multiplication** by the programmer, which is actually defined as addition by C++.

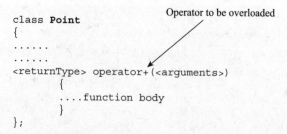

Figure 13.2: Creating operator function as an inline member function of the class

If P1, P2, and P3 are objects of class Point, we can use + with these objects because **operator**+ is defined for class Point.

P3 =P1+P2;

However, the meaning of the above statement will depend on the actual operations that are performed inside the body of the operator function. If the **operator**+ function internally performs multiplication the statement P3 =P1+P2, it will then actually perform multiplication of Point objects instead of addition. This reflects that we have easily changed the meaning or semantic of operator+ for objects of class Point, but the syntax of operator+ still remains unchanged. This action hampers the readability of the program badly anybody who views the statement P3=P1+P2 would get an impression that this is an addition at a first glance, but what actually happens in multiplication! Hence, it is strongly recommended not to change the semantics of an operator when overloading it. The point we have just discussed is illustrated in the Figure 13.3.

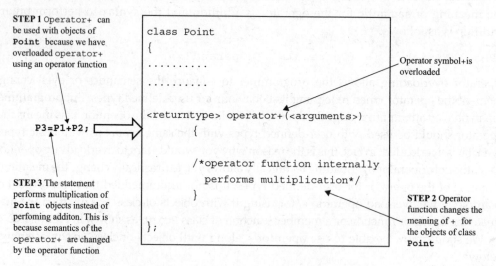

Figure 13.3: Operator function changing the semantics of the operator+

Also, other grammatical rules such as associativity and priority of the operator remain unchanged when an operator is overloaded. This means that C++ always follows the priority and rules of the operator that is actually overloaded, and it is immaterial of the new semantics defined by the programmer. Hence, even if the programmer has changed the semantics of the `operator+` to internally perform **multiplication** of points, C++ will still follow priority, associativity, and grammatical rules of **addition**. This may lead to mathematically incorrect results because multiplication can now be performed with a priority of addition. Operator overloading should not be misused to create such confusions in the program. I emphasize that **the semantics of the operator should not be changed while overloading an operator, although** C++ **allows you to do so.**

The following is the list of C++ operators which can be overloaded using an operator function:

Arithmetic operators:

Binary operators: `+, -, /, *, %, =`
Unary operators: `++, --, -, +`
Shorthand operators: `+=, -=, /=, *=, %=`

Logical operators: `&&, ||, !`

Bitwise operators: `&, |, ~, ^, >>, <<, <<=, >>=`

Relational operators: `>, >=, <, <=, ==, !=`

Parenthesis: `[], ()`

Operators used with pointers: `->, ->*, *(indirection),&`
Dynamic memory allocation: `new, delete`
Others: `Function call operator, type cast operator, comma operator`

13.3   Overloading One's Complement ~ and Minus – Operators: An Example

As an example to understand **overloading of unary operators**, let us overload unary operators ~ (which finds one's complement of a number) and – (which is a unary minus sign used to negate a number). This means that we intend to create a C++ program that will use ~ and – operators with objects of class. To understand this overloading, let us create a class `Data` with two integer members a and b and two member functions `input()` and `output()` for accepting the member variables as input from the user and to print their values, respectively. We will learn to use operators ~ and – with objects of class `Data`. Given that there are two operators which we need to overload, we must create two different operator functions in class `Data`. The job of the operator function **operator~ ()** is to find one's complement of the members a and b using the following statements:

```
Data res;
res.a=~a;
res.b=~b;
return res;
```

The calculated one's complement of members a and b is stored in a local object named res by the operator function, which is then returned to the caller of the **operator~ ()** function. It is clear that the function returns another object of class `Data` as a result of its operation and hence the return type of the function should be `Data`.

Similarly, the job of the operator function `operator-()` is to negate the values of members a and b and return the resultant object back to the caller using the following statements:

```
Data res;
res.a=-a;
res.b=-b;
return res;
```

The following is the full source code which overloads ~ and – operators for objects of class Data.

```
#include<iostream.h>
class Data
{
private:
    int a;
    int b;
public:
    void input()
    {
    cin>>a>>b;
    }
    Data operator~()
    {
    Data res;
    res.a=~a;
    res.b=~b;
    return res;
    }
    Data operator-()
    {
    Data res;
    res.a=-a;
    res.b=-b;
    return res;
    }
    void output()
    {
    cout<<"a="<<a<< " b="<<b<<endl;
    }
};
void main()
{
//Create Objects of class Data
Data d1,d2,d3,d4;
//Take members of d1 and d2 as input from the user
cout<<"Enter members a,b for object d1"<<endl;
```

```
d1.input();
cout<<"Enter members a,b for object d2"<<endl;
d2.input();
//Use operator - with object d1
d3 = -d1;
//Use operator ~ with object d2
d4 = ~d2;
//print the values for d1 and d2
cout<<"Result of unary minus on d1 is stored in d3 as:"<<endl;
d3.output();
cout<<"Result of one's complement on d2 is stored in d4:"<<endl;
d4.output();
}
```

Output

```
Enter members a,b for object d1
10 20
Enter members a,b for object d2
50 60
Result of unary minus on d1 is stored in d3 as:
a=-10 b=-20
Result of one's complement on d2 is stored in d4:
a=-51 b=-61
```

The first statement of main () function.

```
Data d1,d2;
```

creates two objects of class Data named d1 and d2.

The statements

```
d1.input();
```

and

```
d2.input();
```

invoke the member function input () on each of the objects to accept the values of the members a and b as input from the user. Assuming sample user input values, Figure 13.4 shows the state of objects d1 and d2.

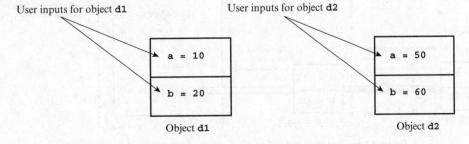

Figure 13.4: State of objects d1 and d2

The statement

```
d3=-d1;
```

applies an operator minus to object d1 and stores the result of operation in d3. First, it is possible to write such a statement only because the operator minus is overloaded by creating an **operator-()** function in class Data. The statement will actually invoke the function **operator-()** to determine the behaviour of unary minus with objects of class Data. As **operator-()** is a member function of class Data, it must actually be invoked using some object of type Data. The compiler internally calls the function **operator-()** using object d1 because the negation is actually applied to object d1. This means that the compiler internally translates the statement.

```
d3 = -d1;
```

as shown below:

```
d3 = d1.operator-();
```

Note that we do not explicitly write the statement **d3 = d1.operator-();** in the program however, the C++ compiler applies this translation to ensure that the member function **operator-** is invoked using object d1. This saves the programmer from writing such a complex statement, thereby retaining the syntax of the operator when it is overloaded.

As the operator function is invoked using object d1, the members a and b of d1 can be directly accessed within the scope of the operator function as shown in the Figure 13.5. The result of the operation is to be stored in the object d3, however it is not accessible inside the **operator-** function. This is because object d3 is created as a local variable of main(). Hence, we create a temporary object named res to store the result after negating the members of d1. The object res is then returned to main() using the return statement in the operator function. Hence, the result gets initialized to object d3 when operator function completes its execution, as shown in Figure 13.5.

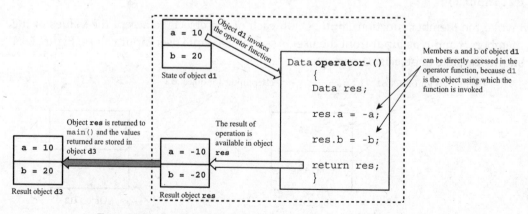

Figure 13.5: Invoking the function operator-() using object d1

Similarly, the next statement

```
d4 = ~d2;
```

applies a ~ operator on object d2, and the compiler internally translates the statement as

```
d4 = d2.operator~();
```

thereby invoking the `operator~` function using object d2. The execution of this statement is exactly same as what is explained for d3 = -d1; with the only difference being that the `operator~` function is used for object d2 which finds the one's complement of each of its member values as shown in the Figure 13.6.

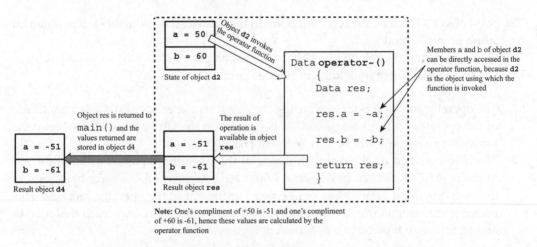

Figure 13.6: Invoking the function `operator~()` using object d2

After the respective operator functions are executed, the new state of the objects d1 and d2 is displayed on the screen by invoking the function `output()` over both the objects.

Can I explicitly invoke operator functions by writing statements d3=d1.operator-(); and d4=d2. operator~(); in the program, instead of writing d3=-d1 and d4=~d2? **?**

Yes you can, but then you are defeating the whole purpose of operator overloading. As mentioned in the beginning of this chapter, operator overloading is essentially used to create programs with a **friendly** syntax by making it possible to use operators with user-defined types in the same way (and with the same syntax) as with basic types. Invoking operator function explicitly is as good as calling any other function and hence is not a good programming practice.

13.4 Overloading Binary Operators Plus + and Minus –

As an example to understand overloading of binary operators, let us create a C++ program to overload operators + and – in binary form to perform addition and subtraction of Point objects. This means that we can now add/subtract objects of class Point in the same way as that of primitive types like integers, floats, and so on. We will reuse the class Point from Chapter 11 which contains two integer members x and y, thereby storing the x and y coordinate values for each of the Point objects. To perform addition and subtraction of Point objects, we have included two operator functions **operator+** and **operator-** as member functions of class Point. Let us concentrate on addition of Point objects, subtraction can be understood similarly.

Overloading operator + will give us an ability to perform addition of Point objects P1 and P2 using the following statement:

```
P3=P1+P2;
```

The point object P3 will be the resultant point in the Cartesian coordinate system obtained by adding points P1 and P2.

When compiling the statement P3=P1+P2, the compiler follows the following rules to invoke the operator function defined in class Point:

1. The operator function is invoked using the object that is written on the left hand side of the operator. In this case, object P1 is present on the left hand side of + hence the function operator+ will be invoked using object P1.

2. The object written on the right hand side of the operator is passed as an argument to the operator function. In this case, object P2 is written on the right hand side of the operator + and hence P2 is passed as an argument to the operator function. This means that the signature of the operator function should be written such that it takes one argument of type Point as shown in Figure 13.7.

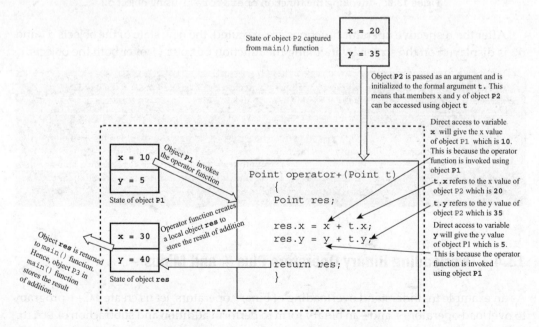

Figure 13.7: Function call to operator+

3. The object required to store the result of the expression is assigned with the return value of the operator function. In this case, object P3 is required to store the result of addition of the points and hence P3 will be assigned a value that is returned by the operator function. This means that the operator function must return the object of type Point as shown in Figure 13.7.

In summary, the compiler internally translates the statement P3=P1+P2; as P3=P1.operator+(P2);

NOTES

Compiler always **invokes** the operator function using the object which appears on the **left hand side** of the operator and passes the object that appears on the **right hand side** as an **argument** to it. For example, if we rewrite the statement P3=P1+P2; as

P3 = P2+P1;

the compiler will invoke the **operator+()** function using object **P2** (because it appears on the left hand side of +) and pass **P1** as an argument to it.

In this case, the results produced by both the statements would be the same because the operator function performs addition which is a commutative operation. However, this is something you should remember when working with operators like subtraction which are **not commutative**. Results produced by P2-P1 will be different then the result produced by P1-P2. Hence, the objects should be carefully placed on left hand side and right hand side of the operator when invoking an operator function which is not commutative in nature.

The following is the full source code overloading operators + and – to perform addition and subtraction of Point objects:

```
#include<iostream.h>
class Point
{
private:
    int x;
    int y;
public:
    void input()
    {
    cin>>x>>y;
    }
Point operator+(Point t)
    {
        Point res;
        res.x=x+t.x;
        res.y =y +t.y;
        return res;
    }
```

```
Point operator-(Point t)
    {
        Point res;
        res.x=x-t.x;
        res.y =y -t.y;
        return res;
    }
    void output()
    {
    cout<<"("<<x<<","<<y<<")"<<endl;
    }
};
void main()
{
Point P1,P2,P3,P4,P5;
cout<<"Enter the x and y values of P1"<<endl;
P1.input();
cout<<"Enter the x and y values of P2"<<endl;
P2.input();
P3 = P1 + P2;
cout<<"Result of addition is:"<<endl;
P3.output();
P4= P1-P2;
cout<<"Result of subtraction is:"<<endl;
P4.output();
P5 = P1+(P2-P3)+P4;
cout<<"Result of the expression is:"<<endl;
P5.output();
}
```

Output

```
Enter the x and y values of P1
10 5
Enter the x and y values of P2
20 35
Result of addition is:
(30,40)
Result of subtraction is:
(-10,-30)
Result of the expression is:
(-10,-30)
```

Most of the program is similar to what is given in Chapter 11, hence we will only concentrate on the overloaded operator functions. Let the user inputs for P1 be (x=10,y=5) and for P2 be (x= 20,y=35). As discussed before, the statement P3=P1+P2 is internally translated by the compiler as **P3=P1.operator+(P2)**, since P1 has invoked the operator function writing x and y in the function body will refer to the x and y values of P1 as shown in the Figure 13.7. The members of object P2 could not be directly accessed inside the operator function because P2 is a local variable of `main()`, and it is not available in the scope of **operator+**. Hence, the object P2 is passed as an argument to the function while making the function call to it. This means that the members of actual argument P2 will be initialized to a formal argument–in this case object t. Therefore, x and y values of P2 can be accessed as `t.x` and `t.y`, respectively, within the scope of operator function, as shown in the Figure13.7.

We need to store the result of addition in the `Point` object P3, however it is not accessible inside the **operator+()** function. This is because object P3 is created as a local variable of `main()`. Hence, we create a temporary object named `res` that stores the result of addition within the scope of `operator+()`. The object `res` is then returned to `main()` using the return statement in the operator function. Hence, the result of addition is initialized to object P3 when operator function completes its execution, as shown in Figure 13.7.

The statement

```
P3.output();
```

will print the resultant x and y values on the computer screen.

Similarly, the statement

```
P4 = P1 - P2;
```

invokes the operator function minus to perform subtraction of two point objects P1 and P2. This statement is internally translated by the compiler as `P4 = P1.operator-(P2);`

At this stage, assuming for P1 as (x=10, y=5) and for P2 as (x=20, y=35), the state of objects P1, P2, P3 and P4 is as shown in the Figure 13.8.

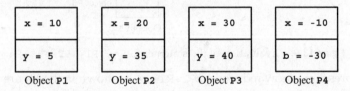

x = 10	x = 20	x = 30	x = -10
y = 5	y = 35	y = 40	b = -30
Object **P1**	Object **P2**	Object **P3**	Object **P4**

Figure 13.8: State of objects P1, P2, P3 and P4

Now, let us understand the statement

```
P5 = P1+(P2-P3)+P4;
```

which makes use of + as well as – operators and stores the result of expression in object P5. As mentioned in section 13.1, we can write such composite statements in the program because the associativity, priority, grammatical rules, and the syntax of the operator remain unchanged when an operator is overloaded. Hence, we will also be able to perform addition of multiple objects within a single expression provided we use correct syntax to code the expression. It is needless to mention that you can use only those operators with objects which you have overloaded. In this case, we have written a mixed statement using + and – because we have overloaded both of them in the program to work with objects of class `Point`. Compiler creates a multiple **temporary nameless** objects for this mixed statement to get executed correctly. Although the objects are nameless, we will name them as R1 and R2 for the sake of explaining the execution of this statement. The execution of the statement is as shown in the Figure 13.9 and is performed as follows.

Step 1: As P2-P3 is surrounded in parenthesis this will be the first part to get evaluated. Hence as a first step, P2 invokes the operator minus function and passes P3 as an argument. The result returned by the **operator-()** function is the temporary nameless object containing the subtraction of P2 and P3. We call this object as R1 as shown in the Figure 13.9.

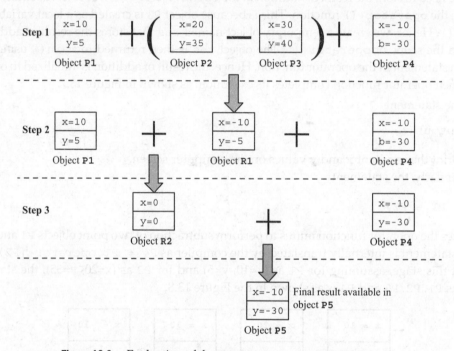

Figure 13.9: Evaluation of the statement P5 = P1+(P2-P3)+P4

Step 2: The expression is now reduced to P1+R1+P4 as shown in the Figure 13.9. Since the operator + is left to right associative, P1+R1 is the first to execute since it is the left most addition. To evaluate the result of P1+R1, the compiler invokes operator+ function using object P1 and passes R1 as an argument to it. The result returned by the **operator+()** function is another temporary nameless object containing the addition of P1 and R1. We call this object as R2 as shown in the Figure 13.9.

Step 3: Finally, objects R2 and P4 are added by invoking an **operator+()** function using object R2 and passing P4 as an argument to it. The result returned by the operator function is stored in object P5 which is the final result of the expression.

The temporary nameless objects are created while executing this expression because one of the overloaded operator functions needs to be invoked at each step using the temporary result of the previous step. This way, P5 contains the final result of the mixed expression preserving associativity and precedence at each step of evaluation. Generating such results without operator overloading is possible but is very cumbersome. Hence, operator overloading gives a huge relief to the programmers if they intend to perform complex mathematical operations with objects.

13.5 Overloading Shorthand Operators: An Example

Recall from Chapter 3, +=, -=, *=, /=, and %= are called as shorthand arithmetic operators in C++. For example, let us overload a shorthand operator += to perform addition of objects of user-defined types. Consider two primitive type variables say a and b then a+=b will perform addition of a and b storing the result back in variable a. This means that the value of the variable which is on the left hand side of the operator is always overwritten so that it contains the result of the shorthand operation. We will write a C++ program showing how to extend the capability of shorthand operators to work with objects.

Let us create a class `Weight` with two integer members `kilogram` and `gram`. This means that we intend to represent all weights in the form of kilograms and grams. Let us perform addition of two `Weight` objects w1 and w2 using += to understand overloading of shorthand operators. This means that we should now be able to write the following statement with objects of class `Weight`:

```
w1+=w2;
```

The statement will perform addition of two `Weight` objects w1 and w2 and store the result of addition back in object w1. In this case, as the operator += is to be overloaded, we include the function **operator+=** as a member function of class `Weight` as seen in the code. Also, we know that when an operator is used with objects, compiler invokes an operator function using the object present on the left hand side of the operator and passes object present on the right hand side of the operator as an argument. Following steps will be performed at the time of compilation of the statement w1+=w2.

Step 1: The function operator+= will be invoked using object w1 because it is present on the left hand side of += in the statement. This means that members of object w1 can be directly accessed within the operator function as `kilogram` and `gram` as shown in Figure 13.10.

Step 2: The object w2 will be passed as an argument to the operator function because it is present on the right hand side. This means that operator+= function must be designed such that it takes one argument of type `Weight` as shown in the Figure 13.10. This means that the members of object w2 can be accessed as t.kilogram and t.gram within the scope of the operator function.

Step 3: Operator function need not return any value because we need to store the result of addition in the same object which invoked the function (which is w1 in this case) and we have clarified in step 1 that the members of w1 can be directly accessed in operator+=() function.

In summary, the compiler internally translates the statement w1+=w2 as
```
w1.operator+=(w2);
```

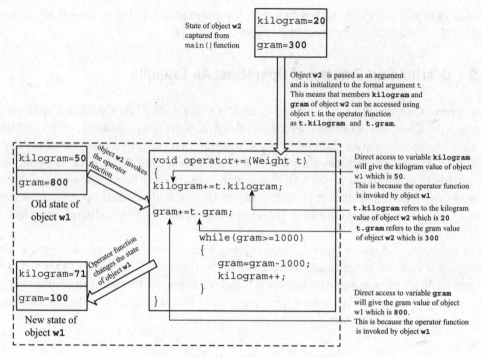

Figure 13.10: Call to operator function

As the constructors are invoked for objects w1 and w2, w1 is set as 50 kgs and 800 grams whereas w2 is set as 20 kgs and 300 grams as seen in the program. Figure 13.10 shows the execution of the operator+= function assuming these sample values.

The following is the source code to overload += with objects of class Weight:

```cpp
#include<iostream.h>
class Weight
{
private:
    int kilogram;
    int gram;
public:
Weight()
{
kilogram =0;
gram =0;
}
Weight(int p,int q)
{
kilogram=p;
gram=q;
}
```

```
void operator+=(Weight t)
{
kilogram+=t.kilogram;
gram+=t.gram;
    while(gram>=1000)
    {
    gram=gram-1000;
    kilogram++;
    }
}
void output()
{
cout<<kilogram<<" kgs and "<<gram<<" grams"<<endl;
}
};
void main()
{
//create Weight objects
Weight w1(50,800) ;
Weight w2(20,300);
//execute operation += with objects
w1+=w2;
//print the result of addition
cout<<"The result Weight :";
w1.output();
}
```

Output

```
The result Weight is :71 kgs and 100 grams
```

The following two statements in operator+=() will perform addition of w1's members kilogram and gram with w2's members t.kilogram and t.gram and store the result back in w1.

```
feet+=t.feet;
inch+=t.inch;
```

After execution of these statements, the value of w1.kilogram is set to 50+20=**70 kilogram** and w1.gram is set to 800+300=**1100 grams** as shown in Figure 13.11.

We realize that the kilogram and gram values of object w1 must be reformatted because the grams value appears to have crossed 1000, which can be easily and part of it can be represented in terms of kilogram. Hence, instead of saying 70 kilograms

Values of members before adjustment is applied by the while loop

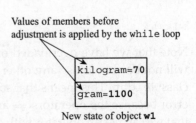

New state of object **w1**

Figure 13.11: State of object w1 before execution of the while loop

and 1100 grams, we can reformat w1 as **71 kilogram and 100 grams.** This formatting is achieved using the following while loop written in the operator function. The while loop basically reduces 1000 from gram till the time gram value is greater than or equal to 1000. Each time gram is reduced by 1000, its value is adjusted in terms of kilogram by incrementing it by 1.

```
while(gram>=1000)
   {
      gram=gram-1000;
      kilogram++;
   }
```

After the execution of the operator function, the state of object w1 is as shown in the Figure 13.12.

New state of object **w1**

Figure 13.12: Object w1

13.6 Overloading Relational Operators: An Example

Recall from Chapter 3, >, > =, <, < =, = =, and ! = are called as relational operators in C++. These operators check if a specific relationship is true between two of its operands and return Boolean values as a result of this check. The relational operator returns 1 if the relationship between the operands is true, and returns zero if the relationship is false. For example, if a and b are integer variables and we apply a check a>=b, then we will get the result as 1 if value of variable a is greater than or equal to b, and we will get a result as 0 if value of a is less than b. As relational operators always return Boolean values (0 or 1), they are generally used as a conditional expression inside a decision making control structure of C++. In this example, we will learn overloading of relational operators to extend its capabilities to work with objects.

Let us use class **Weight** from previous example, with two members of type **int** named as kilogram and gram. We will now compare objects of class Weight using two operators > and <=. This means that we must create two operator functions, **operator>()** and **operator<=()**, inside class Weight. If w1 and w2 are two objects of class Weight, then after overloading these operators we will be able to compare two objects as

w1>w2

or

w1<=w2

Note that we have overloaded only two of the relational operators > and <=. Hence we will not be able to use any other relational operator apart from > and <= with objects of class Weight. This means that some C++ expression like w1==w2 or w1>=w2 will give an error because the operators == and >= are not overloaded. We should always remember that we can use an operator with objects if, and only if, it is overloaded with an appropriate operator function.

The expression

```
w1>w2
```

will invoke `operator>()` function using object w1 by passing w2 as an argument. This is because w1 appears on the left hand side of the operator and w2 on the right hand side.

We know that the result of comparison always has to be a Boolean value (i.e., 0 or 1). Hence the return type of each of the operator functions is set as **int**. If the relation between the two objects is true, the operator function returns1, and it returns 0 otherwise. Since `Weight` is our own class, we can define our own rules on how to compare its objects. Here, each `Weight` object is specified in terms of kilograms and grams; hence, to compare two `Weight` objects w1 and w2, we must first get them into a single unit. The operator function converts both the weights fully into grams and then compares the converted values with each other. Let g1 and g2 be fully converted gram values of weights w1 and w2 then g1 and g2 can be calculated as

```
g1 = w1.kilogram*1000+w1.gram;
g2 = w2.kilogram*1000+w2.gram;
```

If g1>g2, then it implies that the weight object w1 is greater than w2. Hence the `operator>()` function returns 1 if g1>g2 and returns 0 otherwise.

The `main()` function is not bothered about how an operator function internally applies the comparison. The `main()` function simply contains an if block which compares two weights w1 and w2 as shown below:

```
if(w1>w2)
{
cout<<"Condition w1>w2 is TRUE"<<endl;
}
else
{
cout<<"Condition w1>w2 is FALSE"<<endl;
}
```

To evaluate the condition w1>w2, the `operator>()` function will be invoked which is shown in Figure 13.13, which calculates gram values g1 and g2 for weights w1 and w2, respectively. Note that the members of w1 can be directly accessed within the operator function because it is the object which invoked the function. Members of w2 are accessed as **t.kilogram** and **t.gram** because w2 is passed as an argument and initialized to t. The objects w1 and w2 are created by invoking a constructor with two arguments as

```
Weight w1(50,800);
Weight w2(20,300);
```

Therefore,

```
w1 = 50 kilogram and 800 grams
w2 = 20 kilogram and 300 grams
```

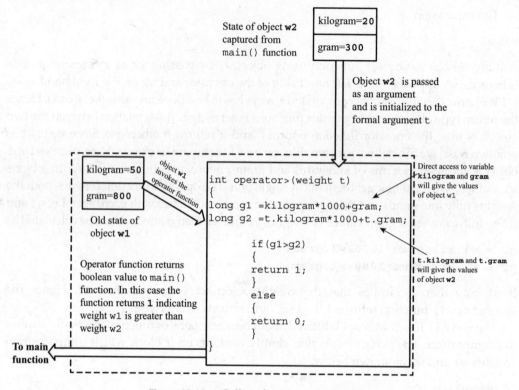

Figure 13.13: Calling function `operator>`

Hence the operator function calculates **g1 = 50,800** and **g2 = 20,300**. As g1>g2 the operator function returns 1, indicating that the weight w1 is actually greater than weight w2. After execution of the operator function, the control is returned to main(), and the condition w1>w2 is identified as true because the operator function has returned 1. This transfers the control inside the if block, thereby printing following message on the computer screen:

```
Condition w1>w2 is TRUE
```

Note that data type of variables g1 and g2 is long to support values which are out of integer range.

The following is the full source code which overloads > and <= to compare Weight objects:

```
#include<iostream.h>
class Weight
{
private:
    int kilogram;
    int gram;
public:
```

```
Weight()
{
kilogram =0;
gram =0;
}
Weight(int p,int q)
{
kilogram=p;
gram=q;
}
int operator>(Weight t)
{
long g1 =kilogram*1000+gram;
long g2 =t.kilogram*1000+t.gram;
    if(g1>g2)
    {
    return 1;
    }
    else
    {
    return 0;
    }
}
int operator<=(Weight t)
    {
long g1 =kilogram*1000+gram;
long g2 =t.kilogram*1000+t.gram;
    if(g1<=g2)
    {
    return 1;
    }
    else
    {
    return 0;
    }
}
    void output()
    {
    cout<<kilogram<<" kgs and "<<gram<<" grams"<<endl;
    }
};
void main()
{
//create Weight objects
Weight w1(50,800) ;
```

```
Weight w2(20,300);
Weight w3(110,100) ;
Weight w4(25,450);
      if(w1>w2)
      {
      cout<<"Condition w1>w2 is TRUE"<<endl;
      }
      else
      {
      cout<<"Condition w1>w2 is FALSE"<<endl;
      }
      if(w3<=w4)
      {
      cout<<"Condition w3<=w4 is TRUE"<<endl;
      }
      else
      {
      cout<<"Condition w3<=w4 is FALSE"<<endl;
      }
}
```

Output

```
Condition w1>w2 is TRUE
Condition w3<=w4 is FALSE
```

Similarly, the next if block compares the two objects w3 and w4 using a <= operator. Hence the compiler will invoke the function **operator<=** using object w3 passing w4 as an argument. In this case, the operator<= function will return 0 because the condition w3<=w4 is false. Hence the control of execution will this time be transferred to the else block, thereby printing the following message on the computer screen:

```
Condition w3<=w4 is FALSE
```

13.7   Overloading Increment/Decrement Operators: An Example

Let us now overload an increment operator (++)to use it with objects of a class. The same approach can also be followed to overload a decrement operator (--). Recall from Chapter 3 that there are two forms of increment/decrement operators in C++, prefix form and the postfix form. When the increment/decrement operators are used in a prefix form (++variableName), the value of the variable is updated first and then the new value is used in the expression, whereas in the postfix form (variableName++), the current value of the variable is first used in the expression and later the variable is updated to reflect the new value. In this section, we will learn how to overload increment operator (++) in prefix as well as postfix form.

Let us create a class Integer with one member of type int say variable a. Hence, every object of class Integer will have member variable a in the object memory. We will overload increment operator (++) to use it with objects of class Integer by creating necessary operator functions.

Let O1 be the object of Integer, then following should work if we overload the increment operator

++O1;

and

O1++;

If the compiler invokes the same operator function for both of the above statements, the operator function will not be able to determine whether the function is invoked by O1 with a prefix notation or a postfix notation. This is because in both the cases, it's the same object O1 invoking the function **operator++**. If this happens, both the statements ++O1 and O1++ would now produce identical results, which is unacceptable. To solve this problem, the compiler passes a dummy argument of type integer when increment operator is used in a postfix form. No dummy argument is passed when the increment operator is used in a prefix form. This means that we must now write two different operator functions inside class Integer:

1. **Operator function that takes no arguments:** This operator function will be called when an increment/decrement operator is used in a prefix form. When we write a statement ++O1, the member function **operator++** that takes no arguments will be invoked by the compiler.
2. **Operator function that takes a dummy integer argument:** This operator function will be called when an increment/decrement operator is used in a postfix form. When we write a statement O1++, the member function **operator++(int)** that takes one dummy argument, will be invoked by the compiler.

If O1 and O2 are objects of Integer, we must also support the following type of statements in the program:

O2=++O1;

OR

O2=O1++;

++ is a unary operator, and hence, in both the cases, the operator function will be invoked using object O1. In the case of prefix notation, O1 will invoke operator function with no arguments, whereas in the case of postfix notation object O1 will invoke operator function with one dummy argument of type integer. Both the statements are required to store the result in object O2; this means that both the operator functions must return the result as another object of class Integer. The object returned by the operator function can then be initialized to O2.

The following is the full source code to overload operator ++ for objects of class Integer

```cpp
#include<iostream.h>
class Integer
{
private:
    int a;
public:
    Integer()
    {
    }
    Integer(int p)
    {
    a=p;
    }
    Integer operator++()
    {
    Integer res;
    res.a = ++a;
    return res;
    }
    Integer operator++(int dummy)
    {
    Integer res;
    res.a =a++;
    return res;
    }
    void output()
    {
    cout<<"value of variable a is:"<<a<<endl;
    }
};
void main()
{
Integer O1(10),O2(20), O3,O4;
O3= ++O1;
O4=O2++;
cout<<"Object O1"<<endl;
O1.output();
cout<<"Object O2"<<endl;
O2.output();
cout<<"Object O3"<<endl;
O3.output();
```

```
cout<<"Object O4"<<endl;
O4.output();
}
```

Output

```
Object O1
value of variable a is:11
Object O2
value of variable a is:21
Object O3
value of variable a is:11
Object O4
value of variable a is:20
```

The first statement in `main()` function

```
Integer O1(10),O2(20),O3,O4;
```

creates four objects O1, O2, O3, and O4 of class `Integer`. A constructor with one argument initializes the a value of object O1 as 10, and a value of object O2 as 20 as shown in the Figure 13.14. The members of object O3 and O4 will not be initialized because the default constructor is called for O3 and O4.

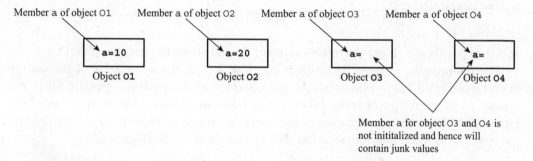

Figure 13.14: Objects O1, O2, O3, O4

The statement

```
O3= ++O1;
```

applies a prefix increment operation on object O1 and stores the result in object O3. As the operator ++ is used with the object of class `Integer`, the compiler invokes an **operator++()** function using object O1. The ++ operator is used in a prefix form, and hence the compiler will invoke an operator function that takes no arguments. The operator function is invoked by object O1, and hence the member variables of O1 can be directly accessed inside the operator function as shown in the Figure 13.15.

The operator function is required to increment the value stored in variable a of object O1 and assign the incremented value to member a of O3 (the prefix form of increment should first update the member of object O1 and then initialize the updated value to member

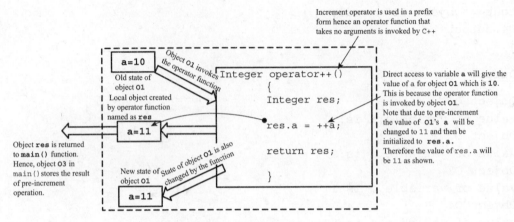

Figure 13.15: Call to operator function

of O3). However, since O3 is a local variable of main(), we create a temporary object res inside the operator function to store the result of pre-increment operation. The value of member a inside object res is set to 11 by the following statement:

```
res.a=++a;
```

The object res is returned by the operator function and its values get initialized to O3 as shown in the Figure 13.15.

The next statement

```
O4= O2++;
```

applies a postfix increment operation on object O2 and stores the result in object O4.

The operator ++ is used with object O2, and hence, the compiler will invoke the operator function using object O2. As the operator ++ is used in a postfix form, the compiler will invoke the operator function that takes **one dummy argument of type int**. Figure 13.16 explains the execution of the operator function. The object res returned by the operator function gets initialized to object O4 as shown in the Figure 13.16.

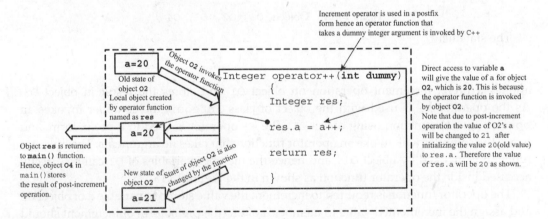

Figure 13.16: Call to operator function

Finally, we invoke `output()` function over each of the objects O1, O2, O3, and O4 to print the value of member a for each of them.

NOTES

The key difference between the implementation of the operator function with no arguments and the operator function with a dummy argument is that the operator function with no arguments calculates member a of result using a prefix notation, as shown below:

```
res.a=++a; //prefix notation
```

whereas, the operator function with dummy argument calculates the member a of result using a postfix notation, as shown below:

```
res.a=a++; //postfix notation
```

Direct access to a, in both the cases, will give the value of member a of the invoking object. The operator function with no arguments is invoked when ++ is used in prefix form on the invoking object, and hence, it applies prefix ++ on **a**, whereas the operator function with a dummy argument is invoked when ++ is used in postfix form on the invoking object and hence it applies postfix ++ on **a**.

Why have we created a dummy argument while defining the operator function for postfix form?   **?**

We need two different `operator++()` functions in the class `Integer`, one for prefix notation and the other for the post fix notation. The rule is that, two different functions can exist in the **single class** only if they have a different **function signature**.

Recall from chapter 11 section 11.25 the, function signature of any function is defined by following 4 properties of the function

1. Name of the function.
2. Number of arguments the function takes.
3. Data type of each of the arguments.
4. Order of the arguments.

You can create two functions in the same class only if at least one of the 4 points is different in each of them. This is because compiler uniquely identifies each member function using its signature. Note that, first point in the function signature is the name of the function and hence two functions with different names can safely coexist in the single class even if they take arguments of same type in the same order. But if the name of two functions is same, then at least one of the remaining points (2,3 or 4) must differ in each of them if they are required to coexists in the same class. The examples of coexistence of two functions when they are overloaded are explained in Chapter 11, section 11.25. Same rules apply for operator functions as well, because operator function is also a member function of class like any other function.

In this case, we have actually overloaded the `operator++()` function in the class `Integer` by implementing it in two different ways for prefix and postfix notations respectively. The two functions should have the same name as `operator++()`, because it is the same operator which is to be used in both the cases. Given that the first operator function does not take any arguments, the only way by which we can make the signature of the second operator function different is by adding a dummy argument to it. When ++ is used with primitive types, compiler handles this situation by passing a dummy parameter of type int to the operator function responsible for giving the postfix implementation. Since we are overloading the operator ++ for objects of class `Integer`, we must do it in the same way in which compiler does for primitive types. Hence we have created a **dummy argument** of type int in the `operator++()` function which gets executed for postfix notation.

13.8 Function Object: Overloading Function Call Operator ()

An object that acts as a function is called as **function object or** a functor. We can use this object as if it is an ordinary function. To create such objects, we must overload the function call operator(), by including operator() as a member function in the class.

Figure 13.17 shows the syntax to overload the operator(). The function can be defined to accept any number of arguments depending on the requirement of the programmer.

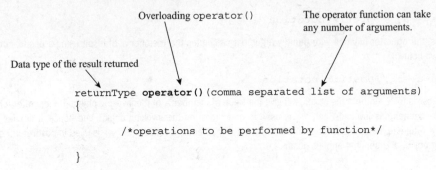

Figure 13.17: Syntax to overload function call operator

As an example, let us consider class Rectangle, which has a single member function that overloads operator(). The function calculates and returns the area of the rectangle based on values of length and breadth passed to it.

```cpp
#include<iostream.h>
class Rectangle
{
public:
    float operator()(float length,float breadth)
    {
        return length*breadth;
    }
};
void main()
{
Rectangle area;
float x = area(10.0, 3.0);
float y = area(15.5, 5.0);
float z = area(3.5, 6.45);
cout<<"Area of rectangle with length=10.0 and breadth=3.0
    is:"<<x<<endl;
cout<<"Area of rectangle with length=15.5 and breadth=5.0
    is:"<<y<<endl;
cout<<"Area of rectangle with length=3.5 and breadth=6.45
    is:"<<z<<endl;
}
```

The requirement here is not to store the lengths and breadths in object memory, but to determine what would be the area of a `Rectangle` object for various different values of lengths and breadth. This can be achieved by creating a single object of class `Rectangle` named as `area`

```
Rectangle area;
```

Although, `area` is an object of class `Rectangle`, we are using it as if it's a simple function taking two arguments and returning a value, as seen in the following statement:

```
float x = area(10.0, 3.0);
```

This statement internally invokes the member function `operator()` defined in class `Rectangle`, taking two arguments of type `float` as `length` and `breadth`. The operator function returns area of rectangle as `length*breadth`. Hence, the value of variable `x` is set to `30.0` in this case.

Similarly, the other two statements

```
float y = area(15.5, 5.0);
float z = area(3.5, 6.45);
```

calculate area with different length and breadth values and store the result in variables `y` and `z`, respectively.

NOTES

area is an object of class `Rectangle`, but we have used it as if it is an ordinary function taking two arguments and returning a result. Hence, area is called as a **function object** because we have **invoked the object** like we invoke functions.

NOTES

Don't confuse between calling a **constructor** and calling an **operator()** function. Constructors are called when an object is **being constructed**, whereas `operator()` is called when an object is invoked **after creation.**
    For example, the following statement will **not** work,

```
Rectangle area(5.1,2.5);
```

because it attempts to call a constructor with two arguments to create object named **area**, but we have **not** defined any parameterized constructor in class **Rectangle**. If you want this statement to work, you must create a parameterized constructor in class `Rectangle`. It is agreed, that there is no point doing so because there are no members in class `Rectangle` that the constructor could really initialize. Hence we did not create our own constructor in class `Rectangle`, at the first place. In this program, we have created the object named `area` as

```
Rectangle area;
```

which invokes the default constructor provided by the compiler. After the object is created, if you use `()` operator with object anytime later in the program, the compiler will invoke `operator()` function. Indeed, constructors are called at the time of creation of the object and not after creation. Hence, the statement

```
float x = area(10.0,3.0);
```

invokes **operator()** function which takes two arguments

13.9 Overloading Subscript Operator []

We can make an object act as an array by overloading operator [] as a member function of the class. You can add many additional functions to these objects to make them as intelligent as possible to suite your business requirement. For example, you may want to add a customized algorithm to search an element in the array, to find element with minimum value, to read elements of the array in a specific approach, checking boundary conditions while accessing array elements, and so on. In this section, we will show one of the examples, to overloading of the subscript operator, but you may overload it for a different reason all together.

As an example, let us consider class Point described in section 13.4 with x and y coordinate values. We will overload the subscript operator [] with class Point to access x and y coordinate values of each of the Point objects.

The operator[] function defined in class Point takes an integer argument index and returns an appropriate member of the invoking object to the caller. If the index=0, x is returned by the function and if index=1, then the function returns y. This means that every object of class Point can be imagined as an **array of two elements** such that the first element is x and the second element is the y. For example, if A is the object of class Point with x value as 10 and y value as 15, then you can access members of A as A[0] and A[1]. When you write A[0] in the code, the subscript operator is invoked using object A, by passing index=0 as an argument. Hence the compiler internally translates A[0] as

A.operator[](0);

As the value of index passed is 0, the operator function returns x of object A as shown in Figure 13.18. Similarly, A[1] will return y of object A.

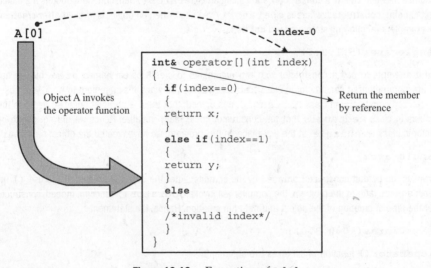

Figure 13.18: Execution of A[0]

NOTES

The operator function returns by reference to make it possible to place its call as a **assignee** in the expression. Recall, Chapter 8, section 8.15 where we have explained that the function call can appear on the left hand side of the assignment if it returns the **address or reference** to a memory location.

NOTES

In summary, we have treated object A as if it's an **array** by accessing its elements as **A[0]** and **A[1]**. In reality, A is just a simple object of class `Point`, but the programmer gets a feeling as if it's an array. This is one of the best examples describing the level of **abstraction** that can be provided in the program by overloading operators in a right way.

The following is the full source code which overloads operator[] with objects of class Point:

```cpp
#include<iostream.h>
class Point
{
private:
    int x;
    int y;
public:
    void input()
    {
    cin>>x>>y;
    }
int& operator[](int index)
{
    if(index==0)
    {
    return x;
    }
    else if(index==1)
    {
    return y;
    }
    else
    {
cout<<"ERROR:: Invalid Array Index "<<index<<" :: Array Index Out
    of Bounds"<<endl;
cout<<"*Results will be incorrect because one of the array
    elements have been accessed wrongly*"<<endl;
return index;
    }
}
```

```
void output()
    {
    cout<<"("<<x<<","<<y<<")"<<endl;
    }
};
void main()
{
Point A,B,C;
cout<<"Enter the x and y values of point A"<<endl;
A.input();
cout<<"Enter the x and y values of point B"<<endl;
B.input();
//Add x coordinates
C[0] = A[0] + B[0];
//Add y coordinates
C[1] = A[1] + B[1];
cout<<"Result of addition is:"<<endl;
C.output();
}
```

The program creates three objects of class Point as A, B, and C and performs addition of points A and B storing the resultant point in object C.

The statement

```
C[0] = A[0] + B[0];
```

invokes the overloaded operator [] function for each objects A, B, and C. We know that, operator function will return x value of the invoking object if index zero is passed to it and return y value if index 1 is passed to it. Hence, this statement adds the x value of A with x value of B and stores the result as x value of C. Note that the subscript operator function is also called on the left hand side of the assignment–to assign the value of x for object C; hence, we have implemented return by reference in the operator function. Return by reference is explained in Chapter 8, section 8.15. Figure 13.19 shows the execution of the statement C[0] = A[0] + B[0];

Similarly, the statement

```
C[1] = A[1] + B[1];
```

adds the y value of A with y value of B and stores the result as y value of C.

NOTES

If an index passed to the operator function is other than 0 or 1 we print an error message on the screen. This error message will help genuine programmers to detect accidental mistakes like typing or logical errors made in the program due to which incorrect index value is generated. These are called as **boundary checks** which should be performed while accessing array elements. As mentioned in Chapter 6, the default array in C++ is not smart enough to generate such error messages and hence many times C++ programmers simply overload subscript operator just in perform **boundary checks**.

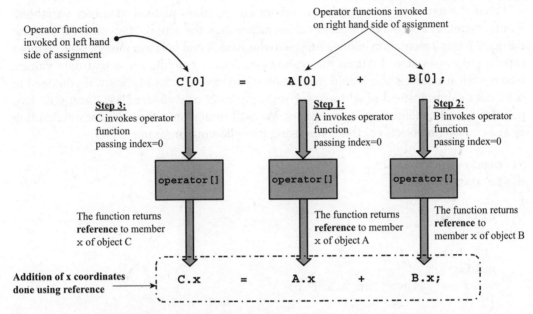

Figure 13.19: Execution of statement `C[0] = A[0] + B[0];`

13.10 Overloading Assignment Operator =

In this section, we will overload assignment **operator** = to work with objects of class. Actually, this operator is already overloaded for every class, by default, by the compiler of C++. This means that the compiler provides `operator=()` function to every class that you create, just like it provides a default constructor to every class. The default implementation of the `operator=` function is such that it does a member-by-member copy when one object is assigned to another. For example, consider class `Point` in section 13.4, we have not overloaded = with it, but still the following statement would work for `Point` objects P1 and P2,

```
P1 = P2;
```

The statement will copy all the members of P2 to the corresponding members of P1; this means that the x value of P2 will be copied to x value of P1 and y value of P2 will be copied to y value of P1. So, if P2's x and y values are 10 and 20, respectively, the same will be copied over as member values of P1 as shown in the Figure 13.20.

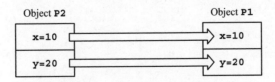

Figure 13.20: Execution of statement `P1=P2`

What if there is a class whose members are pointers instead of direct variables? Pointers contain address of the data values rather than the actual data values. If you use the default implementation of operator= in this case, it will perform member-by-member copy of addresses stored within the pointers instead of copying the actual data values. Under such situations, you would need to overload operator= explicitly, if you need to copy data values instead of addresses. For example, let us consider class Data with two pointers p and q defined as its members. We will understand the effect of overloading operator= with objects of class Data using the following program:

```cpp
#include<iostream.h>
class Data
{
    private:
    int *p;
    int *q;
    public:
    void setValues(int a,int b)
    {
      p= new int(a);
      q= new int(b);
    }
    void changeValues()
    {
      (*p)++;
      (*q)++;
    }
    void printValues()
    {
      cout<<"Value 1 = "<<*p<<" Value 2= "<<*q<<endl;
    }
    void operator=(Data t)
    {
      /*Allocate a different memory to store values for target
    object */
      p = new int;
      q = new int;
      /*copy values from source object to target object*/
      *p=*(t.p);
      *q=*(t.q);
    }
};
void main()
{
```

```
    Data D1,D2;
    D1.setValues(10,20);
    D2=D1;
cout<<"***************Before change****************"<<endl;
cout<<"---OBJECT D1---"<<endl;
    D1.printValues();
cout<<"---OBJECT D2---"<<endl;
    D2.printValues();
    D1.changeValues();
cout<<"***************After change****************"<<endl;
cout<<"---OBJECT D1---"<<endl;
    D1.printValues();
cout<<"---OBJECT D2---"<<endl;
    D2.printValues();
}
```

The first statement in `main()`

```
Data D1,D2;
```

creates two objects of class `Data` named `D1` and `D2`. We have initialized the pointers of object `D1` to point to integer values 10 and 20, respectively, by invoking the `setValues()` function as seen in the code. The members of object `D2` are not yet initialized.

The next statement

```
D2=D1;
```

invokes an `operator=` function defined in class `Data`. It will not invoke the compilers implementation of `operator=` because we have defined our own `operator=` function in class `Data`. In this case, `D1` is the source object, which is present on right hand side of the operator, whereas `D2` is the target object, which is on the left hand side. Hence, the operator function will be invoked using object `D2` passing `D1` as a parameter to it. Since `D2` has invoked the operator function writing `p` and `q` in the function body will refer to members of `D2`, whereas `t.p` and `t.q` will refer to members of `D1`. The `operator=` function works in two steps:

Step 1: Allocate new memory area for target object

The `operator=` function makes the two pointers `p` and `q` of the invoking object (in this case `D2`) to point to new integer blocks using the statements

```
p = new int;
q = new int;
```

This ensures that the data space used by object `D1` is not same as that of the data space used by object `D2`.

Step 2: Copy data values from source object to target object

After allocating a separate data space, the operator function copies the data values pointed by pointers p and q of object D1 to the new data spaces pointed by pointers of D2 using the following statements:

```
*p=*(t.p);
*q=*(t.q);
```

The execution of these steps are as shown in Figure 13.21. If we would not have overloaded the `operator=` function, then the statement `D2=D1;` would have invoked the default implementation provided by the compiler. In this case, the addresses stored within the pointer p and q of object D1 would have copied in pointers p and q of object D2. Hence, the pointers p and q would have shared same data values as shown in the second part of the Figure 13.21. This could have caused accidents since any change applied to D1 would have also changed the data values of D2.

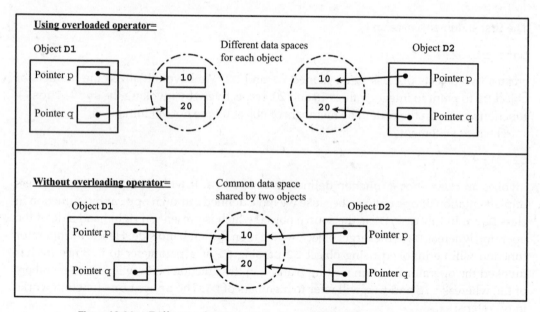

Figure 13.21: Difference between `operator=` written by us and its default implementation of compiler

See the function `changeValues()` which increment the data values pointed by pointers p and q of the invoking object. If we invoke this function using object D1

```
D1.changevalues();
```

it would have also changed the values of D2 because pointers p and q would have pointed to same memory locations **without overloading operator=**. In this case, since we have overloaded `operator=`, `D1.changevalues()` will only change the data values of D1 to 11 and 21, but data values of D2 are not affected as you will see in the output of the program.

13.11   Overloading Type Cast Operator

Like any other operators, we can also overload the type cast operator using an `operator` keyword. Figure 13.22 gives the syntax of overloading type cast operator.

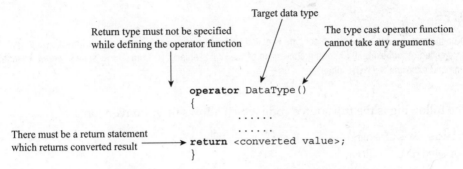

Figure 13.22:   Syntax to overload type cast operator

NOTES

1. The return type should not be specified when defining the operator function which overloads the type cast operator. However, there must be a **return** statement within the operator function which returns the value converted to the target type.
2. Operator function overloading type cast operator **cannot** take any arguments.

There are certain user-defined types that could be fully represented using primitive types. Consider class `Weight` that we have created in section 13.4.1, specifies weight in kilogram and gram. You could also represent this value as a single long number in grams. For example, a `Weight` object with values as 50 kg and 800 g can be represented as a single long value of 50,800 g as shown in Figure 13.23. This means that there is a scope to cash a weight object into a primitive type. You can overload type cast operator in class `Weight` if you would want to allow casting objects of weight to a specific type. In this case, we would want to cast a weight

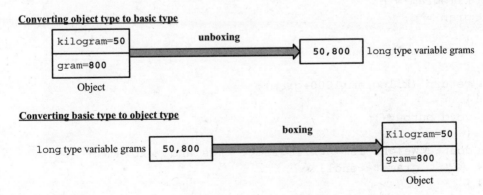

Figure 13.23:   Boxing and unboxing `Weight` objects to/from a long value

object into a long type and hence we will overload the type cast operator for long type with `Weight` class. However, you could also represent a single long value specified in grams into an equivalent Weight object (50,800 g can be represented as 50 kg and 800 g) as shown in the Figure 13.23. In this section, we will lean how to facilitate such conversions.

NOTES

Conversion from primitive type to Object type is called as **boxing**, whereas conversion from object type to primitive type is called as **unboxing**. By allowing conversion of `Weight` objects to/from `long` values, we are essentially boxing and unboxing `Weight` objects.

The following is the full source code which allows these conversions.

```cpp
#include<iostream.h>
class Weight
{
private:
    int kilogram;
    int gram;
public:
    Weight()
    {
    kilogram = 0;
    gram = 0;
    }
    Weight(long g)
    {
    kilogram = g/1000;
    gram = g%1000;
    }
    Weight(int p,int q)
    {
    kilogram = p;
    gram = q;
    }
    operator long()
    {
    return (kilogram*1000+gram);
    }
    void output()
    {
    cout<<"Weight is "<<kilogram<<" kgs and "<<gram<<"
        grams"<<endl;
    }
};
```

```
void main()
{
//create Weight objects
Weight w1(50,800);
/*UN-BOXING from Object to basic value*/
long grams =(long)w1;
cout<<"Weight in grams is "<<grams<<endl;
Weight w2;
/*BOXING: From Basic to Object value using a constructor*/
w2=grams;
w2.output();
}
```

A weight object specified in terms of kilogram and gram can be fully converted into grams as follows:

kilogram*1000 + gram

Hence we have written an operator function in class `Weight` which overloads the type cast operator **long()** as shown below.

```
operator long()
{
    return (kilogram*1000+gram);
}
```

The statement

```
long grams =(long)w1;
```

applies a cast operator to object w1 to convert it into a `long` value. Hence, it invokes the `operator long()` function defined in class `Weight`. Needless to mention that object w1 has invoked this function and hence members kilogram and gram of w1 can be accessed directly within the scope of the function. As w1 has a kilogram value of 50 and gram value of 800, the cast operator function returns 50,800 which is assigned to a `long` type variable grams.

Let us now focus on converting long value to object of `Weight`. In order to achieve this, we have two options:

Option 1: Create a constructor in `Weight` class, which takes one argument of type `long` and initializes the kilogram and gram values as shown in Figure 13.24.

Option 2: Overload `operator=` function in class `Weight`, which allows assigning of `long` values to `Weight` objects. The `operator=` takes a long type argument and assigns the value of members kilogram and gram from it as shown in Figure 13.24.

In the given program, we have implemented option 1, but any of these options can be used interchangeably.

The statement

```
w2 = grams;
```

assigns the value of long type variable grams to a `Weight` object w2. In this case, the compiler invokes a constructor with one argument of type long to initialize kilogram and gram values of w2 as shown in Figure 13.24.

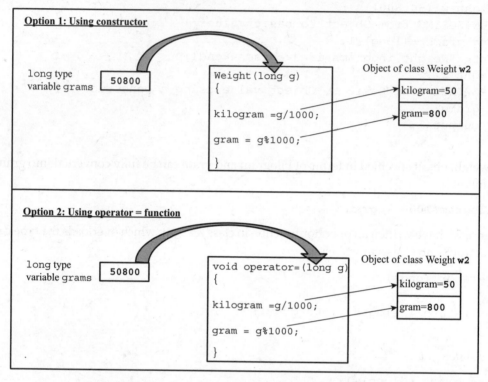

Figure 13.24: Options to convert primitive type to Object type

Instead of constructor, if we would have written an operator function, the statement

```
w2 = grams;
```

would have invoked the `operator=` function defined in the `Weight` class using object w2, passing `long` variable grams as an argument to it.

NOTES

1. Any object type can be converted into primitive type by overloading the **type cast operator function**, just like we have converted `Weight` object to long value.
2. Any primitive type can be converted into an object type using a **constructor or an operator= function**. These options can be used interchangeably.

13.12 Conversion of One User-defined Type to Another

The type cast operator can also be overloaded to convert the object of one class to another. To show the conversion of one object type to another, we have created a class `Gram` with a single member g, to represent the weight value in grams. We will now overload the type cast operator to convert the object of class Weight to an object of class Gram.

The operator function to be written in Weight class; to convert a Weight object to a Gram object is similar to how we handled the conversion of Weight object to a long object except the target type is now specified as Gram as shown in the Figure 13.25.

Specify the target type as Gram

```
operator Gram()
{

    /* return an equivalent Gram object*/

}
```

Figure 13.25: Operator function in Weight class

The casting operator function must always be written in the source class since it is invoked by the source object. In this case, we need to convert Weight object to a Gram object, and hence the cast operator function is written in the Weight class. However, if the requirement would have been to convert Gram object to Weight object, we would have written type cast operator function in Gram class with target type as Weight.

The following is the full source code showing the overloading of cast operator to convert Weight object to Gram object.

```
#include<iostream.h>
class Gram
{
private:
int g;
public:
    Gram(int t)
    {
    g=t;
    }
    void output()
    {
    cout<<"Weight in grams is "<<g<<endl;
    }
};
class Weight
{
private:
    int kilogram;
    int gram;
public:
    Weight()
    {
    kilogram=0;
    gram=0;
    }
```

```
    Weight(int p,int q)
    {
    kilogram=p;
    gram=q;
    }
    operator Gram()
    {
    Gram res(kilogram*1000+gram);
    return res;
    }
    void output()
    {
    cout<<"Weight is "<<kilogram<<" kgs and "<<gram<<"
    grams"<<endl;
    }
};
void main()
{
Weight w1(50,800);
Gram o1 = (Gram)w1;
o1.output();
}
```

The statement

```
Gram o1 = (Gram)w1;
```

applies a cast operator on `Weight` object `w1` to convert it into `Gram` object. Hence, the compiler will invoke the operator function defined in class `Weight` using object `w1`. This function returns a `Gram` object, which is assigned to object `o1`. The members `kilogram` and `gram` of object `w1` can be accessed directly within the operator function because it is the object with which the function is invoked. Hence, the below statement written in operator function creates an object of class `Gram` named `res` by passing the value `kilogram*1000+gram` which evaluates to `50,800` in this case—to a one argument constructor present in class `Gram`.

```
Gram res(kilogram*1000+gram);
```

Hence, the member `g` of object `res` is set to 50,800, which is then returned to `main()` function as shown in Figure 13.26.

Similarly, if we need to cast a `Gram` object back to `Weight` object,

```
w1 = (Weight)o1;
```

following operator function must be defined in `Gram` class

```
operator Weight()
{
    Weight res(g/1000,g%1000);
    return res;
}
```

Execution of statement,
```
Gram o1 = (Gram)w1;
```

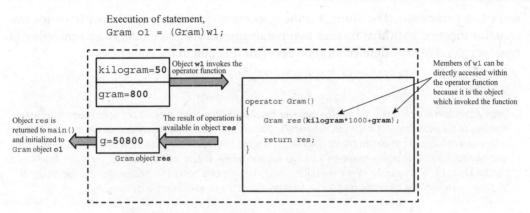

Figure 13.26: Execution of operator `Gram()` function

13.13 Creating Global Operator Functions

All the operator functions we created till now were defined as member functions of a particular class. Operator function can also be defined globally without putting it into any class. Since global operator functions are not the part of any class, the compiler does not need any object to invoke it. Global operator functions are used when we need to perform an operation of primitive type and object type with primitive type appearing on the left hand side of the operator. For example, let us consider a requirement that we need to add 100 g to the weight object w1 and store the resultant weight in w2 using the following statement.

```
w2 = 100+w1;
```

So, we decide to overload operator + to make it work with `Weight` objects. However, we cannot create `operator+` as a member function of class `Weight` because the left hand side of an operator is a constant integer value and the compiler needs an object of a class to invoke a member function. Creating `operator+` as a member function will work if we write the statement other way round:

```
w2 = w1+100;
```

In this case, w1 appears on the left hand side of + and hence the compiler can invoke the `operator+` function using w1 by passing 100 as an argument. The operator function can always return a `Weight` type object as a result, which is assigned to w2. However, writing statements the other way round is not always the solution. What if an operation is not commutative? For example, 100−w1 is not same as w1-100. Hence, the wider problem still remains on how would we make the statement w2 = 100+w1; work. To solve this problem, C++ supports creation of global operator functions. These are the operator functions that do not need any object for their invocation and all the operands are considered as arguments to the function. Hence, if the `operator+` function is defined globally, then for a statement w2 = 100+w1; the compiler will invoke it by passing 100 and w1 as parameters. Therefore, it is the responsibility of the programmer to define this operator function such that it takes two parameters one of type integer and the other of type Weight. We have defined such an operator function in the code below:

> **NOTES**
>
> Since global operator functions are **not the member functions** of the class, they do not have access to **private** members of the class. Hence it is the programmer's responsibility to provide necessary methods in the class using which operator function can access private members, if needed. In the program given below, the **operator+()** function needs access to private members **kilogram** and **gram**. Hence, we have defined two public functions **getKiloGr()** and **getGr()** in Weight class. The **getKiloGr()** function returns the value of kilogram outside the class and **getGr()** function returns the value of member gram.

The following is the full source code which overloads operator + to perform addition of an integer and a Weight object.

```cpp
#include<iostream.h>
class Weight
{
private:
    int kilogram;
    int gram;
public:
    Weight()
    {
    kilogram =0;
    gram =0;
    }
    Weight(int p,int q)
    {
    kilogram=p;
    gram=q;
    }
    void output()
    {
    cout<<kilogram<<" kgs and "<<gram<<" grams"<<endl;
    }
    int getKiloGr()
    {
    return kilogram;
    }
    int getGr()
    {
    return gram;
    }
};
```

```
Weight operator+(int g, Weight& t)
{
   int kilogram,gram;
   kilogram=t.getKiloGr();
   gram=g + t.getGr();/*Add g value to gram*/
    while(gram>=1000)
    {
      gram=gram-1000;
      kilogram++;
    }
    Weight res(kilogram,gram);
    return res;
}
void main()
{
//create Weight objects
Weight w1(50,800),w2 ;
//Adding 100 grams to w1
w2=100+w1;
cout<<"The result Weight :";
w2.output();
}
```

The statement

```
w2=100+w1;
```

invokes an operator+ function by passing 100 and w1 as arguments to it as shown in Figure 13.27. The formal argument g is initialized with 100, and the formal argument t

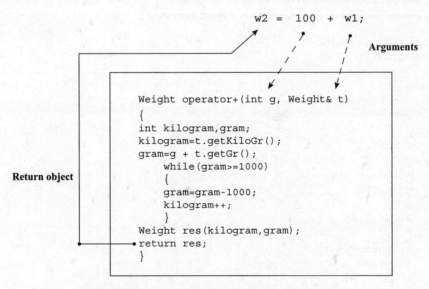

Figure 13.27: Example of a global operator function

is the reference to `Weight` object w1. Hence `t.getKiloGr()` will return the kilogram value of w1 and `t.getGr()` returns the gram value of w1 as shown in Figure 13.27. The operator functions returns an object `res` which is the resultant `Weight` object constructed after adding the 100 g to w1. The object returned by the `operator+` function is assigned to w2 and printed on the computer screen.

Note that the following statement will not work:

```
w2 =w1+100;
```

This is because the order in which the arguments are passed to the operator function is different. In this statement, the first argument is a `Weight` type object, and the second argument is an integer. To support these types of statements, we must define another operator function that accepts `Weight` object as the first argument and an integer as a second argument. Since + is a commutative operation, we simply invoke the `operator+(int,Weight)` from this function as shown below:

```
Weight operator+(Weight& t, int g)
{
Weight res = g+t; /*invokes operator+(int g, Weight& t)*/
return res;
}
```

NOTES

Operator function can also be created as a **friend function**, in this case, there is no need of functions **getKiloGr()** and **getGr()** because the operator function can itself access private members of the class. Recall, from Chapter 11 that creating friend functions is not always a good option because it breaches the principles of data hiding and encapsulation. So you should try to keep the usage of friend functions as low as possible in the program.

As an example, to show the creation of operator function as a friend function, we rewrite the above program by creating the **operator+()** function as a friend function of class `Weight`. The following is the full source code showing the creation of **global operator function** as a **friend function.**

```
#include<iostream.h>
class Weight
{
private:
        int kilogram;
        int gram;
public:
        Weight()
        {
        kilogram 6=0;
        gram=0;
        }
        Weight(int p,int q)
        {
        kilogram=p;
        gram=q;
        }
```

```
      void output()
      {
      cout<<kilogram<<" kgs and "<<gram<<" grams"<<endl;
      }
/*Declare operator function as friend of class Weight*/
friend Weight operator+(int, Weight&);
};
Weight operator+(int g, Weight& t)
{
    int kilogram,gram;
    kilogram=t.kilogram;
    gram=g + t.gram;
      while(gram>=1000)
      {
            gram=gram-1000;
            kilogram++;
      }
      Weight res(kilogram,gram);
      return res;
}
void main()
{
//create Weight objects
Weight w1(50,800),w2;
//Adding 100 grams to w1
w2=100+w1;
  cout<<"The result Weight :";
w2.output();
}
```

13.14 Overloading Insertion and Extraction Operator for `Student` Objects: An Example

We know that cout is an object of class in ostream whereas cin is an object of class istream. Details about built-in stream classes available in C++ are discussed in chapter 16, in this section we will only concentrate on overloading operators << and >> to make them work with objects. We have defined class Student with two private members roll_no and marks. If s1 is an object of class Student, our aim is to directly use extraction and insertion operators with it using the statements below

```
cin>>s1; /*To input members of s1*/
cout<<s1; /*To output members of s1*/
```

The basic principle is that the operators >> and << work with basic data types only and hence we need to extend their capability to directly input or output objects using operator overloading. If you open the header file iostream.h, you will see declarations of operator functions which overload >> and <<. It's a long list to mention all of the declarations, but a few of them have been mentioned below to explain what's happening behind the scene. As you can see, the operators >> and << are already overloaded by C++ for all the basic data types (we just said, only few of them are mentioned below). This explains why operators >> and << work well with basic data types. For instance, when you print an integer value using cout, compiler internally invokes the operator<< function which takes an int argument.

```
ostream& operator<<(short);
ostream& operator<<(int);
ostream& operator<<(long);
ostream& operator<<(float);
ostream& operator<<(double);
istream& operator>>(short &);
istream& operator>>(int &);
istream& operator>>(long &);
istream& operator>>(float &);
istream& operator>>(double &);
```

As we want to use these operators with objects of class Student, we must create operator>>() and operator<<() functions, which can accept an argument of type Student. Before we start creating those, let's have a look at the syntax used to print an integer value a on the computer screen using a cout statement

```
cout<<a;
```

It's clear that object cout invokes the operator<<() function, and the variable a is passed as an argument. As operator function is invoked by object it means that it's a member function of class ostream. istream and ostream are built-in classes, so we cannot just open and edit them. Hence, the only option is to overload operator<< and >> using **global operator functions**. Hence, the statement to print Student object s1

```
cout<<s1;
```

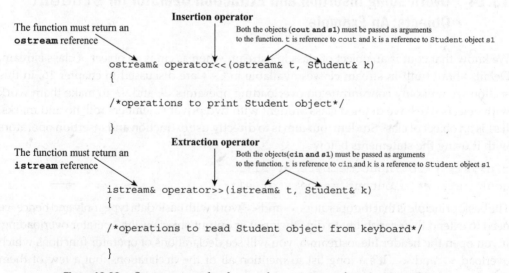

Figure 13.28: Syntax to overload >> and << operators for Student objects

should invoke the insertion operator function by passing both `cout` and `s1` as arguments. Figure 13.28 shows the syntax to overload `<<` and `>>` operators for `Student` objects.

The following is the full source code which shows the overloading of `>>` and `<<` operators for objects of class `Student`.

```
#include<iostream.h>
#include<stddef.h>
class Student
{
    private:
    int roll_no;
    int marks;
    public:
    void setValues(int r,int m)
    {
      roll_no=r;
      marks=m;
    }
    int getRollNo()
    {
      return roll_no;
    }
    int getMarks()
    {
      return marks;
    }
};
    istream& operator>>(istream& t, Student& k)
    {
      int r,m;
      t>>r>>m;
      k.setValues(r,m);
      return t;
    }
    ostream& operator<<(ostream& t, Student& k)
    {
t<<"Roll Number is "<<k.getRollNo()<<" and Marks are "<<k.
    getMarks()<<endl;
return t;
    }
    void main()
    {
      Student s1;
      cout<<"Enter roll Number and Marks of a Student"<<endl;
```

```
    cin>>s1;
    cout<<"** Student details are**"<<endl;
    cout<<s1;
}
```

The statement

```
cin>>s1;
```

invokes the global operator function >> by passing `cin` and `s1` as arguments to it. The formal argument t is a reference to object `cin`, whereas the formal argument k is a reference to object s1 as shown in Figure 13.29. The operator function accepts the values of two local

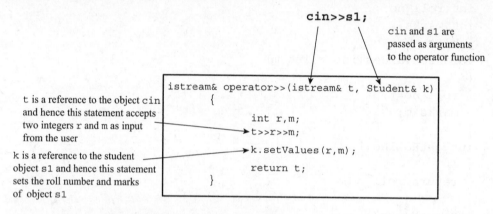

Figure 13.29: Execution of `operator>>()` function

variables r and m as input from the user. These values are the values of `roll_no` and `marks` which we want to set for a `Student` object s1–referred by k. The statement

```
k.setValues(r,m);
```

sets the value of member `roll_no` and `marks` of object s1. Note that we have invoked a public function `setValues()` because we do not have access to private members `roll_no` and marks inside the global operator function.

Similarly, the statement

```
cout<<s1;
```

invokes a global operator function<< by passing `cout` and s1 as arguments. The function internally invokes `getRollNo()` and `getMarks()` to print the value of private members `roll_no` and `marks` of `Student` object.

NOTES

`operator<<()` function returns an `ostream` reference, whereas `operator>>()` function returns an `istream` reference. This is because both the operators support **cascading of their operations**. For example, if we want to print three objects of class `Student`, we can cascade the insertion operator as

```
cout<<s1<<s2<<s3;
```

The operator function is separately invoked for printing each `Student` object. Each execution the operator function returns back an `ostream` reference which is passed as an argument to the next operator function invoked to print the another `Student` object. Similarly, we can justify why `operator>>()` returns an `istream` reference.

13.15   Overloading Operators `new` and `delete`

Operators `new` and `delete` can be overloaded to customize memory allocation and deallocation for objects of a particular class. You may need to customize object creation and deletion for a multiple reasons; for example, let's say that you need to maintain a **pool of objects** in memory and try to make use of an existing object from the pool rather than creating new object each time. In this case, when an object is deleted using `delete` keyword, you want it to be returned to the pool of available objects rather than completely removing it from memory, so that `new` uses this object the next time its invoked rather than creating an object from scratch. This improves the performance and speeds up allocation and deallocation of activities.

NOTES

Recall from Chapter 11 section 11.21, we have used the operators `new` and `delete` extensively to create nodes of a Linked list storing `Employee` objects. Each time data about a particular employee needs to be stored, the program creates a new `Node` object and stores `Employee` data in it. In this case, we are just storing three attributes (id, `name`, and `salary`) of each employee, and hence creating a new node each time may not be that expensive. However, in real practical situations, you may store large number of attributes for a particular object and hence creation of a single `Node` object **will not be quick** as the object is heavy. In such a case, you may **pre-allocate memory** for sufficient number of employees in advance. Hence the behaviour of operator `new` needs to be modified by overloading it, to **pre-create** some objects of `Node` in the object pool. The later invocations to `new` can use the objects from the pool rather than creating a new one each time. When pool is exhausted pre-allocation process can be repeated. This way, the program spends one time effort in pre-allocation, but then it can give quick service to the subsequent employees to be added to the list. This is one of the reasons why you would overload these operators.

Another reason why you might want to overload `new` and `delete` operators is when pointers are defined as members of a particular class rather than data variables. Consider class `Data` defined in the program below with two members `*p` and `*q`. When an object of this class is created using operator `new`, the default implementation of `new` will just allocate the memory for pointers, and it won't create any memory to store data values for the object. For example, the following statement

```
Data *ptr = new Data;
```

will create object of class `Data` using `new` and make the pointer named `ptr` to point to it. If we do not overload `new`, C++ uses the default global implementation of `new`, which will allocate the object memory containing only two pointers p and q as shown in Figure 13.30. Memory to store data values needs to be allocated separately by the programmer, may be inside the constructor or at any other relevant place in the program.

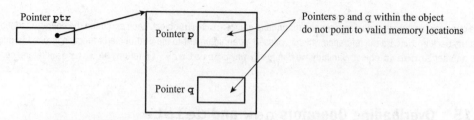

Figure 13.30: Memory allocation of Data objects using default implementation of new

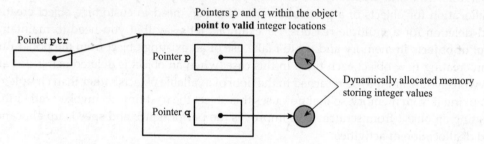

Figure 13.31: Memory allocation of Data objects using overloaded version of new

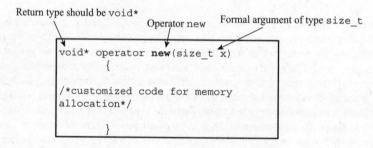

Figure 13.32: Syntax to overload operator new

Rather, it's better from programmer's point of view if creating an object of class Data using new would also allocate the memory to store data values for the object and make pointers p and q to point to the respective data value space as shown in Figure 13.31. So once the object is created, the programmer can directly store the values and perform necessary operations instead of worrying about the memory allocation of individual members. In this section, we will overload operator new, with objects of class Data to achieve this result.

Figure 13.32 shows the syntax to overload operator new. The operator new must take one single argument of type size_t and return a pointer of type void. The pointer returned points to the memory area that is allocated by the operator function.

Similarly, delete needs to be overloaded to delete the memory to which pointers p and q point when an object of class Data is deleted. Figure 13.33 shows the syntax to overload operator delete. The operator function must accept a single void pointer as an argument. This pointer points to the memory area that needs to be deleted.

The following is the source code that overloads operators new and delete for objects of type Data.

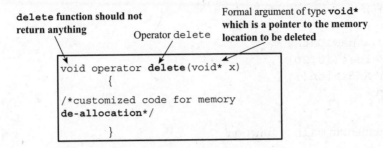

Figure 13.33: Syntax to overload operator `delete`

```cpp
#include<iostream.h>
#include<stddef.h>
class Data
{
    private:
    int *p;
    int *q;
    public:
    void * operator new(size_t x)
    {
      Data *d1 = ::new Data;
      d1->p = ::new int;
      d1->q= ::new int;
      return d1;
    }
    void setValues(int a,int b)
    {
    *p=a;
    *q=b;
    }
    void printAddition()
    {
    cout<<"Value of members *p = "<<*p<<" *q= "<<*q<<endl;
    cout<<"Addition of members is "<<(*p+*q)<<endl;
    }
    void operator delete(void *gen)
    {
    Data *x = (Data*)gen;
    ::delete x->p;
    ::delete x->q;
    ::delete x;
    cout<<"Object fully Destroyed"<<endl;
    }
};
```

```
void main()
{
Data *ptr = new Data;
ptr->setValues(10,20);
ptr->printAddition();
delete ptr;
}
```

The first statement in `main()` function

```
Data *ptr = new Data;
```

creates an object of `Data` using operator new. Since the operator new function is overloaded in class `Data`, this statement invokes the operator function. The operator function invokes the default global implementation of new by using the scope resolution operator `::` as shown in Figure 13.34.

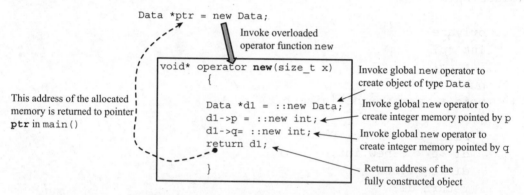

Figure 13.34: Invocation of operator new function

NOTES

`::new` refers to the **global default implementation** of new. And writing **new** without scope resolution invokes the **overloaded operator function** defined in class **Data**. This ambiguity is only in creation of objects of class **Data** because there are two versions of new for type **Data**. One of them is the global implementation of new provided by the compiler, and the other is the overloaded operator function defined by us. Hence, it is absolutely necessary to specify **scope resolution operator :** in the first statement of within the operator function because it attempts to create an object of class **Data**

```
Data *d1 = ::new Data;
```

Writing this statement without scope resolution would result in recursively calling the overloaded version of operator new, thereby taking the program in an infinite loop.
The other two statements,

```
d1->p = ::new int;
d1->q = ::new int;
```

allocate an integer memory and hence there is no ambiguity here. This is because there is only one version of new for integer types which is provided by the compiler, hence specifying scope resolution operator is optional in this case. But it's a good programming practice to always specify the scope resolution operator in cases when we have overloaded new operator. This improves the readability of the program and clearly differentiates between overloaded and global invocations of new.

The first statement in the operator function

```
Data *d1 = ::new Data;
```

creates an object of class `Data`, which is pointed by a pointer `d1`. At this stage, pointers `p` and `q` do not point to valid memory locations. The next two statements

```
d1->p = ::new int;
d1->q = ::new int;
```

make the pointers `p` and `q` to point to valid integer locations as shown in Figure 13.34. The pointer `d1` (of type `Data`), which points to the full structure is returned to the `main()` function and hence `ptr` also points to the same structure as that of `d1`.

The statements, in `main()`

```
ptr->setValues(10,20);
ptr->printAddition();
```

set the value of the pre-allocated data spaces pointer by `p` and `q` to 10 and 20, respectively. The function `printAddition()` just displays the addition of these values on the computer screen.

The last statement

```
delete ptr;
```

invokes an operator function `delete` defined in class `Data`–because the pointer `ptr` is of type `Data`. If you see the function definition of operator `delete`, it first deletes the integer memory allocated for pointers `p` and `q` and then deletes the entire object from memory as seen in the code.

Why are void type pointers used as return type of new and argument to delete operator functions? **?**

Recall from Chapter 7, void type pointers can point to data values of any type. Hence they are used make the **generic function signatures** for new and delete functions which handle memory allocation and de-allocation of different types of memory objects throughout the program. Making a return type of operator new as void*, gives the function an ability to return a pointer of any type. In this case, the operator new() function returns a pointer d1 pointing to Data block. While returning the pointer d1, the operator function implicitly casts the type of pointer d1 to void*. Any pointer can be implicitly casted to void* and hence making the return type void* gives an ability to the function to return a pointer of any type. The statement,

```
Data *ptr = new Data;
```

has an operator new which converts the void* type returned by the operator function back to the type Data*. Note that casting a void pointer back to the Data* is not done in the statement it's just that presence of new keyword takes care of it and hence we do not have to do it explicitly this time. In all the other cases, programmer needs to explicitly cast a void* pointer if it needs to be assigned to any other type.

Similarly, giving a void* type argument to delete function gives a function an ability to accept a pointer of any type thereby making its **signature** generic. The statement,

```
delete ptr;
```

passes a pointer ptr (of type Data) as an argument to delete function which is initialized to the formal argument, gen created as a pointer of type void*. The delete function is required to access members p and q defined in class Data to free up the integer memory pointed by each of them. Hence we type cast the pointer gen to type Data* in the first statement of delete function. As mentioned before, void type pointers must always be explicitly casted before initializing them to any other type

```
Data *x = (Data*)gen;
```

Once casted, the delete function uses pointer x to delete all the memory blocks for the objects of class Data. Although, there is an additional effort involved in casting, this design gives a very big advantage of making the function signatures generic. Let's say, if there is any other delete function in the program to delete objects of some other class, it will also have the same signature, or there is also a possibility to leverage the same delete function by passing different types of arguments to it. Keeping **consistent function signatures** make it easy to override the function when working with virtual functions. We will discuss **function overriding** and **virtual functions** in chapter 14, so don't worry about these terms right now. It is recommended that you revisit this discussion after going through chapter 14.

13.16   Overloading `operator ->`

We can make an object act as a pointer by overloading operator -> as a member function of the class. There could be a multiple reasons you would want to create such objects; for example, if you want to design a customized way to read data from a user-defined collections such as arrays, linked list, and so on or optimize the process that sorts or accesses the collection or perform certain boundary checks while accessing the collection using pointers, etc. In this section, we will show one of the examples to show the overloading of operator ->, but you may overload it for a different reason all together.

Let us consider that we need to store data about multiple students in computer memory. For each student we need to store roll number and marks. So, a simple solution is that we define a class Student with two members roll_no and marks and create an array of objects of type Student. Now, let's say we need this collection to be dynamic and hence array of pointers instead of an array containing direct Student objects. Each element of the array is a pointer that points to one Student object as shown in the Figure 13.35. Actually, we should create a linked list to store Student objects if we need 100% dynamism, but we are here to understand overloading of operator -> and we do not want to put a lot of complexities in the code by creating a linked list of Student. Hence, we compromise by creating array of Student objects. Let us assume that there are 5 students objects pointer by individual pointers in the array. This student data can be represented in tabular format as shown in the Figure 13.35.

Although we have shown sample values of roll_no and marks for each student in the Figure 13.36, the business requirement assures the programmer that every student is uniquely identified by his or her roll number. This means that it is safe to write a program with an assumption that no two students will have a same roll number. Since the size of array of pointers is 5 the index will range from 0 to 4. Given that the name of array is s, each individual element of an array s[0], s[1], s[2], s[3], and s[4] is actually a pointer to object of class Student as shown in the Figure 13.36.

Storage of Student objects using array of pointers

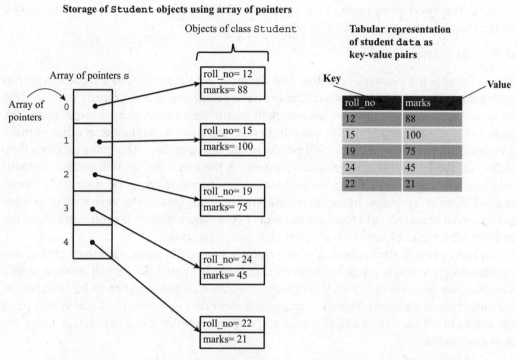

Figure 13.35: Array of pointers to store Student objects in computer memory

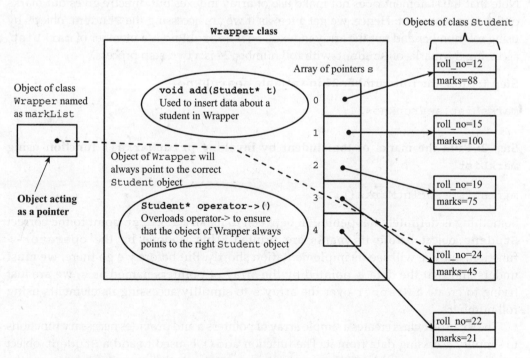

Figure 13.36: Creating a Wrapper class to simplify accessing array of pointers

So if you need print marks of a student with roll number 24, you need to invoke `printMarks()` function in class `Student` as

```
s[3]->printMarks();
```

This is because the pointer at position 3 in the array actually points to a student with roll number 24. How confusing is that! The business requirement is to identify each student by his or her roll number, but we are internally identifying a student by an array index. So, to access marks of a student with roll number 24, you need to remember another number 3 because it's the array index which points to the relevant data. The main problem here is that array elements are always accessed using their indexes. In this section, we will overload the operator `->` to access student information directly using their roll number instead of an array index. In summary, we are targeting creation of new type of pointer (let's name it as `markList`) to access the array of pointers based on the roll numbers of the student rather than built-in indexes provided by the compiler.

As mentioned in the beginning of this chapter, one of the major objectives of operator overloading is to create programs with an user friendly syntax. So we will create a simple variable, say `searchRno`, which will store the value of roll number to be searched in the collection of `Student` objects. And we will overload `operator ->` which will print the marks of the correct `Student` whose roll number is present in `searchRno`, using the statement below:

```
marksList->printMarks();
```

Note that the statement does not make use of array indexes but directly gives out marks of the correct student. Hence, we get a feel as if we are accessing the `Student` objects by using roll number and not the array indexes. So if `searchRno` is a member of `markList`, accessing the marks of `Student` with roll number 24 is a two-step process.

Step 1: Store the roll number 24 in variable `searchRno`

```
marksList.searchRno=24;
```

Step 2: Print the marks of the student by invoking `printMarks()` function using `markList`

```
marksList->printMarks();
```

Something is definitely happening in between to make `markList` point to the correct `Student` object before its marks are printed. This is done by the `operator->` function, and we will see its implementation shortly. But before we go there, we must understand that the data is pointed by the array of pointers named as `s`, we are just trying to create a `Wrapper` over the array `s` to simplify accessing its elements using roll number.

The `Wrapper` class creates a simple array of pointers `s` and provides necessary functions to simplify accessing data from it. The function `add()` is used to add a `Student` object into the wrapper, and the function `operator->` overloads the operator `->` to access the student data based on the roll number. The `operator->` function essentially traverses the array of pointers s to find the address of the correct `Student` object with a matching roll number. Once found, it returns the address to the caller.

In summary, the object of class `Wrapper` provides an additional layer of abstraction on the actual array of pointers, by simplifying the way of accessing it.

```cpp
#include<iostream.h>
class Student
{
    private:
    int roll_no;
    int marks;
    public:
    void input()
    {
      cout<<"Enter Roll Number and Marks of the student"<<endl;
      cin>>roll_no>>marks;
    }
    void output()
    {
    cout<<"Roll Number is "<<roll_no<<" and Marks are
    "<<marks<<endl;
    }
    void printMarks()
    {
      if(marks!=-1)
      cout<<"Marks are "<<marks<<endl;
    }
    friend class Wrapper;
};
class Wrapper
{
    private:
    Student *s[100];
    int size;
    public:
    int searchRno;
    Student temp; // dummy object to be used if Student not
    present in the list
    public:
    Wrapper()
    {
      size=0;
    }
```

```cpp
    void add(Student* t)
    {
       if(size<100)
       {
       s[size]=t;
       size++;
       }
       else
       {
       cout<<"Array is full, Student object cannot be added"<<endl;
       }
    }
    Student* operator->()
    {
       int i=0;
       while(i<size && s[i]->roll_no!=searchRno)
       {
       i++;
       }
       if(i!=size)
       {
       /*Student found*/
       return s[i];
       }
       else
       {
       cout<<"No student found with Roll Number = "
       <<searchRno<<endl;
       /*Returning dummy Student object to avoid NULL pointer
       exception*/
       temp.roll_no=-1;
       temp.marks=-1;
       return &temp;
       }
}
};
void main()
{
Wrapper marksList;
Student s1,s2,s3,s4,s5;
int choice=1;
s1.input();
s2.input();
s3.input();
```

```
s4.input();
s5.input();
marksList.add(&s1);
marksList.add(&s2);
marksList.add(&s3);
marksList.add(&s4);
marksList.add(&s5);
    while(choice==1)
    {
cout<<"Enter the Roll Number of the student whose marks are needed
    "<<endl;
    cin>>marksList.searchRno;
    marksList->printMarks();
    cout<<"Press 1 to continue and any other key to exit"<<endl;
    cin>>choice;
    }
}
```

The first statement in `main()`

```
Wrapper marksList;
```

creates an object of class `Wrapper` named as `markList`. The default constructor of the `Wrapper` initializes the member `size=0` to indicate that there are no `Student` objects currently inside the wrapper, as its just being created. We have created 5 objects of class `Student` [s1, s2, s3, s4, and s5] and invoked `input()` function over each of them to accept roll number and marks as input from the user for each of the students.

We have added each of them to the `markList` wrapper by invoking the `add()` function of the `Wrapper` class. For example, consider the statement `marksList.add(&s1);`

Since the value of variable size is zero at the moment, the `add()` function stores the address of object `s1` in the array at the index zero. It also increments the variable size by 1 to indicate that there is one element in the array now. Hence, variable `size` always represents the number of elements in the wrapper at any point of time. Similarly, the objects `s2`, `s3`, `s4`, and `s5` are added to the array by making call to add function for each of them as seen in the code. The `add()` function also checks the boundary conditions and displays necessary error message to the programmer if the array pointers become full. Note that since we have created an array of pointers with size 100, we will not be able to add more than 100 students inside the wrapper.

Given that we have now stored a sufficient `Student` objects in the wrapper, we will start accessing the marks of the students based on their roll number. The statements

```
cout<<"Enter the Roll Number of the student whose marks are needed
    "<<endl;
cin>>marksList.searchRno;
```

accept the roll number whose marks are to be looked up. We have intentionally created `searchRno` as a public variable of `Wrapper`, so that it can be easily taken as input from the user by the `main()` function.

The statement

```
marksList->printMarks();
```

invokes the operator -> function which searches the exact location in array s, which points to the student with the matching roll number. If the Student object is found, the operator function returns a pointer that Student object. Hence, this statement internally takes the following form after execution of the operator-> function.

(Pointer to a Student Object)->printMarks();

We know that -> in its ordinary usage is used to access the members of the object to which it points. And hence, it invokes the printMarks() function of the Student object with matching roll number. The execution of the operator function is as shown in the Figure 13.37. Note that the operator function can access private members of class Student directly because class Wrapper is created as a friend class of class Student.

Note that if a Student object with a matching roll number is not found in the array, the operator function returns a dummy object of type Student. This is because if it does not return any object and simply returns NULL, it would internally translate the statement marksList->printMarks();as

```
NULL->printMarks();
```

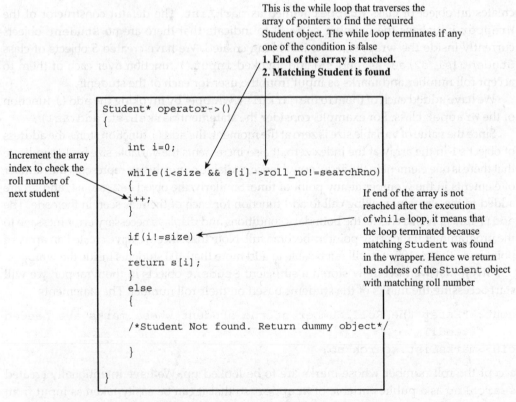

Figure 13.37: Overloaded **operator->()** function

This will produce a runtime error in the program because you cannot access a member of a pointer which is pointing to NULL. Hence to avoid program crashing at runtime in this specific case, we return a dummy Student object with marks = -1, so that the printMarks() function gets correctly invoked. If you see the definition of printMarks() function, it prints the value of variable marks only if it's not equal to -1. This avoids printing marks of the dummy object on the computer screen. This whole process is put in a while loop created in main() so that the user can continue fetching marks of the student by inputting the roll number. User can enter any value of variable choice other than 1 to exit the loop, which will stop the execution of the program.

ONE STEP AHEAD

Advanced programming languages like **Java** support built-in **Wrapper** classes which wrap basic data types into object types to simplify accessing elements from collections. We have designed one of the built-in features of Java in our program because **C++** does not have such wrapper classes in its core libraries. In the above example, we have stored student data as key-value pair, where roll number is a key and marks is the value. A data structure that stores data in this format is called as **Map**. C++ has a standard template library(STL) which supports multiple collections and **Map** is one of them, we have discussed STL in chapter 16. In this program we have achieved effect of **Map** by **overloading ->** and by creating our own wrapper class.

NOTES

If you only look at the main() function, it just creates a Wrapper object named as **markList**, adds Student objects in it and accesses these objects based on roll number. All main() needs to do is to store the correct roll number in the variable searchRno and use the -> operator with the Wrapper object to get the student details.

We have added **additional features** to the arrow operator, which gives the programmers a feeling that **markList** always points to the correct Student object with matching roll number.

All the complexities involved in this access are handled by the Wrapper class. main() need not worry about the internal complexities of the Wrapper but only needs to know how to use it. Hence by making correct use of operator overloading, we have provided a **layer of abstraction** to programmers by hiding the complexities and simplify the coding styles. Currently, we have created the Wrapper class specifically for Student objects, but could generalize it and release it as a library with some documentation, so that others can use our class directly.

Points to Remember when Overloading an Operator

We have overloaded multiple operators of C++ in this chapter to make them work with user-defined data types. We will quickly summarize the rules that must be followed when overloading an operator in C++:

1. There must be an operator function defined for every operator which is to be overloaded.
2. Operator function can be defined as a member function of the class or it can be defined globally.
3. If the operator function is defined as a member function, compiler invokes the operator function using the object that appears on the left hand side of the operator and passes the object on the right hand side as an argument to it.

4. Global operator function does not require any object to invoke it; hence, they are used when the left hand side of the operator in the expression is not an object–for example, if the left hand side of the operator is a constant.

5. Following operators **cannot** be overloaded
   - `sizeof`
   - `?:` (Ternary operator)
   - `.` membership operator
   - `.*` (Pointer to a member)
   - `::` (Scope resolution operator)
   - `static_cast`
   - `dynamic_cast`
   - `const_cast`
   - `reinterprete_cast`

Operator overloading, when used in the right way, can provide a very high degree of abstraction to the programmer in creating programs that need complex operations with user-defined data types. Hence, this feature provided by C++ is widely used by the developers to create programs with a user friendly syntax.

Solved Example 13.1

Write a C++ program to perform concatenation of strings by overloading operator +.

Solution

```cpp
#include<iostream.h>
#include<string.h>
class String
{
private:
char *str;
public:
    String ()
    {
    }
    String(char *p)
    {
    str = new char[strlen(p)+1] ;
    strcpy(str,p);
    }
    String operator + (String t)
    {
    char *res;
    res= new char[strlen(str) + strlen(t.str)+1];
    res = strcat(str, t.str);
    return String(res);
    }
```

```
    void output()
    {
    cout<<str<<endl;
    }
};
void main()
{
cout<<"String Concat using operator overloading"<<endl;
String s1("Computer");
String s2("Programming");
String s3;
s3 = s1+s2;
s3.output();
}
```

Output

```
String Concat using operator overloading
ComputerProgramming
```

SCRATCH PAD

The first statement in `main()`

```
String s1("Computer");
```

creates a `String` object `s1` by invoking a dynamic constructor and passing a string "Computer" as an argument to the constructor. Hence the member `str` of object `s1` will now point to the string "Computer" as shown in the Figure 13.38.

Similarly, the second line in `main()`

```
String s2("Programming");
```

creates a `String` object `s2` by invoking a dynamic constructor and passing a string "Programming" as the argument to the constructor. Hence, the member `str` of object `s2` will now point to the string "Programming" as shown in the Figure 13.38.

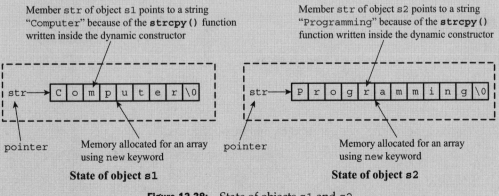

Member `str` of object `s1` points to a string "Computer" because of the **strcpy()** function written inside the dynamic constructor

Member `str` of object `s2` points to a string "Programming" because of the **strcpy()** function written inside the dynamic constructor

str → | C | o | m | p | u | t | e | r | \0 |

str → | P | r | o | g | r | a | m | m | i | n | g | \0 |

pointer   Memory allocated for an array
           using new keyword

pointer   Memory allocated for an array
           using new keyword

State of object s1

State of object s2

Figure 13.38: State of objects s1 and s2

The statement

```
s3 = s1+s2;
```

will invoke an operator function using object s1 and object s2 will be passed as an argument to the function. This means that the member str of object s1 can be directly accessed inside the operator function because the function is invoked by object s1 itself. Also, object s2 is passed as an argument and will be initialized to the formal argument t which is created as a part of operator function, and hence the member str of s2 can now be accessed using object t as **t.str** as shown in the code.

Also, we create a pointer res inside the operator function to point to the resultant String, which should be the concatenation of individual Strings present in objects s1 and s2. This means that the length of the resultant string will be the addition of length of s1's string and length of s2's string. Hence, we allocate the memory for result using the statement below:

```
res= new char[strlen(str) + strlen(t.str)+1];
```

Further, the **strcat()** function used inside the operator function makes the pointer res to point to the concatenation of strings pointed by member str of object s1 and member str of object s2 ("Computer" + "Programming" = "ComputerProgramming"). Also, the object of class String is created using res and returned to the main() function. Hence, the object s3 now contains the concatenation of strings present in s1 and s2 as shown in the Figure 13.39.

The statement s3.output(); invokes the output() function to print the result string stored inside object s3 as seen from the last line of main() function.

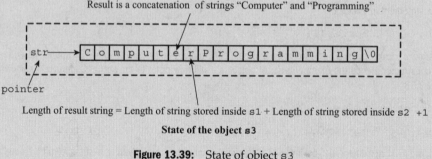

Figure 13.39: State of object s3

Quiz

1. Operator overloading in C++ facilitates.
    (a) Runtime polymorphism
    (b) Compile time polymorphism
    (c) Abstraction
    (d) a and c
    (e) b and c

2. Which of the following operators cannot be overloaded?
    (a) +
    (b) ++
    (c) sizeof
    (d) ->

3. The operator function must return _____ value when an relational operator is to be overloaded.
   (a) Any character value
   (b) Boolean value 0 or 1
   (c) Any integer value
   (d) The operator function should not return any value

4. Operator function can be written as
   (a) Member function of the class
   (b) Friend function of the class
   (c) A global function
   (d) None of the above

5. Which of the following is not included as a part of function signature?
   (a) Name of the function
   (b) Number of arguments the function takes
   (c) Data type of arguments
   (d) Return type of the function

6. If o1 is an object of a class Abc, then in which of the following evaluations it is mandatory to create a global operator function?
   (a) o1*o2
   (b) o1*9
   (c) 9*o2
   (d) None of the above

7. Function overloading facilitates
   (a) Encapsulation
   (b) Compile time polymorphism
   (c) Data hiding
   (d) Runtime polymorphism

8. What will be the number of arguments that the operator function will take when a binary operator is overloaded by creating an operator function as a member function of the class?
   (a) 1   (b) 2   (c) 3   (d) 4

9. What will be the number of arguments that the operator function will take when a unary operator is overloaded by creating an operator function as a global function?
   (a) 1   (b) 2   (c) 3   (d) 4

10. Which of the following statements is correct?
    (a) Early binding is performed for all the operator functions.
    (b) Late binding is performed for all the operator functions.
    (c) The type of binding to be performed depends on the program that we write and there is no general rule for operator function.
    (d) Binding is not performed for operator functions.

Error Finding Exercise

Given are some programs that may or may not contain errors. Correct the errors if they exist in the code and/or determine the output.

Program 1

```
#include<iostream.h>
class DATA
```

```
{
float a;
int b;
public:
    DATA()
    {
    a=0
    b=-10;
    }
    DATA(int p,int q)
    {
    a=p;
    b=q;
    }
    void add(DATA t)
    {
    DATA res;
    res.a=a+t.a;
    res.b=b+t.b;
    return res;
    }
    void output()
    {
    cout<<"a="<<a<<"b="<<b;
    }
    };
void main()
{
DATA d1(10,20);
DATA d2,d3;
d3=d1+d3;
d3.output()
}
```

Program 2

```
#include<iostream.h>
class DATA
{
float a;
public:
    void set_data(int p)
    {
    a=p;
    }
```

```
        int operator<=(DATA t)
        {
        if(a>t.a)
        {
        return 0;
        }
        return 1;
        }
        void output()
        {
        cout<<"a="<<a<<"b="<<b;
        }
};
void main()
{
DATA d1, d2,d3;
d1.set_data(10);
d2.set_data(20);
d3.set_data(30);
        if(d1>d2)
        {
        cout<<"d1 is greater than d2"<<endl;
        }
        else
        {
        cout<<"d1 is not greater than d2" <<endl;
        }
        if(d1<=d3)
        {
        cout<<"d1 is less than or equal to d3" <<endl;
        }
        else
        {
        cout<<"d1 is greater than d3" <<endl;
        }
}
```

Program 3

```
#include<iostream.h>
class DATA
{
float a;
int b;
public:
```

```
DATA()
{
a=50
b=-100;
}
DATA(int p,int q)
{
a=p;
b=q;
}
DATA operator+()
{
DATA res;
res.a=a+d2.a;
res.b=b+d2.b;
return res;
}
void output()
{
cout<<"a="<<a<<"b="<<b;
}
};
void main()
{
DATA d1(10,20);
DATA d2,d3;
d3=d1+d3;
d3.output()
}
```

Program 4

```
#include<iostream.h>
class DATA
{
float a;
int b;
public:
DATA()
{
a=50
b=-100;
}
DATA(int p,int q)
{
```

```
    a=p;
    b=q;
    }
friend DATA operator+(DATA);
    void output()
    {
    cout<<"a="<<a<<"b="<<b;
    }
};
DATA operator+(DATA t)
{
DATA res;
res.a=a+t.a;
res.b=b+t.b;
return res;
}
void main()
{
DATA d1(10,20);
DATA d2,d3;
d3=d1+d3;
d3.output()
}
```

Review Questions

1. Explain operator overloading with appropriate examples.
2. Explain operator overloading for a binary operator with and without a friend function.
3. Write a C++ program to overload operator += to add two objects of class `Time`. Each object of `Time` is specified in terms of minutes and seconds. The program should take two `Time` objects as input from the user and print the result of += operation.
4. What is an operator function? Describe the operator function with syntax and rules of its creation.
5. Write a C++ program to create a class `Date` with members dd, mm, yy. Overload ++ and -- operators to increment/decrement the value of `Date` object. Also, consider the case of leap year while incrementing/decrementing date.
6. Write a program to overload operators +, – and * for performing addition, subtraction, and multiplication of `Matrix` objects respectively. Create a class `Matrix` and overload operators by writing operator functions as friend functions of class `Matrix`.
7. Write a C++ program to overload new and delete operators.
8. What is compile time binding? Explain with examples.

Chapter

14 | Inheritance

14.1 Overview

Inheritance is a relationship between classes wherein one class is derived from another class. The derived class is called child class, and the class from which it is derived is called parent class. Inheritance is also called as parent–child relationship between classes such that child class gives a specialized implementation of parent class. **Reusability** of the code is the key principle of inheritance because the properties defined in the parent class are borrowed by the child class. Inheritance is one of the most important features of object oriented programming, wherein the classes are organized in a **hierarchical** form. The class at the top of hierarchy is called **parent class**, whereas the class at the bottom of the hierarchy is called **child class**. Advantage of inheritance is that the **members** (variables and functions) defined by the parent class are also made available into the child class. This saves the programmers efforts to redevelop logic in child class, which is already implemented in parent class. Along with the properties defined in parent class, the child class can also have additional properties of its own as shown in the Figure 14.1. Hence the parent class is also called **Base class/Super class/Generalized class** and the child class is also called **Derived class/Sub class/Specialized class.**

As seen from the Figure 14.1, the member1 and member2 are defined in the parent class, which are available by default, in the child class. Also, child class can define additional members such as member3 and member4. This means that if you create an object of parent class, it will contain only two members: member1 and member2; whereas, if you create an object of child class, it will contain four members: member1, member2, member3, and member4. Therefore, a parent class should define the common properties that are required by all the child classes, whereas each of child class should define the specialized properties applicable only for that child.

As an example, let's assume that we need to store data about students and professors in a particular institute in computer memory. The requirement is that for every person (a student or a professor)we need to store name, date of birth, and gender. The only attribute difference is that professor has two additional attributes salary and prof_id which student does not, and student has additional attributes marks and roll_no, which professor does not. This means that for every student object, we need to store following information in computer memory:

1. Name
2. Date of Birth(dob)

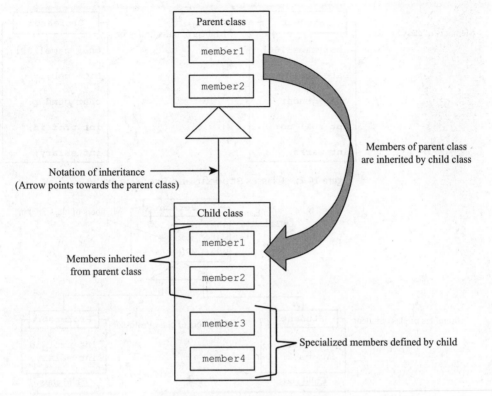

Figure 14.1: Principle of inheritance

3. Gender
4. Roll Number(roll_no)
5. Marks

Also, for every `Professor` object, we plan to store following information in computer memory:

1. Name
2. Date of Birth
3. Gender
4. Professor Identifier(prof_id)
5. Salary

Figure 14.2 shows the attributes of classes `Student` and `Professor` with the attribute differences highlighted in boldface.

Having members `name`, `dob`, and `gender` is a common requirement of `Student` and `Professor` classes. Instead of duplicating this code in both the classes, we can create a common parent class named as `Person` which defines the common members. We then create `Student` and `Professor` as child classes of class `Person` as shown in the Figure 14.3. As we have created a relationship of inheritance, all the child classes will

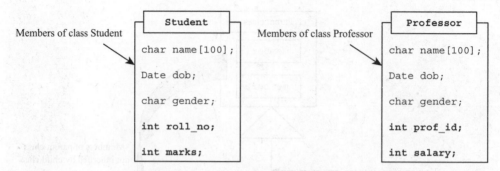

Figure 14.2: Classes Student and Professor

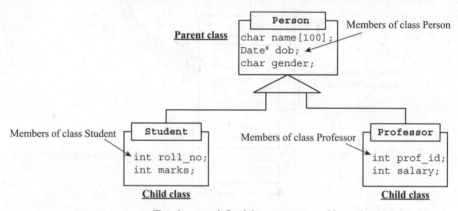

*Date is a user-defined data type as created in section 14.5.

Figure 14.3: Inheritance

by default borrow the members defined in the parent class. This means that we need not create the members name, gender, and dob separately in Student and Professor because they will be inherited from the parent class Person. The child classes Student and Professor should only define the specialized members required by them. This means that, the only members to be defined in class Student are roll_no and marks, whereas those in class Professor should be prof_id and salary as shown in the Figure 14.3. The notation of inheritance is an arrow head drawn from each child which points to the parent class as seen in the Figure 14.3.

Similar to member variables, common member functions can also be defined at a parent level, thereby avoiding duplication of the code in each of the child classes.

Why is the notation of inheritance such that the arrow head points towards the parent class? ?

The arrow drawn from the child class indicates that we can access the members and member functions of the parent class using the object of child class. Note that, the direction of inheritance is always from "parent" to "child", however the arrow head represents the direction of "allowed access" and hence the arrow head is from child to parent. This is a UML notation of inheritance. UML stands for unified modelling language which is used for object oriented analysis and design.

14.2 Creating a Parent–Child Relationship between Classes

Figure 14.4 gives the syntax for creating a parent–child relationship between classes. While defining a child class, we must add a colon followed by the <accessType> and the name of the 'parent' class as shown in the Figure 14.4. The <accessType> can be `private` or `public` or `protected`.

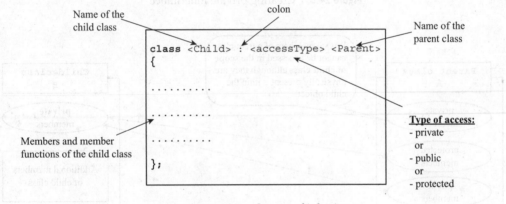

Figure 14.4: Syntax of inheritance

Let class `A` be a parent class and class `B` be a child class, therefore the members and member functions of class `A` will be inherited by class `B`. However, the visibility of the members inherited by class `B` will depend on the <accessType> specified while implementing inheritance. As mentioned earlier, <accessType> can be specified as `private`, `protected` or `public`.

When the <accessType> is specified as `private` while creating the child class `B`, the inheritance is then called **'private inheritance'** as shown in the Figure 14.5.

In case of private inheritance, the public/protected members of parent class `A` will be inherited as `private` members in child class `B`. This means that if any member is defined as `public` or `protected` in a parent class `A`, then it will be treated as if it's a `private` member in the child class `B`. The private members of the parent class `A` can never be accessed inside the child class `B`, although they are inherited and physically present in the object of `B`. Concept of private inheritance is as shown in Figure 14.6.

When the <accessType> is specified as `protected` while creating the child class `B`, the inheritance is then called **'protected inheritance'** as shown in the Figure 14.7.

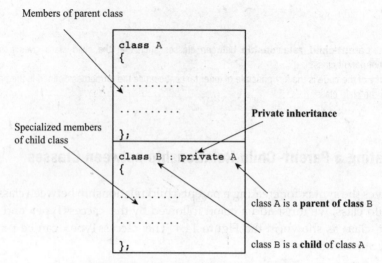

Members of parent class

class A
{
....
....
};

Private inheritance

Specialized members
of child class

class B : private A
{
....
....
};

class A is a **parent of class** B

class B is a **child** of class A

Figure 14.5: Creating private inheritance

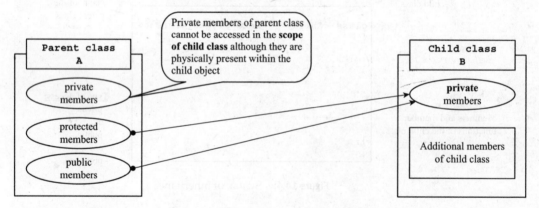

Parent class
A

Private members of parent class
cannot be accessed in the **scope
of child class** although they are
physically present within the
child object

Child class
B

private
members

protected
members

public
members

private
members

Additional members
of child class

Figure 14.6: Private inheritance

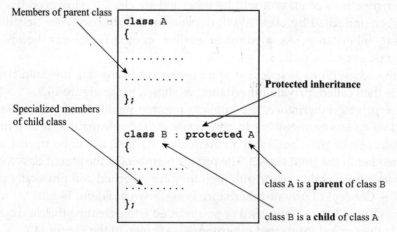

Members of parent class

class A
{
....
....
};

Protected inheritance

Specialized members
of child class

class B : protected A
{
....
....
};

class A is a **parent** of class B

class B is a **child** of class A

Figure 14.7: Creating protected inheritance

In case of protected inheritance, the public/protected members of parent class A will be inherited as `protected` members in child class B. This means that if any member is defined as `public` or `protected` in a parent class A, then it will be inherited as a `protected` member in the child class B as shown the Figure 14.8. Again, the private members of the parent class A can never be accessed inside the child class B, although they are inherited and physically present in the object of B.

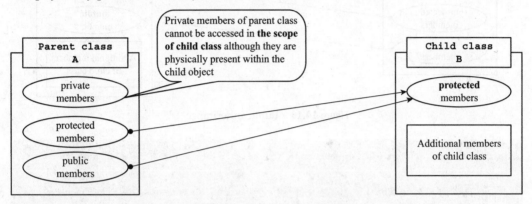

Figure 14.8: Protected inheritance

When the <accessType> is specified as `public` while creating the child class B, the inheritance is then called '**public inheritance**' as shown in the Figure 14.9.

In case of public inheritance, the public members of parent class A will be inherited as `public` members in child class B. The `protected` members of parent class A will be inherited as `protected` members in child class B. As with other types of inheritance, the private members of the parent class A can never be accessed inside the child class B. Concept of public inheritance is as shown the Figure 14.10.

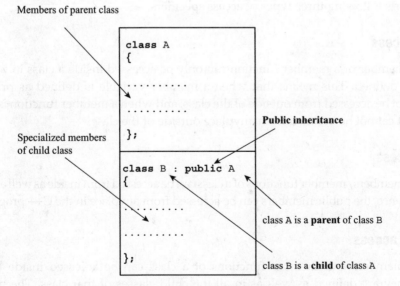

Figure 14.9: Creating public inheritance

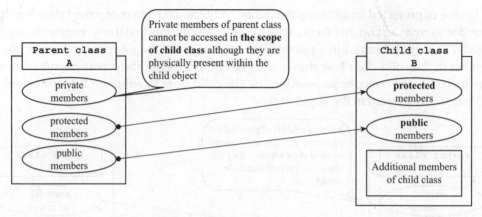

Figure 14.10 Public inheritance

How do I make a choice between private, public and protected inheritance? ?

Selecting between private, public or protected inheritance depends upon the requirements of data hiding to be implemented in the child class. It is recommended to use public inheritance since it preserves the access rules defined by the parent even in the child class. The choice to select appropriate access level for inheritance is still left to the programmer

In this book, we will write all the inheritance programs using **'public inheritance'** because it gives us maximum degree of reusability.

14.3 Access Specifiers in C++: Revisited

C++ supports following three types of access specifiers:

Private access

A private member or a member function can only be accessed inside a class in which the member is defined. This means that when a member variable is defined as private, its value cannot be accessed from outside of the class; and when a member function is defined as private it cannot be invoked from anyplace outside of the class.

Public access

The public members/member functions of a class can be accessed from inside as well as outside the class. Hence, the public members can be accessed from anyplace in the C++ program.

Protected access

Protected members and member functions of a class can be accessed inside the class in which they are defined as well as in all the child classes of that class. The protected members cannot be accessed by any class which is not a child of the class in which they are defined. Hence, a `protected` access is similar to `private` access, with the only difference being that the `protected` members can be accessed by the child classes as well.

As an example, let us create a class Abc with integer members a, b, and c, such that the variable a is private, variable b is protected, and variable c is public. Also, we create public functions setA() and getA() inside class Abc to initialize and return the value of private variable a and public functions setB(), and getB() to initialize and return the value of protected member b. Note that the setter and getter functions for variable c will not be required because c is a public member of class Abc, and it can be directly accessed in child as well as non-child class of Abc.

We create two classes C1 and C2, such that C1 is a child class of Abc, and C2 is a non-child as shown in the Figure 14.11. Both the classes C1 and C2 have a member

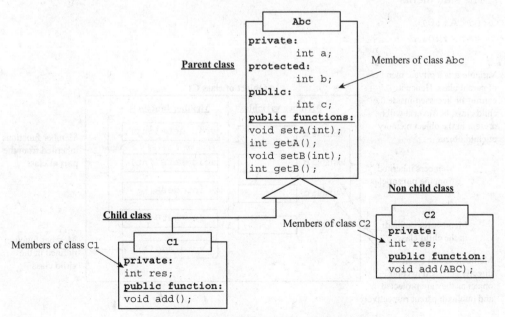

Figure 14.11: Classes Abc, C1, and C2

variable `res` and a member function `add()` as shown in the Figure 14.11. To understand the concept of access specifiers in C++, let us write a code that sets the value of variable `res` in objects of `C1` and `C2`, as the addition of members a, b and c defined in class `Abc`.

As per figure 14.11, `C1` is required to be created as a child class of `Abc`, hence we have defined `C1` as follows in the program:

```
class C1: public Abc /*Create C1 as a child class of class Abc
    using public inheritance*/
{

....... .
....... . .
};
```

The object of class `C1` will inherit the members and member functions of class `Abc` as shown in the Figure 14.12. Along with the inherited members, the object of class `C1` will also contain the member variable `res` and the member function `add()`, which are defined as specialized members of class `C1`.

The statement

```
C1 o1;
```

creates an object of class `C1`, named as `o1`.

As seen, the members/member functions of parent class `Abc` are also the part of child object `o1`. This means that we will now be able to access members of class `Abc` using the `o1`, subject to the controls imposed by access specifiers.

The statements

```
o1.setA(10);
o1.setB(20);
```

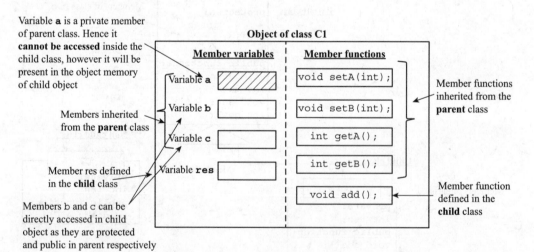

Figure 14.12: Object of class `C1`

invoke public functions like setA() and setB() using object o1. These are public functions invoked to initialize the members a and b. They essentially provide a gateway to initialize the private member a and protected member b from outside class.

As setA() is a member function of class Abc, when o1 invokes the setA() function the control of execution is actually transferred inside class Abc as shown in the Figure 14.13. Given that setA() is defined inside class Abc, we can directly access the **private member** a within the body of function setA(). The function initializes member variable a with an argument passed to it. Hence the following statement:

```
o1.setA(10);
```

will set the value of member a of object o1 as 10 as shown in the Figure 14.13.

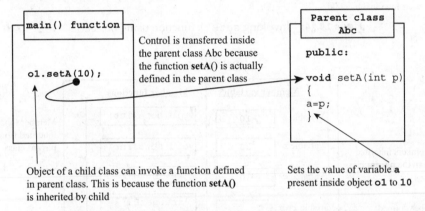

Figure 14.13: Invoking setA() function using object o1

NOTES

o1 is an object of class C1, whereas the function setA() is defined in class Abc, you can still invoke setA() using o1 because C1 is a **child class** of Abc.

Similarly, we invoke a function setB() of a parent class using object o1 to initialize protected member b to 20 as shown in the Figure 14.14. In actuality, there is no restriction imposed by the protected access specifier for us to enter in the scope of parent class to initialize the value of member b, however we are doing it in this case because there is a function named as setB() already defined within the scope of class Abc, and there is no reason for us to create another function for the same reason again in the child class. Yet, if the programmers want to define a function in the child class to do the same job, they are free to do so technically, but this would be silly because you are defining the same thing again in child, which could be rather be reused from parent. Don't forget, **reusability of code** is one of the major reasons of implementing inheritance.

The initialization of the member c can be done directly from the main() function because the member c is the public member inherited by the object o1. Hence, we can initialize the value of member c directly from main() using the statement below:

```
o1.c=30;
```

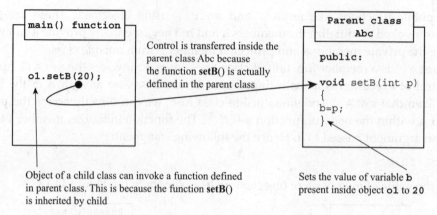

Object of a child class can invoke a function defined in parent class. This is because the function **setB()** is inherited by child

Sets the value of variable **b** present inside object **o1** to **20**

Figure 14.14: Invoking `setB()` function using object `o1`

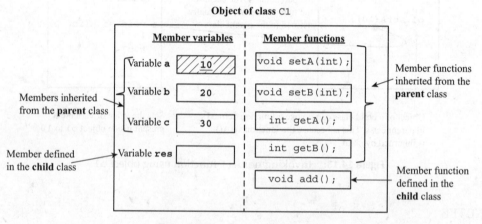

Figure 14.15: State of object `o1`

Figure 14.15 gives the state of child object `o1` with the values of a, b, and c initialized.

Let us invoke a member function `add()` to perform the addition of a, b, and c and store the result in `res`. The outside world can directly invoke a function `add()` because it is a public member function of class C1. Hence, we invoke the function using `o1` as shown below:

```
o1.add();
```

On calling the function `add()` the control of execution will actually be transferred inside child class C1, this is because the member function `add()` is actually defined inside class C1 as shown in Figure 14.16. Variables b and c are `protected` and `public` members of parent class Abc and hence they can be directly accessed inside the child class C1 as shown in the Figure 14.16. However, the member a is a private member of class Abc and hence we cannot directly access its value in the body of `add()` function. This is because the function `add()` is defined in class C1 and member a cannot be accessed at any place outside class Abc.

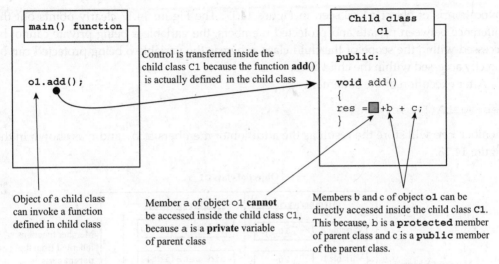

Figure 14.16: Access to members b and c in a member function of child class

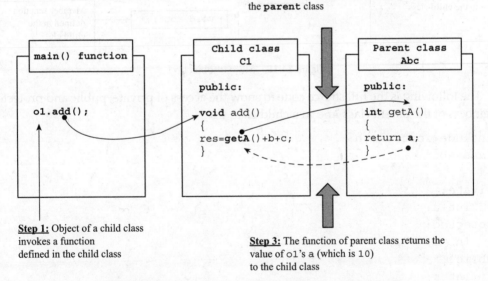

Figure 14.17 Access to member a inside the child class

Although the variable a is present in the object memory of child object o1 it can only be accessed within the body of parent class Abc, because it's defined as private in class Abc.

Therefore, we invoke a member function getA() from function add() which transfers the control of execution inside the parent class Abc as shown in the Figure 14.17. The function getA() can be directly invoked from the body of function add() because getA() in itself is a public function of the parent class Abc, which is inherited by the child. The value of member a of object o1 (which is 10) will be returned by the getA() function because its invocation is of object o1 as seen in Figure 14.17. The Figure 14.17 clearly points out the difference between private and protected members, the variable a being private cannot be accessed within the scope of the child class, whereas the variable b being protected can be directly accessed within the child class.

After execution of the statement

```
res= getA()+b+c;
```

member res will store the result as the addition of members a, b, and c as shown in the Figure 14.18.

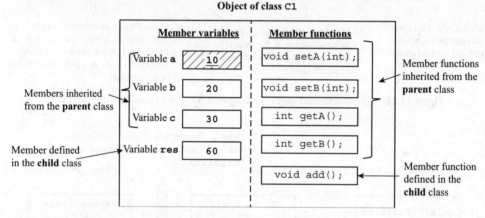

Figure 14.18 State of object o1

The following is the full source code to show the access of private, public and protected members of the parent class Abc in a child class C1.

```
#include<iostream.h>
class Abc
{
private:
    int a;
protected:
    int b;
public:
    int c;
    void setA(int p)
    {
    a=p;
    }
    int getA()
    {
    return a;
    }
    void setB(int p)
```

```
{
b=p;
}
    int getB()
    {
    return b;
    }
};
class C1: public Abc
{
private:
int res;
public:
    void add()
    {
    res=getA()+b+c;
    cout<<"Result of addition is "<<res<<endl;
    }
};
void main()
{
C1 o1;
o1.setA(10);
o1.setB(20);
o1.c=30;
o1.add();
}
```

Output

```
Result of addition is 60
```

Is the private member of parent also present in the memory of child object? **?**

  Yes, the private member of the parent class will also be present in the memory of the **child object** but you cannot access the private member defined by the parent from anyplace in the child class. In the above example we see that the variable a is a private member of the parent class Abc, but still present in the object memory of the child object o1. The statement below applies sizeof operator to determine the size of child object:

```
cout<<"The size of child object is "<<sizeof(o1);
```

We will get the result as 8 bytes because the size of child object is calculated as

```
sizeof(a) + sizeof(b) + sizeof(c) + sizeof(res) = 8 Bytes[1]
```

---

[1] Assuming 16 bit compiler where a single integer is 2 bytes in size.

This proves that member a(which is private) is also present within the memory of child object. However, due to the rules imposed by the private access specifier, we cannot access the value of a inside any function defined in the child class C1.

In order to access the value of member a we must invoke the functions setA()/getA() which are defined in the parent class Abc.

Now, let us create a non-child class C2 with a member res and a member function add(). Obviously, the object of class C2 will not inherit any members or member functions of class Abc because C2 is not a child class of class Abc. This means that the object of class C2 will only contain a member res and a member function add() as shown in the figure 14.19. The statement

```
C2 o2;
```

creates object of class C2 named as o2.

Object of class C2

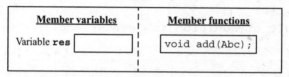

Figure 14.19: Object of class C2

The members a, b and c are not present in the object memory of a non-child object o2, which is a major difference when compared with the object memory of the child object o1, where all the members of class Abc were by default inherited. However, the requirement is that we need to set the value of member res present inside the non-child object o2 as the addition of values of members a, b, and c of class Abc. As these members are not present in the object memory of o2, we will have to create a separate object of class Abc using the statement below:

```
Abc a1;
```

Object a1 will contain members a, b, and c as shown in the Figure 14.20. We will make use of these member variables to perform addition.

Object of class Abc

Member variables

Members variables of class Abc ⟶

Variable **a**

Variable **b**

Variable **c**

Member functions

```
void setA(int);
void setB(int);
int getA();
int getB();
```

Member functions of class Abc

Figure 14.20: Object of class Abc

The statements

```
a1.setA(100);
a1.setB(200);
a1.c=300;
```

initialize the value of members a, b and c for object a1.

Functions setA() and setB() are invoked to initialize the members a and b because these members are private and protected, respectively, and hence they cannot be directly accessed by the outside world. The new state of object a1 will now be as shown in the Figure 14.21:

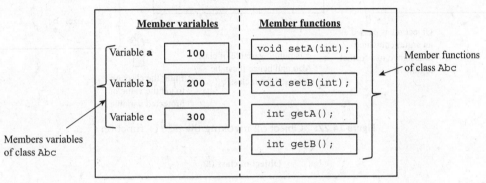

Figure 14.21: State of object a1

The statement

```
o2.add(a1);
```

passes object a1 as an argument to add() function. Hence the members of object a1 can be accessed using object t (which is the name of the formal argument) inside add() as shown in the Figure 14.22.

The members a and b will not be accessible in the non-child class C2; this is because these members are created as private and protected members of class Abc, respectively. I say it once again that the private and protected members of parent class cannot be accessed in any of the non-child classes. Therefore, the only way to access the values a and b in the body of function add() is by invoking the functions getA() and getB() using object t as shown the Figure 14.22. t.getA() and t.getB() will return the value of a(100) and b(200) of object a1, this is because object t is a formal argument corresponding to the actual argument a1. The c value of object a1 can be directly accessed using object t because c is a public variable of class Abc.

After execution of the statement

```
res=t.getA()+t.getB()+t.c;
```

member res of object o2 will store the result as the addition of members a, b, and c of object a1 as shown in the Figure 14.23.

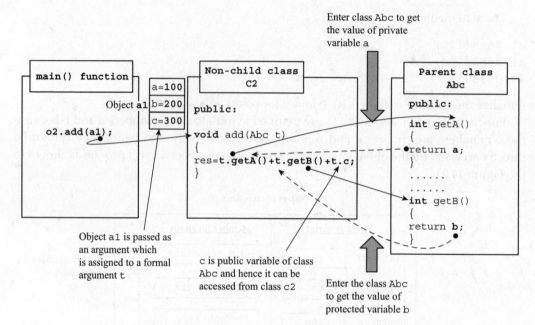

Figure 14.22: Object o2 invoking the add() function

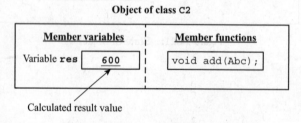

Figure 14.23: State of object o2

The following is the full source code to show the access of private, public, and protected members of the class Abc inside a non-child class C2.

```cpp
#include<iostream.h>
class Abc
{
private:
    int a;
protected:
    int b;
public:
    int c;
    void setA(int p)
    {
    a=p;
```

```
    }
    int getA()
    {
    return a;
    }
    void setB(int p)
    {
    b=p;
    }
    int getB()
    {
    return b;
    }
};
class C2
{
private:
    int res;
public:
    void add(Abc t)
    {
    res=t.getA()+t.getB()+t.c;
    cout<<"Result of addition is "<<res<<endl;
    }
};
void main()
{
C2 o2;
Abc a1;
a1.setA(100);
a1.setB(200);
a1.c=300;
o2.add(a1);
}
```

Output

```
Result of addition is 600
```

Why do we pass the object of class Abc as a argument while invoking the add() function in class C2?
We did not pass any argument while invoking the add() function of class C1.

 C1 is a child class of Abc. Therefore, all the members of class Abc are anyways inherited by C1 and there was no need to pass any separate object when invoking a member function of class C1. However, class C2 does not inherit members and member functions of class Abc because it is not a child of Abc. Hence, we explicitly create an object of class Abc and pass it while invoking the add () function. The relationship between class C1 and Abc is called as IS-A relationship because C1 is a child class of Abc, whereas the relationship between C2 and Abc is called as HAS-A relationship because class C2 has an object of class Abc defined locally in one of its functions. The difference between IS-A and HAS-A relationship is explained in detail in section 14.5. HAS-A relationship does not necessarily mean that the object of one class must always be defined locally within the member function of another class (as in this case); it just means that one class contains object of another class in someway or the other. It is quite possible that object of one class is defined as a member of another class.

14.4 Types of Inheritance

Depending on the structure in which the hierarchy is created, inheritance can be classified into following types:

1. Single level Inheritance
2. Hierarchical Inheritance
3. Multi-level Inheritance
4. Multiple Inheritance
5. Hybrid Inheritance

In this section, we just define each of the inheritance types and we will learn their implementation throughout this chapter.

14.4.1 Single level inheritance

This is a relationship of inheritance created using **single parent and a single child class** as shown in Figure 14.24.

For example, let us consider that we need to store data about students of a particular university in the computer memory. After requirement gathering, it is identified that we need to store following five attributes for each student in the computer memory:

1. Name of the student (character array: name)
2. Date of birth (object: dob)
3. Gender (character variable: gender)
4. Roll Number (integer variable: roll_no)
5. Marks obtained (integer variable: marks)

At this moment, it would be simple to imagine a class Student containing all the five members defined in it. However, we would lack reusability of members if in case we plan to store data about other entities of the university (say professors) in future. Out of the five members, first three (name, dob, and gender) would be relevant to class Professor as well because for every professor, we would also need store to name, gender, and date of birth like for student. These are called as **generic members** because there is a

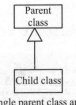

Single parent class and a single child class

Figure 14.24: Single level inheritance

chance to reuse them at a later stage. Whereas, the other two members (roll_no and marks) are specific to class Student, and there is no chance to reuse them. Such members are called as **specialized members**. If we think from the perspective to facilitate reusability in future, it would be a good idea to define the generic members in a **parent class** (named as Person) and keep only the specialized members in the child class Student, as shown in the Figure 14.25. Such an inheritance with a single parent class and a single child class is called **single level inheritance**. Therefore, class Student will have name, dob, gender, roll_no, and marks out of which the members name, dob, and gender are inherited from the parent class Person. We can always create the members name, dob, and gender as **protected** in Person, so that they can be directly accessed in the child class Student. The advantage of this design is that, if we wish to plug one more class in future (say Professor) we can do this by simply creating it as another child class of Person, and it will inherit the generic members without putting any special effort.

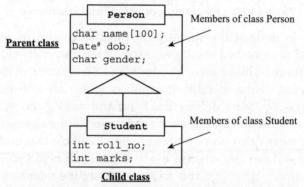

#The implementation of this hierarchy requires class Date to be created as an user-defined data type whose object can store the date of birth. We have implemented class Date in section 14.5

Figure 14.25: An example of single level inheritance

14.4.2 Hierarchical inheritance

This is a relationship of inheritance created with **single parent class having more than one child classes as shown in Figure 14.26.**

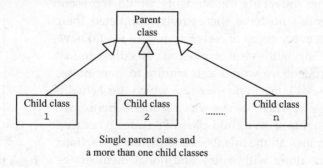

Single parent class and
a more than one child classes

Figure 14.26: Hierarchical inheritance

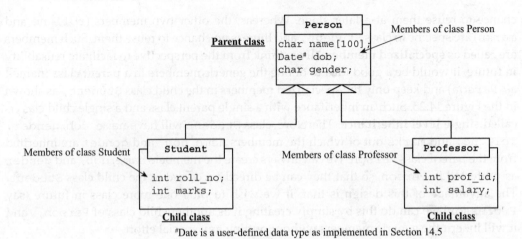

Figure 14.27: An example of hierarchical inheritance

As an example to understand 'hierarchical inheritance', let us modify the design given in Figure 14.27 to store data about professors of the university along with students. Hence, we now create two child classes `Student` and `Professor` of class `Person`. Each of the child classes can define specialized members which are not common among the peer classes, like class `Student` defines `roll_no` and `marks` and `Professor` defines `prof_id` (to store unique identifier for each professor) and `salary` (to store salary of the professor). This means that every `Student` object will contain members `name`, `dob`, `gender`, `roll_no` and `marks`, whereas every `Professor` object will contain members as `name`, `dob`, `gender`, `prof_id` and `salary`, where the members `name`, `dob`, and `gender` are the protected members of parent inherited by each of the child classes.

14.4.3   Multi-level inheritance

This is a relationship of inheritance created when a **class is derived from a child class of some other class.** Structure class of multi-level inheritance as shown in Figure 14.28.

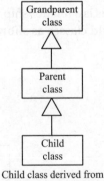

Child class derived from another child class

Figure 14.28: Multi-level inheritance

As an example to understand 'multi-level inheritance', let us modify the design given in Figure 14.28 to store data about ex-students of the university. Ex-Students would represent the set of students who have successfully completed their course, and hence every object of class Ex_student would have a 'final grade' along with 'year of passing'. Needless to say that, for an ex-student we would also require to store `name`, `dob`, `gender`, `roll_no`, and `marks`, which are actually the members present when he/she was a student. Hence, we create class Ex_Student as a child class of `Student` because Ex_Student requires all the members and member functions of class `Student` along with a few additional members as shown in the Figure 14.29. The parent class of Ex_Student is `Student`, which itself is a child of class `Person`, and hence

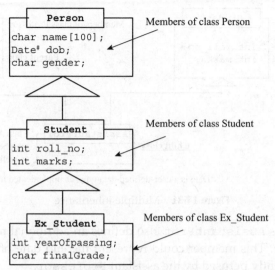

#Date is a user-defined data type as implemented in Section 14.5

Figure 14.29: An example of multi-level inheritance

object of Ex_Student will contain all the members of class Person as well as Student (because Student already inherits members of Person). Such an inheritance is called as multi-level inheritance.

14.4.4 Multiple inheritance

This is a relationship of inheritance created using **multiple parent classes and single child class** as shown in Figure 14.30.

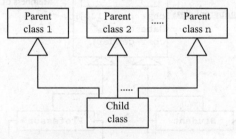

Figure 14.30: Multiple inheritance

To understand this type of inheritance, let us imagine a person in the real world who is both student as well as professor in the same university. This can be a possibility if a person is a teacher for undergraduate courses and pursuing postgraduation at the same time. We designate this category as assistant-professors and create a class named as AssistantProf to represent them. Class AssistantProf should have member's prof_id, salary because he/she is a professor for undergraduate courses and also have members roll_no, marks because he/she is also a student for the postgraduate course. As AssistantProf requires members of Student as well as Professor, it must have two parent classes as shown in the figure 14.31. This example illustrates **multiple inheritance** because AssitantProf is a single child of two parent classes Student and

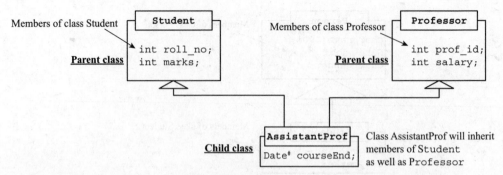

Figure 14.31 Multiple inheritance

Professor. The class AssistantProf also defines an additional member courseEnd which is of type Date. This member could represent the end date of the postgraduation course, which is currently perused by the assistant Professor.

14.4.5 Hybrid inheritance

Combining different inheritance types into a single design is called as hybrid inheritance. The hierarchy in Figure 14.32 is the mixture of multi-level inheritance, multiple inheritance and hierarchical inheritance; this complete example when viewed together illustrates hybrid inheritance as shown in the Figure 14.32. The pattern represents that a Person can either be a Student or a Professor. And a Person who is both Student as well as Professor is called as an AssistantProf.

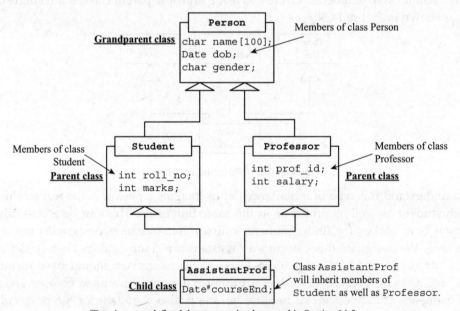

#Date is a user-defined data type as implemented in Section 14.5

Figure 14.32: Hybrid inheritance

How can I determine if two classes are to be related using Inheritance? **?**

 Inheritance should be created whenever there is "IS-A" type of relationship between classes. As an example, lets say we are required to store data about two different types of accounts offered by a Bank:

1. Saving account
2. Current account

We can identify common attributes required by both the accounts and put it in a generic class named as `Account`. We can then apply IS-A relationship and define `Saving` and `Current` as two child classes of class `Account`. The parent class `Account` may define common members like `accountId` (Account identifier), `customerName` (name of the customer holding the account), `balance` (balance funds in the account) etc. because these attributes will be required in both the child classes. These are generic attributes because this information must be stored immaterial of the type of account.

While it is understood that creating inheritance makes sense only when there are common attributes required in multiple child classes, it is equally important to understand that different child classes must be created only if there is at least one **attribute difference** among each of the child classes. When we create two different classes `Saving` and `Current` to represent two different types of accounts, it is indeed very important that there exists some difference in between the two accounts. For instance, saving account pays interest on the balance money which current account does not; whereas current account imposes a rule to its customers to maintain a minimum balance of x dollars which saving account does not. Hence, clearly there is an attribute difference between the two classes, class `Saving` has a specialized member `interest` not present in class `Current`, whereas class `Current` has a specialized member `minBalance` (to represent minimum balance required in account) which is not present in a class `Saving`. Hence it makes a complete sense to create two different child classes `Saving` and `Current` defining specialized members with a common parent class `Account` defining generalized members.

If there had been no difference between saving and current accounts it would not have been possible to identify an attribute which is present in one class but not the other. In fact if both the accounts are exactly same, there would have been no need to create these child classes at all. We could have dumped all the attributes in class `Account` itself. In summary, creating inheritance makes sense only when:

1. There are some common attributes in multiple child classes (which can be declared in a generalized parent class)
2. There is at least one attribute difference among the child classes(peer classes). These specialized attributes specific to a child must be defined by the respective child class.

14.5 IS-A and HAS-A Relationship: An Example

To understand IS-A and HAS-A relationship between classes, let us create a C++ program to implement the hierarchy, which is defined in Figure 14.27. The hierarchy depicts that there are two types of `Person` objects, a `Person` can either be a `Student` or a `Professor`. There are some members such as name, gender, and date of birth, which are relevant for both `Student` as well as `Professor`, hence we define these members in a parent class `Person` and create `Student` and `Professor` as child classes of `Person`. This way we avoid duplication of code because the members defined in parent class will be inherited by each of the child classes. The members name, gender and date of birth will be available in the object memory of `Student` as well as `Professor` without a need to individually define them in these classes because they are defined at parent level.

The child class `Student` defines only those members which are specific to `Student` object such as `roll_no` and `Marks`. These members are not relevant to `Professor` and hence there is no point defining them at parent level. Similarly, class `Professor` defines specialized members such as `salary` and `prof_id` which are not relevant to `Student`. The real world scenario for this is that every student has a roll number and obtains some marks in the examination he appears for. Whereas every professor has a identification number and gets monthly salary for his work.

NOTES

Inheritance should be implemented between classes whenever there exists **IS-A** relationship in real world. For example in this case, we could say Student **IS-A** Person or Professor **IS-A** Person. Hence inheritance is also called as **IS-A** relationship between classes.

Note that one of the members of class `Person` is used to represent 'date of birth' (dob) which in itself is a **composite attribute**. To store date of birth, we actually need to store three different members `dd` (day), `mm` (month), and `yy` (year). Hence, we create another class named as `Date` which contains the members `dd`, `mm`, and `yy` as shown in Figure 14.33. This concept is very similar as described in Chapter 9 where we have created a structure named as Date. In this case, we have created a class `Date` instead of structure to encourage encapsulation and data hiding. Every object of class `Date` will represent one date in the real world. Every `Person` may it be a `Student` or a `Professor` has a date of birth, and hence we create an object of class `Date` in class `Person` to store the date of birth of any `Person`. So when you create object of class `Person` or `Student` or `Professor`, it will have an object of class `Date` embedded in it. Such a relationship between classes is called as **composition.** By definition, when object of one class is required to the part of the object memory of another class such that if the **whole part** is destroyed, then the **subpart** also gets destroyed it is called composition between classes. For example, Figure 14.34 shows one object of class `Student` in memory. This object has an object of class `Date` embedded in it. For some reason, if `Student` object goes out of scope (or gets destroyed), the `Date` object that is contained in it will also be destroyed, hence we say that there is a composition

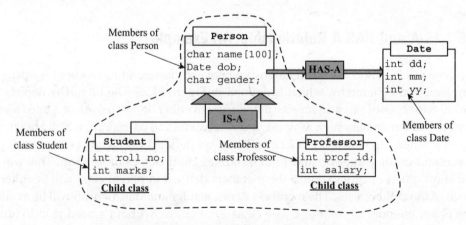

Figure 14.33: IS-A and HAS-A relationship

established between Student and Date classes. Note that, this composition is established indirectly due to inheritance (in actuality, class Person contains object of Date which is inherited by Student).

The following is the full source code to implement the relationships between classes as shown in Figure 14.33.

```cpp
#include<iostream.h>
#include <Windows.h>
#include <stdio.h>
class Date
{
private:
    int dd;
    int mm;
    int yy;
public:
    void inputDate()
    {
      cout<<"Enter dd:"<<endl;
      cin>>dd;
            cout<<"Enter mm:"<<endl;
            cin>>mm;
      cout<<"Enter yyyy:"<<endl;
      cin>>yy;
    }
    void outputDate()
    {
    cout<<"dd:"<<dd<<"-"<<mm<<"-"<<yy<<endl;
    }
    void outputAge()
    {
    cout<<yy<<"years and "<<mm<<" months and "<<dd<<" days"<<endl;
    }
    static Date getCurrentDate()
    {
      SYSTEMTIME system;
      GetSystemTime(&system);
      Date today;
```

```
        today.dd=system.wDay;
        today.mm=system.wMonth;
        today.yy=system.wYear;
        return today;
    }
    Date getDateDiff(Date d)
    {
        Date result;
        if(dd>=d.dd)
        {
            result.dd = dd-d.dd;
        }
        else
            {
                dd=dd+30;
                mm=mm-1;
                result.dd = dd-d.dd;
            }
        if(mm>=d.mm)
        {
            result.mm = mm-d.mm;
        }
        else
        {
            mm=mm+12;
            yy=yy-1;
        result.mm = mm-d.mm;
        }
        result.yy = yy-d.yy;
        return result;
    }
};
class Person
{
    protected:
        char gender;
        char name[100];
        Date dob;
    public:
        void inputPerson ()
        {
            cout<<"Enter Name:"<<endl;
            cin>>name;
            cout<<"Enter Gender:"<<endl;
```

```
      cin>>gender;
      cout<<"Enter Date of birth:"<<endl;
      dob.inputDate();
   }
   void outputPerson ()
   {
   cout<<"Name:"<<name<<endl;
   cout<<"Gender:"<<gender<<endl;
   cout<<"Date of birth is:"<<endl;
   dob.outputDate();
   }
   void calculateAge()
   {
      Date today= Date::getCurrentDate();
      /*Calculate Difference between todays date and date of birth
      to determine the age*/
      Date age = today.getDateDiff(dob);
      cout<<"Age is:"<<endl;
      age.outputAge();
   }
};
class Student:public Person
{
   private:
   int roll_no;
   int marks;
   public:
   void inputStudent()
   {
      inputPerson ();//get generic details
      cout<<"Enter RollNumber:"<<endl;
      cin>>roll_no;
      cout<<"Enter Marks:"<<endl;
      cin>>marks;
   }
   void outputStudent()
   {
      outputPerson ();//get generic details
      calculateAge();//Print age
      cout<<"RollNumber is:"<<roll_no<<endl;
      cout<<"Marks are:"<<marks<<endl;
   }
};
class Professor: public Person
```

```
{
    private:
    int prof_id;
    int salary;
    public:
    void inputProf()
    {
      inputPerson ();//get generic details
      cout<<"EnterProf Id:"<<endl;
      cin>>prof_id;
      cout<<"Enter salary:"<<endl;
      cin>>salary;
    }
    void outputProf()
    {
      outputPerson ();//get generic details
      calculateAge();//Print age
      cout<<"Prof ID is:"<<prof_id<<endl;
      cout<<"Salary is:"<<salary<<endl;
    }
};
void main()
{
cout<<"**************Student******************* "<<endl;
    Student s1;
    s1.inputStudent();
    s1.outputStudent();
cout<<"**************Professor******************* "<<endl;
    Professor p1;
    p1.inputProf();
    p1.outputProf();
}
```

The first statement in main() function

```
Student s1;
```

creates an object of class Student named as s1. This object can store data about one Student in the real world. As Student is a child class of Person, the object memory of s1 will contain members name, dob, and gender inherited from Person along with the specialized member variables (roll_no and marks) as shown in the Figure 14.34. Note that object of Date named as dob, will be the part of object memory of s1 as discussed before. The member functions inputPerson(), outputPerson(), and calculateAge() will also be inherited by class Student and can be accessed directly within the child class as they are defined as public functions in Person. Hence, it would be correct to imagine that the class Student has five functions in all (inputStudent(),

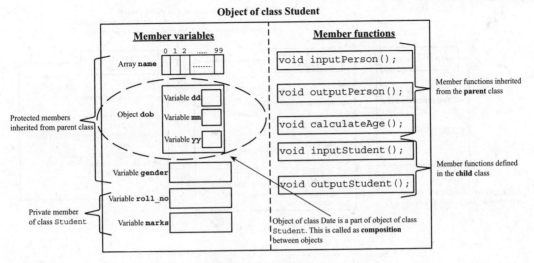

Figure 14.34: Object s1

outputPerson(),calculateAge() inherited from parent class and inputStudent(), outputStudent() defined in class Student itself).

The statement

s1.inputStudent();

invokes the function inputStudent(); using object s1. Since the function is defined in Student the control of execution is transferred within the scope of class Student. The function inputStudent(); is responsible to accept all the member variables relevant to Student object as input from the user. Hence this function in turn calls the inputPerson() defined in class Person which is responsible to accept name, dob, and gender as input from the user. This is one of the best examples of **reusability**, wherein we use the existing implementation in parent class to accept members name, gender, and dob as input from the user instead of writing new set of cin statements again. As mentioned in section 14.1, **reusability of the code** is the key principle of inheritance because the properties defined in the parent class are borrowed by the child class. The function inputPerson() accepts name and gender of s1 as input from the user and invokes inputDate() function, which is defined within the scope of Date class. Note that the function inputDate() is invoked using an object dob (object of class Date) because there is no inheritance between Person and Date. However, while invoking the function inputPerson() from class Student, we did not use any object because Student is a child class of Person and the function inputStudent(); is already invoked by the child object, which can directly access non-private members and member functions defined in parent class. The members roll_no and marks are specialized members of class Student and hence their values are accepted as input from the user by the cin statements present in the function inputStudent(); Figure 14.35 shows the execution flow which takes all the members of Student object as input from the user.

Similarly, the statement

s1.outputStudent();

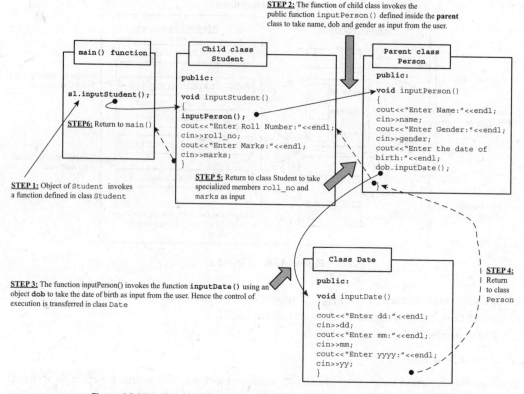

STEP 2: The function of child class invokes the public function inputPerson() defined inside the **parent** class to take name, dob and gender as input from the user.

Figure 14.35: Process to take members of s1 as input from the user

will print all the member values of Student object on the computer screen. This execution flow can be understood in a similar way as we have explained the input logic. The function outputStudent() calls outputPerson() to print name and gender, then calls calculateAge() to print the age of the Student. calculateAge() invokes the getDateDiff() function in class Date which gives the difference between the current date and the date of birth.

Similar to what we have done with the Student object, the statements

```
Professor p1;
p1.inputProf();
p1.outputProf();
```

create an object of class Professor named as p1, input the member variables of p1 and print the details on the computer screen.

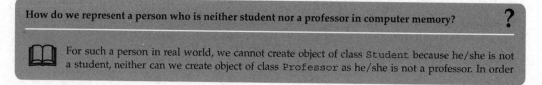

How do we represent a person who is neither student nor a professor in computer memory? **?**

For such a person in real world, we cannot create object of class Student because he/she is not a student, neither can we create object of class Professor as he/she is not a professor. In order to store data about objects which do not belong to any of the child categories we must create an object of a parent class in our program. This is because we know that the real world object just falls in the general category but does not fall in any of the specialized categories. In this case, we know that the real world object is a person but he is neither a student nor a professor of the university. This object may be librarian, clerk or part of any other university staff. In this case, since we do not have the correct child class that can represent this object, we should create an object of a general class(`Person`) using the statement below, to store its data.

`Person p1;`

However, since `p1` contains only three members `name`, `dob` and `gender` we will be able to store only this information for any other object who is neither `Student` or `Professor`. If you need to store any additional information, then it is recommended that you create another child class of class `Person` to represent this category. For example, class `Clerk` may represent all clerks; class `Accountant` may represent all accounts etc. Remember, as mentioned before classes should be plugged into the inheritance hierarchy only if there is a considerable attribute different among them and if the object cannot be represented fully using the generalized class alone.

In some cases, the business logic puts a mandate that all objects must map to at least one child class. This means that there cannot be a situation in business wherein an object does not belong to any of the child categories. In this case your inheritance tree must be complete and there should be child classes created to represent all the possible objects in the scope of business. This way there is no need to create an object of parent class at all. Such a parent class whose object can never be created is called as **abstract class**. Abstract classes are discussed in detail in section 14.14.

14.6 Multi-level Inheritance: Calculator

As an example of multi-level inheritance, let us create a C++ program to design different types of calculators. The requirement is to design three types of calculators:

1. **Basic calculator:** This calculator provides only arithmetic functions like addition, subtraction, multiplication and division with two variables.
2. **Trigonometric calculator:** This calculator provides all the features of basic calculator along with the additional functions to calculate sine, cosine, and tangent of an angle. Since, the trigonometric calculator is required to provide all the features of basic calculator, instead of rewriting them in the `Trigonometric` class, we will create the `Trigonometric` calculator class as a child class of class `Basic`. This way we will only have to define the specialized functions (to compute sine, cosine, and tangent) in the `Trigonometric` class because the functions of `Basic` will be anyways inherited.
3. **Scientific calculator:** This calculator provides all the features of `Basic` and `Trigonometric` class along with the additional functions to calculate natural logarithm and log to the base 10. Although the `Scientific` calculator needs the functions of both `Basic` as well as `Trigonometric`, it is sufficient to create `Scientific` calculator as a child class of `Trigonometric` alone. This is because the `Trigonometric` calculator anyways inherits the features of `Basic` calculator which will be passed on to `Scientific` calculator. Hence we just create the `Scientific` calculator class as a child class of `Trigonometric` calculator. This way, the `Scientific` calculator is only required to define required logarithmic functionalities and the functionalities of `Basic` and `Trigonometric` calculator will be inherited. Required hierarchy of classes is as shown in Figure 14.36.

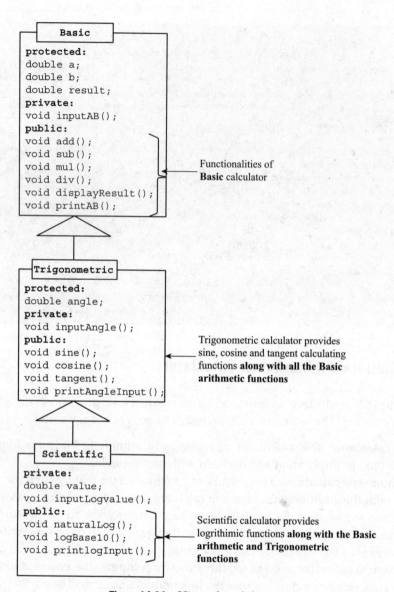

Figure 14.36   Hierarchy of classes

Accidently, if you create the Scientific class as a child class of both Basic as well as Trigonometric, you are creating an ambiguous situation by trying to inherit the features of Basic twice in Scientific class (once through Trigonometric class and the second time directly through Basic class). Compiler does not allow such ambiguities to occur and generates an error complaining that the child class of Trigonometric will anyway contain the features of Basic and hence it should not be specified as another parent explicitly, as shown in the figure 14.37.

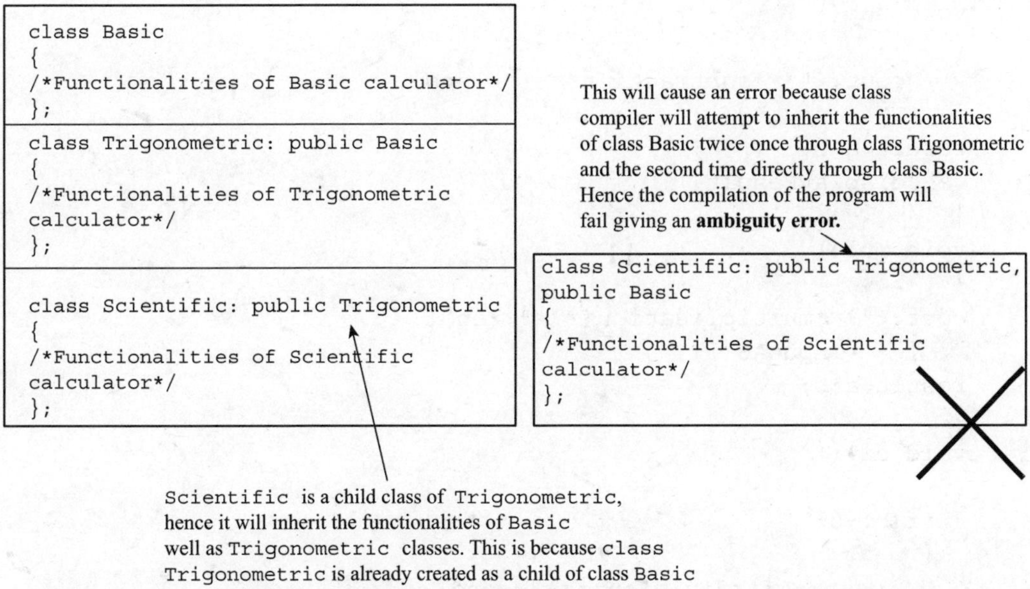

```
class Basic
{
/*Functionalities of Basic calculator*/
};
```

```
class Trigonometric: public Basic
{
/*Functionalities of Trigonometric
calculator*/
};
```

This will cause an error because class compiler will attempt to inherit the functionalities of class Basic twice once through class Trigonometric and the second time directly through class Basic. Hence the compilation of the program will fail giving an **ambiguity error.**

```
class Scientific: public Trigonometric
{
/*Functionalities of Scientific
calculator*/
};
```

```
class Scientific: public Trigonometric,
public Basic
{
/*Functionalities of Scientific
calculator*/
};
```

Scientific is a child class of Trigonometric, hence it will inherit the functionalities of Basic well as Trigonometric classes. This is because class Trigonometric is already created as a child of class Basic

Figure 14.37 C++ syntax to create hierarchy of Basic, Trigonometric and Scientific classes

The following is the full source code for the design given in the Figure 14.36.

```
#include<iostream.h>
#include<math.h>
class Basic
{
    protected:
    double a;
    double b;
    double result;
    private:
    void inputAB()
    {
    cout<<"Enter two numbers"<<endl;
    cin>>a>>b;
    }
    public:
     void add()
     {
     cout<<"***addition****"<<endl;
     inputAB();
     result=a+b;
     displayResult();
     }
```

```cpp
    void sub()
    {
        cout<<"***subtraction****"<<endl;
            inputAB();
    result=a-b;
        displayResult();
    }
    void mul()
    {
    cout<<"***multiplication****"<<endl;
            inputAB();
    result=a*b;
    }
    void div()
    {
       if(b!=0)
       {
           cout<<"***division****"<<endl;
            inputAB();
           result=a/b;
            displayResult();
       }
       else
       {
           cout<<"Division not possible"<<endl;
       }
    }
    void displayResult()
    {
    cout<<"Result is "<<result<<endl;
    }
    void printAB()
    {
        cout<<"Values used by last arithmetic operation:"<<endl;
    cout<<"a="<<a<<"b="<<b<<endl;
    }
};
class Trigonometric: public Basic
{
protected:
double angle;
private:
void inputAngle()
    {
    cout<<"Enter Angle"<<endl;
```

```
        cin>>angle;
        }
public:
void sine()
{
        cout<<"***sine****"<<endl;
        inputAngle();
        result= sin(angle);
        displayResult();
}
void cosine()
{
        cout<<"***cosine****"<<endl;
        inputAngle();
        result= cos(angle);
        displayResult();
}
void tangent()
{
        cout<<"***tangent****"<<endl;
        inputAngle();
        result= tan(angle);
        displayResult();
}
void printAngleInput()
        {
        cout<<"Value used by last Trigonometric operation="
        <<angle<<endl;
        }
};
class Scientific: public Trigonometric
{
private:
double value;
void inputLogValue()
        {
        cout<<"Enter the value for which log needs to be calculated"
        <<endl;
        cin>>value;
        }
public:
void naturalLog()
{
        cout<<"***Log to the base e****"<<endl;
inputLogValue();
```

```
        result= log(value);
        displayResult();
}
void logBase10()
{
        cout<<"***Log to the base 10****"<<endl;
        inputLogValue();
        result= log10 (value);
        displayResult();
}
void printLogInput()
        {
cout<<"Value used by last logarithmic operation="<<value<<endl;
        }
};
void main()
{
        Scientific calculator;
        calculator.add();
        calculator.sub();
        calculator.sine();
        calculator.cosine();
        calculator.naturalLog();
        calculator.printAB();
        calculator.printAngleInput();
        calculator.printLogInput();
}
```

The first statement in the `main()` function

```
Scientific calculator;
```

creates an object of class `Scientific` named as calculator. Given that, calculator is an object of the child most class (`Scientific`), we can access all the member functions of class `Basic` and `Trigonometric` along with those defined in `Scientific` itself.

The statements

```
calculator.add();
calculator.sub();
```

invoke functions `add()` and `sub()` of class `Basic` using the object `calculator` to perform addition and subtraction of two variables a and b. This is possible because the child object can access members defined in any of the parent right up to the root of class hierarchy. Both the functions accept the values of a and b as input from the user before performing the required operation. The function `displayResult()` displays the value of the variable `result` which always stores the result of the last operation. Hence, we have invoked the function `displayResult()` in every function to print the result of operation on the computer screen. So, when the function `add()` invokes the `displayResult()` function, it prints the result of addition of a and b because the variable `result` contains the value of a+b at this point. And when the function `sub()` invokes `displayResult()` function, it prints the value of a-b which is updated in the variable `result` immediately after subtraction is performed.

The statements

```
calculator.sine();
calculator.cosine();
```

invoke sine and cosine functions defined in class `Trigonometric` using the object `calculator`. Note that the user-defined function `sine()` invokes a built-in function `sin()` defined in `math.h`, and the user-defined function `cosine()` invokes a built-in function `cos()`, which is also defined in the header fine `math.h`.

The Table 14.1 gives the summary of different mathematical functions we have created in this program and the built-in functions they call to attain the required result.

Finally, we have invoked the `naturalLog()` function to calculate the log to the base e of the value which is present in the member `value`.

```
calculator.naturalLog();
```

The function `printAB();` prints the last value of variables a and b defined in class `Basic`. Similarly the functions `printAngleInput()` and `printLogInput()` print the last values of variables `angle` and `value` defined in class `Trigonometric` and `Scientific`, respectively.

Table 14.1: Summary of mathematical functions used in the program

User-defined function name	Owning class	Built-in function used from header file `math.h`
sine()	Trigonometric	**sin():** This function gives the sine value of the angle which is passed to it as an argument. The prototype of the function is `double sin(double);` The statement `result= sin(angle);` returns the sine value of the `angle` passed to it in the variable `result`
cosine()	Trigonometric	**cos():** This function gives the cosine value of the angle which is passed to it as an argument. The prototype of the function is `double cos(double);` The statement `result= cos(angle);` returns the cosine value of the `angle` passed to it in the variable `result`

User-defined function name	Owning class	Built-in function used from header file `math.h`

`tangent()`	`Trigonometric`	`tan()`: This function gives the tan value of the angle which is passed to it as an argument.
		The prototype of the function is
		`double tan(double);`
		The statement
		`result= tan(angle);`
		returns the tan value of the `angle` passed to it in the variable `result`

`naturalLog()`	`Scientific`	`log()`: This function gives the log to the base e of the value passed to it as an argument.
		The prototype of the function is
		`double log(double);`
		The statement,
		`result= log(value);`
		returns the log to the base e of the `value` passed to it in the variable `result`

`logBase10()`	`Scientific`	`log10()`: This function gives the log to the base 10 of the value passed to it as an argument.
		The prototype of the function is as follows:
		`double log10(double);`
		The statement
		`result= log10(value);`
		returns the log to the base 10 of the `value` passed to it in the variable `result`

14.7   Resolving Ambiguity in Multiple Inheritance

A relationship of inheritance created using more than one parent class and a single child class is called as a multiple Inheritance as shown in the Figure 14.38. We might face a

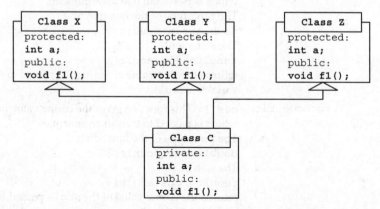

Figure 14.38   Multiple inheritance with ambiguous member variable/member function names

problem in resolving the function calls, if a function with same name is present in more than one parent classes. As an example, let us create three parent classes X, Y and Z with a single child class as C as shown in the Figure 14.38. Further, let us create a function named **f1()** and a variable named **a** in each of the classes in order to understand the resolution of ambiguity in multiple inheritance.

This would mean that the child class C will contain four functions named as f1() and four variables with name a (one from each of the parents and the one defined in class C itself). To avoid confusion, let's concentrate only on the function f1() first.

We create an object o1 of class C and invoke the f1() as shown below:

```
C o1;
o1.f1();
```

In this case, the compiler will correctly invoke the f1() defined in class C because o1 is of type C. As per the principle of early binding, the compiler always determines the function to be invoked based on the data type of the object, which has invoked the function. Therefore, the control is correctly transferred to f1() defined in class C. If we further attempt to make another call to f1() within the scope of class C, the compiler will recursively keep calling the same function f1() again as shown in Figure 14.39. How can we call versions of f1() defined in parent classes X, Y, and Z? This situation is called as **ambiguity in multiple inheritance**, which can be resolved using a **scope resolution operator.**

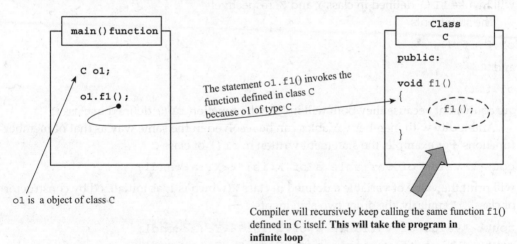

Figure 14.39: Ambiguity in multiple inheritance

We resolve this ambiguity using the scope resolution operator as shown in the code. The statement X::f1() will call the f1() of class X. Similarly, the statements Y::f1() and Z::f1() will invoke function of class Y and Z respectively, as shown in the figure 14.40.

We learnt how ambiguity can be resolved in function calls when a function is called within the scope of the child class. You can also invoke the function defined in any of the parent classes using the child object, directly from main(). The statement

```
o1.X::f1();
```

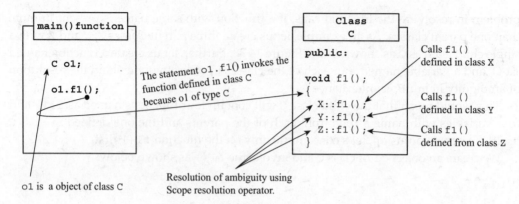

Figure 14.40: Resolution of ambiguity

will invoke the `f1()` defined in class X even if object `o1` is of type C. This is because we have explicitly asked the compiler to invoke function `f1()` within the scope of X using the scope resolution operator.

Similarly, the statements

```
o1.Y::f1();
o1.Z::f1();
```

will invoke `f1()` defined in class Y and Z, respectively.

The statements

```
o1.C::f1();
```

and

```
o1.f1();
```

are equivalent because they both will invoke the function `f1()` defined in class C.

Ambiguity with member variables can be resolved in the same way as that of member functions. For example, the statement written in `f1()` of class C

```
cout<<"Value of variable a of X is:"<<X::a<<endl;
```

will print the value of variable a defined in class X(which is 1, as initialized by constructor of class X). Similarly, the other two statements

```
cout<<"Value of variable a of Y is:"<<Y::a<<endl;
cout<<"Value of variable a of Z is:"<<Z::a<<endl;
```

will print the value of variable a in class Y and class Z, respectively.

The following statement, without any scope resolution operator written inside `f1()` of class C

```
cout<<"Value of variable a of C is:"<<a<<endl;
```

will print the value of variable a of class C itself. This is because we are already in the scope of class C. You can also rewrite this statement by using the scope resolution operator explicitly as shown below:

```
cout<<"Value of variable a of C is:"<<C::a<<endl;
```

The following is the full source code of ambiguity resolution:

```
#include<iostream.h>
class X
{
protected:
int a;
public:
    X()
    {
    a=1;
    }
    void f1()
    {
            cout<<"Function of class X"<<endl;
        cout<<"Value of variable a of X is:"<<a<<endl;
    }
};
class Y
{
protected:
int a;
public:
    Y()
    {
    a=2;
    }
    void f1()
    {
        cout<<"Function of class Y"<<endl;
        cout<<"Value of variable a of Y is:"<<a<<endl;
    }
};
class Z
{
protected:
int a;
public:
    Z()
    {
    a=3;
    }
```

```
    void f1()
    {
       cout<<"Function of class Z"<<endl;
       cout<<"Value of variable a of Z is:"<<a<<endl;
    }
};
class C: public X, public Y,public Z
{
protected:
int a;
public:
    C()
    {
    a=100;
    }
    void f1()
    {
    cout<<"Function of class C"<<endl;
    X::f1();
    Y::f1();
    Z::f1();
    cout<<"Value of variable a of X is:"<<X::a<<endl;
   cout<<"Value of variable a of Y is:"<<Y::a<<endl;
   cout<<"Value of variable a of Z is:"<<Z::a<<endl;
   cout<<"Value of variable a of C is:"<<a<<endl;
    }
};
void main()
{
    C o1;
    o1.f1();
    o1.X::f1();
    o1.Y::f1();
    o1.Z::f1();
}
```

Output

```
Function of class C
Function of class X
Value of variable a of X is:1
Function of class Y
Value of variable a of Y is:2
Function of class Z
Value of variable a of Z is:3
```

```
Value of variable a of X is:1
Value of variable a of Y is:2
Value of variable a of Z is:3
Value of variable a of C is:100
Function of class X
Value of variable a of X is:1
Function of class Y
Value of variable a of Y is:2
Function of class Z
Value of variable a of Z is:3
```

NOTES

If a variable or a function with same name is present in parent as well as child class, then it results in **ambiguity in multiple inheritance**. This ambiguity is resolved using **scope resolution operator : :**

14.8   Virtual Base Class

Let there be a single grandparent class, two parent classes and a single child class as shown in the Figure 14.41.

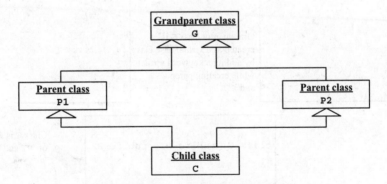

Figure 14.41   Multipath inheritance

In this case members and the member functions of the grandparent class will be inherited by the child class two times, the first time through the path from first parent class (P1) and the second time through the path from second parent class (P2). This means that the child class will contain duplication of inherited members from the grandparent class. This problem can be solved by directly inheriting the members of grandparent class from the grandparent itself, instead of inheriting the members of grandparent from each of the individual parent classes. This means that grandparent class is to be considered as a parent class, so that the child class can inherit the members of grandparent class directly as shown in the Figure 14.42. Such a grandparent class that acts as a parent class to avoid duplication of inherited members in the child class is called as logical parent class or 'virtual base class'.

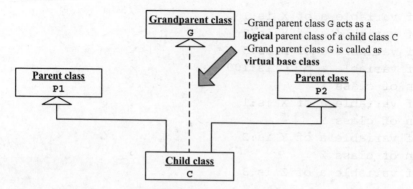

Figure 14.42: Virtual base class

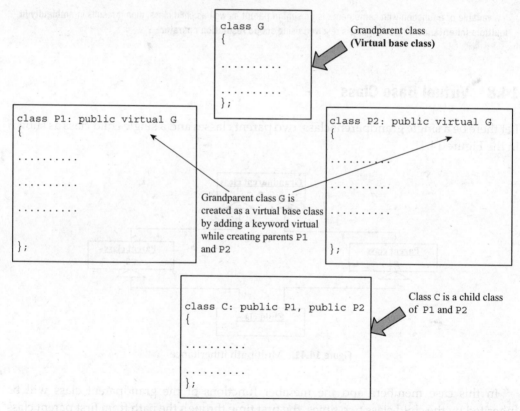

Figure 14.43: Syntax for creating virtual base class

In such a case, the grandparent class(G) should be created as a virtual base class while defining the parent classes P1 and P2 as shown in the Figure 14.43. Note that each of the parent classes (P1 as well as P2) must add a keyword virtual in their definition which will actually create class G as the logical parent of child class C. In actuality, inheritance is all about making instance of parent class available to the child class. In this case, instead of getting the instance of G from P1 as well as P2, class C gets the instance of G from G itself. Adding keyword virtual ensures that a single copy of object of G is maintained within the object of class C. The internal implementation of virtual base classes using pointers is discussed later in this chapter in section14.13.2, don't worry about it right now.

As an example, let us create a C++ program for the hierarchy given in Figure 14.44.

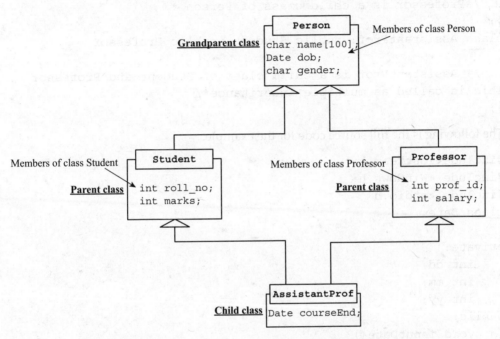

Figure 14.44: Hierarchy showing the usage of virtual base class

The complete hierarchy is very similar as discussed in section 14.4.2 with the only difference being that there is an additional child class named as AssistantProf. The class AssistantProf inherits the features of both Student as well as Professor. This means that an object of AssistantProf represents a Person who is both Student and Professor in the real world. This is a very realistic example because a Person can be a teacher for undergraduate courses and pursuing postgraduation at the same time. This means that members and member functions of class Person would be inherited twice into the class AssistantProf, first time through the path from first parent class (Student) and second time through the path from second parent class (Professor), thereby resulting into ambiguity in inheritance. To solve this problem, we create class Person as a virtual base class by adding keyword virtual while defining the immediate parent classes Student and Professor as shown below:

```
class Person
{
......
};
class Student: public virtual Person
{
...... /*Student is a child class of Person */
};
class Professor: public virtual Person
{
...... /*Professor is a child class of Person */
};
class AssistantProf: public Student, public Professor
{
...... /* AssistantProf is a child class of Student and Professor.
This is called as multiple inheritance*/
};
```

The following is the full source code for the example:

```cpp
#include<iostream.h>
#include <Windows.h>
#include <stdio.h>
class Date
{
private:
    int dd;
    int mm;
    int yy;
public:
    void inputDate()
    {
    cout<<"Enter dd:"<<endl;
    cin>>dd;
        cout<<"Enter mm:"<<endl;
        cin>>mm;
    cout<<"Enter yyyy:"<<endl;
    cin>>yy;
    }
    void outputDate()
    {
    cout<<"dd:"<<dd<<"-"<<mm<<"-"<<yy<<endl;
    }
    void outputAge()
    {
```

```
      cout<<yy<<"years and "<<mm<<" months and "<<dd<<" days"<<endl;
      }
    static Date getCurrentDate()
    {
      SYSTEMTIME system;
      GetSystemTime(&system);
      Date today;
      today.dd=system.wDay;
      today.mm=system.wMonth;
      today.yy=system.wYear;
      return today;
    }
    Date getDateDiff(Date d)
    {
      Date result;
            if(dd>=d.dd)
            {
            result.dd = dd-d.dd;
            }
            else
            {
            dd=dd+30;
            mm=mm-1;
            result.dd = dd-d.dd;
            }
      if(mm>=d.mm)
      {
      result.mm = mm-d.mm;
      }
      else
      {
      mm=mm+12;
      yy=yy-1;
    result.mm = mm-d.mm;
      }
      result.yy = yy-d.yy;
    return result;
      }
};
class Person
{
    protected:
      char gender;
      char name[100];
```

```cpp
    Date dob;
public:
void inputPerson ()
{
  cout<<"Enter Name:"<<endl;
  cin>>name;
  cout<<"Enter Gender:"<<endl;
  cin>>gender;
  cout<<"Enter Date of birth:"<<endl;
  dob.inputDate();
}
void outputPerson ()
{
  cout<<"Name:"<<name<<endl;
  cout<<"Gender:"<<gender<<endl;
  cout<<"Date of birth is:"<<endl;
  dob.outputDate();
}
void calculateAge()
{
Date today= Date::getCurrentDate();
/*Calculate Difference between todays date and date of birth
to determine the age*/
Date age = today.getDateDiff(dob);
cout<<"Age is:"<<endl;
age.outputAge();
}
};
class Student:public virtual Person
{
    private:
    int roll_no;
    int marks;
    public:
    void inputStudent()
    {
      cout<<"Enter Roll Number:"<<endl;
      cin>>roll_no;
      cout<<"Enter Marks:"<<endl;
      cin>>marks;
    }
    void outputStudent()
    {
    cout<<"Roll Number is:"<<roll_no<<endl;
```

```
        cout<<"Marks are:"<<marks<<endl;
        }
};
class Professor:public virtual Person
{
    private:
    int prof_id;
    int salary;
    public:
    void inputProf()
    {
      cout<<"EnterProf Id:"<<endl;
      cin>>prof_id;
      cout<<"Enter salary:"<<endl;
      cin>>salary;
    }
    void outputProf()
    {
    cout<<"Prof ID is:"<<prof_id<<endl;
    cout<<"Salary is:"<<salary<<endl;
    }
};
class AssistantProf: public Student,public Professor
{
private:
Date courseEnd;
public:
void inputAP()
{
inputPerson ();
inputStudent();
inputProf();
cout<<"Enter the Course completion date of Assistant Professor"
    <<endl;
courseEnd.inputDate();
}
void outputAP()
{
outputPerson ();
outputStudent();
outputProf();
calculateAge();
cout<<"Date of Course completion of Assistant Professor
    is:"<<endl;
```

```
courseEnd.outputDate();
}
};
void main()
{
AssistantProf p1;
p1.inputAP();
p1.outputAP();
}
```

The first statement in `main()` function

```
AssistantProf p1;
```

creates an object of class `AssistantProf` named as `p1`. This object represents an assistant professor in real world who is both student as well as professor at the same time. Hence the object inherits the members and member functions of the parent classes `Student` as well as `Professor` as shown in the Figure 14.45. Note that the members of class `Person` are inherited only once because `Person` is created as a virtual base class. The class

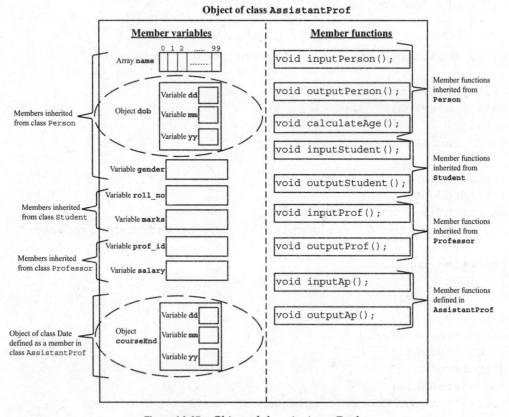

Figure 14.45 Object of class AssistantProf

`AssistantProf` also defines an additional member `courseEnd` which is of type `Date`. The member `courseEnd` represents the end date of the postgraduation course, for an assistant professor.

The statement

`p1.inputAP();`

invokes `inputAP()` function defined in class `AssistantProf`, which in turn invokes the respective input functions to accept members inherited from class `Person`, `Student`, and `Professor` as input from the user. Note that when compared to the code given in section 14.5 we have removed the call to `inputPerson()` from the `inputStudent()` and `inputProf()` functions so as to avoid the execution of `inputPerson()` twice (first time through `Student` class and the second time through `Professor` class).

Along with all the parent function calls the function `inputAP()` also accepts the course end date of the assistant professor as input from the user with the help of the statement

`courseEnd.inputDate();`

which invokes the `inputDate()` function defined in class `Date` using the object `courseEnd`

Similarly, the statement

`p1.outputAP();`

will print all the members of `p1` on the computer screen.

NOTES

The inheritance created using a virtual base class is called as **Virtual inheritance**. Compiler internally creates multiple hidden pointers (called as **virtual pointers**) and hidden tables (called as **virtual tables**) in memory to facilitate virtual Inheritance. Virtual pointers and virtual tables are explained in Section 14.13.

14.9 Function Overriding

When a function is defined in parent class as well as in the child class, the function is said to be overridden. As an example, let us create two classes: class `Person` and class `Student`, such that `Student` is a child class of `Person`, as shown in the Figure 14.46. We will work with simple primitive type members this time to avoid complexities with composite members like Date. We define integer type members `id` and `name` in class `Person` and a single integer type member `marks` in class `Student`.

The class `Person` has members `id` and `name` with following member functions:

1. **inputP()** – Used to accept id and name of a `Person` object as input from the user.
2. **output()** – Used to print the id and name of the `Person` object on the computer screen.

The class `Student` will inherit the members `id` and `name` from class `Person` and has additional member as `marks` with following member functions:

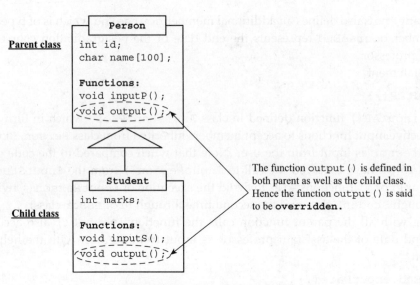

Figure 14.46: Function overriding

1. **inputS()** – Used to accept id, name, and marks of a Student object as input from the user
2. **output()** – Used to print the id, name, and marks of the Student object on the computer screen.

The name of the input functions is intentionally given different in class Person and class Student as inputP() and inputS(), respectively. However, the name and the signature of the output() function is same in parent class as well as the child class, and hence function **output()** is said to be overridden.

```
#include<iostream.h>
class Person
{
protected:
    int id;
    char name[100];
public:
    void inputP()
    {
    cin>>id>>name;
    }
    void output()
    {
    cout<<id<<" "<<name<<endl;
    }
};
class Student: public Person
```

```
{
private:
int marks;
public:
    void inputS()
    {
    cin>>id>>name>>marks;
    }
    void output()
    {
    cout<<id<<" "<<name<<"   "<<marks<<endl;
    }
};
void main()
{
Person p1;
Student s1;
cout<<"Enter id and name of Person "<<endl;
p1.inputP();
cout<<"Person details are "<<endl;
p1.output ();
cout<<"Enter id,name and marks of Student "<<endl;
s1.inputS();
cout<<"Student details are "<<endl;
s1.output ();
}
```

Output

```
Enter id and name of Person
1 John
Person details are
1 John
Enter id,name and marks of Student
2 Jack 90
Student details are
2 Jack 90
```

The main() function creates object p1 of class Person and s1 of class Student using the statements below. Member variables of these objects are as shown in the Figure 14.47.

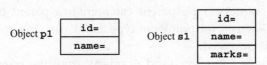

Figure 14.47: Objects p1 and s1

```
Person p1;
Student s1;
```

The function `inputP()` is invoked using object `p1` and `inputS()` is invoked using object `s1` to accept the member variables of both the objects as input from the user.

The following is the description of each of the `output()` function calls made from `main()`:

C++ Statement	Description
`p1.output();`	As `p1` is of type `Person`, this statement calls the `output()` function defined inside class `Person` which prints the `id` and `name` of the `Person` object on the computer screen.
`s1.output();`	As `s1` is of type `Student`, this statement calls the `output()` function defined inside class `Student` which prints the `id`, `name` and `marks` of the `Student` object on the computer screen.

NOTES

Although function `output()` is overridden, compiler correctly calls `output()` function of class **Person** when invoked using **p1** and calls `output()` function of class **Student** when invoked using a **s1**. This is because, the compiler determines which function to call based on the **data type of the object** using which the function is actually invoked.

Are there any rules to be followed while overriding a function? ?

 So as to override a function, the **signature of the function** defined in parent class must be exactly same as the signature of the function defined inside the child class.
The signature of the function includes:

1. Name of the function
2. Number of arguments the function takes
3. Data type of the arguments
4. Order of arguments

If all of the above properties of the function defined in "parent" class exactly match with the function defined in the "child" class then the function is said to be overridden. Note that the return type of the function is not included in the function signature and hence it is possible that the two functions have a different return type in the overriding process.

14.10 Pointers and Inheritance

With inheritance implemented in the program, we can create a 'parent' type pointer or a 'child' type pointer. A pointer of type 'parent' can point to a 'parent' object as well as to any of the 'child' objects. Whereas, the pointer of type 'child' can only point to the object of the same child for which it is created.

Let us reuse the classes `Person` and `Student` from the previous section so as to understand the working of 'pointers' with inheritance.

```
#include<iostream.h>
class Person
{
protected:
    int id;
    char name[100];
public:
    void inputP()
    {
    cin>>id>>name;
    }
    void output()
    {
    cout<<id<<" "<<name<<endl;
    }
};
class Student: public Person
{
private:
int marks;
public:
    void inputS()
    {
    cin>>id>>name>>marks;
    }
    void output()
    {
    cout<<id<<" "<<name<<"   "<<marks<<endl;
    }
};
void main()
{
Person p1;
Student s1;
Person *p;
p=&p1;
cout<<"Enter id and name of Person "<<endl;
p->inputP();
cout<<"Person details are: "<<endl;
p->output ();
p=&s1;
cout<<"Enter id, name and marks of Student"<<endl;
((Student*)p)->inputS();
```

```
cout<<"Student details are:"<<endl;
((Student*)p)->output ();
}
```

Output

```
Enter id and name of Person
1 John
Person details are:
1 John
Enter id, name and marks of Student
2 Jack 90
Student details are:
2 Jack 90
```

As seen from the code we create objects p1 and s1 of type Person and Student, respectively, in the main() function. These objects are as shown in the Figure 14.48. Well, every object we create is stored in memory (RAM) and let the addresses of these objects in the memory be 8000 and 9000 respectively.

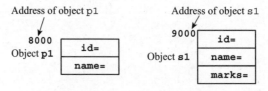

Figure 14.48:   Objects p1 and s1

The statement

```
Person *p;
```

creates a Person type pointer p
    The statement

```
p=&p1;
```

stores the address of a Person object p1 inside the pointer p. This means that the pointer p now points to a Person object as seen in the Figure 14.49a.

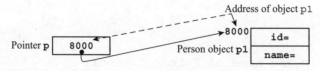

Figure 14.49a: Pointer p points to the parent object p1

The statement

```
p-> inputP ();
```

will invoke inputP() function defined in class Person which will accept the id and name of the Person object p1 as input from the user. Assuming that the sample user inputs are id=1 and name= John, the state of object p1 after execution of this statement is as shown in the Figure 14.49b.

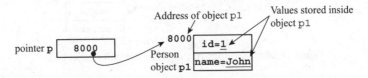

Figure 14.49b: State of object p1 after execution of p->inputP();

Similarly, the statement

```
p-> output ();
```

will invoke the output () function defined in class Person, which will print the id and name of the Person object p1 on the computer screen. Hence, assuming data as per Figure 14.49b, the values 1 and John appear on the computer screen after execution of the output () function.

> **There are two different output() functions, one in class Person and the other in class Student.** ❓
> **How does compiler determine which output() function to call when invoked using a pointer?**
>
> 📖 Complier decides which function to be call based on the type of pointer using which the function is invoked. In this case pointer p is declared of type **Person**, hence the statement,
>
> ```
> p->output();
> ```
>
> invokes the output () function defined in class **Person**.
>   When you compile the program every function you call gets attached to the correct function definition of the function which is to be invoked. In general, the process of establishing a link between a function call and the function definition is called as binding. Binding that happens at the time of compilation of the program is called as **early binding**. Hence a one line answer to this question is that, early binding is responsible to invoke output () function defined in the correct class. This concept is also true for the following statement:
>
> ```
> p->inputP();
> ```
>
> Here, compiler searches and calls the inputP() function in class Person because the data type of pointer p is Person. Its just that we never bothered before about how compiler correctly invokes inputP() function because there is just one point inputP() function throughout the program. But it is equally important to understand that the concept of early binding applies here as well.
>   In principle, early binding is performed for all the functions calls we make in the program (except for function calls to virtual functions). Virtual functions are discussed in detail in section 14.12

The statement

```
p=&s1;
```

makes the pointer p to point to a child object s1 as shown in the Figure 14.50a. This statement will execute successfully because p is a 'parent' type pointer, and it can point to a 'child' type object.

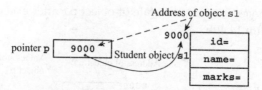

Figure 14.50a: Pointer p points to the child object s1

Let's focus on inputP() for a moment. If we would have written the below statement in the program.

```
p->inputP();
```

it would work correctly and invoke the inputP() function. This is because the function inputP() is defined inside class Person and is also inherited by the Student object. And as the pointer p points to the Student object s1, the statement **cin>>id>>name;** will take only the id and name of s1 as input from the user. You must be thinking what about member marks? This member will be left uninitialized because inputP() does not take care of it. Hence, we do not invoke the function inputP() in our program (even if we can) because it fails to set the value of marks for the Student object (leaving it as junk) as shown in the Figure 14.50b.

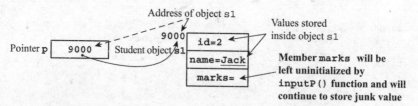

Figure 14.50b: State of object s1 after execution of p->inputP();

Given all of it, we do not want to invoke inputP() function using pointer p this time because it actually points to Student object. So, let's try to invoke the function inputS() defined in class Student using pointer p as

```
p->inputS(); //ERROR
```

This statement will give a compilation error saying **function not found**. I say it again that the compiler decides which function to call based on the data type of the pointer p (which is Person) and not based on the data type of the object to which the pointer points. This means that even if the pointer p is actually pointing to a Student object, the compiler will still search for the inputS() function in class Person because the data type of the pointer is `Person`. And as the function is not present in `Person`, the compilation of the program will fail giving a 'function not found' error.

In reality, we are sure that the pointer p actually points to a `Student` object because we are the one storing the address of `s1` in p. Hence we expect `p->inputS();` to invoke the function `inputS()` of `Student` object, so as to accept the `id`, `name` and `marks` of the `Student` as input from the user. But this does not happen due to the principle of early binding mentioned before. To solve this problem, we have two options:

Option 1: Create another pointer (say q) of type `Student` and store the address of object s1 in q

```
Student *q;
q=&s1;
```

Now, the statement

```
q->inputS();
```

will correctly invoke `inputS()` function defined in class `Student` because data type of pointer q is `Student`.

Option 2: Perform type casting of pointer p

Cast the pointer p to type `Student`, so that compiler searches for the function **inputS()** in class `Student` instead of class `Person`. We can type cast pointer p to `Student` as shown in the statement below:

```
((Student*)p)->inputS();
```

The above statement will also work correctly and invoke the `inputS()` function, which is defined inside class `Student` because the type of p is now converted to `Student`. We have applied this type conversion as we are sure that the pointer p actually points to a `Student` object at runtime of the program.

NOTES

Accidently if you type cast the pointer p to `Student` type when it is **not really** pointing to a `Student` **object,** the compilation of the program will **still succeed** but the program will give a **run time error**. Type casting a pointer is indeed a **very risky** operation and must be performed very carefully; this is because type casting is a check that is qualified at the time of compilation of the program but the pointer **p** is actually initialized to point to **Student object** at runtime. Hence, your mistake may simply go **unnoticed** at the time of **compilation** of the program even if you have performed **type casting wrongly**. Type casting done wrongly could give **bad surprises** to the programmer when the program runs and may require the redesign of full logic of the code; as the core assumption that the pointer is pointing to a specific data type is itself found to be **incorrect**. To avoid this situation, there are a certain cast validating operators like **static_cast** and **dynamic_cast** which the programmer can use to validate if the casting is applied correctly. These operators are discussed in Section 14.15.

In this case, we have correctly applied type casting because pointer p actually points to `Student` object. Hence, the statement **(Student*)p->inputS();** will now accept `id`, `name`, and `marks` of a `Student` object as input from the user. Assuming that the sample user inputs are `id=2, name= Jack,` and `marks=90`, the state of object `p1` after execution of this statement is as shown in the Figure 14.50c.

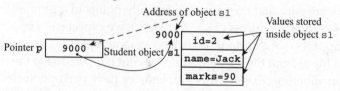

Figure 14.50c: State of object `s1` after execution of `(Student*)p->inputS();`

To confirm our understanding on this topic, let us try to invoke the `output()` function. Note that the function `output()` is overridden, which means that it is present in both parent as well as the child class but this does not change our explanation given before in anyway. Once again, the statement

```
p-> output();
```

will invoke the `output()` function defined in class `Person` because the data type of the pointer `p` is `Person`. The `output()` function will execute a `cout` statement, which will print only the `id` and `name` of the `Student` object. Hence, it would just print value of `id(2)` and `name(Jack)` on the computer screen. We do not want to invoke this `output()` function because it does not print the value of member `marks` at all. However, we are very sure that the pointer `p` is currently pointing to a `Student` object, hence we type cast pointer `p` to correctly invoke `output()` function of class `Student` as shown below:

```
((Student*)p)->output();
```

The above statement will now invoke the `output()` function defined inside class `Student` which will print the `id, name` as well as `marks` of the `Student` object. Assuming data as per Figure 14.50c, the values 2, `Jack` and 90 will appear on the computer screen after execution of the `output()` function.

Can I invoke a function defined in parent class using a pointer of type child? **?**

Of course yes! Don't confuse between early binding and the basic principle of Inheritance. The basic principle of inheritance says that anything that is defined in parent class will be available in child class. Hence, technically all the parent members are available within the child object and they can be accessed using a "child" type variable.

For example, if we create a pointer of type `Student` and make it point to a `Student` object `s1` as shown below

```
Student *q;
q=&s1;
```

you can still invoke function `inputP()` using pointer q as:

```
q->inputP();
```

This is because `inputP()` is a function defined in class `Person` which is anyway inherited by `Student` and hence accessible to `Student` object `s1`. Early binding is not going to change this fact. To explain the same thing in other words, principle of early binding will search the function `inputP()` within type `Student`, because the data type of pointer q is Student. The function `inputP()` will be found in type `Student` because you must understand that although `inputP()` is not defined within class `Student`, it is inherited by class `Student` from its parent `Person`. So, there is no reason why early binding would fail.

NOTES

When a parent type variable is casted to child type so as to access members defined in child class, then it is called **down casting**. Conversely, when child type variable is casted into a parent type then it is called as **up casting**.

Example of Down Casting

The statement

```
((Student*)p)->inputS();
```

converts the type of p to `Student` for correctly invoking the function `inputS()`. The original data type of pointer p is `Person`(parent) which is casted to `Student`(child) to resolve the function call to `inputS()`. Hence this is an example of down casting because we are casting a parent type pointer to a child type. Down casting must always be performed **explicitly** whenever needed.

Example of Up Casting

The statement

```
p=&s1;
```

is an example of up casting, because s1 is of type `Student`(child) whose address is stored in pointer p which is of type `Person`(parent). In this case, up casting is performed **implicitly** without any efforts from the programmer. You can also perform the same action **explicitly** as shown below.

```
p=(Person*)&s1;
```

14.11   Overriding a Function with Different Return Type

Once again, when a function defined in parent class is overridden by the child class, the **function signature** of the functions in parent and child class must exactly match. Function signature of the function includes

1. Name of the function
2. Number of arguments the function accepts as parameters
3. Data type of each of the arguments
4. Order of arguments

Clearly, return type of the function is not the part of its signature, and hence it is possible that the return type of the function overridden by the child class is different than that of the one defined in parent class. Consider an example below, where function add() defined in parent class Abc is overridden by the child class Child. Note that the add() takes two arguments of type integer in both the definitions. However, the return types are different, the add() function in parent class returns void, whereas that of the child class returns int. Having different return types is perfectly fine because there is no mismatch as far as the function signature is concerned. From the given code, we will learn different ways of invoking add() function of parent and child class using pointers.

```
#include<iostream.h>
class Abc
{
```

```cpp
    public:
    void add(int a,int b)
    {
    int res = a+b;
    cout<<"Addition is "<<res<<endl;
    }

};
class Child: public Abc
{
    public:
    int add(int a,int b)
    {
    int res = a+b;
    return res;
    }
};
void main()
{
/*Parent type pointer*/
    Abc *p;
/*Child type object*/
    Child o1;
/*Parent pointer p pointing to child object o1*/
    p=&o1;
/*Calls add function defined in parent class - due to default
    Early Binding*/
    p->add(10,20);
/*Calls add function of child class - due to default Early
    binding*/
    int res1 =((Child*)p)->add(80,85);
    cout<<"Add returned: "<<res1<<endl;
/*Child type pointer q pointing to a child object o1*/
    Child *q = &o1;
/*Calls add function of child class - due to default Early
    binding*/
    int res2 =(q->add(40,45));
    cout<<"Add returned: "<<res2<<endl;
/*Calls add function of parent class - due to Explicit UP
    casting*/
    ((Abc*)q)->add(100,15);
/*Another way to call Parent function using child type pointer q*/
q->Abc::add(200,225);
}
```

The first three statements of `main()` function

```
Abc *p;
Child o1;
p=&o1;
```

create a parent type pointer named as p and make it point to a child object o1.

The statement

```
p->add(10,20);
```

will invoke `add()` defined in parent class which does not return anything. This is because data type of the pointer p is `Abc`, which directs the compiler to invoke `add()` defined in class `Abc` as per principle of early binding.

The next statement

```
int res1 = ((Child*)p)->add(80,85);
```

performs **explicit down casting** of pointer p to `Child*`. Hence, this statement will invoke `add()` defined in `Child` which returns an integer. The result of addition will be stored in `res1`.

The statement

```
Child *q = &o1;
```

creates a `Child` type pointer q and makes it point to the existing child object o1.

The statement

```
int res2 = (q->add(40,45));
```

will invoke the `add()` defined in `Child` which returns an integer value. This is because data type of the pointer q is `Child`, which directs the compiler to invoke `add()` defined in class `Child` as per principle of early binding.

If you need to invoke `add()` defined in parent class using the pointer q, you can perform **explicit up casting** of q to parent type `Abc*`. The statement

```
((Abc*)q)->add(100,15);
```

will invoke `add()` function in parent class that returns `void` because of up casting applied to pointer q. This is one of the cases where up casting needs to be applied explicitly.

Another method to invoke the `add()` function in parent class using a pointer q is with the help of **scope resolution** operator as shown below:

```
q->Abc::add(200,225);
```

This statement instructs the compiler to invoke the `add()` function which is inherited from class `Abc` even if the data type of the q is `Child`.

14.12 Virtual Functions and Runtime Polymorphism

We understand from the previous section that even if the parent type pointer points to a child object, the compiler cannot invoke the functions defined in child class unless **down**

casting is applied explicitly. Although, applying down casting is one of the solutions, it is may not be always possible to implement it. Consider a situation in which you have more than 100 child classes (C1 to C100) and a function f1() of parent, is overridden by each of them. So, when you create a parent type pointer p, it has the ability to point to the parent object and to any of the child objects. Hence, p can mold itself to point to 101 distinct object types (one parent type and 100 different child type objects). This ability of a parent type pointer to take multiple forms is called **polymorphism.**

You are required to design a generic caller code, using a parent type pointer p, which will correctly invoke the function f1() of the right class whose object is pointer by p. The requirement is as shown in the Figure 14.51 where the caller code has an formal argument p which is of type parent, and hence you can pass object of any of 101 classes to it. The question is how would you ensure that f1() of a correct class is invoked using p inside caller?

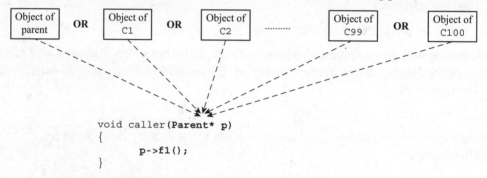

Figure 14.51: Requirement for a generic caller code

The statement

```
p->f1();
```

inside the caller code will always invoke f1() defined in parent immaterial of the type of object passed to it due to the principle of early binding. Also, it is not possible to apply down casting at this stage because we really don't know object of which type will be passed to the caller. Is this really polymorphism? Definitely not, because although we say that the pointer p can point to 101 different types of objects, it can invoke functions defined in one class only. The real issue is that the decision on which function to call is taken at compile time itself (based on type of p), whereas the actual object to which p points known at runtime of the program. Since the decision is taken earlier at compilation stage, even before the target object is known, this type of binding is called as **early binding or static binding**.

The only way to solve this problem is to defer the decision on which function to call at **runtime of the program**. This is because we would know the exact target object to which pointer p points only at runtime of the program (when the object is actually passed to the caller). Such a deferred binding which happens at runtime is called **late binding or dynamic binding**.

The next question is how do we implement late binding? The answer simple: late binding is performed only for special type of functions called **virtual functions**. If you want late binding to happen for a particular function, you must create that function as virtual.

Hence, to solve this problem, we must create f1() as a virtual function, which means that the statement

```
p->f1();
```

will invoke the function in the correct class whose object is pointed by the pointer p.

To create a function as virtual, keyword virtual must be added to the function defined in parent class. There is no need to specify keyword virtual in each of the child classes which override the function. Figure 14.52 gives the syntax of creating f1() as a virtual function.

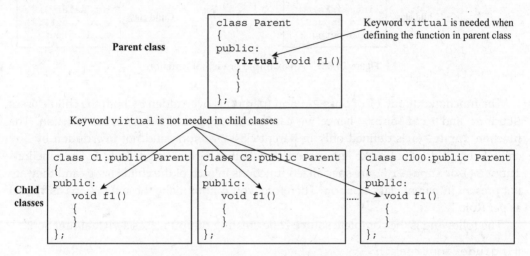

Figure 14.52: Syntax of creating virtual functions

The following are rules for creating virtual functions:

1. A function can be created as virtual only if it is present in parent class. If the function is present only in child class but not in parent, then you cannot make the function as virtual.

2. A child class may or may not override the virtual function defined by parent class. If the child class overrides the virtual function defined in parent, C++ guarantees that the function defined in correct child class will be called, when invoked using a pointer pointing to child object.

3. If the child class does not override the virtual function defined by parent, the function defined in parent class will be called when invoked by a pointer pointing to a child object.

4. It makes sense to create a function as virtual only if it's overridden by at least one child class. If the function is only defined in parent class and no child overrides it, then it means that every child is interested in using the same implementation as that of the parent and function of parent class must be invoked in all cases even if the pointer points to child. This is the default behaviour of early binding anyways; and hence there is no need to create virtual functions in this case.

As an example of virtual functions, let us consider the hierarchy as shown in the Figure 14.53:

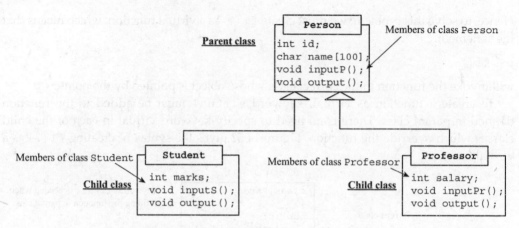

Figure 14.53: An example of virtual function

The function output() of class Person (parent) is overridden by both the child classes Student and Professor, hence we can create output() as a virtual function. The function inputP() is defined only in parent class Person and not overridden by any child, hence it does not make any sense to create it as virtual as per Rule 4. The functions inputS() or inputPr() are specialized functions in each of the child classes and they are not present in parent class Person. Therefore, you cannot make these functions as virtual as per Rule 1.

The following is the complete source code creating output() as a virtual function:

```cpp
#include<iostream.h>
class Person
{
protected:
    int id;
    char name[100];
public:
    void inputP()
    {
    cin>>id>>name;
    }
    virtual void output()
    {
    cout<<id<<" "<<name<<endl;
    }
};
class Student: public Person
{
private:
int marks;
public:
```

```
    void inputS()
    {
    cin>>id>>name>>marks;
    }
    void output()
    {
    cout<<id<<" "<<name<<"  "<<marks<<endl;
    }
};
class Professor: public Person
{
private:
int salary;
public:
    void inputPr()
    {
    cin>>id>>name>>salary;
    }
    void output()
    {
    cout<<id<<" "<<name<<"  "<<salary<<endl;
    }
};
void main()
{
Person p1;
Student s1;
Professor prof1;
Person *p;
p=&p1;
cout<<"Enter id and name of Person "<<endl;
p->inputP();
cout<<"Person details are "<<endl;
p->output ();
p=&s1;
cout<<"Enter id, name and marks of Student "<<endl;
((Student*)p)->inputS();
cout<<"Student details are "<<endl;
p->output ();
p=&prof1;
cout<<"Enter id, name and salary of Professor "<<endl;
((Professor*)p)->inputPr();
cout<<"Professor details are "<<endl;
```

```
p->output ();
}
Enter id and name of Person
1 John
Person details are
1 John
Enter id, name and marks of Student
2 Jack 90
Student details are
2 Jack 90
Enter id, name and salary of Professor
3 Jill 5000
Professor details are
3 Jill 5000
```

The first three statements of main () function

```
Person p1;
Student s1;
Professor prof1;
```

create objects of class Person, Student, and Professor respectively, as shown in the Figure 14.54.

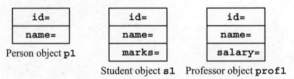

Figure 14.54: Objects p1, s1, and prof1

We create a pointer of type Person (parent type) in the program, using the statement below:

```
Person *p;
```

We can make the pointer p to point to parent object or to any of the child objects.

The statement

```
p=&p1;
```

makes the pointer p to point to Person (parent) object p1. There has to be no confusion at this stage because the type of the pointer is same as the type of the object to which it points to. Hence the statements

```
p->inputP ();
```

and

```
p->output ();
```

invoke the inputP () and output () functions defined in class Person. It is still important to technically differentiate between the two calls: inputP () is not a virtual

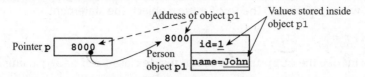

Figure 14.55: State of object p1

function and hence early binding will be performed for resolving its call, whereas output () is a virtual function and hence late binding will be performed for resolving its call. In this case, since the data type of pointer and object is exactly same, it really doesn't matter to us as to which type of binding internally happens but C++ will always perform late binding for virtual functions. Assuming the sample inputs as id=1 and name=John, Figure 14.55 shows the state of object p1 and a pointer p pointing to it.

The statement

```
p=&s1;
```

makes the pointer p point to a Student object s1 as shown in the Figure 14.56. Object of class Student has three members and we need to invoke the function inputS () to accept all the three values as input from the user. We have mentioned before that inputS () is not (and cannot be) created as a virtual function because it is only defined in the child class. Hence the only option to invoke it using a parent pointer p is by **explicitly down casting** the pointer to Student* as discussed in section 14.10. This is as seen in the statement

```
((Student*)p)->inputS();
```

Assuming the sample input values as id=2, name=Jack, and marks=90 the state of Student object s1 will be as shown in the Figure 14.56.

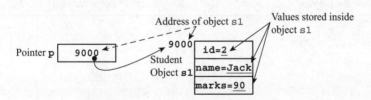

Figure 14.56 State of Student object s1

The statement

```
p->output();
```

will invoke the output () function defined in class Student. This is because the function output () is a virtual function, and the decision on which output () function to call is taken based on the type of the object pointed by p and not based on the type of p; as per the principle of late binding. Therefore, the statement correctly invokes the output () function of class Student because p points to the object of type Student. This will print the values id, name, and marks of object s1 on the computer screen.

Similarly, when p points to the `Professor` object, the statement

```
p->output();
```

will correctly invoke the `output()` function inside class `Professor` using late binding.

NOTES

Binding is a process to attach a function call with the function definition. We have discussed **early binding** in Chapter 11 Section 11.25. In this section, we have explained another type of binding called as **late binding** which is performed only for virtual functions. Given below is the comparison of these two types of bindings performed by C++ in different scenarios and at different times

Early binding	Late binding
This is the binding performed at compile time of the program. This is also called as static binding or compile time binding	This is the binding performed at run time of the program. This is also called as dynamic binding or run time binding
This type of binding is performed in following cases of polymorphism 1. Function overloading 2. Operator overloading 3. Constructor overloading	This type of binding is performed for virtual functions only
This is a basic binding performed by the compiler to resolve any of the function calls made to non-virtual functions	
If p is the pointer invoking the function, then the decision about which function to call is taken based on the data type of p and is immaterial of the data type of the target object to which p points to.	If p is the pointer invoking the function, the decision about which function to call is taken based on the type of target object to which p points to.
This type of binding is used to implement compile time polymorphism in the program	This type of binding is used to implement run time polymorphism in the program

NOTES

When a virtual function is defined in parent class has a return type R, then the return type of the function overridden in child class must be either R or a child of R.

For example, the following overriding of virtual function will give an error because the return type of `output()` defined in parent class P is `int` and it does not match with the return type of `output()` defined in child class C which is `float`.

```
class Abc
{
public:
        virtual int output() //returns int
        {
```

```
        /*virtual function returning an integer*/
        ........................
        ........................
        }
};
class Pqr: public Abc
{
public:
        float output() //ERROR - return types mismatch
        {
        /* function returning a float*/
        ........................
        ........................
        }
};
```

As another example, if class `Student` is a child class of class `Person`, the below overriding of virtual function will work fine without any error. This is because the `output()` function defined in class `Abc` returns an object of class `Person` whereas the return type of `output()` function in class `Pqr` is `Student` (which is child of `Person`)

```
class Abc
{
public:
        virtual Person output() //Returns a Person object
        {
        /*virtual function returning Person object*/
        ........................
        ........................
        }
};
class Pqr: public Abc
{
public:
        Student output() /*This is fine, because Student is a child of
                                                        Person*/
        {
        /* function returning a Student object*/
        ........................
        ........................
        }
};
```

Unlike virtual functions, when a non-virtual function is overridden it does not put any rule on the return types as discussed in Section14.9.

RUNTIME POLYMORPHISM

Clearly, pointer p in this example, has an ability to point to different types of objects thereby taking multiple forms. When,

```
p=&p1;
```

makes the pointer p to point to a generalized object of class `Person`. Hence, p in this case is taking a form of a person in real world who is neither `Student` nor a `Professor`.

When,

```
p=&s1;
```

p is pointing to a Student object thereby taking a form of person who is student in the real world .

And finally, when

```
p=&prof1;
```

p is pointing to a `Professor` object thereby taking a form of a person who is professor in real world.

So who is p, a student, a professor or neither of them? The answer is p takes the form of all of them but one at a time; as and when the program runs. Making `output ()` function as virtual ensures that,

```
p->output();
```

will call the `output ()` function of the correct class whose form is taken by p at a moment.

This ability of a pointer p to take multiple forms during the program execution (at runtime) is called as **run time polymorphism**. Virtual functions are used to implement run time polymorphism. Only making the pointer of type parent without creating necessary virtual functions does not make any sense because you would land up in always accessing parent functions even if the pointer changes its form to one of the child types. Hence, your program must have at least one virtual function if you wish to implement runtime polymorphism. Multiple forms taken by pointer p are as shown in Figure 14.57.

Pointer p taking a form of a Person

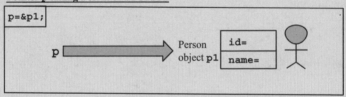

Pointer p taking a form of a Student

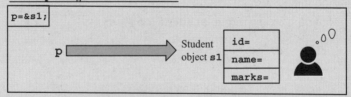

Pointer p taking a form of a Professor

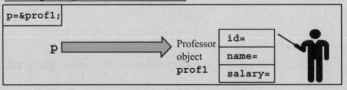

Figure 14.57: Runtime polymorphism

14.13   Virtual Tables

C++ internally creates virtual tables (VTABLEs) to correctly determine which function definition to call when runtime polymorphism is implemented in the code. Runtime polymorphism can only be supported using virtual functions, hence the compiler internally creates VTABLEs in memory only for classes that contain at least one virtual function or classes which derive from them.

Compiler also adds a hidden pointer called virtual table pointer as a member of the class for which a VTABLE is created. This pointer is named as _vptr, and it points to the virtual table of that class.

There can be only one virtual table per class. A virtual table is basically a collection of pointers which point to functions, such that each pointer in the table points to one virtual function of the class. So if the class has x number of virtual functions defined, then the VTABLE will contain x number of pointers. To understand how C++ internally makes use of VTABLEs to facilitate runtime polymorphism, we will revisit our example in Section 14.12. Parent class Person defines a virtual function named as output(), and child classes Student and Professor override it. Therefore, VTABLE is created for each of the classes. The hidden pointer _vptr in each of the class points to the respective VTABLE, as shown in the Figure 14.58. C++ defines the hidden pointer _vptr only in the parent class, the child classes inherit this pointer. The _vptr of a particular class is initialized to point to the virtual table of that class as soon as the object of the class is created.

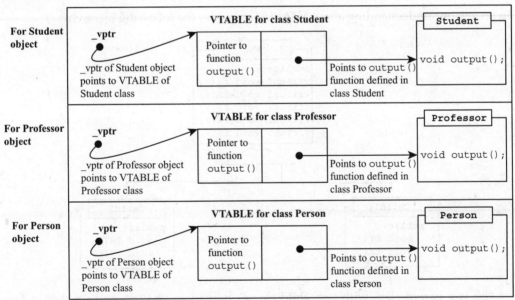

Figure 14.58   VTABLEs for classes Student, Professor and Person

Each of the VTABLES have a pointer to the function output(), which points to the correct output() function to be invoked for the object of the respective class. The pointer to function output() present in the VTABLE of class Student will point to the output() function of class Student, the pointer to function output() present in the VTABLE of class `Professor` will point to the output () function in class `Professor` and same is true for class `Person` as well.

In the program given in Section14.12, we have created a `Person` type pointer p which points to a `Student` type object s1. When `Student` object s1 is created, _vptr for `Student` object is initialized to point to the VTABLE of `Student` class. Also the pointer to function output () in the VTABLE of `Student` points to the output () function defined in class `Student`. Hence the statement

```
p->output();
```

will invoke the output () function defined in class `Student` because the VTABLE of class `Student` contains a pointer to it. Similarly, when the pointer p points to the `Professor` object prof1, VTABLE of `Professor` class is used to resolve virtual function invocations. Hence the statement

```
p->output();
```

will invoke the output () function defined in class `Professor` because the VTABLE of class `Professor` contains a pointer to it.

In summary, virtual tables are used to determine which function definition to invoke when runtime polymorphism is implemented in the program using virtual functions.

14.13.1 Virtual tables: A quick review

To review our understanding about VTABLES consider the following hierarchy:

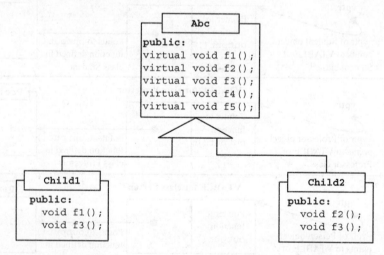

Abc is a parent class with two child classes named as `Child1` and `Child2`. Class Abc defines five virtual functions, f1 () , f2 () , f3 () , f4 () , and f5 () . Class `Child1` overrides functions f1 ()   and f3 () , whereas `Child2` overrides f2 () and f3 () . Compiler will create three VTABLEs for each of these classes as shown in the Figure 14.59. The VTABLE of each class will contain five function pointers because there are five virtual functions in parent class. Each pointer within the VTABLE of a particular class points to correct function to be invoked when runtime polymorphism is implemented in the code.

For example, consider the VTABLE created for class Child1, the pointer to functions f1() and f3() point to the respective function definitions in Child1, whereas the pointers to the remaining functions f2(), f4(), and f5() point to the corresponding function definitions in parent class. This is because class Child1 overrides only two functions f1() and f3(). The thumb rule is that, if a child class does not override the virtual function, then the corresponding pointer present in the VTABLE will continue to point to the parent implementation of virtual function. And if the child class overrides the parent implementation the pointer in VTABLE will point to the function defined in child class. This is as seen in the Figure 14.59. Note that the pointers within the VTABLE of parent class will always point to the functions defined in parent itself.

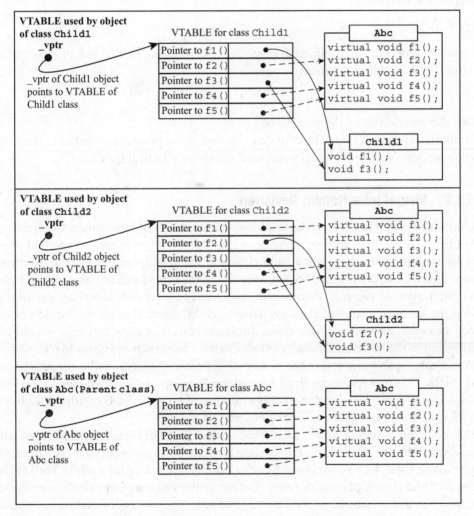

Figure 14.59 VTABLEs for classes Child1, Child2 and Abc

Consider the following statements, where we create a pointer of type parent (Abc) named as p and an object of type Child1 named as o1.

```
Abc *p;
Child1 o1;
```

The moment object of Child1 is created, the virtual pointer (_vptr) for this object is initialized to point to the VTABLE present for class Child1. This VTABLE will now be used for resolving any virtual function invocations with this object.

Let's make the pointer p point to object o1,

```
p=&o1;
```

When we invoke any virtual function using pointer p, it will be resolved using the VTABLE of Child1 (because _vptr for o1 points to it).

Hence, the statement

```
p->f1();
```

will invoke function f1() defined in class Child1, referring to VTABLE of class Child1 in Figure 14.59. And the statement

```
p->f2();
```

will invoke function f2() defined in class Abc.

Similarly, when we create object of Child2 and make pointer p point to it, the virtual function invocations using p will be resolved using the VTABLE for Child2.

14.13.2 Virtual inheritance: Revisited

VTABLEs also play a key role in the implementation of virtual inheritance. Compiler uses VTABLEs to ensure that a single instance of grandparent class is created in child even if there are multiple paths between a child class and the grandparent class. For example, if you see figure 14.44 in Section 14.8, we have made the class Person as a virtual base to avoid duplication of Person members in class AssistantProf. Inheritance is all about making the instance of parent class available in child object. If at all we would not have created Person as a virtual base class, duplicate objects of class Person would have been present in the object of class AssistantProf, as shown in Figure 14.60.

This creates ambiguity errors when accessing Person object within the Assistant Prof class. This problem is resolved by making Person as a virtual base class. Doing so, instructs the compiler to maintain only one copy of Person object within the object of class AssistantProf as shown in the Figure 14.61.

However, the design of AssistantProf object given in Figure 14.61 is not practical because it will create issues during up casting it to one of its parent objects. To understand the up casting issue, let's go to classes Student and Professor for a while. Both of these classes are child classes of class Person and hence the Person object will be embedded with the object of Student as well as Professor. The objects of class Student and Professor are as shown in the Figure 14.62.

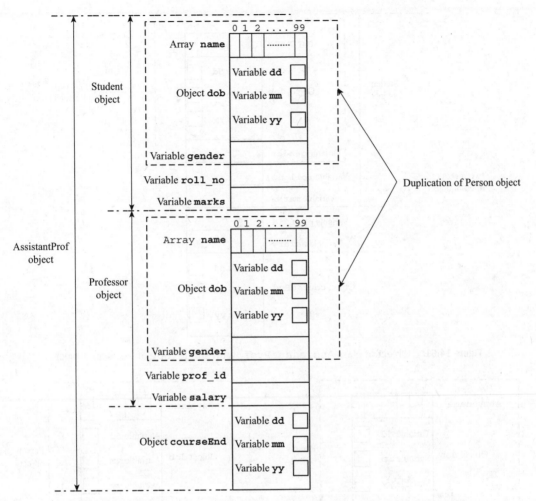

Figure 14.60: Object of class `AssistantProf` with duplication of `Person` object

Up casting is usually performed when you want to use the child object as if it is a parent object. In reality, the parent object is just a sub part of the child object, and hence when you perform up casting, it means that you want to use just one portion of child object (which is the parent object). The principle of inheritance is that the child object contains all the features of parent along with additional functionalities defined in child itself. By up casting child object to a parent object, you are in a way reducing the features you already have. Hence there should not be any case where up casting is not possible. The design of `AssistantProf` object given in Figure 14.63 is not realistic because it does not allow up casting it to a `Professor` object. For up casting operation to be possible the parent object must be stored in contiguous memory locations within the child object because only then it can extract the full parent object from the child object.

If o1 is an object of class `AssistantProf`, the statement

```
Student *p = &o1;
```

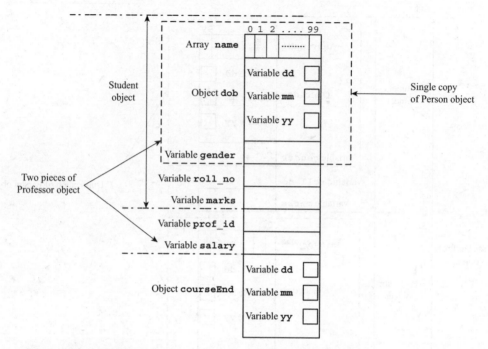

Figure 14.61: Object of class `AssistantProf` with single copy of `Person` object

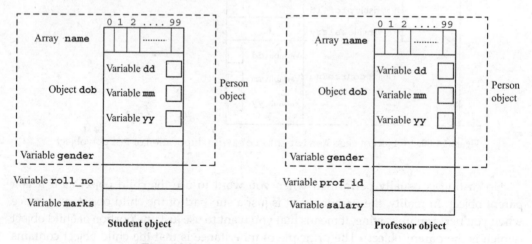

Figure 14.62: `Student` and `Professor` objects

performs up casting by extracting only the `Student` object from the `AssistantProf` object. This is very well possible because the `Student` object is stored at contagious memory locations within `AssistantProf` object as shown in Figure 14.63. However, as seen from the figure, the two pieces of `Professor` object are not stored at contagious memory locations within o1. Hence, it is practically not possible to extract the complete `Professor` object out of o1, which means that you cannot perform up casting to `Professor` type. This is clearly not acceptable; and hence this means that the design given in Figure 14.63 for an object of class `AssistantProf` is wrong and unacceptable.

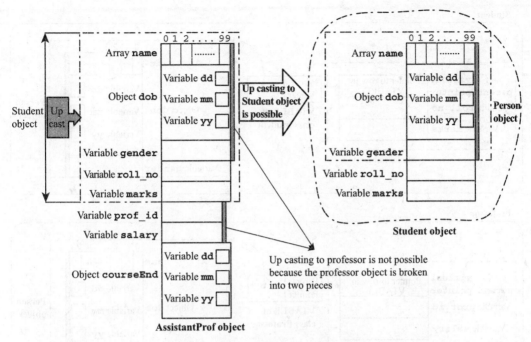

Figure 14.63: Up casting possibilities

How does C++ design the object of class `AssistantProf`? This question still remains unanswered which we will answer now. To correctly design an object of `AssistantProf`, the compiler first changes the design of `Student` and `Professor` objects. Instead of storing `Person` object directly in `Student` object, the compiler creates a virtual parent pointer in `Student` object, which points to the entry in VTABLE that contains the address of `Person` object. The principle is that, instead of storing an object of parent class within the child class, the compiler creates a pointer in child class that points to the parent object (through a VTABLE as shown in Figure 14.64). Similarly the structure of the `Professor` object is also modified as shown in the Figure 14.64.

So, the structure of `Student`/`Professor` objects can be fully represented as a virtual parent pointer followed by the respective specialized members.

Now, let's focus on the structure of the object of class `AssistantProf`. Since this class has two parent classes through which the duplication of `Person` data is possible; the object of class `AssistantProf` will have two different virtual parent pointers (one as a part of `Student` object and the other as a part of `Professor` object). This is because the `AssistantProf` object has both `Student` and `Professor` objects as a part of it. Each of the virtual parent pointers point to a different location in the VTABLE of `AssistantProf` class but both the VTABLE locations point to the same `Person` object as shown in the Figure 14.65. This is how compiler ensures that only one `Person` object is present within the object of class `AssistantProf`.

We can now see that both `Student` and `Professor` objects are now stored in contiguous memory locations, hence we can safely up cast this object to either `Student` or `Professor` types. Hence this design resolves all the issues of up casting we faced before.

Student

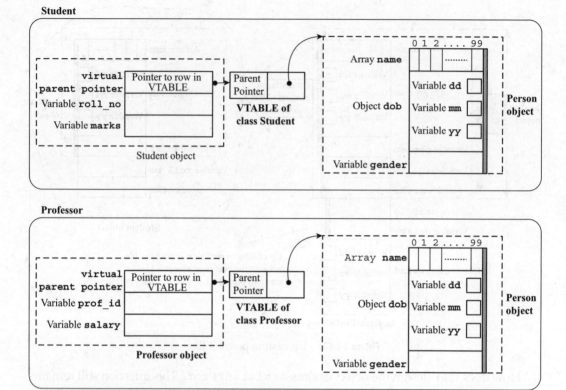

Professor

Figure 14.64: Modified structure of `Student` and `prof` objects

AssistantProf

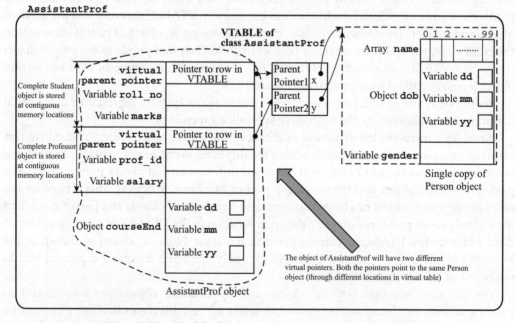

The object of AssistantProf will have two different virtual pointers. Both the pointers point to the same Person object (through different locations in virtual table)

Figure 14.65: Modified structure of `AssistantProf` object

In Figure 14.65, why do the two virtual parent pointers point to a different location in VTABLE given that both the VTABLE entries point to the same Person object? ❓

📖 This is because VTABLE stores relative address (also called as offset) of the Person object. Offset gives the number of bytes you are away from the Person object with respect to the current location. Actually, the Person object is also the part of the same memory as that of the AssistantProf object. The actual Person object is stored at the end within the AssistantProf object. Let the actual location in memory at which the Person object is stored be x bytes away from first virtual pointer and y bytes away from second virtual pointer. These offsets (x and y) are stored at two different entries in VTABLE, and hence the virtual pointers point to two different locations of VTABLE (virtual parent pointer 1 points to the entry where x is stored and virtual parent pointer 2 points to the entry where y is stored in VTABLE).

14.14 Pure Virtual Functions and Abstract Classes

A virtual function with no function body is called a pure virtual function. Just like virtual functions, pure virtual functions are also used to implement runtime polymorphism.

As an example, let us implement hierarchy of classes shown in figure 14.66.

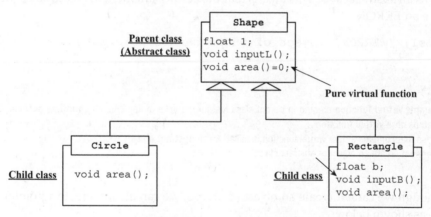

Figure 14.66: Shape and circle

The classes Circle and Rectangle are child classes of class Shape. Parent class Shape defines a member l, which can be used as a radius when computing the area of the circle and can be used as a length of the rectangle when computing the area of the rectangle. To calculate the area of rectangle we also need to store its breadth and hence a variable b is declared in the child class Rectangle as shown in the Figure 14.66.

To implement runtime polymorphism, we create the function area() as a virtual function as seen in the code. However, creating area() as virtual would mean that the function area() must be present in parent as well as the child class. We have created the function area() to a class Circle which calculates the area of circle as 3.14*l*l; as seen in the code. We have also added the function area() in class Rectangle that calculates the `area()` of a rectangle as `l*b` as seen in the code. However, in order to achieve runtime polymorphism, we must define `area()` in parent class `Shape` as well. This is because implementing runtime polymorphism is possible only when the function is created as virtual in parent class and overridden by the child classes. But what would the `area()` function in class `Shape` calculate? The challenge is that class `Shape` does not represent any concrete shape object in the real world. Therefore, we create an **empty virtual function** in class `Shape` just for the sake of implementing runtime polymorphism. Such an empty virtual function is called as a **pure virtual function,** which is defined as shown below:

```
virtual void area()=0;
```

The class that contains at least one pure virtual function is called as an **abstract class**. Abstract class is a class whose object can never be created. This is very reasonable because `Shape` does not have any concrete definition. If I give you pen and paper, can you create a shape? No, you will ask me which shape is to be created. You can draw rectangle, you can draw a circle, but if I ask you to draw just a shape, you can't create it because my question is incomplete. I would put it this way: if you cannot create a shape on paper, C++ should also not allow creating object of class `Shape`; which justifies why `Shape` is created as an abstract class. This means that the below statement to create object of `Shape` will give an ERROR.

```
Shape s1; //ERROR, object of Shape cannot be created
```

NOTES
1. An **empty virtual function** created in parent class just for the sake of implementing **runtime polymorphism** is called as **pure virtual function**
2. A class that contains a pure virtual function is called as an **abstract class**
3. We **cannot** create an object of abstract class.

Although we cannot create an object of `Shape`, we can always create a pointer of type `Shape` as shown below:

```
Shape *p; // This is correct, pointer of type Shape can be created
```

Remember this is a parent type pointer which can take multiple forms, thereby implementing runtime polymorphism. The following is a full source code, which implements runtime polymorphism by creating pure virtual function in class `Shape`

```cpp
#include<iostream.h>
class Shape
{
protected:
float l;
public:
    void inputL()
```

```
        {
        cin>>l;
        }
virtual void area()=0;
};
class Circle: public Shape
{
public:
        void area()
        {
        float a;
        a=3.14*l*l;
        cout<<"Area of circle is "<<a<<endl;
        }
};
class Rectangle: public Shape
{
private:
float b;
public:
        void inputB()
        {
        cin>>b;
        }
        void area()
        {
        float a;
        a= l*b;
        cout<<"Area of Rectangle is "<<a<<endl;
        }
};
void main()
{
Shape *s;
Circle c1;
Rectangle r1;
s=&c1;
cout<<"Enter radius of a circle "<<endl;
s->inputL();
s->area();
s=&r1;
cout<<"Enter length and breadth of a rectangle "<<endl;
s->inputL();
((Rectangle*)s)->inputB();
s->area();
}
```

Output

```
Enter radius of a circle
3.5
Area of circle is 38.465
Enter length and breadth of a rectangle
10 20
Area of Rectangle is 200
```

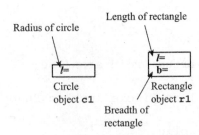

Figure 14.67: Objects c1 and r1

The first two statements in the main() function create the objects of Circle and Rectangle as shown in the Figure 14.67.

```
Circle c1;
Rectangle r1;
```

Note that no type casting is required to invoke a function inputL() using the pointer p because the function inputL() is defined in class Shape and the data type of the pointer p is also Shape. Therefore, the compiler will correctly invoke the function inputL() to accept the radius of the circle as input when the pointer p points to a Circle object and to accept the length of the Rectangle as input when the pointer p points to the Rectangle object.

The statement

```
p->area();
```

will invoke the area() function of the Circle object when the pointer p takes the form of a Circle, and it will correctly invoke the area() function of a Rectangle object when the pointer p takes a form of a Rectangle. This is because area() is declared as a virtual function.

Since the function inputB() is a specialized function defined in Rectangle only, we must perform type casting to Rectangle* when invoking this function using a parent pointer, as shown in the statement below:

```
((Rectangle*)s)->inputB();
```

> **NOTES**
>
> If class contains pure virtual functions, there is a NULL pointer created in a **VTABLE** of the class for each of the pure virtual functions. When concrete child class defines these functions, the corresponding VTABLE of the child class contains the pointer which points to the function defined in child class.

14.15 static_cast **and** dynamic_cast

We have used up casting and down casting extensively in the section 14.10. When the inheritance tree grows large, there are chances that programmers could make mistakes in casting pointer types resulting into a pointer not pointing to the correct type of object.

The operators static_cast and dynamic_cast are validating operators that programmers could use in the program to validate and make sure that the casting applied is correct and error free.

static_cast

The operator static_cast will check if the casting that is applied to the pointers is correct as per their data types at compile time. The operator static_cast will enforce the compiler to throw an error if casting is applied between incompatible data types. This logical error may simply go unnoticed without failing the compilation process if the operator static_cast is not used to validate the operation. Given below is the syntax to use static_cast operator to assign pointer q of type other than T2 to pointer p of type T2 .

```
T2 *p = static_cast <T2*>(q);
```

Consider the example below, which shows the usage of static_cast operator. The classes have been intentionally kept empty so that we focus only on the casting logic of pointers and usage of static_cast operator. There is a class Student , which is a child of class Person. Class Animal is an independent class and does not fall in the inheritance tree. It is neither parent nor child of anyone.

```
class Animal
{
/*..........
..........*/
};
class Person
{
/*..........
.......... */
};
class Student: public Person
{
/*..........
..........*/
};
void main()
{
Student *s = new Student;
Person *p = s; /*up casting*/
Animal *q =(Animal*)s; /* Incorrect casting done. But no compilation
                  error is reported by this statement */
Animal *r = static_cast<Animal*>(s);  /*Applying static_cast  will
fail the compilation process thereby generating an appropriate
error message */
}
```

The first statement in the main() function

```
Student *s = new Student;
```

creates a pointer of type Student, which points to a Student object. There is no casting performed as a part of this statement.

The second statement

```
Person *p = s;
```

assigns a pointer of type Student (named as s) to a pointer of type Person (named as p). This is absolutely fine because we know that the parent type pointer can point to child type object. C++ performs implicit type casting for this statement to execute correctly. This is called as up casting as mentioned in the section 14.10. While we are very confident that this will work correctly, we can always ask the compiler to explicitly validate the casting that we have applied. Hence the statement could be re-written as

```
Person *p = static_cast<Person*>(s);
```

This statement is equivalent to what we have written before, but in this case, the compiler will validate if the casting is applied correct. Given that casting is correct, the compiler will not fail and statement will execute as if it is written as Person *p = s;

The third statement

```
Animal *q =(Animal*)s;
```

performs a cast from Student type to Animal type. Clearly, this is a logically incorrect casting because s is of type Student and in no way related to Animal. However, the compiler does not generate any error at this stage, and this logical error goes unnoticed. In a way, we are fooling the compiler by using the cast operator at the correct place to avoid compile time errors. If the statement had been

```
Animal *q =s;
```

compiler would have generated an error because, in this case, the compiler needs to implicitly perform casting. By doing the casting ourselves, the compiler does not check for data type compatibilities assuming that programmer has taken care of it.

But if you consider statement 4,

```
Animal* r = static_cast<Animal*>(s);
```

it forces the compiler to validate the cast and hence the compiler generates error at this stage, indicating that this is an incorrect casting from type Student to type Animal. Hence static_cast forces the compiler to check logical correctness of casting even if casting is explicitly applied.

dynamic_cast

static_cast performs validations only based on the compile time data types of the pointers. At times this is not sufficient because the pointers may have different data type at runtime. For example, consider the statement

```
Person  *p = new Student;
```

The compile time type of pointer p is Person, but at runtime the pointer actually points to a Student object. Hence, we say that its runtime data type is Student. The validation based on the runtime data types can be performed using dynamic_cast.

To understand this principle, consider the code below:

```
#include <iostream>
class Person
{
public:
    virtual void output()
    {
    cout<<"Output function of class Person "<<endl;
    }
};
class Student:public Person
{
    void output()
    {
    cout<<"Output function of class Student "<<endl;
    }
};
void main()
{
    Person   *p1 = new Student();
    Person   *p2 = new Person ();
    Student  *p3 = dynamic_cast<Student*>(p1);
    if(p3!=0)
    {
    cout<<"Casting operation is correct\n";
    }
    else
    {
    cout<<"Casting operation is wrong\n";
    }
}
```

The statement,

```
p3 = dynamic_cast<Student*>(p1);
```

attempts to initialize pointer p1 to pointer p3. The data type of p3 is Student and pointer p1 also points to a Student object. Hence, this casting is perfectly fine, and as a result of this statement p3 points to the same Student object as p1. If it would have been the case that the dynamic_cast had failed, it would have made pointer p3 to contain zero (point to Null). In this case, since the casting is perfectly Ok, p3 does not point to NULL but points to a valid Student object, thereby printing following message on the computer screen.

```
Casting operation is correct
```

Instead, if we would have attempted to cast pointer p2, using the statement

```
p3 = dynamic_cast<Student*>(p2);
```

the dynamic_cast operator would have failed. This is because at runtime, pointer p2 points to Person object and not to Student object. Hence the program would print, following message on the screen because the operator dynamic_cast will make pointer p3 point to NULL in this case.

```
Casting operation is wrong
```

Note that if we validate this using a static_cast operator (using the statement below)

```
p3 = static_cast<Student*>(p2);
```

it would have been successful because static_cast validates only compile time types and assumes that the programmer will make the pointers point to the correct types at runtime. Hence usage of operator static_cast, in this case, would have given us incorrect results by making pointer p3 to point to a wrong object.

NOTES

dynamic_cast operator is used to validate if run time polymorphism is implemented correctly in the program. The only way to implement run time polymorphism is using virtual functions. Hence, for the dynamic_cast operator to work correctly, the parent class must have **at least one virtual function**. We have therefore created a virtual function named as output () in class Person.

14.16 Constructors and Inheritance

We can use constructors along with inheritance to initialize the members of the object at the time of creation. The object of child class also inherits the members that are defined in the parent class, and hence the constructor defined inside the child class should also initialize the members that are actually defined in parent class. Given below are the set of rules that we should remember when defining constructors in the parent and child class:

Rule 1: Whenever an object of a child class is created, a constructor in the parent class is executed before execution of the constructor in child class. C++ always invokes a default constructor of the parent class before executing the child constructor. If you do not want to invoke a default constructor of parent class when a child object is created, then you must explicitly specify which constructor is to be invoked. We will discuss an example of this case shortly.

Rule 2: If there is no constructor defined in the parent class, then the child class may or may not have a constructor inside it.

Rule 3: If there is a constructor with parameters defined in the parent class, then child class must also contain a constructor with parameters.

Rule 4: In case of multiple inheritance, the constructors in all the parent classes will be executed before a constructor of the child class can execute. The order of execution of the constructors defined in multiple parent classes will be same as that of the order in which the parent classes appear when defining the child class. For example, if C is the child class of three parent classes Px, Py, and Pz defined as follows:

```
class C: public Pz, public Py, public Px
{
............... .
............... .
............... .
};
```

On creation of object of class C, below is the order of constructor execution

Step 1: Execute constructor of Pz
Step 2: Execute constructor of Py
Step 3: Execute constructor of Px
Step 4: Execute the constructor of child class C

Note that the constructor of parent Pz executed first because it appears as first parent in the list of parents when defining class C, the constructor of parent Py is executed next, and so on. The child constructor is always executed at the end after all the parent constructors complete their execution. The only exception to this rule is that if any one of the parents is a virtual base class, then its constructor is always executed first, irrespective of the order. The constructors of remaining parent classes will be executed in an order in which they are specified.

Rule 1 says that C++ always invokes a default constructor of the parent class before executing the child constructor. What if there is no default constructor in the parent class? This could be the case if you have written a constructor with parameters in the parent class without writing any constructor in parent that takes no parameters. In this case, it is the responsibility of the child constructor to explicitly invoke a specific constructor of parent class otherwise compiler will complain throwing an error. So as to handle such a situation, given below is the syntax to explicitly invoke the correct parent constructor from the child constructor. In case of multiple inheritance, there are multiple parent classes and hence which constructor is to be invoked for each parent class is specified as a comma separated list of constructor invocations.

```
child-constructor(<arguments>):<comma separated call to parent
    constructors>
{
/*Initialization of the child members*/
}
```

Let us consider an example below which creates two classes named as P and C such that P is a parent class and C is its child. The parent class P defines two constructors as seen in the code. The first constructor gives a default value to the member a and 20, and the second constructor is a parameterized constructor which could be used to initialize the value of the a. Further, the child class also contains a parameterized constructor to initialize the value of its member b as seen in the code.

```
#include<iostream.h>
class P
{
protected:
    int a;
public:
    P()
    {
      a=20;
    }
    P(int t)
    {
      a=t;
    }
};
class C: public P
{
private:
    int b;
public:
    C(int t)
    {
    b=t;
    }
    void display()
    {
    cout<<"Result is "<<a+b;
    }
};
void main()
{
C o1(50);
o1.display();
}
```

```
Turbo C++ IDE
Result is 70
```

To understand the working of constructors with inheritance, let us understand the given code from the first line of main() function.

The statement

```
C o1(50);
```

creates an object of child class C named as o1. It also invokes a constructor of the child class by passing a value 50 as an argument to the constructor. Note that o1 is an object of child class, and hence the object o1 will have two members a and b in its object memory; where the member a is an inherited from the parent class P. Given below is the sequence that is followed by C++ to initialize the members of the child object o1.

1. The statement, invokes a constructor written inside child class C. This is because we have passed an argument 50 at the time of creating the object o1 .
2. As o1 is the object of child class, before the constructor of child class executes a default constructor of parent class P will be invoked.
3. The default constructor initializes the value of member a of the object o1 to 20.
4. After the parent constructor completes, the control of execution is returned to the child constructor with one argument, thereby initializing the value 50 to the member b present inside the child object.

Hence, the member a of object o1 is initialized to 20, whereas the member b of the object o1 is initialized to 50. Therefore, the function display() prints the result of addition as 70 as seen in the output of the program.

We can also invoke a parent constructor with parameters at the time of creating a child object. In such a case, we must specify the parent constructor to be invoked with a colon at the time of defining the child constructor as shown below.

```
C(int x,int y):P(x)
{
b=y;
}
```

As seen from the constructor definition, the constructor of the child class is defined such that it takes two arguments x and y. The argument x is further passed to the constructor of the parent class P which is invoked after a colon operator as P(x) . This means that the value of x is passed to the constructor P inside parent class, which is then initialized to member variable a. Whereas, the value of argument y is initialized to the member b by the child constructor. Given below is the full source code that invokes a parameterized constructor of the parent class at the time of creating the child object.

```
#include<iostream.h>
class P
{
protected:
int a;
public:
    P()
    {
    a=20;
    }
    P(int t)
```

```
    {
    a=t;
    }
};
class C: public P
{
private:
int b;
public:
    C(int x,int y): P(x)
    {
    b=y;
    }
    void display()
    {
    cout<<"Result is "<<a+b;
    }
};
void main()
{
C o1(50,60);
o1.display();
}
```

To understand the working of constructors, let us understand the given code from the first line of `main()` function.

The statement

```
C o1(50,60);
```

invokes a constructor with two arguments which is written inside the child class C. Hence, the values 50 and 60 are initialized to the formal arguments x and y created as a part of the constructor definition. Before the child constructor executes further, the parameterized constructor of the parent class is invoked by passing a value of variable x as an argument to the constructor. Hence, the value of the member a of object o1 is now initialized to 50 by the parent constructor. After the execution of the parent constructor completes, the control of execution returns to the child constructor thereby initializing the value of the formal argument y to member b. Hence the value of the member b of the object o1 is 60. Therefore, the function `display()` prints the result of addition of members a and b as 110 as seen in the output of the code.

14.17 Working of Constructors with Multiple Inheritance

In case of multiple inheritance, where a child class has more than one parent classes. It is possible to invoke the constructor of each of the parent classes at the time of creation of the child object. The sequence of the parent constructors to be invoked should be specified as a comma separated list at the time of defining the child constructor, as shown in the given program. As seen in the code, the class C is a child class of two parent classes P and Q. Hence, the constructor defined in the child class C specifies the comma separated sequence of the parent constructors to be invoked when a child object is created. As the sequence is specified as P(x), Q(y), it means that the constructor inside the parent class P will be executed first and the constructor of the parent class Q will be executed later.

```cpp
#include<iostream.h>
class P
{
protected:
    int a;
public:
    P()
    {
        a=20;
    }
    P(int t)
    {
        a=t;
    }
};
class Q
{
protected:
int d;
public:
    Q(int t)
    {
    d=t;
    }
};
class C: public P, public Q
{
private:
int b;
public:
    C(int x,int y,int z): P(x),Q(y)
    {
```

```
    b=z;
    }
    void display()
    {
    cout<<"Result is "<<a+b+d;
    }
};
void main()
{
C o1(50,60,100);
o1.display();
}
```

Let us understand the given program from the first line of `main()` function.
The statement

```
C o1(50,60,100);
```

invokes a constructor with three arguments which are written inside the child class C. Hence, the values 50, 60, and 100 are initialized to the formal arguments x, y, and z that are created as a part of the constructor definition. Before the child constructor executes further, the parameterized constructor of each of the parent classes will be invoked by passing a value of variable x as an argument to the constructor of class P and passing the value of variable y as an argument to the constructor of class Q. Hence, the value of the member a of object o1 is now initialized to 50, and the value of member d of the object o1 is initialized to 60 by each of the parent constructors as seen in the code. After the execution of all the parent constructors complete, the control of execution returns to the child constructor thereby initializing the value of the formal argument z to member b. Hence, the value of the member b of the object o1 is 100. Therefore, the function `display()` prints the result of addition of members a, d, and b as 210 as seen in the output of the code.

14.18   Destructors and Inheritance

Destructors execute in the exact reverse order of that of constructors. When a child class object is destroyed, the destructor in the child class executes first and then followed by the destructor of parent class. For example, consider the class hierarchy shown in figure 14.68, wherein P is the parent class, C1 is a child class of P and C2 is a child class of C1. Assuming an user-defined destructor in each of the classes, if the object of C2 is destroyed, the destructors will execute in following sequence:

Step 1: Execute Destructor for class C2.
Step 2: Execute Destructor for class C1.
Step 3: Execute Destructor for class P.

Another important point to note is that, it is optional for any of the classes to contain a user-defined destructor. For example, in the above case if class C1 does not have a user-defined destructor, but if we define destructors in classes C2 and P, then the flow of execution of a destructors will be as follows:

Step 1: Execute Destructor for class C2.
Step 2: Execute Destructor for class P.

In what order the Destructors execute with multiple inheritance? The answer to this question is rather simple. All you should know is the sequence in which constructors execute; you just need to reverse this sequence to determine the sequence of destructor execution.

Consider the code given below, it is the same code as that of section 14.17, with the only difference being that we have added destructors to each of the classes. The code implements multiple inheritance such that C is a child class having two parent classes P and Q. We have explained in sections 14.16 and 14.17 that the flow of constructor execution is as follows:

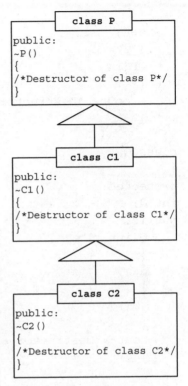

Figure 14.68 Class hierarchy containing destructors

Step 1: Execute **constructor** of class P.
Step 2: Execute **constructor** of class Q.
Step 3: Execute **constructor** of class C.

The destructor execution sequence will be exactly the reverse of the constructor execution sequence. As seen from the output of the code, destructors will execute in following sequence:

Step 1: Execute **destructor** of class C.
Step 2: Execute **destructor** of class Q.
Step 3: Execute **destructor** of class P.

```
#include<iostream.h>
class P
{
protected:
    int a;
    public:
    P()
    {
    a=20;
    }
    P(int t)
```

```
    {
    a=t;
    }
    ~P()
    {
      cout<<"Destructor of parent class P"<<endl;
    }
};
class Q
{
protected:
int d;
public:
    Q(int t)
    {
    d=t;
    }
    ~Q()
    {
    cout<<"Destructor of parent class Q"<<endl;
    }
};
class C: public P, public Q
{
private:
int b;
public:
    C(int x,int y,int z): P(x),Q(y)
    {
    b=z;
    }
    void display()
    {
    cout<<"Result is "<<a+b+d;
    }
    ~C()
    {
    cout<<"Destructor of child class C"<<endl;
    }
};
void main()
{
C o1(50,60,100);
o1.display();
}
```

14.19 Virtual Destructors

In Chapter 11, we have mentioned that destructors can be virtual and constructors **cannot** be virtual. In this section, we will understand the usage of virtual destructors.

A non-virtual destructor does not give proper results when an object of child class is created dynamically with a parent type reference pointing to it. For example, let us consider the following piece of code in which class named Child is a child class of class named Parent. Constructor and destructor are present in both the classes Parent and Child.

```
#include<iostream.h>
class Parent
{
    public:
    Parent()
    {
    cout<<"Constructor of Parent class"<<endl;
    }
    ~Parent()
    {
    cout<<"Destructor of Parent class"<<endl;
    }
};
class Child: public Parent
{
    public:
    Child()
    {
    cout<<"Constructor of Child class"<<endl;
    }
    ~Child()
    {
    cout<<"Destructor of Child class"<<endl;
    }
};
void main()
{
    Parent *ptr = new Child();
    delete ptr;
}
```

The first statement in main() function

```
Parent *ptr = new Child();
```

creates a parent type pointer named as ptr. This pointer points to the object of type child. This is possible as we know that the parent type pointer can also point to any of the child objects.

The new keyword in the above statement creates an object of class Child. Given that the object of child is being created, the constructors are executed in following sequence, as seen in the output of the code:

Step 1: Constructor of Parent class is executed.
Step 2: Constructor of Child class is executed.

The constructor execution sequence is perfectly fine and as expected. Let us now look at the next statement in main() which deletes the child object.

```
delete ptr;
```

We know that the pointer ptr points to the child object. However, in response to this statement C++ will just call the destructor of parent class as seen in the output of the program. This is indeed not what we expect, because technically we are not destroying the parent object, but we are destroying the object pointed by ptr, which is of type Child. But remember that C++ performs **early binding** for all the functions by default, and as per early binding, the compiler decides which function to call based on the data type of the pointer and not based on the data type of the dynamically created object to which the pointer points to. Hence, in response to the delete statement, the compiler will decide which destructor to call based on the data type of ptr which is Parent. Hence, C++ will invoke the destructor of Parent class only, thereby giving incorrect results.

To solve this problem, we must change our code to inform C++ to perform **late binding** for destructors. When we perform late binding, the decision on which function to call is taken based on the data type of the dynamically created object and not based on the data type of the pointer which points to it. Now, the only way we can perform late binding is by creating the destructor function as a virtual function. Hence we can solve this problem by adding a keyword virtual while defining the destructor in the parent class. The modified code is as shown below.

```
#include<iostream.h>
class Parent
{
    public:
    Parent()
    {
    cout<<"Constructor of Parent class"<<endl;
    }
    virtual ~Parent()
    {
    cout<<"Destructor of Parent class"<<endl;
    }
};
class Child: public Parent
{
    public:
    Child()
```

```
    {
    cout<<"Constructor of Child class"<<endl;
    }
    ~Child()
    {
    cout<<"Destructor of Child class"<<endl;
    }
};
void main()
{
    Parent *ptr = new Child();
    delete ptr;
}
```

Since the destructor is made virtual, in response to the statement

```
delete ptr;
```

late binding will be performed to decide which destructor is to be invoked. The data type of the object to be destroyed is Child, and hence the destructor of Child class will be invoked. As per section 14.18, we know that after execution of the child destructor, the parent destructor will be executed anyways. Hence, the flow of destructor execution is as follows:

Step 1: Destructor of Child class is executed.
Step 2: Destructor of Parent class is executed.

In summary, virtual destructors are used to correctly destroy a dynamically created child object which is pointed by a pointer of type parent.

Can we create virtual constructors?   **?**

Constructor in C++ cannot be virtual. In fact there is no need whatsoever for creating a virtual constructor. This is because constructor is always invoked when object is created; no matter if an object is created statically or dynamically (using new keyword).

Solved Example 14.1

An organization wishes to maintain data about its employees. Every employee has a manager to whom the employee reports to. Also, every manager has a set of direct reportees. Store the following details about each employee:

1. ID of the employee
2. Name of the employee
3. Salary of the employee

For every manager store the following information:

1. ID of the manager
2. Name of the manager
3. Salary of the manager
4. Set of employees who report to the manager
5. Number of stocks of the company the manager owns

Create functions to read and display the details of employees and managers on the computer screen. Also, create a function sum() in class Manager that performs the addition of salaries of all employees who report to a particular manager.

```cpp
#include<iostream.h>
class Employee
{
protected:
    int id;
    char* name;
    float salary;
public:
    void input()
    {
    cout<<"Enter the ID, name and salary"<<endl;
    cin>>id>>name>>salary;
    }
    void output()
    {
    cout<<"ID="<<id<<" Name="<<name<<" Salary="<<salary<<endl;
    }
    float get_salary()
      {
      return salary;
      }
};
class Manager: public Employee
{
private:
    int no_of_stocks;
/*e is a array of Employees who report to the manager*/
    Employee e[100];
    int no_of_emp;
public:
```

```
    void input_manager()
    {
    int i;
    /*Input details of Employee*/
    input();
    cout<<"Enter the number of stocks"<<endl;
    cin>>no_of_stocks;
    cout<<"Enter the number of employees reporting to the
    manager"<<endl;
    cin>>no_of_emp;
    cout<<"*****Input the details of each Employee*******"<<endl;
       for(i=0;i<no_of_emp;i++)
       {
       e[i].input();
       }
    }
    void output_manager()
    {
    int i;
    output();
    cout<<"Number of stocks="<<no_of_stocks<<endl;
    cout<<"***** The details of each Employee*******"<<endl;
       for(i=0;i<no_of_emp;i++)
       {
       e[i].output();
       }
    }
    float sum()
    {
    int i;
    float s=0;
       for(i=0;i<no_of_emp;i++)
       {
       s=s+e[i].get_salary();
       }
    return s;
    }
};
void main()
{
Manager m1;
cout<<"***********Manager m1*************"<<endl;
m1.input_manager();
```

```
/*cout<<"**********Calculating sum of salaries of the Employees
    who report to m1*********"<<endl;
m1.sum()*/;
cout<<"**********Printing the details of m1*********"<<endl;
m1.output_manager();
cout<<"***sum of salaries of Employees under m1********"<<endl;
cout<<"Sum is "<<m1.sum();
}
```

Output

```
***********Manager m1*************
Enter the ID, name and salary
1 John 15000
Enter the number of stocks
60
Enter the number of employees reporting to the manager
2
*****Input the details of each Employee*******
Enter the ID, name and salary
2 Jill 5000
Enter the ID, name and salary
3 Jazz 7000
**********Printing the details of m1*********
ID=1 Name=John Salary=15000
Number of stocks=60
***** The details of each Employee*******
ID=2 Name=Jill Salary=5000
ID=3 Name=Jazz Salary=7000
***sum of salaries of Employees under m1********
Sum is 12000
```

NOTES

A seen from the problem statement, the members ID, name and salary are required in both the classes Employee as well as Manager. Class Manager has additional requirement to represent the no_of_stocks owned by the manger and the set of employees managed by the manager. Therefore, we create the class Manager as a child class of class Employee as seen in the code.

We have created an array of type Employee which is named as e inside the class Manager. Each element of the array e will represent an employee who reports to the manager. Hence, we can say that, multiple objects of class Employee will be contained inside a single object of class Manager.

This relationship between a class Manager and class Employee is called as **one to many relationship**, wherein one manager will have many employees under him whereas many employees together will be constrained have a single manager.

Quiz

1. A relationship of inheritance facilitates
   - **(a)** Polymorphism
   - **(b)** Reusability of the code
   - **(c)** Both a and b
   - **(d)** Data hiding and security
2. In case of private inheritance, the public members of the parent class are mapped as _____ members of the child class
   - **(a)** private
   - **(b)** public
   - **(c)** protected
   - **(d)** We cannot create a private inheritance in the program
3. Which of the following members of parent class can be directly accessed inside the child class?
   - **(a)** Private members
   - **(b)** Public members
   - **(c)** Protected members
   - **(d)** Both b and c
4. When object of one class is contained inside another class, then such a relationship between classes is called
   - **(a)** IS-A relationship
   - **(b)** HAS-A relationship
   - **(c)** Realization
   - **(d)** We cannot create an object of one class as a member of another class
5. Which of the following statement(s) is true?
   - **(a)** We can invoke a member function defined inside parent class using the object of child class.
   - **(b)** We can invoke a member function defined inside child class using the object of parent class.
   - **(c)** A member function of a parent class can only be invoked using the object of parent class.
   - **(d)** None of the above are true.
6. Which operator is used to resolve ambiguity in multiple inheritance?
   - **(a)** Arrow operator (->)
   - **(b)** Scope resolution operator (::)
   - **(c)** Membership operator (.)
   - **(d)** Indirection operator (*)
7. Virtual base class in C++ is used to
   - **(a)** implement runtime polymorphism
   - **(b)** implement data hiding
   - **(c)** implement late binding
   - **(d)** avoid duplication of inherited members in the grand child class
8. Inheritance with more than one parent classes and a single child class is called
   - **(a)** Multi-level inheritance
   - **(b)** Multiple inheritance
   - **(c)** Single level inheritance
   - **(d)** Hybrid inheritance
9. Virtual functions are used to
   - **(a)** Implement runtime polymorphism
   - **(b)** Implement data hiding

(c) Implement encapsulation

(d) To avoid duplication of inherited members in the grand child class

10. _____ is performed for virtual functions in C++

(a) Early binding   (c) No binding

(b) Late binding   (d) Static binding

11. A pointer which is of type parent can point to

(a) Parent object only   (c) Both parent as well as child object

(b) Child object only   (d) No such pointer can be created

12. When a function is defined in both parent class as well as child class, then it is called

(a) Function overloading   (c) Function overriding

(b) Function over mapping   (d) None of the above

Error Finding Exercise

Given below are some programs which may or may not contain errors. Correct the error(s) if exist in the code and determine the output.

Program 1

```
#include<iostream.h>
class P1
{
     void callparent()
     {
     cout<<"Inside parent class"<<endl;
     }
};
class P2: public P1
{
     void callchild()
     {
     cout<<"Inside child class"<<endl;
     }
};
void main()
{
P1 o1;
o1. callparent();
o1. callchild();
P2 o2;
O2. callparent();
O2. callchild();
}
```

Program 2

```cpp
#include<iostream.h>
class P1
{
    void callparent()
    {
    cout<<"Inside parent class"<<endl;
    }
};
class P2: public P1
{
    void callchild()
    {
    cout<<"Inside child class"<<endl;
    }
};
void main()
{
P1 *p;
P2 o1;
p=&o1;
p->callparent();
p->callchild();
P1 o2;p=&o2;
p->callparent();
p->callchild();
}
```

Program 3

```cpp
#include<iostream.h>
class X
{
private:
    int a,b,c;
public:
    void set_data(it p,int q,int r)
    {
    a=p;
    b=q;
    c=r;
    }
```

```
    void output()
    {
    cout<<"a="<<a<<"b="<<b<<"c="<<c<<endl;
    }
};
class Y: public X
{
private:
int res;
public:
void add()
{
res=a+b+c;
cout<<"Addition is "<<res;
}
};
void main()
{
Y o1;
o1. set_data(10,20,30);
o1.add();
Y o2;
o2. set_data(100,200,300);
o2.output();
o2.add();
}
```

Program 4

```
#include<iostream.h>
class P: public Q
{
private:
    int b;
    void increment()
    {
    b=a++;
    cout<<"The changed value is"<<b;
    }
};
class Q
{
protected:
int a;
```

```
public:
    void set_data(int p)
    {
    a=p;
    }
};
void main()
{
P o1;
o1.set_data(10);
o1.increment();
Q o2;
o2.set_data(10);
o2.increment();
}
```

Program 5

```
#include<iostream.h>
class P
{
protected:
int a;
public:
    void set_data(int p)
    {
    a=p;
    }
    void display(int p)
    {
    cout<<"a="<<a<<endl;
    }
};
class Q: public P
{
private:
    int b;
    void set_data(int p,int q)
    {
    set_data(p);
    b=q;
    }
```

```
        virtual void display(int p)
        {
        cout<<"a="<<a<<"b="<<b<<endl;
        }
};
void main()
{
Q o1,o2;
o1.set_data(10,20);
o1.display();
o2.set_data(10,20);
o2.display();
}
```

Program 6

```
#include<iostream.h>
class Abc
{
protected:
    int a;

public:
    void inputA()
    {
      cin>>a;
    }
    void outputA()
    {
      cout<<"a="<<a<<endl;
    }

};
class Pqr:public Abc
{
private:
    int a;
    int b;
public:
void inputAB()
    {
      cin>>a>>b;
    }
```

```
      void outputAB()
      {
         cout<<"a="<<a<<"b="<<b<<endl;
      }
};
void main()
{
      Pqr o1;
      Pqr* p;
      p=o1;
      /*Specify if this call works correctly, if justified that
                                              works correctly
      assume any input values and determine the output*/
      p->inputAB();
      p->outputAB();
}
```

Program 7

```
#include<iostream.h>
class Abc
{
public:
      Abc()
      {
         cout<<"Constructor of Abc"<<endl;
      }
      virtual ~Abc()
      {
         cout<<"Destructor of Abc"<<endl;
      }

};
class Pqr:public Abc
{
      public:
      Pqr()
      {
         cout<<"Constructor of Pqr"<<endl;
      }
      ~Pqr()
      {
         cout<<"Destructor of Pqr"<<endl;
      }
};
```

```
void main()
{
    Abc *p = new Abc();
    Abc *r = new Pqr();
    Pqr *s = new Pqr();
    Pqr *t = new Abc();
    delete p;
    delete r;
    delete s;
    delete t;
}
```

Review Questions

1. What is inheritance? Explain the need for inheritance in detail.
2. Explain the different types of inheritance trees supported in C++ with an example
3. What is the difference between private and protected inheritance? Explain with an example.
4. Explain the problem of ambiguity in multiple inheritance with an example.
5. Write a short note on virtual base class. Also give one example of creating virtual base class in C++.
6. What is a difference between early binding and late binding? Explain with an example.
7. What is a difference between compile time polymorphism and runtime polymorphism? Explain with an example.
8. Write a short note on pure virtual functions in C++.
9. Can you invoke a member function of a child class using object of parent class? If yes, write a C++ code to explain this situation.
10. Explain the difference between static cast and dynamic cast.
11. Is it possible to override a function by changing its return type? Demonstrate with example.
12. What are VTABLEs? What is the application of VTABLEs?
13. Explain the rules we should follow when creating constructors in classes with parent child relationship. Consider the case of creating constructors with arguments in parent and child classes.
14. Justify with example need of virtual destructor. Explain why this concept is not applicable to constructors.

Input and Output Streams in C++

15.1   Overview

A **program** is a set of instructions that perform operations on the data to generate a desired output. The data is generally provided to the program from external sources. These sources are called **inputs**, which are given to the program to attain the required results. On receiving the input data, the C++ code must perform necessary computations to generate the results. These results are called the **outputs**, which are either to be stored somewhere or rendered to the user.

It is important to note that a program can take inputs from multiple sources like keyboard, mouse, files, database, and so on. Along the same lines, a program can distribute its output to multiple destinations like computer screen (for rendering), files, database, speaker, and so on. The selection of **input sources** and **output destinations** purely depends upon the business requirements on the basis of which the code is designed.

Given a variety of inputs and outputs possible in today's world, it is important that the programming language makes it easy for the programmer to write a program that can take input from any required source(s) and distribute output to any required destination(s) using a consistent approach. What this means is that, a programming language should offer a layer of **abstraction** to the programmer, so as to hide the complexities of differences in each of the input/output devices. The programmer's job is to only think towards the core business logic of the program and not to worry about the communication with I/O devices. The only way to make this possible is, the programming language must provide a rich **application programming interface (API)** that can handle inputs and outputs in the same way for any I/O device. This API is called a **stream**. An **input stream** is the one that takes data from any of the input devices and transfers it to the program. Whereas, the **output stream** is the one that transfers data/results generated by the program to any of the output devices. By definition, stream is a series of bytes that are transferred between the program and the I/O device. Figure 15.1 shows the role of input and output streams to transfer data between program and external devices.

In reality, different streams are used to handle different types of input and output devices. This is obvious and should not surprise you because every device is different for the other and hence, the type of streams used to communicate with each of the devices will be indeed different. What is important to note is that the approach in which the input

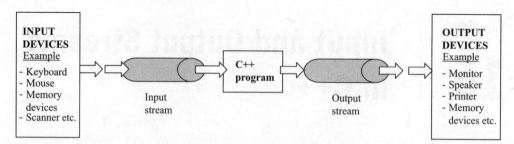

Figure 15.1: I/O streams

is taken and the output is distributed is to be kept consistent across devices. Stream is all about keeping the I/O approach consistent. Streaming I/O API of C++ never says that one type of stream can be used to do everything. The expectation that the programming language could offer such a high level of abstraction is simply unrealistic!

This should not stop you from thinking that there will always be some common elements and components needed, to communicate with different devices, irrespective of the device type. Such components can always be placed together in a parent class and each of the different types of devices can have individual child classes, which only offer the functionalities for that particular device. Needless to say, that the child classes could always override the functionality that is required differently for different device types. Ok, I think you must have already guessed that an API to handle the input and the output will always be a **hierarchy of built-in classes.** Any I/O API uses **Inheritance** and Function overriding (**Polymorphism**), which we have discussed in previous chapters. In this chapter, we will discuss two types of streams, console I/O steam and File I/O stream. There is a different hierarchy of classes, which C++ offers to work with console and File system. These APIs are explained in the later sections of this chapter.

15.2   Types of I/O Streams

C++ supports streaming inputs and outputs to handle variety of I/O devices. This chapter focusses on two types of input streams.

Console I/O stream

A stream used to accept the input from the keyboard is called console input stream, and the stream used to output data to the monitor is called console output stream as shown in the Figure 15.2.

File I/O stream

Instead of always taking the input from the keyboard or distributing the results on the Computer screen, C++ program can also take the input data or distribute outputs to a file that is stored on a disk drive. C++ supports a rich API for file handling, which deals with transfer of data between the program and the file. The process of taking the input data

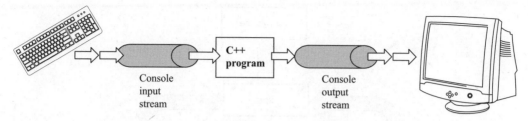

Figure 15.2: Console I/O

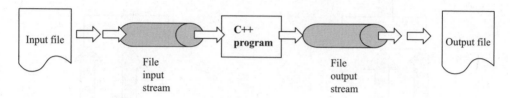

Figure 15.3: File I/O

from the file is called **'reading'** from file and the process of distributing the program results to the file is called **'writing'** to the file. In this chapter, we will discuss the C++ API offered to read/write text files. Figure 15.3 shows a C++ program using streams, which takes input from file using the **file input stream**, and generates output to another file using the **file output stream**.

Is it necessary to have physically different streams for each file? ?

A stream is attached to a single file at a time. You can always reuse the same stream object to get attached to a different file once the current file operation is closed. Unless the current stream is closed, the stream object cannot be attached to a different file. This means that you can have the same stream object pointing to different files at different times of execution of the program, but the stream object can point to only one file at any given point in time. After closing the current stream, a new stream can be created using the same object for a different file.

15.3 Console Input and Output in C++

C++ has a hierarchy of built-in classes to facilitate console input and output. This bundle of classes is shown in the Figure 15.4. As seen from the figure, ios is the parent of all the I/O stream classes, and istream and ostream are immediate child classes of class ios. The class iostream has two parent classes, and hence, it inherits the functionalities of class istream as well as ostream. Further down the hierarchy, there are 'withassign classes' for each of the child class, these classes acts as an operator function = (assignment operator function) to the respective parent classes.

These I/O are defined in the header file **iostream.h.** Hence, it is required to include **iostream.h** in the program before using them. The table 15.1 gives description of each of the classes in the hierarchy:

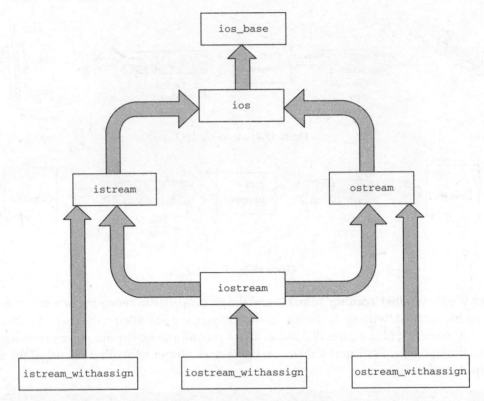

Figure 15.4: C++ console I/O hierarchy

15.4 Formatted v/s Unformatted I/O Operations

Table 15.1 mentions different input and output functions like get(), put(), getline(), write() and so on. Broadly, Input and Output in C++ are classified into two types:

Formatted I/O

An input or output operation, which formats the data into **string** (series of characters) before transferring the data between the program and the I/O device is called **formatted I/O operation**. cin and cout are examples of formatted I/O in C++.

Unformatted I/O

An I/O operation that transfers the direct **binary representation** of data (without applying any conversions) between the device and the program is called **unformatted I/O operation**. The functions get(), put(), getline(), read() and write() are examples of unformatted I/O functions in C++.

Formatted I/O is much user friendly, simple to use and platform independent when compared to unformatted I/O because the formatted I/O functions produce results that

Table 15.1: Input and output functions

Class name	Description
ios_base	This is a parent class in C++ I/O hierarchy. It contains generic functions to configure flags for input and output operations.
ios	This class contains generic features needed for I/O operations and is the parent of all the classes within the console I/O class hierarchy. This class also contains member functions and bit fields for formatting the output and they are discussed in sections 15.5 and 15.6 of this chapter.
istream	This class defines input functionalities. The important input functions defined in this class are 1. Operator function for extraction operator (>>) 2. get() 3. getline() cin is an object of class istream, which we have already used to take values input from the user in the chapters before.
ostream	This class defines the output functionalities. The important output functions defined in this class are 1. Operator function for insertion operator (<<) 2. put() 3. write() cout is an object of class ostream, which we have already used to print values on console, in the previous chapters.
iostream	This is the child class of both istream and ostream and hence, this class provides input as well as output functionalities.
istream_withassign, ostream_withassign, iostream_withassign	These classes add the operator function = (assignment operator function) to the respective parent classes.

are very much user readable and portable. However, formatted I/O operations are slower when compared to unformatted I/O because the execution of the formatted I/O functions requires an additional cost of converting the binary data into a textual form.

15.5 Formatting the Output using Member Functions of Class ios

C++ outputs can be formatted using the functions defined in ios class. Some of these functions are listed in the Table 15.2. These functions are the member functions of the ios class, hence, they need to be invoked using object of class ios. However, we know that the ostream is a child class of ios and hence, we use the object cout to invoke these functions. Also, these functions are mainly used to direct the way the output is produced on the screen and invoking them using cout, improves the readability of the program. Hence, we invoke all these functions using a cout object.

The following is the list of some formatting functions defined in ios class:

Table 15.2: Functions of the `ios` class

ios function name	Function signature	Description

precision	`int precision(int);`	It is used to set the precision for printing floating point numbers. It configures the number of digits to be printed after the decimal point, when printing the value of floating point numbers. The function takes an integer argument, which should specify the new value of precision to be set. The function also returns the previous value of precision that was set, hence, its return type is an integer. For example, if value of variable b is
		
		`float b=4.869218;`
		
		and if the requirement is that, we need to print just 2 digits after the decimal point and we should first set the precision of the output as shown below:
		
		`cout.precision(2);`
		Now, the statement
		`cout<<b;`
		
		will print the value as 4.87. Note that the number is **rounded** to print only 2 digits after the decimal point and hence, the value printed is 4.87 and not 4.86. It is important to note that, if the precision is less than the actual number of digits present after the decimal point, there will be a rounding effect. On the other hand, if the precision set is greater than the actual number of digits after the decimal point, nothing would happen and the number would be printed as it is. (In some cases, Turbo C++ produce unpredictable results, so it is not recommended to set the precision higher than the actual number of digits after the decimal point.)
		    If we look at the value of variable b, the number of digits after the decimal point is 6. Now, if we set the precision as 8, using the precision function:
		
		`cout.precision(8);`
		The statement
		`cout<<b;`
		
		will print the value of b as it is with most of the Turbo C++ versions, as shown below:
		`4.869218`
		The value of the precision once set, is valid throughout, unless it is explicitly changed to any other value.
		    Note that, if you do not set any precision, the default precision of Turbo C++ version 3.0 is 6. The default value of the precision may vary with different versions of C++.

	`int precision();`	This is another version of the precision available in `ios` class. This function does not take any arguments and is just used to return the current value of precision that is set. The function is used, if the programmer wants to determine the current value of precision that is set. If you

ios function name	Function signature	Description
		have not set any value of the precision, the call to this function will return zero indicating that the programmer has not set any value of the precision. On the other hand, it is important to note that the default precision of Turbo C++ version 3.0 is **6**. This means that, although you have not set any value of the precision, all the floating point numbers will be printed up to 6 digits after the decimal point. For example, if the precision is set already set as 8, then the statement `int k = cout.precision();` will assign the value 8 to variable k. If you do not set any precision, this function will return zero, but as said before, floating point numbers will still be printed with a default precision of 6. This function, returning zero only means that programmer has not specified any value of the precision explicitly.

width	`int width(int);`	The function `width()` forces C++ to print the output in the right justified form (when used without `ios::left` flag). By default, C++ prints the values in the left justified form but if the width function is invoked, the next value that will be printed using `cout` will be in the right justified form.
		    This function is used to specify symbol width to be reserved for printing the output. The function takes integer argument, which is used to specify the number of symbol spaces to be reserved to generate the output. The integer value returned by the function gives the width that was set previously.
		    For example, we can set the width as 6 using the following statement:
		`cout.width(6);`
		If the value of variable a is 210, the statement
		`cout<<a;`
		will print the number in the right justified form as shown in Figure 15.5.

			2	1	0

Figure 15.5: Right justified output

Note that there were 6 symbol spaces reserved for printing the value of a, but first 3 were left blank because the output width was set to 6, although there were only three symbols to print.

Remember, the width setting configured is only valid for one specific output, which is generated right after the width is configured. The output behaviour continues to be in its default left justified form for any other subsequent outputs to be printed.

For example, if we set the width, as say 8 and print the values of a and b as shown below:

ios function name	Function signature	Description

int a=102 ,b=215;
cout.width(8);
cout<<a<<endl;
cout<<b<<endl;

The value of variable a will be printed in the right justified form leaving 5 spaces blank in the beginning. But the value of variable b will be printed as default in the left justified form as shown in the Figure 15.6. This is because, the width setting resets to the default value after printing the value of variable a.

					1	0	2
2	1	5					

Figure 15.6: Printing a and b

If every output needs to be in the right justified form, width needs to be set before generating each output as shown below:

int a=102 ,b=215;
cout.width(8);
cout<<a<<endl;
cout.width(8);
cout<<b<<endl

Hence, in this case, values of variables a as well as b will be printed in the right justified form as shown in the Figure 15.7:

					1	0	2
					2	1	5

Figure 15.7: Printing a and b

int width();

This is another version of the width available in the ios class. This function does not take any arguments and is just used to return the current value of width that is set.

For example, if we set the width as 8, then the statement

int k = cout.width();

will assign the value 8 to variable k.

If the width is not set by the programmer, this function will return zero.

fill — char fill(char);

When the width of the output is configured greater than the number of symbols to be printed, the output is right justified with blank area in the beginning. This blank area is actually the number of unutilized symbols spaces in the output. The blank area appears in the beginning, because the default fill character used to fill the unutilized area is **'blank space'**.

The fill character can be configured using the fill() function.

For example, we can set the fill character to $ as follows:

cout.fill('$');

ios function name	Function signature	Description

		Now, if the value of variable a is 210, the below statements
		
		`cout.width(6);`
		`cout<<a;`
		
		will generate the output as shown as shown in Figure 15.8:

$	$	$	2	1	0

Figure 15.8: Working of `fill()` function

ios function name	Function signature	Description
		Note that three dollar symbols appear at the beginning, because the output is right justified, using the `width` function and the fill character is set as $ using the `fill` function. Similar to the width configuration, the fill configuration is only valid for one specific output, which is generated right after the fill is configured.
	`char fill();`	The function gives the current fill character, which is configured. If the fill character is not configured by the programmer, this function will return 'blank space' (ASCII value 32), which is the default fill character. Let us assume that the fill character is already set to $ by the programmer, then the below code: `char k= cout.fill();` will set the value of k as $.

NOTES

Width and the precision of the output can be also be controlled using conventional `printf()` statement and this is explained in Chapter 2 Section 2.6.

15.6 Formatted I/O using `ios` Flags

I/O can be formatted using the flags within the `ios` class. Figure 15.9 lists different `ios` flags along with the description for each of them. `ios` flags are organized into groups, these groups are also called Bit fields. Flags that contradict the behaviour of each other are organized in the same group. Only one flag from each group can be active at a time. If the programmer intentionally makes multiple flags active within the same group, then only the flag that is made active at the end will be considered as an active flag, while others will be considered as deactivated. There are certain flags, which do not fall in any of the groups; these flags can be set or reset independently as their behaviour do not contradict the results produced by other flags.

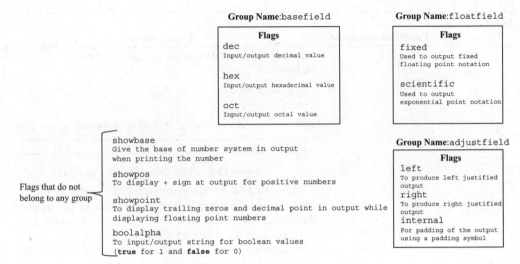

Figure 15.9: ios flags with descriptions

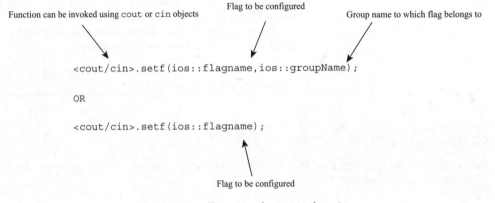

Figure 15.10: Formats of setf() function

The function setf() is used to set these flags. setf() function is defined in the class ios and, hence, can be invoked using cout or cin objects as shown in the Figure 15.10. The function setf() is overloaded in the class ios and is available with two versions. The first version takes two arguments (flag name and the group name), which is used to set the flags that belong to a specific group. The second version of setf(), takes only one argument (flag name) and is used to set the flags that do not belong to any group.

Some of the examples are given below, which will give you an understanding on how to set or reset the flags.

15.6.1 To get the output in octal number system: An Example

If you want to print the result in the octal number system, you will have to set the ios::oct flag that belongs to the group ios::basefield.

The required setf () statement is as below:

```
cout.setf(ios::oct,ios::basefield);
```

Now, the below statements

```
int a =112;
cout.setf(ios::oct,ios::basefield);
cout<<a;
```

will print the value of a as

160

because 160 is an octal representation of 112.

15.6.2 To produce left justified output: An Example

The result of the width function can be made left justified by setting the flag ios::left, which falls in the group ios::adjustfield. The required setf() statement is as below:

```
cout.setf(ios::left,ios::adjusted);
```

Now, the statements below

```
float a =35.468;
cout.width(12);
cout.fill('$');
cout<<a;
```

will generate the output as shown in the Figure 15.11:

$	$	$	$	$	$	3	5	.	4	6	8

Figure 15.11: Output of the left flag set with the width() function

15.6.3 To display the + sign at the output for positive numbers: An Example

Usually, when a number is positive, the symbol + does not appear in the output when we print its value using cout statement. We can make the symbol + to appear in the output value printed by setting the flag ios::showpos. As seen from the Figure 15.9, this flag does not belong to any group. Hence, we need to use the second version of setf(), shown in the Figure 15.10, which takes just one argument. The required C++ statement to set this flag is as below:

```
cout.setf(ios::showpos);
```

The statements below

```
int a=10;
cout.setf(ios::showpos);
cout<<a;
```

will produce the output as

+10

Note, the presence of symbol + in the output that appears, because of setting the relevant flag.

15.6.4 To display trailing zeroes and decimal point in a floating point number : An Example

Consider the following statements:

```
float a=54.210, b =25.00;
cout<<"a="<<a<<endl;
cout<<"b="<<b<<endl;
```

The cout statement will produce the output as

```
a=54.21
b=25
```

Note that the trailing zeros do not appear in the output by default, 54.210 is printed as 54.21 by default. Also, the trailing decimal point does not appear in the output, that is, 25.00 is printed as just 25.

We can make the trailing zeros and decimal point to appear in the output value printed by setting the flag ios::**showpos**

The statements

```
float a=54.210, b =25.00;
cout.setf(ios::showpos);
cout<<"a="<<a<<endl;
cout<<"b="<<b<<endl;
```

will produce the output as

```
a=54.210
b=25.00
```

15.6.5 To display base of the number system in the output: An Example

Consider the statements below:

```
int a=112;
cout.setf(ios::hex,ios::basefield);
cout<<"a="<<a<<endl;
```

The cout statement will print

```
70
```

This is because 70 is hexadecimal representation of 112.

You can force C++ to print the base indicator of the number system at the beginning of the number by setting the flag ios::showbase as shown. The statements

```
int a=112;
cout.setf(ios::hex,ios::basefield);
cout.setf(ios::showbase);
cout<<"a="<<a<<endl;
```

will generate the output as

```
0x70
```

Note, the presence of 0x in the output, which represents that this is an hexadecimal number. Likewise, only symbol 0 (zero) would have been printed had it been an octal number.

15.6.6 Resetting flags

The flag once set remains in effect till the time it is reset. The function unsetf() is used to reset any flag in C++. For example, to reset the hex flag, you can invoke the function as follows:

```
cout.unsetf(ios::hex);
```

This will stop giving hexadecimal outputs and the mode of the output will again return to default, which is the decimal number system.

15.7 Formatted I/O using Manipulators

ios functions are considered to be complex because of their syntax. Hence to make programmers life easy, for each ios function, C++ offers an equivalent manipulator. The advantage of manipulators is that they have a simple syntax compared to the ios functions, and a call to the manipulators can be embedded within the cout/cin statement itself, rather than calling them separately using the cout/cin objects.

Table 15.3 gives the list of I/O manipulators in C++ and their equivalent ios functions. All these manipulators except endl are defined in the header file **iomanip.h**. Hence, the program must include this header file before making use of these manipulators. endl unlike other manipulators is defined in the header file **iostream.h**.

The code below uses ios functions to set the precision as 8 and the width as 10, before printing the value of variable a.

```
float a =20;
cout.precision(8);
cout.width(10);
cout.fill('$');
cout<<a;
```

Table 15.3: I/O manipulators

I/O manipulator	Description
setprecision(int pre)	This is equivalent to the precision() function with 1 argument as described in ios functions
setw(int width)	This is equivalent to the width() function with 1 argument as described in ios functions
setfill(char fillc)	This is equivalent to the fill() function with 1 argument as described in ios functions
endl	Transfers the output cursor on the new line

The same code can be written with equivalent manipulators as shown below:

```
cout<<setprecision(8)<<setw(10)<<setfill('$')<<a;
```

This statement is exactly equivalent to that written using `ios` functions and will produce the same output as that of `ios` functions, as follows:

$$$$$$$20

15.8   Creating your Own Manipulator

You can also create your own manipulator rather than just using the built-in manipulators provided by C++. The following is the syntax to create custom manipulator:

```
ostream& NameOfTheManipulator(Arguments)
{
/*Functionality of the manipulator*/
}
```

Consider the program below, it creates a manipulator for extended tab space and names it as ETAB, which is actually printing 3 tab spaces each time the manipulator is used.

```
#include<iostream.h>
ostream& ETAB(ostream& t)
{
cout<<"\t\t\t";
return t;
}
void main()
{
cout<<"Hello"<<ETAB<<"Bye";
}
```

The function

```
ostream& ETAB(ostream& t)
{
cout<<"\t\t\t";
return t;
}
```

NOTES

It is mandatory for the manipulator function to take an argument of `ostream`, if it is required to work with the `cout` object. This is because `cout` is an object of `ostream`.

contains a cout statement that prints 3 tab characters, hence, each time the manipulator is invoked it will print 3 consecutive TAB spaces.

The statement

```
cout<<"Hello"<<ETAB<<"Bye";
```

in the program invokes the user-defined manipulator ETAB between Hello and Bye. Hence, there will be 3 TAB spaces printed between strings Hello and Bye as shown in the output of the code.

15.9 Passing Arguments to the Custom Manipulator

We have created a manipulator named ETAB in the previous section. This manipulator will always print 3 tab spaces when invoked. However, the number of tabs that we would want to print on the screen might not be always fixed as 3. Programmers would like to have an ability to configure the number of TABs that are printed by this manipulator. In such a case, we will have to create a manipulator that can take a parameter, which defines the number of TABs it should print. Such manipulators are called parameterized manipulators. One of the examples of parameterized manipulator is setprecision(int precision), which takes an integer argument to set the precision for floating point numbers OR setw(int width), which takes width as a parameter to configure the output symbol spacing. Our requirement is that, we should be able to pass an integer parameter to the manipulator ETAB, to determine the actual number of TABs to be printed. For example, the statement

```
cout<<"Hello"<<ETAB(5)<<"Bye";
```

should print 5 TABs between Hello and Bye since we have invoked a manipulator by passing integer constant 5.

Recall the format of creating user-defined manipulators in Figure 15.12, which supports passing custom arguments for parameterized manipulators. In this particular case, we need an additional parameter of type integer, which can give the number of TABs to be printed. Hence, we write the manipulator function, which takes an additional parameter named n.

```
ostream& NameOfTheManipulator(Arguments)

{

/*Functionality of the manipulator*/

}
```

Figure 15.12: Creating user-defined manipulator

```
ostream& ETAB(ostream& p, int n)
{
        while(n>=1)
        {
        p<<"\t";
        n--;
        }
return p;
}
```

The function contains a simple `while` loop that executes n times and hence, it prints n TABs assuming p is set as a reference to the `cout` object during the function call.

It is important to note that, the function ETAB takes two arguments, however, when we use the manipulator in our program, we would just pass a single argument as shown below:

ETAB (5)

Hence, there is a need to create another function that just takes a single argument to resolve this statement; therefore, we overload ETAB function as shown below:

```
MyTab ETAB(int n)
{
return MyTab(ETAB,n);
}
```

Note that the function ETAB returns an object of class `MyTab`, which we created. The class `MyTab` has a constructor that takes two arguments so as to initialize its members, this is because the class has two members:

1. **Pointer to a function named *ptrfn**

   `*ptrfn` is a pointer to the actual manipulator function that takes two arguments and returns an `ostream` reference. The constructor code initializes *ptrfn to point to the ETAB function that prints the tab characters in a `while` loop.

2. **Integer variable named noOfTabs**

   `noOfTabs` is a member variable that contains the value to determine the number of TABs to be printed. This variable is initialized with the value that is passed by the programmer when invoking the manipulator. In the given program, the manipulator is invoked to print 5 tab spaces using the statement below:

   ```
   cout<<"Hello"<<ETAB(5)<<"Bye";
   ```

Hence, the value of member variable `noOfTabs` is set to 5.

The following is the constructor code, used to initialize the value of member variables:

```
MyTab(ostream& (*arg1)(ostream&,int),int arg2)
{
ptrfn=arg1;
noOfTabs =arg2;
}
```

Hence, the overall summary is that the manipulator invocation calls an ETAB function with 1 argument, which returns back an object of class `MyTab`.

Therefore, the insertion operator now has to work with two objects, one of class `ostream` (which is `cout`) and the other of class `MyTab` (which is returned by ETAB function). Hence, the insertion operator function must be overloaded. The operator function, actually invokes the manipulator function with two arguments so as to print the required number of spaces.

```
#include <iostream.h>
#include <iomanip.h>
class MyTab
{
private:
ostream& (*ptrfn)(ostream&,int);
int noOfTabs;
public:
       MyTab(ostream& (*arg1)(ostream&,int), int arg2)
       {
       ptrfn=arg1;
       noOfTabs=arg2;
       }
       friend ostream& operator<<(ostream& arg1, MyTab arg2);
};
ostream& ETAB(ostream& p, int n)
{
       while(n>=0)
       {
       p<<"\t";
       n--;
       }
return p;
}
ostream& operator<<(ostream& arg1,MyTab arg2)
{
       return ETAB(arg1, arg2.noOfTabs);
}
MyTab ETAB(int n)
{
       return MyTab(ETAB,n);
}
void main()
{
       cout<<"Hello"<<ETAB(5)<<"World";
}
```

15.10 Character by Character Unformatted I/O Operations

The functions get () and put () are used to perform character by character I/O operations. This means that, they can only input/output one character at a time. Unlike insertion or extraction operators, which provide formatted input/output, get () and put () provide unformatted I/O operations in C++.

15.10.1 `get()` function

The function `get()` is used to take a single character as an input from the user. It is an unformatted input function defined in class `istream`. There are two overloaded versions of `get()` function present in the class `istream`, as prototyped below:

```
int get();
void get(char&);
```

Any one of the above versions can be used to take a character as an input from the user. Since, `get()` is a member function of the class `istream`, we need an object of class `istream` to invoke it. We know that `cin` is already a built-in object of class `istream` and hence, a `get` function is invoked using `cin` as follows:

```
cin.get(ch);
```
or
```
ch=cin.get();
```

Assuming `ch` is a character type variable, both of the above function calls will take the value of variable `ch` as the input from the user.

The statement

```
cin>>ch;
```

works slightly different as compared to the `get` function call, in a way that the usual `cin` statement with the extraction operator ignores the spaces and the new line characters, but `get` function can accept spaces as well as the new line characters.

Consider a case wherein we need to take a sentence as an input from the user, which is terminated by a full stop and then print the sentence back on the screen. The sentence will obviously have multiple words in it separated by spaces. In such a scenario, we could use the `get()` function in the `while` loop as shown in the program below:

```
#include <iostream.h>
void main()
{
char ch;
ch = cin.get();
    while(ch!='.')
    {
    cout<<ch;
    ch = cin.get();
    }
cout<<".";
}
```

```
***************OUTPUT***********************
This is a sentence.
This is a sentence.
*****************************************
```

The highlighted while loop runs till the time it detects a full stop. Hence, every character that is taken as an input using the get () function is printed back on the screen using the cout statement in the while loop. The process continues till the time user enters a full stop. Therefore, the above program takes the sentence as an input from the user and echo's it back on the screen. Note, that the spaces are preserved in the sentence that is echoed back because the function get () has an ability to take space as an input unlike the cin statement.

If we modify the while loop to make use of a cin statement instead of the get () statement, we will no more have an ability to accept a space or a new line as an input from the user.

```
while(ch!='.')
{
cout<<ch;
cin>>ch;
}
```

With the given while loop, the output of the program will not contain any spaces in the echoed sentence as shown below. This is because the **cin** statement ignores spaces.

Needless to mention, if we hit an enter key in the given program, the value of the variable ch will be set to '\n' if we are using the get () function. However, if we make use of cin instead of the get () function, the new line character will be simply ignored by cin and will be handled just like a space.

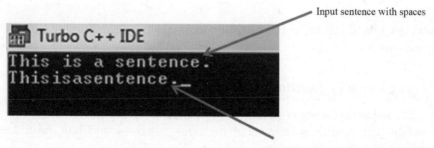

Input sentence with spaces

The string echoed back does not contain spaces because cin statement ignores spaces

15.10.2 put () function

put () is used to print a character on the computer screen. This function is defined in the class ostream. Hence, the function needs to be invoked using cout, which is an object of class ostream. The invocation of put () function to print the value of character variable named ch is as shown below:

```
cout.put(ch);
```

It is important to note that the function put () can be used for character output only, unlike cout, which can output any of the data types.

For example, consider an integer type variable z as shown:

```
int z=65;
```

The statement

```
cout<<z;
```

will print 65 on the computer screen. Whereas, if we use the put function to print z, the statement

```
cout.put(z);
```

will print the upper case character A on the computer screen. This is because 65 is the ASCII value of character A in the upper case.

15.11 Line by Line Unformatted I/O Operations

As we understand from the previous section, get () and put () functions are used to perform character by character I/O operations. Hence, if we need to perform I/O operations with a full sentence, which has multiple characters, we need to execute the get () and put () functions in the loop as described in the previous section.

Although this always remains one of the options to input or output a sentence, C++ has a better way to perform I/O operations of full line of characters. The functions getline () and write () are used to perform line I/O operations in one go, thereby eliminating the need of complex looping.

Similar to get () and put (), getline () and write () functions provide unformatted I/O operations in C++.

15.11.1 getline () function

getline () is used to take a sentence (line of characters) as an input from the user.

The function getline () is defined in the class istream and has the following prototype:

```
istream& getline(char* message, int size, char delimiter='\n' );
```

The function getline () takes two mandatory arguments and one optional argument. The first argument is the message, which is to be taken as an input from the user, and the second argument is the size of the message in terms of number of characters. The third argument to getline () is optional, because it is already supplied with a default value of '\n', which sets the default delimiter for the working of getline () to the new line character. This means the function getline () will take all the characters.

The function can take at the most size -1 characters as an input from the user because 1 character will be occupied by '\n', which is the default delimiter.

Since getline() is a function defined in the class istream, it must be invoked using an istream object. Hence, we can invoke the getline() function using the cin object, as follows:

```
char *p;
cin.getline(p,20);
```

Note that p is a pointer of type character and hence it can point to a string. The function call to getline() will make the pointer p point to the input string. Note that, maximum number of characters, getline() can accept from the user in this case is 19 (since size specified is 20 in the function call).

Hence, if the user enters a string, "Animal Kingdom" as the input, the pointer p will point to the string as shown in Figure 15.13:

Figure 15.13:   Pointer p pointing to the input string after execution of getline()

Needless to say that, instead of using getline(), if we would have used

```
cin>>p;
```

the pointer p would have only pointed to the string, "Animal", since space is considered as a delimiter by cin, and it cannot take space as an input from the user.

Using cin, we would only be able to store a string "Animal", because as soon as the user inputs space, the execution of the extraction operator(>>) terminates and the input characters are stored into the variable p as shown in the Figure 15.14.

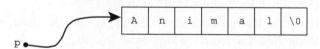

Figure 15.14:   Pointer p pointing to input string after
execution of cin>>p

This way, >> operator, will never give an opportunity to the user to input the remaining part of the input string ("Kingdom") after the user hits the space bar.

15.11.2 write() function

The function write() is used to print a sentence (line of characters) on the computer screen. The function write() is defined in the class ostream and is prototyped as follows:

```
ostream& write(char * message, int size);
```

The character pointer message represents the message to be printed and the size represents the number of characters within the message to be printed on the computer screen. Let us assume that the pointer p points to a string "Animal Kingdom".

```
char *p= "Animal Kingdom";
```

To print this string, the write() function must be invoked using an object cout as shown below:

```
cout.write(p,14);
```

Note that, the length of the string pointed by pointer p is 14 and hence, the second argument is passed as 14 to the function so as to print the full string.

The output will be

```
Animal Kingdom
```

If, we invoke the function by passing a different length say n, then the function will print only the first n characters of the string that is pointed by the pointer p. For example, if we invoke the function by passing length as 5:

```
cout.write(p,5);
```

It will generate the output by printing only the first 5 characters as follows:

```
Anima
```

15.12   File I/O Operations

C++ provides a built-in API, to perform I/O operations with files. Till this point, we have seen how can C++ program take the input from the keyboard and distribute the output on the screen. In this section, we will focus on writing C++ programs, which can perform I/O operations with files instead of console. With the help of file I/O, C++ program can be written to satisfy any one or both of the below requirements:

1. The program can take its input data from the file system that is stored on Hard disk, rather than taking the input from the keyboard.
2. The program can distribute its output data to the file system that is stored on Hard disk, rather than distributing the output on the screen.

Console I/O API is used when the program needs to accept the input from the keyboard and generate the output on the screen, whereas the file I/O API is used when I/O operations are to be performed with files rather than the keyboard or the screen. The process to take the input from the file is called **reading** the file, and the process to generate the output to the file is called **writing** to the file. C++ has a rich API to support read and write operations with files, this API is called **file handling** API of C++.

Given that we have an understanding of console I/O operations, file handling API is simple to learn, because it has an identical syntax and consistent orientation as that of console I/O. Like console I/O, C++ has a building hierarchy of classes to support file handling. Figure 15.15 shows the hierarchy of classes in C++ for file handling. As seen from the figure, all the file handling classes are derived from the classes of the console I/O API.

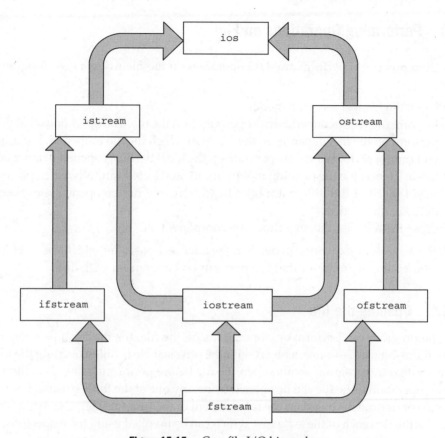

Figure 15.15: C++ file I/O hierarchy

The class ifstream is used to read the data from the file and is derived from classes istream. The class ifstream contains functions required to take the data input from the file. Similarly, class ofstream contains output functions required to write data to the file. The class ofstream is derived from the ostream. We can also perform input as well as output operations on a file at the same time. To support both the input as well as the output operations together, C++ has a built-in class named fstream. This class is derived from iostream class as shown in the Figure 15.15.

In summary, there are three main classes on which you need to focus on to work with the files.

1. ifstream – To be used by the program to read data from the file.
2. ofstream – To be used by the program to write data to the file.
3. fstream – To be used by the program to perform read as well as write operations on the file.

It is important to note that all of the above file handling classes is defined in the header file **fstream.h** and hence, it is very important to include **fstream.h** in the C++ program before using these classes. The next section describes some of the built-in functions defined in each of these classes to perform file I/O operations.

15.13   Performing Operations on File

A three-step process to perform any I/O operation on the file using a C++ program is as follows:

Step 1: Open the file in a required mode.

Step 2: Perform the required read/write operations on the file. The operations that you can perform on the file, depends on the mode in which the file is opened. For example, you cannot perform a write operation on the file if the file is opened in the read only mode. Hence, the file opening mode should be selected carefully when performing step 1. Each of the different modes in which a file can be opened is explained in detail in this section.

Step 3: Close the file after the operations are completed.

Each of these steps are explained in detail in the later sections, after which we will be ready to write some sample programs that can perform I/O operations with files.

15.13.1   Opening the file

Before the program can perform any operations on the file, the file must be opened. The process of linking the C++ stream object with the physical file is called opening the file. It is mandatory, that the program should open the file before performing any streaming input or output operations. The file can be opened using any one of the three streams ifstream, ofstream or ofstream based on the requirement of the programmer. C++ has a function open(), defined in each of these classes, which can be invoked using the respective stream instance.

   When you open the file using the instance of class ifstream, the file is opened in read only mode, this is because ifstream can only perform input/read operations on the file. The code below creates an object of class ifstream and invokes the function open(), to open the file named Employee.dat.

```
ifstream fin; /* fin is created as an object of class ifstream*/
fin.open("Employee.dat"); /*invoke function open(), to open the
file Employee.dat*/
```

The call, fin.open("Employee.dat"); opens the file named Employee.dat present in the current working directory (the directory from which the C++ code is executing). Instead of explicitly invoking the open function, you can also open the file using a constructor present in the class ifstream while creating the object as shown below:

```
ifstream fin("Employee.dat");
```

This is possible, because there exists a constructor with one argument in the class ifstream to which you can pass the file name as a string that internally invokes the open() function. In either cases, the file is always opened in read only mode, because we have used the object of class ifstream.

   Similar to ifstream, the class ofstream also supports two ways to open a file, either using the open() function or using the constructor. As mentioned before, when a file is opened using the ofstream class, the file will be opened in write only mode, because ofstream can only perform output/write operations on the file. The following are the statements to open a file Student.dat in write only mode using an instance of the class ofstream, which we have named fout:

```
ofstream fout; /* fout is created as an object of class ofstream*/
fout.open("Student.dat"); /*invoke function open, to open the file
  Student.dat*/
```

You can also achieve the same effect by opening the file using a constructor as shown:

```
ofstream fout("Student.dat");
```

How to specify the full directory path explicitly when opening the file?   **?**

If you want to specify the full location of the file in windows environment you can do so by using \\ symbol in the directory path. For example, if the actual path of the file is C:\Data\Student.dat, you can specify it as

```
ofstream fout; /* fout is created as an object of class ofstream*/
fout.open("C:\\Data\\Student.dat"); /*invoke function open(), to open the file
  Student.dat*/
```

If the file exists on Linux environment at location \home\Data\Student.dat, then you can specify it as

```
ofstream fout; /* fout is created as an object of class ofstream*/
fout.open("\home\Data\Student.dat"); /*invoke function open(), to open the file
  Student.dat*/
```

We have given the example of ofstream object but similar path syntax works for all other objects to access the file at a specific directory location.

Now that we understand how to open a file using ifstream and ofstream classes, let us understand how to open a file for performing read as well as write operations together. This is possible, because we have a generic class fstream that can support opening of the file in read as well as write operations. However, C++ makes it mandatory for the programmer to specify the mode in which the file needs to be opened and if the file is to be opened using the fstream class. Different modes in which the file can be opened are specified as flags in the ios class as shown in the Table 15.4.

For example, you can invoke a file Employee.dat in read only mode using the class fstream as shown below:

```
fstream file;
file.open("Employee.dat", ios::in);
```

Any of the ios modes can be used in combination with the bitwise or the operator. So, if you want to open a file named Student.dat in read as well as write mode, you can invoke the function open as shown below:

```
fstream file;

file.open("Employee.dat", ios::in|ios::out);
```

Table 15.4: File modes

Mode	Description
ios::in	Read only mode (also called input mode). This is the mode in which the file is opened by default when using the ifstream class.
ios::out	Write only mode (also called output mode). This is the mode in which the file is opened by default when using the ofstream class.
ios::app	Open the already existing file in append mode.
ios::ate	Make the file pointer to point at the end of the file.
ios::nocreate	Do not create a new file, if file is not found while opening it. The open operation to fail if the file does not exist.
ios::noreplace	Create a new file, if file is not found while opening it. The open operation to fail if the file already exists.
ios::trunc	Make the already existing file Empty. This flag actually deletes and recreates the file.
ios::binary	Open the file in binary mode. If the mode is not specified, the file is opened in ASCII mode by default.

How can we check if opening of the file succeeded or failed?

If the opening of the file fails, the stream object points to NULL. So, if the stream object is not NULL after the call to open() method, it means that the opening of the file has succeeded else it has failed. For example, the **if-else** block below implements the check, whether the opening of the file succeeded or failed:

```
fstream file;
file.open("Employee.dat" , ios::in|ios::out);
if(!file)
{
/*Actions to be taken if file opening fails*/
cout<<"Failed to open the file";
}
else
{
/*Actions to be taken if file opening is successful*/
cout<<"File opened successfully";
}
```

15.13.2 Functions to perform read/write operations with files

Once the file is open, it is ready to perform read or write operations. There are three types of I/O operations that can be performed on files using the built-in API of C++. The different types of operations with files are as listed below:

Operation type 1: Formatted I/O using extraction and insertion operator

The extraction and the insertion operators are overloaded in `ifstream` and `ofstream` classes respectively, to perform read and write operations with files.

The insertion operator can be invoked using the object of class `ofstream` and is used to write the data to the file. You can use different manipulators like `endl` to format the output and determine the way in which the data is written to the file.

As an example, let us open file `sample.out` using `ofstream`,

```
ofstream fout("Sample.out");
```

We can now invoke the insertion operator using object `fout` to write the data to the file as shown:

```
fout<<"Hello Everyone,";
fout<<"This is a sample file"<<endl;
fout<<"This message on new line";
```

On execution, the file `Sample.out` will contain the data as below. Note that there is a space after the word `Everyone` because it is as specified in the first `fout` statement. We have used a modifier `endl` after printing the second line and hence, the third message `"This message on new line"` appears on the new line in the file as shown in the Figure 15.16.

```
 File   Edit   Format   View   Help
Hello Everyone,This is a sample file
This message on new line
Value of variable is 10
```

Figure 15.16: Data in the file `sample.out`

Needless to say, you can also print the value of any variable in the file, just as we can do with the console. Below code prints the value of variable `a` on a new line, in the file `Sample.out`.

```
fout<<endl<<"Value of variable is "<<a;
```

The contents of the file are as shown in the Figure 15.16.

You can read the contents of the existing file by invoking the extraction operator, using the instance of the class `ifstream`. To read the contents of `Sample.dat` back, you must open the file in read only mode, which was the default mode selected, when the file was opened using `ifstream` object with the statement below:

```
ifstream fin("sample.dat");
```

We have written a lot of characters in sample.dat to understand how the characters can be read using an extraction operator. Let us try to read back the first line from the file. We know that, the operator >> skips both spaces as well as the new line characters. Hence, it is very difficult to detect the space or a new line using >>. So, reading a file using this approach is slightly complex and is usually not a preferred way of doing the operation unless the data is very much formatted. We create a character pointer named sprt to point to the contents to be read from the file. Because, both spaces and new line characters act as delimiters to the >> operator function, each invocation will extract data up to the first space, thereby extracting one word at a time in this case.

For example, the statement

```
fin>>sptr;
```

will extract Hello (which is the set of characters before the first occurrence of the space) in the pointer sptr. Hence, when we print the contents pointed by sptr on the screen

```
cout<<sptr;
```

it will print Hello on the computer screen.

After execution of the statement fin>>sptr; for the first time, the **file pointer** progresses further to point to the next byte that is to be read from the file. The file pointer is incremented automatically after each read operation to point to the next immediate unread byte. Hence, when we again invoke the >> operator using fin, it will extract the next set of characters after the first space (but before the second space because the >> operator function will again terminate when it gets to the second space).

```
fin>>sprt;
```

sprt will this time point to the string Everyone (which is indeed the second word from the file). This means that, if we want to read back the first full line, we must invoke the extraction operator 6 times, because the first line contains 6 words. If the >> operator is invoked the 7th time using fin, it will extract the first word of the next line. The full source code that invokes >> 7 times and the output is shown with the given program. At this point, it is clear that spaces as well as new lines cannot be handled properly using this approach to read files. Hence, we have to print every word on the new line. This is because there is no way for the program to know when does the line end or when does the word end. The extraction operator simply keeps extracting data word by word and the program keeps printing the values using cout statement.

```
#include<iostream.h>
#include<fstream.h>
void main()
{
char *sptr;
ifstream fin("sample.dat");
cout<<"*******First word from file*********"<<endl;
fin>>sptr;
cout<<sptr<<endl;
cout<<"*******second word from file*********"<<endl;
```

```
fin>>sptr;
cout<<sptr<<endl;
cout<<"*******Third word from file*********"<<endl;
fin>>sptr;
cout<<sptr<<endl;
cout<<"*******Fourth word from file*********"<<endl;
fin>>sptr;
cout<<sptr<<endl;
cout<<"*******Fifth word from file*********"<<endl;
fin>>sptr;
cout<<sptr<<endl;
cout<<"*******Sixth word from file*********"<<endl;
fin>>sptr;
cout<<sptr<<endl;
cout<<"*******First word from the second line*********"<<endl;
fin>>sptr;
cout<<sptr<<endl;
fin.close();
}
```

Output

```
*******First word from file*********
Hello
*******second word from file*********
Everyone,
*******Third word from file*********
This
*******Fourth word from file*********
is
*******Fifth word from file*********
sample
*******Sixth word from file*********
file
*******First word from the second line*********
This
```

What is a file pointer?   **?**

File pointer is a cursor to the file, which is incremented each time a byte is read or written to the file. This is an internally maintained pointer by C++, which keeps track of bytes read/written to the file. Programmers do not have to manage this pointer explicitly, it is the C++ libraries that manage the pointer to ensure that the same byte is not read repeatedly from the file and to ensure that the same location is not overwritten multiple times in the file when read/write operations are performed in iteration.

Note that the last statement of the program invokes a `close()` function using the object `fin`. This disconnects the association between the C++ stream and the file. Even if you do not invoke the `close()` function explicitly, the destructor of the `fin` object will anyways close the stream as and when the object `fin` is destroyed. No further operations can be performed on the file after the stream is closed.

Operation type 2: Character by character unformatted I/O operations with files

As with console I/O, spaces and new line characters can be well detected using `get()` and `put()` functions. The function `get()` is used to read a character from the file and the function `put()` is used to write a character to the file. It is important to note that these functions can read or write one character at a time to/from the file. The function `get()` is defined in the class `ifstream`, whereas the function `put()` is defined in the class `ofstream`.

Assuming, `fin` is an object of class `ifstream` and ch is a character type variable, the statement

```
fin.get(ch);
```

will read a single character from the file represented by `fin` and store in the variable ch. After reading the single character, the file pointer will also be advanced to point to the next unread character.

As an example, let us write a C++ program to read all the characters from the file `sample.dat` (Figure 15.16) using `get()` function. As mentioned before, after reading one character, the file pointer progresses to point to the next unread character in the file, hence, we can read all the characters in the file by simply putting the `get` function in the loop. Every file ends with a special character named end of file (EOF). Hence, it is correct to assume that there will be no data in the file after EOF is detected. Therefore, the loop that is responsible to read the full contents of the file should terminate after it encounters the EOF character. There are multiple ways by which we can detect the EOF character in the program. The different approaches in which the `while` loop can be written are documented in Table 15.5. The table assumes that `fin` is an object of class `ifstream` using which the data from the file is read.

The functions `eof()`, `good()`, and `fail()` are defined in class `ios`, which is present in **iostream.h**. Hence, we must include the header file **iostream.h** before making use of these functions.

In the given program, we use the following `while` loop to read the characters from the file using the `get()` function. As per the description provided in the Table 15.5, the `while` loop will terminate after all the characters are read from the file.

```
while(fin)
{
    fin.get(ch);
    cout<<ch;
}
```

Each iteration of the `while` loop reads exactly one character from the file and stores it in the variable ch. The value of the variable ch is printed on the screen using the `cout` statement.

Table 15.5: Different approaches in which the `while` loop can be written

`while` **loop to detect end of file**	Description

`while(fin)`
`{`
`    ..............`
`}`
	The object of class `ifstream`, `fin` will become 0 when EOF is reached. Hence, this `while` loop will run till the EOF.

`while(!fin.eof())`
`{`
`    ..............`
`}`
	The function `eof()` returns true when EOF is reached. Hence, this `while` loop will run till the EOF, because we have applied a logical operator NOT (`!`) before the condition of the `while` loop.

`while(fin.good())`
`{`
`    ..............`
`}`
	The function `good()` returns false when the EOF is reached. Hence, this `while` loop will run till the EOF.

`while(!fin.fail())`
`{`
`    ..............`
`}`
	The function `fail()` returns true when EOF is reached. Hence, this `while` loop will run till the EOF because we have applied a logical operator NOT (`!`) before the condition of the `while` loop.

As we mentioned before, the file pointer progresses automatically to the next character to be read after completing the current read operation. Hence, when the function `get()` is invoked again in the next iteration of the `while` loop, it will read the next character in variable ch. This way, the loop will read all the characters of file one by one and print it on the screen. It is needless to say that, if we replace the statement `fin.get(ch);` with `cin>>ch;` we will lose all the spaces and new line characters, and this effect is exactly analogous to that of console I/O operations.

The following is the full source code and the output to read the full contents of the file without losing the new line and special characters:

```cpp
#include<iostream.h>
#include<fstream.h>
void main()
{
char ch;
ifstream fin("sample.dat");
    while(fin)
    {
    fin.get(ch);
    cout<<ch;
    }
fin.close();
}
```

Turbo C++ IDE

Hello Everyone, This is sample file
This message on new line.
Value of variable is 10

Analogous to console I/O, there exists a put () function defined in the class ofstream, which is used to write a single character to the file.

Assuming fout is an object of class ofstream and ch is a character type variable, the statement

```
fout.get(ch);
```

will write the character stored in the variable ch to the file, which is represented by the fout.

Operation type 3: Binary mode I/O operations with files

The get () and put () functions perform I/O operations in the ASCII format. This means that if we want to write an integer value, say 132 to the file, it needs to be written in three different symbols '1', '3', and '2' from the complete number. This is because the function put () can only write one character at a time. Each of these three symbols (actually characters) is converted into equivalent ASCII codes. Further, each of the ASCII codes are converted into binary format and written to the stream. Remember, it takes 3 bytes spaces to store an integer value 132 because it is actually converted into 3 characters of 1 byte each.

Instead, it would definitely have been better to write 132 as a single integer constant into the stream, because any integer in reality takes just 2 bytes. If we convert 132 directly into binary and write to the file, we would end up writing just 2 bytes as shown below. This is a straight binary conversion of decimal number 132.

```
0000 0000 1000 0100
```

Hence, binary I/O operations with numeric data are considered better than the ASCII format I/O operations for the following two reasons:

1. The size of the binary converted data is less than the size of ASCII converted data; hence, it helps in saving memory.
2. The I/O stream eventually contains lesser number of bits when reading or writing. Hence, binary I/O is faster than ASCII Input/Output.

C++ supports functions read () and write () to read and write data in the binary format to/from the file respectively. The function read () is defined in the class ifstream, whereas the function write () is defined in the class ofstream. Assuming fin and fout are objects of classes ifstream and ofstream, respectively, the Figure 15.17 shows the syntax to use read () and write () functions to write and read the value of the variable data. Each of the functions takes the following two arguments:

1. Address of the variable whose value is to be written or read to/from the file.
2. Size of the variable (in bytes) whose value is to be written or read to/from the file.

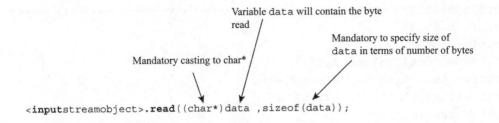

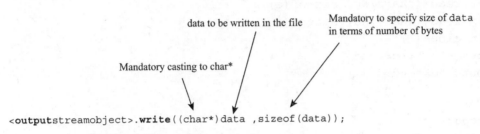

Figure 15.17: Syntax to use read and write functions

It is important to note that, each of the functions require the programmer to cast the address of the variable read/written to be casted into a character pointer. This is because, although we are reading and writing the data in the binary form, the file pointer will still continue to progress byte by byte. Hence, the address of the variable whose value is to be transferred must be casted into a char pointer as char is 1 byte in size. Further, the function will also need to know, how many bytes are to be transferred between the file and the program. Therefore, the second argument should give the size of the variable in bytes to be written or read to/from the file. We will generally use a function sizeof() to determine the size of variable to be transferred as shown in the Figure 15.17.

As an example, the program given below writes the values of two variables a and b to the file named Values.dat, using the write function. The program again opens the same file in the read mode, using ifstream and reads back the values, which were written before into variables c and d. As an evidence, we have read back the values correctly, the program prints the values of c and d on the computer screen using cout. You can see that the first value read from the file goes in the variable c and the second value read from the file goes in the variable d. This is because the value of the variable a was written before the value of the variable b. Hence, you can see in the output that the variable c contains the same value as that of variable a, and the variable d contains the same value as that of the variable b.

```
#include<iostream.h>
#include<fstream.h>
void main()
{
```

```
double a=10.5;
double b=55.5;
double c,d;
ofstream fout("Values.dat");
fout.write((char*)&a, sizeof(a));
fout.write((char*)&b, sizeof(b));
fout.close();
ifstream fin("Values.dat");
fin.read((char*)&c, sizeof(c));
fin.read((char*)&d, sizeof(d));
fin.close();
cout<<"c="<<c<<endl;
cout<<"d="<<d;
}
```

Output

```
c=10.5
d=55.5
```

It must be mentioned that the performance improvements, which are provided by binary I/O operations are majorly applicable for numeric data. If it is required to store string of characters in a file, every character is as such going to take 1 byte and a string will always be stored as series of characters. Hence, it is recommended to use get () and put () functions when operating with text messages.

15.14 Closing the File

The member function close() is used to break the connection between the C++ stream and the physical file. No read/write operations can be performed after the stream is closed. You can invoke the member function close() using instance of any of the three classes (ifstream, ofstream, or fstream). The function close() does not take any arguments and a sample invocation is as shown in the program below. Even if you do not invoke the close function explicitly, the function will be anyways invoked when the stream object is destroyed, because there is a destructor defined in each of the stream classes which invokes close(). Closing a stream is explicitly needed, if you need to share the stream object across multiple files. For example, Figure 15.18 shows the object fin being used to read the data from 3 files. You could see that, before the second file is opened for reading, the stream for the first file is closed.

```
ifstream fin("File1.dat");
/*Read from File1.dat*/
fin.close();
fin.open("File2.dat");
```

```
/*Read from File2.dat*/
fin.close();
fin.open("File3.dat");
/*Read from File3.dat*/
fin.close();
```

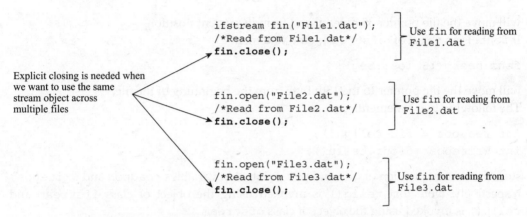

Figure 15.18: `close()` function: Same stream shared across multiple files

15.15   File Pointer Manipulation Functions

We know that, the file pointer is automatically advanced byte by byte after each read or write operation. C++ supports functions to explicitly position a file pointer to a specific byte in the file. The position at which the file pointer needs to be placed can be specified relative to:

Beginning of the file (represented by the ios flag ios::beg)

or

End of the file (represented by the ios flag ios::end)

or

Current position of the file pointer in the file (represented by the ios flag ios::curr)

The function `seekg()` is used to position the `get` pointer, whereas the function `seekp()` is used to position the `put` pointer to a specific byte in the file. You can also determine the current position of the pointer by respective `tell` functions. The function `tellg()` returns the current positon of the `get` pointer, whereas the function `tellp()` returns the current position of the `put` pointer in the file.

Since the functions, `seekg()` and `tellg()` deal with the `get` pointer, they are defined in the class `ifstream` and hence, they must be accessed using an `ifstream` instance. Whereas, the functions `seekp()` and `tellp()` that deal with the `put` pointer are defined in the class `ofstream` and must be accessed using the `ofstream` instance.

The `seekg/p` functions take the following two arguments:

1. Byte number at which the file pointer is to be positioned to.
2. Origin relative to which the pointer needs to be positioned to (ios::beg OR ios::cur OR ios::end). If the origin is not specified, it is defaulted to ios::beg to move the file pointer relative to the beginning of the file by default.

Assuming fin is created as an object of ifstream, the following statement

```
fin.seekg(35,ios::cur);
```

will move the file pointer 35 bytes ahead from its current position.
If fout is an object of ofstream, the statement

```
fout.seekp(15,ios::beg);
```

will move the file pointer to the 15th byte from the beginning of the file.
The following two statements

```
int readpos = fin.tellg ();
int writepos = fout.tellp();
```

store the current position of get and put pointers in variables readpos and writepos, respectively. Note that tellg() is invoked using the object of class ifstream and tellp() is invoked using the object of class ofstream.

Solved Example 15.1

Write a program to demonstrate a file copy operation. Program should copy data from file named as source.txt into another file named as target.txt

```
#include<iostream.h>
#include<fstream.h>
void main()
{
    char value;
    /*open source.txt in read mode*/
    ifstream fin("source.txt");
    /*open target.txt in write mode*/
    ofstream fout("target.txt");
    /*The loop reads all the characters from source.txt and writes
    them to target.txt
    till source file ends*/
    while(!fin.eof())
    {
        /*Read next character from source.txt using input stream
        fin , and store the character in variable named 'value'*/
        fin.get(value);
```

```
                /*Write the character stored in variable 'value' to
                target.txt*/
            fout.put(value);
            }
        fin.close();
        fout.close();
}
```

Output

If the file `source.txt` contains following data

After execution of the program another file will be created in the same directory location named as `target.txt`. The program will ensure that this file contains same data as that of `source.txt`

Solved Example 15.2

Write a program to print all even numbers from 2 to 30 in a file named as `EVEN.txt`

```cpp
#include<iostream.h>
#include<fstream.h>
void main()
{
    /*Open a outputstream for the file */
    ofstream fout;
    fout.open("EVEN.TXT");
    /*The below for loop only writes those values of i which are
    even into the file*/
    for(int i=2;i<=30;i++)
    {
        if(i%2==0)
        {
        /*write i to the file if its even*/
        fout<<i<<endl;
        }
    }
    fout.close();
}
```

Solved Example 15.3

Write a program to open a file in read mode and to count

1. Number of upper case characters in the file
2. Number of lower case characters in the file
3. Number of digits in the file
4. Number of special characters in the file

```cpp
#include<iostream.h>
#include<fstream.h>
void main()
{
    /*Open the source file in input mode*/
    ifstream fin;
    fin.open("source.txt");
    char ch;
    /*set all counts to zero before starting the counting loop*/
    int countUpper=0,countLower=0,countDigit=0,countSpecial=0;
    /*The below loop reads and examines one character at a time
    from input file*/
    while(!fin.eof())
    {
        /*Read a character*/
        fin.get(ch);
        /*Check if the character is upper case based on ASCII
        value ranges*/
        if(ch>=65 && ch<=90)
        {
        countUpper++;
        }
        /*Check if the character is lower case based on ASCII
        value ranges*/
        else if(ch>=97 && ch<=122)
        {
        countLower++;
        }
        /*Check if the character is digit based on ASCII value
        ranges*/
        else if(ch>=48 && ch<=57)
        {
        countDigit++;
        }
```

```
        /*If its not upper case, lower case or digit then it means
        that it is a special character*/
        else
        {
        countSpecial++;
        }
    }
    cout<<"Count of upper case characters is "<<countUpper<<endl;
    cout<<"Count of lower case characters is "<<countLower<<endl;
    cout<<"Count of digits is "<<countDigit<<endl;
    cout<<"Count of special symbols is "<<countSpecial<<endl;
    fin.close();
}
```

Output

```
Count of upper case characters is 2
Count of lower case characters is 45
Count of digits is 4
Count of special symbols is 18
```

NOTES

The given output is assuming following data in the file `source.txt`.

The file contains three full stops and one dollar symbol and hence the count of special characters is 4. Rest of the counts observed in the output are self-explanatory.

```
                                    source - Notepad
File  Edit  Format  View  Help
This is the source file.
This is test data.
25 apples are worth 50$.|
```

Solved Example 15.4

Write a program to count the number of times word `cricket` appears in the input file.

```
#include<iostream.h>
#include<fstream.h>
#include<string.h>
void main()
{
    /*Open the source file in input mode*/
    ifstream fin;
```

```
        fin.open("source.txt");
        char input[100];
        /*set counter to zero before starting the counting loop*/
        int counter=0;
        /*The below loop reads and examines one character at a time
        from input file to determine the type of character*/
        while(!fin.eof())
        {
            /*Read one word at a time using fin object*/
            fin>>input;
            /*compare the read word with cricket(ignoring case)*/
            if(strcmpi(input,"cricket")==0)
                {
                counter++;
                }
        }
        cout<<"Count of word cricket in file is "<<counter<<endl;
        fin.close();
}
```

Output
Count of word cricket in file is 3

NOTES

The given output is assuming following data in the file `source.txt`

Solved Example 15.5

Assume two files containing data named as source1.txt and source2.txt.
    Write a program to create a file target.txt which concatenates the data contained in source1.txt and source2.txt

```
#include<iostream.h>
#include<fstream.h>
#include<string.h>
void main()
{
    char value;
    /*open source1.txt in read mode*/
    ifstream fin("source1.txt");
    /*open target.txt in write mode*/
    ofstream fout("target.txt");
    /*The loop reads all the characters from source1.txt and
    writes them to target.txt
    till source file ends*/
    while(!fin.eof())
    {
        /*Read next character from source1.txt using input stream
        fin , and store the character in variable named 'value'*/
        fin.get(value);
        /*Write the character stored in variable 'value' to
        target.txt*/
        fout.put(value);
    }
    /*close first source file(source1.txt) stream, note that
    target stream fout is still open*/
    fin.close();
    /*open read stream for source2.txt using fin*/
    fin.open("source2.txt");
    /*The loop reads all the characters from source2.txt and
    writes them to target.txt*/
    while(!fin.eof())
    {
    /*Read next character from source2.txt using input stream
    fin , and store the character in variable named 'value'*/
        fin.get(value);
        /*Write the character stored in variable 'value' to target.txt*/
    fout.put(value);
    }
    /*close stream for source2.txt*/
    fin.close();
    /*close stream for target.txt*/
    fout.close();
}
```

Output

If data in source1.txt is as shown below

```
                                    source1 - Notepad
File  Edit  Format  View  Help
This is a data from source1
```

And if data in source2.txt is as shown below

```
                                    source2 - Notepad
File  Edit  Format  View  Help
This is a data from source2
```

Then, program will create a file target.txt with following contents:

```
                                    target - Notepad
File  Edit  Format  View  Help
This is a data from source1

This is a data from source2
```

Solved Example 15.6

Write a program to create a class Employee with three members: id, name and salary. Create three objects of this class and store them in a file named as Organization. txt . Read these objects back from the file using a loop and print on the computer screen.

```cpp
#include<iostream.h>
#include<fstream.h>
#include<string.h>
class Employee
{
private:
    int id;
    char name[100];
    int salary;
public:
        void input()
        {
```

```
        cout<<"Enter id name and salary"<<endl;
        cin>>id>>name>>salary;
        }
        void output()
        {
        cout<<"id="<<id<<" name="<<name<<" salary="<<salary<<endl;
        }
};
void main()
{
    /*Create Employee objects*/
    Employee e1,e2,e3;
    e1.input();
    e2.input();
    e3.input();
    /*Create Organization.txt in write mode*/
    ofstream fout("Organization.txt");
    /*Write three Employee objects into the file Organization.txt
    using fout*/
    fout.write((char*)&e1,sizeof(e1));
    fout.write((char*)&e2,sizeof(e2));
    fout.write((char*)&e3,sizeof(e3));
    fout.close();
        /*Read objects back from file and print on the computer
        screen. We have intentionally created a object temp,
        which will store one employee read from the file in any
        particular iteration of the loop*/
        Employee temp;
        /*Open Organization.txt in read mode*/
        ifstream fin("Organization.txt");
        /*Iterate the file Organization.txt*/
        while(!fin.eof())
        {
        /*Read an Employee object from file and store it in temp*/
        fin.read((char*)&temp,sizeof(temp));
        /*Print the object read from file on computer screen*/
        cout<<"Object read"<<endl;
        temp.output();
    }
fin.close();
}
```

Output

```
Enter id name and salary
10 John 5000
```

```
Enter id name and salary
20 Jack 3000
Enter id name and salary
30 Jill 8000
Object read
id=10 name=John salary=5000
Object read
id=20 name=Jack salary=3000
Object read
id=30 name=Jill salary=8000
```

NOTES

We have to use read() and write() functions to read/write object to the file. This is because every object must be transferred to/from the file in binary format.

SCRATCH PAD

After execution of the program it is recommended that you open Organization.txt and see its data contents. It will all appear as junk to you because this data is written in binary format; however the data has meaning to C++ so please do not attempt to change this file.

Solved Example 15.7

After writing Employee objects in the file named as Organization.txt, change the program given in solved example 15.6 to accept the id of the employee as input from the user and to delete the corresponding Employee object with the matching id from the file.

```cpp
#include<iostream.h>
#include<fstream.h>
#include<string.h>
class Employee
{
private:
    int id;
    char name[100];
    int salary;
public:
        void input()
        {
        cout<<"Enter id name and salary"<<endl;
        cin>>id>>name>>salary;
```

```
        }
        void output()
        {
        cout<<"id="<<id<<" name="<<name<<" salary="<<salary<<endl;
        }
        /*New method added to get the id of the employee object*/
        int getId()
        {
            return id;
        }
};
void main()
{
    /*Create Employee objects*/
    Employee e1,e2,e3;
    e1.input();
    e2.input();
    e3.input();
    /*Create Organization.txt in write mode*/
    ofstream fout("Organization.txt");
    /*Write three Employee objects into the file Organization.txt
    using fout*/
        fout.write((char*)&e1,sizeof(e1));
        fout.write((char*)&e2,sizeof(e2));
        fout.write((char*)&e3,sizeof(e3));
        fout.close();
        /*Take the id of employee to be deleted from the file as
        input*/
        int delId;
        cout<<"Enter the ID of the employee to be deleted from the
        file"<<endl;
        cin>>delId;
    /*Create a temp file to store all records except the record
    which is to be deleted*/
        fout.open("Rec_temp.txt",ios::out);
    /*Read objects back from file and print on the computer
    screen. We have intentionally created an object temp, which
    will store one employee read from the file in any particular
    iteration of the loop*/
        Employee temp;
        /*Open Organization.txt in read mode*/
        ifstream fin("Organization.txt");
        /*Iterate the file Organization.txt*/
        int flag=0;
```

```
    while(!fin.eof())
    {
        /*Read an employee object from file and store it in temp*/
        fin.read((char*)&temp,sizeof(temp));
        /*Check if this is the employee to be deleted*/
        if(temp.getId()==delId)
        {
            flag=1;
            cout<<"Employee Deleted"<<endl;
        }
        else
        {
            /*Write the record in temp file*/
            fout.write((char*)&temp,sizeof(temp));
        }
    }
if(flag==0)
{
    cout<<"Employee with id="<<delId<<"does not exist."<<endl;
}
fin.close();
fout.close();
/*Copy all records from Rec_temp.txt to a new file created
as Organization.txt. Note that, we will create a new file
Organization.txt from scratch which will overwrite the
existing file. Hence the old Organization.txt is deleted and
replaced with new empty Organization.txt*/
fout.open("Organization.txt",ios::out);
/*Open Rec_temp.txt in read mode*/
fin.open("Rec_temp.txt",ios::in);
char value;
    while(!fin.eof())
    {
        /*Read next object from temp file Rec_temp.txt */
        fin.read((char*)&temp,sizeof(temp));
        /*Write the object into temp file - Organization.txt*/
        fout.write((char*)&temp,sizeof(temp));
    }
fin.close();
fout.close();
/*Read back records from Organization,txt to ensure that the
Employee object is not present in the file*/
cout<<"Data in file after deletion is as below"<<endl;
fin.open("Organization.txt",ios::in);
```

```
    while(!fin.eof())
    {
        /*Read an employee object from file and store it in temp*/
        fin.read((char*)&temp,sizeof(temp));
        temp.output();
    }
}
```

Output
```
Enter id name and salary
10 John 2000
Enter id name and salary
20 Jack 4000
Enter id name and salary
30 Jill 5000
Enter the ID of the employee to be deleted from the file
20
Employee Deleted
Data in file after deletion is as below
id=10 name=John salary=2000
id=30 name=Jill salary=5000
```

Review Questions

1. What is streaming input/output? Explain with example.
2. Give a list of streaming classes in C++ for console input/output and file input/output. Explain the purpose of each class in short.
3. Differentiate between formatted and unformatted I/O operations.
4. Differentiate between ASCII mode and binary mode files. Explain how read/write operations are performed in C++ for each of these files.
5. Write a short note on ios flags.
6. Explain the different modes in which file can be opened in C++.
7. Write a program to accept 100 numbers as input from a file. Perform the addition of all the numbers and store the result of addition back in the same file.

16 | Templates in C++

16.1 Overview

Templates in C++ are used to facilitate generic programming by giving the programmer an ability to create generic classes/functions in the program. A component of the program is said to be generic if its functionality remains the same irrespective of data type of the values it operates on. A **generic function** is a function that can work with arguments of any data type, whereas a **generic class** is a class that can work with members of any data type. In this chapter, we will learn creation of generic functions using **function templates** and creation of generic classes using **class templates**.

NOTES

The objective of templates is to create generic components in the program, which can work with different data types. This saves programmers effort to define the same component multiple times and replicating same logic for different type of data values.

16.2 Function Templates

Function templates in C++ enable the programmer to create generic functions. These functions are adaptable to multiple data types and can execute in the same way immaterial of the data type of the values passed to it.

The functions we have written so far in the previous chapters are strictly bonded to specific types. For example, consider the function add() as shown below:

```
int add(int a,int b)
{
    int c = a+b;
    return c;
}
```

The function takes two arguments of type integer and returns the resultant integer, which gives addition of two numbers. This function works well if integer values are passed to it, however the function will not produce correct results if any other type of values are passed to it.

For instance, if we call the function add() by passing float values

```
float k = add(10.2,11.5);
```

the value returned in variable k will not be correct rather truncated. As per the default behaviour of C++, value in variable k will be 21.00 and not 21.7. This means that the function has performed truncation of the resultant value resulting in loss of data. And hence, the function cannot work for float type values.

At times, it is required to implement the same logic for multiple type of values. In such cases, you can use function templates in C++. Function templates enable the programmer to create a function, which can give correct results for different types of data values. The following is the syntax of creating function template:

```
template<class G1,class G2,class G3... class Gn>
```

```
Function Definition of generic function which uses generic types
    G1,G2,G3..Gn
```

Note that the first line in the syntax informs the compiler that G1, G2, G3,... Gn are generic data types which can take different forms when the function call is made. The second line in the syntax then actually defines the generic function.

For example, consider the function definition of generic add() function as shown below:

```
template<class G>
G add(G a,G b)
{
    G c = a+b;
    return c;
}
```

The statement

```
template<class G>
```

informs the compiler that G is a generic type on which the function defined will operate on. Whereas the function add() has a return type as G, and both its arguments a and b are also of type G. The type G will take the correct data type depending on the data type of values passed to function add() when the function is called. The following is the full source code which shows the creation of template function add()

```
#include<iostream.h>
template<class G>
G add(G a,G b)
{
    G c = a+b;
    return c;
}
```

```
void main()
{
int x,y,res1;
float p,q,res2;
cout<<"Enter values of x and y"<<endl;
cin>>x>>y;
res1 = add(x,y);
cout<<"Addition of x and y is "<<res1<<endl;

cout<<"Enter values of p and q"<<endl;
cin>>p>>q;
res2 = add(p,q);
cout<<"Addition of p and q is "<<res2<<endl;
}
```

Output

```
Enter values of x and y
10 20
Addition of x and y is 30
Enter values of p and q
10.3 20.6
Addition of p and q is 30.9
```

In the first function call

```
res1 = add(x,y);
```

type G takes a form of int. This is because the data type of x, y and res1 is int. This means that the function add() performs addition of integers in response to this call. The second function call

```
res2 = add(p,q);
```

makes G to take a form of float because variables p, q and res2 are of type float. Hence, the function call results in correctly calculating addition of two floating point numbers, thereby printing the result without any truncation as seen in the output of the program.

> **CAUTION**
>
> Refer main() function below.
>
> ```
> void main()
> {
> int x;
> float y,res1;
> cout<<"Enter values of x and y"<<endl;
> cin>>x>>y;
> res1 = add(x,y); //ERROR - Incorrect function call
> ```

```
cout<<"Addition of x and y is "<<res1<<endl;
}
```

The call made to add() within main() will not work and raise an error. This is because we have created only one generic type G, and it can take only one form at a time. The function call passes x and y as arguments in which x is of type integer and y is of type float. If you see the function definition of add(), both the arguments must be of a single type G. However, in this case, we have erroneously passed arguments of different types to add() which results into a compilation error. The exact error message is as shown below:

```
[Error]: No matching function for call to 'add (int&, float&)'
```

NOTES

It is possible to create multiple generic types while defining a function. For example, in the code below we have created two generic types G1 and G2, and they can take different forms for a single function call.

```
#include<iostream.h>
template<class G1,class G2>
G2 add(G1 a,G2 b)
{
    G2 c = a+b;
    return c;
}
void main()
{
int x;
float y,res1;
cout<<"Enter values of x and y"<<endl;
cin>>x>>y;
res1=add(x,y);
cout<<"Addition of x and y is "<<res1<<endl;
}
```

Output

```
Enter values of x and y
10 20.5
Addition of x and y is 30.5
```

The function call

```
res1=add(x,y);
```

forces G1 to take the form of int(because x is of type int) and G2 to take the form of float(because y is of type float). Note that the function returns G2 because variable c inside add() is created of type G2. This makes sense because addition of int and float is always a float, and G2 is the generic type which has taken a form of float for this function call.

Had it been that the function call to add() was

```
res1=add(y,x);
```

it would not have resulted into correct result because first argument y, forces G1 to take the form of float, and second argument x forces G2 to take form of int. In the function body, we return c which is the result of addition. The problem is that the data type of result is G2 which is of type int. Hence, this will result into truncation of resultant value. Clearly, this is a logical error because the function call is not made correctly by the programmer. It is the programmer's responsibility to use template functions correctly to avoid such logical errors.

NOTES

It is possible to overload template functions. In the following program, we have defined two versions of add ()
one with template types and other with basic types.

```
#include<iostream.h>
template<class G1,class G2>
G2 add(G1 a,G2 b)
{
cout<<"***Template function called*****"<<endl;
    G2 c = a+b;
    return c;
}
float add(int a,float b)
{
cout<<"****Function in its basic form*****"<<endl;
    float c = a+b;
    return c;
}
void main()
{
int x;
float y,res1;
cout<<"Enter values of x and y"<<endl;
cin>>x>>y;
res1=add(x,y); //calls basic function
cout<<"Addition of x and y is "<<res1<<endl;

float p,q,res2;
cout<<"Enter values of p and q"<<endl;
cin>>p>>q;
res2=add(p,q); //calls template function
cout<<"Addition of p and q is "<<res2<<endl;
}
```

Output

```
Enter values of x and y
10 20
****Function in its basic form****
Addition of x and y is 30
Enter values of p and q
10.4 30.2
***Template function called*****
Addition of p and q is 40.6
```

The statement

```
res1=add(x,y);
```

calls the function add () which takes primitive arguments of type int and float. This is because x is of type
int and y is of type float. Whereas the statement

```
res2=add(p,q);
```

calls a template function because the signature of the primitive function does not match with the signature of the function
call. The variables p and q are of type float, and hence the generic types G1 and G2 take the form of float.

Always remember, if a primitive function is found for a function call, C++ always calls a primitive function.
However, if no matching primitive function is found, then a template function is checked if it can serve the purpose.

16.3   Class Templates

Class templates are used to define generic classes. A generic class is a class which can have generic members and generic member functions. The actual data types which the generic types convert into must be specified while creating an instance of the class.

template<class G1,class G2,class G3... class Gn>

Class definition using generic types G1,G2,G3..Gn

Note that, the first line in the syntax informs the compiler that G1, G2, G3... Gn are generic data types, which can take different forms each time when a class is instantiated. The second line in the syntax then actually defines the generic class. Given below is an example which creates a class Data using two generic types G1 and G2:

```
#include<iostream.h>
template<class G1,class G2>
class Data
{
private:
G1 a;
G2 b;
public:
    void input()
    {
        cout<<"Enter values of a and b"<<endl;
        cin>>a>>b;
    }
    void add()
    {
        cout<<"Addition of a and b is "<<a+b<<endl;
    }
};
void main()
{
    // Addition of two integers
    Data<int,int> o1;
    o1.input();
    o1.add();
    // Addition of one integer and one float
    Data<int,float> o2;
    o2.input();
    o2.add();
    // Addition of two floats
```

```
    Data<float,float> o3;
    o3.input();
    o3.add();
}
```

Output

```
Enter values of a and b
10 20
Addition of a and b is 30
Enter values of a and b
10 30.5
Addition of a and b is 40.5
Enter values of a and b
44.5 44.3
Addition of a and b is 88.8
```

The statement

```
template<class G1,class G2>
```

is present just before defining class Data. This statement informs the compiler that G1 and G2 are two generic types which will be used while defining class Data. In fact, if you see the definition of class Data, it contains members a and b of type G1 and G2, respectively. The member function input() takes the members a and b as input from the user, whereas the function add() performs the addition and prints the result on computer screen.

The first statement of main()

```
Data<int,int> o1;
```

creates an object o1 of class Data. Note that we have specified actual data types in triangular brackets for G1 and G2. The generic tag **<int,int>** informs the compiler that the generic types G1 and G2 should take the form of int, for object o1.

Whereas the statement

```
Data<int,float> o2;
```

creates another object of class Data named as o2. This time, we have specified the tag as **<int,float>** which means that the first generic type G1 will take a form of int and second generic type G2 will take a form of float for this instance. Therefore, the member a of object o2 is an int and member b of object o2 is a float. Whereas both the members of object o1 are integers as shown in Figure 16.1.

NOTES

Objects of same class o1 and o2 have different sizes because the data type of their members is different as shown in Figure 16.1.

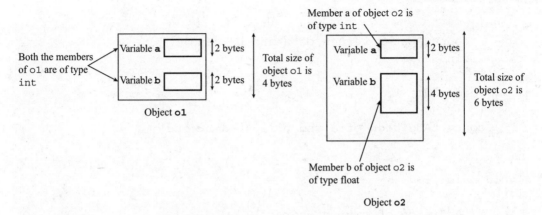

Figure 16.1: Size of objects o1 and o2

The statement

```
o1.input();
```

inputs two integer values a and b for object o1, whereas the statement

```
o1.add();
```

performs the addition of two integers a and b which are members of o1. Similarly, the statement

```
o2.input();
```

inputs one integer(member a) and one float(member b) for object o2, whereas the statement

```
o2.add();
```

performs the addition of member a(int type) and member b(float type) of o2.

NOTES

The program given below creates a class with a single generic type. Under such a design, all the members of this type must be converted to the same data type for a particular instance.

```
#include<iostream.h>
template<class G1> //only one generic type G1 for the class
class Data
{
private:
G1 a;
G1 b;
public:
    void input()
```

```
    {
       cout<<"Enter values of a and b"<<endl;
       cin>>a>>b;
    }
    void add()
    {
    cout<<"Addition of a and b is "<<a+b<<endl;
    }
};
void main()
{
    // Addition of two integers
    Data<int> o1;
    o1.input();
    o1.add();
    // Addition of two floats
    Data<float> o2;
    o2.input();
    o2.add();
}
```

Output

```
Enter values of a and b
10 20
Addition of a and b is 30
Enter values of a and b
11.2 33.4
Addition of a and b is 44.6
```

The statement

```
Data<int> o1;
```

creates an object o1 specifying the generic type as int. This means that members a and b for object o1 will be of type integer as shown in Figure 16.2. Whereas, the statement

```
Data<float> o2;
```

creates object o2 specifying the generic type as float. This means that members a and b for object o2 will be of type float as shown in Figure 16.2.

Note that under this design, it is not possible to have members a and b of different data types for a same object because we have defined just one generic type for the entire class. The generic type can take different forms for different objects, but it can take only one form for one particular object. For object o1, it has taken the form of int, whereas for object o2, it has taken form of float.

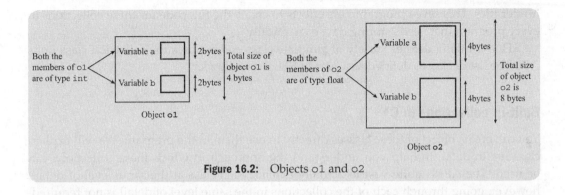

Figure 16.2: Objects o1 and o2

What is the application of templates in C++? ?

Both function templates and class templates, are used to create generic components in the program. Templates are extensively used in creating **collections**. Collection is a data structure used to store multiple values. For example, an array is a collection or a linked list we created in Chapter 10 is a collection. While creating these collections, we define a data type which informs the compiler about the type of values that the collection stores. How different is the program to create and manipulate a linked list that stores integers than the program for a linked list of floats? How different is a function that sorts an array of integers than an array of floats? Basically, everything is same it's just a keyword int replaced by keyword float. However, you will have to copy paste the whole code written for int and create another version for float. And what if we wish to do it for 10 different data types? This means that you will have 10 different versions of the code. This approach will not only increase the length of the overall program but will also make it difficult to maintain. The core application of templates is to give a programmer an ability to define a generic logic and then instantiating it for different types in the program without duplicating the code. For example, we can create a program for linked list using a generic type G1 and then create individual instances of list using specific individual types. If list is the name of the generic class, then

```
list<int> l1;
```

could create a linked list named l1 which can store int types only. Whereas,

```
list<float> l2;
```

could create a linked list named l2 which can store float types.

The complex functions responsible to insert a node into list, delete a node from list, sort the list and so on can be easily defined using generic type within the class list, and hence they can work for objects l1 as well as l2. In practical situations, templates are widely used in creating variety of such collections in the program to make them generic

16.4 Standard Template Library: One of the Applications of Class Templates

Standard template library (STL) is a built-in application programming interface (API) of C++ that defines variety of collections such as linked list, vector, map, stack, queue, and set. Programmers can use these collections directly in the program by including necessary header files. This saves programmers efforts to create the full code for these collections in every program that needs storing data dynamically.

STL essentially defines variety of template class and exposes the collection class in its API. The list of classes defined as a part of STL is as follows.

Built-in collections in C++

You can create object of these classes directly to use them in the program. We will explain class list in detail to help you understand the approach in which these collections can be used. The API is quite vast to actually explain each class at the same level of detail; however, going through each of the collections in the same level of detail is not required. When you understand list, you will have a clear idea of how we can use collections in general.

16.4.1 Linked list

The linked list API is defined in a header file `list.h`, and hence this header file must be included in the program before using the built-in list. This means that the template class `list` is defined in `list.h`.

As `list` is a template class, you can instantiate it using a generic tagged syntax as we did for other template classes. For example,

```
list<int> l1;
```

creates an object `l1` of class `list` forcing the generic type to take the form of `int`. This means that `l1` is essentially a linked list that can store integers. Similarly, the statement

```
list<float> l2;
```

creates linked list `l2` which can store `float` values. Needless to say, you can also create a linked list to store objects of your class. For example, if `Employee` is a class you defined and you want to store a list of employees, you can create a linked list named as say `l3`, which can store `Employee` objects using the statement below:

```
list<Employee> l3;
```

> **NOTES**
>
> The linked list we have implemented in Chapter 10 is a singly linked list in which every node has a pointer to the next node. In a linked list, you can just traverse in one direction as shown in the Figure 16.3.
>
> The built-in class `list` we are talking about is a **doubly linked list**. In this type of list, every node has a pointer to the next node as well as to the node previous to it. So each node has two pointers: one that points to the node before and the other that points to node after. Hence, this list can be traversed in both the directions **forward** (from first node to the last node) as well as **reverse** (from last node to the first node) as shown in Figure 16.4.

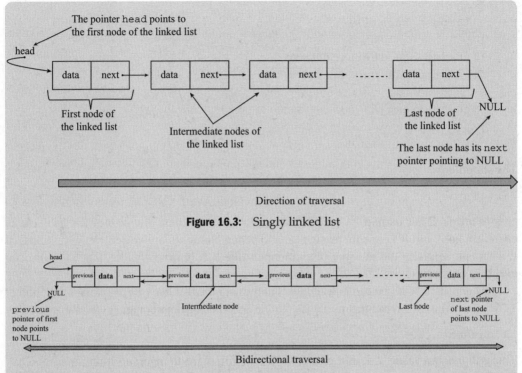

Figure 16.3: Singly linked list

Figure 16.4: Doubly linked list

The design of doubly liked list is complex compared to singly linked list, but it has an advantage that you have an option to go back and forth from any random node. Anyways, we are not really creating a program to implement doubly linked list, it is already present in the header file `list.h`. We are just users of the `list,` and we will use it to store values. This is a very good example of abstraction offered by the API; we really don't care how the list is internally implemented; all we should know is how to use the linked list. Out of interest, readers can go through the header file `list.h` to see the full source code of doubly linked list, but it is not needed at this stage. In this section, we explain how to use the built-in `list` class of STL.

Create and traverse a list

The following program creates a linked list to store `int` values, inserts elements in the linked list, and then traverses the list in forward direction. We will understand this program step by step.

```
#include<list.h>
void main()
{
    list<int> l1;
    int i;
    for(i=0;i<=10;i++)
```

```
  {
    l1.push_back(i);
  }
  list<int> :: iterator temp;
  for( temp= l1.begin();temp != l1.end() ; temp++)
  {
    cout<<*temp<<" ";
  }
}
```

The statement

```
list<int> l1;
```

creates a linked list named `l1` which can store `int` values. The size of the list `l1` is currently zero, but it keeps increasing as and when elements are added to the list. Size of the list is essentially the number of elements in the list. Currently, the list `l1` is empty and hence its size is zero.

One way by which you can add elements to the list is by using a `push_back()` method of `list` class. You can invoke the `push_back()` method using object of list `l1` as shown below:

```
l1.pushback(10);
```

This will insert a value `10` in the list `l1`. Now if you want to insert another value you can invoke `push_back()` on the same object once more.

```
l1.push_back(20);
```

This will insert `20` to the back of `10` and the linked list `l1` will be as shown in Figure 16.5. We will not show the internal pointers to avoid complexity, but as described before each node of the linked list is linked to the next node and to the previous node using internal pointers. Please keep in mind that it is not guaranteed that nodes will be present in contagious memory locations; but they will be linked with pointers.

At this moment, size of list `l1` is `2` because there are two elements in it. If we have four more calls to `push_back()` as below:

```
l1.push_back(30);
l1.push_back(40);
l1.push_back(50);
l1.push_back(60);
```

the value `30` will be inserted to the back of `20`, value `40` will be inserted to the back of `30` in the list and so on. The last element of the list will be `60` and first element of the list is `10` as shown in the Figure 16.6.

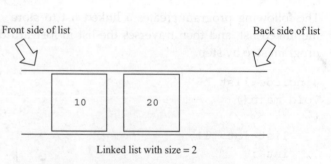

Front side of list   Back side of list

| 10 | 20 |

Linked list with size = 2

Figure 16.5: Linked list `l1` with data values 10 and 20

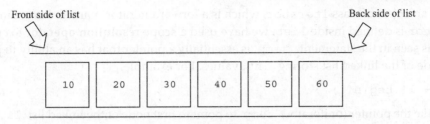

Figure 16.6: Linked list 11 with data values 10, 20, 30, 40, 50 and 60

At this moment, the size of list 11 is 6 because there are overall 6 elements in the list as shown in Figure 16.6.

In the given program, we have written a for loop

```
for(i=0;i<=10;i++)
{
    11.push_back(i);
}
```

which invokes push_back() method 11 times. As the value of i ranges from 0 to 10; the linked list object at the end of the loop will contain values 0 to 10, and hence the size of the list is 11 as shown in Figure 16.7.

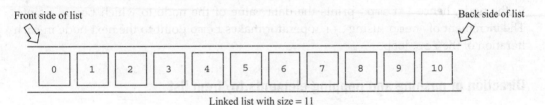

Figure 16.7: Linked list 11 with data values inserted by for loop

iterator

iterator is a built-in object in list which is used to traverse a list. iterator is a general concept and this object is available in all the collections of STL. You can traverse a list in forward as well as in reverse direction. Different types of iterators are

1. Forward Iterator
2. Reverse Iterator
3. Random Iterator (for backward as well as forward movements)

The random iterator is not supported by list but by a different collection called vector which we learn later. Just to understand the concept of using iterator, we will traverse the list object 11 using a forward iterator.

The statement

```
list<int>::iterator temp;
```

creates an object of class iterator, which is a forward iterator named temp. Since class iterator is defined inside list, we have used a **scope resolution operator** to create its object as seen in the statement. temp is essentially a pointer that has an ability to point to any node of the linked list storing int values. For example,

```
temp = l1.begin();
```

will make the pointer (or iterator) temp to point to first node of the linked list l1. When the end of linked list is reached temp is initialized to l1.end().

The method begin() returns a reference to first node of linked list, whereas method end() returns the reference to dummy last node of the list. Dummy last node is a dummy node present after the actual last node of the list. This means that when iterator points to dummy last node, it has already finished scanning the complete list.

The following for loop can be used to traverse the full linked list l1.

```
for(temp = l1.begin();temp != l1.end() ; temp++)
{
    cout<<*temp<<" ";
}
```

Note that the statement

```
cout<<*temp<<" ";
```

prints the contents of node pointed by temp. As mentioned earlier, temp is a pointer to the node, hence *temp prints the data value of the node to which temp points. The increment of temp using ++ operator makes temp point to the next node in each iteration of the for loop.

Direction of pushing and popping elements to/from list

There are two possible ways to push elements into a linked list:

1. You can push elements from front side of the list or
2. You can push elements from back side of the list

push_front(TemplateType)
The function push_front() is used to push an element from front side of the list. The code given below demonstrates the usage of push_front() function.

```
#include<list.h>
void main()
{
    list<int> l1;
    int i;
l1.push_front(50);
l1.push_front(100);
l1.push_front(150);
l1.push_front(200);
```

```
list<int> :: iterator temp;
for(temp = ll.begin();temp != ll.end() ; temp++)
{
    cout<<*temp<<" ";
}
}
```

Output

200 150 100 50

The statement

```
ll.push_front(50);
```

inserts 50 as the first element of the linked list. Then the statement

```
ll.push_front(100);
```

pushes 100 from the front side there by making 100 as the first element of the list and 50 as the second element as shown in Figure 16.8.

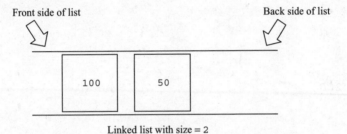

Linked list with size = 2

Figure 16.8: Linked list

Similarly, the statements

```
ll.push_front(150);
ll.push_front(200);
```

push 150 and 200 from the front side of the list. Hence, 200 becomes the first element of the linked list after all the pushes. This is because it was the last element pushed in the program from front side of the list. The linked list is as shown in Figure 16.9.

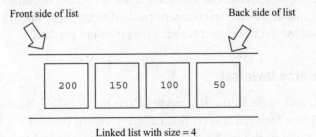

Linked list with size = 4

Figure 16.9: Linked list

push_back(TemplateType)

The function push_back() is used to push an element from back side of the list. The code given below demonstrates the usage of push_back() function.

```
#include<list.h>
void main()
{
    list<int> l1;
    int i;
l1.push_back(50);
l1.push_back(100);
l1.push_back(150);
l1.push_back(200);
    list<int> :: iterator temp;
    for(temp = l1.begin();temp != l1.end() ; temp++)
    {
      cout<<*temp<<" ";
    }
}
```

Output

50 100 150 200

The statement

l1.push_back(50);

inserts 50 as the first element of the linked list. Then, the statement

l1.push_back(100);

inserts 100 from back side of the list, thereby making it as a second element of linked list. The statements

l1.push_back(150);
l1.push_back(200);

inserts 150 and 200 from back side of the list. Hence, 200 becomes the last element of the linked list because it was the last element pushed from back side, whereas 50 remains the first element of the list because it was the first element pushed.

Forward and reverse traversal

A traversal from first node to the last node of the list is called 'forward traversal'. The iterator that supports forward traversal is called 'forward iterator'. A traversal from last node to the first node of the list is called 'reverse traversal', and the iterator supporting reverse traversal is called 'reverse iterator'. The list class of C++ supports both forward and reverse traversal. The following is the code that demonstrates the usage of forward and reverse iterators in the `list`

```cpp
#include<list.h>
#include<iostream.h>
  void main()
  {
        list<int> l1;
        int i;

    l1.push_back(50);
    l1.push_back(100);
    l1.push_back(150);
    l1.push_back(200);
        list<int> :: iterator temp;
    cout<<"Forward traversal"<<endl;
        for(temp = l1.begin();temp != l1.end() ; temp++)
        {
                cout<<*temp<<" ";
        }

        cout<<endl<<"Forward traversal"<<endl;
        list<int> :: reverse_iterator rtemp;
        for( rtemp= l1.rbegin();rtemp != l1.rend() ; rtemp++)
        {
                cout<<*rtemp<<" ";
        }

  }
```

Output

```
Forward traversal

50 100 150 200

Forward traversal

200 150 100 50
```

The statement

```cpp
list<int>::iterator temp;
```

creates an forward iterator named as `temp`. Basically, iterator is an inner class defined inside class `list` which is used for forward traversing.

The `for` loop takes iterator from `begin()` to `end()` of the list and prints each data value by dereferencing `temp` inside the loop. Remember that `l1.begin()` returns the reference to the first node of the list and `ll.end()` returns the reference to the dummy end node of the list. Hence, the `for` loop must terminate when `temp=ll.end()`. The last node is a dummy node that must never be dereferenced because it never contains any valid data value. Hence, the `for` loop for traversal must run only if following condition is true.

```
temp != ll.end()
```

The increment `temp++` takes the iterator `temp` ahead **node by node** in each iteration of the `for` loop. The following is the `for` loop for forward traversal.

```
for(temp = ll.begin();temp != ll.end() ; temp++)
        {
                cout<<*temp<<" ";
        }
```

Just like `iterator` is an inner class of `list` used for forward traversal, `reverse_iterator` is also an inner class of `list` used for reverse traversal. The following statement creates an `reverse_iterator` object named as `rtemp`

```
list<int>::reverse_iterator rtemp;
```

Method `rbegin()` gives the reference to the last node of the linked list and `rend()` gives the reference to the dummy first node of the list. The dummy first node is the dummy node present before the first node of the list. Given below is the `for` loop for reverse traversal:

```
for(rtemp = ll.rbegin();rtemp != ll.rend() ; rtemp++)
        {
                cout<<*rtemp<<" ";
        }
```

Remember that we are working with reverse iterator and `rtemp++` is written as a part of the `for` loop to make the reverse iterator move ahead to point to the next node. Moving ahead from the perspective of `reverse_iterator` means actually moving backward in the list (node by node in each iteration); we have used to term ahead just keep the description of `iterator` and `reverse_iterator` consistent.

Insertion, deletion and size of the list

The following program demonstrates the usage of `insert()`, `erase()` and `size()` functions of the `list` class. The function `insert()` is used to insert an element in the linked list at a specific position. `erase()` is used to delete the element from the list. And the function `size()` gives the size of the list at any point in time. Size of the list is number of elements present in list.

```
#include<list.h>
    void main()
```

```
{
list<int> l1;
int i;
l1.push_back(50);
l1.push_back(100);
l1.push_back(150);
l1.push_back(200);
cout<<"Size of list "<<l1.size()<<endl;
list<int>::iterator temp;
   temp = l1.begin();  // temp points to first position
   temp++; // temp points to second position
   temp++;// temp points to third position
   l1.insert (temp,555);   //555 is inserted to the left of 150

cout<<"Size of list after inserting value 555 is "<<l1.
size()<<endl;
   temp--; // temp points to node with value 555
   l1.insert (temp,444);   //444 is inserted to the left of 555

 cout<<"Size of list after inserting value 444 is "<<l1.
size()<<endl;
cout<<"Full List"<<endl;
   for( temp= l1.begin();temp != l1.end() ; temp++)
   {
        cout<<*temp<<" ";
   }
   cout<<endl;
   temp = l1.begin();   // temp points to first position
   temp++; // temp points to second position
   //delete second element
   temp=l1.erase(temp); // temp now points to element after
deleted hence temp points to 444
   cout<<"Size of list after erasing second element is "<<l1.
size()<<endl;
   temp++;               // temp points to 555
   temp=l1.erase(temp); //delete 555
   cout<<"Size of list after erasing third element is "<<l1.
size()<<endl;
        cout<<"Full List"<<endl;
   for( temp= l1.begin();temp != l1.end() ; temp++)
   {
        cout<<*temp<<" ";
   }
}
```

Output

```
Size of list 4
Size of list after inserting value 555 is 5
Size of list after inserting value 444 is 6
Full List
50 100 444 555 150 200
Size of list after erasing second element is 5
Size of list after erasing third element is 4
Full List
50 444 150 200
```

Following push_back() statements

```
ll.push_back(50);
ll.push_back(100);
ll.push_back(150);
ll.push_back(200);
```

insert these elements. Hence, the linked list is as shown in Figure 16.10.

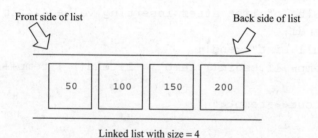

Front side of list   Back side of list

| 50 | 100 | 150 | 200 |

Linked list with size = 4

Figure 16.10:   Linked list ll

At this point, the linked list ll has 4 elements and hence its size is 4. Therefore, the following statement

```
cout<<"Size of list "<<ll.size()<<endl;
```

prints the size as 4 on the computer screen.

The forward iterator temp points to the first node of the linked list due to following statement:

```
temp = ll.begin();   // temp points to first position
```

We have then applied ++ operator twice, taking temp two steps ahead.

```
temp++; // temp points to second position
temp++;// temp points to third position
```

Hence, temp points to the third node of the linked list which currently stores a value 150.

The call to insert() function

```
ll.insert (temp,555);
```

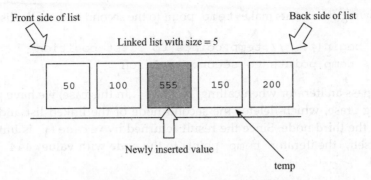

Front side of list

Back side of list

Linked list with size = 5

| 50 | 100 | 555 | 150 | 200 |

Newly inserted value

temp

Figure 16.11: Insertion of 555 in linked list

inserts the data value 555 at the position where temp points to as shown in figure 16.11. The insert() function is designed such that it shifts 150 to the right and inserts the new value (555) at the current position where temp points to as shown in Figure 16.11.

Certainly, each time you insert a new value in the list, the size of the linked list increases. Hence, the size of the linked list 11 is 5 at this point in time. After the insertion, temp continues to point to node with a value of 150 as it was pointing before the insertion.

Applying -- operator on iterator temp takes it behind by one node, and hence it points to the node with data value 555.

```
temp--; // temp points to node 555
```

The following call to insert() function inserts 444 at the position where temp points to and shifts 555 to the right in the list as shown in Figure 16.12. After the insertion, temp will continue to point to the node with data value 555 as it was doing before the insertion.

```
11.insert(temp,444); //444 is inserted to the left of 555
```

The function erase() deletes the current node pointed by the iterator passed to it and returns an iterator that points to the next node of the node which is deleted from the list.

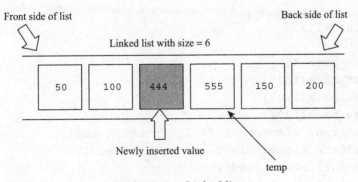

Front side of list

Back side of list

Linked list with size = 6

| 50 | 100 | 444 | 555 | 150 | 200 |

Newly inserted value

temp

Figure 16.12: Linked list

The following statements make `temp` point to the second node of the list.

```
temp = 11.begin();  // temp points to first position
temp++; // temp points to second position
```

We have to pass an iterator when calling `erase()`. In this case, we have passed `temp` while calling erase, which deletes the second node of the linked list and returns the reference to the third node. Since the result returned by `erase()` is initialized back to `temp` itself, the iterator `temp` points to the node with value `444` as shown in Figure 16.13.

```
temp=11.erase(temp); /* temp now points to element after deleted.
     Hence temp points to 444 */
```

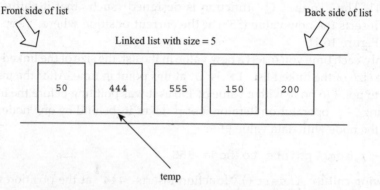

Figure 16.13: Effect of `erase()`: 100 is deleted from list

`front()` and `back()` methods

The function `front()` returns the first element in the list, whereas the function `back()` returns the last element in the list. The program given below demonstrates the results of `front()` and `back()` functions.

```
#include<list.h>
void main()
{
list<int> 11;
int i;
11.push_back(50);
11.push_back(100);
11.push_back(150);
11.push_back(200);
cout<<"Front element is "<<11.front()<<endl;
cout<<"Back element is "<<11.back()<<endl;
cout<<"Full List"<<endl;
    list<int> :: iterator temp;
```

```
for( temp= ll.begin();temp != ll.end() ; temp++)
{
        cout<<*temp<<" ";
}
}
```

Output

```
Front element is 50
Back element is 200
Full List
50 100 150 200
```

The following calls to `push_back()` inserts 4 elements in the linked list as shown in Figure 16.14.

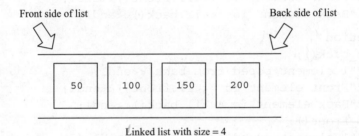

Figure 16.14: Linked list

```
ll.push_back(50);
ll.push_back(100);
ll.push_back(150);
ll.push_back(200);
```

The front element is `50` and the back element is `200`. Hence, the following statement which calls the `front()` function prints `50` on the computer screen:

```
cout<<"Front element is "<<ll.front()<<endl;
```

The below `cout` statement calls `back()` function, which prints 200 on the computer screen.

```
cout<<"Back element is "<<ll.back()<<endl;
```

NOTES

The functions `front()` and `back()` actually return the **data value** of first and last node respectively. Their usage is demonstrated in implementation of stack and queues later in this chapter.

pop_front() and pop_back() methods

The function `pop_front()` deletes the front element of the linked list and the function `pop_back()` deletes the back element of the linked list. Following program demonstrates the usage of `pop_front()` and `pop_back()` functions:

```cpp
#include<list.h>
#include<iostream.h>
    void main()
    {
       list<int> l1;
       int i;
    l1.push_back(50);
    l1.push_back(100);
    l1.push_back(150);
    l1.push_back(200);
    cout<<"Front element is "<<l1.front()<<endl;
    cout<<"Back element is "<<l1.back()<<endl;

    //deletion
    l1.pop_back();
    cout<<"1 element poped from back"<<endl;
    cout<<"Front element is "<<l1.front()<<endl;
    cout<<"Back element is "<<l1.back()<<endl;
    l1.pop_front();
    cout<<"1 element poped from front"<<endl;
    cout<<"Front element is "<<l1.front()<<endl;
    cout<<"Back element is "<<l1.back()<<endl;
    cout<<"Full List"<<endl;
       list<int> :: iterator temp;
       for(temp = l1.begin();temp != l1.end(); temp++)
       {
            cout<<*temp<<" ";
       }
    }
```

Output

```
Front element is 50
Back element is 200
1 element poped from back
Front element is 50
Back element is 150
1 element poped from front
Front element is 100
Back element is 150
Full List
100 150
```

`sort()` method

The method `sort()` is used to sort the elements in the collection in ascending order by default. The program demonstrates sorting of linked list containing integer values.

```
#include<list.h>
void main()
{
    list<int> l1;
    int i;
    for(i=10;i>=1;i--)
    {
       l1.push_back(i);
    }
//sort the elements of the list
    l1.sort();
    cout<<"Sorted list"<<endl;
    list<int> :: iterator temp;
    for(temp = l1.begin();temp != l1.end() ; temp++)
    {
       cout<<*temp<<" ";
    }
}
```

Output

```
Sorted list
1 2 3 4 5 6 7 8 9 10
```

The statement

```
l1.sort();
```

invokes a `sort()` method which arranges the linked list l1 in ascending order.

Defining custom logic for comparison

It is possible to define a custom comparison logic to `sort()` method. An overloaded version of `sort()` is available in STL, which accepts a user-defined function as an argument. This user-defined function can define the logic on how should the `sort()` method perform comparison of any two elements in the linked list.

We have learnt sorting of arrays in Chapter 6 Section 6.2.5, recall that the process of sorting compared two elements at any point in time. Hence, the user-defined function we would create to customize the sorting process must define the logic on how any two elements of the list are to be compared. If the user-defined function returns 1 (true), it means that two elements in the list are in correct order; whereas, if the user-defined function returns 0 (false), it means that the two elements in the list are in the incorrect order and their positions need to be interchanged.

Consider the user-defined function given below:

```
int compareLogic(int firstValue,int secondValue)
{
if(firstValue<secondValue)
return 0;
else
return 1;
}
```

We have named the user-defined function as `compareLogic()`. It takes two integer arguments `firstValue` and `secondValue` which represents two values of the list which are compared by the `sort()` algorithm at any given point of time. We have written the function `compareLogic()`, such that it returns false if `firstValue<secondValue`. This means that for any two values in the list if the value before is less than the value after, then their positions will be interchanged. In summary, this means that all the values that appear before in the list must be greater than all the values that appear after. Hence, our custom logic of comparison forces `sort()` function to arrange the elements of linked list in **descending order**. Recall, the default behaviour of `sort()` is to arrange elements in ascending order.

Given below is the program that demonstrates the usage of `sort()` function with a custom logic for comparison:

```
#include<list.h>
int compareLogic(int firstValue,int secondValue)
{
if(firstValue < secondValue)
return 0;
else
return 1;
}
void main()
{
    list<int> l1;
    int i;
    for(i=10;i>=1;i--)
    {
      l1.push_back(i);
    }
//sort the elements of the list
    l1.sort(compareLogic);
    cout<<"Sorted list"<<endl;
    list<int> :: iterator temp;
    for(temp = l1.begin();temp != l1.end(); temp++)
```

```
    {
        cout<<*temp<<" ";
    }
}
```

Output

```
Sorted list
10  9  8  7  6  5  4  3  2  1
```

The statement

```
l1.sort(compareLogic);
```

invokes the `sort()` function to sort linked list `l1`. Note that we have passed the function name `customLogic` to the `sort()` function as an argument. This informs the `sort()` algorithm to apply comparison of elements as specified in the user-defined function. The `sort()` algorithm will change the position of elements if the user-defined function `compareLogic` returns 0 (false) and keep the two elements intact if `compareLogic` returns 1 (true). Thereby, arranging the linked list `l1` in descending order as seen in the output of the code.

16.4.2 Difference between vector and linked list

`vector` is very similar to linked list with two major differences:

1. Internally, vector is implemented as an array, and hence elements inside vector are stored in adjacent memory location. Whereas linked list is created using different node objects linked to each other using pointers. Hence nodes of linked list are not guaranteed to be in adjacent memory locations.
2. Vector supports random iterator which linked list does not. For example, if `temp` is an iterator object, then following statements are valid in vector but not in linked list.

Iterator expression	Description
`temp=v1.begin()+5`	Makes the iterator `temp` point to 5th element from the beginning in vector named as `v1`
`temp=temp+8`	Moves iterator `temp` 8 steps ahead relative to its current location. So, for example, if `temp` is pointing to the 3rd element in the vector currently, the execution of this statement will make `temp` point to 11th position in the vector
`temp=temp-3`	Moves the iterator 3 steps behind. For example, if `temp` is currently pointing to 4th element of the vector after execution of this statement `temp` will start pointing to 1st element of the vector

It is not possible to have these random movements of iterator in the linked list because linked list only supports two types of iterators:

1. Forward iterator
2. Backward iterator

You can only use ++ or -- operators with the iterator of linked list; this is because linked list iterator can only move one step at a time. The statements given in the table above will not work for linked list iterator but will work for a vector iterator.

Given below is the demonstration of random iterator supported by vector. Note that the for loop has an initialization statement as

```
temp= v1.begin()+5
```

which means that the iteration will start from 6th element of the vector. This means that the first five elements of the vector will not be printed.

```
#include<vector.h>
void main()
{
    vector<int> v1;
    int i;
    for(i=0;i<=10;i++)
    {
      v1.push_back(i);
    }
    cout<<"Printing vector skipping first 5 elements"<<endl;
    vector<int> :: iterator temp;
    for(temp = v1.begin()+5;temp != v1.end() ; temp++)
    {
      cout<<*temp<<" ";
    }
}
```

Output

```
Printing vector skipping first 5 elements
5 6 7 8 9 10
```

16.4.3 Map

Map is a collection which stores data in the form of key, value pairs. You can imagine a map as a table indexed by key and a specific data value which is stored corresponding to each key. Key must be unique for each entry in the map, however it is possible to have same or different value for two different entries of the map.

For example, consider a map that stores roll number and name of students. Here, roll number is a unique identifier and is a key for each entry. Value is the name of the student. It is realistic that two different students have same name in the real world, however their roll numbers will be different. All this means is that, values can have duplicates but key must be unique.

Given below is the program that demonstrates usage of built-in collection map in C++.

```
#include<map.h>
#include<iostream.h>
void main()
{
map<int,char*> students;

//Inserting data into map
students[10]="John";
students[22]="Jack";
students[55]="Jill";

cout<<"Size of the map after insertions = "<<students.
    size()<<endl;

//traversing map using iterator
cout<<"Forward traversal of Map"<<endl;
map<int,char*> :: iterator temp;
for(temp = students.begin();temp != students.end() ; temp++)
        {
    cout<<"Key="<<(*temp).first<<" Value= "<<(*temp).
        second<<endl;
        }
}
```

Output

```
Size of the map after insertions = 3
Forward traversal of Map
Key=10 Value=John
Key=22 Value=Jack
Key=55 Value=Jill
```

The template class map is defined in an header file map.h, hence this header file must be included before using map in the program.

While creating a map object, you have to specify two data types:

1. Data type of the key
2. Data type of the value

Given below is the syntax to create a map object:

```
map<keyDataType,valueDataType> object;
```

In our example, we are storing data about students with roll number as a key and name as a value. Hence, the data type of key is int, whereas the value is array of characters (char*). The structure we created in the program is as shown in Figure 16.15. The statement

```
map<int,char*> students;
```

creates a map named students with data type of key as int and data type of value as char*

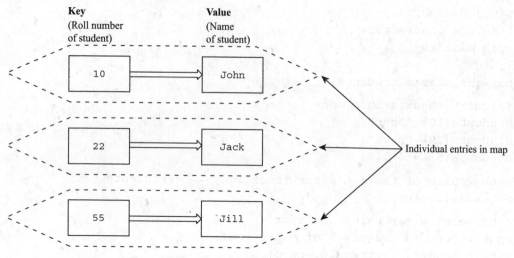

Figure 16.15: Example: map storing students data

Once created, you can insert entries in map using the following syntax:

```
mapName[key]=Value;
```

Following statements create, three entries in the map for three different students.

```
students[10]="John"; /* creates an entry with key=10 and
    value=John*/
students[22]="Jack"; /* creates an entry with key=22 and
    value=Jack*/
students[55]="Jill"; /* creates an entry with key=55 and value=Jill */
```

The data stored in map `students` is as shown in the Figure 16.16.

It is possible to iterate through map in the same way as that of other collections by creating an iterator object. The following statement creates an iterator named as `temp` to iterate through map storing an `int` type key and `char*` type value

Key	Value
10	John
22	Jack
55	Jill

Figure 16.16: Map named `students`

```
map<int,char*>::iterator temp;
```

The `for` loop that iterates through each entry of the map is as shown below:

```
for(temp = students.begin();temp != students.end() ; temp++)
    {
    cout<<"Key="<<(*temp).first<<" Value= "<<(*temp).second<<endl;
    }
```

The iterator `temp` progresses through each entry of the map, step by step in each iteration of the `for` loop. The key of the entry pointed by `temp` is accessed as `(*temp).first` and the data value of the entry is accessed as `(*temp).second`.

One of the important advantages of map is that, it is very easy to search a value corresponding to a given key. For example, if we want to fetch the name of the student with roll number 10 in pointer p, then we can write the following statement:

```
char* p = students[10];
```

In general, if you want to fetch the name of any student with roll number x, you can do so by the statement

```
char* p = students[x];
```

Given below are three sample cout statements that print the name of three students having roll numbers 10, 22 and 55.

```
cout<<"Name of the student with roll number 10 is "<<students[10]<<endl;
cout<<"Name of the student with roll number 22 is "<<students[22]<<endl;
cout<<"Name of the student with roll number 55 is "<<students[55]<<endl;
```

16.5 Implementation of Stack using Linked List: An Example

Stack is a last-in-first-out type of data structure. We can imagine stack as a bucket with one open end as shown in Figure 16.17:

As the structure as only one open end, we can insert/remove elements from it only through one end.

Let us assume we insert first value 10 into stack. The stack is as shown in Figure 16.18.

Now, if you insert second value in stack as 20, it will be on top of 10 as shown in Figure 16.19.

If you insert third value in stack as 30, it will be on top of 20 as shown in Figure 16.20.

The process of inserting elements into stack is called as **pushing**. Whereas, the process of removing elements from stack is called as **popping**.

The pop operation always removes the top most element from the stack. When you execute pop operation, the first element that will be removed is 30, which was inserted last. Hence, stack is called as last-in-first-out type of data structure. After 30 is removed from stack the 20 becomes the top most element and hence the second pop operation will remove 20 from stack. Similarly, the last pop operation will remove 10, thereby making the stack empty because it was the only element in the stack. The effect of pop operations is as shown in Figure 16.21.

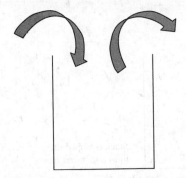

Figure 16.17: Stack with one open end

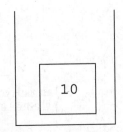

Figure 16.18: Push 10 in stack

Figure 16.19:   Push 20 in stack   **Figure 16.20:**   Push 30 in stack

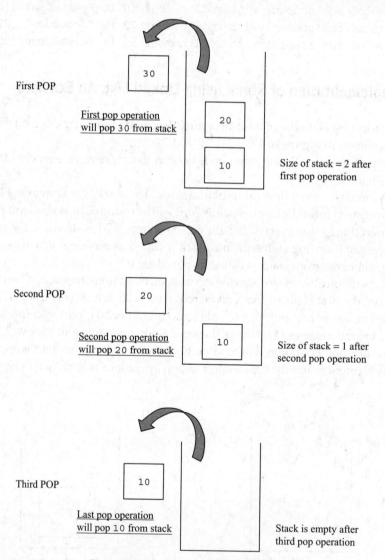

First POP

First pop operation
will pop 30 from stack

Size of stack = 2 after
first pop operation

Second POP

Second pop operation
will pop 20 from stack

Size of stack = 1 after
second pop operation

Third POP

Last pop operation
will pop 10 from stack

Stack is empty after
third pop operation

Figure 16.21:   Pop operations on stack

In the above discussion, we have just pushed and popped integer values to/from stack. We can always implement a generic stack using templates. In this example, we will implement stack using the built-in `list` present in C++.

```cpp
#include<list.h>
template<class G>
class Stack
{
  private:
  list<G> ll;
  int size;
  public:
  Stack()
  {
        size=0;
  }
  void push(G element)
  {
  ll.push_back(element);
  size++;
  }
  G pop()
  {
  G element = ll.back();   //get the top most element
  ll.pop_back(); //delete the element from stack
  size--;
  return element;
  }
  int isempty()
  {
        return (size==0);
  }
};
void main()
{
Stack<int> s;
s.push(10);
cout<<"Pushed 10"<<endl;
s.push(20);
cout<<"Pushed 20"<<endl;
s.push(30);
cout<<"Pushed 30"<<endl;
cout<<"**********Elements popped***************"<<endl;
int temp;
```

```
    while(!s.isempty())
    {
        temp =s.pop();
        cout<<temp<<endl;
    }


}
```

Output

```
Pushed 10
Pushed 20
Pushed 30
**********Elements popped***************
30
20
10
```

In the class Stack, we have created a generic list ll

```
list<G> ll;
```

We will use this list to store the elements of stack. We have created the list ll as a private member of Stack, so the outside world cannot directly access the list ll. Every access to elements of list ll must be passed through the public methods of class Stack. There are two public methods in class Stack.

void push(G element)

This method is used to insert elements into the stack by calling push_back() method of list ll. So this means that all elements which are inserted are only from back side of the list. The push method takes the element to be pushed as input and performs following two steps:

Statement	Description
ll.push_back(element);	Insert the element in linked list ll from the back side.(The back side of the list actually acts as a stack top in our implementation)
size++;	Increase the size of stack by 1

If you refer to the code written in main() method, we have created an object of Stack named as s using the statement below:

```
Stack<int> s;
```

At this stage, the stack is empty because object s is just created.

NOTES

The class Stack has another integer type variable named is size. It is used to represent the size of stack at any point in time. When an object of class Stack is created, the default constructor will be called which sets the size to zero.

We have called push method three times. Each call to push internally calls push_ back() method of the linked list 11. Hence three elements are inserted into the list 11 from the back side.

```
s.push(10);
s.push(20);
s.push(30);
```

Each call to push() also increases the size of stack, and hence after three elements are pushed into the stack, size of the stack is 3.

The method isempty() is used to check if stack is empty. The logic inside this method checks the variable size. Each time you push element into stack, size is increased by 1 using following statement in push() method:

```
size++;
```

Whereas, each time you pop the element from stack, the size of stack is decreased by 1 using following statement inside pop() method:

```
size--;
```

Hence, if size is zero, it means that stack is empty. The isempty() method returns false (0) if stack is not empty and returns true (1) if stack is empty.

G pop()

Since pushing of elements was done from back side of the list popping should also be done from the same side. This is because stack has only one open end by its definition. The pop() method does following 4 steps:

Statement	Description
G element =11.back();	Read the backmost element in list 11 and store it in variable named as element.
11.pop_back();	Actually delete the backmost element in the list. (So this gives the effect as if the top most element of stack is deleted.)
size--;	Reduce the size of stack by 1.
return element;	Return the deleted element to the calling method.

The following loop written in main() method invokes pop() method till the time stack is not empty. The condition of while loop is

```
!s.isempty()
```

This means the while loop will continue to run till the time stack is not empty. Inside the while loop, we have invoked a pop() method, hence the while loop will keep popping elements and printing them on the screen using the cout statement. The loop terminates once all the elements of stack are popped out, thereby leaving the stack as empty.

```
while(!s.isempty())
{
temp =s.pop();
cout<<temp<<endl;
}
```

16.6   Queue using List

Queue is a first-in-first-out type of data structure. Queue has two open ends as shown in Figure 16.22. Elements are inserted in queue through the rear end and removed from the queue through the front end. So the element first inserted is first to come out of the queue.

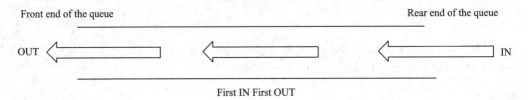

Figure 16.22:   Structure of queue

To understand, let us first insert value 10 in the queue. After the first insertion, the size of queue is 1 as shown in Figure 16.23.

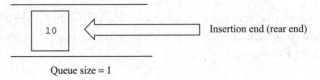

Figure 16.23:   Insertion of 10

If we now insert 20 in the queue, its size becomes 2 and 20 is stored in the queue behind 10 as shown in Figure 16.24.

Inserting a third value 30 in the queue will make the queue look as shown in Figure 16.25. The value 30 will be stored behind 20 because it was inserted after 20.

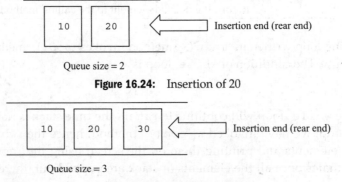

Figure 16.24:   Insertion of 20

Figure 16.25:   Insertion of 30

NOTES

On each insertion the size of the queue increases by 1. We have written a function `add()` in class `Queue` to insert elements in the queue, hence `add()` contains a statement

`size++;`

to ensure that size of the queue is increased by 1 on each insertion. Keep in mind that the default constructor of `Queue` class is only executed once, which gives initial value to variable `size` as `0`.

We will implement a generic queue using a built-in `list` of C++. The implementation of `Queue` is very similar to that of `Stack`, the only point to remember is we should not use the same end for insertion and deletion of elements. If insertion of elements is from the back end of the linked list `ll` then the deletion should be from the front end of the list. In the code below, method `add()` is responsible to add elements to the queue; internally, it invokes `push_back()` method of linked list `ll`. This means that we are inserting from back side of the list.

Now if you see the remove method it uses `pop_front()`, which removes element from front side of the list. Hence the element first inserted will be first to come out. As seen from the output of the program 10 was first added in the queue which is first to come out of the queue.

```
#include<list.h>
    template<class G>
    class Queue
    {
      private:
      list<G> ll;
      int size;
      public:
      Queue()
      {
            size=0;
      }

      void add(G element)
      {
      ll.push_back(element);
      size++;
      }
      G remove()
      {
      G element = ll.front(); //get the front element
      ll.pop_front(); //delete the element from queue
      size--;
      return element;
```

```
        }
        int isempty()
        {
                return (size==0);
        }
    };
    void main()
    {
    Queue<int> q;
    q.add(10);
    cout<<"Added 10"<<endl;
    q.add(20);
    cout<<"Added 20"<<endl;
    q.add(30);
    cout<<"Added 30"<<endl;
    cout<<"**********Order of removing
    elements***************"<<endl;
    int temp;
        while(!q.isempty())
        {
                temp =q.remove();
                cout<<temp<<endl;
        }
    }
```

Output

```
Added 10
Added 20
Added 30
**********Order of removing elements****************
10
20
30
```

Error Finding Exercise

The following are some programs that may or may not contain errors. Correct the errors if they exist in the code and determine the output after applying the corrections.

Program 1

```
template <class G>
int a=10,b=20;
G add(G a,G b)
{
```

```
    G c = a+b;
    return c;
}
void main()
{
int res=add(a,b);
cout<<"Result is"<<res;
}
```

Program 2

```
#include<list.h>
    #include<iostream.h>
      void main()
      {
            list<int> l1;
            int i;
      l1.push_back(50);
      l1.push_back(100);
      l1.push_back(150);
      l1.push_back(200);
            list<int> :: iterator temp;
      cout<<"Reverse traversal"<<endl;
          for(temp= l1.end();temp != l1.begin() ; temp--)
            {
                  cout<<*temp<<" ";
            }
```

Program 3

```
#include<list.h>
    void main()
    {
    list<int> l1;
    int i;
    l1.push_back(50);
    l1.push_back(100);
    l1.push_back(150);
    l1.push_back(200);
    cout<<"Size of list "<<l1.size()<<endl;
    list<int>::iterator temp;
        temp = l1.begin();  // temp points to first position
        temp = temp+5;
        l1.insert (temp,7000);
        temp = temp-2;
l1.insert (temp,9000);
```

```
cout<<"Full List"<<endl;
    for(temp = 11.begin();temp != 11.end() ; temp++)
 {
        cout<<*temp<<" ";
 }
}
```

Program 4

```
using namespace std;
#include<iostream>
template <class G1,class G2>
G2 add(G1 a,G2 b)
{
G2 c = a+b;
return c;
}
template <class G1,class G2>
G2 add(G2 a,G1 b)
{
G2 c = a+b;
return c;
}

void main()
{
int x;
float y,res1;
cout<<"Enter values of x and y"<<endl;
cin>>x>>y;
res1=add(x,y);
cout<<"Addition of x and y is "<<res1<<endl;
}
```

Review Questions

1. Explain with example the usage of class templates and function templates.
2. Explain the difference between vector and linked list.
3. What is a map? What are it's applications?
4. Write a C++ program to create a linked list of Employee objects using a built-in list class. Store salary for every employee and sort the linked list as per salary. Arrange the Employee objects stored in list in ascending order of salary.
5. What is an iterator? What are different types of iterators?
6. What is the difference between stack and queue explain the implementation of both the data structures?

Chapter

17 | Exception Handling in C++

17.1   Overview

Exception is an abnormal situation in the program that can terminate the program if it is not handled by the programmer. Some examples of exception are as follows:

1. If you accidently perform division by zero in the program, then it is called division by zero exception
2. If you access array elements beyond the specific boundaries of an array index, then it is called array index out of bounds exception. For example, if the size of array a is 5 and if you accidently try to access a[7] that does not exist, then it could give logically incorrect results, which is an exception
3. If your program is required to take salary of an employee as input from the user and by mistake the user inputs a negative number, then it is called an invalid input exception
4. If your program is writing to a file but the file is read-only, then there is an access rights violation in performing the output operation, which is also an example of exception
5. In network communication, if you are writing your own C++ client to communicate with the server on the same network and if server is down when you are sending messages through the client program, then it is called 'Resource Not available' type of exception

There are many more specific types of exceptions that may occur in your program from case to case. What is important is to understand what exceptions are and how effectively we can handle them to ensure that the program does not terminate abruptly when exception occurs. It is the programmer's responsibility to create robust programs that do not fail abruptly even if any abnormal situation occurs.

> **NOTES**
>
> There is a difference between an exception and an error. If there is an error in the program, the program will certainly fail. For example, a semicolon missing after a statement is an example of syntax error; program going out of memory while running a large loop is an example of memory error and so on. Errors cannot be handled and hence the program will certainly fail when an error occurs. Whereas, exception is something that can be handled in the program thereby avoiding the abrupt failure of the program. Exception handlers in C++ are used to handle exceptions (not errors). Any exception when appropriately handled will avoid abrupt termination of program even if the exception occurs. However, if an exception is unhandled, it will terminate the program immediately on its occurrence.

17.2 Exception Handler in C++

`try-catch` block is an exception handler in C++. The part of the program that has a possibility of generating an exception must be put in `try` block. `catch` block contains a piece of code that executes only when a specific exception occurs. The following is the syntax of writing `try-catch` blocks in C++:

```
try
{
/*Code which has a possibility of exception*/
}
catch(exceptionType1 variable1)
{
/*Handler for exceptionType1*/
}
catch(exceptionType2 variable2)
{
/*Handler for exceptionType2*/
}
catch(exceptionType3 variable3)
{
/*Handler for exceptionType3*/
}
....... .
catch(exceptionTypeN variableN)
{
/*Handler for exceptionTypeN*/
}
```

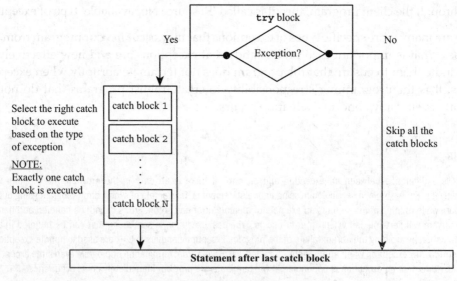

Figure 17.1: Execution of `try-catch`

You can have multiple catch blocks after a single try block. Each catch block is dedicated to handle a specific type of exception. In the above example, if there is an exception of exceptionType3 in the catch block, then the control of execution will be transferred to the third try block, skipping the first two catch blocks.

In summary, this means that the control is transferred to the right catch block depending on the type of exception in the try block. In the best case situation, if there is no exception in try block, then none of the catch blocks will be executed and the control of execution will be transferred to the statement after the last catch block, thereby skipping all the catch blocks as shown in Figure 17.1.

17.3   throw Keyword

throw keyword is used to generate an exception. The syntax of throw statement is

throw <Exception>;

or

throw;

We will see the examples of each of these syntaxes later. For now, the only thing that you must understand is that, whenever you need to generate an exception in the program you must use throw keyword.

17.4   Examples

17.4.1   Array index out of bounds exception: An example

As a first example, let us create a C++ program to handle array index out of bounds exception. Here, we imagine a situation in which the program accidently tries to access an element in the array out of allowed limits of its index. Consider the following program that creates an array a of size 5 using an initializer block. Later, we take value of i as input from the user and print the element in the array at position i.

```
#include<iostream.h>
void main()
{
int a[] ={10,20,30,40,50};
int i;
cout<<"Enter index of an array"<<endl;
cin>>i;
cout<<"Element at position"<<i<<"is"<<a[i]<<endl;
}
```

Output
```
Enter index of an array
7
Element at position 7 is -82103460
```

The program works perfectly fine if the user enters the value of i from 0 to 4, which is the boundary of the array. However, the above program has a risk of failing (generating erroneous results) if the user enters some invalid value of i. For example, let us assume that the user enters value of i as 7 as seen in the output, it generates some junk value which is stored at this location. We know that a[7] does not exist as the size of array is just 5. Hence, the program fails to generate logically correct value at the output. This is called **crashing of program**. We can use **exception handling** to avoid this situation. The following is the program which is rewritten using exception handling:

```
#include<iostream.h>
void main()
{
int a[] ={10,20,30,40,50};
int i;
    try {
    cout<<"Enter index of an array"<<endl;
    cin>>i;
      if(i<0 || i>4)
      {
      throw i;
      cout<<"This statement will not be executed"<<endl;
      }
      else
      {
      cout<<"Element at position "<<i<<" is "<<a[i]<<endl;
      }
    }
    catch(int t)
    {
    cout<<"Invalid array index "<<t<<endl;
    }
cout<<"Good Bye"<<endl;
}
```

Output
```
Enter index of an array
7
Invalid array index 7
Good Bye
```

Statements that have the possibility to generate an exception are put in the try block. The program inputs the value of i using a cin statement. Factually, it does not matter whether the cin statement is inside the try block or outside of it. We have intentionally put it inside the try block because it is the value of i using which we can decide whether an exception is to be generated. The following if block checks if the value of i inputted by the user is a valid index of an array. Since the size of an array is 5, the valid indexes are from 0 to 4. So if the user inputs a value less than 0 or greater than 4, it should result in an exception. This `if` block that checks erroneous conditions must be in the `try` block because this is the piece of code that has a possibility to throw an exception.

```
if(i<0 || i>4)
{
throw i;
cout<<"This statement will not be executed"<<endl;
}
```

The statement

```
throw i;
```

actually throws an exception. Since i is thrown by the `throw` statement and data type of i is `int`, a `catch` block that catches an `int` value will be correctly executed. Therefore, the control of execution is transferred to the following `catch` block; thereby printing a message: Invalid array index 7 (assume the user inputs i as 7) on the computer screen.

```
catch(int t)
{
cout<<"Invalid array index "<<t<<endl;
}
```

NOTES

The `try` block terminates immediately after a `throw` statement is encountered and the control is transferred to the right `catch` block that can handle the thrown exception. Hence, the following statement in the `try` block that appears right after the `throw` statement will never be executed.

```
cout<<"This statement will not be executed"<<endl;
```

In fact, it is not correct to write statements at this place because this part of the code is never reachable. Recent compilers remove such unreachable code automatically as a part of code optimization or generate necessary error/warning messages to the programmer highlighting such unreachable statements.

After the `catch` block completes its execution, the exception is considered to be as handled. Hence, the program continues to execute normally after the `catch` block completes its execution. The following statement is written after the `catch` block:

```
cout<<"Good Bye"<<endl;
```

will get executed in any case, thereby printing Good Bye on the computer screen.

If the user inputs any valid value of i from 0 to 4, then the control of execution will never be transferred in the `if` block and hence the exception will not be thrown. This time the control is transferred in the `else` block because the user has inputted a valid index of an array, thereby executing the following statement, which prints the array element at a specific index i.

```
cout<<"Element at position "<<i<<" is "<<a[i]<<endl;
```

Since there was no exception in the `try` block, the `catch` block will not be executed this time and the control of execution directly jumps to the first statement after the `catch` block, which is

```
cout<<"Good Bye"<<endl;
```

This prints the message `Good Bye` on the computer screen.

> **NOTES**
>
> `catch` block is executed only if there is an exception generated in the `try` block. If there is no exception in the `try` block, all the `catch` block(s) are skipped.

> **NOTES**
>
> Always remember to check the boundary conditions before accessing elements of the array in your program to avoid occurrence of **array index out of bounds exception**. It is a good programming practice to have such proactive checks in the program that deals with arrays.

17.4.2   NULL pointer exception: An example

Let us assume that we have created a pointer in the program, which points to NULL and no valid data value. In this case, dereferencing a pointer makes no real sense because it is not pointing to any valid memory location. However, if the programmer tries to accidently dereference this pointer, then the results will be erroneous, and this exception is called NULL pointer exception.

In this example, we will demonstrate two things together:

1. Handling of NULL pointer exception
2. Generating an exception in the called function and handling it in calling function

```
#include<iostream.h>
void printData(int *p)
{
    if(p == NULL)
    {
    throw 0;
    }
    else
    {
    cout<<"Data is "<<*p<<endl;
    }
}
void main()
{
int *p=0;
int a=10;
/*Following statement is commented*/
```

```
//p=&a;
   try
   {
   printData(p);
   }
   catch(int x)
   {
   cout<<"NULL POINTER EXCEPTION. Pointer is "<<x<<endl;
   }
cout<<"Good Bye"<<endl;
}
```

Output
```
NULL POINTER EXCEPTION. Pointer is 0
Good Bye
```

Let's first look at the printData() function. The function is essentially used to print the data value pointed by the pointer passed to it. If the pointer points to NULL, it throws the exception.

```
throw 0;
```

Otherwise, if the pointer does not point to NULL, then the function assumes it is pointing to a valid memory location and prints its data value using the statement:

```
cout<<"Data is "<<*p<<endl;
```

The call to function printData() is made in the try block because there is a possibility of an exception to be generated within the printData() function. If the printData() function throws an exception, the catch block written inside main() will be executed, because there is no catch block present in printData() to handle this exception. In a worst-case scenario, if main() also does not have the relevant catch block, then the execution of the program will terminate abruptly. In this case, printData() function throws an exception using the statement:

```
throw 0;
```

The value 0 is int and hence the following catch block is executed in main() function, thereby printing a message NULL POINTER EXCEPTION as seen in the output of the program.

```
catch(int x)
{
cout<<"NULL POINTER EXCEPTION. Pointer is "<<x<<endl;
}
```

After the catch block completes its execution, the exception is considered to be as handled. Hence, the program continues to execute normally after the catch block completes its execution. The following statement is written after the catch block

```
cout<<"Good Bye"<<endl;
```

will get executed in any case thereby printing Good Bye on the computer screen.

We have intentionally commented the following line

```
p=&a;
```

to show a demonstration of generating an exception. Now, if you uncomment this line, the printer p will point to a valid data element in memory, and hence it will no more be NULL. In this case, the following statement will be executed to print the value pointed by p, which is 10 in our example.

```
cout<<"Data is "<<*p<<endl;
```

In this case, the function printData() will not throw any exception, and hence, there is no exception in the try block of main() function. Therefore, the catch block will not be executed at all. Hence, the control of execution will directly be transferred to the following statement after the try block completes:

```
cout<<"Good Bye"<<endl;
```

> **NOTES**
>
> Always remember to check whether a pointer is pointing to NULL before dereferencing a pointer. It is a good programming practice to proactively have a NULL check in the program when dealing with pointers.

17.4.3 Arithmetic exception: An example

Arithmetic exception can occur if an illegal arithmetic operation is performed in the program, for example division by zero. The program given below takes values of two variables a and b as input from the user and performs two operations.

1. a/b
2. a+b

Out of the two operations, a/b is risky because it will generate erroneous results if value of b is entered as zero by the user. If this exception is not handled, it will crash the full program. Clearly, it does not make any sense to stop addition operation even if division fails. However, if we do not handle the exception, the complete program will crash and addition will also not be performed. If, we would like addition to be performed in any case whether or not the division fails, then we can implement exception handling as shown in the program below

```
#include<iostream.h>
void main()
{
int a,b,c,d;
cout<<"Enter two numbers"<<endl;
cin>>a>>b;
    try
```

```
    {
        if(b==0)
        {
        throw b;
        }
    c = a/b;
    cout<<"Result of division is "<<c<<endl;
    }
    catch(int t)
    {
    cout<<"Division by zero exception : Operation failed"<<endl;
    }
d = a+b;
cout<<"Result of addition is "<<d<<endl;
}
```

Output
```
Enter two numbers
10 0
Division by zero exception : Operation failed
Result of addition is 10
```

The operation a+b is not a risky one, so there is no need to perform a+b in the try block. In fact, we would like a+b to be performed in any case whether or not the division succeeds. Hence, we put it after the try-catch handler in the code. To understand this code, let us go through the following two cases:

Case 1: Value of b is zero

Let us assume the user inputs value of a as 10 and b as 0. In this case, the following check in the try block will throw an exception:

```
if(b==0)
{
throw b;
}
```

Hence the control will be transferred to the catch block without performing any division. Recall, when the throw is executed, the control exits the try block immediately and is transferred to the matching catch block. The catch block prints the message 'Division by zero Exception : Operation failed' using the following cout statement:

```
cout<<"Division by zero Exception : Operation failed"<<endl;
```

After the catch block completes its execution, the exception is considered to be handled and the rest of the program will now execute normally. Hence the addition operation is successfully performed, which is outside the try-catch handler, thereby printing the result of addition on the computer screen.

```
Result of addition is 10
```

Case 2: Value of b is not zero

Let us assume the user inputs value of a as 10 and b as 2. In this case, the `try` block will not execute the `throw` statement because b is not zero. The division operation will be performed in the `try` block and the `cout` inside the `try` block will be executed printing the following message on the screen:

```
Result of division is 5
```

Since there was no exception in the `try` block, the `catch` block will not be executed, thereby directly transferring the control to the first statement after the `catch` block. Hence, the addition will now be performed printing the following message on the screen:

```
Result of addition is 12
```

NOTES

Always remember to check if denominator evaluates to zero before performing division in the program. It is a good programming practice to have such proactive checks in the program.

17.4.4 Multiple exceptions: An example

It is possible to have multiple `catch` blocks after a single `try` block. You may want to do this if there is a possibility of different types of exceptions being generated in the `try` block and each of them need a different handling process, when it occurs.

The program given below has multiple `catch` blocks after a single `try` block

```
#include<iostream.h>
void printData(int *p)
{
    if(p == NULL)
    {
    throw 0.0;
    }
    else
    {
    cout<<"Data is "<<*p<<endl;
    }
}
void main()
{
int a,b,c,d;
cout<<"Enter two numbers"<<endl;
cin>>a>>b;
int *p=NULL;
/*Following statement is commented */
    // p=&a;
    try
    {
```

```
    if(b==0)
    {
    throw b;
    }
    c = a/b;
    cout<<"Result of division is "<<c<<endl;
    printData(p);
    }
    catch(double x)
    {
    cout<<"NULL POINTER EXCEPTION"<<endl;
    }
    catch(int t)
    {
    cout<<"Division by zero Exception : Operation failed"<<endl;
    }
d = a+b;
cout<<"Result of addition is "<<d<<endl;
}
```

Output
```
Enter two numbers
10 2
Result of division is 5
NULL POINTER EXCEPTION
Result of addition is 12
```

Much part of this code is already explained in examples 17.4.2 and 17.4.3, so we will not go into the details of this program. The `try` block in `main()` does two jobs:

1. Performs the operation a/b
2. Calls `printData()` function to dereference a pointer p

Hence, there are two risks in the code:

1. Risk of division by zero when the value of b is zero
2. Risk of NULL pointer exception when the pointer p is NULL

To handle the possibility of these two exceptions, we have written two different `catch` blocks. The first `catch` block responds to the throw statement that throws an `int` type, when division by zero case happens to be in the program. The `throw` statement in the program responsible to throw arithmetic exception is

```
throw b; /*b is of type int*/
```

The second `catch` block responds to the `throw` statement that throws `double` object 0.0, when NULL pointer exception case happens to be in the program. The `throw` statement in the program responsible to generate the null pointer exception is

```
throw 0.0; /*0.0 is by default considered as double by the
    compiler */
```

NOTES

C++ determines which `catch` block to execute based on the data type of the object that is thrown. In this example, when the `throw` statement throws a constant `0.0`, the `catch` block catching `double` type value will handle the exception. Whereas, when the `throw` statement throwing `int` is executed, the `catch` block catching `int` will handle the exception. Similarly, you can throw and catch object of any other data type including user-defined types. We have intentionally written one integer and one double `catch` block to differentiate the handling of each of the exceptions.

NOTES

In the given program, we throw a dummy value of `0.0`, which is by default considered as double. This value acts as a signal to the calling function that `NULL` pointer exception has occurred within the `printData()`.

NOTES

It is possible to create a generic `catch` block, which can handle all the exceptions that occur in the `try` block. Programmers can follow this approach if all exceptions are to be handled in the same way.

The syntax for creating a generic `catch` block is as follows:

```
catch(...)
{
/*Generic catch block for all types of exceptions*/
}
```

The given program can be rewritten to have a single generic `catch` block instead of writing different `catch` blocks for different types of exceptions. In this case, no matter what type of exception occurs the control will always be transferred to a generic `catch` block that will handle all exceptions. The downside of this design is that you cannot have a specific handling for different types of exceptions. Given below is the program that uses a generic catch block:

```
#include<iostream.h>
void printData(int *p)
{
    if(p == NULL)
    {
    throw 0.0;
    }
    else
    {
    cout<<"Data is "<<*p<<endl;
    }
}
void main()
{
int a,b,c,d;
cout<<"Enter two numbers"<<endl;
cin>>a>>b;
int *p=NULL;
/*Following statement is commented*/
  // p=&a;
    try
    {
```

```
        if(b==0)
        {
        throw b;
        }
        c = a/b;
        cout<<"Result of division is "<<c<<endl;
        printData(p);
    }
    catch(...)
    {
    cout<<"Some exception has occured"<<endl;
    }
d = a+b;
cout<<"Result of addition is "<<d<<endl;
}
```

Output

```
Enter two numbers
10 2
Result of division is 5
Some exception has occured
Result of addition is 12
```

17.5   Order of writing Catch Blocks

If your program has both specialized and generic catch blocks, all the specialized catch blocks must always appear before the generic catch block as shown in Figure 17.2. This is because the generic catch block has a potential to catch all the types of exceptions, and if it is written before the specialized one's, the specialized catch blocks will never get executed as all the special exceptions will also be caught by the generalized catch block itself.

```
    try
    {
     /*Code that may throw an exception*/
    }
    catch(int a)
    {
    /*Special catch block to handle int type objects*/
    }
    catch(char a)
    {
    /*Special catch block to handle char type objects*/
    }
    catch(float a)
    {
     /*Special catch block to handle float type objects*/
    }
    catch(...)
    {
    /*Generic catch block*/
    }
```

Specialized catch blocks

Generalized catch block must be written after all the specialized catch blocks

Figure 17.2:   Order of writing catch blocks

Is it possible to nest try-catch blocks? ?

Yes, you can nest one `try-catch` block inside another. Given below is the syntax of nesting of `try-catch` blocks. If there is any exception in the statements written in the inner `try` block, C++ will first check if there is a `catch` corresponding to the `try` in which the exception occurred. If yes, the respective `catch` block will be executed.

If there is no `catch` block corresponding to an inner `try` block for this type of exception, C++ will check all `catch` blocks corresponding to the outer `try` block to find the best matching handler for the exception. If there is an outer `catch` block corresponding to this exception, it will be executed and the exception will be considered as handled. If there is no matching `catch` block found for an exception, then the exception will be considered as unhandled and the program will crash. The aim of the exception handling is to avoid programs crashing abruptly, and hence it is recommended to handle all the possible exceptions some way or the other to make the program robust.

For instance, if an exception of Type 3 occurs in the inner `try` block, the `catch` block written corresponding to the outer `try` block that handles exception of Type 3 will get executed, and the exception will be considered as handled. If exception of Type 1 or Type 2 is generated in the inner `try` block, the respective inner `catch` block will be executed and the exception will be considered as handled by the inner `try-catch` blocks itself. Remember that if there is an exception generated in the statements of the outer `try` block, then C++ will not handle them using the inner `catch` blocks.

```
try
{
/*statements in outer try block*/
    try
    {
    /*statements in inner try block*/
    }
    catch(Type1 obj1)
    {
    /*To handle exceptions of Type 1 in the inner try block*/
    }
    catch(Type2 obj2)
    {
    /*To handle exceptions of Type 2 in the inner try block*/
    }
    ...... (many inner catch blocks possible)
/*some more statements in outer try block*/
}
catch(Type3 obj3)
{
/*To handle exceptions of Type 3 in the inner and outer try block*/
}
catch(Type4 obj4)
{
/*To handle exceptions of Type 4 in the inner and outer try block*/
}
...... (many outer catch blocks possible)
```

17.6 Catching and Throwing User-defined Objects

Just like we can throw and catch primitive data items, we can also throw user-defined objects. As an example, let us go back to the `Account` class created in Chapter 11, Section 11.7 for managing bank accounts. We will modify the same code to use exception handling.

The `withdraw()` method has a check to ensure that balance does not fall below the allowed limit before allowing withdrawal operation. We will modify `withdraw()` method to throw an exception if such situation happens. We will create a new class named `InsufficientFunds`, and throw the object of this class using the `throw` keyword, and handle it in catch handler to demonstrate catching and throwing of user-defined exceptions. Given below is the full source code to manage bank accounts that is in line with Chapter 11, Section 11.7 except the `withdraw()` method, which is modified to use exception handling features.

```cpp
#include<iostream.h>
class InsufficientFunds
{
public:
    void printMessage()
    {
    cout<<"You do not have sufficient funds in account for this
    operation"<<endl;
    }
};
class Account
{
private:
int acc_no;
char name[100];
float bal;
public:
    void input()
    {
    cin>>acc_no>>name>>bal;
        while(bal<500)
        {
    cout<<"Balance cannot be less than 500, please re-enter its
    value";
        cin>>bal;
        }
    }
    void withdraw(float amount)
    {
        if(bal-amount>=500)
        {
        bal = bal - amount;
        cout<<"New Balance is "<<bal<<endl;
        }
        else
        {
```

```cpp
            throw InsufficientFunds();
        }
    }
    void deposit(float amount)
    {
        if(amount<0)
        {
        cout<<"Amount to deposit cannot be negative"<<endl;
        }
        else
        {
        bal-bal-amount;
        cout<<"New Balance is "<<bal<<endl;
        }
    }
    void output()
    {
    cout<<acc_no<<" "<<name<<" "<<bal<<endl;
    }
};
void main()
{
Account a1,a2;
cout<<"Enter the details of first account"<<endl;
a1.input();
cout<<"Enter the details of second account"<<endl;
a2.input();
cout<<"Withdraw Rs 4200 from John's account"<<endl;
try {
a1.withdraw(4200);
}
catch(InsufficientFunds e)
{
e.printMessage();
}
cout<<"Deposit Rs 2000 in Jack's account"<<endl;
a2.deposit(2000);
cout<<"The account details are"<<endl;
a1.output();
a2.output();
}
```

Output

```
Enter the details of first account
10 john 800
```

```
Enter the details of second account
12 Jack 600
Withdraw Rs 4200 from John's account
```
You do not have sufficient funds in account for this operation
```
Deposit Rs 2000 in Jack's account
New Balance is 600
The account details are
10   john   800
12   Jack   600
```

We have created a class named InsufficientFunds with a simple public method named as printMessage(), which prints the insufficient funds message on the user screen. The withdraw() function in Account class is being modified to throw InsufficientFunds object if operation of withdrawal is not possible as shown below:

```cpp
void withdraw(float amount)
{
    if(bal-amount>=500)
    {
    bal = bal - amount;
    cout<<"New Balance is "<<bal<<endl;
    }
    else
    {
    throw InsufficientFunds();
    }
}
```

We have thrown an object of InsuficientFunds() using the throw statement. This creates an effect of an exception in the program. If this exception is not handled, it will abruptly terminate the program. Hence, we have handled this exception by putting the function call to withdraw() in try-catch block as shown below:

```cpp
try
{
a1.withdraw(4200);
}
catch(InsufficientFunds e)
{
e.printMessage();
}
```

The catch block will be executed only if withdraw() throws an exception of type InsufficientFunds. If the method withdraw() completes successfully without an exception, the catch block will never be executed.

The statement

```cpp
e.printMessage();
```

invokes the `printMessage()` method of class `InsufficientFunds` as the object e is an object of the class `InsufficientFunds`.

NOTES

Specifying throw list for a function

You can optionally specify the list of exceptions that are expected to be generated from the function. This list can be specified using the `throw` keyword while defining the function.

For example, while defining the `withdraw()` function in class `Account` you can specify that it may throw `InsufficientFunds` type of exception as follows:

```
void withdraw(float amount) throw (InsufficientFunds)
{
        if(bal-amount>=500)
        {
        bal = bal - amount;
        cout<<"New Balance is "<<bal<<endl;
        }
        else
        {
        throw InsufficientFunds();
        }
}
```

If it is the situation that a particular function is expected to throw multiple different types of exceptions, then you can specify a comma separated list of different types of exceptions that a function may throw. For example, if a function `void f1()` is expected to throw `int`, `float`, `char` and a user-defined exception named as `XYZ`, then you can optionally specify the list while defining the function as shown below:

```
void f1() throw (int,float,char,XYZ)
{
/*function body*/
}
```

What is the advantage of specifying the throw list? **?**

The throw list gives an idea to the programmer about the risks involved in calling the function. So the programmer is well aware of all the possible exceptions that a function may throw so that he/she can handle them in the calling code. In this case, `f1()` throws 4 different exceptions as per the throw list, and hence the programmer must handle all the 4 exceptions while calling this function.

If the function accidentally throws an exception which is of a different type other than what is specified in the throw list, a built-in function `unexpected()` is called. This function abruptly terminates the program by internally calling the function `abort()`.

17.7   Program Specifying Throw List

As an example, let us create a function `check()` to check the type of input entered by the user. We will ask the user to enter any symbol from 0 to 9, and if the user enters any other symbol apart from 0 to 9, we will throw an exception. If the user enters an upper case character, we will throw an exception named as `UpperCaseException`. If the user enters a lower case character, we will throw an exception named as LowerCaseException. If the user enters a special character, we will throw an exception named as SpecialException. If the user enters a digit from 0 to 9, we will not throw any exception but print the success message. This means that it is possible for check () function to throw any one of the three exceptions depending on the user input. Hence, we have specified them in the throw list while defining the check () function as shown in the code below:

```cpp
#include<iostream.h>
class UpperCaseException { };
class LowerCaseException { };
class SpecialException { };
void check(char ch) throw (UpperCaseException, LowerCaseException,
    SpecialException)
{
    if(ch>=48 && ch<=57)
    {
    cout<<"Correct input - check successful"<<endl;
    }
    else if(ch>=65 && ch<=90)
    {
    throw UpperCaseException();
    }
    else if(ch>=97 && ch<=122)
    {
    throw LowerCaseException();
    }
    else
    {
    throw SpecialException();
    }
}
void main()
{
char ch;
cout<<"Enter a character"<<endl;
cin>>ch;
    try
    {
    check(ch);
    }
    catch( ...)
    {
    cout<<"Invalid Input"<<endl;
    }
}
```

Output
```
Enter a character
a
Invalid Input
```

We have created empty classes `UpperCaseException`, `LowerCaseException`, and `SpecialException` just to demonstrate throwing these exceptions in different cases. The `check()` function takes the input character `ch` as argument and throws `UpperCaseException` if `ch` is upper case, `LowerCaseException` if `ch` is lower case and `SpecialException` if `ch` is a special character. The function does not throw any exception if `ch` is a symbol from 0 to 9.

In summary, there are three different exceptions that the function may throw, and hence they appear in the throw list while defining the function as seen in the program.

You have a choice to handle each exception individually by writing three different `catch` blocks. However, we have just written a generic `catch` block that will handle all the exceptions thrown by the function `check()` as shown below:

```
try
{
check(ch);
}
catch(...)
{
cout<<"Invalid Input"<<endl;
}
```

17.8 C++ Built-in Exception Classes

While we have learnt how to create our own exception class, C++ also has built-in exception classes dedicated to different built-in exceptional scenarios that may occur in the program when using specific functionality.

There is a class named `exception` present in the standard library, which is the parent of all these built-in classes. C++ has a quite an extensive exception hierarchy, and we will just list a few of these exception classes, which are child classes of class `exception`.

- **bad_alloc:** This is a built-in child class of class `exception`. This exception is raised when allocation of dynamic memory fails when using the new operator.
- **overflow_error:** When the result of an arithmetic or logical operation is too large to be stored in assigned memory location. An overflow situation occurs when an object of this class is created.
- **bad_cast:** When casting performed using dynamic_cast operator is incorrect, this exception is thrown.

And there are many more classes. This section is just to give you an idea that there are built-in exception classes in C++ whose objects can be thrown or caught in the same way as we did for primitive types and user-defined classes. The exception hierarchy is quite extensive and going in details of each of the exception classes is beyond the scope this text book.

Error Finding Exercise

The following are some programs that may or may not contain errors. Correct the errors if they exist in the code and determine the output after applying the corrections.

Program 1

```
#include<iostream.h>
void output (int *p)
{
    throw p;
}
void main()
{
int *p = 0;
    try
    {
    output(p);
    }
    catch(int *x)
    {
    cout<<"Pointer catched"<<endl;
    }
}
```

Program 2

```
#include<iostream.h>
void main()
{
long premium;
cout<<"Enter the annual premium of the policy"<<endl;
cin>> premium;
    if(premium >=100000)
    {
    throw 1;
    }
    else if(premium >=75000)
    {
    throw 2;
    }
    else if(premium >=50000)
    {
    throw 3;
    }
    else
```

```
    {
    cout<<"All is OK. This is a REGULAR policy"<<endl;
    }
}
```

Program 3

```cpp
#include<iostream.h>
void main()
{
int a,b,c;
cout<<"Enter two numbers"<<endl;
cin>>a>>b;
    try
    {
      if(b==0)
      {
      throw b;
      }
    c = a/b;
    cout<<"Result of division is"<<c<<endl;
    }
    catch(…)
    {
    cout<<"All exceptions"<<endl;
    }
    catch(int t)
    {
    cout<<"Division by zero Exception : Operation failed"<<endl;
    }
d = a+b;
cout<<"Result of addition is"<<d<<endl;
}
```

Program 4

```cpp
#include<iostream.h>
void main()
{
    try {
throw "testmessage";
    }
    catch(char *x)
    {
    cout<<x;
    }
}
```

Program 5

```
#include<iostream.h>
class A
{
};
class B: public A
{
};
class C: public B
{
};
void myException()
{
    throw C();
}
void main()
{
int *p = 0;
    try
    {
    myException();
    }
    catch(A obj1)
    {
    cout<<"Block1"<<endl;
    }
    catch(B obj2)
    {
    cout<<"Block2"<<endl;
    }
    catch(C obj3)
    {
    cout<<"Block3"<<endl;
    }
}
```

Program 6

```
#include<iostream.h>
void main()
{
    try {
    throw 1;
    }
```

```
cout<<"I am here"<<endl;
    catch(int x)
    {
    cout<<x;
    }
}
```

Quiz

Choose the correct statement(s):
1. Exception handling is used to
    (a) Avoid crashing of the program in case of exception
    (b) Avoid crashing of the program in case of error
    (c) Successful compilation of the program even if there are syntax errors
    (d) None of the above
2. Which of the following is not the keyword of C++?
    (a) try   (c) throw   (e) finally
    (b) catch   (d) throws
3. throw is used to
    (a) Handle the exception
    (b) Generate the exception
    (c) Generate an error
    (d) Both b and c
4. Which of the following is/are correct statements?
    (a) You can have single try and multiple catch blocks in a single handler.
    (b) You can have multiple try and multiple catch blocks in a single handler.
    (c) There should not be any statement after end of try and before beginning of catch block.
    (d) You can throw an exception from catch block.
5. If the function throws an exception which is not specified in the throw list then
    (a) There is a compilation error in the program
    (b) The program will crash abruptly and the exception will not be handled
    (c) Program runs successfully and the exception is ignored
    (d) None of the above

Review Questions

1. Explain the usage of try-catch blocks in C++.
2. Explain the usage of throw statement with examples.
3. Describe the significance of throw list in C++.
4. Explain how you can catch and throw an object of a user-defined class with an example.

5. Explain Array index out of bounds exception and NULL pointer exception with an example.

6. Create a function f1() with an empty throw list specified while defining the function as shown below. Attempt to throw a integer type exception from f1().

```
void f1() throw()
{
/*throw integer exception here*/
}
```

Write a main() function to call f1(). State the error/output that you get and justify the same.

ASCII Values

ASCII value	Character symbol	Description
0	NUL	Null character
1	SOH	Start of header
2	STX	Start of text
3	ETX	End of text
4	EOT	End of transmission
5	ENQ	Enquiry
6	ACK	Acknowledgement
7	BEL	Bell
8	BS	Backspace
9	HT	Horizontal tab
10	LF	Line feed
11	VT	Vertical tab
12	FF	Form feed
13	CR	Carriage return
14	SO	Shifting out
15	SI	Shifting in
16	DLE	Data link escape
17	DC1	Device Control 1
18	DC2	Device Control 2
19	DC3	Device Control 3
20	DC4	Device Control 4
21	NAK	Negative Acknowledgement
22	SYN	Synchronous idle
23	ETB	End of transfer blocks
24	CAN	Cancel
25	EM	End of medium
26	SUB	Substitute character
27	ESC	Escape

ASCII value	Character symbol	Description
28	FS	File separator
29	GS	Group separator
30	RS	Record separator
31	US	Unit separator
32		Space
33	!	Exclamation
34	"	Double quote
35	#	Hash
36	$	Dollar
37	%	Percentage
38	&	Ampersand
39	'	Apostrophe
40	(	Open Parenthesis
41	)	Close Parenthesis
42	*	Asterisk
43	+	Plus
44	,	Comma
45	-	Minus
46	.	Dot
47	/	Slash
48	0	Digit
49	1	Digit
50	2	Digit
51	3	Digit
52	4	Digit
53	5	Digit
54	6	Digit
55	7	Digit
56	8	Digit
57	9	Digit
58	:	Colon
59	;	Semicolon
60	<	Less than
61	=	Assignment
62	>	Greater than
63	?	Question mark
64	@	At sign

ASCII value	Character symbol	Description
65	A	Upper case character
66	B	Upper case character
67	C	Upper case character
68	D	Upper case character
69	E	Upper case character
70	F	Upper case character
71	G	Upper case character
72	H	Upper case character
73	I	Upper case character
74	J	Upper case character
75	K	Upper case character
76	L	Upper case character
77	M	Upper case character
78	N	Upper case character
79	O	Upper case character
80	P	Upper case character
81	Q	Upper case character
82	R	Upper case character
83	S	Upper case character
84	T	Upper case character
85	U	Upper case character
86	V	Upper case character
87	W	Upper case character
88	X	Upper case character
89	Y	Upper case character
90	Z	Upper case character
91	[	Open rectangular bracket
92	\	Backslash
93	]	Close rectangular bracket
94	^	Caret
95	_	Underscore
96	`	Back quote
97	a	Lower case character
98	b	Lower case character
99	c	Lower case character
100	d	Lower case character
101	e	Lower case character

ASCII value	Character symbol	Description
102	f	Lower case character
103	g	Lower case character
104	h	Lower case character
105	i	Lower case character
106	j	Lower case character
107	k	Lower case character
108	l	Lower case character
109	m	Lower case character
110	n	Lower case character
111	o	Lower case character
112	p	Lower case character
113	q	Lower case character
114	r	Lower case character
115	s	Lower case character
116	t	Lower case character
117	u	Lower case character
118	v	Lower case character
119	w	Lower case character
120	x	Lower case character
121	y	Lower case character
122	z	Lower case character
123	{	Open Curly bracket
124			Pipe
125	}	Close curly bracket
126	~	Tilde
127	DEL	Delete

II | List of Keywords in C++

and	const	float	operator	static_cast	using
and_eq	const_cast	for	or	struct	virtual
asm	continue	friend	or_eq	switch	void
auto	default	goto	private	template	volatile
bitand	delete	if	protected	this	wchar_t
bitor	do	inline	public	throw	while
bool	double	int	register	TRUE	xor
break	dynamic_cast	long	reinterpret_cast	try	xor_eq
case	else	mutable	return	typedef	
catch	enum	namespace	short	typeid	
char	explicit	new	signed	typename	
class	extern	not	sizeof	union	
compl	FALSE	not_eq	static	unsigned	

Software Development Life Cycle

Any software system to be developed (using any of the programming languages) must go through a series of steps before the system is deployed and released on to the production environment. The software development life cycle (SDLC) defines the stages involved in the software development process, so as to develop a particular application. One of the models that are followed in the development of a software application is called as a 'waterfall' model, which is shown in Figure A3.1.

The figure shows a series of steps that we must follow in the software development process. The meaning of each of the phases is as explained below:

Analysis: This is a phase in software development where the software engineer understands the exact requirements of the software to be developed. The requirements of the application to be developed are captured from the end users of the application and a 'Business requirements document' is prepared, which describes the answers to the following questions:

1. What are the inputs to the system to be developed?
2. What is the processing to be performed by the system to be developed?
3. What are the outputs of the system to be developed?

'Analysis' is the detailed study of the requirements that are received from the business users for a particular software system to be developed under a given set of constraints.

Design: Software 'design' is a process to create 'model' of the system to be developed thereby finalizing the complete approach of development. The models created during the 'design' phase should define the following attributes:

1. The detailed software architecture of the system to be developed.
2. The detailed procedure/algorithm of each functionality which is required to implement the solution.
3. The specifications of the data models to be implemented for the system to be developed.
4. Other software system and integrity constraints.

The 'feasibility study' is also done in the design process so as to determine if the requirements are possible to be implemented under a given set of constraints. If any of the requirements is found to be unfeasible, the development process may be reiterated from the analysis phase where the requirements for the system are redefined. It is important to note that the 'waterfall'

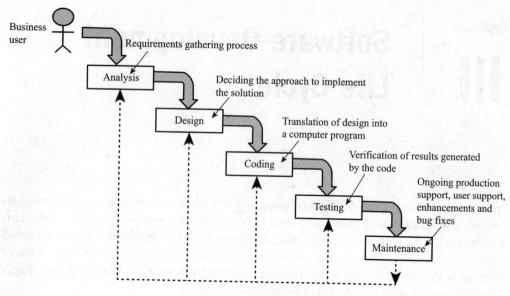

Figure A3.1: Waterfall model

model is an iterative model which means that we can go back to the previous stage at any time during the development process so as to reinitiate the required stages in the model. The functional specifications and design documents are prepared by the technical team at the end of the design phase. These documents give complete descriptions of the approach to be followed in the development process describing the 'algorithms', flowcharts', 'data models', etc., which are required to be followed to implement the solution for a given problem statement.

Coding: The 'coding' phase refers to the translation of the design into a computer program. If the design is explained and accurate, coding will just be a mechanical task because all the algorithms and data models are finalized in the design process itself.

Testing: Software testing is the process to compare the results produced by the system with the 'Business Requirements Document', so as to ensure that the code produces correct output. The testing and the quality assurance of the system are performed in this phase of the software development. There are two types of testing performed on the system which is under development, first comes the 'alpha' testing and then comes the 'beta' testing. The 'alpha' testing is the testing that is performed by the 'technical' team of the application whereas the 'beta' testing is the testing that is performed by the end users of the application. The 'beta' testing is also called as a 'user acceptance testing' when in the users of the application rigorously test the system for verifying the correctness of the results produced by the system.

Maintenance: After the software system is being released and deployed into production, it may still require some enhancements or corrections. The maintenance phase of the waterfall model defines the approach to implement the enhancements and changes to the software system which has been already released into production. The system which is already released into production may be required to go through changes due to any of the following reasons:

1. Change in user requirements.
2. To fix a bug in the system that was not detected at the time of testing.
3. Change in the production environment over which the system is deployed.
4. Enhancements to be made to the existing system in production.

It is recommended that each phase of the SDLC produces necessary documents and reports providing the details of each activity that is executed in the respective stage. This makes the maintenance of the application an easy and quick process.

Bibliography

Aho, Alfred V., Monica S. Lam, Ravi Sethi, and Jaffrey D. Ullman. 2011. *Compilers: Principles, Techniques and Tools*. 2nd edition. New Delhi: Pearson.

Eckel, Bruce. 2000. *Thinking in C++, Volume 1: Introduction to standard C++*. 2nd edition. Upper Saddle River, NJ: Prentice Hall PTR.

Gottfried, Byron. 1996. *Schaum's outline of theory and problems of programming with C*. 2nd edition. New York: McGraw Hill.

Hall, Douglas V. 2006. *Microprocessors and Interfacing: Programming and Hardware*. 2nd edition. New Delhi: Tata McGraw Hill Edition.

Hearn, Donald, and M. Pauline Baker. 2011. *Computer graphics C version*. 2nd edition. New Delhi: Pearson.

John Donovan. 1991. *Systems Programming*. Tata McGraw Hill edition. New Delhi: Tata McGraw Hill.

Langsam, Yedidyah , Moshe J. Augenstein, and Aaron M. Tenenbaum. 1996. *Data Structures using C and C++*. 2nd edition. Upper Saddle River, NJ: Prentice Hall PTR.

Nagler, Eric. 1994. *Learning C++; A Hands-on Approach*. Delhi: Jaico Publishing House.

Pimparkhede, Kunal. 2012. *Computer Programming 1*. New Delhi: Tata McGraw Hill Pub. Pvt. Ltd.

Silberschatz, Abraham, Henry F. Korth, and S. Sudarshan. 2002. *Database System Concepts*. 4th edition. New York: McGraw-Hill, Inc.

Stroustrup, Bjarne. 2013. *The C++ Programming Language*. 4th edition. Reading Mass: Addison Wesley.